ECONOMIC EDUCATION FOR CONSUMERS

3rd Edition

Roger LeRoy Miller

Alan D. Stafford

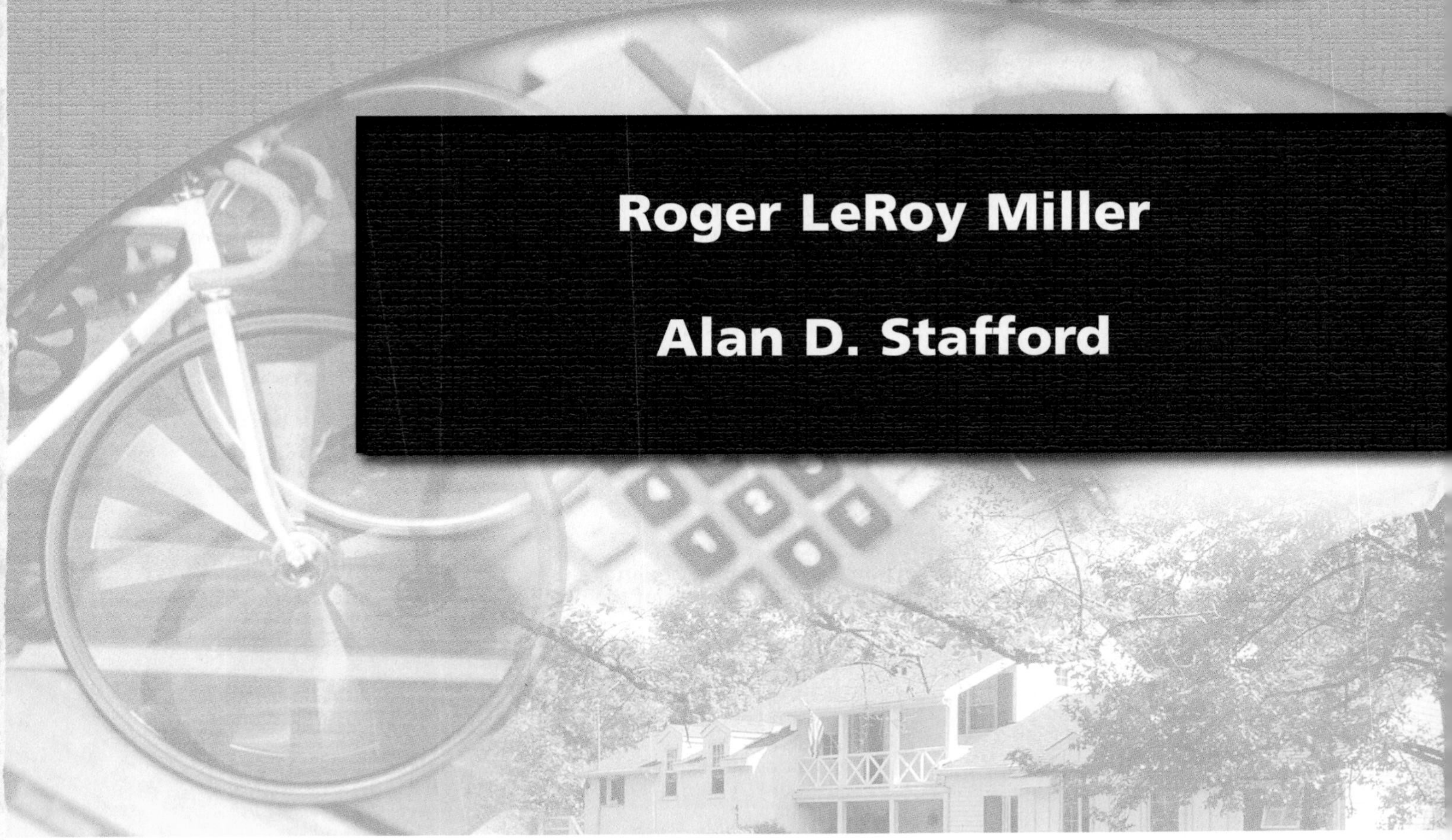

THOMSON

SOUTH-WESTERN

Australia · Canada · Mexico · Singapore · Spain · United Kingdom · United States

Economic Education for Consumers 3e

VP/Editorial Director
Jack W. Calhoun

VP/Editor-in-Chief
Karen Schmohe

Acquistions Editor
Marilyn Hornsby

Project Manager
Enid Nagel

Production Manager
Patricia Matthews Boies

Production Editor
Cami Cacciatore

VP/Director of Marketing
Carol Volz

Senior Marketing Manager
Nancy Long

Marketing Coordinator
Angela A. Russo

Editorial Assistant
Linda Keith

Manufacturing Coordinator
Kevin Kluck

Art Director
Stacy Jenkins Shirley

Cover and Internal Designer
Joseph Pagliaro
Graphic Design

Compositor
Navta Associates, Inc.

Printer
Quebecor World
Dubuque, Iowa

The names of all companies or products mentioned herein are used for identification purposes only and may be trademarks or registered trademarks of their respective owners. South-Western disclaims any affiliation, association, connection with, sponsorship, or endorsement by such owners.

ASIA (including India)
Thomson Learning
5 Shenton Way
#01-01 UIC Building
Singapore 068808

CANADA
Thomson Nelson
1120 Birchmount Road
Toronto, Ontario
Canada M1K 5G4

AUSTRALIA/NEW ZEALAND
Thomson Learning
Australia
102 Dodds Street
Southbank, Victoria 3006
Australia

UK/EUROPE/MIDDLE EAST/AFRICA
Thomson Learning
High Holborn House
50-51 Bedford Road
London WC1R 4LR
United Kingdom

LATIN AMERICA
Thomson Learning
Seneca, 53
Colonia Polanco
11560 Mexico
D.F.Mexico

SPAIN (includes Portugal)
Thomson Paraninfo
Calle Magallanes, 25
28015 Madrid, Spain

Don't Settle for the Status Quo

Financial Math Review

Learn all about basic math topics within the context of daily financial exchanges. *Financial Math Review* covers arithmetic, fractions, statistics, ratios, and proportions. Students can relate to the real world examples as they improve their knowledge and skills and prepare for algebra instruction. Students learn math skills that prepare them for standardized testing and allow them to become smart shoppers, valued employees, and informed taxpayers.

TEXT 0-538-44021-X

Investing in Your Future 2E

Start students on the path to dollars and sense. Use NAIC's respected Stock Selection Guide process to teach smart saving, investing, and planning. Students learn how to analyze the value of stocks and mutual funds. Company Profiles introduce every chapter and the lesson-plan approach makes material easy to comprehend.

TEXT 0-538-43881-9
MODULE (ExamView, Instructor's Resource CD, Video, Annotated Instructor's Edition) 0-538-43885-1

Banking Systems

Explore the principles and practices of banking and credit in the United States. This exciting new text guides users through an overview of financial services, mortgage lending, negotiable instruments, employment, security and ethics, and money and interest. Appropriate for the National Academy Foundation's Academy of Finance courses.

TEXT 0-538-44089-9
MODULE (ExamView, Instructor's Resource CD, Video, Annotated Instructor's Edition) 0-538-44094-5

Fundamentals of Insurance

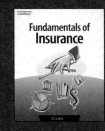

Explore health and property insurance, insurance rates, claims procedures, careers in insurance, and annuities. The extensive use of hands-on activities helps students understand the importance of insurance and how it affects them today and through their retirement years. Appropriate for the National Academy Foundation's (NAF's) Academy of Finance courses.

TEXT 0-538-43201-2
MODULE (ExamView, Instructor's Resource CD, Video, Annotated Instructor's Edition) 0-538-43248-9

Family Financial Management 7E

This hands-on, money management simulation is presented in an extended family setting, presenting situations from young adult to preparing for retirement. Students calculate net worth, plan monthly budgets, complete banking transactions, pay utility bills, perform credit transactions, make housing payments, and reconcile monthly bank statements. Spreadsheet files allow students to use commercial software to work with budgets and financial statements.

ENVELOPE SIMULATION 0-538-43804-5
DATA CD (Windows/Macintosh) 0-538-43842-8

INSTRUCTOR SUPPORT AND OTHER MATERIALS AVAILABLE

THOMSON
SOUTH-WESTERN

Join us on the Internet at www.swlearning.com

CONTENTS

CONTENTS

CHAPTER 5

Income Taxes – How Much Will You Keep? 158

Decision Making Project – Tax Your Dream Job 159, 165, 175, 180, 185, 189

CHAPTER 6

Budgeting – How Will You Use Your Money? 190

Decision Making Project – All in the Family 191, 197, 203, 209, 215, 219

CHAPTER 7

Banking Services – Where to Stash Your Cash 220

Decision Making Project – Check it Out 221, 234, 241, 247, 253, 257

CHAPTER 8

Saving - Plan for Financial Security 258

Decision Making Project - Save Yourself 259, 263, 269, 281, 285

CHAPTER 9

Investing – Prepare for Your Future 286

Decision Making Project – Invest in Yourself 287, 293, 315, 321, 325

CHAPTER 10

Credit – You're in Charge 326

Decision Making Project – Give Yourself Credit 327, 333, 347, 353, 359, 363

CHAPTER 11

Budget Essentials – Food, Clothes, and Fun 364
Decision Making Project – Shop 'til You Drop 365, 377, 383, 389, 393

CHAPTER 12

Transportation – How Will You Get There? 394
Decision Making Project – Got to Get There 395, 407, 415, 421, 427, 431

CONTENTS

CHAPTER 13

Housing - A Place to Call Home 432

Decision Making Project - Rule Your Own Roost 433, 439, 459, 463

CHAPTER 14

Automobile and Home Insurance – Sharing the Risk 464

Decision Making Project – Cover Your Wheels 465, 479, 486, 493, 497

CHAPTER 15

Health and Life Insurance – Your Personal Security 498

Decision Making Project – An Apple a Day 499, 517, 524, 531, 535

CHAPTER 16

Choose Services – When You Need Help 536

Decision Making Project – Is There a Doctor in the House? 537, 545, 553, 559, 563

CONTENTS

About the Authors

Roger Leroy Miller, Center for University Studies, Arlington, Texas. Dr. Miller was a Woodrow Wilson Honor Fellow, National Science Foundation Fellow, and Lilly Honor Fellow while pursuing his graduate degree in economics. Since then he has taught at the University of Washington, the University of Miami, and Clemson University. Among the more than 100 books he has written or co-authored are works on economics, statistics, law, consumer finance, careers, and government. Dr. Miller has also operated several business and served as a consultant to government agencies, private corporations, and law firms.

Alan D. Stafford, Niagara County Community College, Sanborn, New York. Professor Stafford is a Professor Emeritus of Economics and the former Director of Planning for Niagara County Community College. He has earned an MBA and MEd in Social Studies Education from the State University of New York at Buffalo. Professor Stafford taught secondary social studies for fourteen years before joining the faculty of NCCC. He is the author or co-author of a variety of economics and consumer education texts and received the New York State Chancellor's Award for Excellence in Teaching in 1998.

REVIEWERS

Jean A. Abbott
Teacher, Family and Consumer Science
Ben Davis High School
Indianapolis, Indiana

Robert J. Acosta
Consumer Economics Teacher
Chatsworth High School
Chatsworth, California

Wendy J. Baron
Life Management Educator
Kentwood Public Schools
Kentwood, Michigan

Cynthia Bertrand
Consultant, Vocational Education
Calcasieu Parish School Board
Lake Charles, Louisiana

Ron Caulford
Teacher, Marketing/Business
Mountain High School
Kaysville, Utah

Rebecca A. Cernoch
Teacher and Coordinator, Marketing
Education and Career and Technology
La Grange High School
La Grange, Texas

Linda L. Crouch
Teacher, Business Department
Wheeler High School
Fossil, Oregon

Lupe Ferran Diaz
Chairperson, Business Technology and
Marketing Education
Miami Beach Senior High School
Miami Beach, Florida

Gloria Green
Teacher, Business Education
Lonoke High School
Lonoke, Arkansas

Mary Jane Hoag
Curriculum Consultant
Bryan, Texas

Jacob Jackson
Teacher, Business
Eastmont High School
East Wenatchee, Washington

William O. King
Director, Academy of Finance
Cumberland County Schools
Fayetteville, North Carolina

Beverly M. Moore
Teacher, Family and Consumer Science
Westminster High School
Westminster, Maryland

Richard Reding
Tax Accountant
Cincinnati, Ohio

Jerry Sax
Teacher, Consumer Education
Gridley High School
Gridley, Illinois

Josephine Sicurella
Teacher, Business Department
Henry P. Becton Regional High School
East Rutherford, New Jersey

Janell Stewart
Teacher, Social Studies Department
Bryan County High School
Pembroke, Georgia

Gemelia Tyler
Teacher, Work and Family Life
Hillsboro High School
Hillsboro, Ohio

Gary G. Vink
Teacher, Business Department
James Buchanan High School
Mercersburg, Pennsylvania

TO THE STUDENT

When you're in a class, do you often wonder, "What does this have to do with anything?" Sometimes a class can seem like it has nothing to do with your life outside of school. But this class is different.

What Is a Consumer?   A consumer is anyone who buys or uses a product. If you buy a jacket at a store, you are acting as a consumer. If your brother borrows your jacket (hopefully with your permission), then your brother is acting as a consumer as well. With such a broad definition, almost anything you do can be considered a consumer action.

Rational Buying Decisions   The most important thing for a consumer to know is how to make rational buying decisions. Think about what you do when you want to buy something. Do you think of what you need or want? Do you consider all of your options? Do you look at the trade-offs you have to make because you can't have everything you want? Do you look back on a buying decision and realize that you learned something from it?

Decision Making   This is the beginning of a step-by-step process called a decision making process, and it works well in consumer and many other types of situations. When you take the time to think through important decisions, you are less likely to do or buy something you'll regret later.

Rights and Responsibilities   It is important for all consumers to know their rights and responsibilities. For example, you have the right in most states to return a sweater to the store that sold it to you for a full refund if it isn't damaged, you have your receipt, and it is within a certain amount of time. Your responsibility is to make sure the sweater isn't damaged, you have a copy of your receipt, and you know how long you have to return it.

Financial Decisions   The global economy holds endless possibilities for financial success and financial pitfalls. Good financial decisions now, such as staying out of credit card debt and investing wisely can give you a good start into your adult life. Some bad financial decisions made while you are young, such as credit card debt and no retirement savings, can take time and money to straighten out.

Valuable Information   Every chapter will give you valuable information you will need to make some of the most important consumer decisions of your life. Some information you can use today. Some information you can probably use in a year or two. Some information you will have more use for in about 10 years. All of it is here to introduce you to the impact that being a consumer will have on your life, and what an impact being a consumer can have in your local, state, and national economy.

FEATURES TO MAKE YOU A "SUPER-INFORMED" CONSUMER

Buy the Numbers Learn to evaluate the information in ads to make rational consumer decisions.

Consumer Action These are consumer situations that you will probably find yourself in one day.

Consumer Alert Scams can be found anywhere, but this feature will give you tips to help you avoid them.

Cyber Consumer Learn to use the Web to help you find answers to questions about consumer issues.

Exploding Myths Test what you know, or rather what you think you know.

Guess What? These are interesting and little known consumer facts.

What in the World? Learn about consumers in other countries who have different choices.

CONNECT CONSUMER ISSUES TO OTHER CURRICULAR AREAS

Journal Journey Write about what you know before you read each chapter.

Journal Recap After you have finished the chapter, look at what you wrote. Do you think what you wrote before is still true?

Vote Your Wallet Why should you bother voting once you turn 18? Read this feature and discover how much local, state, and national elections affect your life and lives in your community. You can make a difference.

Math of Money Review the basic math skills you need to make rational consumer decisions.

Communicate Write about consumer issues.

Primary Sources Read these historical accounts of consumer situations, and compare them to your experience.

LOADS OF ACTIVITIES

Life-Span Plan Project This capstone project incorporates materials developed throughout the course into one comprehensive life-span plan.

Decision Making Project Every chapter contains a project that will help you and a group of other students through the decision making process.

In Class Activity These activities in every lesson can be completed in class with a group or by yourself to help you understand the lesson.

Internet Activity These activities in every chapter give you an opportunity to use the Internet and e-mail your classmates.

TECHNOLOGY

Planning Tools CD This CD provides a calculator to help you calculate college, savings, loans, and retirement expenditures.

Data CD This CD provides additional computer activities for each chapter.

Web site The web site *www.ee4c.swlearning.com* provides additional Internet activities and crossword puzzles for each chapter.

Interactive Study Guide This electronic study guide provides additional help for studying each chapter.

CNN Video This video provides short real-life videos to introduce each chapter.

JUMP$TART COALITION FOR PERSONAL FINANCIAL LITERACY

The text correlates to the Jump$tart Standards for Personal Financial Literacy to indicate the knowledge and skills you should possess as a confident consumer.

TEST YOUR UNDERSTANDING

. . . of the lesson

Checkpoint   These short questions within the lesson ask you about what you just read.

Try These   Do you understand the lesson? If so, you are able to answer these basic, informational questions about the lesson.

Think Critically   Can you apply what you learned in the lesson? If so, you are able to answer these critical thinking exercises.

. . . of the chapter

Key Ideas   An overview of the main points in the chapter.

Terms Review   This is a matching vocabulary exercise.

Consumer Decisions   Answer questions about real-world consumer situations and explain your answers.

Think Critically   These questions about real-life consumer situations have you applying higher-level thinking skills.

Look It Up   Find information about consumer topics using the newspaper, the library, or the Internet and evaluate what you found.

Which Is the Best Deal?   You have three choices in this real-life consumer situation. Evaluate your alternatives, make a decision, and explain how you made that decision.

Inside the Numbers   Analyze the data in this real-life consumer situation and figure out what it means.

Curriculum Connection   Discover how subjects you study in other classes are intertwined with consumer issues.

Chapter 1

CONSUMERS
THE ENGINE THAT RUNS THE ECONOMY

WHAT'S AHEAD

EXPLODING MYTHS

Fact or Myth?
What do you think is true?

1. When you buy a product, your cost is just the price you pay for the item.

2. As a consumer, you don't have much influence on the products that businesses make and offer for sale.

3. You are wise to ignore advertising. Businesses just use it to get you to buy products you don't really need.

JOURNAL JOURNEY

WRITE IN YOUR JOURNAL ABOUT THE FOLLOWING.

MAKE DECISIONS How do you decide what to buy? Do you consider different options before you decide? Do your friends or family influence your choices?

ADVERTISING Does advertising help you make better decisions? If so, how? Has advertising ever misled you? Give an example.

PROTECT THE ENVIRONMENT What do you do in your daily life that harms the environment? How can you do things differently to help protect the environment?

DECISION MAKING PROJECT

SPECIFY ● **SEARCH** ● **SIFT** ● **SELECT** ● **STUDY**

GET OUT OF TOWN You and three friends have saved up $3,000 to take a trip during your spring break. You want to stay a week. Keep in mind that you have to stay within your budget.

GOAL

To learn about the decision making process by planning a vacation

PROJECT PROCESS

SPECIFY	Lesson 1.2
SEARCH	Lesson 1.3
SIFT	Lesson 1.4
SELECT	Lesson 1.6
STUDY	Chapter Assessment

GOALS

DESCRIBE
values, goals, and
opportunity costs

EXPLAIN
the difference between
a need and a want

© Corel

1.1 Decisions, Decisions

You've Got the Power

Have you ever heard the phrase *the customer is always right*? If businesses want to make a profit, they have to give customers what they want. If they do not give customers what they want, the customers will go to another business or not buy at all. A business cannot succeed without customers.

You have the power to choose what you buy and where you buy it. You can choose not to buy from businesses whose products you don't like and instead buy mostly from your favorite businesses. Businesses spend lots of money each year taking surveys to find out what customers want.

Values

You have the power to make so many decisions that you may wonder where to start. Knowing your values is a good place to begin. **Values** are your principles—the standards by which you live. When you list your values, you are making

CONSUMER ACTION

Anthony saved every penny he could to buy a classic 1957 Chevy. Last year, he had $8,000 in his savings account. Anthony's mother can't afford to pay for any more educational expenses. If he wants education after high school, he will have to pay for it himself. Anthony wants to become a computer programmer. What should he do?

judgments. You decide what is right or wrong, good or bad, important or unimportant for you.

Life values are the principles that are most important to you in life. Wanting to spend time with your friends and family is an example of a life value.

Work values are the principles that are important to you in your work. Wanting to earn a living by working with people you like is an example of a work value.

Cultural values are principles that are important to you because of your ethnic heritage or religion. Wanting to practice your religion or dress in clothing that shows your heritage are examples of cultural values.

Social values are principles that are important to you because of the community in which you live. Wanting to help your community have good government or working to keep it clean and safe are examples of social values.

Demographic values are principles that are important to you because of how and where people live. *Demography* is the study of population trends. When people in a community grow older, have

children, or move to obtain employment, their values change. In the 19th century, many Americans moved west because they valued open spaces and the opportunity to start a new life.

© Getty Images/PhotoDisc

Values Change   Values are not constant. Your values change as you learn and grow. This is also true for societies as a whole.

In the 1950s, for example, many people held the social value that women should stay at home to raise their children. Since then, this social value has changed for many Americans. Today, more families place a high value on a mother's contribution to the household income.

Different People, Different Values   Suppose you have $20. You want to buy a new CD. Your best

What In The World?

Values can vary greatly among different countries and cultures. The cow is sacred to Hindus in India. Eating a beef hamburger in India would be considered a sin. To Indian Muslims, eating pork is offensive. To sell fast food in India, McDonald's had to replace its U.S.-style hamburger with a burger made of lamb and add many vegetarian items.

© Getty Images/PhotoDisc

friend would spend the money on a baseball cap. Different people make different choices. This does not mean that one of you is right and the other is wrong. It just means that people value different things. Before you make a decision, consider what you value most.

What are some of your values? Make a list of values and what they mean to you.

Goals

The things you want to accomplish in your life are **goals**. They come from your values, your needs and wants, and your hopes and dreams.

For example, you may be determined to graduate from high school. This is a goal you have set for yourself. Your goals can be influenced by something you see or read. Your family or experiences you have had can also influence your goals.

© Getty Images/PhotoDisc

Needs and Wants

Needs are the things you can't live without. Everyone needs a minimum amount of food, water, clothing, and a place to live. Needs include having food in the house and having a warm coat for the winter.

Wants are the things that you would like to have but can live without. A want might be a new interactive game system or a new team jacket.

Sometimes people confuse needs and wants. For instance, you may need a warm coat for winter. This does not mean that you *need* the same coat that your friends are wearing. You may need food, but you do not *need* junk food.

Hopes and Dreams

What do you want to do for a living after you graduate? What do you want to own in the future? What kind of person do you want to be?

These are important questions. The answers can be your goals. For example, you may want to be a computer programmer, a doctor, or a race car driver. You may want to have a nice home and a good car someday. You may want to be a leader in your community.

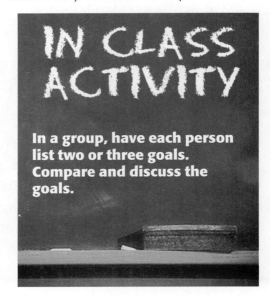

IN CLASS ACTIVITY

In a group, have each person list two or three goals. Compare and discuss the goals.

Your Life Span

Birth					Death
Infancy	Childhood	Young Adult	Mature Adult	Retired	Elderly

School Job Career Travel
Advanced Education Care for Parents
Raise Children Community Service
Home Ownership Medical Care

EVENTS IN YOUR LIFE CYCLE

A Life-Span Plan

You should expect the things you want most in your life to change as you grow older. Today you might believe that owning a nice car is your most important goal. In ten years you may be more concerned with buying a home or saving for your children's education. Even later you will want to have a rewarding retirement. Important events in your life, such as preparing for a career, raising a family, or enjoying retirement, are parts of your **life cycle**.

When you are young, you will set **long-term goals** that you want to achieve over a period of years during your life span. Your **life span** is the time from your birth to your death. It includes the events that make up your life cycle. You may think of your life span as a straight line that contains the events of your life cycle.

The life-span timeline at the top of this page can help you understand the relationship between a life span and events in a person's life cycle. It shows a life span as a straight line

along the top of the figure. Events in the life cycle appear beneath the time in a person's life when they might happen. If you construct a figure like this for yourself, it will have different events taking place at different times.

Life-span goals are long-term goals that you want to reach during your life. They may include earning a college degree, owning a business, raising a family, or achieving financial security. In this class, you will be asked to choose life-span goals. These goals will become part of a **life-span plan** that you may use to help make important choices in the future.

In the Life-Span project that follows Chapter 17, you will be asked to construct your own life-span plan. As you read each chapter in this textbook, you will gain knowledge about yourself that will help you develop your life-span plan. Throughout the chapters, topics and features that may help you complete the life-span project will be identified with a life-span icon, as shown next to the life-span timeline.

© Getty Images/PhotoDisc

Short-Term Goals

To help you achieve your life-span goals you will set many short-term goals. **Short-term goals** are things you hope to accomplish within a year. Your short-term goals should contribute to achieving your life-

span goals over time. Suppose your most important life-span goal is to become a computer programmer. A short-term goal you could set now would be to save $1,000 this year to help pay college expenses later. Achieving this short-term goal will not make you a computer programmer. But, it will make it easier to achieve your life-span goal in the future. To reach your goals, either life-span or short-term, you must identify what you want from your life. It is difficult to work hard if you don't know why you are working.

Plan to Reach Your Goals

Knowing your goals is just the first step. The next step is to plan how you will reach them. Again, suppose that one of your life-span goals is to be a computer programmer. In addition to saving, you can register for

COMMUNICATE

Write a paragraph about each of your goals, values, hopes, and dreams. Why do you think it is important to know your goals, values, hopes, and dreams when making decisions? What are some consequences of losing sight of these things?

© Getty Images/PhotoDisc

programming courses at your high school, community college, or other training centers. You can ask computer programmers how they got started and whether they have any advice to help you.

Make a plan and stick to it. Set short-term goals that will help you achieve the things you want most in your life span. Make a budget and follow it. Save the money, earn the grades, or gain the knowledge you need to succeed. Planning will help you reach your goals.

CheckPoint

Why should people set short- and long-term goals? How are needs different from wants? Why are hopes and dreams important?

Opportunity Cost and Decisions When making a decision, consider the things you have to give up or not have. Is the price too high? The opportunity cost of buying a CD, for example, could be the baseball cap you also wanted, but you didn't have money for both.

Is It Worth It? Ask yourself if the reward is worth the cost. You

CYBER CONSUMER

A wide array of merchandise can be purchased on the Internet. Locate a few online retailers and research the price of a CD you want to purchase. Then research the price of a ball cap you might also like to purchase. Explain how opportunity cost may be a factor if you are unable to afford both.

Opportunity Cost

Having a plan is a great way to reach your goals. But what about the things you have to give up? If you become a full-time student, you won't have as much time to have a job and make money. The income you give up while you're in school is your opportunity cost.

Opportunity cost is the value of your next best alternative whenever you make a choice. Because different people value different things, your opportunity cost may not be the same as a friend's may be for the same situation.

© Getty Images/PhotoDisc

© Getty Images/PhotoDisc

may decide that it is. For instance, you may think that it is better for you to be a full-time student than to have a job right now.

Consider Other Options Perhaps you have been working and saving for two years without a vacation. It might be worth it to you to take an inexpensive vacation with your savings, or reduce other spending to allow for a vacation. Goals can change just as your values can change. After you achieve a short-term goal, set some more goals for yourself. Consider your values, your needs and wants, your hopes and dreams, and your opportunity costs. Then make a plan to achieve your life-span goals!

CheckPoint

What decision have you made within the last week? What was the opportunity cost of that decision?

TRY THESE

1. What does "the customer is always right" mean?

2. What is the difference between a need and a want?

3. Why do businesses spend millions of dollars a year to find out what customers want?

4. What are values? Give an example.

5. What are short-term goals?

6. How are cultural, social, and demographic values formed?

7. What does the term *life span* refer to? What is a life-span plan?

8. What is opportunity cost? Give an example.

THINK CRITICALLY

9. **CONSUMER ACTION** Anthony had to make a choice. If you were Anthony, what would you choose? What are your values that support your decision? Think of the option given up. What are some benefits you could have received from the option you did not choose?

10. Describe a need and a want in your life. Why is one a need and the other a want?

11. **COMMUNICATE** Write about a financial decision you made based upon your values. How did you arrive at this decision? What values (cultural, demographic, social) influenced your choice?

12. How important are life-span goals? How do priorities change over the life span?

13. List some opportunity costs of having a job after school.

14. How do customers have power over businesses?

© Getty Images/PhotoDisc

GOALS

EXPLAIN
how to use
a decision making
process

DESCRIBE
the benefits
of making rational
buying decisions

1.2 Make Decisions

Decision Making Process

Now that you are aware of your values and goals, how do you use this knowledge to make consumer decisions? You can follow a five-step decision making process. If you follow this decision making process whenever you make a consumer choice, you will make a rational buying decision. A **rational buying decision** is a choice made in an organized, logical manner. Choices made this way will most likely fulfill your needs or wants.

Decision Making Process

▶ **SPECIFY** Identify the need or want that you are trying to fulfill. Determine your goals.

▶ **SEARCH** Plan specific steps to gather information.

▶ **SIFT** Look at all your options. Look at your opportunity costs.

▶ **SELECT** Make a choice and act on it.

▶ **STUDY** Evaluate the result.

CONSUMER ACTION

Clara is thinking about buying a new camera. She found a discontinued model she likes offered for half price. The store, however, has only one left. If she wants the camera, she must buy it immediately. How should she make her decision?

© Getty Images/PhotoDisc

Specify

Most people go to a store or mall to buy something specific. You have probably done the same. You probably shop to fill a need or want. But before you go shopping, you should identify the particular need or want that you are looking to fill. For example, focus your thinking from just "going shopping" to "going shopping to buy shoes."

Need or Want? Footwear is a common need. However, you probably don't want just something to protect your feet. You want shoes that are affordable and stylish. If your sandals have holes in the soles, you might need new ones. But what kind of sandals do you want? What style? What color?

Goals Identifying your needs and wants leads to your goals for this shopping trip. You want to buy sandals. That is one of your goals. You look into your wallet and find only $30 left from your paycheck. Another goal, then, is to buy sandals for $30 or less. And you don't want just any style. You want sandals that go with your summer clothes. So, you really have three goals in fulfilling your need for footwear.

Goals

1. You want to buy sandals.

2. You want sandals for $30 or less.

3. You want them to go with your summer clothes.

Values In determining your goals, consider your values. You could have asked a friend or your parents for more money, but perhaps you value your independence. You earned the $30. So, you decide not to spend more money than you have.

Goals and values may be different for different people. Suppose your friend Tina also wants a pair of sandals. She doesn't have a job, so she asks her mother for the money to buy sandals. This does not mean that one of you is right and the other is wrong. You and Tina have different values, even if your goals are similar.

Values are the principles that work best for the person who holds them. Some values, such as honesty, last a lifetime. Some values change as the person changes. After Tina has a job and can pay for her own purchases, her values may change. She will use her own money instead of asking her mother for money.

CheckPoint

Think about the last purchase you made. What need or want were you fulfilling? What were your goals? What values contributed to your goals?

Search

Having a plan will help you make a rational buying decision. You know that only four stores in your town sell shoes in your price range. So, you plan to go to each store. You decide ahead of time that you won't buy until you have seen all the sandals.

Plan Your Search   You have outlined some good steps to get information for your purchase. Comparing the sandals from four stores will help you make a rational buying decision. You will know your options.

Impulse Purchases   Many times people make impulse purchases. An *impulse purchase* is a purchase made on a whim, without using a decision making process. In other words, you see something that you *must* have, so you buy it.

Sometimes impulse buying is a wise choice. If you see a product you use regularly at a low price or that is hard to find, buying it then might be a rational decision.

An impulse purchase can turn out to be a good choice, but often it isn't. You may go to another store and find the same thing at a better price. Or, you may discover that you wish you had spent your money on something else. Having a plan and sticking to it can help you control the urge to buy on impulse.

Sift

The next step is to look at all your options. You went to four shoe stores. You saw a nice pair of black leather sandals for $28 at the first store. The other pair you liked was at the last store you visited. The sandals were a plain tan fabric and cost $25 on sale. All other sandals were either out of your price range or you didn't like them.

Look at Your Options
Making a decision without considering all your options can cost you. For instance, you go shopping for a shirt. You buy a shirt at the first store you visit. At the third store, you find a better shirt at a lower price. You buy it, but now you have to go back to the first store to return the first shirt you bought. You wasted time you could have spent doing something else.

Look at Your Opportunity Costs   Evaluating the benefits and costs of all your options is an important step in the decision making process. By doing so, you are making a rational choice, not an impulse purchase.

Let's say that you are leaning toward buying the leather sandals, because you think leather will last

GUESS WHAT

Retail and grocery stores place small, inexpensive items near the checkout counter because they know customers will buy them on impulse.

© Getty Images/PhotoDisc

longer than fabric sandals. One opportunity cost of these sandals is the second best use for the $3 that would be in your pocket if you bought the $25 fabric sandals instead of the $28 pair. You could use that $3 to rent a video. By buying the leather sandals, you would be giving up the benefits of the $3—renting the video.

© Getty Images/EyeWire

A trade-off of choosing the fabric sandals is the shorter time you can use them. If the fabric sandals wear out quicker than the leather ones, you will get less use out of them than you would the leather sandals. Plus, you may have to spend money to buy new sandals before the summer is over.

You have evaluated all the benefits and costs of each option. Now you are ready to make a rational buying decision.

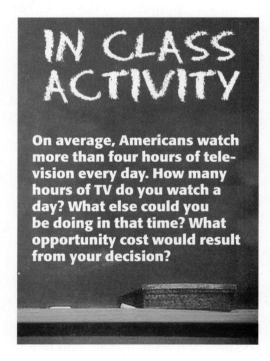

IN CLASS ACTIVITY

On average, Americans watch more than four hours of television every day. How many hours of TV do you watch a day? What else could you be doing in that time? What opportunity cost would result from your decision?

Select

This is it! This is why you have gone through the steps in the decision making process. Compare the benefits and costs of each option, and decide.

Let's say you decide to buy the fabric sandals. You go to the store and buy the sandals for $25. Then you go to the video store and rent a video. You invite a few friends over to watch the video, and you wear your new sandals. You are happy with your decision.

CheckPoint

Have you ever looked at the costs of a choice and decided against it? Why?

Study

Learning is an ongoing process. You can learn important lessons from the results of your actions. Would you do the same thing again? If so, why? If not, what would you do differently?

Suppose that a month after you buy the sandals, you are no longer happy with your selection. The sandals already look worn out, and it is the middle of summer. Study your decision. Should you have bought the leather sandals instead, even though they cost more? Maybe they would have lasted longer. Now you have to save to buy another pair.

Buyer's Remorse At some point, you will regret a purchase decision you made. Even though you made a rational buying decision, given the information you had at the time, a product still might not live up to your expectations. If you had known the fabric sandals would last only a month, you probably would have chosen differently.

You have learned something, though. Buying the lowest priced item isn't necessarily the best choice in all situations. Maybe next time you will choose durability over price for products you want to last a long time.

You can also learn from purchase decisions that you don't regret. Think about what went right, and do it again next time. By using the decision making process, you will increase your chances of buying the product that fits your needs and wants best.

CheckPoint

What important lesson have you learned from a buying decision you made?

MATH OF MONEY

You have a part-time job at a discount store that pays $7 per hour after taxes. Your boss asks you to work next Sunday. You will be paid an overtime rate if you accept (1.5 times your regular rate of pay). However, you have a big math test on Monday, and you were planning to study on Sunday. How much will you earn if you agree to work eight hours on Sunday? What are the opportunity costs of each option?

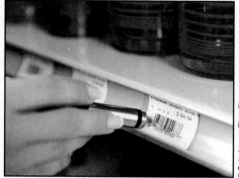

© Getty Images/PhotoDisc

SOLUTION

You will earn $84 if you work eight hours on Sunday.

$7.00 × 1.5 × 8 = $84

If you choose to stay home and study, the opportunity cost of this decision is the $84 you are giving up and all the benefits the money would bring you.

If you choose to work on Sunday, the opportunity cost of this decision is the better grade you could earn on the math test.

TRY THESE

1. Define each step in the decision making process in your own words.

2. What is the difference between a rational buying decision and an impulse purchase?

3. What is the difference between "focusing on your needs, wants, and goals" and "just shopping"? What could happen if you don't identify your needs and wants or determine your goals before you go shopping?

4. Think of a particular product you would like to buy. What kinds of information would you gather about your options?

5. What is the purpose of studying your buying decisions?

THINK CRITICALLY

6. **CONSUMER ACTION** Clara must decide whether or not to buy the discontinued camera she saw offered at half price. She must decide now. If you were Clara, how would you go about making this decision? What additional information would you want before you could make a rational buying decision? What decision would you make? Why?

7. **COMMUNICATE** Think of a purchase decision you have to make. Follow the decision making process, and write what you would do at each step. Be sure to list the opportunity cost of each option as well as the price.

8. **MATH OF MONEY** Tara volunteers at a neighborhood assisted-living home. She reads stories and talks with senior citizens. She hopes to be a director of this kind of facility someday. To volunteer, Tara gave up a job that paid her $6.50 per hour. She usually worked 12 hours a week. How much income has Tara traded for her experience as a volunteer? Do you believe she made a rational choice? Why?

9. Think of something you bought on impulse. Would you have bought it if you had gone through the decision making process? What would you have discovered from the process that you didn't know before you made the impulse purchase?

DECISION MAKING PROJECT

SPECIFY   **SEARCH**   **SIFT**   **SELECT**   **STUDY**

SPECIFY Write out your goals for your trip with three other people. For instance, you might all want to go to a beach or to another country. To put together this trip, your group has to agree on where you would go, where you would stay, what you would want to do there, and so on. List four places that you would want to go that might also fit your budget.

© Getty Images/PhotoDisc

GOALS

DESCRIBE
four economic
systems

EXPLAIN
how demand and
supply work

1.3 Understand Economic Systems

Economic Systems

Every nation has an economic system. An *economic system* is the way a nation uses resources to produce goods and services. **Production** is the creation of goods and services. Manufacturing products, such as cars or pencils, is production. Providing services, such as dry cleaning, is production, too. A dry cleaner's product is clean clothes.

Producing goods and services requires resources. **Resources** are things that are used to create other goods or services. Experts sometimes divide resources into two groups: human and nonhuman resources. *Human resources* are the skills, training, and abilities people have to complete tasks that result in the production of goods or services. *Nonhuman resources* are the raw materials, tools, and manufactured products, such as oil, tractors, and lumber, that are used to make goods and services.

Car manufacturers, for example, need the metals, plastics, and other materials to make a car. They also

CONSUMER ACTION

Pablo is the assistant manager of the Double Dip ice cream shop. Another ice cream shop just opened up in town. Pablo noticed that Double Dip is losing customers to the other ice cream shop. What actions should Pablo consider to win back customers?

need special equipment, workers trained to run the equipment, and large buildings for the equipment and workers. After the cars are built, they are shipped to various car dealerships where salespeople sell the cars to consumers. These are just a few of the human and nonhuman resources required to produce the car you want to buy.

Economics is the study of how economic systems work. In this lesson, you will learn about four types of economic systems. These are traditional, command, market, and mixed economies.

Traditional Economy

Through most of human history, people have lived in traditional economies. In a **traditional economy**, the ways to produce products are passed from one generation to the next. Parents teach children how to produce goods and services. Children pass these methods on to their children.

© Corel

Tribes in remote areas of the world still live in a traditional economy. Parents teach children how to produce hunting tools as well as how to hunt, weave baskets, and create jugs to carry water.

Our society still contains some elements of a traditional economy. Your parents probably taught you how to cook, clean, and use a bank account.

Command Economy

Through most of the 20th century, several nations had command economies. In a **command economy**

the government owned most resources and made most economic decisions. Each company received a government plan that told it what to produce. The government determined all prices, styles, colors, and even the amounts of products produced.

Individuals within a command economy had no say in production and often not even their role in it. If the government told you that you would be an assembly-line worker, then that is what you would be.

The former Soviet Union was one of the best-known countries with a command economy. In the late 20th century, the Soviet Union broke up into different countries and moved toward a market economy. Now the best-known command economies are North Korea and Cuba.

CheckPoint

What is a traditional economy? What is a command economy? Choose a product and describe how that product might be produced differently in these two economic systems.

Market Economy

The primary economic system in most industrialized countries is a market, or *capitalist,* economy. Under a **market economy**, people, rather than the government, own the resources and run the businesses. The purpose of most businesses operating under a market economy is to earn a profit.

Profit is the difference between the money received from selling a product and the cost of producing that product.

Profit = Price − Cost

Individuals, not the government, make most economic decisions in a market economy. Businesses are free to choose which products to produce and how to produce them. They can set their own prices.

Customers are free to buy any goods and services they choose. Buyers and sellers are free to make transactions among themselves, without government interference.

VOTE Your Wallet

Suppose a foreign country has companies that manufacture widgets. Because there are low wages, they are able to sell their widgets at a very low price. To keep out competition, there is a hefty tax on products from other countries.

A plant in your community manufactures similar widgets. The United States has no trade barriers and imposes no taxes on products from the foreign country. The foreign companies are allowed to sell their widgets at a lower price to your customers. When you try to export your widgets to the foreign country, the foreign country taxes your products at a high rate. Because of this competition, the plant in your community loses sales and might have to shut down.

Would you ask your representative in Congress to support import taxes on widgets from the foreign country? Why or why not? What are some possible long-term consequences of this action?

Mixed Economy

The economic system in the United States is not a pure market economy. Our government does control the economy in some ways. For example, it sets the rates that public utilities, such as electric companies, can charge consumers.

For the good of society, the government also sets limits on what businesses and individuals may do. For example, no one is allowed to discard hazardous waste into a river. Also, a business may not make false claims about its products.

Because our economy is a mixture of a market economy with some aspects of a command economy (government control), our system is really a **mixed economy**. A market economy, however, is the dominant economic system in the United States.

© Getty Images/PhotoDisc

CheckPoint

What is the purpose of running a business in a market economy? Why do nations with a market economy really have a mixed economy?

© Getty Images/PhotoDisc

Demand and Supply

The basic problem facing every economy is scarcity. **Scarcity** is the situation in which consumers' wants are greater than the resources available to satisfy those wants. Resources are required to produce goods and services, and resources are limited. Resources used for one product can't then be used for another. Every society must decide what it will use its scarce resources to produce.

In a market economy such as in the United States, the choices individual consumers make every day determine how society's scarce resources will be used. By your choices, you and every other consumer determine what will be produced, how much will be produced, and what the prices will be. Your choices, together, create the market forces of demand and supply.

Demand

Demand is the quantity of a good or service that consumers are *willing* and *able* to buy at various *prices* during a given *time* period. So to be included in the overall demand for tacos, you must first have enough money to buy them (the *ability*). Then you must be willing to spend your money for tacos instead of for something else (the *willingness*).

Say you have the money and are willing to spend it on tacos. You might buy four of them each week if they cost $1 each. Your quantity demanded for tacos would then be four per week.

But how many would you buy at different *prices*? Say the price went up to $2 apiece. Maybe now you would buy only two tacos a week. The *law of demand* says that consumers will demand more of a product at a lower price than at a higher price.

When the relationship between price and quantity demanded is shown on a graph, it is called a *demand curve.*

In the demand curve graph, notice that the demand curve slopes downward from left to right. This means that as the price goes up (along the vertical *y*-axis), the quantity demanded goes down (along horizontal *x*-axis). As the price of tacos goes up, consumers will buy fewer of them.

to make available for sale at various prices over a given time period. The *law of supply* says that producers are willing to offer more of a product for sale at a higher price than at a lower price. As the price rises, the quantity supplied increases.

This relationship between price and quantity supplied, shown on a graph, is the *supply curve.*

Demand Curve

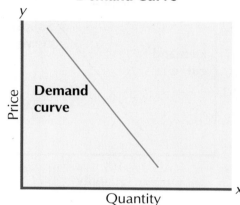

Supply Curve

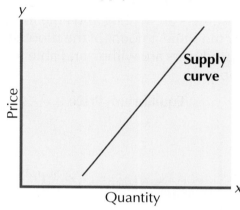

Supply

Supply is the quantity of a product that producers are willing and able

Notice that the supply curve graph slopes upward. As the price of a product goes up, producers will supply more of that product for sale.

Equilibrium

By combining the supply and demand curves on the same graph, you can see how supply and demand together determine how much of a product will be produced and the equilibrium price. The **equilibrium price** for a product is the price at which the quantity supplied exactly equals the quantity demanded of that product.

That is, at the equilibrium price, consumers are willing and able to buy the same amount of the product as producers are willing and able to supply.

Equilibrium Price

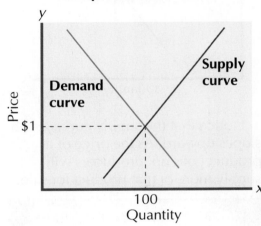

In the graph, the equilibrium price is the price at which the supply and demand curves cross. For this example, suppose that when tacos are offered for sale at $1 apiece, consumers will buy 100 of them. At this price, producers supply exactly the same number of tacos to the market.

Surplus What happens if taco producers raise the price to $2 apiece? According to the law of demand, consumers will buy fewer tacos.

In the surplus graph, the price of $2 corresponds to a quantity of 50 on the demand curve. In this case, at $2, consumers will demand only 50 tacos. Maybe they will choose to buy hamburgers or pizzas with their money instead. But at $2 on the supply curve, taco producers will choose to supply 150 tacos. The higher prices encourage them to make more tacos in the hope of earning a greater profit per taco.

Surplus Graph

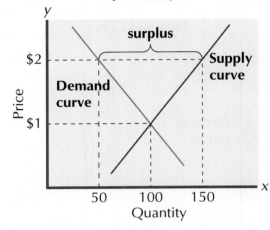

The result, however, is a surplus of 100 tacos. Producers supply 150 tacos, but consumers buy only 50. This excess quantity supplied, or *surplus,* will eventually force producers to lower the price so they can sell their overstock of tacos.

As the price comes down, consumers will buy more tacos until the price returns to the equilibrium price. At the equilibrium price, the quantity demanded equals quantity supplied.

Shortage   The market forces of supply and demand cause prices to reach equilibrium no matter which way they go.

In the shortage graph, you can see the result if prices fall below the equilibrium price.

Suppose that the price of tacos is $0.50 apiece. Consumers will be willing to buy more of them. But producers receive less per taco, encouraging them to use more of their resources to make something else that they hope will be more profitable. They will supply fewer tacos for customers to buy. In the shortage graph, the price of $0.50 corresponds to a quantity of 125 tacos on the demand curve. But at $0.50 on the supply curve, producers are supplying only 75 tacos. There is a shortage of 50 tacos.

IN CLASS ACTIVITY

Suppose you owned a restaurant. Create an economic scenario like the taco example used in this lesson. Use a product and draw graphs to represent what you think would be the supply, demand, and equilibrium price for this product.

This shortage creates upward pressure on the price. Consumers are willing and able to buy more tacos than are available for sale. To take advantage of this excess quantity demanded, producers will start raising the price, until it again reaches equilibrium.

These examples show how demand and supply work together to determine how much of a product is produced and at what price. As you can see, the buying decisions you and other consumers make influence how the economy works.

Shortage Graph

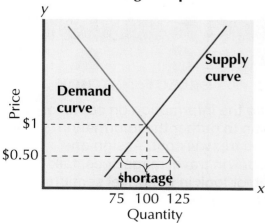

CheckPoint

How do demand and supply work together to determine prices and how much producers will produce?

1. What is the difference between human and nonhuman resources?

2. Describe the four economic systems identified in this chapter in your own words.

3. Why do governments limit individual freedoms in the marketplace?

4. Why are many nations really operating as a mixed economy?

5. Why does a demand curve normally slope downward from left to right?

6. When the demand and supply curves are on the same graph, how do they show the equilibrium price?

THINK CRITICALLY

7. CONSUMER ACTION Pablo is facing competition from another store. Make a list of questions you might ask Pablo to discover how the competitor is able to win over his customers.

8. COMMUNICATE Write about a purchase you recently made. How did you benefit from this purchase? How did the seller benefit?

9. Draw a flow chart to illustrate the production of a product you know something about or that you can imagine. Start with bringing together the raw materials, production, distribution, and the sale to the customer. Label the human and nonhuman resources for each step.

10. Think of a successful business in your neighborhood. How does this business serve its customers? How do its customers help make it a success?

11. COMMUNICATE Imagine what it would be like to be a manager of a factory in a command economy. Write a paragraph describing your responsibilities. Then imagine what it might be like to be a manager in a similar factory in a market economy. Write a paragraph describing these responsibilities. Then write a paragraph about the differences you notice between the two economic systems.

12. Suppose the equilibrium price for tickets to first-run movies is $9. In terms of supply and demand, explain what happens if theaters raise their price to $12 per ticket.

DECISION MAKING PROJECT

SPECIFY   **SEARCH**   **SIFT**   **SELECT**   **STUDY**

SEARCH   Write a plan for gathering the information on costs for your group trip. Then follow your plan to gather the information you need to determine how much the trip will cost. Assign one place to each person to research. Look in travel magazines, talk to a travel agent, get on the Internet, or look in the travel section of your local paper. Don't forget about meals!

© Getty Images/PhotoDisc

GOALS

DEFINE
the profit motive

EXPLAIN
the role of consumers
in a market economy

1.4 Consumer's Role in the Economy

Making Decisions in a Market Economy

In a market economy, customers and businesses operate without much government interference. Consumers are free to buy. Producers are free to sell. Both buyers and sellers gain in a transaction because they both get what they want.

Suppose you spent $60 for a wool sweater at a store. You bought the sweater because you valued it more than the $60 you spent to get it. The store sold the sweater for $60 because it could make a profit at that price. Both buyers and sellers benefit when they make exchanges in a market economy.

Information for the Economy

Exchanges in a market economy do more than benefit buyers and sellers. They also provide information that helps the economic system work.

CONSUMER ACTION

Yolanda paints houses to earn money while she is going to school. She is concerned, because after she pays for the paint, brushes, and gas to get to the job, she doesn't earn much per hour for her work. What can she do to help her business be more profitable?

25

The Store When customers buy items, stores gain information about customers' buying habits. If more people buy the same sweater that you did, the store will order more sweaters from the manufacturer.

The Manufacturer The store's request for more sweaters might cause the manufacturer to place new orders for wool. If lots of consumers buy wool sweaters, then sweater manufacturers might hire additional workers to make more sweaters. Your consumer decision helped to determine what the manufacturer would make and what the store would offer for sale.

© Getty Images/PhotoDisc

Prices

Prices also provide information that influences a market economy. Let's say Company A sets a higher price for similar products than Company B. Most consumers will buy from Company B, so Company A will make few sales. The lack of sales tells Company A that it must change if it wants to stay in business.

Profits are up!

© Getty Images/PhotoDisc

Company A has three basic choices.

1. Lower the price.

2. Convince customers to pay the higher price.

3. Stop offering the product for sale.

The owners of Company A will make the choice they think will lead to the greatest profit.

The Profit Motive

The most important reason to run a business in a market economy is to earn a profit. Companies that do not earn a profit will not last. They can increase profits in three ways.

1. **Reduce Costs** They might find less expensive raw materials or buy machines that are more efficient.

2. **Change Price** By changing prices, the company may increase profits. It could lower prices to gain more sales. Or, it could raise prices and earn a larger profit on each sale.

3. **Increase Quantity of Products Sold** Businesses often use advertising to encourage consumers to buy their products.

CheckPoint

What role does profit play in a market economy? How do your consumer decisions help the economy work?

Consumer Economics

A **consumer** is anyone who buys or uses products. Most of the time, consumers purchase the products they consume. In some cases, consumers use products bought by others. You might ride your friend's bicycle or watch your brother's television.

These are acts of consumption. It is more the act of use that makes you a consumer than the act of buying. **Consumer economics** is the study of the role consumers play in an economic system.

Consumers in Charge

More than 200 years ago, a British economist, Adam Smith, described an idea he called *consumer sovereignty.* The word *sovereignty* means to be in charge of something. Smith argued that in a market economy, consumers are in charge. Consumer choices determine what goods and services are produced.

Consumers Determine Products

Profits result from selling products for more than it costs to make them. A business that sells no products will earn no profit. To earn a profit, businesses must produce products that consumers buy. Therefore, when consumers spend their money, they determine what products are produced.

Suppose two restaurants open near your school. One sells pizza, and the other sells sandwiches. You and your friends prefer to buy pizza rather than sandwiches. If many consumers prefer pizza over sandwiches, can the sandwich shop stay in business? You and your friends, along with other consumers in your area, have the power to decide which restaurant will succeed. In an economic sense, the consumer rules.

Benefits of Competition

Competition is the contest among sellers to win customers. Competition exists when several companies offer similar products for sale. When you buy an apple, you probably don't care where it was grown. You care about its price and quality. A farmer who offers apples for a higher price than other farmers won't sell many. Or, if the farmer's apples are of poor quality compared to other farmers' apples, customers will buy from the other farmers.

Serve Consumers

Competition is at the heart of capitalism and mixed economies. Competition forces businesses to serve consumers. The only way companies can earn a profit is to offer good quality products that consumers want to buy at a fair price. Business owners may think they are working for themselves, but they are really serving consumers.

© Getty Images/PhotoDisc

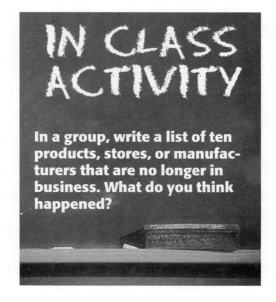

IN CLASS ACTIVITY

In a group, write a list of ten products, stores, or manufacturers that are no longer in business. What do you think happened?

© Getty Images/PhotoDisc

CheckPoint

What does *consumer sovereignty* mean? How do consumer choices help determine which businesses thrive or fail? How does competition benefit consumers?

Efficiency and Profits

Businesses use resources to create goods and services, and resources cost money. Companies must pay workers and buy raw materials and equipment.

As companies compete, they must find ways to use their resources efficiently. In other words, they must produce products at low costs so they can sell the products at a price consumers are willing to pay and still make a profit.

Suppose that two companies produce skateboards. Company A is very efficient and produces high-quality skateboards at a low cost. Company B is not efficient and produces low-quality skateboards at higher costs. Since Company A produces at a lower cost, it can offer its skateboards to consumers at a lower price and still make a profit.

If you have a choice of buying a better skateboard at a lower price from Company A, you will most likely buy from Company A. Most consumers will not buy from Company B, so Company B won't make a profit.

Eventually, Company B will go out of business.

Profitable companies are doing these three things.

1. Selling products consumers want to buy.

2. Selling products at a price consumers are willing to pay.

3. Taking in more money from sales than the company spends to produce the products.

Profits also influence how people make their spending decisions. A firm that is profitable is better able to pay for new tools or hire more skilled workers. This can help it make even more desirable products. It can also buy more advertising to influence consumers.

As a consumer, you play a vital role in our economic system. As you buy goods and services, you create sales that provide profit. To carry out your role in the economy, you need to make good choices.

GUESS WHAT

In a recent year, more than 16 million businesses were owned by individuals in the United States. Of these, only about 12 million earned a profit.

CheckPoint

Why must companies operate efficiently? What three things must companies do to earn a profit?

TRY THESE

1. How do both buyers and sellers gain when they complete transactions?

2. How do prices and transactions between buyers and sellers help the economy work?

3. What three choices does a failing company have for trying to increase its profits?

4. What does the term *consumer sovereignty* mean?

5. List three things that a profitable company does.

6. Why do companies fail that do not serve their customers?

THINK CRITICALLY

7. **CONSUMER ACTION** Yolanda wants to find a way to make her house-painting business more profitable. If you were Yolanda, what alternatives would you consider for increasing your profits? What choice would you make? Why? If your choice didn't result in greater profits, what alternatives would you consider?

8. Identify a local business that you believe is profitable. Describe how its profits allow it to serve you better and influence your spending decisions.

9. In what ways is the *consumer in charge*? When you are in a store, do you think that you are in charge of the transaction? Why or why not?

10. **COMMUNICATE** Think of two stores that compete with each other to sell similar products to you. Write about how they compete and how these stores try to convince you to buy their products.

11. What are some actions that businesses take to increase efficiency? Think of a business in your community that you know has increased efficiency. What did the business do?

12. Recall a recent purchase you made. What information did you provide the seller? What do you think is a possible consequence of the seller having this information?

DECISION MAKING PROJECT

 SPECIFY   SEARCH   **SIFT**   SELECT   STUDY

SIFT Now that your group has gathered information about costs for your trip, you can evaluate your options. Write down and discuss the benefits, costs, and opportunity costs for each option. Also, record your preferences for mode of transportation, lodging along the way, or any other details of the trip.

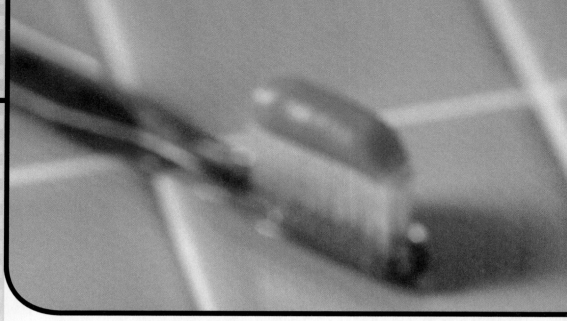

1.5 Advertising and Consumer Decisions

Types of Advertising

Businesses advertise to encourage consumers to buy their products so the businesses can make a profit. Different types of ads try to influence in different ways. Some want to make you aware of new products or brands. Others inform you about product features. Still others compare their products to competitors' products to try to convince you that theirs are better.

The information in ads can help you make a rational decision. Ads can also entertain you while they sell their product. The customer is in charge, so businesses want to let you know about their products. More customer awareness can lead to more sales.

CONSUMER ACTION

Emil saw an ad on TV for a tooth-whitening paste. The ad said that the product would make his teeth three shades lighter. Emil wanted whiter teeth, so he bought the toothpaste. He brushed with the toothpaste for two months and didn't notice any change in the color of his teeth. What decision making mistakes did Emil make? On what kind of ad did he base his decision?

© Getty Images/PhotoDisc

Brand Advertising

The purpose of *brand advertising* is to cause you to remember a particular brand name. The advertisers hope that if you remember the brand name, you will be more likely to buy the product when you shop.

This type of advertising is often used to introduce new products to consumers or to reinforce consumer loyalty to an existing brand. For example, think of soft drinks. If you usually buy the brand you think of first, then brand advertising has influenced your buying decisions.

Jingles and Slogans   Advertising jingles or slogans are an effective type of brand advertising. Have you ever caught yourself humming a jingle from a radio ad? These catchy tunes entertain you, so you remember the brand.

Benefits of Brands   A benefit of brands is that if you like the product quality when you buy it the first time, then you can usually depend on getting the same quality the next time you buy that brand. You won't have to spend as much time looking for the quality you want.

Costs of Brand Advertising

To pay the cost of advertising, businesses may have to increase the price of the product. If you look at all your options, you will notice that often the price of the familiar brand is higher than the price of unfamiliar brands or products that carry the name of the retail store.

The unfamiliar brands and unbranded products could have the same quality as the familiar brand, yet cost less. Shop around and evaluate your options.

CheckPoint

Why is brand advertising a good way to introduce new products?

Informative Advertising

Informative advertising is designed to influence you to buy a product by educating you about the product's benefits. This type of ad is often used for complex or highly technical products that consumers may not understand, such as computers and automobiles.

Buy the Numbers?

A company selling satellite television service made this claim in a newspaper ad.

What factual information does this ad provide? What questions would you want the company to answer before you purchase its service? What else would you do before signing up with this service?

> *You can enjoy hundreds of television channels for about the same cost as renting one video tape each day.*

For example, an ad for a car may explain the benefits of features, such as anti-lock brakes, fuel-injection systems, or side impact air bags.

Informative Ads and Decision Making Informative advertising provides information that helps you make a good buying decision. After all, you need to know what anti-lock brakes do before you can decide if you want them.

But keep in mind that the purpose of any advertisement is to sway you toward buying the advertised product. No ad will tell you about the downside of the product or about the lower price at a competitor's store.

CheckPoint

Why do sellers of complex or technical products often use informative advertising?

Comparative Advertising

Some advertising tries to win your favor by comparing its product's qualities to those of a competing product. This is *comparative advertising*. The purpose of the ad is to convince you

to buy the advertised product instead of the targeted competing product.

To accomplish this goal, comparative ads will always be slanted in favor of the advertised product. For instance, fast-food chain A may advertise that it offers a healthier menu than does fast-food chain B. This may be true. Chain A's burgers might also taste like hockey pucks, but their comparative ad will not mention this.

Comparative Ads and Decision Making Comparative ads supply useful information. From them, you can learn what the advertiser considers the best qualities of its product. If you value these qualities, you might evaluate the product further.

Comparative ads also tell you the

Check the labels of the leading detergents! Only Kleen has the patented stain-fighting enzymes to get your wash extra- *KLEEN!*

LAUNDRY DETERGENT
25% more!
KLEEN
which sock is the KLEEN sock?

Which sock is the KLEEN sock?

We get your whites whiter!

competitor's weaknesses. Though the weaknesses may be exaggerated, at least you know what to investigate when you evaluate the competing product.

Defensive Advertising

To counter attacks from comparative ads, businesses often use *defensive advertising* to respond to claims made by the other companies.

If the producer of Brand X detergent claims its product removes stains better than Brand Y, the producer of Brand Y may respond by pointing out that its product is color-safe and will not cause clothing to fade after repeated washings the way Brand X does.

Don't be fooled by other detergent claims!
Only Kleen detergent has the patented stain-fighting enzymes at the best price.

KLEEN!

Which sock is the KLEEN sock?

Defensive Ads and Decision Making
Defensive advertising does not provide a complete or balanced picture of a product any more than comparative advertising does. The company is trying to convince you that its product is the best choice.

Just recognize comparative and defensive advertising for what they are. Use the information they supply along with other information you gather when you evaluate your alternatives.

CheckPoint

What is comparative advertising? Why does it cause other companies to run defensive ads?

Persuasive Advertising
Persuasive advertising is designed to appeal to your emotions to influence you to buy, but it doesn't provide much useful information. The ads try to convince you that owning a particular product will make you happier, more successful, or more satisfied. The ads focus on creating a desire in you to buy the product rather than on providing information that might help you evaluate it.

Persuasive ads often portray attractive people who appear happy or popular because they are using the advertised product. The ads are trying to suggest that you will be as happy or popular as the people in the ads if you use this product.

Persuasive Ads and Decision Making
Most cosmetics are advertised in this way. Consider the cosmetics ads you have seen recently on television. You probably cannot

GUESS WHAT

Nearly 160,000 Americans join the military each year. The military runs ads during sports programs.

identify much factual information in them.

When you evaluate a product, remember that owning a particular product is not likely to change your life in any significant way. Ignore persuasive ads in your decision making process.

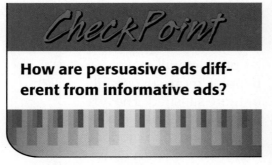

CheckPoint

How are persuasive ads different from informative ads?

Benefits and Costs of Advertising

Businesses spend over $250 billion each year trying to influence your buying decisions. Businesses advertise because they believe it will help them earn a profit.

No matter what you think of the advertising that you see every day, you and other consumers are paying for it directly or indirectly. Companies won't spend a dollar for advertising unless they believe it will help them earn a profit. The cost of advertising

is then built into the price you pay when you buy goods and services.

How Consumers Benefit from Advertising Consumers may benefit from advertising because the increased sales generated by advertising allow businesses to produce a higher volume of products. Higher volume often means lower production costs, and the lower costs may be passed on to consumers in the form of lower prices. This consumer benefit from advertising may or may not happen.

No matter what, businesses will continue to advertise to try to influence your decisions. Your best choice is to learn to use the information that advertising provides to help you make rational buying decisions.

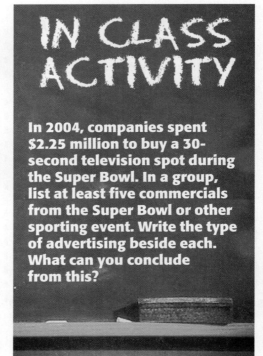

IN CLASS ACTIVITY

In 2004, companies spent $2.25 million to buy a 30-second television spot during the Super Bowl. In a group, list at least five commercials from the Super Bowl or other sporting event. Write the type of advertising beside each. What can you conclude from this?

Deceptive Ads Versus Puffery

It is often difficult to draw a line between which advertising is deceptive and which is not. Advertising does not give a totally balanced presentation of a product. To sell their products, advertisers try to make them look as good as possible, which can involve some exaggeration. The difference between legitimate and deceptive advertising is that *deceptive advertising* is deliberately designed to mislead you.

Puffery

The trick in evaluating advertising is to know how to distinguish innocent exaggeration, called *puffery,* from truly false claims. Puffery is legal. Deceptive advertising is not.

Factually Wrong

Advertisements that contain factually wrong statements are deceptive. If a company advertises that its vitamin supplement will "cure" arthritis, its advertisement is deceptive unless the company has proof that the statement is true. Often, this proof must come from scientific studies.

The government has the power to require companies to stop advertising

A Minnesota car dealer recently placed ads that offered cars for "half price." The attorney general of Minnesota sued him for false advertising. The dealer explained that the advertised cars were being leased, and the cost of a three-year lease was about half of the price of buying a car. He argued his ads were correct and honest. The courts did not agree and required him to stop using the ads. Do you believe the courts were right? Why or why not? Would you be suspicious of any ad that offered a car for half price? How would you check it out?

deceptively by imposing heavy fines if they don't stop. The government has difficulty enforcing this law, however, because businesses can make small changes in their ads to avoid regulation.

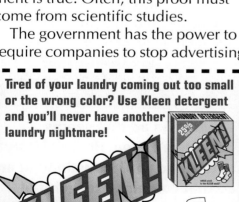

Tired of your laundry coming out too small or the wrong color? Use Kleen detergent and you'll never have another laundry nightmare!

Which sock is the KLEEN sock?

KLEEN! is the best detergent available to whiten your whites, brighten your brights!

Which sock is the KLEEN sock?

If the vitamin advertiser claims only that its supplement will make people "feel younger and more limber," the advertisement is perfectly legal. The phrase "feel younger and more limber" is so vague that it is difficult to prove in court that the claim is false.

Exaggerated Claims Are Legal

Exaggerated claims can mislead you yet still be legal. One common practice is to advertise sales with enormous markdowns of 50 percent or more. Claims like this may mean that the business first marked the products way up so it could then mark them down 50 percent and still earn a large profit.

This practice is legal. To avoid being misled by this gimmick, always compare prices among stores. Don't assume that a sale is really a sale without checking prices at other stores.

Is It Free?

Some advertisements offer *gifts* to customers who buy a particular product. Courts have ruled that it is deceptive to say a gift is *free* if customers are required to buy something else to receive it.

It is relatively easy to get by this rule. An ad could say *all expenses paid* instead of *free.* Or, the advertiser could use a photograph.

Suppose a car dealer offers a trip to Florida to any customer who buys a new car. Advertising the trip as free could be ruled deceptive. But a photograph showing a person receiving a ticket to Florida in front of a car dealership may not be ruled deceptive. The photo made no misleading *statement,* but the message would be clear.

Protecting Yourself from Deceptive Advertising

To avoid being deceived by advertising, always use the decision making process. The decision making process helps you approach buying decisions in an organized, logical manner. It recommends you gather information from several sources so that you don't make your decision based on an advertisement alone. The process also reminds you to evaluate the information and consider alternative choices.

CheckPoint

Think of an ad that seems deceptive to you. How did it try to mislead you? Now think of an ad that contains exaggerated claims. What is the difference between the two ads?

TRY THESE

1. Why do businesses advertise?

2. What are brand name products? What are the benefits and costs of brands for consumers?

3. How can informative advertising help you make good buying decisions?

4. Who pays for advertising?

5. How does advertising benefit consumers?

6. What makes an advertisement deceptive?

7. How can using the decision making process help you avoid being misled by deceptive advertising?

THINK CRITICALLY

8. **CONSUMER ACTION** Emil bought a toothpaste that an ad told him would make his teeth three shades whiter. But, the product didn't live up to its advertising claim. What decision making mistakes did Emil make? What kind of ad did he base his decision on? If you were Emil, what would you do differently next time to make a more rational buying decision?

9. What do you think of the advertising that bombards you every day? Does it help or confuse you? Do you believe it is a reliable source of information, or do you just ignore it?

10. How does an advertising jingle contribute to the goal of an ad? Let's say that you can easily remember the tune but not the name of the product. Would the jingle accomplish its goal?

11. Look at the ad on page 31. What type of advertising is being used? List the characteristics the ad has that tell you what type of advertising it is.

12. Look at the ad on page 32. What type of advertising is being used? List the characteristics the ad has that tell you what type of advertising it is.

13. Look at the ad on page 33. What type of advertising is being used?

List the characteristics the ad has that tell you what type of advertising it is.

14. Look at the table of TV advertising costs below. Why might advertisers have been willing to pay much higher prices to place ads during the Super Bowl or American Idol than for spots they could have purchased on typical daytime television shows? What do you suppose these advertising prices are based on? Why?

Cost of a 30-Second Major Network Advertisement in 2003–2004	
SHOW	**COST OF A 30-SECOND AD**
2004 Super Bowl	$2,250,000
American Idol	400,000
Who Wants to Be a Millionaire?	250,000
Oprah Winfrey Show	60,000
The Jerry Springer Show	13,500

15. Look at the ad on page 34. What type of advertising is being used? List the characteristics the ad has that tell you what type of advertising it is.

16. One of the ads on page 35 is illegal and one is legal. Identify which is which and explain why.

17. Look at the ad on page 36. What type of advertising is being used? List the characteristics the ad has that tell you what type of advertising it is.

© Getty Images/PhotoDisc

1.6 Be a Responsible Consumer

Consumers in Society

As an American, you have the freedom to make many decisions. You make choices for your own benefit. But the decisions you make can also have an impact on the lives of others.

For example, consumers who bought women's hats used to prefer hats with feathers of wild birds as decorations. To meet this consumer demand, hat manufacturers paid hunters to shoot birds for their feathers. Now, some of those species are extinct. Consumers' decisions to buy hats with feathers led to the birds' extinction.

You live in a community that you share with other people. In fact, you live in a worldwide community as well as your local community. Your actions affect other people. Your actions can even affect communities

CONSUMER **ACTION**

Gretchen lives in Reno, Nevada. She is proud of the rose garden she has grown. To keep her flowers healthy, she waters them for two hours every morning. For $3,000, she can buy an automatic watering system. It would reduce the amount of water she uses by 70 percent. What should she consider as she decides whether to purchase this system? How may her choice affect other consumers?

around the globe and, in the future, in space. The best decisions benefit the world community as well as you and your local community.

Sharing Limited Resources

Society can produce only so many goods and services. If a product is in short supply, who should receive the available product? The available product will be in demand, and the price will be high. Since wealthy people can pay more for the product, should they be allowed to buy all they want?

During World War II, most of the gasoline the country produced had to be used in the war effort. There wasn't enough gasoline left for everyone else who wanted to buy it.

The government could have allowed the price to increase. Instead, the government required the price to remain reasonable and limited everyone to three gallons per week. No matter how much money consumers had, they could buy only three gallons per week.

Suppose heating oil was scarce today. In cold climates, heating oil can mean the difference between life and death. Heating oil that you buy could mean that another family would freeze. Because resources are scarce, your buying decisions affect everyone else in your community.

Clean air is a scarce resource, too. Your decision to drive a car or mow your lawn contributes to the pollution in the air. In fact, the pollution in some American cities, such as Los Angeles, travels over mountains and pollutes other communities. Every day, consumer decisions affect people in other parts of the world.

Protecting Public Safety

Society places limits on individuals' freedom of choice. The government usually sets these limits, based on community values. Your rights to use your property as you like do not include actions that endanger other people.

Suppose you bought a car that could go 140 miles per hour. It is illegal for you to travel at this speed because it would be unsafe for other drivers as well as for yourself.

© Getty Images/PhotoDisc

CheckPoint

How can your consumer choices affect the people around you? Why does the government need to limit freedom of choice?

Using Natural Resources

Natural resources are precious and limited. Resources such as oil, coal, natural gas, forests, and plant and animal species take hundreds or even thousands of years to create. Once used, they cannot be replaced quickly. In some cases, they can't be replaced at all.

Your consumer choices often involve use of natural resources. You can choose to use resources in moderation or consume them without regard for future generations. Here are some examples of how consumer choices impact limited natural resources.

© Getty Images/PhotoDisc

Resource Consuming Products

Part of the American dream is to own a car. In a recent year, U.S. consumers bought more than 2 million sport utility vehicles (SUVs). SUVs have many desirable features.

Their greatest drawback is low gas mileage. Most SUVs get about 17 miles per gallon (mpg), compared to about 26 mpg for the average family car. The consumers who buy them are willing to pay for the extra gas they use.

The extra gas SUVs consume uses up the earth's supply of oil more quickly than other vehicles. SUVs emit more pollution into the atmosphere. Their large size creates more wear on public roads.

When you make your buying decisions, consider how your choice will impact the earth's resources. Use resources in moderation. Remember, the scarcer the resource, the higher the price in dollars and perhaps on the environment.

GUESS WHAT

In Las Vegas, more than half the water consumed is used for fountains, pools, and plantings. Water conservation has become a top priority as Las Vegas continues to expand.

Water

In recent years, the population in southwestern cities, such as Phoenix, Albuquerque, and Las Vegas, has grown rapidly. Many of these communities are having trouble supplying all the water their residents want. An important question is, "How much water do consumers really *need*?"

The southwestern states don't get much rainfall. Many people there have lawns and gardens that consume thousands of gallons of water each year.

Needs or Wants? Water is a *need*. We all need it to live. Yet, much of the water we consume every day we do not really need to live. We use water mostly for wants. Think about your showers or the times you leave the water running in the sink when you are doing something else.

Use water in moderation and don't pollute it. Water is as important to your pocketbook as it is to your body. If water were to become very scarce, costs of everything from utilities to dining out would skyrocket.

CheckPoint

What are some ways that you use natural resources to satisfy your wants instead of your needs? What decisions can you make in your daily life to use resources more responsibly?

Forest Products

Trees are used for many consumer products, such as paper, pencils, lumber for building, and furniture. Oxygen released by forests helps to clean the air.

In the past 20 years, some of the world's forests have been destroyed. As a result, thousands of the plants and animals that depend on the forests have become endangered or extinct.

PRIMARYSOURCES

R ead the following historic account of legislation to create a clean water supply in Boston. What does this tell you about the priorities of the community? What would you think if this Board came to buy your land? What would you do?

"The Metropolitan Water Act, Chapter 488 of the Acts of the year 1895, approved June 5, 1895, provided. . . that the Metropolitan Water Board was given broad powers, not only for the construction of the works, but also for the taking of property, for the changing of highways and railroads, and for the conduct of such operations as should be deemed necessary for protecting and preserving the purity of the water."

Forests benefit everyone, so use their products in moderation. Recycle paper products. Used paper and cardboard can be made into other useful products or reused.

The Environment

The environment in which you live affects your health and quality of life. Your decisions can help or harm your environment.

Garbage Americans, as a group, produce more than 1 billion pounds of trash each day. Trash buried in landfills takes hundreds of years to break down to become part of the soil. Some never will break down and will remain buried forever.

Trash that isn't buried is burned. Burning releases pollutants into the atmosphere. Burning fuel, such as gasoline, releases nearly 1.5 billion tons of carbon dioxide into the atmosphere per year in the United States alone.

Also, about 16 tons of waste is dumped into our nation's waterways every minute of every day.

Other Pollutants Some chemicals released into the atmosphere appear to have harmed the earth's ozone layer—the part of the earth's atmosphere that protects us from the sun's rays. Without the ozone layer, humans may get skin cancer at an alarming rate.

CYBER CONSUMER

Use the Internet to find at least two suppliers of recycled paper products. Compare the prices of the products they offer with those of products made from new resources. How may these prices affect people's willingness to buy recycled products?

Encourage Business Responsibility

As a group, you and other consumers have great power to influence businesses to operate in socially responsible ways. If many consumers buy more fuel-efficient cars, then car manufacturers will design cars to be more fuel efficient.

You can also encourage businesses to avoid polluting or wasting resources by buying products produced in environmentally responsible ways. Lists of businesses that produce responsibly are available from many sources. One list is the *National Green Pages,* prepared each year by CO-OP America.

Dispose of Waste Responsibly

We all want to live in a clean world, free of disease-causing pollution. You can help by deciding not to pollute any more than necessary in your daily life. Recycle what you can.

Recycling programs reduce the amount of trash discarded into the environment. As a consumer, you can encourage recycling by buying products made from recycled materials.

When you finish using products, dispose of them in a responsible way. Many states require businesses that sell potentially hazardous products, such as car batteries and motor oil, to accept these used products from consumers and dispose of them properly.

Most communities have special collection programs for hazardous household waste, such as old paint or cleaning products. Contact your local government offices for the programs in your area. Never pour solvents or oil down the sink or in the storm sewer.

© Getty Images/PhotoDisc

INTERNET ACTIVITY

More than 75 million tons of trash are recycled in the United States each year. Search the Internet for more recycling facts and recycling tips. Cite four recycling facts you discovered. Then list ten ways you and your family can reduce or recycle the trash you produce. E-mail your lists to your teacher.

Obey smog alert instructions. Sometimes your local government may ask you not to put gas in your car or drive in the middle of the day if you can avoid it. Pollutants from burning fuel can disperse more easily in the evening. Your local government may ask you not to mow or water your lawn on certain days to limit pollution and water consumption.

Respect Your Neighbors

You live in a world community. What you do affects people around you and sometimes people around the world. Consume responsibly. Conserve. You and consumers like you can save the earth's limited resources for future generations.

CheckPoint

How can your consumer decisions influence businesses to operate responsibly? What recycling programs does your community offer?

TRY THESE

1. How can your consumer decisions affect people in your local community and world community?

2. Give three examples of the rights of an individual consumer conflicting with the rights of others in the community.

3. What are some scarce natural resources? What goods and services do you buy that use these resources?

4. What decisions can you make to conserve natural resources?

5. How can you dispose of waste responsibly?

6. Why is it important to dispose of waste responsibly?

7. How can you encourage businesses to operate more responsibly?

THINK CRITICALLY

8. **CONSUMER ACTION** Gretchen is trying to decide whether or not to buy an automatic watering system. Write a one-page essay identifying the benefits and costs of each option. Be sure to identify some opportunity costs. Evaluate how her choice would affect other people in her community. Do you think the benefits are worth the costs Gretchen would pay? Explain.

9. What could you and your family do to protect the environment?

10. List some consequences to the environment and humans if waste is not disposed of properly. Use a real-life example if possible. Suggest some ways to prevent improper disposal of waste.

11. **COMMUNICATE** Call your local government offices and find out what programs your community offers for recycling and disposing of hazardous products. Write down what you find out and present it to the class.

12. Using the Internet or your local library, find two laws that require businesses to operate responsibly. What do these laws require businesses to do? How do these laws protect you and your community?

13. **COMMUNICATE** Suppose a news program reported that a business in your community had been dumping hazardous waste in a local river. Write a paragraph on what you would do.

DECISION MAKING PROJECT

SPECIFY · SEARCH · SIFT · **SELECT** · STUDY

SELECT Now that your group has evaluated your options for the trip, make your decisions. Prepare a presentation to the class. Present your work at each step in the decision making process. Display the ads you gathered. Tell the class what you decided to do for each aspect of the trip. Justify your decisions with the information you gathered.

ASSESSMENT

KEY IDEAS

Decisions, Decisions

1. As a consumer, you have the power to influence how businesses operate.
2. Values are your principles — the standards you use to judge what is right and wrong or good and bad. Values are often based on cultural, social, and demographic factors.
3. Needs are things you can't live without. Wants are things you would like to have but can live without.
4. Over your life span, your goals will change. Your life cycle is made up of important events that take place during different phases of your life. To achieve your life-span goals, you should set short-term goals.
5. Opportunity cost is the value of the next best alternative that you give up when you make a choice.

Make Decisions

6. A decision making process is a logical step-by-step process that will help you make rational buying decisions.
7. The steps in a good decision making process are Specify, Search, Sift, Select, and Study.
8. Your needs, wants, and values all enter into your buying goals.
9. To evaluate your options, identify the benefits and costs (including opportunity costs) of each option. Then compare and select the option that has the most benefits and least costs for you. Study your choice later to learn from your decisions.

Understand Economic Systems

10. Production is the creation of goods and services. To produce goods and services, businesses use both human and nonhuman resources.
11. Different nations have had traditional, command, market, or mixed economies.
12. Scarcity exists when consumers' wants are greater than the resources available to satisfy those wants.
13. Demand is the quantity of a good or service that consumers are willing and able to buy at various prices during a given time period.
14. Supply is the quantity of a product that producers are willing and able to make available for sale at various prices over a given time period.
15. The equilibrium price for a product is the price at which the quantity supplied exactly equals the quantity demanded of that product.

Consumer's Role in the Economy

16. Profit is the difference between the cost required to create a product and the money received from selling it. Profitable firms are often able to influence consumers' spending habits.
17. A consumer is anyone who buys or uses a good or service.
18. Competition, a contest among sellers to win customers, forces businesses to serve customers.

Advertising and Consumer Decisions

19. Brand advertising tries to make you remember the brand name.
20. Informative advertising encourages you to buy a product by educating you about its benefits.
21. Comparative advertising compares one product's qualities to those of another. Targets of unfavorable comparative ads often respond with defensive advertising.

22. Persuasive advertising tries to encourage you to buy but doesn't provide useful information.
23. Advertising can benefit consumers by increasing sales and reducing production costs and prices of products.
24. Advertising can be misleading yet still legal. If an ad is deliberately misleading, it is deceptive advertising.

Be a Responsible Consumer
25. The earth's natural resources are limited and not quickly replaced. Use resources in moderation and recycle to conserve them.
26. Dispose of waste responsibly. Encourage businesses to act responsibly.

TERMS REVIEW

Match each term on the left with its definition on the right.
Some terms may not be used.

a. command economy
b. consumer
c. consumer economics
d. demand
e. economics
f. equilibrium price
g. goals
h. life cycle
i. life span
j. life-span goal
k. life-span plan
l. long-term goal
m. market economy
n. mixed economy
o. need
p. opportunity cost
q. production
r. profit
s. rational buying decision
t. resource
u. scarcity
v. short-term goal
w. supply
x. traditional economy
y. value
z. want

1. a person who buys or uses a good or service
2. the time between a person's birth and death
3. the value of the next best alternative that is given up when a choice is made
4. the price at which the quantity of a product supplied exactly equals the quantity demanded
5. what businesses use to produce goods and services
6. what a decision making process will help you make
7. the government owns most resources and makes most economic decisions
8. a plan to reach long-term goals within a person's life
9. the quantity of a product that consumers are willing and able to buy at various prices during a given time period
10. a system that has characteristics of a market and a command economy
11. the difference between the cost of creating a product and the income received from selling it
12. something you would like but can live without
13. something you want to accomplish within a year
14. the creation of goods or services
15. study of how economic systems work
16. standard by which you live

CONSUMER DECISIONS

17. You often disagree with other members of your family about what to watch on television. How would you decide whether to buy a second television for your home?

18. You like a shirt that's $35. You have the $35 but want to use it to go out next weekend. How would you decide whether to buy the shirt?

19. You have been offered a job at a community health clinic after school. It doesn't pay much, but it would be good experience because you want to be a nurse. If you take the job, you won't be able to play on your school's basketball team. How could your life-span goal help you make this decision?

20. How would you decide whether to drive to work or take the bus? How might your decision affect other people and the environment?

THINK CRITICALLY

21. You are thinking about joining a CD-of-the-month club. The club offers your choice of three CDs for just $1 each, plus $3.99 shipping and handling for each order, regardless of the number of CDs shipped. To get these low-priced CDs, you have to agree to buy at least five additional CDs for $15.99 each, plus shipping and handling, during your first year of membership. When you buy CDs at your neighborhood store, you typically pay $14.99 each. Would you join the club? Why or why not? What other factors would you consider?

22. On one graph, draw a demand curve and a supply curve that represent the demand for and supply of a particular video game. Make the equilibrium price $30 and the equilibrium quantity 500. Suppose the game's manufacturer just raised the price to $40. On your graph, show what happens to quantities demanded and supplied. Make up numbers as needed. Then write an explanation of what happens and why.

LOOK IT UP

23. Identify a product that has become more popular recently. Investigate what type of advertising has been created to encourage its sales.

24. Find out what detergent your family often buys. Identify two competing products. Find information about these products and evaluate their quality. Will your family continue to buy the product it always buys or switch?

WHICH IS THE BEST DEAL?

You need to have your house painted. You've gotten the estimates below. What is the most it would cost to have Franklin & Sons paint your house? What other factors would you consider? What decision would you make? Explain.

Alternative 1 Paint Unlimited offers to do the job for $2,200, all costs included.

Alternative 2 Franklin & Sons, Inc. will charge $20 per hour plus $14 for each gallon of paint used. Mr. Franklin estimates that it will take 80 to 90 hours and 20 gallons of paint to do the job. He has committed to staying within his estimate.

Alternative 3 Your neighbor's son has offered to paint your house for $8 an hour, if you provide the paint. He doesn't know how long it will take him.

POINT YOUR BROWSER TO

www.ee4c.swlearning.com
Complete the activity for Chapter 1.

25. The government has established a rule for advertising that may appear on Saturday morning children's television programs. Find out what the rule is. Does it make sense to you?

26. Investigate laws that have been passed in your community to protect its environment. Do these laws seem reasonable to you? How do they limit individual freedoms?

INSIDE THE NUMBERS

27. About 290 million people live in the United States. Each person, on average, produces 4.4 pounds of trash each day. How much trash is produced in the U.S. in a year? Nearly 30 percent of this trash is recycled. If we could increase this to 40 percent, how much less trash would we discard? What would Americans have to do to accomplish this recycling goal?

28. Suppose you were offered two different summer jobs. One is working at a concession stand at a ballpark. It would pay $8 per hour for 20 hours per week. The other job is a sales associate at a clothing store. That job pays $7 per hour for only 16 hours a week, but it also pays a 5 percent commission of any sales you make. You think you could sell $100 worth of clothing an hour. Which job would you take to earn the most income possible? What other factors should you consider when you choose?

CURRICULUM CONNECTION

29. **ENGLISH** Upton Sinclair wrote *The Jungle* soon after 1900. In this book, he described unhealthy conditions in the meat-packing industry. This book led to the passage of the Pure Food and Drugs Act in 1906. Find Sinclair's book in a library and read several chapters. What did the book reveal that probably influenced the government to pass a law to require food manufacturers to operate more responsibly?

30. **SCIENCE** Many different types of scientists are involved in working to recycle the products we use. Look on the Internet or in the library to find job titles for five scientists that work with recycled products. What do they do? What classes did these scientists have to take?

JOURNAL RECAP

31. After reading this chapter, review the answers you wrote to the questions in Journal Journey. Have your opinions changed?

SPECIFY   SEARCH   SIFT   SELECT   STUDY

STUDY After your presentation, ask the class to identify something that could mess up your trip. Then use the information you have already gathered to describe a way around this problem so that your trip will be a success.

Chapter 2

BUYING TECHNOLOGY PRODUCTS
LET'S TALK TECH

WHAT'S AHEAD

EXPLODING MYTHS

Fact or Myth?
What do you think is true?

1. When a new technology-based product comes out, you should buy it right away.

2. Advertising on the Internet benefits only the advertisers. It is just a pain for everyone else.

3. If you don't give out information about yourself over the Internet, then your privacy is safe.

JOURNAL JOURNEY

WRITE IN YOUR JOURNAL ABOUT THE FOLLOWING.

TECHNOLOGY-BASED PRODUCTS How confident are you in your ability to evaluate technology-based products, such as a computer? What would you look for? What questions would you ask?

USING THE INTERNET What is your opinion of the Internet? Is it fun? Helpful? Does anything worry you about being online? If so, what?

INTERNET SHOPPING How does Internet shopping compare to an evening at your local shopping mall? What is better about shopping online? What is better about shopping at the mall?

DECISION MAKING PROJECT

SPECIFY   **SEARCH**   **SIFT**   **SELECT**   **STUDY**

GET INTO THE INFORMATION AGE You have $1,200 to buy a computer system. Learn what you need to run word processing and spreadsheet applications, send e-mails, play games, and surf the Internet while staying within your budget.

GOAL

To learn how to shop for a computer, peripheral devices, and software.

PROJECT PROCESS

SPECIFY	**Lesson 2.3**
SEARCH	**Lesson 2.4**
SIFT	**Lesson 2.5**
SELECT	**Chapter Assessment**
STUDY	**Chapter Assessment**

2.1 Technology and Consumer Choice

Choosing Technology-Based Products

You are living in the 21st century—a time of new ideas and new technologies. Some people worry that they may not be able to keep up with all the changes. Consider the products you can buy. Compare them to those your parents or grandparents could buy when they were young. Some have stayed about the same. Other products you use did not exist 25 or 50 years ago. Or, they were different from the kinds available today.

Automobiles Cars produced in the 1960s were simple by today's standards. They had an engine, transmission, drive train, brakes, and four wheels. That was about all.

Today's cars have on-board computers that operate many of the car's systems. They are likely to have fuel injection, cruise control, air bags, and automatic braking systems. When consumers purchase a new car, they often don't really know what they are buying. Totally

CONSUMER ACTION

Larry likes to be first at everything. When a new product hits the market, you can be sure he will be first in line to buy one. He bought a PlayStation 2 system as soon as a local store had one. Did Larry make a rational buying decision? What benefits did Larry get from buying this new product right away? What were the drawbacks for Larry in buying now instead of waiting?

understanding modern automobiles is beyond the ability of most consumers. Also, people who repair today's cars need regular training to keep up with changing technologies.

Technology Challenge

New technology has changed consumers' ability to evaluate the goods and services they buy. How many of the technology-based products that you use can you honestly say you understand? How many could you repair if you wanted?

Decision Overload Change is good, but it also makes consumer decisions more difficult. The complexity of products has created a new problem—"decision overload." Consumers may feel overwhelmed by decisions they must make. As a result, they may not try to make *rational decisions*. They might think, "I can't figure it out. I don't know what's best. What's the use in trying? I'll just do what feels right and not worry about it."

This attitude is understandable but can lead to costly mistakes. Technology-based products are often expensive, so you have more to gain from a good decision and more to lose from a poor one. Careful evaluation of alternatives is the best way to get the most from your money.

CheckPoint

Why do consumers sometimes buy technology-based products without carefully evaluating their alternatives?

Obsolescence

With new technologies developing so rapidly, products bought only months ago may already be "old" or "obsolete." Do you remember the first video game you ever played? It was exciting at the time. But now, new technologies have improved video games so much that those old games seem prehistoric.

If you bought one of those old games when it first came out, you probably don't use it much now. You've moved on to new, more exciting games. When new technology makes products based on old technology out-of-date, this is called **technological obsolescence**.

© Getty Images/PhotoDisc

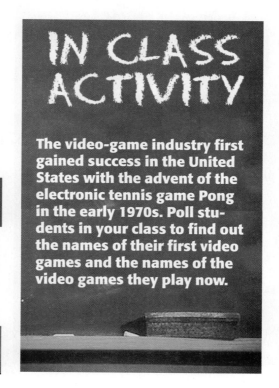

IN CLASS ACTIVITY

The video-game industry first gained success in the United States with the advent of the electronic tennis game Pong in the early 1970s. Poll students in your class to find out the names of their first video games and the names of the video games they play now.

Depreciation

New technologies can also cause products to decline in value. Products can lose value from wear and use. They can also lose value because technological advances make them obsolete. Older products can become worthless even when they work perfectly.

Suppose someone purchased a new, state-of-the-art computer for $2,500 in 1998. The owner became ill and never took the computer out of its box. How much would this "brand new" computer be worth today? Remember, the best measure of anything's value is the amount someone else is willing to pay for it. Would you be willing to pay $2,500 for a computer that can't run today's software? A decline in a product's value is called **depreciation**.

© Getty Images/PhotoDisc

Search for Information

You can gather information about technology-based products from many sources: magazines, newspapers, television, and the Internet. Unfortunately, information you find today may be out-of-date in only a few months. Suppose you spend hours evaluating new computers. You decide to wait because you don't have enough money saved. When you are finally ready to buy, the information will be out-of-date. You will have to search again.

From Businesses Information is also available from businesses that offer technology-based products for sale. Businesses, however, might not provide a balanced presentation. Naturally, they want to encourage you to buy their products instead of a competitor's.

Service Consumers who purchase technology-based products often must rely on the seller for help with the product. When it comes to new technology, service is important. If you buy something you don't understand, buy from an established business with a record for standing behind its products. These businesses value their reputations. If you need help with a product, a company that wants to keep your business will probably give you the most help.

CheckPoint

Why should you consider obsolescence when buying a computer?

© Getty Images/PhotoDisc

When Should You Buy?

If everyone in your class had a new computer program, would you rush out and buy it? If you did, would you be making a rational choice? Before you make this type of decision, be sure to give the process some time and thought. One problem with new technology is that it's hard to decide when to buy.

Out-of-Date Technology

If a product is likely to be out-of-date soon, should you put off buying it? Suppose you know that an MP3 player you want is likely to be improved. Would you buy it now, wait until it is on sale, or wait for the new model? Suppose you wait six months. How would you know that it wouldn't be better to wait nine months instead? If you wait, you can't use the MP3 player now. That is one cost of putting off your decision. What is the value of the effort you make trying to find the right time to buy? Is it possible that you might never buy the player?

High Price of New Technology

Prices charged when a product is new are usually the highest they will ever be. Companies spend large amounts of money to develop new products. The reward for companies that are first to bring a new product to market is the high price they can charge. Since no other company yet offers the product, consumers who want the product must buy from the company that introduced it. This premium price helps the company recover the costs of developing the product. Later, competition from other firms will likely force the original company to reduce its price.

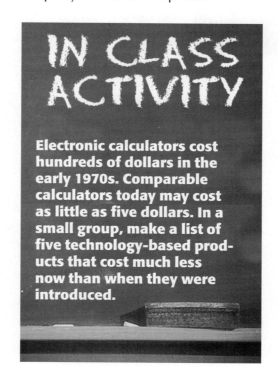

IN CLASS ACTIVITY

Electronic calculators cost hundreds of dollars in the early 1970s. Comparable calculators today may cost as little as five dollars. In a small group, make a list of five technology-based products that cost much less now than when they were introduced.

Product Quality of New Technology

Technology-based products are likely to have the most defects when they are first available. No amount of testing can uncover every "bug" in a new product. The computer operating system called Windows XP was introduced in 2001. Soon after its introduction, Microsoft's consumer help lines were flooded with calls from purchasers. Many users could not operate the program successfully. Six months later, most of the problems were solved. This did not provide satisfaction to consumers who bought the program early and were not able to use it, however.

As a general rule, "When in doubt, wait." It is almost always better to let others experience the difficulties of new products. Just a few months is usually enough time to make the difference.

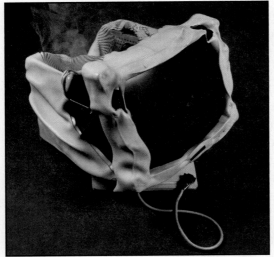
© Getty Images/PhotoDisc

Safety Hazards and New Products

"**B**ugs" found in new products can affect how well they work. When some operating systems were first introduced, there was a programming loophole. The loophole allowed access to a user's hard drive through the Internet. It became easier for hackers to do damage. Consumers who put off buying the systems avoided the problems. If you are not sure a new product is safe, you probably should wait to buy until you are sure.

Is It Ever Smart to Buy Now?

So, you should always wait to buy new products, right? Well, not always. Sometimes buying now is your best choice. Every purchase has an opportunity cost. Suppose a new product offers benefits important to you. You should not automatically avoid buying one just because it is new.

For example, the first home computers became available in the late 1970s. They were expensive and limited compared to those of today. But their ability to store and retrieve data made them very valuable to many people. People who ran home businesses or kept complicated financial records wanted them. They purchased the computers regardless of their high price and limitations. For these consumers, the value of the benefits outweighed the cost.

Rational Decision Whether your choice involves new or old technologies, you can make a rational purchase decision that is good for you by using the decision making process. The more complicated the product, the more important it is to evaluate your alternatives carefully. In this way, you can make the best possible decisions.

CheckPoint

Why can companies charge a high price for new products they develop and market first?

TRY THESE

1. How has technological change made it difficult for consumers to make rational decisions?

2. Why is technological obsolescence a problem for consumers?

3. Why do technology-based products often depreciate rapidly?

4. Why are new technology-based products often expensive?

5. How can you find up-to-date information about technology-based products?

6. What steps can you take to make rational choices when you buy new technology-based products?

7. When might buying a new product now be the best choice?

THINK CRITICALLY

8. **CONSUMER ACTION** Larry always wanted to be first to buy a new product. Explain the consequences for Larry of being first to buy the PlayStation 2 system. What are the benefits of buying the system right away? What are the drawbacks?

9. **CONSUMER ACTION** Assume that a few months after Larry bought a PlayStation 2, a competing firm brought out a new video game system. Should Larry buy the new system? How would you advise Larry to make a rational decision?

10. Choose a technology-based product you have used that did not meet your expectations. Write an e-mail to the manufacturer clearly explaining the problem and suggesting how you would like to see it resolved. Send this e-mail to your teacher.

11. **COMMUNICATE** Think of a technology-based product that you would really like to have. Search for information about that product, including price, features, and options. Use the decision making process to decide whether to buy now or wait. Write a paragraph explaining your decision.

12. Suppose that the manufacturer had already planned to have the functions you wanted in the new software upgrade. Would you buy it right away once it was available or would you wait? Why?

13. Write a paragraph about a purchase you made that was affected by "decision overload." Describe what happened. What did you learn?

© Getty Images/PhotoDisc

GOALS

IDENTIFY
equipment you need
to access the Internet

EXPLAIN
the trade-offs you must
consider in shopping
for an Internet service
provider

2.2 Move Into Cyberspace

Explosive Growth of the Internet

New technologies have introduced many exciting innovations. One that has brought the world into our homes is the **Internet**. Not many years ago, few people had ever heard of the Internet. Now, millions of people worldwide use the Internet daily.

Start of the Internet The Internet began in the 1960s as a project to link computers, funded by the U.S. Department of Defense. The purpose was to create a nuclear-attack-proof communications system for people working in defense research. Soon, other researchers began to use it. Sharing information made research more efficient. Before long, the Internet grew beyond the needs of the government. Its funding and administration were passed to private organizations.

Growth of the Internet An early limitation of the Internet was

CONSUMER ACTION

Lisa's Internet service is very slow. It takes several minutes to download files, and sometimes she can't get online. Her friends subscribe to an Internet cable service. They say it is very fast, and they never have trouble getting online. However, it costs twice as much as her telephone-line Internet service provider (ISP). How should Lisa decide whether to replace her current ISP with the cable service?

56

that only highly trained technicians were able to use it. In 1990, the development of a new computer coding system called **HyperText Markup Language (HTML)** permitted the use of graphics on the Internet. From this innovation, the World Wide Web grew. The **World Wide Web (WWW** or simply the **Web**) is an information retrieval system that organizes the Internet's resources in a graphical fashion. Web pages can link to other web pages anywhere in the world.

Consumers Use the Internet

In 1993, the creation of Mosaic, the first **web browser**, gave ordinary people the ability to search the Web. Users no longer needed technical knowledge. They could move among web pages with the click of a mouse.

Internet technologies have continued to evolve. New web browsers have made surfing easier and more enjoyable. New computer languages have expanded the capabilities of HTML. New methods for transferring data have increased surfing speeds. Today, the Internet is a worldwide network of millions of computers. People all over the world can share information through computers linked on the "information super-highway."

Advances have improved the efficiency of the Internet, but they have not changed its basic character. It is still the most common method of linking computers to share information. Technological advances will continue to expand the Internet. More changes will result from people finding new ways to use the powerful potential of the Internet.

Access to the Internet

Most people use a personal computer (PC) and a modem to connect to the Internet. A **modem** is a device that allows computers to communicate over telephone lines or television cables. You also need to subscribe to an **Internet service provider (ISP)**. ISPs are businesses that relay messages across the Internet from computer to computer.

Web-TV Services In the late 1990s, Web-TV services provided an alternative to using computers to access the Internet. This type of service allows consumers to reach the Internet by using a special keyboard and their television. The televisions are linked to the Internet through a cable TV service or telephone line. This type of connection to the Internet is less expensive because you don't need to buy a computer. Web-TV has not grown rapidly, however. This may be because it does not offer many of the advantages of owning a computer.

GUESS WHAT

Did you know that the Internet was called the *Information Superhighway* by former Vice President Al Gore?

CheckPoint

What is the Internet? What was its original purpose? What innovations made the Internet accessible to the average consumer?

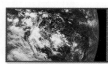

What In The World?

Today, over 60 percent of U.S. households have access to the Internet. This is among the highest access rates in the world. One possible reason for a high U.S. access rate may be the lower prices charged for Internet access in this country. In many countries, ISPs are quite costly. As recently as the year 2000, the access rate in France was just 20 percent. At that time, the cost of an ISP in France was only a little higher than in the United States. But, because most French ISPs used telephone lines, the total cost was much higher.

You probably pay a fixed amount each month to make as many local calls as you want. In France, local calls are timed, and customers are charged an amount per minute used. When a French consumer accessed the Internet, the cost of using the telephone line was often more than the cost of the ISP. As cable ISPs became available in France, they were even more expensive. Suppose your cost of accessing the Internet doubled. Would you continue to subscribe to an ISP? If many Americans stopped using the Internet, how might it affect our economy?

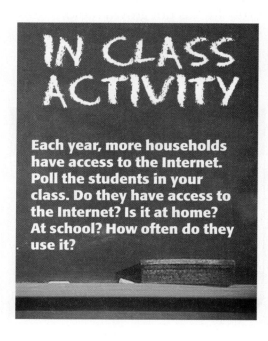

IN CLASS ACTIVITY

Each year, more households have access to the Internet. Poll the students in your class. Do they have access to the Internet? Is it at home? At school? How often do they use it?

© Getty Images/PhotoDisc

Choosing an Internet Service Provider

Assume that you have purchased your computer system. Now what? Your next step is to get connected to the Internet. For this, you need to subscribe to an Internet service provider (ISP). There are three common types of ISPs available for most homes. In the beginning, most ISPs provided access to the Internet over ordinary telephone lines. In recent years a different alternative has been offered by TV cable services. In some areas a third type of high-speed ISP is available called Digital Subscriber Line (DSL). This type of ISP uses telephone lines that are specifically dedicated to each customer. All ISPs offer access to the Internet for a price. But, the ease of getting there and what you find when you arrive can vary from service to service.

Telephone-Line-Based ISPs

Some telephone-line-based ISPs offer their services throughout the nation. These include America Online (AOL), MSN, EarthLink, and AT&T. There are many smaller telephone-line-based ISPs that offer similar services, often at a lower price than national providers. Most national providers charge a monthly fee of about $25 for unlimited access to the Internet. To consumers who spend only an hour on the Internet per month, this may seem expensive.

When you investigate telephone-line-based ISPs, be sure to find out whether they provide access through a local phone number. If your computer must make a long-distance call every time you go online, you can end up paying more in long-distance charges than you do for your ISP service. Your telephone bills can get out of hand in a hurry!

© Getty Images/PhotoDisc

Cable-Based ISPs Consumers who use a cable-based ISP are automatically connected to the Internet when they turn on their computers. There is no waiting for it to dial up a connection. Cable Internet connections are made over the same lines that bring cable television to your home. They are able to carry more data than most telephone connections. Although cable systems can "go down," they generally provide access to the Internet that is faster than an ordinary telephone connection. People who want to download large files or send images online benefit from the speed of cable connections.

One problem with cable ISPs is their higher cost. A cable connection typically costs about $50 per month. If you are also required to subscribe to the firm's cable TV service, the cost of these services can total as much as $100 a month or more.

DSL Connections Digital Subscriber Line connections are not available in all parts of the country.

CYBER CONSUMER

Consumers can connect to the Internet in different ways. One type of connection is through television cable lines. Investigate a cable ISP by visiting its web site on the Internet. How does it try to convince you to purchase its service? How much does it charge? Do you believe that its service is worth the cost? Explain your answer.

Where they are available, they are quite expensive. This type of connection should be considered by people who need rapid speed and easy access. Subscribers should also be able to pay the higher fee without giving up other goods or services they want.

© Getty Images/PhotoDisc

Investigate Your Alternatives

The key question you must answer when you choose an ISP is whether it will allow you to access the Internet when you want at a price you can afford. Any system that has more subscribers than it is able to handle will provide unreliable service. This is true for cable services just as much as for telephone-line-based ones. When some cable systems first offered Internet access, they signed up more people than their equipment could serve. Subscribers paid higher prices for service that they often did not receive. Most of these problems have been solved, but you should still investigate any ISP you might use. Ask other people who live in your community about the quality of service they receive from their ISPs.

For national providers, you can check in a variety of publications. Magazines such as *PC World* and *Smart Computing* rate ISPs on ease of access and other considerations. These reviews also tell you what you should expect to spend for different services. The time you use to choose the best provider will be well spent.

CheckPoint

Why is it important to find out about access limitations of an ISP?

TRY THESE

1. What is the Internet?

2. Who first used the Internet?

3. What two important pieces of information do you need to know about any ISP you are considering?

4. What were some major milestones in the growth of the Internet?

5. What does a web browser allow you to do on the Internet?

THINK CRITICALLY

6. **CONSUMER ACTION** Lisa wants to get online faster but doesn't know how. What does Lisa need to buy to get a quicker connection? Describe the steps Lisa should take in making her buying decisions. Discuss the opportunity costs.

7. Most telephone-line-based ISPs offer their service for about $25 per month. A typical cable service is priced around $50 per month.

Suppose you subscribe to a telephone-line-based ISP but are considering upgrading to cable. Write a paragraph that discusses the benefits and costs of making this choice. E-mail your answer to your teacher.

8. **COMMUNICATE** Write a short paragraph on what impact the Internet has had on your life, and what impact it might have on your life over the next ten years.

2.3 Choose a Personal Computer

Consider Your Choices

The first step toward accessing the Internet is buying a personal computer. When considering your choices, remember that you can use your computer for many purposes. Any computer you buy should be able to carry out the other tasks you want it to do, besides connecting to the Internet.

Computer Uses Today you may be interested in using a computer only to write assignments for school using a word processing program. Perhaps you want to store and send images using a digital camera. You may also want to play interactive games or send electronic mail (e-mail) to your friends. Before you choose a computer and software, know what you want to accomplish with them.

Future Uses No matter how you plan to use your PC today, you will probably find other uses in the future. You may need a spreadsheet application for an accounting class. You might need to create a database of names and addresses to complete a marketing course. It is difficult to predict how you will use your computer in the future. People and their technology needs change.

CONSUMER ACTION

Jamie needs a new computer. His current one is so old he can't run some of his new games. When surfing the Internet, he waits minutes as he moves between screens or as he downloads files. Jamie knows what he wants in a computer but doesn't have a lot of money. How should Jamie decide which computer to buy?

In a few years, you may be attending college or a trade school. You may be required to investigate assignments on the Internet. You might even be taking classes over the Internet through distance learning. It is important to buy a computer that will meet your current needs as well as future needs. To accomplish this, identify and rank these needs before you go shopping for a computer and its software.

What Should You Look For?

When choosing a computer system, you need to know what to investigate. The heart of any computer is its **central processing unit (CPU)**. This is the device that converts data into electronic codes. It uses these codes to complete calculations, transfer information or images, or create sound.

Modern CPUs have **microprocessors** that carry out these functions. The speed of a computer's microprocessor determines how quickly it can work. Microprocessor speed can be measured in gigahertz (GHz). The higher the gigahertz, the faster the computer can work. In 2004, the Pentium 4 3.6-GHz chip was state-of-the-art for new PCs. Better, faster chips are certain to be available in the future.

More speed means higher cost, so don't assume that you need the fastest computer available. Slower machines are often less expensive, and the difference in speed may not be noticeable to the average user. Reviews in computer magazines such as *PC World* and *PC Magazine* can help you decide how much speed you need.

Memory Another important feature of a computer is its **random access memory (RAM)**. RAM is the computer's main workspace. Computers with more RAM are able to run more complex programs. Having more RAM is particularly important if you plan to run more than one program at a time. Like microprocessor speed, more RAM means higher cost.

For most computers, it is relatively easy to purchase additional RAM. Find out how much RAM can be added to the computers you are considering. Can you add enough to meet your future needs? If so, maybe your best choice is to buy what you need now and upgrade later.

© Getty Images/PhotoDisc

CheckPoint

What function does a microprocessor perform? Why do you need to know about memory?

CYBER CONSUMER

Companies that sell computers on the Internet sometimes allow consumers to select the components they want. Search for the Gateway or Dell Computer Corporation site. Surf to the company's desktop computer information page. Click on one of the computers to read detailed information about it. Then surf to the page where you can customize the computer. You may need to click on a button that says *customize* or *select and price*. In the form provided, try selecting different options. Then, see how your selections affect the price.

Data Storage

A computer's ability to store data or programs is important for running computer applications. All new computers have a **hard drive** that stores massive amounts of electronic data. PC storage space is usually stated in megabytes (MB) or gigabytes (GB). A byte is a unit of storage space. A megabyte is 1 million bytes. A gigabyte is 1 billion bytes. A hard drive with 40 to 120 gigabytes of memory is typical for new computers.

Floppy disks A **floppy disk** can hold up to 1.44 MB of data, which is small for today's technology. It works best for storing smaller files.

CD-ROM A third type of storage device is the **CD-ROM**, a disc on which most computer games and programs are sold. CD-ROM drives may come in various speeds, such as 32X or 48X. The higher the number, the faster the drive can call up information from the disc.

Most new computers that have CD-ROM drives are also able to record or "burn" data onto the disc. This ability is particularly useful for backing up operating systems and data files that would otherwise require many floppies to copy. CDs are also a good place to store digital photographs and images that require large amounts of computer memory. Once recorded, these images are easy to access from the CD and can be eliminated from your computer's hard drive to free its space for other uses.

DVD-ROM A new type of storage device called a DVD-ROM became available in 1997. A **DVD-ROM** is a disc like a CD-ROM, but it can store much more data. Video requires lots of storage space. DVD-ROMs can store entire movies and run them with theater-quality video and sound. To use these discs, you need a DVD-ROM drive on your computer or a special DVD-ROM disc player for your TV.

Peripheral Devices

The value of a computer system also depends on the peripheral devices you choose. A **peripheral device** is any hardware connected to the CPU. Some peripherals you really must have, such as a keyboard, monitor, and mouse. Others, such as a printer or scanner, are optional, depending on your needs.

Monitors   Evaluate monitors by how clear and easy-to-read they are. Larger monitors are more expensive but can help reduce eye strain. Flat screen monitors take up less space but are more expensive than ordinary monitors.

Scanners   A scanner will enable you to put images into your computer. You can scan in your favorite photos for storage. Then, you can send them to a friend over the Internet if you like.

Printers   You will probably want a printer for your computer. Black-and-white laser printers can print good quality copies at high speed. Some laser printers can print in color too. Ink jet printers are less expensive and can print nicely in black and white or color. Ink jets are slower than lasers but are still fast enough for most uses. Replacement cartridges for ink

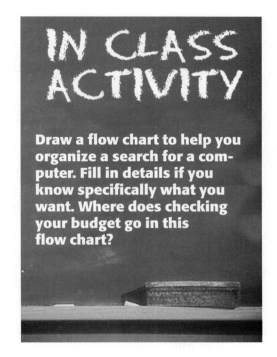

IN CLASS ACTIVITY

Draw a flow chart to help you organize a search for a computer. Fill in details if you know specifically what you want. Where does checking your budget go in this flow chart?

jets are roughly one-third of the cost of laser printer cartridges.

Software

Most new computers sold today come with many types of software already installed. These usually include a word processing program and often a spreadsheet application. Database programs may also be installed.

Subscriptions to a virus protection service and programs that allow you

Buy the Numbers?

This advertisement is typical of ads you see every day. Do you believe that buying this computer would really save you $300? How might this figure be misleading? What should you do to check out this offer?

$300 BONUS REBATE

EVERY COMPUTER WE SELL THIS WEEK COMES WITH A $300 BONUS CERTIFICATE THAT MAY BE USED TO PURCHASE OTHER ELECTRONIC EQUIPMENT AT OUR STORE.

Why pay extra somewhere else?

to download music or digital photographs may also be available. The fact that some of these programs are provided with your computer does not mean they are the best ones for your needs. You may want to buy and install other software. Suppose you use the Lotus spreadsheet program at work. It would make sense to have Lotus on your home computer as well, even if your computer came with Microsoft Excel already loaded.

Laptop Computers

If you travel in your job or just like to work with your computer at school, at the library, and at home, you may want to consider a portable computer. Portable computers are usually called **laptop** or **notebook computers**. Laptops come in various sizes, but most weigh less than 6 pounds and can fit into carrying cases the size of a briefcase.

Higher Cost There are trade-offs to consider when shopping for laptops. To get the convenience of portability, you will have to pay significantly more than you would for a desktop computer. Often, the price is 50 to 75 percent more for the same capabilities. For the same money, you can get many more features on a desktop system, so you need to decide how important portability is to you.

Other Trade-Offs The small size of laptops requires some trade-offs in other ways too. Usually, the keyboard is smaller than desktop keyboards. If you have large hands, you might look for a laptop that has the same size keys as

© Getty Images/PhotoDisc

desktops. Also, the screen of the laptop will be smaller. If you spend hours at a time at your computer, the small screen may make your eyes tired, so you may want to consider spending more to get a laptop with a larger screen. If you travel often, weight may be important. Usually, the smaller the laptop, the more it costs.

Laptops can be as powerful as desktop systems, with as much memory and speed and with similar peripherals. Adding more memory usually costs more for laptops than for desktops, however. Also, laptops can be more limited than desktops in the amount of additional memory they can hold. If you think you will need to add memory to your computer later, find out the limitations of the laptops you are considering.

More Choices for the Future

Technology marches on. In the future, your alternatives will surely expand. Selecting a computer will always involve trade-offs between capabilities and price. The more you want (speed, storage space, peripherals, and so on), the higher the price. So, approach your decision by asking yourself what you need, not just what you want.

CheckPoint

What are the major trade-offs to consider when buying a laptop?

TRY THESE

1. What should you do before you start shopping for a PC?

2. Where can you find information to help you evaluate computer choices?

3. What are some trade-offs you must consider when buying a computer?

4. What are peripheral devices?

5. Why is memory important?

6. List benefits and limitations of laptop computers.

THINK CRITICALLY

7. CONSUMER ACTION Jamie knows what he wants his new computer to do. List the steps he should take to purchase the right computer.

8. COMMUNICATE Computers can be used for more subjects than just computer programming. Think about the classes in which you could benefit from using a computer to perform word processing and spreadsheet applications or to access the Internet. Write a letter to your school's administration to persuade them to provide a laptop computer for every student in your school. Send this letter to your teacher by e-mail.

9. Let's say you have your heart set on a laptop computer. You like to get together with friends to do homework or play computer games, so you want a computer that's mobile.

Make a list of what you would like to do on the computer now and what you think you will do with it in the future. Assume that you have money only for a medium-priced computer, so you can't have everything. What are some of your trade-offs?

10. Use the Internet to research the difference between two models of laptops and two models of desktops in price, power, memory, and speed. Make a chart with your findings.

11. Many word processing software packages have the capability to help you create web pages. Use a template from one such package and create a web page for this class.

12. What is the major difference between CD-ROMs and DVD-ROMs? Why would you need a DVD-ROM instead of a CD-ROM?

DECISION MAKING PROJECT

 SPECIFY   **SEARCH**   **SIFT**   **SELECT**   **STUDY**

SPECIFY   You have decided to buy a new computer. Make a list of what you want to accomplish with it, such as using it as a communication tool. Then make a list of the computer's specifications, peripheral devices, and software needed to achieve your goals. Set a reasonable budget for your purchases.

© Getty Images/PhotoDisc

2.4 Shop on the Net

Ups and Downs of Internet Shopping

Connecting to the Internet is not the same as visiting a shopping mall. Still, the difference between these alternatives is becoming smaller every day. By the year 2000, almost every large retailer in the United States maintained a web site, and most of them offered products for sale over the Internet. Retail web sites allow you to shop 24 hours a day, 365 days a year. Experts believe you can find better prices and quicker service on the Internet—without leaving the comfort of your home. The variety of choices offered over the Internet does not change a basic consumer rule: Always use the decision making process when you shop.

Surveys show that since the turn of the 21st century, someone in more than half of all American families has shopped on the Internet and made purchases online. Consumers receive many benefits from shopping online, but there are some disadvantages as well.

CONSUMER ACTION

Keith has a problem when he goes shopping. He can't seem to make up his mind. He visits many stores, but he can't keep track of their prices. When he goes to the next store, he can't remember the first store's products well enough to compare. On top of these problems, he wears an unusual size. If he finally decides to buy something, the store may not have his size. He often comes home with nothing. How can Keith benefit from shopping on the Internet?

Getting the Best Deal

Most Internet shoppers rate convenience as the most important benefit of shopping over the Internet. Running a close second is the ability to comparison-shop. It takes only a few clicks of your mouse to visit retail web sites. You can find pictures of products with written descriptions of their styles and qualities. You can learn about guarantees, service, return policies, and shipping costs. By visiting competing web sites, you can find the best deal for a product you want to buy.

Variety of Choices

Retail stores are limited in many ways. Stores have only so much space to display and store products. They cannot maintain inventories of every product, style, or size consumers might want. When retail stores sell a product, they cannot replace it immediately. Most of these limitations do not exist for Internet retailers.

When you see the wide array of products displayed on web sites, you might think that Internet retailers keep massive inventories. This is not the case. Many Internet retailers have no inventory at all. They send orders electronically to suppliers, who ship directly to consumers.

Any Style or Size Internet retailers can fill orders from Internet customers for almost any style or size. This individualized service is important for many consumers. People who want products that are unique in style, size, or quality often have difficulty shopping. Some people, for example, have very wide feet. These

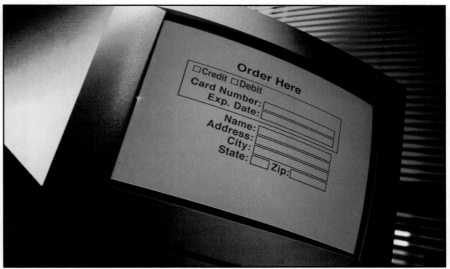

consumers once found buying comfortable shoes difficult or impossible. Now they can order the size they want on the Internet.

Special Sales Another advantage to Internet shopping is the access it provides to special sales. Many reduced-price goods are never sold at retail stores. If a company has too many products of a particular style or size, it marks them down. In recent years, many companies have chosen to sell these products only over the Internet. This is less expensive and quicker than sending them to retail outlets.

Auctions Some businesses market products through electronic auctions (e-auctions). They place a picture and a description of a product they wish to sell on their web page. Then, they sell it to the person who offers the most money within a specific period of time.

You Can't Try It On

An important problem of Internet shopping is that you cannot see, touch, use, or try on products. You can do these things only when you receive your order. Clothes bought over the Internet may not fit. Clothes that look wonderful in a picture may not look so good on you. A coat may fit but be poorly constructed. Or, its color may be different from the one that appeared on your computer. If you don't like the product, you must go to the trouble of sending it back.

Return Policies Before you buy any product over the Internet, investigate the company's return policy. Getting answers to the following questions before you buy can save you frustration later.

▶ Can you send a purchase back just because you don't like it?

▶ Does the product have to be defective to return it?

▶ Is there a time limit for returns?

▶ Who pays for the cost of return shipping?

▶ Can you get a refund or just a credit to buy something else from that company?

▶ If you have a problem, can you talk to a company representative?

▶ Is the phone number toll-free?

© Getty Images/PhotoDisc

The Junk-Mail Hassle

When you place an order over the Internet, you must give your address and pay with a credit card. Providing this information may create problems. All retailers maintain lists of their customers for their own use. They want to be able to mail advertising or contact customers if there is a problem. This is a reasonable use of consumer information. Some retailers, however, sell this information to other organizations. Information about you can end up in places you don't want it to be.

Suppose that you bought a backpack from a sporting-goods Internet retailer. You used a credit card, so the retailer has your address

© Getty Images/PhotoDisc

CheckPoint

Have you ever visited a store to buy an item on sale, only to find the store didn't have it in your size? Why don't stores always have all sizes in stock? Why would an Internet retailer be more likely to have your size?

along with a record of your purchase and most likely your e-mail address. Other retailers that sell similar products would like to be able to contact you, since you have shown interest in sporting goods by your purchase. These stores might buy your contact information. As a result, you might receive advertisements in the mail or by e-mail for tents, hiking boots, guided hiking trips, and other goods and services. Since you have no control over which organizations buy your information, many other types of organizations could have you in their files.

CheckPoint

What are some advantages to buying products over the Internet? What are some disadvantages?

Buying Services over the Internet

Many companies use the Internet to market services instead of goods. These businesses offer to do something for you for a price. You can buy banking services, tickets to concerts, travel services, subscriptions for news delivered over the Net, and many other services. You may find it difficult to make rational choices when you shop for services over the Internet. You may not understand what you are buying, and there is no one to talk to. If you buy a service on the Internet, be careful. Investigate the offer to be sure it is

legitimate. Also, be sure you understand the deal before you agree to it.

Banking on the Net

Many banks maintain web sites that consumers may use to complete financial transactions. From the bank's web site you can transfer funds from one account to another or pay bills. Also, your employer might deposit your paycheck directly into your account electronically. One banking transaction you can't complete online is withdrawing cash. This you must still do in person or at an automated teller machine (ATM).

VOTE Your Wallet

Political parties, like businesses, provide information and advertise on the Internet. In 2004, both the Bush and Kerry campaigns created official presidential election web sites. Thousands of voters visited these sites each day. They found information and registered their opinions. The data gathered helped the candidates prepare speeches and guided their campaigns. Search the Internet for the site of either the Democratic or Republican national parties. Many state and local politicians maintain sites. If the site you visit offers an opportunity to tell your representative how you feel about an issue important to you, do so. Your opinion counts!

Suppose you want to open an online bank account. You would go to your bank to fill out the necessary forms. The bank would assign special codes to your account, so that no one else can access it. That's it. You're on your way! Any time, day or night, seven days a week, you can do your banking. Just access your account electronically and tell your computer what you want to do.

Fewer Employees Banks provide online services to help them earn a profit. Part of that profit may come from fees paid by people who use the service. Banks benefit

CYBER CONSUMER

If you could go anywhere on vacation, where would you go? Surf the Net to find out as much as you can about this place. What would it cost to buy tickets to fly there? How much would a hotel room cost?

most, however, from being able to employ fewer people. Online transactions you complete do not require the help of bank employees. Since salaries and benefits are a large part of a bank's cost of doing business, fewer employees means reduced costs. From the bank's point of view, lower costs lead to higher profits.

Travels in Cyberspace

Another type of business that was quick to use the Internet is the travel industry. All major airlines and many travel agencies maintain web sites. Popular travel destinations often have sites managed by the local tourist bureau. It is now possible to book hotel rooms and buy airline, train, or bus tickets over the Internet.

Some travel specialists on the Internet help you shop for the best prices. You can search in the "Travel" category of your favorite search engine. You can probably find a travel agency that will notify you by e-mail of the lowest airfares each week to your favorite destinations.

© Getty Images/PhotoDisc

INTERNET ACTIVITY

In groups, use the Internet to identify products and services that are and are not offered for sale online. Share your lists through e-mails and have one person compile a final list. What characteristics are shared by the products on these two lists?

Web Advertising

In 1997, when web advertising was fairly new, American businesses spent $3 billion to place advertisements on the Internet. By 2002, this amount had grown to over $6 billion, and experts estimated the total would reach $8 billion by 2006. Businesses are willing to pay for Internet advertising because they believe it will help them earn better profits. Consumers also benefit from advertising. Like other forms of advertising, Internet ads can be a source of information to help consumers make rational decisions.

Business Web Sites A business web site is often mostly advertising. For businesses, the Internet is another advertising medium, such as billboards or radio. The site's main purpose is to sell products.

Advertising Space Owners of popular web sites often sell advertising space on their web pages. Like advertising in newspapers or magazines, ads can appear anywhere on the web page. Usually, you can click on these ads to get an expanded ad or to visit the advertiser's own web site. The next time you surf the Internet, notice how many ads you see.

Buying Advertising A large share of American businesses buy advertising on the Internet. Although this spending is expected to grow over time, it actually fell in 2001. General Motors, for example, cut its Internet spending in 2001 to about $26 million from over $50 million in 2000. This decline was the result of an economic downturn. It will probably be reversed as the economy improves.

Do you find advertising on the Internet distracting? You might think it would be good to eliminate most of these ads. But advertising pays a large part of the cost of maintaining the Internet. The more businesses spend to place their ads on the Internet, the less ISPs need to charge you for your access. A little more than half the cost of operating the typical ISP is paid through advertising.

GUESS WHAT

Did you know that you can have your own web page? Many ISPs offer space on their web server for their customers' web pages.

CheckPoint

Why would companies spend millions of dollars to advertise on the Internet?

SMATH OF MONEY

When businesses purchase Internet advertising, they hope to increase their sales and profits. There is, however, a limit to the amount businesses are able to spend on all types of advertising. Dollars spent on Internet advertising cannot be spent on advertisements in other media. In 2003, $248 billion was spent on advertising. iMedia Connection Online estimated that total spending for advertising in all media would grow at an average rate of 4.9 percent in each of the following three years. It also projected that in 2004 and 2005, 2.6 percent of all advertising dollars would be allocated to Internet advertising. By 2006, the portion of Internet advertising was expected to grow to 2.8 percent.

Use these data to calculate the total amount of spending for Internet advertising in the three years of 2004, 2005, and 2006, assuming iMedia projections are correct. Explain why businesses need to carefully evaluate their advertising alternatives.

▌SOLUTION

Multiply the amount of advertising spending in 2003 by a factor of 1.049 to project the total spending in the year 2004. Do the same for 2005 and 2006. Multiply these values times 0.026 to find the amounts spent for Internet advertising in 2004 and 2005. Do the same for 2006, but use a factor of 0.028. Add the amounts of Internet advertising spending for all three years to find the total.

Year	Billions Spent in Previous Year		Growth		Total Spent This Year		Proportion Spent on Internet Ads		Billions Spent on Internet Ads
2004	$248.00	×	1.049	=	$260.15	×	0.026	=	$ 6.764
2005	$260.15	×	1.049	=	$272.90	×	0.026	=	7.095
2006	$272.90	×	1.049	=	$286.27	×	0.028	=	8.016
Total Billions of Internet Spending Projected for Three Years									$21.875

Businesses need to evaluate their advertising spending to ensure that the right mix of advertising media is used to reach the greatest number of their target customers. If their product is mainly sold to professionals of high income who are likely to use computers and the Internet on a daily basis, they may wish to allocate a larger proportion of funds to Internet advertising. Internet advertising may include e-mail campaigns of upcoming specials to consenting current customers.

TRY THESE

1. Name two advantages and two disadvantages of shopping on the Internet.

2. Why is it important to check the company's return policies before you buy over the Internet?

3. What services can you buy over the Internet?

4. Why do businesses offer some products at sale prices over the Internet?

5. Why do companies advertise on the Internet?

6. How does Internet advertising benefit you as a consumer?

THINK CRITICALLY

7. **CONSUMER ACTION** In one page or less, explain to Keith how the Internet might be the answer to his shopping problems. Be sure to address each of Keith's problems.

8. Surf the Internet and list five sites where you found ads. For each site, describe the kinds of content the site contained. What products were advertised on each site? Why do you think these advertisers chose to advertise on these sites?

MATH OF MONEY **Use the table to answer exercises 9 and 10.**

9. In 2000, the population of California was 33,872,000. How many people owned computers in California that year?

10. What percent of people who owned computers in Texas in 2000 were also connected to the Internet?

11. In 2000, 23.6 percent of Hispanic Americans were connected to the Internet compared to 46.1 percent of White Americans. There were 199,414,000 White Americans and 38,168,000 Hispanic Americans in 2000. How many more White Americans were connected to the Internet than Hispanic Americans in 2000?

12. In 2000, 68.4 percent of all web pages in the world appeared in English. Only 2.42 percent were in Spanish. How might this have affected Hispanic people's willingness to subscribe to ISPs?

13. Suppose you wanted to advertise healthcare services for people who are economically disadvantaged. Would you place these ads on the Internet?

PERCENT OF POPULATION THAT OWNED A COMPUTER/ WERE CONNECTED TO THE INTERNET IN CALIFORNIA AND TEXAS IN 2000

STATE	OWNED A COMPUTER	CONNECTED TO THE INTERNET
California	56.6%	46.7%
Texas	47.9%	38.3%

DECISION MAKING PROJECT

SPECIFY **SEARCH** SIFT SELECT STUDY

SEARCH Write a plan for shopping for your computer and comparing three models. Follow your plan and list your findings.

© Getty Images/PhotoDisc

2.5 Protect Yourself on the Internet

Privacy Issues on the Internet

Years ago Americans became alarmed by personal information gathered by the government. They pressured Congress to pass laws to protect their privacy. In 1966, the Freedom of Information Act was passed. It gave people the right to examine and challenge information about them in government files.

Americans have the right to see federal government information that involves them. They do not have the right to remove this information. This right does not extend to personal data gathered by states. Some states sell information about their residents to private companies.

Right to Privacy Although the Constitution doesn't guarantee a right to privacy, the Supreme Court has ruled that such a right exists. Invasions of personal privacy can result when technology changes more rapidly than the law.

The Privacy Act of 1974 regulates access to and the use of personal

CONSUMER ACTION

Juan has placed many orders for products over the Internet. He likes the convenience and ease of Internet shopping. But he worries about the information he gives over the Net. Could it be used in ways that could harm him? How can he tell that an offer is genuine? What happens when he is connected to another computer on the Net? What precautions should he take to protect himself while shopping on the Internet?

information kept in computer files. Much of the use of such information is still unprotected by law, however. At the start of the 21st century, few laws addressed Internet privacy problems.

Internet Information New technology makes it possible to gather information about people over the Internet. It is difficult to know how your personal data are collected and used.

You must take precautions to protect your privacy when you use the Internet. You can be sure that information about you will be stored in computer files in several places. And this information is available to other people and organizations. Your files are likely to include the following.

▶ your health, credit, marital, educational, and employment histories

▶ records of purchases you have made over the telephone or Internet

▶ your financial transactions with banks and insurance companies

▶ any use you have made of credit cards, checks, or wire transfers of money

▶ your history of e-mail and telephone messages

CheckPoint

What sorts of personal information can be gathered about you, and how can it be used?

Your Cookie Jar

Cookies are files that hold information about you. The web sites you visit store cookies on your hard drive. When you return to those web sites, the sites will be able to access the information again.

To find out if you have any cookies, you can go to your computer's file manager. Use the "Find File" command and type "cookie." Open the cookie file. If you have surfed the Net much, you will probably see a long list of file names you can't identify.

© Getty Images/PhotoDisc

How Cookies Happen

Here's how cookies work. When you visit a web site, your computer exchanges information with another computer. Part of the message sent from the web site may be an instruction to record information about you. This file is then placed on your computer's hard drive.

IN CLASS ACTIVITY

Many commercial web sites in the U.S. have a policy that concerns the privacy of their customers. Find an Internet site that has a policy on security. Print it out, and compare yours to others in a group. How will these policies protect you?

Cookies Can Be Good

Most of the time, cookies are harmless, even helpful. Sites you visit may use them to record your browsing habits—the products you looked at and the routes you took through the site. If an Internet store knows your product preferences, it can personalize pages for your next visit.

For example, the site might tell you that a product you viewed last visit is on sale. When you register at a site, the cookie will allow the site to recognize you when you return. You don't have to sign in every time.

Shopping Baskets Cookies also make "shopping baskets" possible. When you decide to buy a product at many Internet stores, you can select the item for your shopping basket and continue browsing. The cookie keeps track of your selections. When you are ready to check out, you can pay for all your purchases at once.

Cookies Can Be Bad

Unfortunately, the information cookies collect can be used in ways you may not like. If you shop on the Internet, providing personal information is unavoidable. Without your address, the company wouldn't know where to send your purchase. Also, you must supply your credit card number to pay for the purchase.

No Control Once your information is collected, you have no way to control its use. The company may sell your data to other companies. Your credit card number could be used by

© Getty Images/PhotoDisc

criminals. Although such cases are rare, the results can be devastating.

Even seemingly harmless information, such as a log of your site visits, can be used against you. Suppose you have a serious disease. You visit web sites that provide information about the disease. Would you want your employer or medical insurance company to know of your visits?

Erase Those Cookies You can erase the cookies in your cookie file. Some programs even warn you when a cookie is stored in your computer. This can allow you to accept or reject the cookie. Remember that most cookies serve useful purposes. Rejecting a cookie may end your visit to a web site you wish to explore. Also, the site may not work properly without the cookie.

If you are concerned about cookies, there is software available that can limit information that a cookie can access.

CheckPoint

What are cookies? How can cookies make Internet shopping easier? What are some potential dangers of cookies?

Internet Scams

The power of the Internet can be used to cheat people. In the few years the Net has been widely available to consumers, thousands of schemes have been hatched.

I Can Make You Rich

You can surf the Net and see messages that promise great rewards for little cost. There are many offers for consumers to make a quick buck by forwarding a chain letter. You may see ads that offer "free" trips or luxury products, if only you send in some money for a chance in a drawing.

Whenever you see an offer on the Internet that seems too good to be true, it probably is. Be suspicious.

Check Them Out Don't send money to anyone you contact through the Internet without checking them out thoroughly first. Check out companies with organizations such as the Better Business Bureau. Also, your state attorney general's office keeps records of charges filed against businesses. Another way to check out a company is to require it to give you its address and telephone number. You can even check out Internet scams by searching the Net using the keyword *scam.*

I Can Make You Well

People who are ill are prime targets of Internet con artists. Dishonest businesses create web sites pretending to represent hospitals or doctors who don't really exist. They may offer people miracle cures—for a price. People desperate for a cure send money that they could spend for actual medical care.

I Can Be Your Friend

Unfortunately, the Internet has given criminals a new way to prey on victims. When you exchange messages with a stranger on the Internet, you have no way of knowing who that person really is. A person might represent himself as an 18-year-old

student. In reality this person could be 40 years old and interested only in taking advantage of you. More often, what they deliver is danger.

Never agree to meet anyone you have gotten to know on the Internet. If someone you encounter on the Internet asks to meet you in person, the best thing to do is to tell your parent, teacher, or the police. You will not only protect yourself, but may also save someone else who is less careful.

© Getty Images/PhotoDisc

Spam Is a Four-Letter Word

Like most households, your family probably receives lots of junk mail. Unwanted advertising can also bombard you through e-mail. Internet users call it **spam**.

Consumer
ALERT

Send me a dollar!
Get a dollar, put it in an envelope and send it today to:

Send me a dollar!
P.O. Box ABC
Our Towne, ST 12345

(Please, no checks)

Here is an advertisement like one found on the Internet. Do you think this is legitimate? How would you check it out?

The Internet is an easy, inexpensive, and highly efficient way to distribute information. It's not surprising that advertisers are tempted to use it to reach potential customers.

Non-profit organizations and small businesses often don't have the money to advertise the way big companies do. For them, the Internet offers a way to tell people about their products.

Spam can also come from disreputable sources, however. "Get-rich-quick" schemes and offensive materials are often distributed this way. By 2003, millions of U.S. computer users reported they received as many as a hundred or more unwanted e-mails each day. They demanded that Congress take action. Finally, in November of that year President Bush signed the Controlling the Assault of Non-Solicited Pornography and Marketing Act (better known as the Can-Spam Act) into law.

The Can-Spam Act requires that unsolicited commercial e-mail messages be labeled and include opt-out instructions and the sender's physical address. It prohibits the uses of deceptive subject lines and false headers. The fact that this type of spam is against the law does not mean that it has ceased to exist. The Federal Trade Commission (FTC) was authorized to establish a national "do-not-e-mail" registry but declined to create it, stating that it was afraid spammers would obtain copies of the list and use it to spam everyone who had signed up to avoid spam. Spam continues to be an irritating and largely unavoidable problem for Internet users.

CheckPoint

Why do you think consumers fall victim to scams on the Internet? How can you protect yourself from scams?

© Getty Images/PhotoDisc

PRIMARY SOURCES

Read the following selection from the Penalty section of the Controlling the Assault of Non-Solicited Pornography and Marketing Act of 2003. This law states that in addition to jail terms of up to five years, judges are instructed that those who are found guilty of breaking the law should be punished in the following ways. Do you believe these are appropriate punishments? Why or why not?

(1) IN GENERAL—The court, in imposing sentence on a person who is convicted of an offense under this section, shall order that the defendant forfeit to the United States—

   (A) any property, real or personal, constituting or traceable to gross proceeds obtained from such offense; and

   (B) any equipment, software, or other technology used or intended to be used to commit or to facilitate the commission of such offense.

TRY THESE

1. In what ways can use of the Internet threaten personal privacy?

2. Why do businesses create and use cookies?

3. What benefits could you lose if you refused cookies?

4. What is spam? What are some of the difficulties in trying to restrict spam?

5. How can you protect yourself from improper use of your personal information collected over the Internet?

6. What are some of the scams that have found their way to the Internet?

7. How can you use the decision making process to avoid the scams you identified in exercise 6?

THINK CRITICALLY

8. **CONSUMER ACTION/ COMMUNICATE** Juan was concerned about several potential problems that his Internet shopping could cause him. In one page or less, describe some things Juan needs to watch for as he uses the Internet. Explain to him what he can do to reduce his risk. Send your advice to your teacher in an e-mail.

9. Open the "cookie" folder on your computer. If you don't have any cookies, work with a friend who does. Try to identify where one cookie came from. The file names often contain abbreviations of the sites that created them. Go to that site and look around to see how the site operates. What do you think the cookie does to help you use the site? Leave the site and then delete that site's cookie from your computer. Now return to the site and look around again. If the site offers you a cookie, refuse it. Does the site operate differently? Can you identify what the cookie did?

10. Think about the scams discussed in this lesson. Con artists operate similar scams by telephone, in print media (magazines and newspapers), and in person. Compare how these schemes might be carried out on the Internet versus these other methods. What characteristics of the Internet can be used to a con artist's advantage in pulling off such scams? How can you use the Internet to protect yourself from scams?

DECISION MAKING PROJECT

SPECIFY   **SEARCH**   **SIFT**   **SELECT**   **STUDY**

SIFT In a group, compare your findings and discuss pros and cons of the alternative choices. Create a table to compare features, benefits, and costs of each product and compare this with what you want from your new computer and software. Identify trade-offs you need to make to stay within your budget. Can you achieve everything you want without spending more than $1,200? If not, what items would you cut?

ASSESSMENT

KEY IDEAS

Technology and Consumer Choice

1. New technology has made products more complex and difficult for consumers to evaluate.

2. Technological change causes products to depreciate and become obsolete rapidly, making it difficult for consumers to decide when to buy.

3. New technology products may contain more bugs and be more expensive when they are first introduced. In time, the bugs will be worked out, and competitors will drive prices down.

Move into Cyberspace

4. To connect to the Internet, you need a personal computer and an Internet service provider (ISP). Most connections are through telephone lines or television cables.

5. In evaluating an Internet service provider, you need to find out if it gives you access when you want it. Cost and speed are important factors, but there is little value in having an ISP that is not reliable.

Choose a Personal Computer

6. When choosing a personal computer and software, consider what you want to use them for, both now and in the future. Spreadsheet, database, and word processing applications can be just as important as accessing the Internet.

7. More speed, features, and peripherals on a computer mean more cost, so approach your decision by asking yourself what you *need,* not just what you *want.*

Shop on the Net

8. Internet shopping offers consumers the convenience of buying without leaving home, a large inventory, and the ability to comparison-shop, but there are opportunity costs as well.

9. The Internet is also a convenient source of consumer services, such as online banking, travel arrangements, and concert tickets.

10. The Internet offers businesses another medium for advertising their products, and advertising helps to pay for the Internet service you are enjoying.

Protect Yourself on the Internet

11. Use of the Internet enables companies and other users to gather information about you that can be distributed without your knowledge.

12. Cookies are files that hold information about you. Web sites you visit store the files on your hard drive and access them next time you visit.

13. Scams are as numerous on the Internet as they are in the rest of the marketplace.

© Getty Images/PhotoDisc

TERMS REVIEW

Match each term on the left with its definition on the right.
Some terms may not be used.

a. CD-ROM

b. central processing unit (CPU)

c. cookies

d. depreciation

e. DVD-ROM

f. floppy disk

g. hard drive

h. HyperText Markup Language (HTML)

i. Internet

j. Internet service provider (ISP)

k. laptop or notebook computer

l. microprocessor

m. modem

n. peripheral device

o. random access memory (RAM)

p. spam

q. technological obsolescence

r. web browser

s. World Wide Web (WWW or Web)

1. the heart of a computer that converts data into electronic codes and uses these codes to complete calculations, transfer information or images, or create sound

2. any hardware connected to the CPU

3. the computer's main workspace

4. unwanted advertising distributed through e-mail

5. the process of new technology making products based on old technology out-of-date

6. program that gives users the ability to search the Web for information with just the click of a mouse button

7. a decline in a product's value because of wear and use or technological obsolescence

8. a worldwide network of millions of computer networks

9. files containing information about you that web sites store on your hard drive

10. computer coding system that enables the use of graphics on the Internet

11. business that relays messages across the Internet from computer to computer

12. information retrieval system that organizes the Internet's resources in a graphical fashion

13. a data storage disc that holds much more data than a CD-ROM

14. device that allows computers to communicate over telephone or cable lines

15. computer's main storage area for electronic data

16. device within a computer's CPU that carries out the computing functions

CONSUMER DECISIONS

17. All purchases involve trade-offs between benefits and costs. What does this mean in terms of your consumer decision making process?

18. How would you go about buying a personal computer? What would you do first? What features would you consider in evaluating your alternatives?

19. How can shopping on the Internet make your consumer buying decisions easier? How can it make the buying process more difficult?

20. What are some ways that consumers can get into trouble on the Internet? What can you do to protect yourself from these dangers?

THINK CRITICALLY

21. You would like to buy a computer, but you are worried that it will rapidly become obsolete. So, you are thinking about leasing a PC. You can buy the computer system you want for $1,299. Or, you can lease the same system by paying $49 each month for the next two years. At the end of that time, you would give the system back. You could then lease a newer system if you wanted. Which choice would you make? Why? What else would you consider in this decision besides cost?

LOOK IT UP

22. Select a product based on new technology that just has come on the market. What bugs are people finding in the product?

23. Find out what model and brand of computer is the smallest on the market today. How small is it?

24. Compare the cost and services of a local ISP with a national organization such as AOL. Are there differences in their services? What is the monthly cost of each? Which would you choose? Why?

25. Go to the home page of an Internet service provider. What services does the ISP provide to its customers besides connecting them to the Internet?

26. Find two Internet shopping sites that sell similar products. Select a product and compare the features and prices at both sites. Where would you buy this product? Why?

27. Find an article in a newspaper or magazine that concerns rights to privacy on the Internet. Do you agree with the article's point of view on this subject? Why or why not?

INSIDE THE NUMBERS

28. In 1993, the federal Uniform Crime Report showed that, on average, for every 100,000 Americans, 306 were involved in criminal activity. In the year 2004, 150 million Americans were Internet users. If the 1993 ratio of criminality is accurate, how many Internet users were involved in criminal activity in 2004? Does this number change what you think about safety on the Internet?

WHICH IS THE BEST DEAL?

You have investigated a new computer system and found that to purchase the equipment you want, you would have to spend about $1,500. This is more than the $800 you have saved. You have identified the four alternatives described below. Use the decision making process to choose the alternative that is best for you. Explain how you made your choice.

Alternative 1 Borrow the extra $700 you need from your brother and pay him back $75 each month for the next ten months.

Alternative 2 Wait and buy the computer eight months from now after you have saved the extra $700 you need.

Alternative 3 Buy a less expensive computer now with less power and speed than you really want.

Alternative 4 Buy a used computer from your neighbor for $300 that is good enough for your current needs but probably won't have enough memory for your needs a year from now.

POINT YOUR BROWSER TO

www.ee4c.swlearning.com
Complete the activity for Chapter 2.

CURRICULUM CONNECTIONS

29. SCIENCE The science of computer chip technology is fascinating and ever-changing. What is a computer chip? Go to your local library or to the Internet and find out! Write a one-page paper explaining what a computer chip is and what's happening with chip technology right now. Hint: You can start by looking up a company called Intel.

30. HISTORY When looms (fabric-weaving machines) were first used in England, this new technology put many people out of work. Investigate the workers' reactions and the results of the pressure they put on the English government. Write a one-page paper describing what this event shows about people's resistance to changes in technology. Give an example of how some people are resisting the changes brought about by the Internet.

31. CULTURE Technology has had an impact on American society. One school of thought considers advances in technology to be good. The world seems to get a little bit smaller with each advance. This school of thought also believes that technology has broken down barriers between people and nations. Another school of thought believes advances in technology lead to a more isolated society, one in which people would rather communicate via computer than face-to-face. Which school of thought makes the most sense to you? Why?

32. BUSINESS Internet shopping has become so popular that some retail industry analysts are worried. If people shop at home over the Internet rather than visiting actual showrooms or stores, what might happen to the stores as we know them? Will store sales increase or decrease? Why? What do you think an increase in Internet shopping might do to shopping malls? What might Internet shopping mean for people whose jobs are in retail sales? What kinds of jobs might Internet shopping create? Why?

JOURNAL RECAP

33. After reading this chapter, review answers you wrote to the questions in Journal Journey. Have your opinions changed?

DECISION MAKING PROJECT

○ SPECIFY ● SEARCH ● SIFT ◉ SELECT ◉ STUDY

SELECT Decide which computer, peripheral devices, and software programs you would buy. Be sure to stay within the budget you set earlier. As a group, write an essay that explains your choices.

STUDY Suppose that in six months you discover that your computer does not have enough RAM to run some new programs. Explain how to avoid this type of problem when you choose your next computer.

Chapter

3

CONSUMER PROTECTION
RIGHTS, RESPONSIBILITIES, RESOLUTIONS

WHAT'S AHEAD

EXPLODING MYTHS

Fact or Myth?
What do you think is true?

1. You can depend on the government to protect your consumer rights.

2. People who get "taken" by con artists deserve what they get.

3. When you are dissatisfied with a product, you should go straight to the top to seek satisfaction.

JOURNAL JOURNEY

WRITE IN YOUR JOURNAL ABOUT THE FOLLOWING.

CONSUMER RIGHTS AND RESPONSIBILITIES
What do you think you have the right to expect from the products you buy and the companies that sell them to you? What responsibilities do you have in return?

DECEPTION AND FRAUD How can you tell a good deal from a scam? What clues make you suspicious about an offer? Should all deceptive selling practices be illegal? Why or why not?

RESOLVE CONSUMER PROBLEMS When you are dissatisfied with a product you purchased, what do you do about it? Were you ever frustrated in your attempts to exchange a product or get a refund? What happened?

DECISION MAKING PROJECT

SPECIFY **SEARCH** **SIFT** **SELECT** **STUDY**

DISSATISFIED? DO SOMETHING ABOUT IT! Your group will use a real-life example from someone in the group who was dissatisfied and wants to complain to the seller or manufacturer. The group will plan to file a complaint about the product or service.

GOAL
To learn
how to complain
successfully

PROJECT PROCESS
SPECIFY	Lesson 3.1
SEARCH	Lesson 3.2
SIFT	Lesson 3.3
SELECT	Lesson 3.4
STUDY	Chapter Assessment

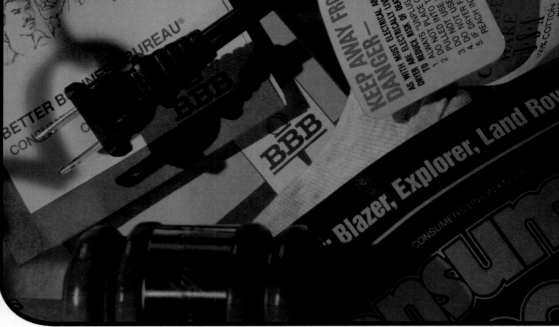
© Getty Images/PhotoDisc

GOALS

DESCRIBE
your rights as a
consumer

EXPLAIN
responsibilities that
come with your rights

3.1 Consumer Rights and Responsibilities

A Consumer Bill of Rights

As an American consumer, you expect certain things in exchange for your money. When you buy a product, you expect to receive a fair value for the price. You expect to be treated with respect and honesty. You expect products to be reliable and safe. If a product is defective, you expect to be able to exchange it or get a refund. Most American businesses are fair and work to meet consumer expectations. Unfortunately, some businesses do not.

In 1962, President John F. Kennedy established a set of four fundamental consumer rights. Later, three more rights were added, creating the *Consumer Bill of Rights* shown on the next page.

CONSUMER ACTION

Shauna bought a game of yard darts for her ten-year-old brother, Tyler. He loved the game and soon had several friends with him in the back yard, all throwing the foot-long darts at plastic rings on the ground. According to the instructions, everyone was supposed to stand behind the dart thrower. Shauna noticed that some kids were standing near the target ring while another child was tossing. Someone could be seriously injured if hit by a dart. Shauna wondered what to do. What were her options? How should she decide the best course of action?

Consumer Bill of Rights	Consumer Responsibilities
1. **Right to Safety** Products must not endanger consumers' lives or health.	1. **Responsibility to Use Products Safely** Consumers are responsible for following the manufacturer's instructions for proper use and maintenance of the products.
2. **Right to Be Informed** Businesses must provide accurate information in advertising, labeling, and sales practices.	2. **Responsibility to Use Information** Consumers are responsible for using the information to evaluate product choices.
3. **Right to Choose** Consumers should have a variety of goods and services from which to choose.	3. **Responsibility to Choose Carefully** Consumers should take advantage of product variety by considering many options and making rational choices.
4. **Right to Be Heard** The government must consider consumer interests when creating laws.	4. **Responsibility to Express Satisfaction or Dissatisfaction** Consumers should tell their elected officials their opinions on consumer issues and inform them of improper business practices.
5. **Right to Redress** Consumers should be able to obtain fair remedies to consumer problems.	5. **Responsibility to Seek Redress** Consumers should inform businesses of product defects and unfair practices. Consumers should pursue remedies.
6. **Right to Consumer Education** Sufficient information should be available for consumers to make rational decisions.	6. **Responsibility to Be an Educated Consumer** Consumers should take advantage of opportunities to gather information and learn how to make rational buying decisions.
7. **Right to a Healthy Environment** Businesses should avoid polluting the environment and should contribute to the welfare of the community in which they operate.	7. **Responsibility to Contribute to a Healthy Environment** Consumers should support businesses that operate responsibly and report environmental abuses to authorities.

Rights Carry Responsibilities

With rights come responsibilities. No amount of consumer information will help you make rational decisions if you don't gather and use the information. Elected officials cannot create laws in your best interest if you don't tell them what you need. Also, a product may not function properly if you use it incorrectly.

Look at the responsibilities that you as a consumer share as a fair exchange for the rights you enjoy.

Right to Safety

You have the right to expect that the products you buy won't endanger your life or health. Your stove should cook your food without causing a fire. Toys should not be designed in a way that could harm

IN CLASS ACTIVITY

Read each right carefully. Then, in a group, select a consumer right. Make a list of how this consumer right affects producers of goods you buy. Give specific examples.

VOTE Your Wallet

Recently, the U.S. Department of Agriculture (USDA) changed its rules governing what can be advertised as *organic*. Before this, the USDA had received more than 200,000 letters, faxes, and e-mails from consumers stating their opinions on products that should or should not be labeled organic.

The public doesn't vote when government agencies set rules, but public opinion does play a role. Before making such important rules, agencies gather public opinion and consider it with data from field experts.

The USDA defines many terms advertising food products, such as *from scratch*, *natural*, and *all natural*. Write your definitions, and then visit the USDA web site to compare the definitions. Are they about the same or quite different? Would you be willing to register your point of view when the USDA sets rules for food products?

children. In exchange, you should accept the responsibility to use products as intended and according to instructions.

For example, when microwave ovens were first introduced, a man tried to dry his shoes by placing them in his oven. When they melted, he complained to the manufacturer. As a consumer, you should use common sense and good judgment in the use of products.

© Getty Images/PhotoDisc

Right to Be Informed

Businesses must supply you with accurate information about their products. Advertising should not be misleading. Food labels must accurately state the ingredients. Where appropriate, labels should contain clear instructions about proper use and storage. As a consumer, you are responsible for using the information to learn how to use products properly.

Right to Choose

You must have the opportunity to choose among competing products.

Without choices, you would have to pay whatever price the store demanded or go without the product. Your responsibility as a consumer is to take advantage of this variety.

Competition is a contest among sellers to win customers. Competition helps keep prices reasonable.

Competitors know that if their prices get too high, you will buy from someone else.

Competition also encourages manufacturers to keep improving their products. They know that if they can satisfy your needs better than their competitors, they will most likely win your business.

In 2000, Microsoft was ruled a **monopoly**—a company which had an unfair advantage over competitors in an area of business. Without competition, there is less incentive for a company to listen to consumers because there are fewer choices consumers can make.

Right to Be Heard

You have the right and responsibility to state your point of view when lawmakers are considering consumer issues. Consumers elect their government officials to carry out their wishes. However, lawmakers

cannot carry out their responsibilities unless they know what consumers want.

© Getty Images/PhotoDisc

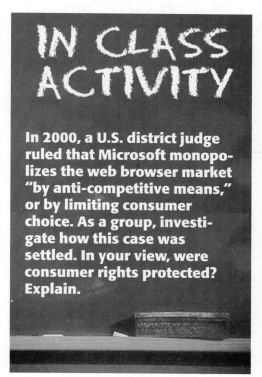

In 2000, a U.S. district judge ruled that Microsoft monopolizes the web browser market "by anti-competitive means," or by limiting consumer choice. As a group, investigate how this case was settled. In your view, were consumer rights protected? Explain.

The following is information from the web site maintained by the Attorney General's office of the state of Maine.

"Odometer fraud occurs when the true mileage of a vehicle is intentionally hidden from the consumer." It is a crime for a person or dealer to alter the odometer reading with the intent to deceive.

Odometer fraud affects you in two ways. First, you may pay considerably more than the vehicle is worth. Second, you will believe that you have purchased a safe, low-mileage vehicle when in fact the vehicle has high mileage and may not be safe at all, especially since you will service and maintain it as if it were a low-mileage vehicle. Thus, your life, the lives of your family, and the lives of others are placed in jeopardy by the odometer–fraud criminal.

What consumer rights does odometer fraud violate? To find out how to avoid fraud when you buy a used car, visit your state Attorney General's web site to find what protections it offers.

Buy the Numbers?

If you wanted to buy carpet and you saw this advertisement, how would you evaluate the information it provides? How would the following facts influence your decision?

1. The store runs this promotion at least once a month.
2. The store defines an average room as 12 feet by 12 feet. It will provide up to 432 square feet at this price.
3. You must choose from a specified group. No carpet in this group has a normal price over $11.99 per square yard.
4. Although you won't pay a penny until next year, you will be charged 18 percent interest, which will increase the amount you owe.

Explain why you should ask questions about advertisements before acting on them. Does this type of advertisement respect consumer rights?

> **COME TO**
> ## CARPETOWN'S
> ## ONE-DAY SALE!
>
> **For *one day* only — Saturday**
>
> You can carpet three rooms for only $799. You choose the carpet. We'll install it free. You won't pay a penny until next year.
>
> Don't Miss Your Big Chance!

© Getty Images/PhotoDisc

Right to Redress

If a product breaks or doesn't live up to your quality expectations, you have the right to **redress**— to seek and receive a remedy, such as money or other compensation. Talking with a company representative and agreeing on an acceptable remedy can solve most problems. In fact, as a responsible consumer, you should seek redress when you are dissatisfied. Most companies want an opportunity to fix the problem. In the case of dangerous products or unethical business practices, authorities need to know so they can protect other consumers.

If you can't work out a solution with the company or if the problem is bad enough, you have the right to sue. For example, if a defective product physically harmed you, then settling on a suitable remedy might require a lawyer's help. Bringing suit should be a last resort. Lawyers are expensive, and court proceedings can be time consuming.

Right to Consumer Education

You have the right to sufficient information to help you make rational buying decisions. You also have the responsibility to use this information to learn how to be an informed consumer. There is a lot of product information out there. Take advantage of it to get the best value for your money.

Right to a Healthy Environment

You have a right to live in an environment free of pollution and dangers to your life and health. You also have a right to expect businesses operating in your area to avoid polluting the environment.

For example, if an airport wants to add a new runway, it should consider the effects of noise pollution on the surrounding community. Perhaps the airport should consider other alternatives.

CheckPoint

What responsibilities do companies have toward you, the consumer? What responsibilities do you have in return?

TRY THESE

1. What are the seven consumer rights established by American presidents?

2. How does competition benefit you as a consumer?

3. What is a monopoly, and why is it considered unfair to consumers?

4. How are businesses responsible for maintaining a healthy environment?

THINK CRITICALLY

5. **CONSUMER ACTION** If you were Shauna, what would you do first? What are her rights and responsibilities? How would the situation change if someone were injured playing the game?

6. For each consumer responsibility, describe a situation in which you exercised that responsibility. Explain what you did.

7. **COMMUNICATE** In a one-page essay, describe an unsatisfactory product you bought, and explain how you resolved the problem. E-mail it to your teacher.

DECISION MAKING PROJECT

SPECIFY   SEARCH   SIFT   SELECT   STUDY

SPECIFY Get into a group. Talk about times when you were so dissatisfied with a product or a service that you wanted to complain. Choose one real product or service to take through the complaint process. Identify what you want the seller or manufacturer to do in response. Be realistic!

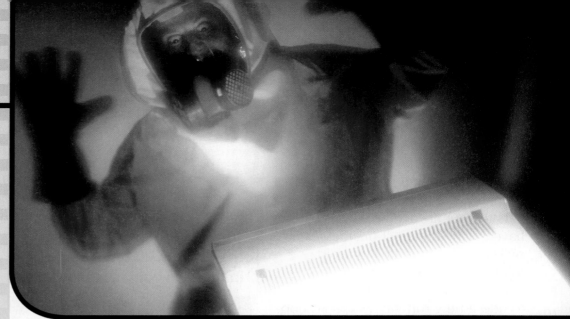

3.2 Government and Consumer Protection

The Rise of the Consumer Movement

The first steps toward consumer protection took place soon after the American Revolution. In the late 1700s, states enforced weights and measurement standards so that consumers could be sure that, for example, they got a pound of corn when they paid for a pound of corn.

Later, the federal Interstate Commerce Act of 1887 prevented railroads from setting unreasonable rates. Since railroads were the major means of transporting products to market, railroad rates were a great concern in the economy.

Most of the early laws, though, were intended to regulate how businesses operated rather than to protect the individual consumer.

Consumerism as a grass-roots movement really began in the early 1900s. Public pressure at that time

CONSUMER ACTION

Jessica ordered a new pool table and was told it would be delivered in six weeks. She paid a $500 deposit and agreed to make her final payment when the table arrived. For eight weeks she heard nothing. Yesterday, she called the store, only to hear a recording that said the store's phone was no longer in service. What should Jessica do? Where can she go for help? The store gave Jessica a three-year full warranty on the pool table. Can this warranty help her in this situation?

brought about passage of laws that set standards in the production of food and drugs. Consumerism grew during the Depression of the 1930s and then exploded into a major national concern in the 1960s.

A Growing Concern

Two hundred years ago, most products consumers bought were simple and easy to understand. Consumers might buy corn or a coat, and they were able to evaluate these products through experience.

Today, you buy many products you don't understand. You may have a general idea of how a television or a computer works, but you are probably not able to build or repair one. Most consumers do not understand the medicines they buy. The foods you eat are prepared by others—frozen, packaged, and often treated with preservatives.

A Growing Awareness

Two landmark books published in the 1960s shocked the nation into awareness of the serious need for

© Getty Images/PhotoDisc

better consumer protection. Published in 1962, Rachel Carson's book *Silent Spring* predicted a world without birds, exterminated by the widespread use of pesticides.

Three years later, Ralph Nader published *Unsafe at Any Speed*, exposing the dangers of many of the automobiles produced and sold in the United States. These national best-sellers and other publications awakened consumers to the need to organize to protect their interests.

The Consumer Movement

As products become more complicated, it is more difficult to evaluate them and protect yourself from poor-quality or even dangerous products. Consumer groups try to influence the government to pass laws to keep dangerous or defective products off the market. They also want laws passed that require businesses to provide information to help consumers evaluate the products they sell.

The **consumer movement**, or consumerism, seeks to protect and inform consumers by requiring such practices as honest advertising, product warranties, and improved safety standards. The consumer movement grew out of the consumers' desire for government intervention on their behalf.

CheckPoint

What is the purpose of the consumer movement? How did it start? Why did it explode in the 1960s?

Out of class, look for reports about unsafe products in newspapers, magazines, or on the Internet. Summarize your findings, and e-mail them to other members of your group. Agree on the most dangerous product. E-mail your teacher a product summary, and explain how consumers can protect themselves from this product.

Government Protection

Today, consumers and businesses are more equal in power in the American economy than at any other time in history. Government protection has helped to level the playing field. Federal, state, and local governments pass laws to protect consumers. Various federal agencies are responsible for enforcing federal laws.

Federal Trade Commission

The **Federal Trade Commission (FTC)**, created in 1914, is the most important federal consumer protection agency. The FTC is responsible for protecting consumers from unfair or deceptive business practices, such as misleading information in advertising or on product labels.

For example, suppose you saw a TV ad for a simulated-gold sculpture. You sent $79 for one. When it arrived, you found it was only three inches high and seemed to be made out of gold-colored plastic. If this happened to you, you could file a complaint with the FTC.

When the FTC receives many complaints about a product, it investigates. If it determines that a company is using deceptive advertising, it issues a **cease-and-desist order**. This order requires the company to stop using the advertisement. Continued use of the ad would result in a stiff fine.

The FTC has offices in most large cities. Your local FTC office can answer your questions and help you solve consumer problems.

Consumer Product Safety Commission

The **Consumer Product Safety Commission (CPSC)** was created in 1972 to protect consumers from dangerous products. Although other laws were passed earlier to protect consumers, the CPSC was the first federal agency with power over *all* consumer products. The CPSC can set safety standards for any consumer product and ban those that it considers hazardous.

UNITED STATES CONSUMER PRODUCT SAFETY COMMISSION

HOTLINE

To report a safety problem with a consumer product, CALL US!

1-800-638-CPSC

The CPSC also provides data about product safety to consumers. Each year, the CPSC prepares a list of hazardous products, based on data it collects from hospital emergency rooms.

Environmental Protection Agency

The federal **Environmental Protection Agency (EPA)** was created in 1970 to enforce laws that protect our environment. The EPA makes sure that businesses safely dispose of hazardous waste produced during manufacturing. The EPA also sets standards for air and water quality and monitors businesses for compliance with these standards.

The EPA's operations help protect the environment. Nothing is free, however. To comply with EPA environmental standards, businesses may have to add special equipment to remove dangerous gases before releasing smoke into the atmosphere. Businesses pass on to consumers the cost in the form of higher prices.

State and Local Protection

In most cases, federal agencies work to solve national consumer issues. State and local governments protect consumers in local situations. Sometimes state and local standards are even stricter than federal standards. For example, in southern California, where smog is a major problem, local governments may limit lawn mowing to certain times of the day, when mower emissions can be more easily dispersed in the atmosphere.

Most companies accused of cheating consumers are prosecuted under state laws. States often deal with disputes over credit rights and

CYBER CONSUMER

The government provides special consumer protection for different population groups. The CPSC has rules for toys, and the EPA sets higher standards for gasoline quality in major cities than in rural areas. Local governments use zoning ordinances to keep factories out of residential areas. Visit the CPSC or EPA web sites to find out how to report a dangerous product or a situation that concerns you. Will these consumer issues likely be the ones that you will care about in the future? E-mail a summary of what you find to your teacher.

insurance agreements. Health and sanitation standards are set and enforced by state and local governments. State consumer protection agencies are usually part of the Attorney General's office. Many local governments have consumer affairs departments as well.

CheckPoint

How does the FTC protect consumers? What does the CPSC regulate? Why is environmental protection a consumer issue?

Warranties

Most companies want you to trust that the products they sell will meet your quality expectations. One way for companies to gain your trust is by offering a written guarantee or warranty. A **warranty** is a company's promise that the product will meet specific standards over a given time period, or the company will repair or replace it, or give a refund.

Warranties from reputable companies reduce your risk because if the product is defective, you will be able to remedy the situation without much trouble. Remember that only the company that provided it backs a warranty. If the company goes out of business or turns out to be nothing more than a post office box, the warranty is worth no more than the paper it is printed on.

The Magnuson-Moss Warranty Act

Before 1975, warranties often were vague and difficult to understand. Many left out critical information,  such as the name and address of the company, the product or part covered, and the length of warranty coverage. Some did not even say what the company would do to remedy a problem. Such warranties did little to protect consumers because they would not hold up in court.

To protect consumers from worthless warranties, Congress passed the Magnuson-Moss

IN CLASS ACTIVITY

Bring in copies of warranties from home. In a group, discuss each warranty. Is the warranty limited or full? What are your responsibilities for the proper use of the product?

Warranty Act in 1975. Although the law does not require all products to carry warranties, it specifies how a warranty must be written if a company offers one. Under this law, all warranties are divided into two groups, full warranties and limited warranties.

A **full warranty** is a very specific written guarantee. It must promise that the company will repair or replace a defective product within a specified time period at no charge. It must also explain how to file a claim and how to return the product to the business. The consumer must receive satisfaction within a reasonable period of time.

A **limited warranty** is a written warranty that does not meet the standards of a full warranty because of specified limitations. The limitations must be explained in the warranty. Like full warranties, a limited warranty must also specify the coverage time period, explain how to make a claim, and promise a solution within a reasonable time period.

Implied Warranties

You are entitled to some warranty rights, even when the company offers no written warranty. Every product carries at least an **implied warranty**— an unwritten guarantee that the product is of sufficient quality to fulfill the purpose for which it was designed. If you buy a hammer, you expect that it won't break when you hammer a nail into wood. If it does break, you have the right to return it, even if the hammer came with no written warranty. Selling a hammer implies that it will not break when used for its intended purpose.

Consumer Movement Today

Today, the consumer movement is alive and well. Organizations such as the Sierra Club work to protect the environment. The Consumer's Union tests products and reports on the results in *Consumer Reports,* a popular consumer magazine. Most newspapers, news media, and magazines have articles on consumer topics. State organizations investigate consumer problems and encourage state governments to pass and enforce laws. You can take an active role in protecting your own interests by joining and supporting consumer organizations.

CheckPoint

What is a warranty? Why was warranty legislation needed? What are the requirements of a full warranty? What does an implied warranty promise?

MATH OF MONEY

Suppose you could purchase a three-year service contract for a $200 DVD player for $30. The DVD player already has a one-year full warranty, so the $30 adds only two more years of protection. If 1 of every 40 DVD players fails in its second or third year of use, how much profit can the store expect to gain from selling 40 service contracts? Assume the average cost of repairing a DVD player is $75.

▌SOLUTION

The store will receive $1,200 from the sales of 40 service contracts.

$30 × 40 = $1,200

The store expects to repair one DVD player at a cost of $75.

$1,200 − $75 = $1,125

So, the expected profit is $1,125. Why do you think stores encourage consumers to buy service contracts?

TRY THESE

1. What is the consumer movement?
2. How do consumer groups benefit consumers?
3. How has government leveled the playing field for consumers?
4. Name two of the federal consumer protection agencies and explain their functions.
5. Why was the Magnuson-Moss Warranty Act passed?
6. What is a warranty?
7. What is the difference between a full and a limited warranty?
8. What is an implied warranty?

THINK CRITICALLY

9. **CONSUMER ACTION** Jessica paid a $500 deposit for a pool table from a store that closed soon after her purchase. If you were Jessica, what would you do? What government agency might be able to help? Can the three-year full warranty on the pool table help in this situation?

10. When Frank purchased his lawn-mower, he paid an extra $49 to extend its one-year service warranty to five years. The extended warranty included a long list of things Frank was required to do. Three years later, the mower's engine broke. When he took it to the store, a mechanic told Frank he hadn't changed the oil often enough. Overall, did the warranty save Frank money? Why would the store owner offer extended warranties?

11. **COMMUNICATE** Should the government be involved in protecting consumers? Can't they look out for themselves? Answer these questions in an essay and e-mail it to your teacher.

12. **COMMUNICATE** You have just invented the ultimate mousetrap. Since you are new to the mousetrap business, you want to assure your customers that you will stand behind your product. Write a full warranty to offer to customers who buy your mousetrap. Make sure you include all the requirements for a full warranty.

DECISION MAKING PROJECT

SPECIFY   SEARCH   SIFT   SELECT   STUDY

SEARCH Meet with your group again to talk about the complaint you will file. List all the facts about the purchase and what it was that went wrong. Brainstorm for ideas about what steps you could take to file a complaint. What can you do if you are not satisfied with a seller or manufacturer's response to your initial complaint?

© Getty Images/PhotoDisc

GOALS

IDENTIFY deceptive and fraudulent selling practices

EXPLAIN how to protect yourself from deception and fraud

3.3 Deception and Fraud

Deception

Sometimes the products you buy don't meet your needs or they fall short of your quality standards. You may also encounter problems that don't relate directly to the product—problems such as deceptive or fraudulent selling practices.

The difference between deception and fraud is a matter of degree. Advertising becomes deceptive when it misleads. Deceptive advertising or selling practices taken to unlawful extremes become fraud.

Legitimate selling practices are not deceptive. Most advertising provides accurate product information. Salespeople usually try to help you find the product that best meets your needs. However, exaggerated claims and misleading prices are deceptive practices.

CONSUMER ACTION

Patrick received a letter in the mail offering him a chance to earn $900. All he had to do was send $100 to a post office box in Canada. Then he could mail ten letters to friends, asking them to send him $100. The letter explained that he would receive $100 from each of his ten friends, or $1,000 total. After subtracting his initial $100 investment, he would make a total of $900 in "profits." His friends, in turn, would send letters to ten other people to make the same profit. It sounded like a great deal! How could he lose? Still, Patrick had doubts. Should he do it?

Trading Up

You've seen the advertising and you've decided to buy it. When you get to the store, however, the salesperson tells you that the product really isn't much good. What you really need is this more expensive model. The practice of pressuring consumers to buy a more expensive product than they intended is called **trading up**.

Trading up is not illegal. Maybe you really should buy the more expensive product. But it's possible that you don't need all those extra features. Will you actually use all the programming options on the DVD player, or do you just want to put in a DVD and watch it?

Salespeople can be a great help to you in evaluating products. They can explain the differences among alternatives and the benefits of each one. Just remember that the salesperson's job is to sell you something. Often, salespeople earn more income if they can influence consumers to spend more. Use the decision making process to buy what meets your needs, not what the salesperson says you should buy.

Sale Price

A sale is a sale only if the price is below the usual price. If the store recently sold the product at a higher price, then the lower price can

legally be called a sale. Sale prices can be deceptive, though. Suppose the store offered the product at the higher price for only one day. Would the lower price really be a sale price?

Suggested Retail Price

Prices can be deceptive in other ways, too. A manufacturer's suggested retail price is sometimes higher than any retailer expects to actually get for the product. For example, most car dealers expect you to negotiate down from the manufacturer's suggested retail price shown on the sticker.

Beware of retailers' claims about having the lowest prices in town. Maybe they do, and maybe they don't. The only way to know for sure is to shop and compare.

Loss Leader

Sometimes a retailer's goal is to get you into the store. Once there, maybe you will buy other items that you hadn't originally intended to buy. To attract you to the store, the retailer may price an item below the cost of buying the item from the manufacturer. The retailer will lose money if you buy only that item. But, if you buy other items at the store, then the technique has worked. The retailer made a profit on the other items you bought. The item priced below cost to attract you to the store is called a **loss leader**.

A loss leader is a legal and perfectly acceptable selling practice. You get the benefit of a really low price on that product. Just be careful to use the decision making process when you consider other items in the store. They may be priced higher than usual to make up the profit lost on the loss leader.

© Getty Images/PhotoDisc

Fraud

When selling practices go beyond deceptive into illegal, they become fraud. **Fraud** is deliberate deception, designed to secure unfair or unlawful gain. In short, fraud means cheating the consumer. According to law, a statement is fraudulent if it meets these two conditions.

1. The person who made the statement must know it is false.

2. The purpose of the statement must be to cause others to give up property that has value, such as money.

Proving these conditions exist can be difficult. To succeed, you must show what the person who made the statement had in mind. How can you prove it wasn't just a mistake or a harmless attempt to promote a product? Is it possible that no one intended to do any harm? Without written evidence or witnesses, fraud is hard to prove.

Your best protection against fraud is to avoid it. You need to learn how to distinguish between honest and dishonest offers. When an offer seems too good to be true, it may be fraud.

Bait and Switch

Trading up is a legitimate, though possibly deceptive, selling practice. Trading up moves into the more serious realm of fraud when the store never intended to sell the advertised product. Suppose you arrive at the store to buy the advertised product. It is out of stock or sold out. Then, the salesperson leads you over to the much better, more expensive, and available option. This practice of baiting consumers with an advertised but nonexistent bargain and then switching them to a more expensive product is called **bait and switch**.

Use the decision making process to make a rational buying decision. Don't just buy the more costly product because you came to the store ready to buy the similar, advertised product.

Pyramid Schemes

Have you ever received a chain letter that asked you to mail a dollar to the top person on the list and send copies of the letter to ten friends? If so, you were the target of a pyramid scheme.

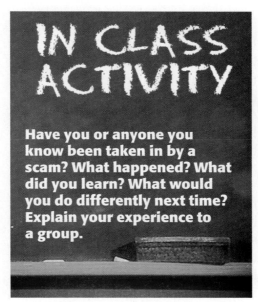

IN CLASS ACTIVITY

Have you or anyone you know been taken in by a scam? What happened? What did you learn? What would you do differently next time? Explain your experience to a group.

What In The World?

Since the breakup of the Soviet Union in the early 1990s, products produced in Western countries have been in great demand there. As their own economy struggles to switch from a command economy to a market economy, consumers are looking for the reliable quality of Western-made products.

However, Western products are often expensive and in short supply in the former Soviet Union. This combination of high demand and short supply affords a prime opportunity for fraud.

Also, the nations of the former Soviet Union do not have many consumer protection laws. Those that do exist are not well enforced. Consumers often cannot tell if a product was produced in the West or not. Without consumer protection laws, they cannot trust the information on labels, in advertising, or from salespeople. Unfortunately, many products being sold as Western are actually low-quality counterfeits. Without laws to protect them, consumers in this region have nowhere to turn for help.

Why do you think products from the West are in demand in the former Soviet Union? Why do you think they are expensive there? If you were a Russian citizen, how would you protect yourself from fraud?

© Getty Images/PhotoDisc

A **pyramid scheme** is a type of financial fraud in which people pay to join an organization in exchange for the right to sell memberships to others. The difference between a pyramid and a legitimate multi-level marketing organization is that the pyramid sells no legitimate product.

In a typical pyramid scheme, a few people at the top of the pyramid begin by convincing new recruits to send money to join. Those people then recruit others to send money. Recruits are promised large sums of money if they bring in others who pay to join the pyramid. In the end, the pyramid falls apart, and the only people who get the big payoff are the people at the top.

CheckPoint

What is the difference between deception and fraud? At what point does trading up turn into bait and switch?

PRIMARYSOURCES

The famous magician, Harry Houdini, enjoyed exposing the frauds that some psychics and mediums performed. Read this passage from 1923 which describes one such fraud. How believable would a person be who could produce the fingerprints of someone who was dead?

"In (a) sequence of photographs Houdini demonstrated how spirit hands that appeared at seances were made by less ethereal beings. In 'A magician among the spirits' Houdini described the mediumistic fraud known as 'finger-printing a spirit.' A mold of a dead person's hand would be carefully prepared and, during a seance with the believed relatives, fingerprints of the deceased would appear on a lampblacked trumpet. In his book Houdini stated the following: 'There are two cases on record where fortunes were at stake because of this sort of fraud. In one case five hundred "thousand" dollars changed hands upon the recognition of the fingerprints of a man who had died two years before.'"

Airport One pyramid scheme, called Airport, had each person who joined pay $1,500 to buy a square (membership). This gave that person the right to sell 8 squares to others for $1,500 each. Members who found eight people to buy squares earned $10,500 in profit.

Income: $1,500 \times 8 = $12,000

Income − Cost = Profit

$12,000 − $1,500 = $10,500

They could then "fly away" with the profits, hence the name Airport. The scheme worked well for the people who started the scheme or joined early. But, in a pyramid scheme, someone always loses. The winners' profits are everyone else's losses. People who bought their squares late received nothing. Pyramid schemes, like many other deals that offer large profits for little effort, are fraud.

Telephone Fraud

The telephone offers many advantages to con artists. You can't see them, so you can't tell if they are calling from a legitimate business or from a phone booth.

Also, you can't use body language cues to help judge truth from lies, and you won't be able to visually identify them to police. Here are some clues to listen for.

▶ They offer a deal that seems too good to be true.

▶ They ask for your credit card or Social Security number to verify your identity.

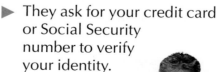

© Getty Images/PhotoDisc

► You must buy something to get something else of greater value for free.

► They refuse to send you a written copy of a sales agreement before you agree to buy.

► They demand that you act now or the offer will expire.

► They refuse to identify themselves or their organization.

► They refuse to provide a telephone number and address where you can reach their organization.

People who carry out telephone fraud play on your emotions. They have scripts that tell them what to say in almost any situation. In the chart below are some examples of persuasive techniques that telephone con artists use.

Remember that you don't really have to buy now. Legitimate business callers will give you the information you need to evaluate the offer. They will be happy to call you back later if you want time to consider the offer.

The Many Faces of Fraud

Covering all the many fraudulent schemes would fill a whole book. Here are some other scenarios that should bring out the healthy skeptic in you.

1. Healthcare products that promise to cure incurable diseases.

2. Home-improvement contractors who want you to pay most of the cost before they do any work.

3. Vacation clubs that require you to send money to join with the promise of inexpensive first-class vacations later.

© Getty Images/PhotoDisc

Technique	Example
Try to impress you by using names of famous people.	"When I had lunch with Senator Smith last week, he told me what a good deal this is."
Call you by your first name, use a term of endearment, or call older victims mom or dad.	"May I call you mom? I lost my mother a few years ago, and you remind me of her so much."
Suggest you don't have the power to make choices on your own.	"Should I be talking to your mother or father about this?"
Try to make you feel guilty if you decide not to buy.	"Now, I've spent a lot of time with you. A lot of other people are waiting to hear from me, but I put them off so I could talk to you."
Try to pressure you to make quick decisions.	"We have only two left. I don't know how much longer I can hold one."

© Getty Images/PhotoDisc

Dishonest people have learned a new way to take advantage of consumers. They target people who have already been victimized over the telephone. Here's how it works. A con artist convinced an elderly widow to charge $10,000 worth of products to her credit card. Some of the products never arrived. Others came but were not as they had been described. When the consumer tried to return the goods, she could not reach the business.

About a month later, a "helpful young man" called and offered to recover the money for $750. The consumer paid him but never received any money. He was part of the *piggyback swindle*. Today, she continues to receive telephone calls for bogus offers. Criminals who specialize in fraud share names and phone numbers. Consumers who have been victimized are likely to become victims again.

Imagine how the phone conversation might have gone between the con artist and the victim in this scam. List some statements that the con artist might have said to entice this woman to charge $10,000 worth of products. Include some statements that might also be part of a legitimate business offer. What key statements would alert you that the deal might possibly be fraud?

4. Repair work offered at well below the going rate.

5. Weight-loss programs that promise unrealistic results.

Protect Yourself from Deception and Fraud

Your first step in protecting yourself from deception and fraud is to recognize it when you see it. Learn to be skeptical. Check out unfamiliar companies before buying, especially companies that sell sight-unseen.

Ask questions about offers that seem too good to be true, and then carefully evaluate the responses. Understand the product or service you are buying. Make decisions with your head, not your emotions. Above all, use the decision making process to evaluate your options. Buying without careful consideration is the easiest way to become a victim.

GUESS WHAT

Recently, the FDA ruled that manufacturers of "dieter's teas" had to explain on their labels that the weight loss they provided was caused by water loss.

CheckPoint

What kinds of offers should make you suspicious? How can you protect yourself from deceptive and dishonest selling practices?

TRY THESE

1. Explain this statement: "The difference between 'deception' and 'fraud' is a matter of degree."

2. Describe three legal selling practices that could be deceptive.

3. When is a sale not a sale?

4. What two conditions are necessary for a statement to be fraudulent?

5. Why is it difficult to prove fraud?

6. How does a pyramid scheme work?

7. What characteristics should alert you that a telephone offer may be fraudulent?

8. What tactics do telephone con artists use to convince people to send them money?

9. What are some ways you can protect yourself from deception and fraud?

THINK CRITICALLY

10. **CONSUMER ACTION** Patrick was trying to decide whether to mail $100 to someone for the a chance to gain a $900 profit. Does this offer seem legitimate, deceptive, or fraudulent? If you think it is a scam, what kind? How could Patrick lose in such a deal? If you were offered this deal, would you take the risk? Justify your answer.

11. **COMMUNICATE** An oil company wants to build a refinery in your town. You believe it would pollute the environment and be a danger to those who live nearby. Use a word processing program to write a letter urging your neighbors to attend a meeting to oppose the refinery. Give the location and time. E-mail the letter to your teacher and two classmates.

12. Describe three offers that you have seen recently that you think might have been fraudulent. What made you suspicious? How would you go about verifying their legitimacy?

13. **COMMUNICATE** Define the difference between fraud and deception using examples. These examples can be from your experience or you can create them.

14. **COMMUNICATE** Using your answer to exercise 13, list ways you can avoid being cheated by each example you discussed.

DECISION MAKING PROJECT

SPECIFY   SEARCH   SIFT   SELECT   STUDY

SIFT Discuss the ideas from your brainstorming with your group. Have someone in the group list the pros and cons of each idea for filing a complaint. Keep in mind what you want the seller or manufacturer to do.

© Getty Images/PhotoDisc

GOALS

DESCRIBE
how to complain
successfully

IDENTIFY
government programs
and consumer-
oriented organizations
that can help resolve
consumer problems

3.4 Resolve Consumer Problems

Prepare to Make a Complaint

Sometimes products simply don't meet your needs or expectations. Perhaps the sweater you bought didn't match the pants you wanted to wear it with. Maybe when your concert tickets arrived, the seats were not together, as you had requested. What do you do?

Resolve the Problem The purpose of your complaint is to resolve the problem. The best way to accomplish this is to have your facts straight before you begin the complaint process. You also need documentation, such as the sales receipt and warranty. Get into the habit of saving your receipt whenever you make a purchase. Then, if you have a problem with the product, the receipt will prove where you bought it and the price you paid.

CONSUMER ACTION

Claudia bought a desk chair from a furniture store and arranged to have it delivered to her home. When the bill arrived, she discovered that she was charged an extra $50 for delivery and set-up. The salesperson did not mention any additional charges, so she felt deceived. Also, the additional $50 made the chair cost more than she wanted to spend, so now she wants to return the chair for a refund. What should she do first? How should she go about getting the refund she wants? Should she report the deception? If so, to whom?

Write down the facts of the situation on a piece of paper. Also, list the resolutions that you would accept. These are the kinds of information to include on your list of facts.

1. The date and location of the transaction.

2. A description of the product you purchased. Be as specific as possible. Include the model number, color, size, and so on. For complicated products, such as computers, include the options you selected and identifying specifications, such as speed and memory.

3. The product's price and your method of payment, such as credit card, check, or cash.

4. A specific explanation of what is wrong with the product.

5. A statement of how you want the problem resolved. Do you want the product repaired or replaced, or do you want a refund? Be reasonable. The resolution should be fair for both you and the store.

© Getty Images/Digital Vision

CheckPoint

Why should you always keep sales receipts? Why should you gather the facts before beginning the complaint process?

The Complaint Process

Consumer problems come in all shapes and sizes. Some are as small as a shirt that doesn't fit and needs to be exchanged. Other problems are more serious, such as a defective product that could cause injury.

Most businesspeople are honest and want to earn a profit by providing reliable products at fair prices. If you are dissatisfied with a purchase, give the business an opportunity to correct the problem.

Start with the Seller The best approach for resolving any consumer problem is to start with the seller. Progress toward more serious actions only if you don't reach an acceptable resolution with the seller.

With the product, receipt, and list of facts in hand, you are ready to make your complaint. For best results, be rational, not emotional. People are usually more willing to give you what you want if you present the problem calmly, without a verbal attack.

Here is a process you can follow to resolve your consumer problem.

1. Return to the store. Explain the problem to a salesperson in the appropriate department or to a customer service representative. Ask for the person's name, and write it down. You may need to talk to that person again later or

COMMUNICATE

You bought an expensive digital camera from Delta Cameras, Inc. You paid for it with your MasterCard. When the camera arrived, the package had been crushed. Although the camera did turn on, it made only a clicking sound when you tried to use the zoom lens.

You are willing to let the company repair the camera if the repair can be completed in three weeks. You are going on vacation then and want to take the camera with you. Write a letter to the company, clearly stating the problem and how you want it to be resolved.

refer to the conversation in later steps in the complaint process. Ask this person for the resolution you think is fair.

2. If the salesperson or customer service representative can't resolve the problem, ask to speak to a manager.

3. If the manager can't help, write to the manufacturer. Describe the problem clearly and honestly, but not emotionally. Do not overstate. State what you are seeking. Include information about how to contact you. Enclose a copy (not the original) of the sales receipt and warranty. Keep a copy of all written correspondence.

4. If you are still not satisfied, your next step is to contact a consumer group or professional organization, such as the Better Business Bureau or your local chamber of commerce. You may also contact your state's attorney general's office or your city or county consumer division for assistance.

5. Your last resort, if all else fails, is to bring a lawsuit.

CheckPoint

Why does the complaint process start with the store? Why not just start with the highest authority? Why should you state your complaint calmly, without attacking?

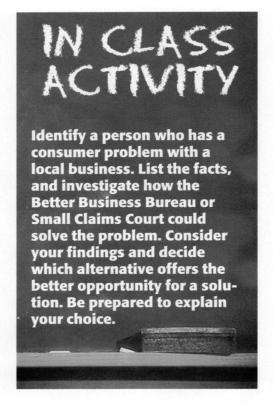

IN CLASS ACTIVITY

Identify a person who has a consumer problem with a local business. List the facts, and investigate how the Better Business Bureau or Small Claims Court could solve the problem. Consider your findings and decide which alternative offers the better opportunity for a solution. Be prepared to explain your choice.

Seek Help from Consumer Organizations

Several organizations help consumers resolve problems. One of the best known is the **Better Business Bureau (BBB)**. The BBB is a nonprofit agency with offices across the country, each sponsored by local businesses. The BBB helps consumers in the following ways.

1. Helps resolve disputes between consumers and sellers.

2. Keeps a file of complaints against local businesses and supplies this information to consumers who ask for it.

3. Educates consumers by providing information in printed tip sheets and booklets and on the Internet.

4. Promotes honest advertising and selling practices.

The Better Business Bureau has no legal power to force a decision on either a consumer or a business. However, most BBB offices will contact businesses about consumer complaints and help the two sides reach an agreement. If you want to check a company's reputation, call your local BBB and ask if it has any complaints about this company on file.

Arbitration Many business groups, particularly in the appliance and automobile industries, have created panels to resolve consumer complaints. The DaimlerChrysler Customer Arbitration Board, for example, has the power to decide what the DaimlerChrysler Corporation will do when it receives a complaint. The board's decision is binding on DaimlerChrysler but not on the customer. Consumers have the right to take their case to court.

Media Help Other resources include consumer help services operated by many newspapers and television and radio stations. These businesses often help resolve consumer problems to gain stories for their news reports. Although they benefit from their efforts, they can also help you solve your consumer problem.

CheckPoint

How can the Better Business Bureau help with consumer problems? Name three examples of situations in which you would seek help from the BBB.

Government Efforts to Help Consumers

Our government has taken a variety of steps to help people with consumer problems. A number of these steps are intended to keep consumer problems from ever taking place. Others help consumers gain satisfaction in disputes over defective or misrepresented products.

Truth in Information

Consumer protection laws require businesses to supply accurate, honest information about their products to consumers. For example, laws require businesses to label food ingredients accurately and to tell consumers how to use products safely.

Enforcement Is Difficult

Enforcing these laws is difficult. The government must first identify businesses using an illegal practice before it can require them to stop. Individual people generally do not have the resources to take businesses to court. They must rely on the government to prosecute dishonest businesses. Identifying and prosecuting dishonest businesses across the country is an enormous task.

Use Common Sense

As a consumer, your best defense is to apply your own common sense to advertising messages and other information from businesses. If the information makes you suspicious, check it out before spending.

Cooling-Off Periods

The federal government and many states have established cooling-off periods for some consumer purchases. A **cooling-off period** is a specified period of time within which a consumer can back out of an agreement to buy something. Often the specified period is three days from the agreement date. The Federal Trade Commission has made a rule that consumers can cancel contracts they sign in their homes within three days of contract signing. This rule is designed to protect

© Getty Images/PhotoDisc

consumers from high-pressure door-to-door salespeople. After the specified cooling-off period, consumers are bound by the contracts they signed.

Reporting Consumer Problems

Every state has an attorney general and a consumer affairs office that are responsible for enforcing consumer-protection laws. You can register complaints with either of these offices. Although these offices cannot follow up on every complaint, they will look into cases in which many people file the same complaint.

These offices may not be able to get the resolution you want, but they can force offending businesses to close or clean up their act. Your complaint may protect other consumers from the problems you experienced.

Using Small Claims Courts

After you have tried every other option in the complaint process without success, your last resort is to bring suit. If your claim is small, you can take your case to **small claims court**. Small claims courts exist in all states. Each state establishes the maximum claim size that its small claims court will handle. In most states, the maximum ranges from $1,000 to $10,000. The small claims

court will handle disputes involving any amount below the maximum.

The advantages to small claims court are:

1. You don't need a lawyer. In fact, lawyers are not allowed to represent clients in small claims court.

2. Court costs are low, usually under $200.

3. Most cases are resolved quickly.

To begin a suit in small claims court, take all the information you have about the problem to the courthouse. The clerks there will tell you how to proceed.

Be sure to exhaust all other options before deciding to sue. Remember that you may not win. If you don't win, you may be required to pay the defendant's costs.

Also, a small claims court will not collect the judgment for you. Even if the court finds in your favor, it will do nothing if the defendant chooses not to pay. To collect, you may have to hire a lawyer and take your case to a higher court. When your loss is small, taking the matter to a higher court can cost you more than you might win.

CheckPoint

What is the purpose of a cooling-off period? Why should you report dishonest business practices to the attorney general or consumer affairs office? What are the advantages and disadvantages of small claims court?

TRY THESE

1. What kinds of information and documentation do you need before you start the complaint process?

2. What are the steps in the complaint process?

3. What is the Better Business Bureau? How can your local BBB help you as a consumer?

4. What is a cooling-off period? How does it protect consumers?

5. What are the two state offices that enforce consumer laws?

6. What is small claims court, and what are its advantages for consumers? Why should it be a last resort in the complaint process?

THINK CRITICALLY

7. **CONSUMER ACTION** Claudia felt deceived by the extra $50 charged to her for delivery and set-up of her new desk chair. Also, the chair now costs more than she wants to spend, so she wants a refund. If you were Claudia, how would you prepare to make your complaint? What steps would you follow to seek a refund? Where could you go for help with the complaint? Would you report the deception? Why or why not?

8. Think about a product or service you bought recently that disappointed you. If you haven't been dissatisfied with a product or service lately, choose one you bought and imagine a problem with it. Make a list of the specific information about this product or service that you would need before beginning the complaint process.

9. **COMMUNICATE** Referring to exercise 8, assume that you were unable to come to a satisfactory agreement with the store or service provider about the problem. Write a letter to the manufacturer or to the president of the service company, explaining the problem and asking for a reasonable resolution. Be direct but not emotional or attacking. Send your letter to your teacher by e-mail.

10. The Better Business Bureau is sponsored by local businesses. How might this sponsorship benefit you as a consumer? How might it cause a conflict of interest that may not benefit you?

DECISION MAKING PROJECT

SPECIFY   SEARCH   SIFT   SELECT   STUDY

SELECT After looking at the pros and cons of all the ways you could file your complaint, plan the steps you would take toward a resolution. Be specific. Draw a flow chart to illustrate your steps.

KEY IDEAS

Consumer Rights and Responsibilities

1. For the seven consumer rights you enjoy, you have seven corresponding responsibilities.
2. Competition among companies for your business helps to keep prices reasonable and product quality high.

Government and Consumer Protection

3. The consumer movement seeks to protect and inform consumers by requiring such practices as honest advertising, product warranties, and improved safety standards.
4. The FTC protects consumers from unfair or deceptive business practices. The CPSC protects consumers from dangerous products. The EPA enforces regulations to protect the environment. State and local governments offer many types of consumer protection.
5. Written warranties can be full or limited. Limited warranties must explain their limitations. Implied warranties are unwritten guarantees that the product will work for the purpose intended.

Deception and Fraud

6. Deceptive advertising or selling practices, taken to an unlawful extreme, become fraud.
7. Some legal selling practices, such as trading up, loss leaders, and sale pricing, may seem deceptive.
8. Fraud is deliberate deception, designed to secure unfair or unlawful gain.

9. Fraud comes in many forms, but some of the most popular are bait and switch and pyramid schemes.
10. Your first step in protecting yourself against deception and fraud is to recognize it and use the decision making process to evaluate all offers.

Resolve Consumer Problems

11. When you are dissatisfied with a product or service, your first step is to write down the facts and gather the sales documentation.
12. The complaint process begins with the store where you bought the product and progresses toward more serious actions to seek a resolution to a consumer problem.
13. Local business-sponsored Better Business Bureaus help resolve disputes between buyers and sellers, keep files of complaints lodged against local companies, and offer consumer educational information.
14. Laws protect consumers from inaccurate or misleading information.
15. The federal government and many states provide for a cooling-off period, in which consumers can back out of a sales contract without obligation.
16. A consumer's last resort in resolving a dispute is to sue. Small claims courts offer an inexpensive way to resolve complaints. However, small claims courts do not collect judgments for consumers.

TERMS REVIEW

Match each term on the left with its definition on the right.
Some terms may not be used.

a. bait and switch

b. Better Business Bureau (BBB)

c. cease-and-desist order

d. competition

e. consumer movement

f. Consumer Product Safety Commission (CPSC)

g. cooling-off period

h. Environmental Protection Agency (EPA)

i. Federal Trade Commission (FTC)

j. fraud

k. full warranty

l. implied warranty

m. limited warranty

n. loss leader

o. monopoly

p. pyramid scheme

q. redress

r. small claims court

s. trading up

t. warranty

1. responsible for protecting consumers from unfair or deceptive business practices

2. agency that protects consumers from dangerous products

3. order that requires the company to stop using an advertisement

4. agency that enforces laws that protect the environment

5. a company's promise that the product will meet specific standards over a given time period

6. an unwritten guarantee that the product is of sufficient quality to fulfill the purpose for which it was designed

7. a company that has an unfair advantage over competitors in an area of business

8. to seek and receive a remedy to the problem

9. item priced below cost to attract you to the store

10. pressuring consumers to buy a more expensive product than they intended

11. deliberate deception, designed to secure unfair or unlawful gain

12. a nonprofit agency that helps to resolve disputes between consumers and sellers

13. specified period of time within which a consumer can back out of an agreement to buy something

14. handles disputes involving smaller dollar amounts

CONSUMER DECISIONS

15. You bought a chain saw that came with a booklet explaining how to use the saw safely. You really don't want to plow through a lot of manufacturer's warnings. You just want to cut up some firewood for tonight. Besides, the store wouldn't sell the saw if it weren't safe to use. What are your rights and responsibilities in this case? What would you do?

16. The warranty you received with your new exercise machine didn't seem to cover everything. What elements would you look for to make sure it meets the requirements for a valid warranty?

17. When a telephone salesperson is explaining a deal to you, what cues would you listen for to try to determine if the deal is really fraud?

18. Your new bike broke after one use, and you are really mad. How would you approach the salesperson who sold it to you? Would you verbally attack the salesperson to show how angry you are? Why or why not?

LOOK IT UP

19. Find advertisements for a similar product from three different companies. Do the ads provide evidence of competition among the companies for your business? How does the competition benefit you as a consumer?

20. Explore how to protect an elderly person from dangerous medications. Contact the FDA at its web site www.fda.gov.

21. Find an advertisement in a magazine or on the Internet that you think is fraud. What clues made you suspicious?

22. Find out about your local Better Business Bureau. What is its stated mission? What services does it offer to consumers? What consumer information publications does it have?

INSIDE THE NUMBERS

23. You have been looking for living room furniture for your first apartment. You found two sets that you like at different stores. Both sets have a list price of $1,599, which is more than you can pay in cash. One store offers to rent its set for $40 a week for the next year. The business would own the furniture until you have made all the rental payments. Then, the set becomes your property. If you miss two payments in a row, the store will take the furniture back. The other store offers to sell its set for $599 down and $300 per month for the next four months. You can afford either of these arrangements. Which is the better deal? What should you consider in the first store's offer in addition to the cost?

24. When you buy an Apple iPod player, the salesperson asks you if you would like to purchase an extended warranty for $15. The

WHICH IS THE BEST DEAL?

You feel out of shape. You weigh more than you would like and you don't get much exercise. You finally decided to do something about your condition. What benefits and costs would you consider as you make your decision? What would you do?

Alternative 1 Buying a membership at one health club would cost $199 for the next year and $4 per hour each time you visit the club. By joining, you would have use of the exercise equipment, the club pool, and the advice of a professional exercise instructor.

Alternative 2 Buying a membership at another health club would cost $50 a month. The second health club also offers the use of the exercise equipment, the club pool, and the advice of a professional exercise instructor.

Alternative 3 Buying your favorite exercise machine, a treadmill machine, would cost $1,200.

POINT YOUR BROWSER TO

www.ee4c.swlearning.com
Complete the activity for Chapter 3.

current warranty lasts for three months. You have never heard of an iPod player breaking down, but the salesperson points out that just to have the player inspected, not fixed, costs $20. What will you do? What additional information can help you make a rational buying decision?

THINK CRITICALLY

25. Calvin collects baseball cards. His favorite team is the New York Yankees. He has cards for the entire 1996 World Series winning team except for John Wetteland, who was voted most valuable player. Calvin found a baseball card dealer who has one of these cards in good condition that he will sell for $50. Last week, Calvin visited a baseball chat-room on the Internet. One of the other people in the conversation offered to sell him a John Wetteland card if Calvin would send him $25 in the mail. How should Cal decide which card to buy?

CURRICULUM CONNECTION

26. **GOVERNMENT** Locate a copy of the first ten amendments to the Constitution. These amendments are the Bill of Rights. Read through them and identify ways in which these amendments defend consumers' rights. Write a one-page paper

describing how these rights apply to consumers.

27. **BUSINESS** Select a product or service that you like. Write a brief advertisement for it. The goal of your ad is to entice people to buy the product or service, so make it enthusiastic and convincing. It must accurately describe the features of the product or service without being deceptive.

28. **WRITING** Think of a product or service that you believe is dangerous. Describe the product or service and why you think it is dangerous. Do you think a government regulatory agency should take action to ban this product or service? Do you think your state's attorney general should know about this product or service to press charges in court against the person producing the product or service? Would you join a consumer group to press for regulation or other government intervention? Why or why not?

JOURNAL RECAP

29. After reading this chapter, review the answers you wrote to the questions in Journal Journey. Have your opinions changed? How would you use available resources to resolve consumer problems?

DECISION MAKING PROJECT

SPECIFY SEARCH SIFT SELECT STUDY

STUDY Present your situation and plan to the class. See if anyone in the class has any other suggestions. If someone in your group follows the steps you planned, tell the results and what you learned.

CHOOSE A CAREER

GET A JOB

WHAT'S AHEAD

EXPLODING MYTHS

Fact or Myth?
What do you think is true?

1. A career is something you do to make money for your real life outside of work.

2. It is better to accept a job that is offered than to hold out for the one you want.

3. Success in a career depends mostly on luck or knowing the right people.

JOURNAL JOURNEY

WRITE IN YOUR JOURNAL ABOUT THE FOLLOWING.

UNDERSTAND YOURSELF What do you value most in your life? What interests you? What do you do well? How would you describe your personality?

IDENTIFY A CAREER GOAL What do you think you want to do for a living? What do you like about this career? What don't you like about it? What do you need to do to prepare for this career?

LOOK FOR A JOB What could you do to find a job or a better job? What could you do to convince an employer that you are the best person for the job?

DECISION MAKING PROJECT

● SPECIFY ● SEARCH ● SIFT ● SELECT ● STUDY

GET A JOB! Start thinking now about the kind of job or career you would like to have! You will analyze your skills, aptitudes, interests, and personality, as well as the job market.

GOAL

To learn how to find a career that is right for you

PROJECT PROCESS

SPECIFY	Lesson 4.1
SEARCH	Lesson 4.2
SIFT	Lesson 4.3
SELECT	Lesson 4.4
STUDY	Chapter Assessment

© Getty Images/PhotoDisc

GOALS

DESCRIBE
what is important in
your life

IDENTIFY
interests, aptitudes,
and personality traits
that will influence your
career choice

4.1 Get to Know Yourself

What Do You Value?

Suppose you found Aladdin's magic lamp. What would you wish for: fame, fortune, or power, something for today or something to last for life? Choosing a career is much like finding a way to fulfill your wishes. Choices you make now will likely affect you during your life span. Choose wisely!

If you had to choose between a job that you enjoy and one that you don't enjoy but pays more money, which would you choose? Useful career plans include a clear idea of your values, aptitudes, skills, interests, and personality.

As you plan your career, consider your life-span goals. A career plan is important but is only one part of a life-span plan.

CONSUMER **ACTION**

Carlos always did well in school, but he wasn't sure what he wanted to do for a living. His best friend wanted to be an accountant and told him that accountants make good money. So, after graduating from high school, Carlos enrolled in accounting courses at his community college. Very soon, however, Carlos discovered he didn't like accounting. He didn't know where to turn for career help. Many of his friends had used career exploration books. So Carlos went to a bookstore, but there were so many books, and they were expensive. What should Carlos do?

Life Values

Recall from Chapter 1 that *values* are your principles—standards you live by. *Life values* are the most important principles in your life. If you value being with family, taking a job in Spain is likely a mistake. For someone who values travel and learning about other lands, a job in Spain might be perfect.

Work Values

Work values are the principles most important to you in your work. Suppose you value travel and learning about other lands, and you want to be a lawyer. Spain doesn't have the same legal system as the United States does. A law career in Spain might not be the perfect choice.

Understand Your Values

Career planning starts with understanding your values. To be a good choice for you, a career must closely fit with your life and work values.

INTERNET ACTIVITY

How can the social, cultural, and demographic values you learned about in Chapter 1 help you choose a career? Using e-mail, exchange your thoughts with a classmate and evaluate this student's ideas. Use the comments you receive to write an essay on the importance of these values. E-mail it to your teacher.

Life and Work Values

▶ **Income and wealth** How much is enough for you? How high a priority do you put on wealth?

▶ **Security** Do you want the security of keeping the same job for many years? Or would you rather change jobs and do new things throughout your work life?

▶ **Independence** Is it important to you to be able to choose how you do your job? Or would you rather follow company guidelines in doing your job?

▶ **Physical risk** Would you take a job with only little physical risk? Or do you like adventurous jobs that require physical risk?

▶ **Recognition** How important is gaining other people's respect?

▶ **Creativity** How important is developing new ideas and ways of doing things?

▶ **Personal growth** Do you prefer jobs that give you an opportunity to gain additional skills, training, or education? Or would you rather become the best you can be in the skills required in one job?

▶ **Family** How important is it to have regular time with your family? Would you like to stay close to your family or establish your life elsewhere?

▶ **Community** How important is sharing time with other members of your community?

▶ **Location** How important is the place where you live? If you could live anywhere, where would you choose?

Interests, Aptitudes, and Personality

Suppose you accept a job when you are 18 and work 40 hours a week until you are 65. If you do, you will work more than 90,000 hours! This is a long time to do something that doesn't interest you. You will be happier if you choose a career doing something you enjoy.

What Are Your Interests?

Your personal interests go beyond the passing enjoyment you feel when you listen to a CD. **Personal interests** are activities you find rewarding over an extended period of time.

To determine your interests, identify things you do that hold your attention. You might like using machines or tools. Taking and developing photographs might be your hobby. Being a member of the school debating team may bring you satisfaction.

© Getty Images/PhotoDisc

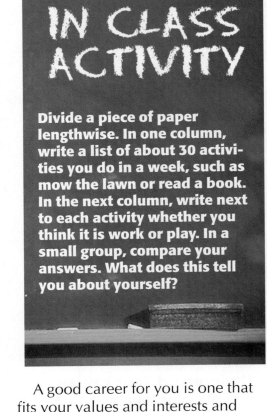

IN CLASS ACTIVITY

Divide a piece of paper lengthwise. In one column, write a list of about 30 activities you do in a week, such as mow the lawn or read a book. In the next column, write next to each activity whether you think it is work or play. In a small group, compare your answers. What does this tell you about yourself?

A good career for you is one that fits your values and interests and provides enough income to support you and your family. Does this sound like a lot to ask of a career? It is—which is why you must plan for your future now.

What Are Your Aptitudes?

Your interests may lead you toward particular careers, but success in a career requires aptitudes and skills. An **aptitude** is a natural talent for learning some skills over others. Math may come easily to you, but you really have to work at learning to write well. Your best friend may learn new languages with ease but considers history a chore. Everyone finds some things easier to learn than others. Different people have different aptitudes for learning new tasks. Everyone has aptitudes—including you. You just need to discover what they are.

Common Aptitudes

▶ **Verbal aptitude** is the ability to write in a clear and interesting manner and to explain ideas so that others can understand them. People with a verbal aptitude may be successful in a career in writing, editing, or teaching.

▶ **Numerical aptitude** is the ability to work with numbers quickly and accurately. Careers in science, math, finance, or accounting may be good choices for people with this aptitude.

▶ **Spatial aptitude** is the ability to "see" what something will look like from a verbal description or a flat drawing or photograph. People with a spatial aptitude are often successful in careers in graphic arts, design, or architecture.

▶ **Manual dexterity** is the ability to fix and build things and to do other physical work. People with this aptitude may succeed in a career in the building trades, such as carpentry or plumbing, or in repair jobs, such as computer or car repair.

▶ **Physical coordination** is the ability to execute precise muscle movements. This aptitude could lead to success in sports training, physical education, or coaching.

Turn Aptitudes into Skills

Success in a career requires developing aptitudes into **skills** through training and experience. People must develop **transferable skills** allowing them to complete specific tasks in various careers. Learning to write clearly, for example, can lead to success as a business manager, a newspaper reporter, or an English teacher. Using a spreadsheet program is necessary for an

VOTE *Your Wallet*

Oregon's rivers provide much of our salmon supply. Logging harms these rivers and makes them less suitable for salmon habitat.

Environmentalists want the government to reduce logging to restore the salmon habitat. The drop in salmon has put many fishers out of work, but to stop logging will jeopardize loggers' jobs.

What are the conflicting values in this issue? How would you vote? How would you vote if you were a fisher? A timber company executive?

accountant as well as a research scientist.

Developing one skill isn't the key to career success. If you have developed your verbal aptitude into leadership skills, you still need financial skills to be a manager.

COMMUNICATE

Think about the aptitudes listed. What others do you have that aren't on the list? Write a letter to a friend describing your aptitudes.

Life-Span Plan

$MATH OF MONEY

You decide to buy a DVD of your favorite movie. A store near your school sells it for $20.00. A discount store five miles away sells the same DVD for $15.00. What is the discount? What is the discount as a percentage of the more expensive price?

SOLUTION

The discount is $5.00. The discount is 25% of the more expensive price.

$$\begin{array}{r} \$20.00 \\ -\ \ 15.00 \\ \hline =\ \$\ \ 5.00 \end{array}$$

$$\frac{\$5}{\$20} = 0.25 = 25\%$$

If you can do this problem in your head, you may have an aptitude for working with numbers.

What Is Your Personality?

You are unique. No one else in the world is like you. Your **personality** is the unique blend of qualities that defines you as an individual based on what you think, feel, and believe. Others judge your personality by your behaviors.

Each career option fits better with some personalities than others. If you like to be with people, a job requiring you to work alone may not suit you. Whatever your personality, you can find a career that matches it. To do this, first identify your personality type.

Career Goals Preparing for a career requires setting short-term and life-span goals. If your life-span goal is to own and operate a successful electronics store, first set short-term goals. For example, your choice of classes or a job can help you reach that life-span goal. Your personality will influence your career goals.

IN CLASS ACTIVITY

Choose a friend as a partner. Make two lists—one, a self-assessment of your values, aptitudes, and personality traits, and the other, a list of the same items for your friend. Compare your lists. What do they say about how others see you? How can self-assessment help you make a better career choice?

PRIMARYSOURCES

Read this excerpt from a short autobiographical story called *New Way Dry Cleaning and Laundry*. What type of personality is described here? Would you be comfortable taking a risk like this?

"He made about $75 a week at the job. In June of 1931 we moved back to town so we could be near his work. He continued his work at this laundry about a year, then decided if he could make that much for the other fellow, he could do even better for himself.

He went into partnership with another man and rented a building a couple of blocks up the street from where we are now. As soon as the machinery was installed, we opened up for business. The first week we took in exactly $218."

© Getty Images/PhotoDisc

Personality Types

▶ **Realistic** people like to know what's really going on around them. They like to know what's true, even if the truth is unpleasant. They make lists and put people, events, and objects into groups. Realistic people are often successful in business careers.

▶ **Investigative** people like to know why things happen. They enjoy gathering and analyzing information to find solutions. Investigative people are often successful in careers in the sciences.

▶ **Creative** people like to be involved in free, unrestricted activities. They like an atmosphere free of rules so they can be inventive. Creative people often are successful in careers in art, theater, or music.

▶ **Social** people like to work with other people and prefer group activities over solitary activities.

Social people often are successful in careers in sales, teaching, or health care.

▶ **Enterprising** people like to lead and direct others in achieving a goal. They enjoy taking risks and like to develop plans and carry them out. Enterprising people often use leadership skills to gain success and public approval. They have management or political careers or operate a business.

CheckPoint

When a friend asks you to describe someone's personality, how do you know what to say? Why is personality important in career planning?

TRY THESE

1. Give three examples of values and career options that would fit well with these values.

2. What is the difference between liking something and being interested in something?

3. Why do you need skills as well as aptitudes to succeed in a career?

4. Why should you consider your personality in your career planning?

5. Why do people who carefully set short-term goals often achieve their life-span career goals?

6. What might be some good career choices for an enterprising personality? Explain your reasoning.

THINK CRITICALLY

7. **CONSUMER ACTION** Carlos didn't like his accounting courses, so he wondered how to look for a new career. Write a letter to Carlos advising him about how to look for a new career. Use what you know about his values and personality. Suggest career options that might be better for him.

8. What aptitudes do you have that you believe could be developed into job skills? Give three career options that your aptitudes and skills would fit.

9. Draw an object in your room from memory. What does your drawing tell you about aptitudes you either have or do not have?

10. **COMMUNICATE** In an e-mail to a classmate, identify a career you would like to follow. Explain how your values, interests, personality, and aptitudes make it a good choice. Evaluate the classmate's e-mail you receive. Is the other student's choice a good one?

11. Have you ever taken a personality test? If so, what personality type are you? If you have not taken a personality test, ask your guidance counselor for one, and take the test. What can you learn about yourself?

DECISION MAKING PROJECT

○ SPECIFY   ○ SEARCH   ○ SIFT   ○ SELECT   ○ STUDY

SPECIFY Start thinking about a career you might like. Consider the lists you have made in this lesson of your values, interests, aptitudes, and personality. Use a word processing program to organize these lists on a sheet of paper. Make another list of short-term and life-span career goals you might set to succeed in the career you have chosen. Save these lists. You will use them to complete this project.

© Getty Images/PhotoDisc

4.2 Explore Careers

Job or Career Information

Accepting a job is quite different from choosing a career. A **job** is the set of tasks you accomplish as you work. You may have a part-time job that is important to you because it provides spending money and work experience. If you don't intend to stay in that employment field for a large part of your life, then it is a job—not a career.

A **career** is an occupation to which you have made a long-term commitment. To achieve a career requires planning, education, and preparation. You must want the career enough to be willing to make sacrifices to achieve your goal. A career is a serious commitment. Choose it carefully.

Almost everyone begins a career by accepting an entry-level job. Over time, you may gain skills and experience in your career field and move up to positions of more

CONSUMER ACTION

Jalisa is looking forward to her graduation from high school next year with joy and dread. What will she do then? She has always been good at science in school, especially biology, and she loves animals. What can she do with this aptitude to make a living? She doesn't even know how to start thinking about a career. Her uncle offered her a job as an assistant in his pet grooming business. This isn't exactly the job of her dreams, but should she take it anyway?

responsibility. Or you may discover other avenues within your field that you want to try. For example, after a few years of working in software development, you might decide to use your expertise to market software.

During your lifetime, you may even switch career fields. Changing career fields may be difficult. You might have transferable skills required for the new career field, but you would probably have to gain many more.

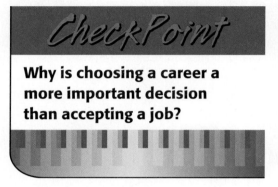

CheckPoint

Why is choosing a career a more important decision than accepting a job?

Identifying Possible Careers

After getting to know yourself and what you want in life, your next step is to identify and investigate career alternatives that interest you.

First, you can look at what careers are available. You can find sources of career information by visiting your school's guidance office. You can also find information at public libraries or on the Internet. No matter what career interests you, there is plenty of information to be found.

Federal Sources of Information

Most libraries have career information sections containing hundreds of information sources. Instead of checking publications randomly, you might want to review these federal government publications first.

Occupational Outlook Handbook (OOH) *OOH* describes about 250 occupations that you can use to identify general fields of interest to investigate further.

Occupational Information Network (O*NET) O*NET is a comprehensive database of the job characteristics, skills, and knowledge that are required for most jobs. It has replaced the *Dictionary of Occupational Titles* that had been printed in book form in the past.

Occupational Outlook Quarterly and Monthly Labor Review These two federal publications provide specific information about careers. They contain articles about job opportunities and working conditions in different careers. Although they go into greater depth, they do not cover as many careers as other sources.

These publications will not tell you everything you need to know about any career. They can, however, help you narrow your search to just the careers that might interest you.

© Getty Images/PhotoDisc

CYBER CONSUMER

The Internet offers abundant sources of career information. Use the keyword "careers" or "jobs" to search the Net. You will find lots of links to follow. Try narrowing your search by adding keywords of professions that interest you, like "law" or "wildlife management."

You will also find many sites where employers list job openings. Also, if you check out the web site of a particular company, often you will find a description of jobs with that company.

seekers. It also provides many links to other related sites. There are many other web sites that provide general or specific career information that can be found through an Internet search using the keywords *career* and *information*. You may also search using a specific career title that interests you.

For more career information sources, you can ask your guidance counselor or librarian or visit your local bookstore. The telephone book and the Internet are additional sources of career ideas.

Private Sources of Career Information

You can also find non-government sources of career information.

U.S. News Work and Career Web Site   *U.S. News and World Report* maintains a commercial work and career web site that provides access to articles dealing with careers and employment. It also has links to a wide variety of other sites that you may find useful in your career search. These articles are not likely to provide extensive information about specific careers but will help you gain a general understanding of employment trends and career opportunities.

Mapping Your Future

Mapping Your Future is an organization that maintains a web site that furnishes extensive advice for job

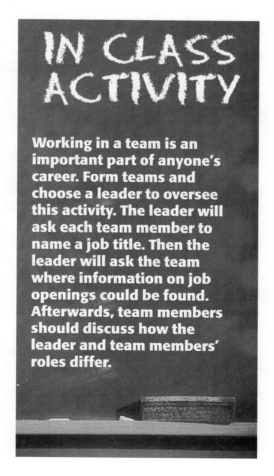

IN CLASS ACTIVITY

Working in a team is an important part of anyone's career. Form teams and choose a leader to oversee this activity. The leader will ask each team member to name a job title. Then the leader will ask the team where information on job openings could be found. Afterwards, team members should discuss how the leader and team members' roles differ.

CAREER CLUSTERS

There are fifteen career clusters identified by
the United States Office of Education

AGRIBUSINESS AND NATURAL RESOURCES

Farmer, food
processor, chemist,
commodities analyst

BUSINESS AND OFFICE TECHNOLOGY

Office manager,
executive assistant,
human resources staff,
clerical staff

HEALTH AND MEDICINE

Nurse, orderly,
doctor, insurance
adjuster, admissions
clerk, dentist,
physical therapist

PUBLIC SERVICE

Police, armed
services, political office
holder,
post office worker

ENVIRONMENTAL SCIENCES

Biologist, engineer,
park ranger,
environmental historian

COMMUNICATIONS AND MEDIA

Computer, network,
Internet
programmer,
broadcast journalist,
cable installer

HOSPITALITY AND RECREATION

Hotel desk clerk,
travel agent,
chef,
restaurant server

MANUFACTURING TECHNOLOGY

Quality assurance
specialist, line manager,
line crew,
industrial safety
technician

MARKETING AND DISTRIBUTION

Sales manager,
warehouse manager,
inventory specialist,
market research
specialist, forklift driver

MARINE SCIENCE

Diver, treasure
explorer, marine
biologist, hatcheries
manager,
ecologist

PERSONAL SERVICES

Manicurist,
salon stylist,
massage therapist

CONSTRUCTION TECHNOLOGY

Site supervisor,
architect, electrician,
plumber, general
contractor

TRANSPORTATION TECHNOLOGY

Truck driver,
train conductor,
airplane pilot,
air traffic controller

FAMILY AND CONSUMER SCIENCE

Teacher, interior
designer, consumer
product analyst

FINE ART AND HUMANITIES

Ballet dancer,
conductor, costume
designer, musician,
actor, painter

COMMUNICATE

Compare the *Family* and *Consumer Science* career cluster on the preceding page with the *Business and Office Technology* cluster. Find information you need by using *OOH* or *O*NET*. Write an essay that explains which of these clusters offers careers that fit in best with your personality, aptitudes, and values. Do any of these careers offer entrepreneurial options?

Private Employment Agencies

Most private employment agencies do not counsel you about a career. They match your existing skills with the needs of employers and leave the rest to you.

Private employment agencies earn income by charging a fee to match workers with jobs. If you have a skill that is in demand, employers pay the fee. But if you have no special skills or knowledge, the employment agency charges you the fee.

Be sure that you don't have to pay the fee until *after* you accept a job offer. When you pay first, you may receive little or nothing for your money. Be sure to check with the Better Business Bureau to learn about any private employment agency you consider.

Make a Career Connection

Talking to someone working in a career that interests you is an excellent way to learn about it. Most people are willing to talk to students. The meeting you have with someone who works in your career of choice is a **career connection**. Before making one, prepare clear, well-thought-out questions and be aware of the person's time demands. Observing someone at work for a day is a good way to learn about a career.

Volunteer

Another useful way to investigate a career is to volunteer or seek a job that supports people who work in that field. Suppose you think you might like to be a doctor or nurse. If you volunteer to answer the telephone in a hospital, you will be able to observe what doctors and nurses do. This experience may help you decide whether you want to prepare for a career in medicine.

Some careers are glamorized in television shows. Volunteering can help you see what everyday life is like in these professions. For example, most lawyers don't ever set foot in a courtroom. Perhaps, after finding this out, you might choose not to go to law school.

CheckPoint

What federal publications should you check first in your job search? Why? What can you learn from talking to people or observing them at work that you won't get from publications?

Plan Your Career

If a goal is important to you, planning will increase your chances of achieving that goal.

Determine Skills, Training, and Education Required

Most careers require certain skills, knowledge, and experience. The higher you hope to go in a career, the more you must improve your skills. Steps to reach your goals vary, but many require completing some higher education or training.

Consider Your Family

Your career choice also affects other lives. A low-wage position could force your spouse to work more hours or take a job only for more money. You might have to live far from your relatives. A career that requires long days or travel could prevent much family time. When you plan your career, keep family in mind. A career plan is only part of your life-span plan.

Finance Your Plans

Preparing for a career requires paying for classes, training, and even equipment such as carpentry tools. Career preparation also has an opportunity cost, such as the lost income from a part-time job you quit to attend a class or training program. Thus, you need a long-term financial plan.

Investigate state schools and programs. Many offer excellent education at lower costs than private schools. Most have financial aid offices to help students. Many companies offer tuition assistance to employees.

CheckPoint

Where can you look for financial help with your education or training?

What In The World?

Apprenticeship programs are an excellent way for young people to earn money and investigate careers. The government in Germany pays businesses to operate apprenticeship programs. Almost two-thirds of all German high school graduates work as apprentices.

The problem now is that there are more students than the programs can take. Businesses have become more selective in the students they choose. If you were a German student, how could you make yourself more attractive to a business in your field?

TRY THESE

1. What is the difference between a job and a career?

2. What federal publications can help you narrow your career search to just the options most worth further investigation?

3. What is O*NET and how can it help you with your career research?

4. Why should you talk to people working in the career field you are considering?

5. What is the purpose of taking a job that supports people working in the career you think you want?

6. Why is planning an important part of achieving your career goals?

THINK CRITICALLY

7. **CONSUMER ACTION** Jalisa doesn't know how to start planning a career that uses her biology aptitude and interest in animals. What should she do first? Write a plan for her to investigate careers in biology. Could a job in her uncle's pet-grooming business help her achieve her career goals?

8. **COMMUNICATE** Identify a career that you think might interest you. Assume that a family friend works in that field and would be happy to talk with you. Prepare eight questions to ask this person. Ask questions that will give you the clearest picture of this career.

9. Consider a career as a teacher. E-mail a teacher asking about the career's benefits and costs. Is he or she happy with this choice?

10. You have saved $2,000 in an account that pays 5 percent interest to help pay for the two-year college you hope to attend in three years. The annual cost will be $6,000. You want to save enough now that you won't need to work while you go to school. Use the College Planner to calculate how much you need to save in each of the next three years to pay for your training.

SPECIFY **SEARCH** **SIFT** **SELECT** **STUDY**

SEARCH Gather information about three careers in order of interest that fit well with the goals you set in *Specify.* Write a plan to find more information about these careers. List the types of information you need: pay, work hours, job duties, chances for advancement, and geographic location. Arrange a *career connection* interview with someone employed in the career that interests you the most.

Remember that your career choice will affect others. How would it affect your parents, spouse, children, or friends? Would it provide a secure retirement? Make notes about the information you find to use in the next step in the decision making process.

© Getty Images/PhotoDisc

4.3 Apply for a Job

Look for Job Openings

When you are looking for job openings, you have many avenues to explore. People, companies, newspapers, employment agencies, and the Internet can inform you about job openings in your field.

People You Know

Think of all the people you know. Friends, parents of friends, acquaintances, relatives, and their friends—all might know of job openings. Ask people who work in your field if they know of any job openings.

Studies show that as many as 40 percent of all employees found their first job though a referral. A **referral** is the recommendation of a person for a job given to an employer by someone the employer knows.

Referrals from successful employees at the company are especially

CONSUMER ACTION

Brenda wants to be an architect. She is looking for a part-time job to save for college. She applied several places and received two offers. One is to be a waitress for $95 a week. The other is to be a file clerk for a construction company for $50 a week. How should Brenda decide which job offer to accept? What are the trade-offs she must consider?

powerful. Managers know that if a successful employee recommends a job candidate, that person is likely to be a successful employee too.

© Getty Images/PhotoDisc

CheckPoint

List five working adults whom you know. What companies do they work for? Pick one of these companies that most interests you. What part-time job could you seek that might lead to a career at this company?

Potential Employers

Most businesses keep files of applications that they use when they have job openings. Most employers do not advertise their job openings. They don't need to because they already know of many qualified people who would like to work for them. Make sure that businesses you would like to work for have your application on file.

Be Selective In deciding which potential employers to contact, don't apply at random. Apply for jobs related to your chosen career field. Suppose you want to own a day care center some day. To gain valuable experience, apply for a caregiving job at a day care facility, for a job as a teacher's aid at an elementary school, or for an assistant job in the children's ward of a hospital.

Newspapers

Your local newspaper can alert you to job openings. Although most businesses never advertise their openings, many do. Check the

newspaper's help-wanted ads. You are most likely to find entry-level jobs in want ads.

Look At Ads Also check the newspaper for product advertisements. From these ads, you can find the names and locations of the companies that placed them. If any of these companies interest you, apply—even if they currently have no openings. Next week, they may.

Employment Agencies

Employment agencies are government or private organizations that help people find jobs. Every state operates employment offices that keep lists of job openings from employers who choose to submit them. You can check the list of openings for free.

The selection may be limited, however. Many businesses don't tell state offices when they have job openings. Those that do often are having trouble finding employees because they do not pay well or have poor working conditions.

Private employment agencies are run to earn a profit for their owners. They charge fees to applicants, employers, or both. Many of these businesses are listed in your telephone book. Be sure you understand what fee you must pay and what services to expect for this fee.

GUESS WHAT

Private employment agencies earn over $10 billion per year in fees.

Temporary Agencies

Temporary agencies are private companies that specialize in supplying short-term employees to businesses. Accepting work from a temporary agency allows you to

sample many types of jobs and often leads to full-time employment. The pay, however, is often low, and the agency may provide no benefits, such as health insurance or sick leave. Still, temporary work is a good way to investigate a number of career possibilities in a short time.

Jobs Online

Online job search sites are some of the most visited sites on the Web. These sites will search for job openings in your field across the country and even globally. Often you can post your resume at the site. Employers post job openings on these search sites as well. Two of the largest online job-search services are monster.com and CareerBuilder.com.

Companies often advertise their job openings on their own web sites. You can search the Web for sites of companies that interest you. Even if a company has no openings now, the site may describe jobs at the company to help you decide if you would like to work there in the future.

CheckPoint

How can temporary employment lead to full-time employment? How can the Internet aid your job search?

Application Process

During the application process, you must sell yourself. You must convince the employer that you are the best person for the job.

IN CLASS ACTIVITY

Write a list of jobs that you could learn about by being an apprentice, a temporary employee, or a volunteer. List the benefits of learning about a career this way.

Everything you say or do in the application process will affect your chances of getting the job.

Preparing a Resume

Your first task in applying for a job is to prepare a resume. A **resume** is a brief summary of your job qualifications, including your education and training, job skills, and work experience. Your resume includes information similar to the information requested in a job application. But, with a resume, you have an advantage. You write it before actually applying for a job, so you can emphasize your strengths.

Here are some guidelines to help you prepare an impressive resume:

▶ Express yourself clearly.

▶ Be brief. Most resumes should be limited to one page. Include only information relevant to your qualifications for the job. Employers don't have time to read a lot of words to get to the important points.

► Use dynamic words that demonstrate your accomplishments—words such as *directed, improved, planned,* and *organized.*

► Always tell the truth. Emphasizing strengths is fine, but lying is not.

► Check your resume carefully. If you make an error on your resume, an employer might think you would not be a careful worker.

► Ask someone who has experience with resumes to read and evaluate your resume before you send it.

RESUME

Brenda Ramirez
123 Home Street
Hometown, ST 12345
(123) 555-1234

YOUR INFORMATION

Objective
Part-time, entry-level office position in construction

Qualifications
Aptitude with numbers
Able to follow directions
Computer skills, including CAD

Employment History
Summer 2004   Summer intern. Charles Blueprints, Inc. Hometown, ST
        Delivered bluprints to offices and job sites
        Completed clerical work on word processor, spreadsheet, and CAD programs

Summer 2003   Cashier. Pop's Dairy Store, Hometown, ST
        Performed cash register responsibilities
        Stocked shelves
        Answered customer questions
        Made ice cream cones, malts, and shakes

INCLUDE EXPERIENCE
SHOWING SKILLS

Other Experience
Spring 2004   Volunteer. Oak Forest Home, Hometown, ST
        Volunteered for a program that taught elderly residents how to use computers and the Internet

Education
June 2005   Graduated from Hometown High School, Hometown, ST
        Achieved 3.0/4.0 GPA
        President of Computer Club

References available upon request.

INCLUDE
ANY
SPECIAL
HONORS

COVER LETTER

DATE, CONTACT PERSON AND ADDRESS

YOUR INFORMATION

Brenda Ramirez
123 Home Street
Hometown, ST 12345
(123) 555-1234

March 15, 20--

Mr. A.J. Smith
Smith Construction, Inc.
123 Business Street
Hometown, ST 12345

Dear Mr. Smith

POSITION YOU ARE SEEKING

I am interested in the part-time file clerk position that was advertised in the *Hometown Post.* You will note from my resume that I have office experience. I also have experience working with blueprints, computers, and construction sites. Past employers will tell you I am an honest, hard-working employee.

REQUEST AN INTERVIEW

I would like to arrange an interview. I can be reached at 555-1234, or by e-mail at bramirez@abcdef.hometownnet.com.

Thank you for your consideration. I look forward to meeting you.

Sincerely

Brenda Ramirez

Brenda Ramirez

encl.

Writing a Cover Letter

Send your resume to prospective employers along with a cover letter. A **cover letter** is your letter of introduction. The purpose of the cover letter is to encourage the employer to read your resume and ask you for an interview. In your cover letter, explain why you are applying for the job and how your services will benefit the employer. Mention the strengths that will be most important to the employer.

CheckPoint

How does a resume help you sell your services to an employer? What is the purpose of a cover letter?

Completing the Application

When you apply for a job, you will probably have to complete a written application form. Be prepared. Have necessary information with you on a data sheet. Most applications require you to provide the following.

1. Your name, address, telephone number, and Social Security number.

2. Information about your education and training.

3. A list of your work experience, including company names and addresses, dates of employment, supervisor names, and reasons for leaving.

4. The name of the job you are applying for and the salary you expect to receive.

Application for Employment		
Please print		

Position applied for	Full, Part or Shift?
File clerk	Part-time

Last Name	First Name	Middle Initial
Ramirez	Brenda	N

Address	City	State	Zip code
123 Home Street	Hometown	ST	12345

Telephone Number(s)	Social Security number
(123) 555-1234	123-12-1234

	Name and Address of School	Course of Study	Years Completed	Type of Diploma or Degree Received
High School	Hometown High School Hometown, ST		4	Graduated
College				
Graduate				
Other				

List all past and present employment, including part-time or seasonal, beginning with the most recent.

Company	Employment Dates and Salary	Describe the work you did	Reason for leaving
Name Charles Blueprints, Inc. Address 123 Charles Street Phone 555-1266 Supervisor Ben Charles	From June 2004 To August 2004 Salary $7.50/hr.	Clerical work Deliveries	School
Name Pop's Dairy Store Address 100 Charles Street Phone 555-1255 Supervisor "Pop" Jiminez	From June 2003 To August 2003 Salary $6.00/hr.	Cashier Stocked shelves	School

Are you a veteran of the United States military? ☐ Yes ☒ No
If yes, what service branch?_____ Service Dates From:_____ To: _____

Are you a U.S. citizen or otherwise authorized to work in the U.S.? ☒ Yes ☐ No
(Proof of citizenship or immigration status will be required within three business days of employment.)

Please indicate other abilities, skills, experience, or special knowledge which you feel would qualify you for the type of work for which you are now applying Experience with word processor, spreadsheet, and CAD programs

　　I authorize the investigation of all statements in this application, and I understand that any false statements or deliberate omissions on this application will be cause for my discharge.

Signature of Applicant _Brenda Ramirez_　　Date _March 20, 20—_

WE ARE AN EQUAL OPPORTUNITY EMPLOYER

Read the entire application before you write anything. Then follow all directions exactly. Work slowly and be careful not to make mistakes. Be neat. If you make a mistake, ask for another form.

You must use a pen to fill out a job application. Ask if the application is available online. If so, you can key the application using a word processor. This will make it more readable.

Answer all questions that apply to you. Spell words correctly. If you have trouble with spelling, bring a pocket dictionary or use an electronic speller. Check your work when you are finished.

References

Prospective employers usually want you to supply a list of references. **References** are people the employer can contact to verify your training, experience, or character.

Select three or four people who you know will recommend you. Keep in mind that many employers request that your references don't include members of your family. Always ask people for permission to list them as references *before* you give their names to an employer. Your supervisors in previous jobs make good references, since they can verify your job skills. Include each person's phone number and address in your data sheet.

Once you get a job, make sure you let your references know. You might send a thank-you letter. They have done you a great favor by informing potential employers that you can do what you say you can.

COMMUNICATE

Write your resume using the skills and experience you have right now. Don't forget to include part-time or volunteer positions. Because you might not have much experience, you might want to highlight your aptitudes for certain classes you are taking or have taken in high school, which may benefit potential employers.

CheckPoint

Why would a previous supervisor be a good reference for you?

Buy the Numbers?

Suppose you could prepare your own resume if you worked for about three hours, or you could hire a professional service that advertises to do the job for $60. The service claims that its resumes give people a better chance of gaining employment. Do you believe this claim is correct? Besides no spelling errors, what else does your resume need to show? Will you prepare it yourself, or will you hire the service to do it for you? Why?

TRY THESE

1. List five sources that can help you find job openings.

2. Why are job referrals valuable to both job seekers and employers?

3. Why is it important to fill out job applications completely, neatly, and accurately?

4. What is the purpose of a resume?

5. What is the purpose of a cover letter?

6. Why are references important?

7. Why would you send a thank-you letter to a reference?

THINK CRITICALLY

8. **CONSUMER ACTION** Brenda is looking for part-time work to save for college. Reread the scenario. What benefits would she receive from each job? What is the opportunity cost of each option? If you were Brenda, which choice would you make? Why?

9. Search the Web to find monster.com and CareerBuilder.com. What services do these two sites offer? Which services are free and which are not?

10. **COMMUNICATE** Prepare a resume for yourself. Assume that you want to apply for a part-time job at a fast-food restaurant while you attend school. Think about what the employer would want in an ideal employee for that job. Then emphasize your strengths that best fit that ideal employee.

11. **COMMUNICATE** Prepare a cover letter to the manager of the fast-food restaurant you chose in exercise 10. Remember that the purpose of the cover letter is to encourage the manager to read your resume and ask you to fill out an application. Send your letter to your teacher by e-mail.

12. Most word processing programs contain templates for resumes. All you have to do is fill in your information. What are some benefits of using a resume template? What are some reasons you might want to stay away from these resume templates?

13. Many people post their resumes on their own web sites. Investigate how you could create your own resume web site. Look at resume web sites that other people have created. Create your own resume web site, or create a document showing what you would do with your resume web site.

DECISION MAKING PROJECT

SPECIFY   SEARCH   SIFT   SELECT   STUDY

SIFT Evaluate the career information you gathered. List the benefits and costs (including opportunity costs) for each choice. Rank the careers in order of their fit with your life-span plan. Are you willing to make sacrifices now to achieve your future goals?

4.4 Interview Successfully

The Important Interview

Each employer has a process to screen resumes, and few get through this process. Now that you have made it to the interview phase, prepare thoroughly!

A face-to-face meeting with an employer, called an **interview**, is often the final step in a successful job search. Your interview is your chance to "close the deal." It can also sink your chances to get the job.

The interview is important because it gives an employer a chance to ask you questions to see if you and the position are a good fit. Do you have the skills, attitude, and personality needed to be a successful team member? Because an interview is so important, sometimes employers may ask you for more than one interview. They may also have you interview with more than one person.

Another reason that interviews are important is that they give you the chance to interview the company. You should ask questions to

CONSUMER ACTION

Joe knew that he was not good on job interviews. He would say inappropriate things, fidget, and forget the questions that he was being asked. Joe saw a commercial for a book and video that guaranteed a successful interview if he followed all their "success steps." He knew he needed something to help him on interviews, but was this it?

determine if the position and the company are right for you.

CheckPoint

Why are interviews important to employers? Why are they important to you?

Pre-Interview Checklist

Be on Time   It seems like common sense to be on time, but many first-time job seekers are late to interviews. Be sure to call ahead to confirm the time of the interview and ask for any directions.

Know Your Resume   Know the information you have provided in your resume and application. Be able to talk about anything you wrote.

Know the Company   Many employers complain that first-time job seekers don't know much about the companies with which they interview. After all, how can applicants really want to work somewhere that they don't know much about?

For information about a company, you can go to your local library and

© Getty Images/PhotoDisc

ask the reference librarian for help. You might look up old newspaper articles about the company. You might also talk to current or past employees. Once you have this information, you can better explain what you can do for the company.

Anticipate Questions
Practice answering questions in a positive way. Here are some popular interview questions.

▶ How can your skills and experience benefit the company?

▶ How would this job fit in with your long-range career goals?

▶ Why do you want to work here?

▶ What were your major responsibilities in your last job?

▶ What did you like best about your last job? What did you like least?

▶ Describe a situation where you had to manage conflicting priorities.

Answers to Hard Questions
Anticipate tough questions the interviewer might ask and be prepared to answer them. For example, if you lost a job, the interviewer will probably ask why.

Also, the interviewer might ask what your greatest weaknesses are. Be honest. You might explain what you are willing to do to overcome a weakness. For example, if a job requires proficiency with a computer program and you are really a beginner, you might offer to take additional courses to achieve proficiency.

Do a Practice Interview   Ask a friend or family member to act as the interviewer and ask you realistic questions. Practice answering each question slowly and thoughtfully.

Prepare Questions Prepare questions that you have about the job. Bring your list of questions, as well as a few extra copies of your resume, with you to the interview. Rather than ask about pay or benefits, ask questions that will help you decide if this job would be a good fit for you.

▶ Describe a normal workday.

▶ To whom would I report? Will I meet this person before the interview process is over?

▶ What are the opportunities for advancement?

Dress for Success Dress appropriately for the interview. If you are applying for an office job, wear something appropriate to an office setting, such as a suit or dress. If you are applying for manual labor, wear clean, dressy casual clothing.

Women should avoid using too much makeup, heavy perfume, and flashy jewelry. Men should remember to be well groomed and shaven. The interviewer can better focus on you if there are few distractions.

CheckPoint

How should you prepare for an interview? List at least five steps.

In the Interview

It will be very important to leave your interviewer with a favorable impression of you. Here are some tips.

Be Polite Remember to be polite to every person you meet, and remember their names if you can, so you can thank them later in a follow-up letter. Don't forget that if you are rude to the receptionist, he or she might tell your interviewer. In a tight contest between you and another candidate, this could weigh against you.

Nonverbal Communication Unspoken messages you send can sometimes speak louder than your voice. You could be the best candidate for the job, but if your body language offends your interviewer, you probably won't get the job. These are some suggestions.

▶ Shake hands firmly with your interviewer(s).

▶ Think through each answer before responding. Keep your answers brief. Speak slowly and clearly. Use good grammar, not slang. Don't interrupt or chew gum.

▶ Sit up straight and look the interviewer in the eye as you answer questions. Be confident.

▶ Don't cross your arms. This tells the person across from you that

CYBER CONSUMER

Visit the web sites of online clothing retailers. Download an image of clothing appropriate and inappropriate for a job interview. Write a brief essay about the appropriateness of each.

you are uncomfortable and don't want to be there. Folding your hands is acceptable.

▶ If you know you have a nervous habit that might come out in an interview, try to train yourself out of it. Going through a mock interview with a friend might help.

▶ Use proper etiquette. Be polite and respectful.

Other Tips A common mistake that job seekers make is to say something negative about a former employer or teacher. This will make you look bad to the interviewer. Try to make only positive remarks.

Let the interviewer lead the conversation, but don't forget to bring up the skills and experience you have that would fit the position. Also, remember to ask the questions that you brought with you.

When the interview is over, and it is time to leave, thank the interviewer. Again, let the interviewer know you would like the position.

© Getty Images/PhotoDisc

The Rehabilitation Act of 1973 protects those with physical or mental disabilities from discrimination in the hiring process.

You should answer questions directly related to the job or its requirements. You have the right to refuse to answer questions that ask for information that could lead to discrimination in the hiring process. Here are some examples of inappropriate questions.

▶ Have you ever seen a therapist?

▶ Are you planning to have kids?

▶ What is your medical history?

▶ You're a Christian, aren't you?

▶ What country are you from?

CheckPoint

Why is it important to pay attention to your body language in an interview?

What They Can't Ask You

The Equal Employment Opportunity Act of 1964 forbids discrimination by potential employers or their agencies on the basis of race, age, color, religion, gender, or national origin.

CheckPoint

Why is it important to know what an interviewer cannot ask you in an interview?

Write a Follow-Up Letter

As soon as you get home from the interview, you should write a follow-up letter to the interviewer. This letter can be handwritten, typed, or word processed. Most importantly, it must be clean, legible, and free of errors. Make sure you send it no later than a day after your interview.

Follow-up letters are important because they keep your name in front of the interviewer and act as a reminder of your interest.

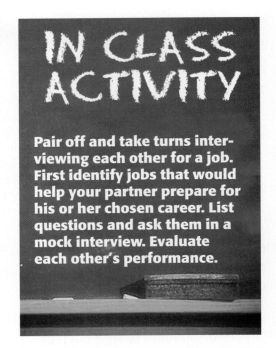

IN CLASS ACTIVITY

Pair off and take turns interviewing each other for a job. First identify jobs that would help your partner prepare for his or her chosen career. List questions and ask them in a mock interview. Evaluate each other's performance.

INTERVIEW FOLLOW-UP LETTER

YOUR INFORMATION →

Joseph Smith
1213 East Street
Hometown, ST 12345
(123) 555-7890

April 2, 20- -

Ms. Jane Manager
Big Corporation, Inc.
123 Business Street, Suite 100
Hometown, ST 23456

← **CONTACT PERSON, ADDRESS AND DATE**

Dear Ms. Manager

← **THANK THE INTERVIEWER**

Thank you so much for the opportunity to meet with you to discuss how my skills and enthusiasm can benefit Big Corporation, Inc., as a sales associate. ← **POSITION YOU ARE SEEKING**
I enjoyed listening to your plans for expanding your sales effort into a new marketing area, and I hope to be a part of it.

I look forward to hearing from you soon. Thank you for your consideration. ← **REPEAT YOUR INTEREST**

Sincerely

Joseph Smith

Joseph Smith

TRY THESE

1. Why are interviews important to employers?

2. Why are interviews important to you?

3. How should you prepare for an employment interview?

4. Why can't employers ask any questions they want to ask?

5. Why is it important to use good etiquette in an interview?

6. Why is nonverbal communication a factor in an interview?

7. Why should you write a follow-up letter after an interview?

8. Why is it important to be well-groomed for an interview?

THINK CRITICALLY

9. **CONSUMER ACTION** Joe is considering buying a book and video to help him with interviews. What would you advise Joe to do before buying this program?

10. Write a list of questions you think should not be asked during a job interview. After each question, state why it shouldn't be asked. What would you say to an interviewer who asked you an inappropriate question?

11. **COMMUNICATE** People who are successful in sports or business often claim that before a successful game or meeting, they visualize how they could be successful in the game or meeting. Visualize yourself going for the interview for your dream job with your dream company. Write a few paragraphs about how you would prepare for this interview, what questions the interviewer might ask, and what your answers would be.

12. **COMMUNICATE** Write a follow-up letter for the interview from exercise 11. Send your letter to your teacher by e-mail.

13. Consider the type of job you would want in your chosen career. Write a list of questions you would want to ask at an interview for this job.

14. Consider the type of job you would want in your chosen career. Write a list of questions that you expect your interviewer to ask you. Then write your responses to those questions.

DECISION MAKING PROJECT

SPECIFY   SEARCH   SIFT   SELECT   STUDY

SELECT Use the lists you have made to help pick a career that you feel is best for you. Keep your values, personality, abilities, and aptitudes in mind. Remember, you aren't locked into this choice for your life. Use your choice to set several short-term goals to achieve now to help you reach your future career goals.

GOALS

EXPLAIN
why it is important
to perform all job
duties well

IDENTIFY
ways of being
prepared for
career changes

© Getty Images/PhotoDisc

4.5 Prepare for the Future

A Job Well Done

A job you accept early in your career is likely to be a stepping stone toward your career goals. Success in your first job will provide good training, experience, and references for your next job application.

Be a Part of the Team On the job, you and your coworkers are a team, all working toward accomplishing company goals. You must be able to get along with your coworkers. When they need help, help them. They will likely return the favor when you need it. Accept differences among people. Treat others with respect and consideration.

Being part of the team means dressing and acting appropriately. Employees meeting the public, for example, must be particularly careful how they dress. Wearing a dirty T-shirt and old jeans is a mistake if you want to convince customers to buy fine furniture. Using proper

---

CONSUMER **ACTION**

Gina hated her job at the grocery store. She didn't get along with the other people who worked there. She really wanted to work as a manager in a clothing store, even though she knew she didn't have the skills or experience. She heard about a course in retail merchandising at a local community college. What could Gina do?

etiquette is just as important. There is a big difference between "How may I help you?" and "Whatdayawant?"

Take Direction   When you are new, you will know less than anyone else about what to do. To succeed, you *must* be willing to take directions. Ask for help when you need it.

Always arrive at work on time. Be enthusiastic and honest. Honesty includes doing an honest day's work for your pay. If you make a mistake, accept responsibility and learn how to do it better next time. No one expects you to be perfect when you are new. They do expect you to learn.

CheckPoint

Why is it important to get along with your coworkers?

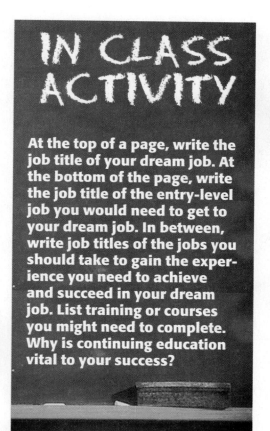

IN CLASS ACTIVITY

At the top of a page, write the job title of your dream job. At the bottom of the page, write the job title of the entry-level job you would need to get to your dream job. In between, write job titles of the jobs you should take to gain the experience you need to achieve and succeed in your dream job. List training or courses you might need to complete. Why is continuing education vital to your success?

Know When It's Time to Move On

Changing Careers   Statistics show that average American workers will hold seven jobs in their adult working lives. At some point along your career path, you will probably want to change jobs. Maybe you need more training or greater challenges than the current job can provide. Maybe you want to start your own business or you discovered another job with a brighter future.

Getting Downsized   You may be forced to leave a job because of circumstances outside your control. Your employer may not be doing well and may have to terminate employees to cut expenses. This practice is called **downsizing**. You might be a valued employee and still lose your job.

If this happens, accept any assistance your employer offers. Many large businesses help former employees find new jobs. Sometimes employees are given **severance pay**, a sum of money for which they are eligible upon termination. Be sure to get a written recommendation to clarify for potential employers that you left because of downsizing, not poor performance.

GUESS WHAT
Recently, 54 percent of the 88 million places in college adult education courses were taken by people to advance their careers.

Getting Fired You might also leave a job because it is not a good fit for you. If you are having trouble performing job tasks up to expectations, discuss the problems with your supervisor. Your supervisor probably has already observed your problems. You may be able to work out solutions to your job problems.

Make sure you are doing all you can to succeed in the job. If you cannot solve the problems, quit before your employer fires you.

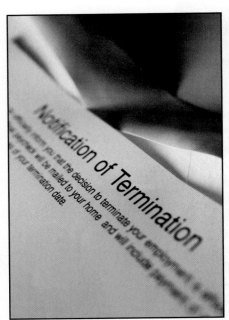
© Getty Images/PhotoDisc

Remember, though, that poor job performance will harm your chances for future jobs.

Work hard in every job and try to succeed. This way, your current employer can write you a good recommendation for another job. Then you can leave each job on good terms.

© Getty Images/PhotoDisc

Consumer ALERT

Recently, Ellen lost her job as a manager when the store she worked for closed. She searched for a new position for more than three months with no success. Although she received several job offers, they all paid less than her old job. Ellen finally visited a private employment agency. This agency promised to find her three job offers that would pay at least 90 percent as much as her old job. They made no other promises about the jobs they would find. To receive this service, Ellen must pay the firm $3,000 immediately. How should Ellen decide whether to employ this agency?

Leave on Good Terms

No matter what your reason for leaving a job, always be considerate of your current employer's needs. A good recommendation from this employer can help you get future jobs. When you decide to leave a job, always give notice to your current employer. **Notice** is your official written notification that you are leaving the company. It should include the date you are leaving. You should usually turn in your notice at least two weeks before you leave. This gives the employer time to look for or to train your replacement.

Be Prepared

Most people who are fired or down-sized have a pretty good idea before-hand that they will soon be unemployed. The time to plan is before being officially notified. Update your resume and start thinking about what you want for your next job.

Plan Your Finances   Many financial planners agree that you should have enough in savings for up to six months of your expenses. In case of a job change, whether voluntary or involuntary, this will give you at least six months to find another job.

If you know you would like to change careers or professions, investigate the qualifications. Will you need to go back to school? Will you need to go back and start at entry level? Can you live on entry-level wages?

If you have financial obligations, such as children or mortgages, it is even more important for you to plan ahead for changes that may upset your family.

CheckPoint

Why should you always leave a job on good terms? What can you do to be prepared for career changes?

TRY THESE

1. Why are getting along with co-workers and taking directions well vital to your success on any job?

2. Why should you always do your job well, even if you hate your job?

3. How can you prevent getting fired from a job?

4. What is downsizing?

5. Why should you get a recommendation from your employer before you are downsized?

6. Why should you always give notice when you plan to leave a job?

THINK CRITICALLY

7. **CONSUMER ACTION**   Gina would rather work as a store manager than as a grocery store clerk. Her skills are limited, but there are courses available. Write a list of two or three ways that Gina can achieve her dream job.

8. You have been offered a job you would like to accept. But you must start immediately if you take it. To do this, you would have to quit your current job without giving any notice. What would you do? Explain.

9. List some examples of teamwork in a work setting.

10. **COMMUNICATE**   The unemployment rate represents people not working to support their families. Write an essay on how unemployment affects families, communities, and the nation. Use personal experience if you can. E-mail the essay to your teacher.

ASSESSMENT

KEY IDEAS

Get to Know Yourself

1. Career planning starts with understanding your values, including your attitudes on topics such as wealth, independence, security, family, and location. Remember that your career plan is just one part of your life-span plan.

2. Personal interests are activities you find rewarding over an extended period of time. A good career for you is one that fits your values and interests and provides enough income to support you and your family.

3. An aptitude is a natural talent for learning skills. To prepare for a career, identify your aptitudes and develop them into skills.

4. Your personality is your unique blend of qualities that defines you as an individual. Find a career that harmonizes with your personality.

5. Your career choice will affect your family, friends, and community. You should keep others in mind as you make your decision.

Explore Careers

6. A job is a set of tasks you accomplish while you work. A career is a long-term commitment to an occupation. A career requires planning, education, and preparation.

7. You can find out what careers are available from your school's guidance office, a library, or the Internet. The federal government publishes a number of references.

8. To find out what a career is really like, make a career connection. Also try volunteering or seeking a job that supports people who work in that field. You can then observe people who work in the career.

9. Succeeding in your career choice takes planning. You must acquire the knowledge, skills, and experience that the field requires and plan a way to pay for them.

Apply for a Job

10. People, companies, newspapers, employment agencies, and the Internet can alert you to job openings. Many people find their first job through referrals.

11. Prepare a resume, a summary of your job qualifications. Send the resume along with a cover letter to the employer.

12. You will need to complete an application form. Complete the application honestly and completely. Always check for errors.

Interview Successfully

13. Before the interview, review your resume so that you can answer questions about it. Prepare answers to tough questions. Learn what the company does and how your skills can contribute.

14. Wear appropriate clothes to the interview, and pay attention to your nonverbal communication.

Prepare for the Future

15. It is important to get along with your coworkers and learn from them. Always work hard to be successful in the job. When it is time to leave, leave on good terms. If you are downsized, take advantage of job-search help the company offers.

TERMS REVIEW

Match each term on the left with its definition on the right.
Some terms may not be used.

a. aptitude

b. career

c. career connection

d. cover letter

e downsizing

f. interview

g. job

h. notice

i. personal interest

j. personality

k. reference

l. referral

m. resume

n. severance pay

o. skill

p. temporary agency

q. transferable skill

1. aptitude developed through training and experience
2. unique blend of qualities that defines an individual
3. set of tasks you accomplish while you work
4. official written notification that you are leaving the company
5. recommendation of a person for a job
6. private firm that specializes in supplying short-term employees to businesses
7. natural talent for learning some skills over others
8. brief summary of your job qualifications
9. letter of introduction sent with your resume to a potential employer
10. activity you find rewarding over an extended period of time
11. occupation to which you have made a long-term commitment
12. person the employer can contact to verify your training, experience, or character
13. face-to-face meeting with a potential employer to discuss your job qualifications
14. terminating employees to cut expenses

CONSUMER DECISIONS

15. What aptitudes do you have? What can you do now to help develop these aptitudes into valuable job skills?

16. Why should you find the *right* job rather than accept the *first* job offered to you? Why might you accept a job offer with lower pay than you could earn in another job?

17. What can you do as a student to make your resume more attractive to an employer? Are good grades all you should work to achieve in school?

THINK CRITICALLY

18. You have received two similar job offers. One is from a business located a few hundred yards from your home. It pays $500 a week. The other is located on the other side of town. It pays $575 a week. To reach this second job, you would have to take a 50-minute bus ride to and from work each day at a cost of $2 each way. Which job would provide the most income after you pay your travel expenses? What other factors would you consider in making your choice? Which job would you accept? Why?

LOOK IT UP

19. The U.S. Department of Labor maintains a web site at www.ajb.dni.us, where it provides access to national and state employment data. Select a career that interests you. Then visit this site and find out what types of job opportunities exist in that field.

20. *The Wall Street Journal* and other financial publications print advertisements for executive job openings. Find one of these ads. Write a description of the career path someone might take to become qualified for this job.

21. Identify a recent technological breakthrough. Investigate the career opportunities that this advancement has created. What occupations may no longer be available because of this breakthrough?

22. Look in the *Yellow Pages* of your telephone book to identify an employment agency you could use to find a job. Call the company and ask what services it provides and what it charges for these services.

How could this agency help you find a job? Do you think the services are worth the price?

23. Contact an online employment service. Find out what you would need to do to file an online resume or job application. Does this seem to be a reasonable method for you to carry out a job search? Explain your answer.

INSIDE THE NUMBERS

24. The government reported that 136 million Americans were employed in 2002, and 8.4 million were looking for work. Of that number, over 2 million had been out of work for more than 15 weeks. In a one-page essay describe reasons for extended unemployment. What can you do now to prevent being unemployed in the future? Why is retraining an important part of most career plans?

25. Suppose you are looking for a part-time job for the summer. One job at a fast-food restaurant would pay $6.00 an hour. You would work mostly weekend nights and around

WHICH IS THE BEST DEAL?

Shelly would like a promotion to a job that requires an associate degree. Shelly already has finished about half of her coursework. Explain what you think Shelly should do. What other factors should Shelly consider besides her spending and income?

Alternative 1 She believes she could complete the degree in three years by taking evening classes.

Alternative 2 She could take an unpaid leave of absence from her job and finish her degree in one year. To do this, she would have to borrow $10,000 to pay her bills. If she receives a promotion, she would earn $3,800 more each year.

Alternative 3 She could consider another career that doesn't require an associate degree.

20 hours a week. You are given one meal for each 5-hour shift. A video store has a part-time position open that would pay $5.50. You would also have to work mostly weekend nights for up to 15 hours a week. You could have three free video rentals a month. Which part-time job would pay more? Which would you take? Why?

CURRICULUM CONNECTION

26. **WORLD STUDIES** In many nations, students take a test after they complete eighth grade. Their grade on this test determines much of their future. For example, students who score high in science or mechanical aptitude may become engineers. Students who score lower are placed in apprenticeship programs and do not continue with academic studies. Write a one-page essay that evaluates this system. What are some advantages and disadvantages of this system?

27. **MATH** People with an aptitude in math have more career options than you might think. Check the *OOH* and O*NET for careers in math. Also check several online sources of job information. Make a list of the career choices you found.

28. **CAREER STUDIES** There are people whose job it is to predict trends in the job market. If you were to make some predictions about where there would be many jobs in the future, in what industries would these be, and why do you think they would need more workers?

JOURNAL RECAP

29. After reading this chapter, review the answers you wrote to the questions in Journal Journey. Have your opinions changed?

DECISION MAKING PROJECT

SPECIFY   SEARCH   SIFT   SELECT   STUDY

STUDY The decision making process isn't over yet! Go back to the Select step and make a plan for gaining the skills you need to get into the career you want. What training do you need? Where can you get it? How much will it cost? Where can you get the money?

Once you are happy with your plan, start taking your first steps toward getting into the career you want. Your priorities for a career may change as you get older and gain more experience. If you find that the career choice you made here no longer interests you, simply go through the decision making process again and plan steps toward a new career goal. You are not locked in—there are always other options.

Chapter 5

INCOME TAXES
HOW MUCH WILL YOU KEEP?

WHAT'S AHEAD

EXPLODING MYTHS

Fact or Myth?
What do you think is true?

1. A good way to save is to have more income than necessary withheld from your paychecks, so you will receive a big tax refund at the end of the year.

2. The tax system is too complicated for ordinary taxpayers to understand.

JOURNAL JOURNEY

WRITE IN YOUR JOURNAL ABOUT THE FOLLOWING.

TAXES How are they collected? How are they used?

COMPLETING INCOME TAX RETURNS What kinds of information do you need to complete your income tax return?

DECISION MAKING PROJECT

SPECIFY SEARCH SIFT SELECT STUDY

TAX YOUR DREAM JOB You and your group will create a scenario for a student who is 17 years old and must file a federal tax return. You will create a Form W-4, a Form W-2, and fill out a Form 1040 EZ for the student that may be filed online.

GOAL
To learn how to fill out a Form 1040EZ

PROJECT PROCESS
SPECIFY	Lesson 5.1
SEARCH	Lesson 5.2
SIFT	Lesson 5.3
SELECT	Lesson 5.4
STUDY	Chapter Assessment

© Getty Images/PhotoDisc

5.1 Taxes and Your Paycheck

Payroll Taxes

The federal government receives the largest part of its revenue from income and payroll taxes. **Payroll taxes** are taxes based on the payroll of a business. All payroll taxes are based on employee total earnings. These taxes are paid to the government by you and your employer. An example of payroll taxes is social insurance taxes.

Income taxes are taxes you pay on most types of income you receive. Income taxes are not a fixed percent-age of income that all Americans pay. The amount varies, depending on each taxpayer's financial and family situation. You are responsible for calculating the tax you owe.

Some taxes on income support social programs. **FICA**, which is the abbreviation for **Federal Insurance Contributions Act**, is the law that requires workers to contribute to Social Security and Medicare. You will learn more about these programs in Chapters 15 and 16.

CONSUMER ACTION

Kelly found a part-time job after school that pays $7.50 per hour. She wants to take home at least $50 per week, so she agreed to work seven hours each Saturday. She expected her first paycheck to be $52.50. She was surprised to find it was only $40.39. Why wasn't Kelly's check larger?

The Video Store, Inc. 494 Main Street Hometown, ST 12345			CHECK NO. **06825**	

Employee Name:	Kelly O'Rourke	**Employee social**		**Check date:**	09/15/--
Employee Address:	188 Oak Street Hometown, ST 12345	**security number:** 127-83-4545		**Pay period ending:**	09/15/--

EARNINGS		DEDUCTIONS			
Hours	7	**Federal Income Tax**	$ 7.88	**Gross Pay**	$52.50
Rate	$ 7.50	**Social Security Tax**	$ 3.26	**Total Deductions**	$12.11
Gross Pay	$52.50	**Medicare Tax**	$ 0.76	**Net Pay**	$40.39
		State Tax	$ 0.21		
		Local Tax	$ 0.00		
		Total Withholding	$12.11		

Withholding

Your employer collects payroll taxes by deducting or **withholding** money from your wages. Income withheld from your paycheck goes to prepay your federal income tax and social insurance taxes. Withholding enables the government to collect taxes at a steady rate rather than all at the end of the year. Withholding also makes it more likely that people will pay their taxes.

As a taxpayer, you benefit from withholding because your tax payments are spread out over time. You pay a little tax with each paycheck, so you don't face a huge tax bill at the end of the year.

Your Paycheck Stub

Attached to your paycheck is a stub that shows your gross income and different types of withholding. **Gross income** is the amount you earn before taxes are withheld. For Kelly, the gross income was $52.50. **Net income** is the amount you receive after withholdings are subtracted from your gross pay. For Kelly, the net income was $40.39.

Your paycheck stub also shows you how much was withheld for each tax. You will see amounts for federal income taxes as well as Social Security taxes. Your city or state may also require withholding.

CYBER CONSUMER

The IRS maintains a web site devoted to providing individual and business taxpayers with information and assistance. At this easy-to-navigate site, you can learn how to e-file your tax return online, get answers to tax questions, and find out how to request an extension of the April 15 filing date. Visit this web site at www.irs.gov to investigate the types of tax forms you may download. Why do you think the IRS has placed so much information online?

CheckPoint

How does withholding money from your paycheck benefit you? How can you find out the amount of money being withheld from your pay?

Form W-4

The amount of income tax you owe depends on several factors—your gross income, the number of people you support, and other expenses.

When you are hired, your employer will ask you to complete federal Form W-4, which is required by law. **Form W-4** provides the information your employer needs to determine the proper amount to withhold from your paycheck. A sample Form W-4 is shown below.

Your Responsibility for Proper Withholding

You are responsible for the consequences if the information on your W-4 is incorrect and causes withholdings to be too small. If the amount withheld from your paycheck during the year is not close to the total tax you owe, the Internal Revenue Service may fine you. The **Internal Revenue Service (IRS)** is the federal agency that collects income taxes.

Sample Form W-4

Personal Allowances Worksheet (Keep for your records.)

A   Enter "1" for **yourself** if no one else can claim you as a dependent . . . .   **A** _____

B   Enter "1" if:
- You are single and have only one job; or
- You are married, have only one job, and your spouse does not work; or
- Your wages from a second job or your spouse's wages (or the total of both) are $1,000 or less.

   B   **1**

C   Enter "1" for your **spouse**. But, you may choose to enter "-0-" if you are married and have either a working spouse or more than one job. (Entering "-0-" may help you avoid having too little tax withheld.) . . . .   **C** _____

D   Enter number of **dependents** (other than your spouse or yourself) you will claim on your tax return . . . .   **D** _____

E   Enter "1" if you will file as **head of household** on your tax return (see conditions under **Head of household** above) .   **E** _____

F   Enter "1" if you have at least $1,500 of **child or dependent care expenses** for which you plan to claim a credit . .   **F** _____
    (**Note:** *Do **not** include child support payments. See **Pub. 503**, Child and Dependent Care Expenses, for details.*)

G   **Child Tax Credit** (including additional child tax credit):
- If your total income will be less than $52,000 ($77,000 if married), enter "2" for each eligible child.
- If your total income will be between $52,000 and $84,000 ($77,000 and $119,000 if married), enter "1" for each eligible child plus "1" **additional** if you have four or more eligible children.

   G _____

H   Add lines A through G and enter total here. **Note:** *This may be different from the number of exemptions you claim on your tax return.* ▶   **H**   **1**

For accuracy, complete all worksheets that apply.
- If you plan to **itemize or claim adjustments to income** and want to reduce your withholding, see the **Deductions and Adjustments Worksheet** on page 2.
- If you have **more than one job** or are **married and you and your spouse both work** and the combined earnings from all jobs exceed $35,000 ($25,000 if married) see the **Two-Earner/Two-Job Worksheet** on page 2 to avoid having too little tax withheld.
- If **neither** of the above situations applies, **stop here** and enter the number from line H on line 5 of Form W-4 below.

- - - - - - - - - - Cut here and give Form W-4 to your employer. Keep the top part for your records. - - - - - - - - -

Form **W-4** Department of the Treasury Internal Revenue Service	**Employee's Withholding Allowance Certificate** ▶ Your employer must send a copy of this form to the IRS if: (a) you claim more than 10 allowances or (b) you claim "Exempt" and your wages are normally more than $200 per week.	OMB No. 1545-0010 **20—**

1 Type or print your first name and middle initial: **Kelly A.**   Last name: **O'Rourke**   **2** Your social security number: **127 83 4545**

Home address (number and street or rural route): **188 Oak Street**

3 ☒ Single ☐ Married ☐ Married, but withhold at higher Single rate.
Note: *If married, but legally separated, or spouse is a nonresident alien, check the "Single" box.*

City or town, state, and ZIP code: **Hometown, ST 12345**

4 If your last name differs from that shown on your social security card, check here. You must call 1-800-772-1213 for a new card. ▶ ☐

5 Total number of allowances you are claiming (from line **H** above **or** from the applicable worksheet on page 2)   **5**   **1**

6 Additional amount, if any, you want withheld from each paycheck . . . .   **6** $ _____

7 I claim exemption from withholding for 2004, and I certify that I meet **both** of the following conditions for exemption:
- Last year I had a right to a refund of **all** Federal income tax withheld because I had **no** tax liability **and**
- This year I expect a refund of **all** Federal income tax withheld because I expect to have **no** tax liability.

If you meet both conditions, write "Exempt" here . . . . ▶   **7**

Under penalties of perjury, I certify that I am entitled to the number of withholding allowances claimed on this certificate, or I am entitled to claim exempt status.

Employee's signature
(Form is not valid unless you sign it.) ▶ *Kelly A. O'Rourke*   Date ▶ **Sept. 4, 20—**

8 Employer's name and address (Employer: Complete lines 8 and 10 only if sending to the IRS.)   **9** Office code (optional)   **10** Employer identification number (EIN)

Fill out a worksheet for the W-4 form and a W-4 form for yourself.

Allowances

A worksheet provided with your W-4 tells you how to calculate the number of allowances you should claim. An **allowance** is a number that reduces the amount of money withheld from your pay. The more allowances you claim, the smaller is the amount withheld.

The number of allowances you claim will not change the amount of tax you owe. Suppose you claim five allowances on your W-4 when you should only claim one. Your employer might withhold $500 from your pay over the year, but you may owe $3,000 in taxes. You have to pay not only the rest of the taxes, but also interest and possibly a fine because the amount withheld was not close enough to the tax owed. You alone are responsible for calculating the amount of income tax you owe.

Adjusting Your Allowance

Sometimes, the allowance you calculate using the W-4 worksheet does not result in the proper amount of withholding. The W-4 does not consider special situations.

Withholding Too Much

Students often have too much withheld, because they usually work more hours during the summer than during the school year. Suppose you work five hours a week during the school year and earn $35. But in the summer, you put in 40-hour weeks and earn $280. The amount withheld during the summer will be much larger than during the rest of the year. Your

What In The World?

Taxes may seem high in the United States, but they are much higher in other developed nations. One way to measure the impact of taxes is to calculate the percent taken of the total income in a nation's economy. In 2001, all taxes in the United States took 28.9 percent of its total income. The percent of income taken in Sweden was the highest at 51.4 percent. Other nations in Europe were close behind with 49.4 percent in Denmark, 45.0 percent in Germany, and 42.0 percent in Italy. Only Japan and South Korea had smaller tax burdens at 27.3 and 27.2 percent, respectively. Why do other nations have such high taxes? How might the tax revenue collected be used?

© CORBIS

total withholdings will be too large because the withholding is based on a 40-hour workweek all year long.

Withholding Too Little The allowance calculated on the W-4 worksheet may also result in withholding too little. Suppose you hold a job during the week *and* are self-employed painting houses on weekends. Your weekday employer might not withhold enough for your painting income as well.

You can avoid paying a large tax bill—and maybe a fine—at the end of the year by

1. Sending extra tax payments to the IRS.

2. Claiming fewer allowances.

3. Specifying an extra amount to be withheld from each paycheck on your W-4.

CheckPoint

What is the purpose of Form W-4? What happens if you increase the number of allowances?

Overwithholding as a Way to Save

Some taxpayers choose to have extra income withheld from their wages to force themselves to save. By claiming too few allowances, they can be sure they will receive a refund at the end of the year. From a financial point of view, this is a bad decision.

Suppose you need to have $75 withheld from each biweekly paycheck to pay the income tax you owe. By claiming no allowances, you increase the amount withheld to $100. At the end of the year, the government refunds you $650. The government used your funds for much of the year and paid you nothing for the privilege. A bank would pay you interest.

Buy the Numbers?

George has received job offers from two firms located in different states. The part of his income that would be taxed in one state is $25,000. That state charges 3 percent for its income tax. He would also pay a 1 percent local income tax. If he took the job in the other state, his taxed income would be $30,000. That state's income tax rate is 4 percent and the local tax is 2 percent. How much state and local income tax would George pay in each of these states? How might this information influence which offer George chooses to accept?

You can reduce your withholding to bring it more in line with the tax you will owe for that year by claiming additional allowances. As long as the amount withheld is close to the tax you owe, the IRS won't fine you.

Your goal in completing your W-4 is to make your withholdings almost exactly equal to the tax you owe.

CheckPoint

Should you reduce your allowances to force yourself to save? Why or why not?

TRY THESE

1. How do you and other taxpayers benefit from the taxes you pay?

2. What are payroll taxes?

3. In the sample paycheck stub, what is the amount withheld for federal income tax? For Social Security tax? For Medicare tax? For state tax? For local tax?

4. What is the purpose of Form W-4?

5. What is an allowance on Form W-4?

6. In what types of situations should you consider claiming extra allowances?

7. What is your main goal in determining how many allowances to claim?

THINK CRITICALLY

8. **CONSUMER ACTION** What did Kelly misunderstand about her paycheck? What options should Kelly consider to help her reach her goal of taking home at least $50 per week?

9. **COMMUNICATE** Explain how you and the government benefit from the system of withholding. How might you get into financial problems if this system did not exist?

Send your answer to your teacher by e-mail.

10. **MATH OF MONEY** Prepare a paycheck stub with gross earnings of $250. Use $36.04 for federal income tax and $12.26 for state tax withheld. Calculate Social Security tax at 6.2 percent and Medicare tax at 1.45 percent of gross pay. What is the net pay?

DECISION MAKING PROJECT

 SPECIFY   **SEARCH**   **SIFT**   **SELECT**   **STUDY**

SPECIFY Create a scenario for a 17-year-old student. Assume that this student qualifies to use a Form 1040EZ and that he or she will work only in the summer months of June, July, and August. What does this student do for income? Fill out a Form W-4 for this student.

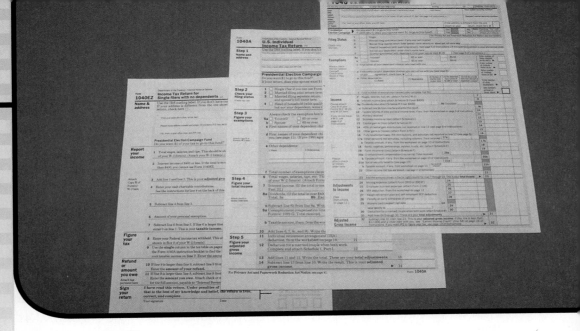

GOALS

IDENTIFY
the information you
need to complete your
income tax return

DEMONSTRATE
an ability to complete
a Form 1040EZ

5.2 File a Tax Return

Your Income Tax Return

If you have income above a minimum set each year by the government, you must fill out a tax return. A **tax return** is a set of forms that taxpayers use to calculate their tax obligation.

If your tax return shows that your withholding wasn't enough to cover your taxes, then you must send the remaining amount to the government. If your return shows that your withholding more than covered

your taxes, then the government will send you a refund for the extra amount.

Income For tax purposes, income is more than just your wages. The tips you receive as a restaurant server are income. Interest on your savings is income. The amount you earn by doing odd jobs in your neighborhood is income. Basically, most income you receive from wages, tips, and interest will be taxed.

CONSUMER ACTION

Ezra has never filled out a tax return. He knows he will probably have to file one because he had a summer job. Ezra doesn't even know where to get the tax forms. He heard there are books and software that can help him fill out tax returns. He went to his local bookstore, but the books did not seem like they were for people filing a tax return for the first time. When he went to the software store, he found the same thing to be true. What should Ezra do?

You may fill out your tax return yourself or hire a professional tax preparer. In either case, you are responsible for the accuracy of the return.

Sources of Information for Your Tax Return

Form W-2 Most young employees can complete their tax returns with just the information sent to them from various sources. One source is your employer. By January 31, employers must mail their workers a Form W-2. **Form W-2** is a summary of your earnings and withholdings for the year for a job. A sample Form W-2 is shown below. You will get a W-2 from each job you held during the year.

When you file, or send in, your tax return, you must enclose a copy of your W-2 form. Your employer also sends a copy to the IRS. If you fail to report your earnings, you will hear from the IRS. The IRS will know about your income from the W-2 it receives from your employer, as well as from the tax that was withheld.

Form 1099-INT You will also receive a record of the interest you earned on money you deposited in a bank. Banks are required to send depositors a Form 1099-INT.

Form 1099-INT is a statement of the interest your bank paid on your savings that year. As employers do with Form W-2, the bank sends a copy of the Form 1099-INT to the IRS. Information from Forms W-2 and 1099-INT is enough for most young people to complete their income tax returns.

GUESS WHAT

The Sixteenth Amendment to the Constitution in 1913 allowed the current income tax system to be established.

Sample Form W-2

a Control number 22222 Void ☐	For Official Use Only ▶ OMB No. 1545-0008	
b Employer identification number 94-18643	**1** Wages, tips, other compensation 525.00	**2** Federal income tax withheld 57.80
c Employer's name, address, and ZIP code The Video Store. Inc. 494 Main Street Hometown, ST 12345	**3** Social security wages 525.00	**4** Social security tax withheld 32.55
	5 Medicare wages and tips 525.00	**6** Medicare tax withheld 7.61
	7 Social security tips	**8** Allocated tips
d Employee's social security number 127-83-4545	**9** Advance EIC payment	**10** Dependent care benefits
e Employee's first name and initial Last name	**11** Nonqualified plans	**12a** See instructions for box 12
Kelly A. O'Rourke 188 Oak Street Hometown, ST 12345	**13** Statutory employee ☐ Retirement plan ☐ Third-party sick pay ☐	**12b**
	14 Other	**12c**
		12d
f Employee's address and ZIP code		

15 State	Employer's state ID number	**16** State wages, tips, etc.	**17** State income tax	**18** Local wages, tips, etc.	**19** Local income tax	**20** Locality name
ST	94-18643	525.00	2.10			

Form **W-2** Wage and Tax Statement   20—   Department of the Treasury—Internal Revenue Service

Copy A For Social Security Administration — Send this entire page with Form W-3 to the Social Security Administration; photocopies are **not** acceptable.

Cat. No. 10134D

For Privacy Act and Paperwork Reduction Act Notice, see back of Copy D.

Income Tax Forms

All taxpayers must use one of the three basic forms for filing federal income tax returns. Forms 1040, 1040A, and 1040EZ are available at local libraries or on the Internet at the IRS web site. Instructions with each form provide a checklist of qualifications for using the form.

The EZ Way Most young people qualify to use the simplest of these forms, **Form 1040EZ**. To qualify to use Form 1040EZ, you must meet the following criteria.

▶ you are single or married and filing jointly with your spouse

▶ you have no **dependents** (people you support financially, such as children)

▶ you and your spouse are under 65

▶ neither you nor your spouse is blind

▶ you have a taxable income of less than $50,000

▶ you earned no more than $1,500 in interest

▶ you had no income other than wages, interest, tips, scholarships, or unemployment compensation

Form 1040 When you are older, your financial life is likely to be more complicated. You may own a home, invest in the stock market, or run a small business. Then you may be required to use Form 1040. In fact, you could benefit from using this form because it allows you to itemize deductions. **Deductions** are expenses you can legally subtract from your income when figuring your taxes.

CheckPoint

What is the purpose of an income tax return? What forms do you receive from your employer and your bank? What information do these forms contain?

How to Complete a 1040EZ

Tax forms can appear more difficult than they really are. A copy of Form 1040EZ appears on page 169. Follow along on the form as you read the instructions.

Identify Yourself

At the top of the form are spaces to write your name, address, and Social Security number. Your **Social Security number** is unique. No one else has it. The government uses this number throughout your life to identify you as a taxpayer and keep track of your earnings and tax records. Memorize this number. You will have to write it on many official documents during your lifetime.

Below your identification information on Form 1040EZ is a checkbox for presidential election campaigns. If you check "Yes," your contribution will not increase your tax or decrease your refund.

Income

Total Wages, Salaries, and Tips The number you will need for this can be found in box 1 on your W-2 form(s).

Taxable Interest Income Fill in the amount from the interest reported on your 1099-INT form(s).

Form
1040EZ

Department of the Treasury—Internal Revenue Service
**Income Tax Return for Single and
Joint Filers With No Dependents** (99) **20—**

OMB No. 1545-0675

Label

(See page 12.)
**Use the IRS
label.**
Otherwise,
please print
or type.

L A B E L   H E R E

Your first name and initial	Last name	Your social security number
JAMES	LIN	123 : 32 : 1234
If a joint return, spouse's first name and initial	Last name	Spouse's social security number

Home address (number and street). If you have a P.O. box, see page 12.   Apt. no.
101 OAK STREET

City, town or post office, state, and ZIP code. If you have a foreign address, see page 12.
HOMETOWN, IL   12345

▲ Important! ▲
You **must** enter your
SSN(s) above.

**Presidential
Election
Campaign**
(page 12) ▶

Note. Checking "Yes" will not change your tax or reduce your refund.
Do you, or your spouse if a joint return, want $3 to go to this fund? . . . . . . ▶

	You		Spouse	
	☒ Yes	☐ No	☐ Yes	☐ No

Income

**Attach
Form(s) W-2
here.**
Enclose, but
do not attach,
any payment.

1 Wages, salaries, and tips. This should be shown in box 1 of your Form(s) W-2.
Attach your Form(s) W-2.   **1**   35,223 | 00

2 Taxable interest. If the total is over $1,500, you cannot use Form 1040EZ.   **2**   200 | 00

3 Unemployment compensation and Alaska Permanent Fund dividends
(see page 14).   **3**

4 Add lines 1, 2, and 3. This is your **adjusted gross income.**   **4**   35,423 | 00

**Note. You
must** check
Yes or No.

5 Can your parents (or someone else) claim you on their return?
Yes. Enter amount from
☐ worksheet on back.
No. If **single,** enter $7,800.
☒ If **married filing jointly,** enter $15,600.
See back for explanation.   **5**   7,800 | 00

6 Subtract line 5 from line 4. If line 5 is larger than line 4, enter -0-.
This is your **taxable income.** ▶ **6**   27,623 | 00

**Payments
and tax**

7 Federal income tax withheld from box 2 of your Form(s) W-2.   **7**   4,526 | 00

8 **Earned income credit (EIC).**   **8**

9 Add lines 7 and 8. These are your **total payments.** ▶ **9**   4,526 | 00

10 **Tax.** Use the amount on **line 6 above** to find your tax in the tax table on pages
24–28 of the booklet. Then, enter the tax from the table on this line.   **10**   3,794 | 00

Refund

Have it directly
deposited! See
page 19 and fill
in 11b, 11c,
and 11d.

11a If line 9 is larger than line 10, subtract line 10 from line 9. This is your **refund.** ▶ **11a**   732 | 00

▶ **b** Routing number   ▶ **c** Type: ☐ Checking ☐ Savings

▶ **d** Account number

**Amount
you owe**

12 If line 10 is larger than line 9, subtract line 9 from line 10. This is
the **amount you owe.** For details on how to pay, see page 20. ▶ **12**

**Third party
designee**

Do you want to allow another person to discuss this return with the IRS (see page 20)? ☐ **Yes.** Complete the following. ☐**No**

Designee's
name ▶   Phone
no. ▶ ( )   Personal identification
number (PIN) ▶

**Sign
here**

Joint return?
See page 11.
Keep a copy
for your
records.

Under penalties of perjury, I declare that I have examined this return, and to the best of my knowledge and belief, it is true, correct, and accurately lists all amounts and sources of income I received during the tax year. Declaration of preparer (other than the taxpayer) is based on all information of which the preparer has any knowledge.

Your signature	Date	Your occupation	Daytime phone number
James Lin	4/14/--	SALES	( )
Spouse's signature. If a joint return, **both** must sign.	Date	Spouse's occupation	

**Paid
preparer's
use only**

| Preparer's
signature ▶ | Date | Check if
self-employed ☐ | Preparer's SSN or PTIN |
|---|---|---|---|
| Firm's name (or
yours if self-employed),
address, and ZIP code ▶ | | EIN | |
| | | Phone no. ( ) | |

For Disclosure, Privacy Act, and Paperwork Reduction Act Notice, see page 23.   Cat. No. 11329W   Form **1040EZ**

Unemployment Compensation Fill in the amount of any unemployment compensation you received.

Adjusted Gross Income When you add the income from all sources, the total is your *adjusted gross income.* This is your total income before subtracting any deductions or exemptions.

Determine Your Deduction If your parents or guardian claim you as a dependent, you may not claim yourself too. If this is your situation, then you should check the "Yes" box on the form. Then complete the worksheet on the back of the tax form to determine the amount you can deduct. If no one else can claim you as a dependent, then you should check "No" on the form and enter the amount specified.

Most young people are claimed as dependents by their parents or guardians who file their tax returns on Forms 1040A or 1040. These forms allow taxpayers a deduction for each dependent. This deduction reduces the gross adjusted income.

A *standard deduction* is an amount you may subtract from your adjusted gross income, which is not based on how many dependents you have.

When you check the "No" box, the amount the form tells you to enter is the total of your exemption and standard deduction. When you check the "Yes" box, the worksheet on the back of the tax form will help you determine your standard deduction and exemption, if any.

Your Taxable Income After you subtract the exemptions and deductions from your adjusted gross income, the result is your

taxable income. This is the income figure used to determine your taxes.

Payments and Tax

Federal Income Tax Withheld Your next step is to enter the amount of federal income tax that was withheld from your paychecks. Your employer sent the withholdings to the government to pay your taxes. The total withholding for the year appears in box 2 on your Form W-2 for each job.

Earned Income Credit Some workers with low incomes qualify for an earned income credit. This amount is treated as if it were an additional tax payment made. The instruction booklet for Form 1040EZ provides the qualifications and directions for calculating this credit.

Total Payments For Line 9 of the form, you will add the withholdings and earned income credits. The result is the total amount of your taxes that you have already paid.

Tax The instruction booklet for Form 1040EZ contains a table that tells you your total tax for the year.

Part of this tax table is shown on this page. The tax table lists income ranges—"at least" this number "but less than" that number.

Your taxable income will be recorded on Line 6. On the table, you would locate the two numbers within which your taxable income falls. Then you would read across that row to the column under "single" or "married, filing jointly," whichever is appropriate for you. The number in the correct range and appropriate column would be your total tax.

For example, look at the tax table on this page. If you are single and your taxable income was $27,623, your tax would be $3,794. You would record your tax on Line 10.

If you had made no payments to the IRS during the year, you would owe the full amount of the tax shown in the table. In this example, you would owe the IRS $3,794.

If Form 1040EZ, line 6, is—		And you are—	
At least	But less than	Single	Married filing jointly
		Your tax is—	
27,000			
27,000	27,050	3,704	3,354
27,050	27,100	3,711	3,361
27,100	27,150	3,719	3,369
27,150	27,200	3,726	3,376
27,200	27,250	3,734	3,384
27,250	27,300	3,741	3,391
27,300	27,350	3,749	3,399
27,350	27,400	3,756	3,406
27,400	27,450	3,764	3,414
27,450	27,500	3,771	3,421
27,500	27,550	3,779	3,429
27,550	27,600	3,786	3,436
27,600	27,650	3,794	3,444
27,650	27,700	3,801	3,451

$MATH OF MONEY

Use the tax table above. Your W-2 form reports that your total wages were $34,539. Your W-2 form reports that $4,053 was withheld from your wages for federal income tax. You receive a 1099-INT from your bank that tells you your interest income was $281. You are single and are not claimed by any other person as a dependent.

1. How much is your adjusted gross income?

2. How much is your taxable income?

3. What is your total tax for the year?

4. What is the amount of your payment or refund?

SOLUTION

1. Add your total wages to your taxable interest.

   $34,539 + $281 = $34,820

2. Subtract $7,800 from your adjusted gross income.

   $34,820 − $7,800 = $27,020

3. Look on the tax table at the row for $27,000–27,050 and match it with the amount in the corresponding column for single people: $3,704

4. Subtract your tax from your total tax payments. You paid $349 too much.

   $4,053 − $3,704 = $349

Consumer ALERT

Recently, a tax preparation service advertised that it would prepare Form 1040EZ for $35. The IRS predicted it would take a taxpayer less than two hours to complete this form. Would you buy this service? How could you benefit from doing your own tax return?

Refund

Because of withholding, however, you would have already paid most or all of this amount. If your withholding totaled more than $3,794, you would receive the difference as a refund. You would write in the difference on Line 11a.

Deposit Your Refund Electronically If you are owed a refund, you have the option of having it deposited electronically. The routing number is your bank's electronic address for funds transfers. Your bank will tell you its routing number. Your employer uses the same routing number if your paycheck is directly deposited.

Check the type of account and write your account number. The IRS will deposit your refund into that account once it processes your return.

Amount You Owe

If your withholding totals less than the tax you calculated for Line 10, you would record the amount you still owe in Line 12. You then have to pay the rest of the amount owed.

Sign Here

You must always remember to sign your return and fill in the date and your occupation. The IRS won't consider your tax return filed unless it is signed. By signing the form, you are declaring (under penalty of perjury) that the information on the form is true.

Check for Accuracy and File Your Return

Always check your tax forms for accuracy before you send them to the IRS. If you make a mistake, you may have to pay a penalty or you may receive a lower refund than you deserve.

© CORBIS

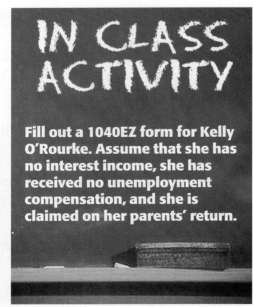

IN CLASS ACTIVITY

Fill out a 1040EZ form for Kelly O'Rourke. Assume that she has no interest income, she has received no unemployment compensation, and she is claimed on her parents' return.

When you are sure you have completed your return correctly, write a check or make a credit card payment to the IRS (if you owe money). Write your Social Security number and the year of your income tax return on the memo line of your check. Send the form along with your Form(s) W-2 and your check (if necessary) to the IRS. Keep a copy for your records. The deadline is April 15!

Self-Employment Tax

Remember, the amount of earnings a person is paid is much less than the total earnings. This happens because the employer withholds Social Security, Medicare, and income tax from the person's paycheck.

Do people who work for themselves (that is, are self-employed) pay income tax and, if so, how? What about young adults who make significant income from providing lawn mowing, snow removal, and baby-sitting services and from computer-related jobs?

Paying on a Quarterly Basis
When a person is self-employed and makes more than $400 in a year, he or she must file using Form 1040. The burden of paying self-employment taxes is left to the individual taxpayer. Self-employed individuals pay estimated taxes in quarterly installments to the U.S. Treasury. The amount is based on the income they received during the quarter. Many newly self-employed people are surprised at the taxes they owe at the end of the year if they haven't made quarterly payments. Failure to pay estimated taxes subjects the person to underpayment penalties in addition to the tax owed.

CheckPoint

What do you subtract from your total tax to determine your refund or tax still owed?

Schedule C (1040) A person who is self-employed must complete and attach Schedule C, Profit or Loss From Business, to his or her 1040 form. Self-employed persons must keep detailed records of their income and expenses to determine their income tax liability accurately on Schedule C. The amount determined as net income or loss on Schedule C is then entered on line 12 of Form 1040.

© Getty Images/PhotoDisc

A self-employed person pays the same taxes that any employee pays: the regular income tax based solely on the business income plus the tax for Social Security and Medicare (both the employee's and employer's portions). The big difference is that self-employed people must "with-hold" their own taxes and make the payments themselves.

IN CLASS ACTIVITY

What self-employed jobs can you think of? In a group, list as many as you can name.

© Getty Images/PhotoDisc

CheckPoint

What are the differences in the way company-employed and self-employed people pay their taxes?

Online Payment

No matter which form you use, you may file your tax return online. According to the IRS, more than 40 percent of all individual returns were filed electronically in 2003. Probably the greatest advantage to filing online is getting your refund faster. Most electronic filings take about three weeks or less to be processed. Paper returns can take six weeks or more. You may learn how to file online by visiting the IRS web site at www.irs.gov.

Many taxpayers purchase software to help them prepare their tax returns. These programs help you organize your returns and allow you to enter your tax information electronically. They do not eliminate the need to keep accurate and complete financial records. Among the most popular programs are *TurboTax*® and *TaxCut*®. Other programs are available at most software and larger bookstores.

Many individuals and small businesses use programs marketed at the *Quicken* web site for simple tasks such as writing checks to more complex ones of paying employees and filing various tax forms.

CheckPoint

How can you file your tax return online? What is the advantage of filing online?

TRY THESE

1. What information do you need to complete a Form 1040EZ, and where does it come from?

2. What must you include as income for your tax form?

3. Why don't most young people claim themselves as a dependent?

4. What is the difference between adjusted gross income and taxable income?

5. How do your withholdings affect your taxes?

6. Why should you check your work before filing your tax return?

THINK CRITICALLY

7. **CONSUMER ACTION** Write an explanation to Ezra about how the tax return process works. Include a brief explanation of the forms containing the information he needs and the sources of these forms. Would you advise him to buy a book or software?

8. **COMMUNICATE** Write one or two paragraphs on how to fill out Form 1040EZ. How is your description

different from the one in the tax instruction booklet? E-mail your explanation to your teacher.

Look at the Form 1040EZ on page 169. Answer the following questions.

9. Is James Lin single or married?

10. How much was withheld from James' paycheck for federal taxes?

11. Will he receive a refund or will he have to write a check to the IRS?

DECISION MAKING PROJECT

SPECIFY · SEARCH · SIFT · SELECT · STUDY

SEARCH Consider your student's job. How much does it pay per hour? How many days per week would this student work? Based on this income information, what federal, state, or local taxes would the student have withheld from each paycheck? Calculate the biweekly paycheck for the student. Then work together with your group to calculate the student's Form W-2.

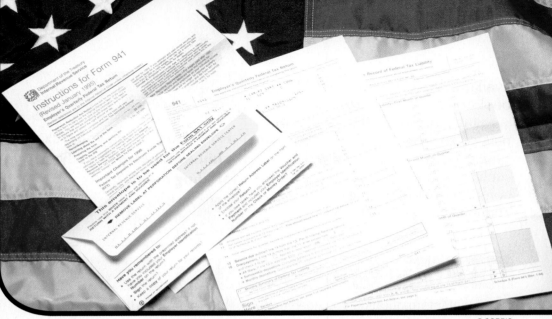

© CORBIS

5.3 Taxes and Government

Federal, State, and Local Government Income

More than 20 percent of all income in the United States flows into the federal government each year. The government receives funds from taxes and borrowing. The borrowing is in the form of government bonds, which will be discussed later.

The federal government receives the largest part of its income from income taxes, which account for close to 43 percent of the federal government's tax revenue. Social Security and Medicare taxes bring in another 35 percent of the total. About 14 percent of federal tax revenue comes from other types of taxes, and 8 percent is borrowed to cover the deficit.

Social Security and Medicare

Both employers and employees pay Social Security and Medicare taxes.

CONSUMER ACTION

Raj lives near the border between two states. In his state, the gas prices are much higher than in the neighboring state. He knows that the taxes from the sale of the gasoline benefit his state somehow, but the difference in gas prices means he will be paying much more for gas if he bought it in his state instead of crossing the border to buy gas. What should Raj do?

The amounts withheld for these taxes may appear under the amount labeled FICA on your paycheck stub.

Contributions to Social Security Under FICA regulations, workers' wages are taxed at a rate of 6.2 percent. This percentage is collected on gross income up to a maximum level that is adjusted each year. In 2004, the maximum income taxable for Social Security was $87,900.

Contributions to Medicare An additional 1.45 percent is taken on *all* earned income to pay for the Medicare program. Adding these percentages together, the total most people pay for Social Security and Medicare is 7.65 percent of gross income.

Your Employer's Contribution Employers match employees' payments for Social Security and Medicare. For each dollar you earn up to a maximum amount, 15.3 cents goes to the government for these taxes. Half comes from you. The other half comes from your employer. If you are self-employed, the government requires you to pay the entire 15.3 cents.

CheckPoint

What are some taxes that are deducted from your paycheck?

Classifying Taxes

A good way to understand how you are taxed is to learn different ways in which taxes are classified. Three common ways are to group taxes according to their principles, the share of income they take, and the way in which they are collected.

Principles of Taxation

The principles of American democracy demand that every taxpayer should be treated equally under the law. This does not mean, however, that all taxpayers should pay the same amount of tax. Principles of taxation suggest that some should pay more than others.

Under the *benefit principle,* those who use a good or service provided by the government should pay for it. Toll roads are an example of this principle. Those who drive on the road pay the tolls.

Under the *ability-to-pay principle,* those who have larger incomes should pay a larger share of what they receive. Federal income taxes are an example of this principle. As people's taxable income grows, the rate of this tax increases from 10 percent to 35 percent.

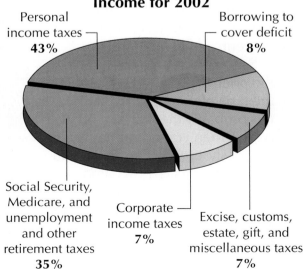

Sources of Federal Government Income for 2002

Personal income taxes **43%**

Borrowing to cover deficit **8%**

Social Security, Medicare, and unemployment and other retirement taxes **35%**

Corporate income taxes **7%**

Excise, customs, estate, gift, and miscellaneous taxes **7%**

Taxes and Income

Taxes are classified in three ways depending on the share of income they take of different levels of yearly income.

Progressive taxes take a larger share of higher incomes. Ray's income tax rate increased from 15 to 25 percent when his earnings went from $24,000 to $32,000 per year.

Regressive taxes take a smaller share of higher incomes than of lower incomes. Many U.S. state and local taxes are regressive. Suppose that Louisa earns $16,000 a year compared to Ray's $32,000. Both buy a used car for $10,000 and pay an 8 percent sales tax. The $800 tax is 5 percent of Louisa's income but only 2.5 percent of Ray's.

Proportional taxes take the same share of all incomes. If all people were taxed 10 percent of all their income, this would be a proportional tax. No perfect examples of proportional taxes exist, however, in our economy.

A person with a high income can pay more dollars with a regressive tax than a person with a small income. Remember that the *number* of dollars taken in tax is not what makes the difference. Whether a tax is regressive, progressive, or proportional depends only on the percentage of different incomes that it takes.

How Taxes Are Collected

Direct Taxes *Direct taxes* such as income and property taxes are paid directly to the government.

Indirect Taxes Taxes included in the cost of a good or service are *indirect taxes.* For example, part of the rent tenants pay is used by their landlords to pay property taxes.

Pay-as-You-Earn Taxes

Taxes that are paid as you earn income are pay-as-you-earn taxes. Federal withholding is an example of this type of tax payment. As you receive a paycheck, the government takes its cut.

Types of Taxes

Income Taxes Most states and some cities have income tax systems patterned after the federal system. State and local income taxes may be withheld from your paycheck.

As with federal tax, you are responsible for calculating the amount of income tax you owe. Information you provide on your Form W-4 provides the information your employer needs to determine state and local withholdings.

The most apparent difference between state, local, and federal income taxes is the tax rate. State and local income tax rates are much lower. Federal income tax rates ranged from 15 to 39.6 percent in 2000. A law passed in 2001 and amended in 2003 lowered the maximum rate to 35 percent. Most state income tax rates are less than 10 percent. Local government taxes are typically between 1 and 2 percent.

Sales Taxes Taxes added to the price of goods and services at the time of purchase are **sales taxes**. It is probably the first tax you ever paid. When you buy a magazine, a pair of shoes, or a computer, you pay sales taxes. The tax amount appears on your sales receipt. Funds collected from sales taxes are normally divided between state and local governments.

Property Taxes

Property taxes are taxes on the value of real estate property. Government workers estimate the value of a piece of land, structure, or other type of property. The tax is a percentage of that value. These taxes are most often used by local governments and school districts.

Often property taxes are added to your home loan payments. The financial institution collects your taxes from your payments to pay the property taxes.

Excise Taxes

An **excise tax** is collected on the sale of specific goods and services. States place excise taxes on items such as tobacco, gasoline, and alcoholic beverages. The federal government imposes excise taxes on oil products, firearms, and air travel. Unlike sales taxes, excise taxes are included in the price charged to consumers. If you pay $1.99 for a gallon of gasoline, the price includes both federal and state excise taxes.

INTERNET ACTIVITY

Most gasoline used in the United States is made from imported oil. If a large tariff was placed on imported oil forcing the price of gasoline up $1 per gallon, how would this affect you? Make a list. Working with another student, identify five important impacts of the new tariff, and e-mail the list to your teacher.

Estate and Gift Taxes

When a person dies, there may be **estate taxes** on the property that is received by those legally entitled to the estate. Only estates higher than a certain amount are taxed.

Gift taxes are taxes that the giver of gifts may pay. Federal law allows people to make some gifts that are not taxed. The maximum value of untaxed gifts is $11,000 per year. This amount is periodically increased to account for inflation.

 PRIMARYSOURCES

In a 1938 interview, Arthur Botsford, a Connecticut clockmaker, had this to say about taxes.

"Democracy is goin' downhill. Taxes on this house used to be $19 once—now they're a hundred and thirteen.... You got to pay income tax on a thousand dollars, and if you got money in the bank, they want to know just how much, and how much interest is comin' on it.... Call that freedom?"

Write a paragraph about Mr. Botsford's attitude toward taxation and freedom. Do you think he would vote for any tax increases? By what percent did Mr. Botsford's property taxes increase?

Business and License Taxes

To operate certain kinds of businesses, companies or individuals must have a license, permit, or stamp. A **business** or **license tax** is paid for this certification, which may be accompanied by a test. For instance, to be licensed to practice medicine in your state, your doctor had to pass some certification tests.

Customs Duties and Tariffs

To control the flow of products that are imported into the United States, **customs duties** or **tariffs** are imposed on some imports. This sometimes results in items from abroad being sold at higher prices than similar American-made products.

CheckPoint

What is the main difference between state or local taxes and federal income taxes?

TRY THESE

1. What is the largest source of federal government revenue?
2. Which governments benefit from sales taxes?
3. What are the principles of taxation?
4. What is the difference between sales and excise taxes?

THINK CRITICALLY

5. **CONSUMER ACTION** Raj is torn between buying cheaper gas or higher priced gas that supports state programs. Write a paragraph advising Raj and e-mail it to your teacher.

6. **COMMUNICATE** Suppose you could vote on a proposal for a property tax increase to raise money for local law enforcement. You own property worth $100,000, and the current property tax rate is 2 percent. If this proposal passes, the new property tax rate would be 2.5 percent. Would you vote for the increase? Why? What would it cost you if the proposal passed?

DECISION MAKING PROJECT

SPECIFY   SEARCH   SIFT   SELECT   STUDY

SIFT Fill out a Form 1040EZ for the student using Form W-2. Assume another person claims the student as a dependent and that there is no taxable interest income, unemployment compensation, or earned income credits to report. What is the taxable income? Does the student have to pay the IRS or can the student expect a refund? How can this return be filed online?

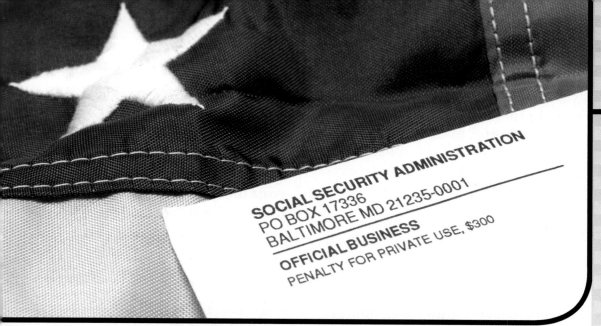

© CORBIS

5.4 Government Spending

The Power to Influence

Governments use taxes not only to bring in revenue but also to influence consumers' buying decisions. Taxing a good or service generally means fewer consumers will buy it. The higher the tax, the more it influences consumer decisions. You can find examples of ways the government uses taxes to affect consumer decisions throughout your community.

"Sin" Taxes Some goods are harmful to your health, yet they are legal. For example, adults can legally buy and use tobacco products, even though these products are harmful to their health. The government requires producers to place warning labels on tobacco products. Millions of Americans buy and use them anyway.

CONSUMER **ACTION**

Tara wants to build a cabin on land her family owns. Her father said that she has to get building permits, follow specific building codes, and pass inspections along the way. Tara wonders why all this hassle is necessary. It will certainly raise the cost of the cabin to follow building codes. She knows the cabin will be safe the way she wants to build it, so why does the government get involved?

To discourage such sales, federal and state governments tax tobacco products. The governments hope that fewer people will smoke because cigarettes are expensive.

Tax Cuts

Lower taxes encourage consumers to make beneficial choices. In 2001 and 2003, President Bush led Congress to reduce income tax rates by roughly 10 percent. The idea was to encourage consumer spending to improve the economy.

Many local governments in areas with high unemployment reduce property taxes for businesses that operate there. They hope that the lower taxes will entice more businesses to open facilities in their area and employ their workers.

Charities The government may allow you to deduct your contribution to a charity from your adjusted gross income. This tax break influences people to give to charities.

As you can see, governments can use taxes to raise money and influence your consumer decisions.

CheckPoint

How can taxes influence your buying decisions? How can your local government use taxes to help local workers?

Government Spending

The federal government spends more than $2.4 trillion each year. State and local governments together spend nearly two-thirds as much. Added together, these amounts work out to roughly $17,000 per year for every American.

Most of the government's income pays for goods and services that benefit all Americans. These **public goods** include roads, schools, national defense, and services of various regulatory agencies.

Few people could afford to pay for these goods and services on their own. Still, people want and need them. To make them available, the government must provide them. Your tax dollars are used in six major areas.

Social Security, Medicare, and Other Retirement The largest portion of your federal taxes goes to fund programs such as Social Security and Medicare.

U.S. Government Spending for 2002

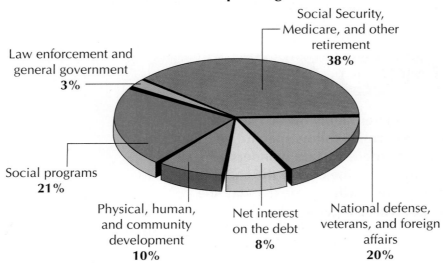

- Social Security, Medicare, and other retirement **38%**
- Law enforcement and general government **3%**
- Social programs **21%**
- Physical, human, and community development **10%**
- Net interest on the debt **8%**
- National defense, veterans, and foreign affairs **20%**

Social Programs The second largest portion of federal spending goes to fund programs such as Medicaid, food stamps, unemployment compensation, and social services.

National Defense, Veterans, and Foreign Affairs The third largest portion of federal dollars is spent to fund our military, our foreign embassies, and to support veterans who have served our country.

Physical, Human, and Community Development A large portion of federal spending goes to agricultural programs, primary and secondary education, direct assistance to college students, and job training programs. Space, energy, and general science programs are also in this category.

Net Interest on the Debt Another portion of federal government spending goes to pay the interest on the national debt.

Law Enforcement and General Government The smallest portion of federal spending pays

© CORBIS

for all federal law enforcement agencies as well as government offices. It also funds agencies responsible for collecting the taxes that support all categories of spending.

Debt Reduction In the late 1990s and 2000, the federal government received more tax revenue than it spent. It used these funds to pay down the national debt. By 2002, the federal government had a deficit so no funds were used to reduce the national debt.

What State and Local Governments Provide

Think about the goods and services that state and local governments provide. Here are examples.

▶ building and maintaining roads

▶ operating police and fire protection services

▶ maintaining a criminal justice system

▶ building and staffing schools

▶ building and operating state colleges and universities

▶ supporting medical facilities

▶ constructing and operating sewage treatment plants

▶ operating unemployment compensation programs

COMMUNICATE

Look at the two pie charts on pages 177 and 182. One shows where the federal government's income comes from, and the other shows where it goes. What do you think these say about the priorities of our nation? Write a letter to your Congressperson or Senator expressing your opinions and recommendations.

VOTE Your Wallet

Every year, many school districts across the country ask voters to approve a tax increase or "levy." Schools ask for these funds to help pay for building repairs, more teachers, after-school activities, and books. Most people would say that they want their community to have good schools. So why do voters reject many school levies?

Find out from your teacher or a school official when your school last had a tax levy on the ballot. Look for articles in the newspaper or on the Internet about the school levy. How did the school plan to use the funds? What were supporters doing to try to get the levy approved? Did students participate? What were opponents saying? Did it pass? If not, what were the consequences for the school?

Now step into the shoes of a voter in your school district. Would you have voted for the levy? If you were 60 years old and had no children in school, would you have voted for it? What other ways might your school get the money it needs?

© CORBIS/ James L. Amos

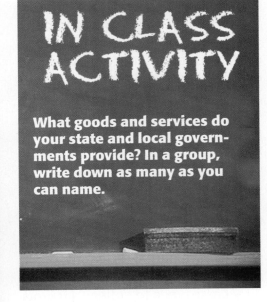

IN CLASS ACTIVITY

What goods and services do your state and local governments provide? In a group, write down as many as you can name.

State and Local Government Regulations

Many rules are written into laws and enforced by state and local governments. For instance, to drive a car, you must obtain a driver's license. To build a house, you need a building permit and must follow local building codes that make sure your home is safe.

Regulations like these create order and safety in your state and local community. For example, your driver's license verifies that you have passed the driver's test so you have the skills to drive safely. Your state and local tax dollars keep these programs running.

CheckPoint

What state or local programs benefit you most? How do state and local regulations help keep you safe?

TRY THESE

1. List the major categories of federal government spending.

2. In what category does the federal government spend the most money?

3. What category of federal spending supports space programs, such as NASA?

4. What category of federal spending supports public schools?

5. What are public goods and how are they paid for? Who can use them?

6. How can taxes be used to discourage you from buying some products?

7. How can taxes be used to encourage some types of spending decisions?

8. Why should you follow government regulations?

THINK CRITICALLY

9. **CONSUMER ACTION** Tara has to follow lots of government regulations to build her cabin. Tara wants to know the point of all this regulation. Write a one-page note to Tara, explaining how the regulations benefit consumers. What might happen without them?

10. Look at the pie chart on page 177 that shows the sources of federal government tax dollars. Are there any sources that surprise you? What changes would you make in how taxes are collected if you could? Explain your feelings in a one-page essay. Send your essay to your teacher in an e-mail.

11. Federal, state, and local governments support programs that employ many people. Write a list of titles of government jobs in your area.

12. **COMMUNICATE** Is there a category whose portion of federal spending is much larger than you thought it was? If so, which category is it and why are you surprised?

13. Identify a public good that you used today. Explain why this good would probably not exist if the government did not collect taxes to pay for it.

14. Federal, state, and local governments support programs that benefit people in your community. Write a list of goods and services that benefit your community.

15. Your state and local governments enforce traffic laws and administer driver's licenses. List two laws or regulations you must follow to get your driver's license. Why do you think these laws or regulations are in place?

DECISION MAKING PROJECT

SPECIFY   SEARCH   SIFT   **SELECT**   STUDY

SELECT Compare completed Form 1040EZ returns. Check each other's forms. Choose which return you think is correct, and prepare a presentation describing the process of filling out a return for the student you created.

ASSESSMENT

KEY IDEAS

Taxes and Your Paycheck

1. Income taxes are taxes individuals pay on funds they receive from sources such as wages and interest. Social insurance taxes are taxes that support programs that provide social benefits, such as Social Security and Medicare.

2. The government requires your employer to withhold money from your paychecks to pay taxes. Your paycheck stub shows your gross pay (earnings before withholding), the amounts withheld for each type of tax, and your net income (the amount you take home).

3. Form W-4 provides the information your employer needs to determine the proper amount to withhold from your paycheck.

4. You can calculate your allowances on the W-4 using the worksheet attached to it. You can claim more or fewer allowances, but the number of allowances you claim will not change the amount of tax you owe.

File a Tax Return

5. If your income exceeds a certain minimum, you must complete a tax return. In January, your employer will send you a Form W-2 summarizing your income and withholdings. Your bank will send you a Form 1099-INT showing the interest you earned on your savings. Most young people can fill out their tax returns with just the information on these forms.

6. For tax purposes, income is more than just your wages. Most income you receive from wages, tips, and interest will be taxed.

7. All taxpayers must use one of the three basic forms for filing income tax returns. Young people living at home usually qualify for Form 1040EZ. You may file your tax return on paper or online.

8. Your Social Security number identifies you as a taxpayer. The government will use this number throughout your life to keep track of your earnings and tax records.

9. On the tax form, when you total your income, the result is your adjusted gross income. From this figure, you subtract your exemptions and deductions to arrive at your taxable income. The lower your taxable income, the lower your taxes.

10. To find your total tax, locate your taxable income on the tax table. Your withholdings and earned income credit, if applicable, are the tax payments you made during the year. By subtracting these payments from your total tax, you will determine your refund or amount owed.

Taxes and Government

11. State and local governments collect most of their revenue from four types of taxes: income, sales, property, and excise taxes. Sales taxes are added to the price of products at the time you buy them. Property taxes are taxes on the value of property you own. Governments raise the price of some products by adding an excise tax directly into their prices.

12. Other taxes are estate, gift, business, and tariffs.

Government Spending

13. State and local governments pay for most programs that benefit you directly, such as schools and police protection. State and local regulations, such as building codes, bring safety to your community.

14. The government uses sin taxes on harmful but legal products such as alcohol and tobacco to discourage sales of these products. Governments can also cut taxes to encourage spending.

TERMS REVIEW

Match each term on the left with its definition on the right.
Some terms may not be used.

a. allowance

b. business or license tax

c. customs duty or tariff

d. deduction

e. dependent

f. estate tax

g. excise tax

h. FICA (Federal Insurance Contributions Act)

i. Form 1040EZ

j. Form 1099-INT

k. Form W-2

l. Form W-4

m. gift tax

n. gross income

o. income tax

p. Internal Revenue Service (IRS)

q. net income

r. payroll tax

s. property tax

t. public good

u. sales tax

v. Social Security number

w. tax return

x. taxable income

y. withholding

1. a form that you fill out to provide the information your employer needs to determine the proper amount to withhold from your paycheck

2. the pay you earn before taxes are withheld

3. goods and services provided by the government that benefit all Americans

4. for tax purposes, a person you support financially

5. a statement of the interest your bank paid on your savings that year

6. a set of forms that taxpayers use to calculate their tax obligation

7. a share of workers' earnings paid to the government by workers and their employers

8. a number that you calculate on a Form W-4 that reduces the amount withheld from your pay

9. a tax included in the price of certain goods and services

10. employer deductions from employees, earnings to pay employees' taxes

11. all the wages, tips, and interest on which you pay taxes

12. tax paid by the giver of gifts worth more than $11,000

13. the number that the government uses to identify you as a taxpayer

14. the simplest of the basic income tax forms

15. a tax added to the price of a product at the time of purchase

16. tax that is imposed on imports

17. a summary of your earnings and withholdings for the year from your employer

18. a tax on the value of real estate

19. an amount that you may subtract from adjusted gross income on your tax form

187

CONSUMER DECISIONS

20. You have a thriving snow-removal business this winter and have lots of lawn-mowing business lined up for the summer. You expect to make a lot of money this year. Since you are self-employed, no one is withholding money from your earnings to pay taxes. What would you do? Why?

21. A friend tells you that you can get more money in your paycheck if you claim 10 allowances on your W-4. Should you do this? Why or why not?

22. You have just started a job at a restaurant as a server. You get generous tips. A veteran server takes you aside and says, "All the servers here claim on our tax returns no more than $20 in tips a week. This way, we all get tax-free income. You should do this, too. If you claim the full amount of your tips, the IRS might suspect the rest of us. Besides, tips don't show up on your W-2, so the IRS has no way of knowing what you make." What would you do? Why?

23. You can buy a pair of shoes at your local mall or you can buy the same pair of shoes in another state and have them sent to you. By having them sent, you could avoid paying local sales tax. What would you do?

THINK CRITICALLY

24. Suppose you will be able to vote on several tax proposals. One is a sales tax to rebuild schools. Another is a state income tax increase to repave major highways in the state. The last is an increased excise tax on cigarettes. You know that you want to vote for only one tax increase. Which one would you vote for? Why? How would your parents vote? Why?

25. Suppose you could vote on a tax to fund the local animal shelter. If the proposal doesn't pass, there would be no local animal shelter. What would you do?

LOOK IT UP!

26. Find the following amounts for the most recent tax year.
   a. the amount that can be deducted from adjusted gross income for each dependent
   b. the amount of the standard deduction for single and married people who file jointly

27. Investigate local gasoline taxes. What percentage of the price per gallon do the federal and state excise taxes represent?

28. Investigate property tax rates in your community. Have these rates declined, remained stable, or

WHICH IS THE BEST DEAL?

Terrell paid a professional tax consultant to prepare his income tax return. He will receive a $400 refund. He is having a party at his house next weekend and would like to use the refund to buy a CD player and some CDs for the party. What are the costs and benefits of each choice for Terrell?

Alternative 1 The tax consultant offered to pay Terrell $380 now and take his $400 refund when it arrives in about six weeks.

Alternative 2 Terrell's tax consultant will electronically file his return for a $15 fee. He should receive the return in half the time.

Alternative 3 Terrell can wait six weeks for the $400.

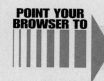

POINT YOUR BROWSER TO

www.ee4c.swlearning.com
Complete the activity for Chapter 5.

increased in the past three years? What reasons can you identify for any changes?

INSIDE THE NUMBERS

29. You want to know what share of your total income goes to taxes. Your adjusted gross income last year was $23,173.40. According to your records and estimates, you paid the following taxes.

   Federal income tax—$2,145.67
   FICA taxes—$1,772.76
   State income tax—$732.18
   Property tax—$955.32
   Sales tax—$800.00 (estimated)
   Excise tax—$350.00 (estimated)

   a. What was the total amount of tax you paid?
   b. What percentage of your adjusted gross income did you pay in taxes?

30. Estimate the taxes you expect to pay from your summer job. Decide where you would like to work this summer. How much will it pay? How many hours a week will you work? How many weeks of the summer will you work? Based on this, estimate your gross income. Fill out a Form 1040EZ for your summer job, assuming that no taxes are withheld from your paycheck. Subtract any deductions that are appropriate. Go to the library or Internet to find a current tax table.

Find your tax. Then figure the total income tax you will have to pay.

CURRICULUM CONNECTION

31. **MATHEMATICS** Alex has been offered a new job. If he takes it, he would earn another $6,000 in taxable income next year. This additional income would be taxed at a 25 percent federal tax rate, a 5 percent state income tax rate, 6.2 percent for Social Security, and 1.45 percent for Medicare. How much of his increased income would Alex keep? How might taxes influence Alex's decision about taking the new job?

32. **HISTORY** Throughout the history of our nation and the history of other nations, citizens have protested their taxes. Write a one-page paper about a famous tax protest. What was the tax? How did citizens protest? What was the result?

33. **CAREERS** Every April, tax preparers of all sorts are very busy. Write a list of job titles for anyone who might prepare tax returns for a fee. What are the qualifications for these jobs?

JOURNAL RECAP

34. After reading this chapter, review the answers you wrote in the chapter-opening Journal Journey questions. Have your opinions changed?

DECISION MAKING PROJECT

SPECIFY   SEARCH   SIFT   SELECT   STUDY

STUDY Each group should present its student profile and its completed Form 1040EZ return. Did you later find you had made mistakes? Would you complete your own returns in the future?

BUDGETING
HOW WILL YOU USE YOUR MONEY?

WHAT'S AHEAD

EXPLODING MYTHS

Fact or Myth?
What do you think is true?

1. Financial success depends on luck more than planning.

2. Spending small amounts of money now will not affect your life-span financial success.

3. Your spending decisions do not affect anyone but yourself.

JOURNAL JOURNEY

WRITE IN YOUR JOURNAL ABOUT THE FOLLOWING.

SPENDING Do you often buy things you want without considering their costs? How could money you spend now affect your ability to buy things you want in the future?

KEEPING FINANCIAL RECORDS How do you keep track of where all your income comes from or how you spend it? What is the value of keeping financial records?

CREATING A BUDGET Have you ever been unable to buy something you really wanted because you ran out of money? How can a budget help you?

DECISION MAKING PROJECT

SPECIFY   SEARCH   SIFT   SELECT   STUDY

ALL IN THE FAMILY Small groups collect information about short-term goals, life-span goals, and monthly costs for a family making $3,500 per month. They look into the trade-offs that must be made. Then they create a budget based upon their priorities.

GOAL

To learn how to create a family budget

PROJECT PROCESS

SPECIFY	Lesson 6.1
SEARCH	Lesson 6.2
SIFT	Lesson 6.3
SELECT	Lesson 6.4
STUDY	Chapter Assessment

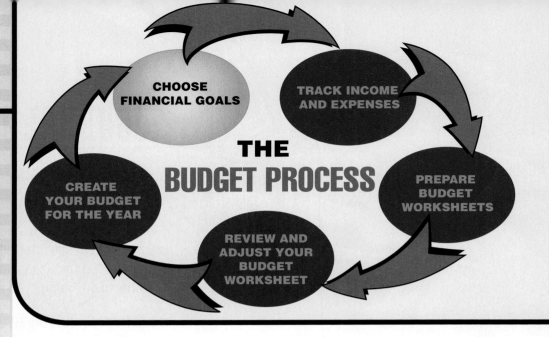

THE BUDGET PROCESS

- CHOOSE FINANCIAL GOALS
- TRACK INCOME AND EXPENSES
- PREPARE BUDGET WORKSHEETS
- REVIEW AND ADJUST YOUR BUDGET WORKSHEET
- CREATE YOUR BUDGET FOR THE YEAR

6.1 Choose Financial Goals

Types of Financial Goals

In some way, most things you want in life require money, which you receive as *income.* It gives you the power to buy cars, TVs, and clothes. It allows you to take vacations, support your family, continue your education, and prepare for retirement. Almost everything you do requires income.

Things you value most are worth working for. Making and following a financial plan, or budget, is part of that work. A **budget** is a plan for

dividing income among spending and saving options. It can help you achieve more of what is important to you during your life span.

Most budgets are based on short- and long-term financial goals. The first step in budgeting is to consider the important goals you have set in your life-span plan.

Short- and Long-Term Financial Goals You have learned that short-term goals are things you hope to achieve within a

Life-Span Plan

CONSUMER ACTION

Kerry would like to open a restaurant some day. He has a part-time job after school and gets a paycheck each week. But he never has any income left at the end of the week. What short-term goals can he set now to help him reach his life-span goal? How can his life-span goal affect his family and community?

year, such as spending $200 to visit a friend who moved away. A neighbor might want to spend $200 to buy a new TV. These are short-term goals that can be achieved quickly with limited planning and do not involve large amounts of spending. But spending on short-term wants adds up. You should avoid spending so much on short-term wants that you are unable to achieve the long-term goals that are part of your life-span plan.

Things that you want to achieve over more than a year are long-term goals. Long-term financial goals are always important parts of life-span plans. Life-span goals usually require more money than people can set aside from current income. To pay for goals such as college, a home, and care for elderly parents, you need savings. To save income over time, you need a life-span financial plan.

© Getty Images/PhotoDisc

Balancing Short-Term Spending with Long-Term Success

Achieving your life-span plan depends on many things. Controlling short-term spending, which may not seem to matter much, is one of the most crucial. Short-term choices are steps to long-term success or failure. Saving now for a computer class or college can help you reach your life-span goals. Spending only to satisfy short-term wants can take you in the wrong direction. People who evaluate each small step are likely to reach their intended goals.

Suppose an important part of your life-span plan is to become a computer programmer. To help achieve this, you set a short-term financial goal of saving $50 per week from your part-time job. If instead of saving, you spend the $50 each week on clothing and entertainment, you could have to

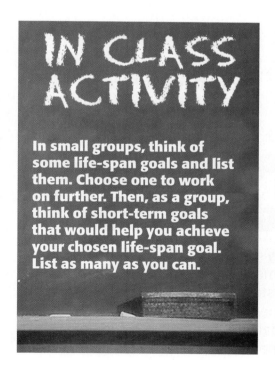

IN CLASS ACTIVITY

In small groups, think of some life-span goals and list them. Choose one to work on further. Then, as a group, think of short-term goals that would help you achieve your chosen life-span goal. List as many as you can.

GUESS WHAT

In a recent study by researchers at Cornell University, several hundred high school graduates ranked their desire for financial success highly. Ten years later, on average, these students earned 20 percent more than other students in the study.

give up your life-span plan or find another way to pay for it.

When you consider satisfying a short-term want, think about how your choice can affect your future. Suppose you want to buy a new DVD player. It costs only $150, but that's three weeks of your planned savings. If spending now prevents you from reaching your long-term goal of paying for your education, the better choice may be to wait.

Spending for short-term wants doesn't always stop you from reaching life-span goals. You might be able to set aside $20 per week to buy "extras" such as a new DVD player. Even with this spending, you can save $50 each week for your life-span goal. Buying the DVD player will neither help nor hinder your ability to become a computer programmer. What is important is to create and follow a budget. A good one allows you to enjoy yourself now and helps you achieve what you want most over your life span.

Budgeting, like other consumer decisions, requires trade-offs and opportunity costs. To make good budget decisions, you need to understand your life-span goals

clearly. Then you must prioritize, or rank, them from the most to least important. Focus your budget on your most important financial goals.

CheckPoint

What is a budget? How do your financial goals impact your budget? How do short-term goals lead to long-term success?

Your Goals Affect Others

Humans are social beings. They live together in families and communities. Almost every decision you make affects other people. When you make a budget, consider other people's goals as well as your own.

Your Family and Your Goals
Your Current Family Your career goal of being a computer programmer will be easier to achieve if

Buy the Numbers?

Hari buys his lunch at a diner most days that he works. The diner's manager advertised a special offer. Customers may pay $20 for a book of 20 coupons. Each coupon entitles the customer to a 25 percent discount on any food or drink order. Hari usually spends about $5 for his lunch. Does the coupon book sound like a good deal? Do you think it would help Hari achieve his financial goals? What money-saving alternatives does he have?

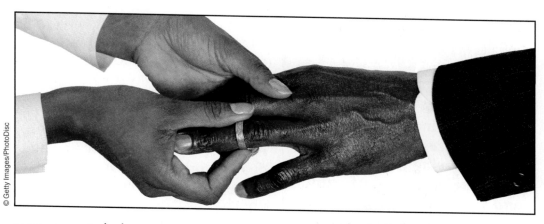

your parents help you pay your costs for training. You may be able to save $50 a week. But that simply is not enough. You ask your parents to loan or give you $20,000. If they agree, how will their choice affect them? Will they be able to reach their own life-span goals?

Many parents take out loans to pay for their children's education. They go far into debt. It could take many years to pay off their loan. How might this financial burden change their lives? How should you consider their goals when you ask for help?

CYBER CONSUMER

How much does it really cost to go to college? Find out on the Web! Hint: Search for the National Center for Educational Statistics or the U.S. Department of Education. Or, check out the web sites of schools that interest you.

Your Future Family Most people your age are not married. But statistics show an 80 percent chance that you will marry before you reach the age of 25. Decisions you make in the next few years could affect the person you marry as much as they affect you.

It is common for young people to go into debt. You have limited income when you first set up your household. Often the only way you can buy expensive items is to borrow.

Loans must be repaid over time. When you borrow to get what you want now, you must make loan payments each month. These loan payments are money you can't spend for something else. By borrowing, you give up future spending for current spending.

As long as you borrow responsibly, borrowing makes sense. Problems occur, however, if you borrow so much that you are unable to pay your bills. When you marry, your new family will share your financial burden.

Your Community and Your Goals

People who are successful in their personal lives also contribute to the welfare of their community. Suppose you work, save, and study for many years. Finally, you achieve your career goal of being a computer

Life-Span Plan

Communicate

COMMUNICATE

Make a list of your current long-term financial goals. Write a paragraph about how achieving your goals will benefit you, your family, and your community.

programmer. You earn a good salary and have a nice home. You marry, raise children, and save for retirement. You are not the only person who benefited from your effort.

You earn a good salary because your work has value. Suppose a pharmaceutical company employs you to help run drug studies, which will help the company achieve its goals. Suppose these studies help the company to discover a cure for a terrible disease. As a result, the pharmaceutical company earns a larger profit. Your community has a new cure. You benefit, but so do the company and your community.

Your community will benefit from your success. If your life-span goal is to operate a picture-framing shop, your customers will benefit from the quality work you do. Or if you are a plumber, your customers will benefit from having faucets that do not leak.

While you are achieving your life-span goals, you are helping others along the way.

CheckPoint

How could your goals affect your parents or guardians? your future spouse and family? your community?

What In The World?

In Japan, it is legal to charge interest rates as high as 29.2 percent. At that rate, it takes about two years and nine months for a borrowed amount to double.

Consider Toru Okada, a 50-year-old banker in Tokyo. He earned 12 million yen a year ($60,000 U.S.) but racked up debts of 11.8 million yen that he could not afford to repay. He borrowed more money to make payments until he was forced to file bankruptcy. His financial problems also cost him his job, because his employer said his lack of financial responsibility reflected poorly on the bank.

Would you ever agree to borrow money at 29 percent interest? Why or why not?

TRY THESE

1. Why should people consider their life-span goals when they decide whether to satisfy a short-term want?

2. How can short-term goals lead to achieving long-term goals?

3. Why should you prioritize your goals?

4. How do your personal goals affect your family and your community?

5. What is a budget?

THINK CRITICALLY

6. **CONSUMER ACTION** Kerry wants to open a restaurant some day but isn't making much progress toward this goal. What short-term goals can help him get there? What can he do now to make progress? How might his goal affect his family and community?

7. What life-span goals do you have that would be easier to achieve if you begin to save now?

8. **COMMUNICATE** What goals could you achieve with a trade-school or community college education? Select a goal that interests you. Find a trade school or community college web site and read about programs it offers that might help you achieve your goal. Compose a letter to the school, stating your goal and asking for information about its

programs. Be sure to ask for specific financial information that could help you decide whether or not to attend that school.

9. Make a list of your current short-term financial goals. Compare them with a life-span goal that is important to you. Which of your short-term goals will help you achieve your life-span goal? How could you revise your short-term goals so that some are steps toward your larger goal?

10. It is not always possible to work toward all of your life-span goals at once. You need to prioritize. List three life-span goals in priority order. Write a paragraph explaining how you decided where each goal should go on your list. E-mail it to your teacher.

DECISION MAKING PROJECT

SPECIFY   SEARCH   SIFT   SELECT   STUDY

SPECIFY Give each person in a group a role as a family member: parent/guardian, infant, elementary or secondary age student, and at least one grandparent. This family has after-tax income of $3,500 a month. Agree on reasonable costs for housing, food, clothing, and other basic needs. Have each person then list specific short-term and life-span goals and the expenses for these different life cycle stages (tuition, housing, or retirement). Make a family budget with these goals and costs.

Life-Span Plan

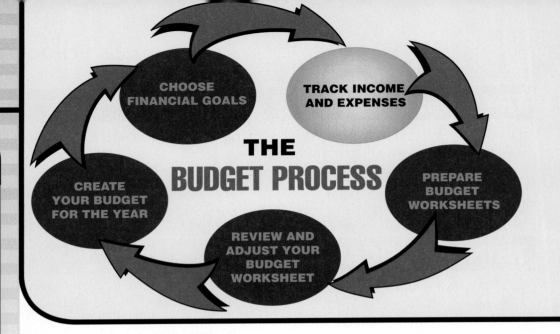

CHOOSE FINANCIAL GOALS

TRACK INCOME AND EXPENSES

THE BUDGET PROCESS

CREATE YOUR BUDGET FOR THE YEAR

PREPARE BUDGET WORKSHEETS

REVIEW AND ADJUST YOUR BUDGET WORKSHEET

6.2 Track Income and Expenses

Keep Financial Records

After determining your goals, list your income and expenses. You aren't likely to know what these will be in the future, but you can find out what they are now. By keeping records, you can see where your money goes. Then you can reasonably estimate your income and spending for your budget. Using a computer spreadsheet program, such as Lotus 1-2-3 or Microsoft® Excel, can help you accomplish this task.

Track Your Income   A paycheck is a source of regular income. The paycheck stub serves as a record of that income. A weekly allowance from your parents is also a source of regular income, but it comes with no written record. In cases like this, you need to make written records by listing your income and its sources.

Keeping track of your income would be easy if you always received the same amount at the same time throughout the year. However, you probably receive income from various sources at

CONSUMER ACTION

Mary's only regular source of income is from her part-time job. She earns $65 a week. She never pays attention to how she spends it. All she knows is that after a few days, it's gone. How can Mary keep track of her spending? She has seen various books and software on budgeting. What should she do?

different times during the year. For example, you may cut your neighbor's lawn to earn $25. Your aunt may send you $30 for your birthday. If you have a savings account, you will earn different amounts of interest.

For income you receive in cash or by check, simply note the amount and source on your list of income. Your bank will send you a statement of the interest you earn on savings.

Track Your Spending Your spending records include sales receipts, credit card statements, and your checking account statement sent to you by your bank. If a receipt or check doesn't show what it was for, simply note on it what you bought before filing it.

Establish a Filing System

An easy way to keep your records straight is to establish a filing system. You can label file folders for different categories of expenses, such as *clothes*, *CDs*, and *entertainment*. For income, you probably need folders labeled *paycheck stubs*, *bank statements*, and *miscellaneous income*.

As you receive income or buy something, simply file your receipts, stubs, and notes about income or purchases in the appropriate folders. If you find you need another category, just make up a new folder. Once you have set up your system, filing your records is easy! Remember that these tasks can be done using a computer spreadsheet application.

When you make good record keeping a regular habit, you will be able to take control of your financial life. You can plan your spending so that you don't spend more than you earn. You can plan for vacations, major purchases, and long-term expenses, such as education. You can make sure you spend on the things you value most.

Effective Record Keeping

To be useful, your filing system needs to be organized, complete, and easy to find. Be sure to file each record as you receive it or enter it on

PRIMARY SOURCES

Read this quote from Margie Rushing, a textile worker in Huntsville, NC in 1939. What are her financial goals? Are they very different from financial goals that a young family might have today? Why or why not?

"You know, it's right hard to decide what to spend your money for when you want so much...I've seen so many people nearly dead with (disease) around these mills just because they cut down on their grocery bill in order to have money to run around and have a good time. Lots of them buy a new car almost every year and are not planning to ever own a home. We keep an old cheap car that is just barely able to carry us to the mill and back, but we'll have a nice home before we think about a fine car."

your computer. Receipts and other records must be available when you prepare your budget. If you lose some records or forget where you spent some cash, your budget won't be accurate or useful. If you use a computer, be sure to back up all files on a separate disk.

Also, find a good place to keep your files. If you don't have a filing cabinet, a plastic filing crate is a good alternative. It is designed to hold file folders, is inexpensive, and is available at most stores that sell business supplies. You can also stand your files upright in a cardboard box.

The important thing is to keep all your records in files and all your files in one place.

© Getty Images/EyeWire

CheckPoint

How can you estimate your income and spending for the near future? What financial records do you need to keep? What are the characteristics of a good filing system?

MATH OF MONEY

Suppose you want to estimate the amount you will budget to spend on entertainment. You recorded the amounts you spent on entertainment for the last six months. The amounts were $40.95, $29.54, $35.25, $38.96, $28.65, and $32.74. You want to take the average amount spent in the last six months to be your new budgeted amount. What will be your budgeted amount for next month's entertainment?

SOLUTION

You would budget $34.35 for entertainment.

$40.95
29.54
35.25   Add the amounts
38.96   from the last six months.
28.65
+ 32.74
$206.09

Then divide this total by the amount of months, which is six, to get the average.

$206.09 ÷ 6 = $34.348333, or $34.35 rounded to the nearest cent.

How to Use Financial Records

The purpose of keeping financial records is to use them to help you plan. By studying records of your income and spending, you will get to know your "financial self." You have identified your goals and decided which are most important to you. With good financial records, you can compare what you want to do with your income and what you actually spend. You can control your spending to reach your goals.

© Getty Images/EyeWire

Why is it important to know your "financial self"?

Fixed and Flexible Expenses

Some types of spending you must do no matter what. Other types of spending you can choose to do or not to do. Both types of spending are important and should be included in your budget. Each type affects your budget differently.

Fixed Expenses

Suppose you own a car. You must make payments on it each month. Your car payment is a fixed expense. **Fixed expenses** are amounts you have already committed to spend. You have no choice. You must pay these expenses when they are due.

When you finish school and set up your own household, you will have more fixed expenses than you have now. If you live in an apartment, your monthly rent is a fixed expense. You must pay it or you will be evicted. If you own a house, your mortgage and property taxes are fixed expenses. Your homeowner's insurance is a fixed expense as well.

One good thing about most fixed expenses is that you know how much you have to pay and when you have to pay it. So, you can plan ahead to save the money to pay these bills when they are due.

For example, most car insurance payments are due once or twice a year. If you must pay $600 for your insurance every six months, you need to put aside money to total $600 by the time the payment is due. In your budget, you can plan to save $100 each month for this payment.

GUESS WHAT

In 1995, U.S. consumers saved 5.6 percent of their after-tax income. By 2003, this saving rate was only 2.1 percent.

© Getty Images/PhotoDisc

IN CLASS ACTIVITY

In a small group, list luxury products in each of the following categories.

Jeans	**Stereos**
Athletic Shoes	**Computers**
Watches	**Jackets**

Flexible Expenses

At this time in your life, most of your spending is likely to be for flexible expenses. **Flexible expenses** are amounts that you can choose to spend or not to spend. You can choose to buy a jacket or a sweater, or you can choose not to buy anything at all. You do not have to buy designer clothes, but you must have clothes to wear. You can do without the latest new basketball shoes, but you must wear shoes.

The cost of luxury goods is almost always a flexible expense. **Luxury goods** are goods that have special qualities that make them more expensive than alternative goods. A new sports car is much more expensive than a used compact car. The sports car may be stylish and may impress your friends, but either car is a means of travel. The sports car is a luxury good. When you buy a luxury good, you are giving up more things you want than you would be by buying a less expensive alternative.

You can choose among many flexible spending options. You have to prioritize your options and determine the ones you can and want to afford.

CheckPoint

How do fixed expenses affect your spending plan? How do flexible expenses affect your spending plan?

TRY THESE

1. What is the purpose of keeping financial records?

2. What income records should you keep?

3. What spending records should you keep?

4. Describe how to set up an effective filing system.

5. What is the difference between fixed and flexible expenses?

6. What are possible opportunity costs of buying luxury goods?

THINK CRITICALLY

7. **CONSUMER ACTION** Mary's $65 weekly wage disappears in a few days. Explain to Mary how to track her spending. Tell her how she would benefit from record keeping.

8. **COMMUNICATE** Write a plan for creating your own record keeping system. What categories would you use for your file folder labels? What would you use to keep your files together? Where would you put the filing system? Would you store your records on a computer?

9. Why is the difference between fixed and flexible expenses important to your spending plan?

10. **MATH OF MONEY** Suppose you must make a $750 car insurance payment every six months. You deposit your savings in an account that pays 5 percent interest. Use the Savings Planner to calculate the monthly contribution you should budget to be able to make your insurance payment.

11. List three luxury goods that you have purchased and the cost of each. Next to each item, list a less expensive alternative and its cost. What do you notice?

12. If you wanted to use a computer to help track your income and expenses, how would you set it up? What software could you use? How would you customize it?

13. List jobs whose main responsibilities include accurate record keeping. List why each job would require accurate record keeping. E-mail your answer to your teacher.

 DECISION MAKING PROJECT

SPECIFY   **SEARCH**   SIFT   SELECT   STUDY

SEARCH Each family member will investigate the expenses that are incurred on a monthly basis for someone that age. Make a list of the fixed and flexible expenses for each role. Also, each person must investigate and list the costs of his or her short-term and life-span goals.

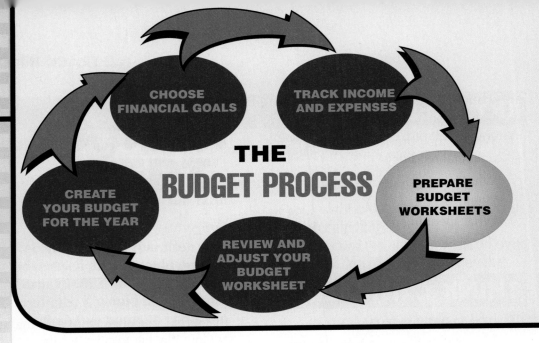

THE
BUDGET PROCESS

CHOOSE FINANCIAL GOALS

TRACK INCOME AND EXPENSES

PREPARE BUDGET WORKSHEETS

REVIEW AND ADJUST YOUR BUDGET WORKSHEET

CREATE YOUR BUDGET FOR THE YEAR

6.3 Your Budget Worksheet

Create Your Budget Worksheet

Your income is a limited resource. You can probably think of more ways to spend your income than you have income. So you have to make trade-offs. Buying one thing means giving up something else. You can make sure you are using your money for the things you want most by making a plan.

Suppose you have been spending $50 a month for entertainment. When you look at your spending records, you realize you cannot afford the new bike you want because you spend your money on movies and pizza. You decide to spend only $20 on entertainment next month and to save the remaining $30 for the bike. Once you know how you use your money, you can make decisions that better fit your priorities.

Steps in Preparing Your Budget Worksheet

To get the information you need to plan your future spending and saving, you need to investigate your current spending habits. To do this, you can build a budget worksheet.

CONSUMER ACTION

Emilio wants to save for a new computer system. But at the end of the month, he discovers that he has saved nothing. His goal is to save $800 in the next 12 months so he can buy the computer system. How can Emilio plan to achieve his goal?

© Getty Images/PhotoDisc

A **budget worksheet** is a planning document on which you record your expected and actual income and spending over a short time, usually one month.

How much income do you expect to receive from all sources? What fixed expenses will you have? What do you expect to buy that month? About how much will your purchases cost? What do you plan to save? All this information goes into your budget worksheet.

A budget worksheet is a way to compare how you think you spend your income with how you actually spend it. You may find that you spend your money in ways you never realized.

Step 1: Create a Worksheet

To get started, divide a sheet of paper or an electronic spreadsheet into four columns as shown in the model on page 207. The first column is for listing your sources of income and categories of spending and sav-ing. You can personalize your worksheet. Just add other categories.

The second column is for recording the amounts you expect to receive, spend, or save during the month. The third column is for recording the amounts you actually receive, spend, or save. The fourth column is for recording the difference.

Step 2: Estimate Your Income

It's easy to estimate income that occurs in the same amounts and at regular time periods throughout the year. If you kept good records of your previous income, you can base your estimates on these records. Be sure to use *net income* from your paycheck stubs—the income you bring home. This is the income that is actually available to you.

Estimate Uneven Income
Your income may not be the same every month. You may expect to receive $200 in cash gifts on your birthday. Your employer may tell you that if the company does well this year, all employees will get a $100 bonus at the end of the year. If you have a savings account, your bank may pay you different amounts of interest each month, depending on the amount in your account.

Be Sure the Income Is Real
When you create your budget, try to think of all sources of income during the year, including these uneven income flows. Remember, though, you can't spend or save what you don't have. Include only income that you really think you will receive.

For example, if you include in your budget $20 a week from mowing lawns, you must be com-mitted to making that $20.

Otherwise, you will plan to spend or save income you won't have. Be reasonably sure that you can really make $20 per week mowing lawns. If you have done it before, then you can estimate from what you made previously. If you haven't, ask friends how much they receive for mowing, or start lining up your jobs to make sure you will earn $20.

Add your expected income and write the result in the Total Income row in the Expected Amount column. This is the money you expect to receive.

Step 3: Estimate Your Expenses and Savings

Look in your records for your fixed and flexible expenses. List fixed expenses first because you have committed to pay them. You will usually have to pay the same amounts each month.

Next, list your flexible expenses. These expenses usually vary from month to month. If you are unsure of how much you expect to spend, look

© Getty Images/EyeWire

into your records for the last few months. You can calculate the average amount you spent and use this average as your expected amount.

Plan for Uneven Expenses
Expenses can occur unevenly throughout the year, too. Many fixed expenses are paid only once or twice a year. Car insurance payments may be due every May and November. Income taxes are due every April 15.

Add your expected expenses and enter the sum in the Total Expenses row in the Expected Amount column. This is what you expect to spend.

Plan Your Saving Saving needs to be planned as part of your expenses. It should not be just the amount that's left over at the end of the month. When you subtract expected spending from expected income, you may end up with zero saving or worse, negative saving. Negative saving means that you may have to dip into your savings for money to pay your expenses that month. Adjust your spending to achieve your saving goals.

Add your expected savings and write the result in the Total Savings row in the Expected Amount column. This is the money you expect to save.

Finally, add your expenses and savings and write the result in the Expenses and Savings row in the Expected Amount column. Subtract your total expected expenses and savings from your total expected income. Adjust this amount so that it equals your income. You may want to increase your savings if your income is more than your spending.

Step 4: Record Your Actual Income and Expenses

As you receive income or make purchases during the month, file your records in your filing system. At the end of the month, get out your records and your budget worksheet. Then record your actual income, expenses, and savings in the Actual Amount column of the worksheet.

If you do your banking online, the banking software will keep track of your actual income and expenses as you enter each transaction in your electronic checkbook register. It can even put each amount into income or expense categories for you.

Sample One-Month Budget Worksheet

Income	Expected Amount	Actual Amount	Over (+) or Under (−)
Paycheck	_____	_____	_____
Allowance	_____	_____	_____
Cash Gifts	_____	_____	_____
Interest on Savings	_____	_____	_____
	_____	_____	_____
Total Income	_____	_____	_____
Fixed Expenses			
Housing	_____	_____	_____
Utilities	_____	_____	_____
Telephone	_____	_____	_____
Car Payments	_____	_____	_____
Car Insurance	_____	_____	_____
Medical Insurance	_____	_____	_____
	_____	_____	_____
Flexible Expenses			
Groceries	_____	_____	_____
Restaurants	_____	_____	_____
Clothes	_____	_____	_____
Laundry	_____	_____	_____
Transportation	_____	_____	_____
Medical	_____	_____	_____
Entertainment	_____	_____	_____
Personal Care Items	_____	_____	_____
Total Expenses	_____	_____	_____
Savings			
Car	_____	_____	_____
College	_____	_____	_____
Total Savings	_____	_____	_____
Expenses and Savings	_____	_____	_____

Step 5: Calculate the Differences

Now compare your expected amounts with your actual amounts. Subtract the expected amount from the actual amount in each row. In the Over or Under column, record the differences. If the result of your subtraction is a positive number, put a + sign next to it in the Over or Under column. This means that you spent or received as income more than you expected in that category.

If the result is a negative number, put a − sign next to it in the Over or Under column. This means that you spent or received less than you expected in that category.

CheckPoint

What is a budget worksheet? How do you estimate expected income and expenses? What does subtracting expected amounts from actual amounts tell you?

Budget Pitfalls

Despite the fact that all consumers can benefit from having a realistic budget, few consumers have realistic budgets. Here are some reasons for this.

1. Some people get too specific, and the level of detail becomes too much trouble. Keep your budget simple.

2. Some people don't predict the correct amount of their flexible expenses. Good record keeping

IN CLASS ACTIVITY

In a group, list reasons for and against creating a budget and sticking to it.

can help you investigate your flexible expenses. If you know what you paid and when you paid it, you can be more accurate.

3. Some people lump too many expenses under *miscellaneous.* If a large portion of your expenses is not in a category, it will be hard for you to plan your spending.

4. Some people give up on budgets because they think it takes too much time and effort to create and maintain them. If you set aside an hour each week, you can easily maintain your budget. Keeping a budget takes commitment, but it will help you achieve your life-span goals.

CheckPoint

What are some reasons that people don't maintain their budgets?

TRY THESE

1. What is the purpose of a budget worksheet?

2. How does preparing a budget worksheet involve trade-offs?

3. What are the steps in preparing a budget worksheet?

4. How would you use your previous income and spending records to prepare a budget worksheet?

5. What does the Over or Under column of the worksheet tell you?

THINK CRITICALLY

6. CONSUMER ACTION Emilio needs to save $800 in 12 months. What would you advise Emilio to do? What should he do if his expected monthly spending doesn't leave enough savings to achieve his goal?

MATH OF MONEY Using the table, answer questions 7–12.

7. What was your total income for October?

8. How much did you spend in October?

9. How much did you save in October?

10. What income amounts can you count on receiving every month?

11. Which of your expenses were flexible expenses?

12. If you want to save $10 more each month, what expenses would you reduce? Explain.

YOUR INCOME AND EXPENSE RECORDS FOR OCTOBER				
Date	Income Source	Purchase	Income	Expenses
10/3	pay from job		$63.25	
10/5		movie		$ 9.00
10/5		new shoes		$76.00
10/7	allowance		$25.00	
10/15		lunch		$ 6.25
10/17	pay from job		$63.25	
10/21		new shirt		$38.00
10/21	allowance		$25.00	
10/29	birthday present		$50.00	
10/30		repay loan*		$20.00

*You owe your brother $360.

13. Suppose that at the end of a month, you calculated the following amounts in the Over or Under column on your worksheet.

Entertainment: −$35

Savings: +$110

What do these amounts tell you? Would you adjust your worksheet for next month? If so, how? If not, why not?

DECISION MAKING PROJECT

SPECIFY   SEARCH   SIFT   SELECT   STUDY

SIFT Using the information each family member gathered, start to fill in the budget worksheet. Create more than one budget. Make sure you do not spend more than your family income!

Life-Span Plan

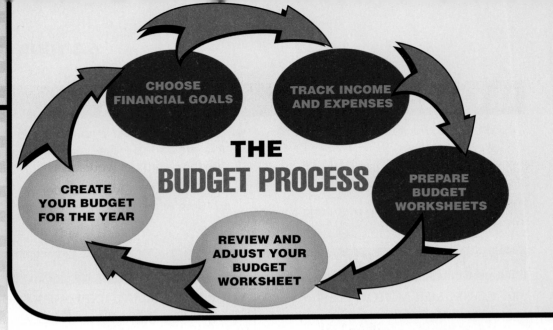

THE
BUDGET PROCESS

CHOOSE FINANCIAL GOALS

TRACK INCOME AND EXPENSES

PREPARE BUDGET WORKSHEETS

CREATE YOUR BUDGET FOR THE YEAR

REVIEW AND ADJUST YOUR BUDGET WORKSHEET

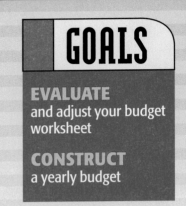

GOALS

EVALUATE
and adjust your budget worksheet

CONSTRUCT
a yearly budget

Life-Span Plan

6.4 Create Your Budget for the Year

Evaluate Your Budget Worksheet

After you complete your budget worksheet, evaluate what it tells you. The purpose of a budget worksheet is to help you divide your income among the spending and saving options that will help you meet your goals. It is a plan, not just information.

Adjust Your Spending

Remember, when you reduce spending, you can cut back only on flexible expenses. Fixed expenses are costs you have already committed to pay, so you must pay them. Flexible expenses are costs you can choose to pay or not pay.

Suppose you spent more than you expected this month. What should you do? You have two choices. You can change your future spending to match the expected spending you estimated for your worksheet, or you can adjust your spending estimates and make a new worksheet to reflect your new plan. Choose the option that best meets your goals.

CONSUMER ACTION

Carmen wants to take her family to the seashore. She prepared a budget for the year to help her save for the trip. Carmen is pleased because she has put aside $2,000. Unfortunately, no one else in her family likes her budget. Her children complain that they have nothing new to wear. Her husband would prefer to eat steak more often. How can Carmen budget and keep her family happy at the same time?

In the example in Lesson 6.3, you were spending $50 a month on entertainment. You want to cut this spending to $20 so that you can save $30 toward a new bike. In your new worksheet, you would record the $20 under Expected Amount in the flexible expense row for entertainment and $30 in the savings row for a bike.

Make Several Plans Complete several budget worksheets to see the results of different choices. Each new worksheet represents a plan for dividing your income among spending and saving options. You can follow the worksheet that uses your income for what you want most.

Remember there is no one *right* way to use your income. The best way for you depends on your goals and those of your family.

CheckPoint

What does a completed budget worksheet tell you? How can you benefit from preparing several budget worksheets?

Businesses that lend money to consumers sometimes do not require monthly payments. They may send customers a letter that says something like this: "We would like to give you a special opportunity. You may skip this month's payment without any penalty. Interest will continue to accumulate on your balance." Does this sound like a good deal? How could accepting this offer make it more difficult for you to stick to your budget?

Budgeting for the Year

Budget worksheets help you understand your spending and saving habits. You can use budget worksheets to plan how to use your income over a short time, such as a month. However, to reach life-span goals, you need a life-span plan.

Budgeting for a year at a time can help you plan steps toward major goals that may take many years to achieve. A yearly budget is a summary of all your budget worksheets for 12 months. One way to create a budget is to first do a worksheet for each month of the year. Then combine them into a budget for the year.

An example of a budget for one year appears on the next page. It is arranged in two parts. One is for your income, and the other is for spending

Sample Budget for a Year

Income		Expenses and Savings	
Source	*Amount*	*For*	*Amount*
Paychecks	$1,625.00	Clothing	$ 800.00
Allowance	1,000.00	Entertainment	500.00
Gifts/Bonus	600.00	Repay loan	240.00
Interest	40.00	New bicycle	600.00
Total	$3,265.00	Miscellaneous	225.00
		College savings	900.00
		Total	$3,265.00

and saving. Like budget worksheets, estimates of income from all sources go on the income side. Estimates of all fixed and flexible expenses go on the spending side. Savings appear on the spending side because they represent a use of your income.

You can calculate fixed expenses the same way you calculate your income. Suppose your car payment of $168 is due each month. Also, your car insurance of $549 is due twice a year. You can calculate these fixed expenses for the year as follows:

$$\$168 \times 12 \text{ payments} = \$2,016$$
$$\$549 \times 2 \text{ payments} = \$1,098$$
$$\text{Total fixed expenses} = \$3,114$$

When you make a budget for the year, plan for uneven expenses. You may have to pay for car insurance only every six months, so a good plan is to set aside money for this fixed expense every month. Otherwise, you may not have the money when the payment is due.

Review and Adjust Your Budget

Notice the total for income is the same as the total for expenses and savings in the sample budget shown above. Income received either goes out as expenses or is saved.

Total Income = Expenses + Savings

If your budget doesn't allow you to buy those products you want most, you should adjust it. Suppose you add up your budgeted expenses, and the total shows that you plan to spend $500 more than your expected income. What can you do? One choice is to borrow $500. This loan is $500 in income to you. However, it is also a fixed expense of $500 plus interest over the next several months.

Another option to balance your budget is to reduce your expenses or savings in your budget. Reducing your expenses is the least expensive option. If you reduce your savings, you are giving up the interest you can earn. You can also choose to do a little of both.

Relate Your Goals to Your Budget The purpose of creating a budget is to help you achieve your life-span goals. Include your goals at the top of your budget. Being

GUESS WHAT

In 2003, American workers received an average weekly wage of $517.36.

reminded of your life-span goals can help you stick to your budget.

Adjust to Changing Goals Everyone changes over time. Your goals may be different in five years than they are today. When your goals change, your budget should change, too. Plan to review your budget at least once a year, and adjust the uses of your income to achieve your new goals. Treat your budget as a flexible tool to help you get what you want.

© Getty Images/PhotoDisc

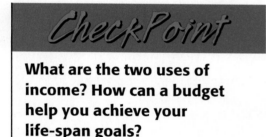

What are the two uses of income? How can a budget help you achieve your life-span goals?

Family Budget

Many people live in families that share income. The way one family member spends often affects others. If your parents choose to buy a car, they may not be able to buy you the new coat you want. Buying an expensive coat for you may prevent other family members from having things they want.

Planning Together Creating a family budget involves many important choices. Often, family members want more products than their family income can buy. Trade-offs have to be made. When families work together to create a budget, they can decide on the trade-offs together.

Suppose your family decides that the new coat you want is too expensive for the budget. But if you know how much the family budgeted for your coat, you could choose to contribute some of your own savings or choose a less expensive coat.

Compromising Suppose your life-span goal is to attend college, but you can't pay the costs. You might want your family to help pay your tuition, but doing so might prevent other family members from reaching their goals.

The best way to deal with these situations is to talk about them. Decide what you want most and what things you would be willing to give up.

List five long-term financial goals for your family. Use the Internet to research the potential costs of achieving these goals. Compare your list to other students' lists. Which goals are similar? Why do many U.S. families have similar long-term financial goals?

Suppose you want your parents to contribute $2,000 to your college fund. In exchange for their help, be willing to help them. To reduce family expenses, you could do household jobs or watch younger siblings when your parents are gone. Be willing to give something of value to receive something you want.

The Budget Cycle

The importance of maintaining and adjusting a budget cannot be overstated. If followed, the budget is an important tool in achieving your life-span financial goals and safeguarding against going into too much debt. In Chapter 9, you will learn that financial planning is another tool to use to reach your financial goals.

CheckPoint

How do your goals affect other members of your family? How can a family benefit from working on the family budget together?

VOTE Your Wallet

For many years, the federal government spent more than it received from taxes. To make up the difference, it borrowed funds. This created a net public debt that reached a total of about $4.4 trillion in 2004. This debt forced the government to make large interest payments even in years with a budget surplus. Some government leaders believe the government should pay off its debt to reduce its interest payments. To do this, however, spending must be kept below the amount of tax revenue the government collects. Would you vote for a politician who was in favor of cutting spending to pay off part of the debt? What types of spending do you think could be reduced?

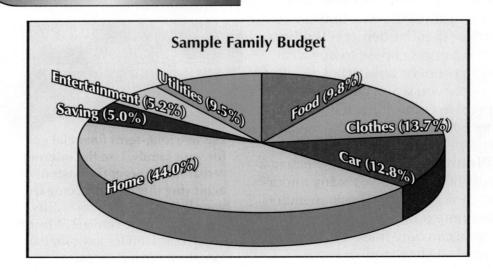

Sample Family Budget

Entertainment (5.2%)
Utilities (9.5%)
Saving (5.0%)
Food (9.8%)
Clothes (13.7%)
Car (12.8%)
Home (44.0%)

TRY THESE

1. Why must your budget balance?

2. What can you do to adjust your budget if it doesn't balance?

3. Why should you review your budget at least once a year?

4. What are the benefits of planning a family budget together?

5. What is the value of compromising as you plan with your family?

6. How can budget worksheets help you create a budget for the year?

7. How should you decide what uneven income flows to include in your budget?

THINK CRITICALLY

8. **CONSUMER ACTION** Carmen created and followed a budget to save for a family vacation. Other family members didn't like the trade-offs. How can Carmen save for her goal and keep her family happy?

9. **MATH OF MONEY** You expect to have the following income and expenses for next year. Create a budget using a computer spreadsheet application and these figures. Make sure your budget balances!

▶ You earn $60 every two weeks from a part-time job.

▶ Your boss promised all employees a bonus of $100 at the end of the year if the company doubles sales this year. You expect this to happen.

▶ Aunt Emily usually gives you $20 on your birthday and your mom and dad usually give you $50.

▶ Buy two pairs of jeans at $35 each.

▶ Buy five CDs at $15 each.

▶ Buy a swimsuit at $45.

▶ Buy a pair of hiking boots for $59.

▶ Go to 10 movies this year at $9 each.

▶ Rent 12 videos for $3 each.

▶ Go to the local water park 5 times with a $15 admission each time.

▶ Eat out 25 times at an average of $5 each time.

10. **MATH OF MONEY** Use the budget you created in exercise 9. Suppose that your goal is to save $150 for the year to buy in-line skates. How would you adjust spending to meet this goal? How can you adjust income to reach your goal? E-mail your answers to your teacher.

DECISION MAKING PROJECT

● SPECIFY ● SEARCH ● SIFT ● SELECT ● STUDY

SELECT With these sample budgets, decide which will be the monthly budget for the family. Make a list of the reasons why you chose the short-term and life-span goals that are in your budget.

ASSESSMENT

KEY IDEAS

Choose Financial Goals

1. A budget is a plan for dividing income among spending and saving options. It can help you achieve more of what is important to you in your life span. Your budget is based on your financial goals and life-span plan.

2. Short-term goals are things you hope to achieve within a year. Short-term goals don't usually require lots of money and don't have a great impact on your life. But, short-term goals can be used as steps toward achieving a life-span goal.

3. Long-term goals are things you hope to achieve in more than a year. You need to prioritize your goals to focus on those most important to you.

4. The goals you set affect your family, future family, and community. When you set your goals, consider their impact on other people.

Track Income and Expenses

5. By keeping records of your spending and income, you can see where your money goes. With this information, you can estimate your income and spending for your budget.

6. Your paycheck stub is an income record. Some income has no written record, so you need to make one by listing your income and the sources of it. Your spending records include sales receipts, credit card statements, and your checking account statement sent to you by your bank.

7. To keep your records straight, you should establish a filing system. To be useful, your filing system needs to be organized, complete, and easy to find. Spreadsheet applications are helpful in doing this.

8. Expenses are either fixed or flexible. Fixed expenses are amounts you have already committed to spend. You have no choice but to pay them. Flexible expenses are amounts you can choose to spend or not to spend.

9. The purpose of keeping financial records is to use them to help you plan. With good financial records, you can compare what you want to do with your income and what you are actually doing.

Your Budget Worksheet

10. Your income is a limited resource. You can't buy everything you want. A budget will help you use your money for the things you want most.

11. A budget worksheet is a short-term planning document that usually covers one month. You record your expected and actual income and spending for the month. Then you compare to see if your estimates closely match your actual income and spending.

12. The steps for completing a budget worksheet are (1) create a worksheet, (2) estimate your income, (3) estimate your expenses and savings, (4) record your actual income, spending, and saving, and (5) calculate the differences between expected and actual amounts.

Create Your Budget for the Year

13. Evaluate your completed worksheet to see how you are using your income. Make adjustments

if necessary. Remember that when you reduce spending, you can cut back only on flexible expenses.

14. Create several worksheets so that you can choose from several plans. There is no one *right* way to use your income. The best way for you depends on your goals.

15. To achieve life-span goals, you need a long-term plan to project income and spending for a year or more. One way to create a budget is to first do a worksheet for each month of the year. Then combine them into a budget for the year.

16. Your income and spending may not be the same each month. Include these uneven cash inflows and outflows in your budget only if you are reasonably sure they will occur.

17. If you live in a family, you most likely share the family income. You will probably have to compromise. Planning the family budget together can give everyone a voice in the trade-offs the family makes.

TERMS REVIEW

Match each term on the left with its definition on the right.
Some terms may not be used.

a. budget
b. budget worksheet
c. fixed expenses
d. flexible expenses
e. luxury goods

1. amounts you have already committed to spend
2. a plan for dividing up your income among spending and saving options
3. amounts that you can choose to spend or not to spend
4. planning document on which you record your expected and actual income and spending
5. goods that have special qualities that make them more expensive than other alternative goods

CONSUMER DECISIONS

6. Have you ever had to give up buying something important because you ran out of money? If you had known this ahead of time, would you have given up something else to buy the important item?

7. Your record keeping is a mess. You kept some paycheck stubs but not all of them. Receipts are scattered all over. You did some work for your neighbors and got paid in cash, but now you can't remember how much you made. Explain the steps you would take to get organized using a computer spreadsheet application.

8. When you estimated your income and spending for next month, you discovered that you would save only $20 that month. Your goal is to save $50 per month toward your college tuition. How could you adjust your budget worksheet to achieve your saving goal?

9. Suppose a gold chain is marked down 50 percent and now costs $200. Will you buy it? Why or why not? How might such a purchase affect your ability to buy other things you want?

THINK CRITICALLY

10. Assume that your total income for next month will be $500. On a sheet of paper, list everything you think you will spend money on next month. Be specific! Then estimate what each thing will cost and add up your expenses. Prepare a budget worksheet for the month, showing your expected income and expenses. Make adjustments to your spending and saving options to balance your budget.

11. Many young people experiencing independence for the first time tend to spend their money on luxury goods. Imagine that you just got your first real job and you have to furnish your new apartment and purchase new work clothes. Write a list of guidelines you would need to follow to keep your budget balanced as you face these decisions.

LOOK IT UP

12. Many Internet sites provide information about budget creation. Find two helpful sites and record their web addresses on a sheet of paper. Next to each address, describe three pieces of helpful information you found on that site.

13. A life-span goal many young people have is to go on to higher education after high school. Find books or magazine articles that suggest ways to plan financially for school. Do the suggestions make higher education seem realistic for you? What sources of income can you count on to help achieve your goal?

14. Many books offer advice on how to create a budget. Visit your library and examine three of these books. What helpful advice did you find in each book? List at least two pieces of advice from each book.

15. Search the Internet or a local newspaper for information about apartments that are available to rent in your community. Identify one you believe you might like to rent when you graduate from high school. How much does it cost? How would renting this apartment for one year affect your budget?

16. Various organizations offer to help people plan their finances. Look in your local telephone book and call

WHICH IS THE BEST DEAL?

You want to buy a new pair of boots. You found a pair you like that is marked down from $150 to $120. You have only $50 right now, but you can save an additional $20 per month. Your sister offered to lend you the $70. She would require you to pay $20 each month for four months to repay her. If you accept her offer, you will pay your sister $10 in interest to use her money. ($20 × 4 months = $80 repaid. $80 − $70 borrowed = $10 interest.) What choice would you make? Explain your decision.

Alternative 1 Wait until you can save enough to buy the boots.

Alternative 2 Agree to your sister's terms and borrow the money.

Alternative 3 Look for a pair of boots that costs only $50.

POINT YOUR BROWSER TO

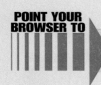

www.ee4c.swlearning.com
Complete the activity for Chapter 6.

community agencies to find sources of budget assistance in your community. List the names of three that you identified. What services does each one offer?

17. Many organizations help people in financial trouble. Contact or look up a web site for one such organization. What does it recommend you do to avoid financial trouble?

INSIDE THE NUMBERS

18. A recent study investigated 1,800 high school students who held part-time jobs. The study related hours of work with students' grades. The grades of working students were compared to the average for all students. The study found that students who worked fewer than 20 hours a week got better grades than the average. Students who worked more than 20 hours a week earned lower grades than the average. Identify and explain possible reasons for these findings.

CURRICULUM CONNECTION

19. **HISTORY** Benjamin Franklin is known for saying, "A penny saved is a penny earned." Explain what you think he meant by this saying. Do you believe he was correct? Do you practice his philosophy in your life? Why or why not?

20. **GOVERNMENT** The budgets of all school districts may be obtained from their boards of education. Get a copy of your school district's budget and evaluate it. Do you think your school district is using its funds wisely? Do you think a budget is important for a school district? Why or why not?

JOURNAL RECAP

21. After reading this chapter, review the answers you wrote to the questions in Journal Journey. Have your opinions changed? How?

DECISION MAKING PROJECT

SPECIFY   **SEARCH**   **SIFT**   **SELECT**   **STUDY**

Life-Span Plan

STUDY Create a PowerPoint slide of your budget. Present your budget to the class. Have each member of your "family" explain how he or she came up with the monthly costs, short-term goals, and life-span goals. Be prepared to explain the process your "family" went through to create this budget. What were the trade-offs? How were you able to reach a compromise? How did you prioritize your goals? What did your "family" learn about budgets during this process?

Answer any questions from the class. Re-evaluate your budget. Based upon feedback from your classmates or your teacher, would you make any adjustments to your budget? If so, what are they?

BANKING SERVICES
WHERE TO STASH YOUR CASH

WHAT'S AHEAD

EXPLODING MYTHS

Fact or Myth?
What do you think is true?

1. Funds deposited in a bank are no more secure than the money you keep in your sock drawer.

2. Checks have no advantages over cash. Both will pay your bills.

3. Personal checks are accepted as payment anywhere.

JOURNAL JOURNEY

WRITE IN YOUR JOURNAL ABOUT THE FOLLOWING.

ROLE OF BANKS   How does a bank benefit you now? How do you think you will use one in the future? If banks didn't exist, how do you think your life would be different?

CHECKING ACCOUNTS   What do you have to do to cash a check? How do you deposit one? How can you make sure you have enough money in your account to pay for the checks you write?

ELECTRONIC BANKING   What is an ATM? What do you have to do to use one? What transactions would you make with an ATM?

DECISION MAKING PROJECT

SPECIFY   SEARCH   SIFT   SELECT   STUDY

CHECK IT OUT!   Your group will look at checking accounts available in your area to see which would be best for you and your money.

GOAL

To learn how to choose a checking account

PROJECT PROCESS

SPECIFY	Lesson 7.2
SEARCH	Lesson 7.3
SIFT	Lesson 7.4
SELECT	Lesson 7.5
STUDY	Chapter Assessment

GOALS

EXPLAIN
how banks operate
and how they
benefit consumers

DESCRIBE
the benefits of using
a checking account

© Getty Images/EyeWire

7.1 How Banks Work

The Role of Banks

Your city or town probably has several banks. Most communities do. Banks are more than just a place to keep your money. Banks provide many vital services that benefit consumers and the economy.

Banks Are in Business to Earn a Profit

Banks are private businesses. They work to earn a profit by selling financial services. Most income that banks earn comes from the interest they charge when they lend money. The money they lend comes mostly from deposits made by consumers and businesses.

Banks pay depositors interest on most types of accounts. The interest rates depositors receive are lower than the interest rates banks charge borrowers. The difference between these rates is the banks' income.

Suppose you deposit $100 in your bank account. The bank pays you 2 percent interest to use your money. The bank lends your $100 to a business and charges 6 percent interest. The 4 percent difference between what the bank pays for your deposit and what it charges for the loan is its income. This income allows the bank to pay its costs and earn a profit.

CONSUMER ACTION

Kevin wants to buy a computer. For the past three months, he has put aside $25 each week. He is pleased because he now has $300. Kevin keeps his money in a box in his bedroom closet. What advice would you give Kevin? What risks is he taking? How could he earn additional income from his savings?

Banks have many other sources of income. They charge consumers fees for credit cards and checking accounts. Some banks help consumers create financial plans for a fee. Still, most bank income comes from interest charged on loans.

Banks Provide Security

You might deposit your money in a bank because you want to earn interest. However, another important reason to keep your money in a bank is that banks provide security. They have vaults, employ guards, and use electronic surveillance systems. If money is stolen, banks have insurance to cover the loss. Money kept in your home is not safe. The $300 Kevin keeps in a box in his closet may be lost, stolen, or subject to mishap.

Protect Your Money's Purchasing Power   There is another important reason not to keep extra money at home. When prices go up, the amount of products you can buy with your money goes down. Suppose you saw a pair of in-line skates you want for $150. After saving for a year, you have $150 in an envelope. When you go to the store, you discover that the skates now cost $154. Your $150 no longer buys what it used to buy. When the price went up, the **purchasing power** of your money went down.

Now suppose you put your $150 in the bank at 3 percent interest per year. At the end of the year, you will have $154.50. You can now buy more than you could if you left the $150 in an envelope. The interest you receive from your bank deposit helps protect the purchasing power of your money.

Banks Are Regulated   There are more government rules and regulations for banks than for almost any other type of business. The government works to protect both depositors and borrowers. For example, bank owners are required to put some of their own money in their business. If a bank loses money, it will lose the owners' money first.

Banks must set aside part of the money they receive in deposits. They may not spend or lend this money. This helps ensure that depositors will be able to withdraw their money whenever they want.

© Getty Images/EyeWire

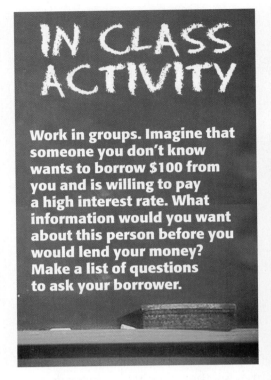

IN CLASS ACTIVITY

Work in groups. Imagine that someone you don't know wants to borrow $100 from you and is willing to pay a high interest rate. What information would you want about this person before you would lend your money? Make a list of questions to ask your borrower.

Most Deposits Are Insured

Banks provide another type of security if they belong to the **Federal Deposit Insurance Corporation (FDIC)**. The FDIC is an organization created by the federal government. It insures deposits in most banks up to a maximum of $100,000. If a bank fails and is not able to pay its depositors, the FDIC will pay instead. There is almost no chance of losing money that you deposit up to $100,000 in a FDIC-insured bank.

Banks Make Borrowing Easier

Some people save money. Other people and businesses want to borrow. But savers and borrowers generally do not know each other.

VOTE Your Wallet

Some elected officials want to eliminate FDIC insurance. They make the following argument.

FDIC insurance makes most deposits in any bank safe. Consumers might only consider interest rates when they deposit money. Banks could make risky loans to earn more income and pay higher interest rates. This could cause more banks to fail. Then the FDIC would have to pay their depositors. This would be bad for the economy and expensive for the government. We should eliminate FDIC insurance.

Do you believe these arguments make sense? Would you vote for a politician who held this position? Explain your answer.

Without help, savers are not likely to lend money to borrowers.

Banks help money flow from savers to borrowers. Savers have no way of knowing if it is safe to lend their money to someone else. Banks are equipped to evaluate borrowers.

Banks buy financial information about people who ask for loans. They can judge who is a good risk and who is not. This helps both savers and borrowers. Savers deposit their money in banks where it is safe

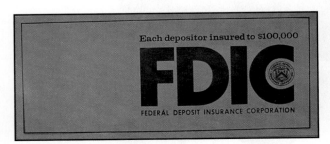

Each depositor insured to $100,000

FDIC
FEDERAL DEPOSIT INSURANCE CORPORATION

and they can earn interest. Banks lend the money to reliable borrowers who pay interest to use it.

Banks help people pay for many of their most important possessions. Few people could manage to buy a house without borrowing. Most cars are purchased with borrowed money. Businesses borrow to pay for new equipment and buildings. Banks help state and local governments borrow. By helping money flow from savers to borrowers, banks make our communities better places to live.

© Getty Images/PhotoDisc

Money and Financial Transactions

What if money didn't exist? How could you buy things? You could trade something you have for something you want. Trading goods and services without using money is called **barter**.

Barter might work as long as you have something to trade that the other person wants. Suppose you have a CD that your friend wants, and she has a CD that you want. You could trade, and both of you would be happy.

But what happens if the things you have to trade don't have the same value? Suppose you want your friend's CD, but all you have to trade is a DVD player. Would you make this trade? The DVD player is probably worth more to you than the CD. How could you barter?

This is when bartering gets complicated. To get your DVD player, maybe your friend is willing to throw in her backpack and softball bat along with the CD. Now would you make the trade?

Money allows you to compare the value of one product to the value of another. Also, with money, you can get the product you want without having something of equal value to trade that the other person wants. You can pay your friend for the CD. If she still wants the DVD player, she can pay you for it, and you can pocket the difference.

CheckPoint

How do banks earn income? How do banks protect your money? If you want to buy a car but you don't have the money, what would you have to do to get the car if banks did not exist? How do banks aid the borrowing process?

© Getty Images/PhotoDisc

Types of Money

Transactions like buying and selling are easier to make using money. Money comes in two forms. But when you think of money, you probably think of currency.

Currency is paper money and coins used for financial transactions. When you buy your lunch or go to a movie, you probably pay with currency. In the United States, most payments are made with currency. But these payments are usually small. Most large payments are made with another form of money—checks.

A **check** is an order to a bank to pay a specified sum to the person or business named on the check—the **payee**. When you write a check to someone and the payee cashes the check, the bank withdraws the amount from your account.

CheckPoint

What is the difference between currency and a check?

Advantages of Using Checks

Safety Probably the greatest advantage of checks is their safety. You write a check to a specific person or organization. If the check is lost or stolen, no one else can cash it. If someone does cash your check illegally, as the check writer you are not responsible. The money will not come out of your account. The bank or business that cashed the check suffers the loss. To protect themselves from someone cashing a check illegally, banks ask for identification before cashing a check.

Checks that are lost or stolen may be replaced. Suppose you lose a check made out to you. Since you are the payee, no one else may legally cash it.

Now suppose you had cashed your check and lost the currency instead. Then you could do nothing about it.

Convenience Checks are convenient for making payments, particularly large ones. If you want to buy a car, you would have to carry a lot of currency to the dealer if you could not pay by check.

Business and government transactions involve enormous amounts of money. Most of these payments are made with checks. Although most transactions in the United States are made with currency, the largest amounts of money change hands through checks.

Checks are safer to send through the mail than cash. Suppose you want to send $100 to your sister who lives in another state. If you could not mail a check, you might have to travel there to hand over the cash.

© Getty Images/PhotoDisc

Records of Your Transactions

You have learned the importance of keeping records of your spending. Checks automatically serve as records of your transactions. When you write a check and the payee cashes or deposits it at a bank anywhere in the world, that bank will return the check to your bank for payment.

Banks keep records of all checking transactions their customers make. Each month, your bank sends you a **statement**, which is a written record of all your transactions. With this statement, some banks also return your checks to you for filing in your record keeping system.

Records such as your checks and bank statements provide proof of transactions. Suppose you paid your monthly apartment rent with currency. Later, your landlord said you never made the payment. If you had paid with a check, you could prove you made the payment. But unless you have a written receipt for your cash payment, you could be forced to pay again.

CheckPoint

What are three main benefits of having a checking account?

TRY THESE

1. How do banks earn most of their income?

2. How can banks help protect the purchasing power of your money?

3. What benefits do you receive from depositing your money in a bank?

4. How do banks make borrowing easier?

5. What is the FDIC? What does it do?

6. What are two forms of money? What are the benefits of each?

THINK CRITICALLY

7. **CONSUMER ACTION** Kevin has set aside $300 that he keeps in a box in his closet. What risks is he taking by keeping his money in his closet? What could he do with his money that would be a better choice? Why?

8. **COMMUNICATE** Explain why banks pay a lower interest rate to account holders than they charge borrowers of that money.

9. Why do banks make loans to people and businesses?

10. Do you think your money is safe if you deposit $200,000 into a checking account at an FDIC-insured bank? Why or why not?

11. Bartering is not a popular way to conduct financial transactions. Why do you think this is true?

12. When do you use currency? When would you use checks in the future? What would determine whether you would use currency or a check?

13. **COMMUNICATE** Describe which advantage of using checks is the most important to you. Explain your reasons in an e-mail to your teacher.

GOALS

DEMONSTRATE
an ability to write,
endorse, record, and
deposit checks

EXPLAIN
types of checking
accounts and checking
account fees

7.2 Use Your Checking Account

Your Checking Account

A bank account that allows depositors to write checks to make payments is a **checking account**. Checking accounts from different banks have small differences, but they all work in basically the same way.

Open a Checking Account

If you are 18 or older, you can open a checking account. You complete the signature card for the bank, show the bank representative valid identification, and make an initial deposit.

The signature card is the bank's record of your signature. If someone else tries to write a check on your account with another signature, your bank normally will not accept it.

The bank provides you with checks, usually for a fee. Companies other than banks can offer to print checks for you, sometimes at a lower cost. You can then fill out these checks to make payments, as long as you don't exceed the amount deposited in your account.

CONSUMER ACTION

Marcy opened her first checking account a week ago. Now she is in Video Land and wants to write a check for $20 to buy a video. But she doesn't know how. What should she write on the check? How can she remember what she spent? How will she know if she has enough in her account to buy something else next week?

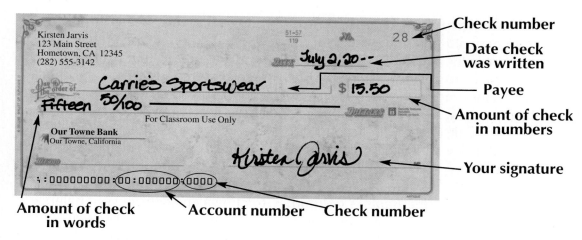

Check number

Date check was written

Payee

Amount of check in numbers

Your signature

Amount of check in words

Account number

Check number

Write a Check

Always fill out checks in ink so that no one can erase or change them. Write clearly. When you write the amount in words, show cents as a fraction. To make sure no one can alter your amount, start writing at the left of the amount spaces. After you write the amount in words, fill the rest of that space with a line. You must fill out these parts: (1) the date you write the check, (2) the name of the payee, (3) the amount of the check, written in numbers and words, and (4) your signature.

To help you remember what you used the check for, you can write a brief description in the memo space.

Record Checks in Your Check Register

In the box with the checks you receive, you will find a booklet, called a **check register**, for recording your transactions. Many computer programs provide an electronic check register for you to enter and store records of your checking transactions.

Record Each Transaction

A good habit is to write the amount of any check or deposit in your check register before you finish the financial transaction. This will ensure that your check register is up to date.

Record Interest If you receive interest on your checking account deposits, the interest is credited, or added, to your account. Your bank statement shows how much interest you received for the month. When you receive your statement, record the interest in the *Deposit/Credit* column of your register.

Sample Check Register

PLEASE BE SURE TO **DEDUCT** CHARGES THAT AFFECT YOUR ACCOUNT

NUMBER	DATE	DESCRIPTION OF TRANSACTION	SUBTRACTIONS PAYMENT/DEBIT (−)		✓ T	(−) FEE IF ANY	ADDITIONS DEPOSIT/CREDIT (+)		BALANCE	
28	7/2	Carrie's Sportswear	15	50		.20			36	70
									15	70
									21	00

Calculate Your New Balance

Your **account balance** is the total amount in the account at a specific date. At the top of the *Balance* column, record the amount in your account before you make any transactions. When you first open your account, the balance is your initial deposit.

Then as you record each check, deposit, interest, or fee, calculate a new amount in the *Balance* column. Subtract the amounts of checks and fees from your previous balance, and record the new balance in the *Balance* column. Add deposits and interest to calculate the new balance. When you turn to a new page in the register, carry the balance forward by recording the current balance at the top of the new page.

Record Check Numbers

Your checks are numbered in sequence. Record the number of each check you write in the *Number* column of your check register. This helps you see at a glance that you have recorded every check.

If your register shows an entry for check 28 and then check 30, you know that you forgot to enter a check. You can call your bank to find the amount of the check so that you can subtract it from your balance.

Overdrawing means writing a check for more than you have in your account. When your bank receives a request to pay the check for which you have insufficient funds, it may refuse to pay and charge you a fee.

Forgetting to record a check is one of the most common causes of overdrawing an account. Without subtracting a check from your balance, you think you have more deposited in your account than you do.

CheckPoint

What parts of a check must you fill out? How do you calculate a new balance in your check register?

Cash Checks or Transfer Them to Someone Else

Cash a Check To cash a check, take it to your bank. Sign your name on the back of the check. Give it to the bank teller, along with your photo identification, to exchange it for currency.

Your signature on the back of a check is called an **endorsement**. When you endorse the check, you are acknowledging that you received the money or transferred your right to the money to someone else. Don't sign the back of your check until you get to the bank. Anyone may cash the check once it has been endorsed!

You can also get cash from your checking account by writing a check to Cash. Then you endorse it with

your signature on the back and give it to the bank teller with your ID for payment. Be careful, though! Anyone can cash a check made out to *Cash.* It is better to make the check out to yourself and then endorse it.

Transfer a Check When you receive a check made out to you, you may want to sign it over to someone else—to Jason Jarvis, for example. To do this, you write "Pay to the order of Jason Jarvis" on the back of the check and then sign your name below that. This is called a **third party check.** Some banks do not accept third party checks.

Deposits

When you receive a check, you may deposit all or a part of it into your account. Suppose you just received your paycheck for $153.20. You want to deposit most of it into your checking account, but you need $20 in cash. As long as you already have at least $20 in your account to cover the amount you want, you can make this transaction.

Deposit Form At the back of your book of checks, you will find deposit forms preprinted with your name and account number. If you don't have preprinted deposit forms,

you can use a blank form available at your bank.

Write the amount of the check in the blank space next to the word *checks.* If you have more than one check, record the amount of the second check below the first. If you also want to deposit cash, write that amount in the *currency* space.

To get the subtotal, add the amounts of all checks and currency. In this example, you have only one check, so your subtotal is the same as the check amount. Then record the $20 you want in cash in the *Less cash received* space. Write the date in the appropriate spot. Since you want cash back, you must also sign the deposit form and have a photo ID ready.

Endorse your check as usual. Give the check, your ID, and deposit form to the bank teller. The teller will check your account balance to make sure you have enough to cover the $20. If so, the teller will give you $20 and a deposit receipt. This is your record of the transaction. File it in your record keeping system.

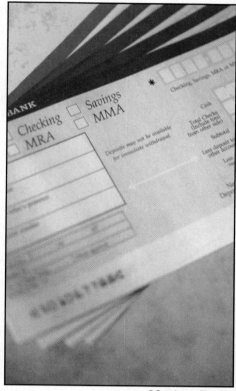

© Getty Images/PhotoDisc

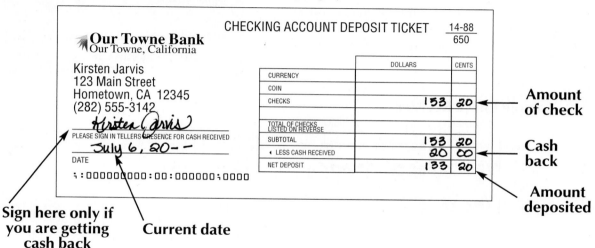

CHECKING ACCOUNT DEPOSIT TICKET 14-88 / 650

Our Towne Bank
Our Towne, California

Kirsten Jarvis
123 Main Street
Hometown, CA 12345
(282) 555-3142

Kirsten Jarvis
PLEASE SIGN IN TELLERS PRESENCE FOR CASH RECEIVED
July 6, 20--
DATE

⑆ :000000000:00:000000;0000

	DOLLARS	CENTS
CURRENCY		
COIN		
CHECKS	153	20
TOTAL OF CHECKS LISTED ON REVERSE		
SUBTOTAL	153	20
◂ LESS CASH RECEIVED	20	00
NET DEPOSIT	133	20

Amount of check ←
Cash back ←
Amount deposited

Sign here only if you are getting cash back **Current date**

For Deposit Only If you want to deposit an entire check without receiving any cash back, you can endorse the check by writing "For deposit only" before your signature.

Record Your Deposit Don't forget to enter every transaction into your check register, including deposits. As soon as you make a deposit—before you even leave the bank—record the transaction in your check register. Write the date you made the deposit. In the *Description of Transaction* column, write "Deposit."

The amount of the deposit goes in the *Deposit/Credit* column. Note that this is the amount you actually deposited, not the amount of the check. Remember, you kept $20 of it in cash. To calculate your new balance, add the amount of the deposit to the current balance, and record the total in the *Balance* column.

The Check-Clearing Process When you deposit a check, you can't withdraw the money immediately unless you already have enough money in your account to cover the check. The check must "clear" first. Your bank will send the check or transmit an electronic image of it to the check writer's bank for payment. That bank will subtract the amount of the check from the check writer's account and send this amount to your bank as payment for the check.

When your bank receives payment, the check has cleared, and the money is available for you to use. Due to recent legislation that allows the use of electronic check images, this process can occur overnight.

CheckPoint

How do you fill out a deposit form? How do you endorse a check that you want to deposit if you don't want any cash back?

IN CLASS ACTIVITY

Suppose your starting balance is $50.87. Use the appropriate forms to deposit $24.35 into your checking account, pay Barry's CDs and More $15.47 for a CD, and get $30.00 in cash. Then calculate your new balance including any fees.

Sample Check Register

PLEASE BE SURE TO **DEDUCT** CHARGES THAT AFFECT YOUR ACCOUNT

NUMBER	DATE	DESCRIPTION OF TRANSACTION	SUBTRACTIONS PAYMENT/DEBIT (−)		✓ T	(−) FEE IF ANY	ADDITIONS DEPOSIT/CREDIT (+)		BALANCE	
									36	70
28	7/2	Carrie's Sportswear	15	50		.20			15	70
									21	00
	7/6	Deposit					133	20	133	20
									154	20

Checking Account Types and Costs

Banks expect to earn a profit from checking accounts. A large part of their income from checking accounts comes from the fees they charge. The fees depend on the type of account.

Checking Account Types

Interest-Bearing Checking Accounts Banks lend money deposited in checking accounts and receive interest income from these loans. Therefore, banks sometimes pay interest on checking accounts. However, they usually require depositors to keep a large minimum balance in the account at all times to qualify for interest. The minimum amount to earn interest varies.

If the account balance becomes less than this required minimum, a fee is usually charged. The account might not be eligible for interest payments until the account's balance meets the required minimum again.

Noninterest-Bearing Checking Accounts If you don't have a large sum to keep in a checking account, you will probably have to open a checking account that pays no interest. The bank will be able to earn income by using funds deposited in your checking account without paying you interest.

Checking Account Fees

Banks charge two types of fees on most checking accounts. The monthly *maintenance fee* is charged no matter how many checks you write. This is a flat fee to cover the costs of maintaining your account.

The other fee is a *service charge* for each check you write. An example of recording this fee is shown in the check register on page 232. If you don't write many checks, then the service charge may be lower than the maintenance fee. The exact fees vary for types of accounts and banks. Investigate the fees charged by competing banks to find the best deal before opening your account.

$MATH OF MONEY

Lisa wants to open a checking account. She thinks she will write an average of ten checks per month. She may choose either of two accounts. One has a $5 monthly maintenance fee and charges $0.15 per check. The other has a $3 monthly maintenance fee but charges $0.25 per check. How much would Lisa pay in fees for these different accounts?

SOLUTION

Account 1 would cost $6.50 per month	$5 + (10 \times $0.15) = $6.50
Account 2 would cost $5.50 per month	$3 + (10 \times $0.25) = $5.50

Banks set rules for your checking account. If you do not follow these rules, you may be charged special fees. The most common special fee is the one you will be charged for overdrawing your account. The payee will also be charged a fee that you will be expected to pay. You could pay as much as $70 in total for each "bad check" you write!

CheckPoint

What costs should you expect to pay to use your checking account?

TRY THESE

1. How should you write a check?

2. How do you make a deposit in your checking account?

3. What is the purpose of a check register?

4. Which types of transactions should you record in the *Payment/Debit* column of your check register? Which types go in the *Deposit/Credit* column?

5. What happens to a check after you cash it?

6. How does a bank earn income from checking accounts?

THINK CRITICALLY

7. CONSUMER ACTION Explain to Marcy how to write a check, record it, and determine her balance.

8. MATH OF MONEY Burg Bank offers a checking account with a maintenance fee of $4.75 and a per-check fee of $0.20. You expect to write 7 checks per month. How much would your monthly fees be? Towne Bank charges a $5 maintenance fee and $0.15 per check. Which is the better deal? Why?

9. Referring to exercise 8, suppose you have a checking account at Burg Bank, but you might switch your account to Towne Bank. What should you consider in this decision? E-mail your answer to your teacher.

DECISION MAKING PROJECT

SPECIFY **SEARCH** **SIFT** **SELECT** **STUDY**

SPECIFY Decide how you want to use a checking account. What type of checking account do you want? What do you think your average daily balance will be? Estimate how many bank transactions you expect to make per month.

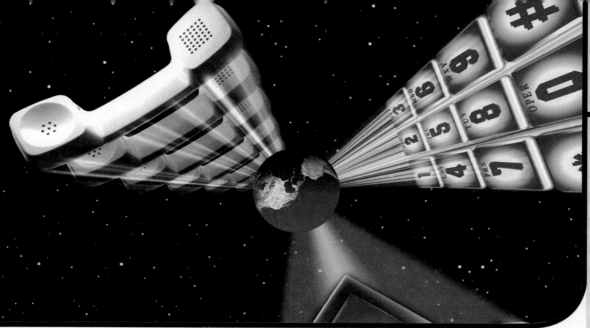
© Getty Images/Digital Vision

7.3 Electronic Banking

Electronic Funds Transfer and ATMs

GOALS

DESCRIBE
electronic transactions you can make

DISCUSS
your rights and responsibilities in electronic transactions

Banks allow consumers to move money from one account to another by computer. This movement of money is called **electronic funds transfer (EFT)**. You don't need checks or currency. A computer sends an electronic message to another computer, telling it to deduct money from one account and add it to another.

EFTs are quicker and less expensive for banks to complete than paper transactions. They reduce the chance of losing money. Also, they create an electronic record of the flow of money. EFTs are commonly made through automated teller machines, direct deposits, debit cards, automatic bill payments, and online banking.

Automated Teller Machines

The most popular way to transfer money electronically is through an **automated teller machine (ATM)**. An ATM is a computer terminal that

CONSUMER ACTION

Beth has a job in a rural area. Her bank has no branches near her work, so she has difficulty visiting it during business hours. She would like to be able to cash her paychecks or make deposits. She would also like to shop at stores without carrying her checkbook or lots of cash. How could Beth solve these problems by using electronic banking?

you can use to make deposits, withdraw cash, transfer money between accounts, check your account balance, and pay some kinds of bills. In fact, an ATM can make most of the financial transactions that a human teller can.

Your ATM Card and PIN

To use an ATM, you must have an ATM card. Banks issue these cards to their depositors. ATM cards have a strip of tape on the back that contains electronic code. When you insert your card into an ATM, the code identifies you and your accounts.

To use an ATM, you must also have a **personal identification number (PIN)**. Your PIN is your secret number that identifies you to the ATM as the owner of the card. When you insert your card and enter your PIN on the ATM keypad, the machine identifies you as the card owner and authorizes you to make transactions. Banks usually allow you to choose your own PIN.

ATM Transactions

ATMs are located just about anywhere. You can use an ATM at any time, day or night.

The ATM screen gives you step-by-step instructions. To begin your transaction, insert your ATM card. The screen will then prompt you to enter your PIN. Next, the ATM will ask you what type of transaction you wish to make.

ATM Deposit

You may deposit money in your savings or checking account at an ATM. To make a deposit, you must place your endorsed check in a special envelope available at the ATM. You will have to write information on the envelope about your transaction, so have a pen with you. After you insert your card and enter your PIN, the ATM screen will guide you through the process. It will then record your deposit and print a receipt. Always keep this receipt and enter the transaction in your check register under *Deposit/Credit.*

Different states have different laws regarding ATM deposits into accounts across state lines. Be careful to ask about these laws if you wish to use ATMs in different states.

ATM Withdrawal

To withdraw money from your savings or checking account, just follow the instructions on the screen. ATMs dispense paper currency only—no coins, so your

© Getty Images/EyeWire

request must be in dollars. Usually, only tens and twenties are dispensed. Keep your receipt of the transaction and record it under *Payment/Debit* in your check register.

ATM Costs   Your bank may charge fees for using ATMs. The most common fee is a fee per use. This fee can range from $1.00 to $4.00 per transaction, depending upon which ATM you use. Many banks maintain their own ATMs. You do not have to use your bank's machines. You may use almost any ATM, but your fee will be higher than when you use your bank's machines.

Suppose you use an ATM that belongs to another bank. The owner of the ATM may charge your bank a fee. Your bank will pass this fee on to you along with its own fee. Typical

Suppose you visit your bank's ATM. A uniformed man near the ATM introduces himself as a bank security officer. He tells you he is investigating a problem with the bank's computer system. He asks to watch you make your transaction to see if the ATM works correctly. Should you cooperate with this request? Why or why not?

What In The World?

Imagine going shopping without cash, checks, or credit cards. What could you accomplish? If you had a *smart card* and lived in Western Europe, the answer would be, "Quite a lot." Smart cards contain an imbedded microchip that your bank "loads" with your deposit amount. When you buy something, the card is swiped through a machine that deducts money from your balance and credits it to the store's account. The process is fast and convenient, relieves you of the need to carry currency, and prevents you from overdrawing your account or exceeding your credit card's borrowing limit.

Smart cards have been common in Western Europe since the mid 1990s. In 2004, more than 50 million were in use, and that number was growing by 10 percent each year. Do smart cards sound like a good idea to you? What advantages do they have over cash? If you could obtain one, would you?

© Getty Images/PhotoDisc

fees are from $1 to $2. Some non-bank ATMs charge as much as $4. Record these fees with any ATM withdrawal under *Fees*.

Some banks charge fees for using tellers to encourage customers to use ATMs. Banks save money when customers use ATMs. ATMs must be serviced regularly, which creates a cost for banks. However, the cost of an ATM is much less than the cost of a teller's salary. Banks have reduced the number of tellers they employ by almost half in the past 15 years because consumers are making more transactions through ATMs, saving banks billions of dollars.

Use ATMs Responsibly

Although ATMs offer many benefits, they involve some dangers as well. Dishonest people need only your PIN and ATM card to steal money from your accounts. When you use an ATM, be sure no one sees you enter your PIN. Never give your PIN or card to anyone else. In case of theft, do not write your PIN on your card or anywhere in your wallet.

If you lose your ATM card, report it immediately. Banks provide toll-free numbers to report lost or stolen cards. Your bank will issue you a new card in a few days. This is a small inconvenience compared to losing your money.

You could be robbed when using an ATM. To reduce risk, use ATMs with a friend or when others are nearby. Avoid using ATMs at night or in isolated or high-crime areas. Use common sense. If an ATM is located where you would be afraid to carry cash, don't use the ATM.

CheckPoint

Suppose you have a checking account and you want to be able to use an ATM. What would you need to do this? How would you deposit money using an ATM? What costs might you pay?

Uses of Electronic Funds

Electronic funds transfers have expanded beyond the use of ATMs. Now you can use direct deposit, debit cards, and automatic payments, as well as online banking.

Direct Deposit

Many employers offer the option of having paychecks deposited directly into employees' checking accounts on payday. This is called **direct deposit**. If you have your paycheck directly deposited, you will receive a regular pay stub and *a non-negotiable check,* which does not have value and cannot be deposited.

Other businesses and government agencies use direct deposit. For instance, the IRS allows you to have your income tax refund directly deposited. Also, Social Security will directly deposit benefit checks.

Debit Cards

Many stores now accept **debit cards**. These cards, sometimes called *check cards,* operate like electronic checks. You can use a debit card to make purchases, and the payments are electronically transferred from your checking account to the store's account.

Like ATM cards, debit cards have a strip of tape containing electronic code that identifies you and your account. The store clerk runs the card through a special terminal that reads the code and transmits it to your bank along with information about the sale.

When your bank's computer receives the message, it checks the balance in your checking account to make sure you have enough to pay for the purchase. Then it subtracts the amount of your purchase from your account and adds it to the store's account. The bank's computer sends an electronic confirmation to the store. The store's terminal prints a record of the transaction as your receipt. This whole transaction takes only seconds.

Debit Cards and Checks

Debit cards work much like checks, but they have several advantages over checks. You don't have to carry or write checks. Since the bank's computer verifies your account balance before completing the transaction, you will not be able to spend more than you have on deposit. Stores often prefer debit card transactions because they receive payment immediately. But, like any

Make a list of the pros and cons of using ATMs. The Internet may provide you with additional ideas. Share your list with another student by e-mail. Reach an agreement with the other student as to the most important advantage and disadvantage of this type of financial transaction. Explain your choice in an e-mail to your teacher.

other transaction you make, always keep the receipt and record the transaction in your check register.

Automatic Bill Payments

Pay by Phone   After you establish your own household, you will have to pay certain bills every month. Bills for housing, electricity, heat, telephone, a car loan, and cable television are typical monthly bills for most families. Many banks offer a system for paying these recurring bills by phone.

First, inform the bank that you wish to be able to pay your bills by phone. You may have to pay a fee for this service. Procedures for setting up automatic bill payment by phone vary from bank to bank. Once set up in your bank's computer, dial the phone number given to you by your bank and make your transactions. Most banks will give you a confirmation number for each transaction. Be sure to record the transaction and confirmation number in your check register.

Automatic Withdrawals In some cases, you can arrange for your bank to pay bills automatically from your account without having to phone the computer. For example, suppose you own a house and your mortgage payment of $850 is due on the first of every month. You can ask your mortgage company if it will set up an **automatic withdrawal** from your bank account each month to pay this bill. The company must set it up directly with your bank.

Once the automatic withdrawal is arranged, your bank will withdraw $850 from your account on the first of every month and send it to the mortgage company. Remember to record this transaction in your check register. Your automatic withdrawals will appear on your monthly statement, but you may get no notification or receipt when the transaction occurs. Usually, though, the mortgage company will send a reminder notice to you.

© Getty Images/PhotoDisc

Online Banking

Many banks have web sites at which consumers may complete transactions online. To use this service, you must register with your bank. There is often a monthly fee for usage.

Once you learn to access your account information online, you can add online payees. Then you may pay bills and transfer money over the Internet. Online payments may not be deducted right away.

Contact your bank to find out how long it takes for a transaction to be completed.

CheckPoint

How do debit cards work? If you use an automatic system for paying your bills, what should you do to make sure you don't overdraw your account?

Consumer Protection and Responsibilities

In 1978, Congress passed the Electronic Fund Transfer Act (EFTA) to protect consumers who make electronic transactions. This law requires banks to inform customers of fees

CYBER CONSUMER

Online banking is relatively new to the banking industry. Search the Internet for recent news articles about online banking. Write a report describing the latest trends in online banking. What services are banks offering online now? What new services are on the horizon? What problems are banks facing in online banking?

associated with EFTs. The bank must offer customers a receipt to verify every electronic transaction.

The law also requires consumers to use EFTs responsibly. If you lose your ATM card, you must report the loss within two business days. Then, if someone uses your card, the most you could lose is $50. If you don't report the loss within two business days, you could lose as much as

$500. After 60 days, you would be responsible for all losses.

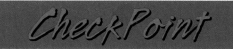

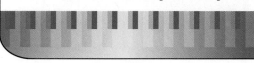

How does the EFTA protect you?

TRY THESE

1. What is an EFT?

2. What is a PIN and what is it for?

3. How does using an ATM help you and the bank?

4. What should you do to protect your money when using an ATM?

5. What is a debit card?

6. What is automatic bill paying and how does it work?

7. How is the Internet becoming part of banking now and in the future?

8. What are your rights and responsibilities under the Electronic Funds Transfer Act?

THINK CRITICALLY

9. **CONSUMER ACTION** Beth's bank has no branches near her job. What electronic options does Beth have for solving her problems? What does she have to do to start using these options?

10. **COMMUNICATE** Would you use automatic bill paying? Explain your reasons in an e-mail to your teacher.

11. What problems can occur from banking electronically? What can you do to avoid these problems?

DECISION MAKING PROJECT

SPECIFY   SEARCH   SIFT   SELECT   STUDY

SEARCH Assign a local bank to each group member. Each person should find out the following from the assigned bank.

1. How many kinds of checking accounts the bank offers.

2. List the check and ATM fees for using each account.

3. List any other terms for using checking accounts at that bank.

© Getty Images/PhotoDisc

7.4 Balance Your Checkbook

Your Bank Statement

At the end of the month, your bank sends you a statement showing all your transactions and bank fees for the month.

This is when careful record keeping pays off. Compare your check register to the bank statement to make sure that neither you nor the bank made a mistake. This comparison is called *balancing* or *reconciling* your account.

Confirm Transactions To make comparing easy, start with the first transaction on your statement and go down the statement one transaction at a time. Make a check mark in your register next to each entry that is on your statement.

After you have checked off everything listed in the statement, look for any entries that you did not check off. Notice that check 31 does not have a check mark in the example. The statement's date is July 23. Check 31 was written on July 28, so it wasn't cashed before the statement was printed. It will probably be on next month's statement.

CONSUMER ACTION

Anna is having trouble with her checking account. She has received overdraft notices from her bank for "bad checks." The amount in her check register never matches the amount on her bank statement. What should Anna do?

STATEMENT OF ACCOUNT

Our Towne Bank
Our Towne, California

Kirstin Jarvis
123 Main Street
Hometown, CA 12345

Account Number 07227679
Statement Date: July 23, 20--

Balance Last Statement	Total Deposits	Total Payments	Bank Fees	Balance This Statement
36.70	266.40	62.70	4.60	235.80

Check Number	Amount	Date Cashed
28	$15.50	7/03/--
29	22.05	7/22/--
30	25.15	7/25/--

Deposit Amount	Date of Deposit
$133.20	7/06/--
133.20	7/22/--

Bank Fee Type	Date	Amount
Check fee	7/03/--	$0.20
Check fee	7/22/--	0.20
Check fee	7/25/--	0.20
Service charge	7/28/--	4.00

Check Register

PLEASE BE SURE TO **DEDUCT** CHARGES THAT AFFECT YOUR ACCOUNT

NUMBER	DATE	DESCRIPTION OF TRANSACTION	SUBTRACTIONS PAYMENT/DEBIT (−)	√ T	(−) FEE IF ANY	ADDITIONS DEPOSIT/CREDIT (+)	BALANCE
							36 70
28	7/2	Carrie's Sportswear	15 50	√	.20		15 70
							21 00
	7/6	Deposit		√		133 20	133 20
							154 20
29	7/20	The Ticket Source	22 05	√	.20		22 25
							131 95
30	7/22	Bell's Department Store	25 15	√	.20		25 35
							106 60
	7/22	Deposit		√		133 20	133 20
							239 80
31	7/28	Northwoods Campground	15 00		.20		15 20
							224 60

CheckPoint

What is the purpose of comparing your statement to your check register?

The Account Reconciliation Form

With your statement each month, your bank will probably enclose an account reconciliation form, usually on the back of your statement. This form helps you find any differences between the statement and your check register.

Statement Column

Balance from Statement

Enter the amount that your statement shows as your current balance. In the example, this amount is $235.80.

List Deposits Not on Statement Deposits after the statement date won't appear on this statement. Record these deposits on the form. In the example, there were no deposits after the statement date, so this amount is 0.

Total Statement Balance and Deposits Add your statement balance and deposits that are not on your statement, and enter the result. In the example, this is $235.80.

List Checks Not on Statement Record transactions that were not on your statement (the entries in your check register that you did not check off). Record any fees not on your statement. In the example, the amount is $15.20 for check 31 and its $0.20 fee.

Total Checks Add the checks and fee amounts, and enter the result. In the example, this amount is $15.20.

Statement Balance Write down the amounts you calculated for *Total statement balance and deposits* and *Total checks*. Subtract *Total checks* from *Total statement balance*

Reconciliation Form

Statement		Checkbook	
Balance from statement	235.80	Balance from checkbook	224.60
List deposits not on statement	0	List deposits not in checkbook	0
	(+)		(+)
Total statement balance and deposits	235.80	Total checkbook balance and deposits	224.60
List checks not on statement	15.20	List fees not in checkbook	4.00
	(+)	Enter interest payment	(+) 0
Total checks	15.20	Total fees and interest	4.00
Total statement balance and deposits	235.80	Total checkbook balance and deposits	224.60
Total checks	(−)15.20	Total fees and interest	(−) 4.00
Statement balance	220.60	Checkbook balance	220.60

and deposits. In the example, this is $220.60, the balance that will be in the account after check 31 is paid.

Checkbook Column

Balance from Checkbook Enter the balance from your check register. In the example, notice that the checkbook balance doesn't match the statement balance.

List Deposits Not in Checkbook If you forgot to enter any deposits in your check register that appeared on your statement, list any amounts on these lines. In this example, there were no deposits on the statement that were not in the register, so this amount is 0.

Total Checkbook Balance and Deposits Add the *Balance from checkbook* with the deposits not in your checkbook, and enter the result. In the example, this is $224.60.

List Fees Not in Checkbook A monthly maintenance fee may show up under *Service Charge* on your statement. Enter this service charge on the form and in your check register. In the example, a monthly maintenance fee of $4 from the statement is entered.

Enter Interest Payment Your statement will show any interest paid to your account. In the example, the account is noninterest bearing, so 0 is recorded for interest paid.

Total Fees and Interest Add the fees not in your checkbook and the interest payment, and enter the result. In the example, this is $4.00.

Checkbook Balance Write the amounts for *Total checkbook balance and deposits* and *Total fees and interest.* Subtract *Total fees and interest* from *Total checkbook balance and deposits,* and record the result. In the example, *Statement balance* and *Checkbook balance* now match! This means that all transactions are accounted for, and the account is balanced.

CheckPoint

Why should you fill out the account reconciliation form?

Buy the Numbers?

Suppose you have an after-school job in a shopping mall. You receive your paycheck every other week. You use an ATM in the mall to deposit your check and get cash when needed. This ATM does not belong to your bank, so you pay a $2 fee for each transaction. Last month you completed five transactions at this ATM. You could use one of your bank's ATMs for free, but the closest one is nearly one mile from your school and two miles from your house. Assume you complete the same number of ATM transactions every month for the next year. Calculate the annual cost of using the other bank's ATM and describe alternative choices that would cost less.

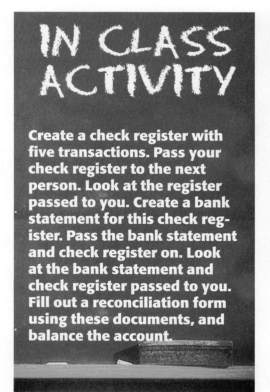

IN CLASS ACTIVITY

Create a check register with five transactions. Pass your check register to the next person. Look at the register passed to you. Create a bank statement for this check register. Pass the bank statement and check register on. Look at the bank statement and check register passed to you. Fill out a reconciliation form using these documents, and balance the account.

Make Adjustments

Be sure to record any maintenance fees and interest earned in your check register. Then determine your

Describe a plan for keeping up to date with your checking account. How often will you enter transactions in your check register? How will you make sure all your ATM transactions will be recorded in your check register? How often will you balance your checkbook?

new balance. Your check register balance should now match that indicated on your reconciliation.

What If the Bank Made an Error?

Banks don't often make mistakes, but it happens. Suppose your statement shows a deposit for $123.20 instead of $133.20. What should you do? First, go to your filing system and get

PRIMARY SOURCES

Read the following account from James A. Burns' *Native Sons of New Mexico* from 1936. Do you think that a bank today could make the same mistake? What is different about our banking practices now? Could Read Larkin cash a check for someone else today?

"One day, needing currency for some purpose, the Governor sent Larkin across the Plaza to the bank with a check for $150. The cashier, in the rush of business and not knowing what the Governor wanted the money for,

glanced at the check, and going back to the vault, made up a bundle of currency amounting to $1,500.00 and gave it to young Read. Larkin thought there was something wrong but took the money back to Governor Giddings and called his attention to the mistake. The Governor counted out the $150 he had sent for and told the boy to return the rest of the money to the banker who had not realized his error. He thanked Larkin profusely...."

your deposit receipt. Take this receipt and your statement to the bank, and explain the problem to a teller. Be polite. If the teller agrees, he or she will adjust your account. Be sure to check your next statement to ensure the adjustment was made correctly.

File Your Records

Although it is becoming less common, the bank may return your **canceled checks** with your statement. Each check will have *Canceled* stamped on it to indicate that the check has been paid. A canceled check serves as proof of a transaction. Even if your bank does not return your checks, you can request a copy of any canceled check. Check copies are stored at your bank.

Keep your canceled checks, statements, and reconciliations. File them by date for easy retrieval should you need to refer to them later.

CheckPoint

What should you do if your statement shows a fee that you forgot to record in your check register?

TRY THESE

1. What does your bank statement tell you?

2. Why should you compare your check register entries to your bank statement?

3. What is the purpose of completing an account reconciliation form?

4. What records serve as proof of a checking account transaction?

THINK CRITICALLY

5. **CONSUMER ACTION** Anna is having problems with her checking account. Describe for Anna how she can keep better track of her account balance.

6. What is an entry you might need to make in your check register only after you receive your bank statement? Why would you have to wait to enter this amount?

DECISION MAKING PROJECT

SPECIFY   SEARCH   SIFT   SELECT   STUDY

SIFT Have each group member present one type of checking account from the bank assigned to them. This account should best fulfill the requirements the group has set for using a checking account with the lowest fees.

© Getty Images/PhotoDisc

7.5 Other Banking Services

Different Checks for Different Purposes

Accepting a personal check can be risky for a business. Your personal check does not guarantee that you have enough on deposit to cover the check. Until a personal check clears, the business won't know if your check is "good." If it isn't, the bank will not pay the check, and the business may not be able to recover the money. Banks offer a variety of checks to solve special payment problems.

Certified Checks

Businesses that sell expensive products, such as cars, are taking a risk if they accept a personal check as payment.

A **certified check** is a personal check that has been stamped and signed by a bank officer. The stamp and signature guarantee that your account has the money to cover the check. Like any other personal check, you write a certified check to

CONSUMER ACTION

Last spring, Corey finally booked his dream vacation to Acapulco. He took $500 with him in cash, which he carried in his wallet. One day when he reached for his wallet to pay for a purchase, he discovered that it was gone. Someone had picked his pocket. Corey's mother mailed him a check the next day to help him out, but his vacation was almost over before he received it. What could Corey have done to protect his money? How could he have replaced the lost money more quickly?

a specific payee. No one else may legally cash it.

To obtain a certified check, you must pay a fee that typically ranges from $5 to $20. When the bank certifies your check, it withdraws the money from your account to cover the amount of the check and the fee. Since you can no longer access this money, the bank and the business know the money will definitely be available to pay the check.

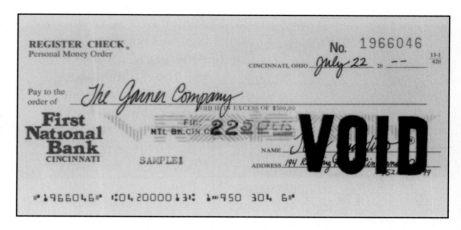

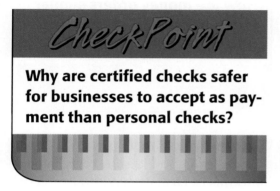

CheckPoint

Why are certified checks safer for businesses to accept as payment than personal checks?

Cashier's Checks

Another way to guarantee payment is with a cashier's check. A **cashier's check** is a bank's own personal check signed by the bank's cashier. Payment of this check comes from the bank's own money. To make a purchase that requires a guarantee of payment, you can buy a cashier's check. The bank then makes out the cashier's check to the payee you specify and the cashier signs it.

The amount you pay for the cashier's check is the amount you want on the check plus a fee of approximately $25. You can pay for the cashier's check with cash or by authorizing the bank to withdraw the money from your account. The bank then takes responsibility for payment of the check.

Businesses are willing to accept certified or cashier's checks because they know that a bank, instead of a person, is responsible for payment. These checks are often required when payments are made to buy homes or other valuable property.

Money Orders

Perhaps you don't have a checking account, or you need to make a small payment to a business that doesn't accept personal checks. You don't want to pay the fee required for a certified check or cashier's check. For this situation, a money order may be a good option.

A **money order** is a check that draws on the money of the bank or other financial business that issued it. In this way, it is like a cashier's check, but there are two main differences. A number of companies, not just banks, sell money orders and take responsibility for paying them. Also, your name, not a bank's name, appears on the money order.

Like a cashier's check, you pay for a money order up front, including a small fee of approximately $1 to $10. You can buy a money order from a bank, the post office, a check-cashing business, or another financial business such as Western Union or American Express.

The company then makes out the money order to the payee you specify, and only the payee may cash it. The payee can be fairly sure that the money order will be paid because payment will come from an established company, not from an individual's bank account.

Suppose you want to order a replacement part for your bicycle through the mail. If you send a check, the business will not send the part until it is sure your check is good. This might take a week or two. Meanwhile, you can't ride your bike.

Using a money order can speed your order. When the business receives your payment, it will send the part immediately because it knows the money order is good. If you want to get the part as soon as possible, you might be willing to pay an extra dollar or two for a money order.

CheckPoint

How are money orders similar to cashier's checks? How are they different?

Traveler's Checks

It is never a good idea to carry large amounts of cash. You could lose it or be robbed. If you are traveling, some local businesses won't accept checks from an out-of-state bank. So how can you safely take enough money with you when you travel? A good solution to this problem is traveler's checks.

Traveler's checks are checks that you pay for in advance, and if they are lost or stolen, the company that you bought them from replaces them. You can buy traveler's checks in many locations, such as banks, American Express offices, some travel agencies, and the American Automobile Association. They are generally sold in amounts of $20, $50, or $100. The fee is usually 1 percent of the amount of the checks, so $500 worth of traveler's checks would cost you a total of $505.

Traveler's checks have two signature lines. When you purchase

© South-Western

traveler's checks, you must sign the top line of each one in front of the employee who sells them to you. You then receive a receipt that doubles as a check register. It contains the serial numbers of the checks. When you travel, always keep this list with you in a safe place, separate from the checks.

To spend or cash a traveler's check, you sign the bottom signature line in front of the person you want to pay. Often some form of ID is required. Businesses are usually willing to accept traveler's checks because payment is guaranteed by the organization that issued them.

After you spend each check, record the serial number, date spent, and payee in the register that comes with the checks.

The most important advantage of traveler's checks is that you can get them replaced quickly if they are lost or stolen. If this happens, you must contact an office of the company that issued the checks. Large companies that issue traveler's checks have offices all over the world that can issue replacement checks for you, usually in a day or two.

To get your new checks, present the list of serial numbers in the check register that shows which checks you spent. From these records, the company can issue replacement checks.

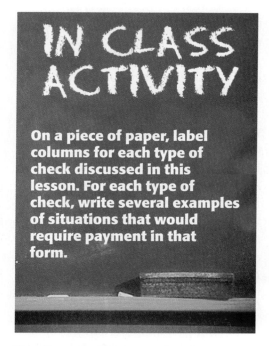

IN CLASS ACTIVITY

On a piece of paper, label columns for each type of check discussed in this lesson. For each type of check, write several examples of situations that would require payment in that form.

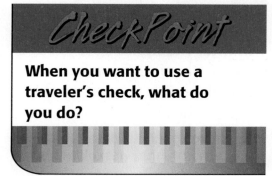

CheckPoint

When you want to use a traveler's check, what do you do?

Other Services

Banks and other financial businesses offer other services besides checks. In an emergency, you can transfer money to someone immediately by using a wire transfer. If you need a safe place to keep important documents, a safe deposit box at your bank is a good option.

Wire Transfers

Most large transfers of money between distant locations take place through wire transfers. A **wire transfer** is an electronic communication that moves money from an account in one bank to an account in a different bank. Wire transfers happen instantly.

Suppose a computer company orders thousands of monitors from a company in Japan and agrees to pay $28,000,000. Such a huge sum would earn substantial interest every day in a bank account or other investment. Companies don't want to lose this interest during the time it takes for a check to go through the mail. For distant transactions, the mail could take a week or more. These companies are much more likely to use a wire transfer to complete the transaction.

Although consumers do not use wire transfers often, wire transfers can be useful in emergencies. Imagine that you are on vacation, and you have car trouble. Your car is towed to a garage, where you discover that the engine needs a new alternator. It will cost $300 to replace. You don't have that much cash with you, and you need to have the car fixed now.

Your bank can arrange to have money wired from your account to pay for your car's repairs. Banks typically charge a fee of $20 to $40 for wire transfers. Other financial organizations, such as Western Union and American Express, also provide wire transfer services.

Wire transfers are most useful when you need to move money quickly. Wired money can get to its destination in minutes.

Safe Deposit Boxes

Most adults have important papers and small possessions they want to protect. Birth certificates, wills, deeds to property, car titles, or stock certificates can be difficult to replace if they are lost or stolen. If you own a coin collection or valuable jewelry, you may want to keep it someplace safer than your home. One way to protect important documents and property is to use a safe deposit box.

Safe deposit boxes are boxes with individual locks that you may rent from a bank. They are located in a vault, where their contents are safe from fire, theft, and loss. The cost of

© Getty Images/EyeWire

renting a small safe deposit box is typically between $30 and $40 a year. Larger boxes are more expensive, but most consumers find small ones to be large enough.

When you rent a safe deposit box, you sign a card, show a valid ID, and receive a key to the box. Each time you want to get into your box, you must sign in, show your ID, and give your key to a bank employee. The employee will compare the signature on your card with the signature you wrote when you signed in. This process protects you by preventing someone else from gaining access to your box. The bank also has a key. The bank representative must use both keys to open the box for you.

CheckPoint

In what situation might you use a wire transfer? If you had a safe deposit box, what would you put in it?

TRY THESE

1. Why might a business be unwilling to accept a personal check as payment for a purchase?

2. How is a certified check different from a cashier's check?

3. Why might you use a money order to make a small payment by mail?

4. How do traveler's checks work?

5. If you lose your traveler's checks, what must you do to get replacements?

6. In what situation might a wire transfer be a better choice than sending a check through the mail?

7. How does a safe deposit box protect your important papers and valuable possessions?

THINK CRITICALLY

8. **CONSUMER ACTION** Corey's trip was ruined when someone stole his wallet. Explain how Corey could have avoided this problem and how he could have replaced his lost money.

9. Imagine that you own a sailboat that you want to sell. A person you don't know responds to the ad you placed in a newspaper. He offers to pay your $5,000 price with a personal check. Should you accept this offer? What could you ask the buyer to do to assure you that his payment is good?

10. **COMMUNICATE** Name five types of checks. For each type, describe a situation in which you would use that type of check, and explain why.

11. **COMMUNICATE** Suppose that you own property that you want to sell.

Two people have offered to buy your property. Charlie lives nearby and is willing to pay $30,000 immediately. He will retract his offer if you don't accept within two days. Glenda lives more than 1,000 miles away. She has offered to pay $35,000. Unfortunately, she will not be back in town for a month. Write an e-mail message to Glenda explaining the situation. Describe why the use of a wire transfer of funds would allow you to sell her the property.

12. David collects baseball cards. He has more than a thousand cards and estimates their total worth to be more than $10,000. How could he protect his collection? What could happen to his collection if he kept them in his home? E-mail your answer to your teacher.

DECISION MAKING PROJECT

SPECIFY **SEARCH** **SIFT** **SELECT** **STUDY**

SELECT Now that you have researched your checking account needs and what checking accounts are available, discuss your findings with your group. Decide which you think will best fulfill your needs. Write a short paragraph stating how your group chose a checking account. Use a mathematical example of how your chosen account will save you money over the next best alternative.

ASSESSMENT

KEY IDEAS

How Banks Work

1. Banks pay interest on deposits and charge interest when they loan this money to borrowers. The difference in interest rates is the bank's income.
2. Banks provide a safe place to keep your money. The FDIC insures most bank deposits. Banks also protect the purchasing power of your money by paying interest on your deposits.
3. Currency and checks are both forms of money. Without money, you would have to barter.
4. Checks provide safety, convenience, and written records of transactions.

Use Your Checking Account

5. To write a check, you must fill in the current date, name of the payee, amount written in numbers and words, and your signature.
6. As soon as you write a check or make a deposit, record the transaction in your check register. Then calculate your new balance.
7. To cash a check, endorse it with your signature on the back. To get cash out of your account, write a check to yourself or to Cash and sign it.
8. To deposit money, fill out a deposit form from the back of your book of checks or use a form from the bank.
9. You will probably have to pay a maintenance fee each month and a service fee for each check. You can either have an interest-bearing or noninterest-bearing checking account.

Electronic Banking

10. An electronic funds transfer (EFT) is the movement of money from one account to another by computer.
11. An automated teller machine (ATM) is a computer terminal that you can use to make deposits, withdraw cash, transfer money between accounts, and check your account balance.
12. You can use a debit card to make purchases without having to write checks or carry large sums of cash.
13. You can use automatic bill paying and automatic withdrawals to pay bills on a regular basis.
14. You can pay some bills by phone from your checking account. Also, many banks offer their customers online banking.

Balance Your Checkbook

15. When your bank statement arrives each month, check off each transaction in your check register.
16. Fill out the account reconciliation form. The adjusted statement balance and adjusted checkbook balance should match. Enter adjustments in your check register as necessary. File your canceled checks, statement, and reconciliation form.

Other Banking Services

17. A certified check is a personal check that has been stamped and signed by a bank officer as a guarantee that your account can cover the check.
18. A cashier's check also guarantees payment because payment comes from the bank's own money.

19. A money order is similar to a cashier's check. The bank or business that issues the check takes responsibility for paying it.

20. Traveler's checks are a good alternative to carrying cash when you travel.

21. A wire transfer is an electronic communication that instantly moves money from an account in one bank to an account in a different bank.

22. You can rent a safe deposit box in your bank to keep important papers and valuable possessions safe.

TERMS REVIEW

Match each term on the left with its definition on the right.
Some terms may not be used.

a. account balance
b. automated teller machine (ATM)
c. automatic withdrawal
d. barter
e. canceled check
f. cashier's check
g. certified check
h. check
i. check register
j. checking account
k. currency
l. debit card
m. direct deposit
n. electronic funds transfer (EFT)
o. endorsement
p. Federal Deposit Insurance Corporation (FDIC)
q. money order
r. overdrawing
s. payee
t. personal identification number (PIN)
u. purchasing power
v. safe deposit box
w. statement
x. third party check
y. traveler's check
z. wire transfer

1. paper money and coins used for financial transactions
2. an order to a bank to pay a specified sum to the person or business named
3. the person or business to whom a check is written
4. writing a check for more than is deposited in your checking account
5. a federal government agency that insures deposits in banks
6. a written record from your bank of all the transactions involving your account
7. a booklet for recording your checking account transactions
8. the total amount in your bank account
9. your signature on the back of a check
10. a check with the bank's stamp on it, indicating that it has been paid
11. the movement of money from one account to another by computer
12. a computer terminal that you can use to make deposits, withdraw cash, transfer money between accounts, and check your account balances
13. a secret number that identifies you to an ATM as the owner of the ATM card
14. a card used to transfer money electronically from your checking account to the store's account to pay for a purchase
15. a check that draws on the money of the bank or other financial business that issued it
16. a check that you pay for in advance that is replaceable if lost or stolen.

CONSUMER DECISIONS

17. You are trying to save to buy a TV for your room. You have been keeping your savings in a drawer. At the rate you are saving, you think you'll have the money you need in a year. Is it worth the hassle of opening a bank account for your money if you plan to collect it for only a year? Nobody is allowed in your room anyway, so maybe the money is safe in your drawer. What decision would you make? Why?

18. You love the convenience of your checking account. Unfortunately, you keep overdrawing and getting hit with big fees. Maybe you should just give up your checking account and use money orders instead. What are the pros and cons of each option? What would you have to do to avoid overdrawing your checking account? Would you be willing to do these things to keep the checking account, or would you choose to pay bills by money order? Why?

19. You have heard about debit cards and are thinking about getting one from your bank. What advantages and potential problems of a debit card would you consider in your decision? What could you do to avoid the problems?

THINK CRITICALLY

20. Juan has a debit card for his checking account. His bank charges no fee when he uses it. It does charge a $0.20 fee when he writes a check. Juan used the card 16 times last month, so he saved $3.20 in fees. There is a problem, however. He accidentally spent so much with his debit card that he was not able to pay several bills on time. He then had to pay $20 in late fees. What would you suggest to Juan to solve his problem? What could happen if he continues operating this way?

LOOK IT UP

21. The first bank to operate on the Internet was Security First Network Bank. Then other major banks, such as Wells Fargo and Bank of America, went online. Search the Net for one of these online banks. List the kinds of transactions you could make online with this bank.

22. Different banks charge different fees for use of ATMs, and their ATMs are located in different places. Ask two banks in your area for lists of their ATM fees and their ATM locations. Which

WHICH IS THE BEST DEAL?

Your bank is located near your job. You can easily use its ATM for free during your lunch hour. A different bank is running a special promotion. It offers people a chance to win a vacation to Hawaii each time they use its ATM. Because this is not your bank, it would cost you $1 to use its ATM. But if you had an account at the other bank, you could use its ATM for free. This other bank is located five blocks from your job. What would you do? Explain.

Alternative 1 Use the other bank's ATM and pay the $1 fee.

Alternative 2 Open an account at the other bank so you can use its ATM for free.

Alternative 3 Forget about the special offer and keep using your own bank's ATM on your lunch hour.

bank has the most convenient ATM locations for you? Which charges the lowest fees? Which bank would you choose based on the ATM information? Why?

23. At a library or on the Internet, look for two recent news articles about new electronic funds transfer services. What new types of EFTs are on the horizon? What benefits do these new EFT services offer consumers?

INSIDE THE NUMBERS

24. Suppose you have a noninterest-bearing checking account. Your account balance on your statement is $1,000. Your check register says you have $1,006. You have entered all your check fees. You have checked off every transaction in your check register. What could account for the difference?

25. Suppose you have a noninterest-bearing checking account. The balance on your bank statement is $342.56. You made no deposits that were not on your statement. There were two checks that were not on your statement. One was for $20.00, and the other was for $25.89. You have a per check fee of $0.20. Your checkbook balance is $291.27. All of your deposits have been recorded in

your check register. You have not yet recorded your monthly maintenance fee of $5. Fill out a reconciliation form. Does your checkbook balance?

CURRICULUM CONNECTION

26. **HISTORY** Money has changed many times throughout history. Look up *greenback* in a history book or encyclopedia. Write a one-page paper on the history of the greenback. What was it? When was it issued? Why was it called a greenback? Is it still used today?

27. **ENGLISH** You are probably familiar with Charles Dickens' short story about Ebenezer Scrooge in *A Christmas Carol.* If not, read this short tale about a man obsessed with money. What does this story tell you about money and happiness in life? How could you apply the lesson Scrooge learned to your financial life?

JOURNAL RECAP

28. After reading this chapter, review the answers you wrote to the questions in Journal Journey. Have your opinions changed? How?

SPECIFY   SEARCH   SIFT   SELECT   STUDY

STUDY Present your paragraph on the process your group went through to choose a checking account. Did any other group have the same requirements of a checking account that your group had? Did any other group choose the same account but for different reasons?

Chapter

8

SAVING
PLAN FOR FINANCIAL SECURITY

WHAT'S AHEAD

EXPLODING MYTHS

Fact or Myth?
What do you think is true?

1. The only reason to save is to be able to pay for something you want but cannot yet afford.

2. All banks pay the same rates of interest.

3. If you deposit funds in a bank and the bank fails, you will lose your money.

JOURNAL JOURNEY

WRITE IN YOUR JOURNAL ABOUT THE FOLLOWING.

TO SAVE OR NOT TO SAVE Do you think saving is important? For what would you save? What problems might you face in the future if you don't save?

SAVING OPTIONS What options do you have for saving? How would you evaluate your options? What would you consider in choosing a way to save?

IMPORTANCE OF INTEREST What is compound interest? Does the way interest is calculated matter to your savings plan? Why or why not?

DECISION MAKING PROJECT

SPECIFY   **SEARCH**   **SIFT**   **SELECT**   **STUDY**

SAVE YOURSELF Your group will decide the best place to put $2,000. You will have to decide what financial institution and what type of savings you will use and how long you will let your savings grow. How much will your money earn?

GOAL

To learn how to choose a savings plan

PROJECT PROCESS

SPECIFY	Lesson 8.1
SEARCH	Lesson 8.2
SIFT	Lesson 8.4
SELECT	Chapter Assessment
STUDY	Chapter Assessment

GOALS

EXPLAIN
how you can benefit
from saving regularly

DESCRIBE
strategies you can use
to meet your saving
goals

© Getty Images/PhotoDisc

8.1 Why Save?

Benefits of Saving

Sometimes your paycheck may seem to be written in disappearing ink. First, the government takes its piece as income tax and other withholding. Then, you must pay your living expenses—rent, car payment, food, and so on. But, after you have met all of your financial obligations, the remainder of your paycheck is yours to spend or not spend.

Saving is a trade-off. When you save, you trade spending now for the ability to spend in the future. You can choose to buy that new outfit now or save the money to buy

something else later. Some future expenses you can anticipate and plan for, such as college or a new car, but you can't foresee some expenses, such as fixing your car after an accident or replacing that window you broke with your home run. The purpose of saving is to cover future expenses whether you can see them coming or not.

Save for the Unexpected

You can be sure that your future will include some unexpected expenses. Accidents happen. Things get lost or

CONSUMER ACTION

Vera wants to save $2,000 to make a down payment on a used car next year. Much of her income as a server in a restaurant comes from tips. Since her tips vary from day to day, she never knows what her income will be for the week. This uncertainty makes it hard for Vera to plan her saving. What could Vera do to help herself achieve her saving goal? How could saving benefit her in other ways?

broken. Major purchases, such as a car, sometimes need unexpected repair. If you save, the money will be there when you need it.

If you lose your job or if you can't work for a while, you still have to pay your fixed expenses, such as your rent and car payment. The money you decide to save now can carry you through such times.

Save for Opportunities

Savings can allow you to take advantage of opportunities. Say you have been saving a little from each paycheck for a couple of years. You have always wanted a car, but most were too expensive.

Then your neighbor said that she would like to sell her old car. To sell it quickly, she offered it to you for a price you can afford. Because you saved, you can buy the car.

Save for Major Purchases

If you want something expensive, such as a home theater, a car, or a house some day, you need to start saving now. Saving a few dollars from each paycheck may not seem

like much, but over time and with interest, you should eventually be able to afford the expensive item you want.

Save for Flexibility

Savings can give you some flexibility in your life choices. If you have money saved, you can choose to quit a job you don't like to take another that pays less now but has better prospects. If you have savings, you can choose to rent an apartment that is a bit too expensive for you now but you know you can afford when you get your next pay raise.

Save to Achieve Your Goals

Your life-span goals will most likely involve large amounts of money. The sooner you start saving, the better are your chances of achieving your goals.

Saving is easier if you are saving for a reason that is important to you. A life-span goal such as a college education is an enormous expense. To get there, though, you can break it down into smaller, more manageable short-term steps. Set goals such as saving $100 each month. When you get a pay raise, you might revise your short-term goal to save $125 a month.

© Getty Images/PhotoDisc

CheckPoint

In what way is saving a trade-off? How can saving benefit you in the future?

COMMUNICATE

Think of a major purchase you would like to make if you had the money. Write a plan for saving for this purchase. Be as specific as you can. How much do you need to save? How long do you think it will take you to save that amount? What saving strategy will you use?

Saving Strategies

Most people, both young and old, find saving a challenge. The best way to save is to have a strategy.

Pay Yourself First A good way to save is to make a deposit in your bank account when you pay your bills or cash your paycheck. In effect, you are paying yourself just as you pay your bills. Consider this deposit to be a required payment. Then leave it in the bank. If you don't have this money in hand, you are less likely to spend it.

Save by the Numbers Many people don't earn the same amount from week to week. If you are a server in a restaurant, you receive most of your income from tips. Tips can vary from one week to the next. Because of this uneven income, you might not be able to save the same amount every week. You could choose to save a certain percentage of your take-home pay, such as 10 or 15 percent, no matter how much you earn each week.

Reward Yourself An effective strategy to reinforce good habits is to reward yourself. Think of things you like to do that don't cost much, such as taking long walks or playing ball. Each time you make a deposit to your savings account, give yourself rewards that don't cost much. Costly rewards would ruin your saving strategy.

Saving and Values You can decide not to buy an item you want now to get something you value more later. Suppose you are saving $20 a week to have $400 for a vacation. You see a jacket for $190. If you buy it, you would be giving up the vacation you want later for the jacket you want now. If you value the vacation more, you won't buy the jacket.

Automatic Saving

Payroll Deductions Find out whether your employer has a payroll deduction plan. Authorizing a deduction of a specific amount from your paycheck to be deposited into your savings account is an easy way to save. The saving comes out of your paycheck before you receive it.

INTERNET ACTIVITY

Make two lists, one with reasons young people don't save and the other with reasons they should begin to save. Search the Internet for data that will help you make your lists. Write a paragraph, citing the data you uncovered on the Web, that would convince more students to begin to save. E-mail it to your teacher.

Checking Account Transfers

You can authorize your bank to transfer a certain amount each month from your checking account to your savings account. Be sure to record these transactions in your savings and checking registers.

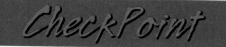

CheckPoint

How can having a strategy help you save? What saving strategies can help you save regularly? How can you set up an automatic saving plan?

TRY THESE

1. How can your savings give you flexibility in your life choices?

2. How do you follow the pay-yourself-first saving strategy?

3. What is a good saving strategy to use if your income is uneven?

4. How do values affect a savings plan?

THINK CRITICALLY

5. **CONSUMER ACTION** How can Vera plan her saving? What strategies could she consider? Aside from her goal of saving for a car, how else would regular saving benefit Vera?

6. Why do you need to save for both expected and unexpected expenses?

7. **MATH OF MONEY** Molly has a part-time job that pays her a gross income of $135 each week. Her withholding each week is $59.50. She also baby-sits. Her saving strategy is to deposit 20 percent of what she takes home. This week she earned $35 from two baby-sitting jobs. How much should she deposit in her account?

8. What saving strategy would work best for you? Why?

9. **COMMUNICATE** To make a class trip to Washington, D.C., at least 60 students must be able to pay the $500 cost. Write a letter to classmates to encourage them to commit to this trip and to explain some saving strategies they can use. E-mail it to another student and your teacher.

DECISION MAKING PROJECT

 SPECIFY   **SEARCH**   **SIFT**   **SELECT**   **STUDY**

Life-Span Plan

SPECIFY What do you want from a savings plan? List things you would save for. How long would you be willing to wait for each thing you want? Which of these are life-span goals?

© CORBIS

GOALS

DESCRIBE
differences among
types of savings
institutions

EXPLAIN
how to select the
savings account
that is right for you

8.2 Savings Institutions and Accounts

Savings Institutions

In the U.S. economy, you can choose among four basic types of financial businesses for depositing your savings: commercial banks, savings banks, savings and loan associations, and credit unions. At one time, these institutions were quite different from each other, and some differences still exist. In recent years, these differences have become smaller. Today, the institutions appear to be much the same.

Commercial Banks

When you think of a bank, you are probably thinking of a commercial bank. A **commercial bank** is a financial institution that serves individuals and businesses. Its wide variety of services includes savings and checking accounts, consumer and business loans, and some types of investment services.

Commercial banks are the largest savings institutions in the United

CONSUMER ACTION

Lisa has set a goal of saving $100 every month. She knows she should deposit this money where it is safe and she can earn interest. She also wants to be able to withdraw her money whenever she wants. Lisa's community has several types of savings institutions, but she doesn't know the differences among them. What should she consider in deciding where to deposit her money? How should she select the type of account that is right for her?

States. Many have offices throughout the country. Most communities have branches of at least one national commercial bank. Although commercial banks serve both consumers and businesses, they are the main source of loans for businesses.

Savings Banks

Savings banks are financial institutions owned by their depositors. As owners, depositors earn dividends instead of interest. A **dividend** is actually a share of the company's profits. The amount of the dividend depends on the how much of the company you own—that is, the size of your deposit. In practice, if you deposit money in a savings bank, you probably will see no difference between earning dividends there or earning interest at a commercial bank.

There are fewer than 500 savings banks in the United States. Most exist in the northeast. Savings banks were established to loan small amounts of money to consumers. Now savings banks offer a wide range of banking services, and many have been reorganized as commercial banks.

Savings and Loan Associations

Saving and loan associations (S&Ls) have existed for many years. These financial institutions became popular during the Great Depression of the 1930s. At that time, many commercial banks suffered losses on consumer loans that had not been repaid, so they began to specialize in business loans. Consumers found it difficult to get the financial services they wanted from commercial banks. As a result, they turned to savings and loan associations.

Savings and loan associations are financial institutions that specialize in lending money to consumers to buy homes. Like savings banks, some S&Ls are owned by their depositors. S&Ls accept deposits and pay interest or dividends on them.

Today, S&Ls offer most of the services that used to be available only from commercial banks. They provide checking and savings accounts and make loans to businesses. Most S&Ls are still relatively small and remain the chief source of home loans for consumers.

Credit Unions

Credit unions are financial institutions that offer memberships to people who share a common bond, such as people in a particular

© Jeff Greenburg

profession, company, church, or labor union. When you deposit money in a credit union, you become a member and owner of the financial institution.

Not for Profit   Credit unions do not operate for a profit. They exist solely to provide saving and lending services to their members. They offer savings and checking accounts and make loans. Credit unions generally pay slightly higher interest rates to depositors than do other financial institutions. They also charge lower rates to borrowers.

There are a few limitations on the services credit unions offer. They do not allow all consumers to join. People who are not part of the group that formed the credit union are not able to use its services. Credit unions do not make business loans. Still, high interest rates for deposits and low rates for loans make credit unions a good choice for people who qualify to be members.

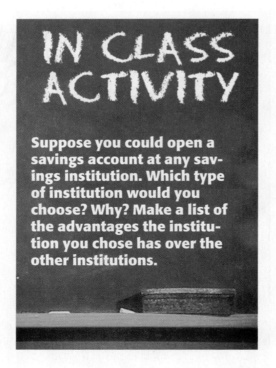

Suppose you could open a savings account at any savings institution. Which type of institution would you choose? Why? Make a list of the advantages the institution you chose has over the other institutions.

In the past, some banks refused to lend money to people who lived in poor or high-crime areas of cities. This practice was called *redlining.* Banks argued that property values in these areas were going down and they were afraid loans they made would not be repaid. Laws have been passed to try to stop redlining, but they have not been totally successful. Do you think all consumers should have an equal opportunity to borrow? Why or why not?

Deposit Insurance

A major reason for depositing money in a financial institution is safety. Financial institutions, like any other businesses, can fail. If your savings institution goes out of business, what happens to your deposit?

Most deposits in savings institutions are insured by agencies of the federal government. The Federal Deposit Insurance Corporation (FDIC) insures money deposited in most commercial and savings banks. Deposits made in S&Ls are insured by the Saving Association Insurance Fund (SAIF). The National Credit Union Share Insurance Fund (NCUSIF) provides the same protection for deposits in credit unions.

Consumers who deposit $100,000 or less in insured accounts have essentially no chance of losing their savings. If the institution fails, the insuring agency will repay depositors. When you shop for a financial institution, ask about its deposit insurance. An institution that is insured by a government agency is generally safer than one insured by a private organization.

CheckPoint

What is the difference between commercial banks and savings and loan associations? What are the advantages of a credit union? What makes savings deposits safe?

Savings Accounts

Savings accounts are accounts offered by any banking institution in which you can deposit money,

earn interest on your deposits, and withdraw your money at any time. Banking institutions offer an array of account options to fit different saving habits. You need only a small deposit to open an account—often as little as $50 or $100.

No matter what savings account you choose, you will be able to withdraw your money at any time. You will also earn interest on your deposit for the length of time you leave it in the account.

Interest Rates

One major consideration in selecting a savings account is the interest rate. In general, if you can keep $1,000 or more in a savings account, you can get a higher interest rate than if you can keep only a small balance.

Some accounts are designed so that people who save regularly can build an even larger balance. To encourage regular saving, these accounts might offer an interest rate that increases when your balance

reaches higher levels. If you plan to save this way, then consider this type of account after you accumulate the minimum required balance.

Fees and Restrictions

Besides the interest rate, accounts differ in their fees and restrictions. For example, some accounts charge a fee for using a teller rather than an ATM to withdraw money. If you plan to make several withdrawals per month using a teller, you may want to select an account that allows several free withdrawals or the smallest fee for withdrawals.

PRIMARY SOURCES

Read the following account of Raymond Tarver's life at the beginning of the Depression. During the Depression, many banks were closed and people lost their savings. Raymond Tarver worked as a clerk in a bank that was closed when there was no deposit insurance.

"Well, my turn came to be laid off. On my desk one morning I found a letter to that effect. Of course it read, 'With appreciation for my valuable service, deep regret, best wishes, etc.' But that didn't help my feelings much. My job was gone and my savings too. Except for the time I served during the war, that was the first day I was without a job since I was just a boy."

What would happen to his savings today if his bank were closed? What do you think happened to depositors in the 1980s who had savings in S&Ls?

TRY THESE

1. What are the four basic types of savings institutions in the U.S.?

2. Why did savings and loan associations grow in popularity during the Great Depression?

3. Why might a credit union be a good choice for your savings if you can qualify to be a member?

4. Why are deposits in savings institutions so safe?

5. What should you consider when choosing the bank and savings account that are best for you?

6. Why do savings accounts play a key role in an overall saving plan?

THINK CRITICALLY

7. **CONSUMER ACTION** Lisa wants to save regularly and to deposit her money where it will be safe and earn income. She also wants to be able to withdraw her money at any time. How should she choose a savings institution? What kinds of savings accounts should she consider?

8. In recent years, different types of savings institutions have become more alike in the kinds of services they offer. Why do you think this trend is happening?

9. Why do you think savings institutions sometimes charge fees for using tellers instead of ATMs to make savings account transactions?

10. **COMMUNICATE** What should you consider in selecting a savings institution? If your town has a small local bank and a branch of a large national bank, what would you consider in making your choice? Explain your reasoning in an e-mail and send it to your teacher.

11. Make a chart comparing the various types of institutions that offer savings accounts. Compare the interest rates, accessibility, and other features of the savings institutions.

DECISION MAKING PROJECT

SPECIFY   **SEARCH**   SIFT   SELECT   STUDY

SEARCH Assign a local savings institution to each group member. Each person should find out the following from the assigned institution.

1. How many kinds of savings accounts the institution offers
2. The fees for using each account
3. Any other terms for using savings accounts at that institution
4. The current interest rate on each type of account and on government bonds if the institution sells them

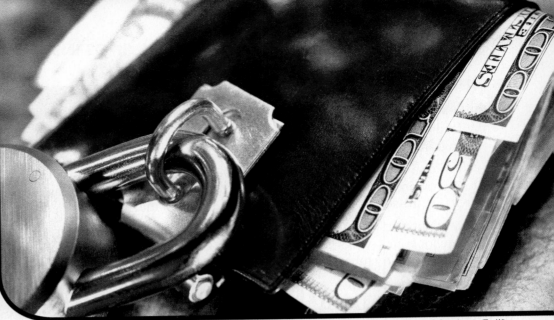

© Getty Images/EyeWire

8.3 Save with Safety

Savings Options

Savings accounts are a safe way to save and earn interest. Banks offer other accounts that are as safe as savings accounts but pay higher interest, however. The most common are certificates of deposit and money market accounts.

Certificate of Deposit

When you make a deposit in a savings account, your bank doesn't know how long it will have use of this money. You might leave your money there for months or years or for only a few days. Therefore, your bank is limited in what it can do with this money. It can use the money to make short-term investments, so that it has the money available for you whenever you decide to withdraw it. The bank can't earn as much from these short-term investments as it could from longer investments, so it pays you a relatively low interest rate for your savings account deposit.

If your bank knew that it would have your deposit for a long period of time, it could invest the money in

CONSUMER ACTION

Fernando recently inherited $5,000. He plans to use this money to help pay his college expenses in two years. He has no other savings. He does not want to risk losing any part of his inheritance. Still, he would like to earn more than a savings account pays. What alternative ways to save can he choose?

ways that would earn higher income. For this reason, banks pay you a higher interest rate if you promise to leave your money on deposit for several months or years.

A **certificate of deposit (CD)** is a deposit in a savings institution that earns a fixed interest rate for a specified period of time. Banks offer CDs for various time periods, ranging from a few months to several years. During the specified time period, you may not withdraw your money without paying a substantial penalty.

Interest Rate In exchange for your commitment to leave your money on deposit in the CD, the bank pays you a higher interest rate than it pays on regular savings accounts. For most CDs, this rate remains the same throughout the term of the CD. In general, the longer the time period of the CD you choose, the higher the interest rate.

The fixed interest rate is good news and bad news. The good news is that you are guaranteed this rate. If interest rates for other saving options go down during your CD's term, your rate stays high. The bad news is that if interest rates for other saving options go up during this time, you can't move your money to a higher interest option without paying a penalty.

Minimum Deposit CDs also require a minimum deposit. This amount may be as little as $500 or as much as several thousand dollars. In general, the larger the minimum deposit required by the CD, the higher the interest rate.

Penalty for Early Withdrawal When you purchase a CD, you agree to leave the money on deposit for the time specified. If you must withdraw

© Getty Images/EyeWire

your money early, you can do so. But the penalty is substantial—often as much as six months' interest.

Safety Most CDs are insured by the FDIC or other organizations for amounts up to $100,000. This makes them as safe as deposits in regular savings accounts.

Money Market Account

A **money market account** is a deposit for which the interest rate changes over time. The bank uses the money to make short-term investments. As interest rates in the economy change, the income the bank can earn on its investments also changes. When rates go up, the bank makes more and will pay you more for your money market account deposit. When the rates go down, the bank makes less and pays you less for your deposit.

Interest Rate In general, money market accounts pay higher interest rates than regular savings accounts, but they pay lower rates than certificates of deposit. Banks may also offer several money market accounts that pay different interest rates, depending on the amount deposited. The more you keep in the account, the higher the interest rate.

Minimum Deposit Money market accounts usually require a substantial minimum deposit—often as much as $1,000 to $2,000 to open an account. For the higher interest levels, the minimum might be $5,000 or more.

Flexibility The major benefit of a money market account is that you may withdraw your money at any time without penalty. Some banks even offer a money market checking account so that you can withdraw your money by writing checks. Most likely, though, your checking activities will have restrictions. For example, you may be able to write only a certain number of checks per month.

Safety In most banks, your deposit in a money market account is insured by the FDIC, so the only risk you take with a money market account is that the interest rate might go down. Your earnings may go down at times.

CheckPoint

Why might you choose a money market account over a CD?

Annual Percentage Yield

At one time, it was difficult to compare interest rates among accounts. Different banks had different ways of figuring the interest rates they paid. For example, some banks paid interest four times a year. Others paid interest every day.

Buy the Numbers?

Suppose you have $2,000 to deposit in a bank. This is all the money you have, so you know you will have to pay your bills with at least some of this money. You have a job, so money is coming in. Still, you would feel more comfortable if you have $1,000 of this money available to pay living expenses.

Your bank offers a CD with a $1,000 minimum deposit at 4 percent interest for six months. The bank also offers a money market account that pays 2.5 percent interest right now. A regular savings account pays 2 percent interest.

With the money market account, you can withdraw funds three times per month without a fee. Additional withdrawals have a $2 fee. The bank's regular checking account pays no interest. You can write checks in any amount, and you can write as many as you want without fees.

What would you do with your $2,000? There is no one right answer in this situation. Explain what you considered in making your decision. Why did you make the choice you did?

© Getty Images/EyeWire

Suppose you had money in an account that paid 4 percent interest. A bank down the street also paid 4 percent. The accounts paid the same, right? If your bank paid the interest four times per year and the one down the street paid it every day, then you would actually earn more by switching banks.

This situation confused depositors. They could not determine which accounts actually paid more. To solve this problem, Congress passed the Truth in Savings Act in 1993.

This law requires banks to report the **annual percentage yield (APY)** for their accounts. The APY is the actual interest rate an account pays per year. All banks are required to figure this rate in the same way. Now you can compare account options easily. If your bank pays 4 percent APY and the bank down the street pays 4 percent APY, then the accounts really do pay the same.

CheckPoint

Why do you need to know the APY on the accounts you are considering?

Government Bonds

The U.S. government gets the money it spends from taxes and borrowing. The government has often spent more than it has collected in taxes. To make up the difference to be able to pay for its programs, the government has had to borrow the amount. Where does the government borrow money? Some of it comes from consumers like you!

Governments and businesses borrow money by selling bonds. A **bond** is a written promise to pay a debt by a specified date. When you buy a bond from the U.S. government, it owes you the amount you paid plus interest.

Most bonds are issued for a specified time or *term.* The term may be as little as three months or as long as ten years. At the end of its term, the bond has matured and the government repays it. You don't need to own your bond for its entire term. You can sell it at any time.

U.S. government bonds are almost absolutely safe. They will be paid as long as the United States is a nation.

Treasury Securities

U.S. Treasury securities are usually sold in amounts of $5,000 or more. These investments are safe and often pay higher interest rates than CDs.

There are two types of Treasury securities that have different terms.

▶ *Treasury bills* have terms of less than one year.

▶ *Treasury notes* have terms that last from one to ten years.

CYBER CONSUMER

You can find out how much a savings bond is worth fast . . .online. Go to the U.S. Treasury's Kids site at www.ustreas.gov/kids. Click the link to the bond calculator. Then you can enter different dates of purchase and see how fast the bond grows over time.

IN CLASS ACTIVITY

Create a table showing each savings option and how it compares with other savings options. List the savings options in one column, and use characteristics of savings options as row headings. Compare your table to those of other students or groups in your class.

Savings Bonds

Even if you have only a little money to save, you can buy savings bonds.

The U.S. government sells Series EE and I **savings bonds** in amounts of $50 to $10,000 through commercial banks, savings and loans, credit unions, and post offices.

Series EE Savings Bonds

These bonds are available in amounts from $50 to $10,000. The amount printed on a bond is its **face value**. EE bonds actually sell for only half of their face value. If you buy a $50 bond, you pay $25.

The U.S. Treasury determines EE bonds' interest rate, which varies and is paid every six months.

You must own an EE bond for at least one year. The longer you own it, the more value it has. Over time, it will reach its face value. If you keep it, the bond continues to earn interest for up to 30 years. You can't sell it, but you can cash it in at any bank.

Series HH Savings Bonds

Until August 2004, HH bonds could be exchanged for EE bonds that had matured. Their interest rate was fixed and paid twice each year. The Treasury stopped issuing HH bonds because very few people traded their EE bonds for them. Those who already hold HH bonds will continue to receive interest and be repaid when they mature.

I Savings Bonds These bonds pay interest adjusted for inflation,

from which the name comes. The government sets a new rate every six months equal to the rate of inflation plus a fixed amount, which recently has been 1.0 percent. This set rate assures savers that the interest they earn on I bonds will always be higher than the inflation rate. Rates for any savings bond are available at the government web site at www.savingsbonds.gov.

Why Buy Government Bonds?

Government bonds have tax advantages. Owners must pay federal, state, and local government taxes on the interest of most saving options, but there are no state or local taxes on government bond interest. The federal tax on Series EE and I savings bonds is due only when they are cashed. Interest on savings bonds may not be taxed if the funds pay for higher education. It is easy to trade bonds for cash. The federal government doesn't pay off its bonds before their terms end, but they can be sold before their terms are up.

Government bonds are among the safest investments since the federal government guarantees payment.

CheckPoint

Why would you want to lend money to the government?

TRY THESE

1. Why might you choose not to invest in a certificate of deposit?

2. What trade-offs do you make when you choose a CD instead of a savings account?

3. Why do money market account rates change over time?

4. Why might you select a money market account over a CD?

5. What does the Truth in Savings Act of 1993 require banks to provide?

6. What is a bond?

7. What causes many savers to buy I savings bonds?

THINK CRITICALLY

8. **CONSUMER ACTION** Fernando wants to save his inheritance with little risk. Write a paragraph explaining some savings options. What should he consider?

9. Which savings options would you consider if you need the flexibility to withdraw money whenever you want?

10. Why do you think CDs, money market accounts, and savings bonds pay higher interest rates than savings accounts?

11. Which savings options would you consider if you don't plan to use the money for at least a year?

12. **COMMUNICATE** Write a paragraph explaining the trade-offs in selecting a CD, money market account, or savings bond over a savings account. E-mail your answer to your teacher.

© Getty Images/PhotoDisc

8.4 Simple and Compound Interest

Simple Interest

The way your bank calculates interest on your savings helps determine how fast your savings will grow. The money you have on deposit in a savings account, CD, or other savings option is called the **principal**. Interest is calculated on the principal.

After the bank pays the interest to your account, you can choose to withdraw it or leave it in the account. If you leave it in your account, then the interest is added to the principal.

The result is your new principal for the next period.

Simple interest is interest paid one time a year at the end of the year on the average balance in a savings account. It is the amount you earn on just the money you deposit, not on any previous interest earned.

Suppose you deposit $100 in an account that pays 6 percent simple interest per year. At the end of the year, the bank will pay you $6 interest, $100 × 0.06 = $6.

CONSUMER ACTION

Carl has $1,500 he wants to save for college. As he is shopping for an account to open, he encounters many options. Some offer simple interest. Others offer compound interest. Some compound monthly. Others compound daily. All the explanations just confuse him. Does the way interest is calculated really matter? What should he look for in selecting an account?

If you leave the interest in your account, your new principal would then be $106.

$100 deposit + $6 interest = $106

Often, interest rates are stated in fractions, such as $\frac{1}{2}$ percent and $3\frac{1}{2}$ percent. To calculate the interest using fractions, first convert the fraction to a decimal.

$\frac{1}{2}\% = 0.5\%$ $3\frac{1}{2}\% = 3.5\%$

Then, move the decimal point to the left two places to change the percent to a decimal.

$0.5\% = 0.05$ $3.5\% = 0.035$

Now you are ready to calculate simple interest as you did earlier. If you deposit $100 at $3\frac{1}{2}$ percent simple interest per year, your calculations would look like this.

$100 × 0.035 = $3.50 interest

At the end of the year, your new principal would be $103.50.

$100 + $3.50 = $103.50

CheckPoint

What is simple interest? How do you calculate simple interest expressed as a fraction?

Compound Interest

Compound interest is interest paid on the principal and on previously earned interest, assuming that the interest is left in the account. It is interest you earn not only on the money you deposit but also on the interest your money earned previously. For example, suppose you earned $6 of interest last year on your $100 initial deposit at 6 percent simple interest. If you leave the interest in the account, it will be added to your $100 principal. Your new principal would be $106.

$MATH OF MONEY

Suppose you have $750 to deposit into a savings account at the given simple interest rates per year. In each case, how much would you have in your account at the end of the year?

SOLUTION

Deposit	Rate	Amount of Simple Interest	New Principal After 1 Year
$750	3%	$750 × 0.03 = $22.50	$750 + $22.50 = $772.50
$750	$4\frac{1}{2}\%$	$750 × 0.045 = $33.75	$750 + $33.75 = $783.75
$750	$6\frac{3}{4}\%$	$750 × 0.0675 = $50.63	$750 + $50.63 = $800.63

The following year, the 6 percent interest rate would be applied to this new principal. Your earnings would be *compounded* because you would receive interest on the $6 interest earned last year as well as on your $100 initial deposit.

Interest can be compounded in several ways.

► annually—every year

► semiannually—every six months

► quarterly—every three months

► monthly

► daily

The more often interest is compounded, the more interest your money earns.

Compound Annually

The $6 of interest was added to the account at the end of the year. In this case, the interest was *compounded annually.* If you left the interest in your account each year, you would have $112.36 at the end of two years.

Year One
$100.00	principal
× 0.06	interest rate annually
6.00	interest, first year

$100.00	principal
+ 6.00	interest, first year
$106.00	principal, end of first year

Year Two
$106.00	principal, end of first year
× 0.06	interest rate annually
$6.36	interest, second year

$106.00	principal, end of first year
+ 6.36	interest, second year
$112.36	principal, end of second year

Compound Semiannually

Interest rates are stated as annual rates. To calculate interest compounded more than once a year, you must divide the annual rate by the number of times during the year that interest will be compounded.

Suppose the annual rate is 6 percent. If interest will be compounded twice a year, or semiannually, then divide the rate by 2. You would multiply your principal by 0.03 or 3 percent.

Year One
$100.00	principal
× 0.03	interest rate for ½ year
3.00	interest, first ½ year

$100.00	principal
+ 3.00	interest, first ½ year
$103.00	principal, end of first ½ year

$103.00	principal
× 0.03	interest rate for ½ year
$3.09	interest, second ½ year

$103.00	principal
+ 3.09	interest, second ½ year
$106.09	principal, end of first year

Year Two
$106.09	principal
× 0.03	interest rate for ½ year
$3.18	interest, third ½ year, rounded

$106.09	principal
+ 3.18	interest, third ½ year
$109.27	principal, end of 1½ years

$109.27	principal
× 0.03	interest rate for ½ year
$3.28	interest, fourth ½ year, rounded

$109.27	principal
+ 3.28	interest, fourth ½ year
$112.55	principal, end of second year

© Getty Images/PhotoDisc

In this example, the difference between annual and semiannual compounding resulted in more in your account at the end of two years.

$112.55   principal semiannual
−112.36   principal annual
  $0.19   more earned with semiannual

Compound Daily

Most banks compound daily, sometimes stated as *continuously*. This means that your interest is calculated and added to your principal each day. Then, the next day's interest is calculated on the new principal. You get interest each day on the previous day's interest. With daily compounding, your savings will grow the fastest. In addition, if you make regular deposits during the year, compound interest will increase these savings as well.

As the amount you have saved grows, you can move some money to higher-paying investments. Regular saving, high interest rates, and frequent compounding are key elements of a successful saving plan.

What In The World?

In 2005, many banks in Japan paid as little as 0.5 percent simple interest on savings deposits each year. If you lived in Japan and made a deposit of 10,000 yen (the Japanese currency), how many yen would you receive in interest at this rate? What might this interest rate do to the willingness of Japanese people to save?

Calculate Compound Interest Using a Table

Banks use computer programs to calculate compound interest. You can simplify your calculations by using a compound interest table.

The table lists the value of one dollar at several percentage rates, compounded daily for different periods of time. You can calculate the new value of your principal with one simple calculation.

Suppose you deposit $2,000 at 10 percent compounded daily. You plan to withdraw the money in four years. How much money will you have in your account after four years?

Read down the 10 percent column and across the row for four years. The number is 1.492. Multiply your $2,000 deposit by this value.

$$\$2,000 \times 1.492 = \$2,984$$

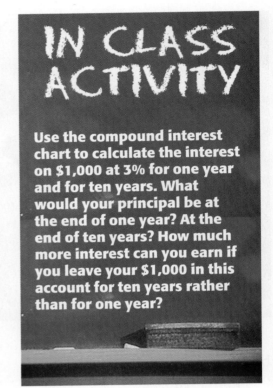

IN CLASS ACTIVITY

Use the compound interest chart to calculate the interest on $1,000 at 3% for one year and for ten years. What would your principal be at the end of one year? At the end of ten years? How much more interest can you earn if you leave your $1,000 in this account for ten years rather than for one year?

The result, $2,984, is the money you will have in your account after four years. To find out how much interest you will have earned in four years, subtract your original deposit from the final amount.

$$\$2,984 - \$2,000 = \$984$$

COMPOUND INTEREST TABLE Value of $1 at 3%, 6%, and 10% Interest, Compounded Daily			
Year	3%	6%	10%
1	1.030	1.062	1.105
2	1.062	1.127	1.221
3	1.094	1.197	1.350
4	1.127	1.271	1.492
5	1.162	1.350	1.649
6	1.197	1.433	1.822
7	1.234	1.522	2.014
8	1.271	1.616	2.225
9	1.310	1.716	2.459
10	1.350	1.822	2.718

The Rule of 72

One of the easiest ways to calculate the effects of compounding is the *Rule of 72*. This rule says that if an asset grows x % a year, its value will double in $72 \div x$ years. So to find how long it takes an investment to double, divide 72 by the annual rate of return. For example, how long will it take for an investment earning an annual rate of return of 10 percent to double in value?

$$72 \div 10 = 7.2 \text{ years}$$

Use APY to Evaluate Options

Different methods of compounding previously made it difficult for consumers to compare accounts offered by different banks. Now they can easily compare by using the bank's annual percentage yield.

It makes no difference how often interest is compounded. By comparing APYs, you can evaluate differences between account rates easily.

CheckPoint

Does it matter how often your bank compounds the interest on your account? Why or why not?

TRY THESE

1. What is an account's principal?

2. What is the difference between simple and compound interest?

3. Why does an account that compounds interest daily pay more interest than an account that compounds monthly?

4. How does APY help you evaluate saving options?

THINK CRITICALLY

5. CONSUMER ACTION Carl is confused by all the ways interest is calculated. What should he look for in judging his account options? Explain the differences among compounding methods.

6. MATH OF MONEY Suppose you open a savings account that pays $4\frac{3}{4}$ percent simple interest annually on a $75 deposit. How much money will you have at the end of the year?

7. MATH OF MONEY Calculate the simple interest you would earn on $8,000 deposited for one year at 6 percent interest. Then use the compound interest table to calculate the interest you would earn on $8,000 deposited for one year at 6 percent interest that is compounded daily for one year. Calculate the difference between the interest earned using simple versus compound interest.

DECISION MAKING PROJECT

 SPECIFY   **SEARCH**   **SIFT**   **SELECT**   **STUDY**

SIFT   Have each group member recommend one method of saving from the assigned savings institution. The presentation should demonstrate how this method will fulfill your specified needs for a savings method and earn the most for your money.

Chapter 8

ASSESSMENT

KEY IDEAS

Why Save?

1. Saving is a trade-off. You trade spending now for the ability to spend in the future. The purpose of saving is to cover future expenses whether you can see them coming or not.

2. Your future will include many unexpected expenses and opportunities. You can save for a major purchase or save to give yourself flexibility in your life choices. Saving will help you meet your goals in life.

3. Having self-control can help you save. One saving strategy is to pay yourself first. Another is to reward yourself for each deposit. If your income is uneven, plan to save a percentage of your income rather than a specific amount.

4. You may be able to set up an automatic saving plan with your employer or bank.

Savings Institutions and Accounts

5. Commercial banks offer the widest range of financial services.

6. Savings banks are small savings institutions that are owned by their depositors.

7. Savings and loan associations specialize in lending to consumers to buy homes. They now offer a wide array of banking services similar to commercial banks.

8. Credit unions exist to provide financial services to their members.

9. Savings accounts are accounts offered by any savings institution into which you can deposit money, earn interest, and withdraw your money at any time.

Accounts differ in their interest rates, fees, and restrictions.

10. Almost all deposits are insured by a federal government agency.

Save with Safety

11. Certificates of deposit and money market accounts pay higher interest. Both CDs and money market accounts require a minimum balance. A CD requires you to keep the money on deposit for a specified time or pay a substantial interest penalty for early withdrawal.

12. CDs offer a fixed rate of interest. A money market account's interest rate changes, but you can withdraw your money at any time. Some banks even offer money market checking accounts, but there may be high minimum balance requirements.

13. The Truth in Savings Act of 1993 requires banks to report the annual percentage yield (APY) for their accounts. APY is figured the same way by all banks.

14. The U.S. government borrows money by selling bonds. A bond is a written promise to pay a debt by a specified date.

15. Savings bonds are U.S. government bonds issued for amounts of $50 to $10,000. You can buy Series EE or I savings bonds. Other government bonds include Treasury bills and Treasury notes.

16. The major advantages of government bonds are their safety, tax savings, and ease of converting to cash.

Simple and Compound Interest

17. An account's principal is the amount on deposit. Simple interest is the amount you earn on only your principal, not on any interest earned previously. To calculate simple interest, multiply the deposit by the interest rate. To determine the amount in the account at the end of the interest period, add the simple interest to the initial deposit.

18. Compound interest is interest on interest. It is interest you earn not only on your principal but also on the interest your money earned.

19. Interest can be compounded annually, semiannually, quarterly, monthly, or daily. The more often interest is compounded, the more interest you make.

20. To calculate compound interest, divide the annual rate by the number of times the interest will compound per year. Multiply the resulting rate by your principal to get the interest for that period. Add the interest to the principal to find the new principal for calculating the next period's interest. You can also use a compound interest table to do the calculations.

21. The higher the rate of interest, the more interest your money will earn.

22. You can evaluate savings account options by using the APY.

TERMS REVIEW

Match each term on the left with its definition on the right.
Some terms may not be used.

a. annual percentage yield (APY)

b. bond

c. certificate of deposit (CD)

d. commercial bank

e. compound interest

f. credit union

g. dividend

h. face value

i. money market account

j. principal

k. saving

l. savings account

m. savings and loan association

n. savings bank

o. savings bond

p. simple interest

1. deposit in a savings institution that earns a fixed interest rate for a specified period of time

2. interest paid on the principal and on previously earned interest, assuming that the interest is left in the account

3. financial institution that serves individuals and businesses with a wide variety of savings accounts, loans, and other services

4. portion of a company's profits paid to the owners

5. financial institution that is owned by its depositors

6. interest paid one time a year at the end of the year on the average balance in a savings account

7. financial institution that specializes in lending money to buy homes

8. the dollar value printed on a bond

9. financial institution that offers memberships and provides services to its members

10. trading current spending for the ability to spend in the future

11. written promise to pay a debt by a specified date

12. account at a savings institution in which you may deposit money, earn interest, and withdraw your money at any time

13. the actual interest rate an account pays per year

14. money on deposit

CONSUMER DECISIONS

15. Suppose your take-home pay from your part-time job is $50 a week. How much of this amount would you choose to save each week? Why would this be the right choice for you?

16. You would like to save $25 from your paycheck each week. What strategy would you use to encourage yourself to save regularly? Why would this strategy work for you?

17. Assume that you have been working full time for four years and have accumulated $5,000 in your savings account. You would like to save some or all of this money in other ways that earn more interest. Which saving options would you choose? How much money would you put in each saving option? Why?

LOOK IT UP!

18. The interest rates banks pay have changed considerably over the years. Find the *Statistical Abstract of the United States* in your public library. Use this publication to find the rate banks have paid on one-year CDs in five recent years. Use these data to construct a graph that shows changes in interest rates.

19. Investigate the interest paid by competing local banks for savings accounts. Are these rates almost the same or quite different? Are you surprised by what you found? Why or why not?

20. Many compound interest calculators are available on the Web. Search using the key words *interest calculator* to find one. Plug in a principal of $5,000 at 8 percent interest compounded monthly. Then calculate the balance for each after 5 years, 10 years, and 15 years. What do your results tell you about the effects of compounding over longer time periods?

INSIDE THE NUMBERS

21. Suppose you have $1,000 you could deposit. Your bank is now paying 5 percent interest on a one-year CD, 6 percent on a five-year CD, and 4½ percent on a money market account. Which choice would you make? Why?

22. Suppose you have $1,000 to deposit. One account offers 6.1 percent interest compounded once a year. Another account offers 6 percent compounded daily. Use the table on page 280 and the process from page 278 to calculate how much each account would have at the end of four years. What do your answers tell you about the power of compounding?

WHICH IS THE BEST DEAL?

Assume that you want to deposit $2,000 in a savings account for two years. Your community has two banks:

Bank A This bank pays interest at a rate of 3 percent that is compounded once a year. It is located across the street from your home.

Bank B This bank pays interest at a rate of 3 percent that is compounded daily. It is located two miles from your home.

How much would your savings be worth after two years at each bank? What else would you consider in your decision? Which bank would you choose? Why?

23. Suppose you want to buy a laptop computer for college in three years. You believe you will be able to buy a good one at that time for $1,600. You have saved $1,400. A local bank is offering a three-year CD that pays 6 percent interest, compounded daily. Use the Savings Planner to determine whether you will have $1,600 to pay for your computer in three years if you deposit your $1,400 in this CD now. How much more or less will you have?

24. Suppose you had $1,000 that you could put into a savings option. Create the characteristics of this savings option, such as its interest rate. How much interest would you earn after five years?

THINK CRITICALLY

25. Suppose you have $2,000. Your bank pays 6 percent interest compounded daily on three-year CDs. Your brother wants to borrow your $2,000 and offers to pay you $2,500 at the end of three years. Which use of your money would earn the most interest? Which option would you choose? Why?

CURRICULUM CONNECTION

26. **HISTORY** In Europe in the Middle Ages, paying or receiving interest was thought to be immoral. Investigate how changes in this attitude contributed to the beginning of the Renaissance.

27. **HISTORY** Investigate the history of deposit insurance. Find out why the Federal Deposit Insurance Corporation was established in the 1930s. How does the FDIC benefit consumers today?

28. **BUSINESS** Banking is a very competitive industry. How do banks try to attract customers? Find advertisements for three different banks. How is each bank portrayed by its ad? What main benefits do they seem to be offering potential customers?

JOURNAL RECAP

29. After reading this chapter, review the answers you wrote to the questions in Journal Journey. Have your opinions changed?

DECISION MAKING PROJECT

SPECIFY   **SEARCH**   **SIFT**   **SELECT**   **STUDY**

SELECT Decide which saving method you think will best fulfill your needs. Write a short paragraph stating how your group chose a saving plan. Show how your chosen method will earn you more interest than the next best alternative.

STUDY Present your paragraph on the process your group went through to choose a savings method. Did any other group have the same requirements of saving that your group had? Did any other group choose the same method? Did they have the same or different reasons?

Chapter

9

INVESTING
PREPARE FOR YOUR FUTURE

WHAT'S AHEAD

EXPLODING MYTHS

Fact or Myth?
What do you think is true?

1. If you invest carefully, you don't have to take risks.

2. If you invest in corporate stocks, you will always earn more than if you deposit your money in a bank.

3. The only way to invest in an assortment of stocks and bonds is to have lots of money.

JOURNAL JOURNEY

WRITE IN YOUR JOURNAL ABOUT THE FOLLOWING.

YOUR RISK PROFILE What are some choices you made lately? Did you take the more risky or less risky options? How does your level of comfort with risk affect the choices you make in your life?

MAKING INVESTMENT DECISIONS Would you study investment options before making your own decisions? Or would you rather pay someone else to manage your investments? Why?

INVESTING IN REAL ESTATE If you had the opportunity to buy a cabin in the mountains that you could rent to other people, would you buy it? How could the cabin benefit you? What problems could it cause you?

DECISION MAKING PROJECT

SPECIFY   **SEARCH**   **SIFT**   **SELECT**   **STUDY**

INVEST IN YOURSELF Your group will decide the best place to invest $2,000. Establish your investing goals, discover your risk tolerance, research investment options, and devise your investment strategy.

GOAL

To learn how to choose investments

PROJECT PROCESS

SPECIFY	Lesson 9.1
SEARCH	Lesson 9.4
SIFT	Lesson 9.5
SELECT	Chapter Assessment
STUDY	Chapter Assessment

9.1 Investing Basics

What Is Investing?

There are many ways to save, including tossing money into your sock drawer. If you choose to save in a way that earns income, you are **investing**.

Savings accounts, CDs, money market accounts, and government bonds are all forms of investing. You also have a wide variety of other investment choices that have potential for earning more than these options, but, as with other consumer choices, investment decisions involve trade-offs. To have a chance to make more income on your investments, you must be willing to accept more risk.

Risk and Rate of Return

The chance that an investment will decrease in value is **risk**. All investments involve some risk, although bank accounts and government bonds are nearly risk free. If you

CONSUMER ACTION

Tyra has been saving regularly since she started working. Now she has $20,000 in her savings account, which pays 3 percent interest. Tyra thinks it is time to invest her savings in some way that earns more income. But how? She doesn't like to take big risks, but she is willing to take an informed risk to earn more. What should she consider in making her investment decisions? How can she minimize her financial risk?

deposit money in an FDIC-insured savings account and the bank fails, the FDIC will return your deposit.

If you invest in a business, there is no guarantee that the business will earn a profit. In fact, if the business fails, you could lose your entire investment. You will not receive a set interest rate. If, however, the business does well, your investment will probably earn more than would a savings account.

The income you earn on an investment is called your **return**. Rate of return is measured as a percentage of the amount invested. Suppose you invest $1,000 in a bicycle repair business. At the end of one year, you receive $100 as your share of the company's profit. The $100 is 10 percent of your $1,000 investment.

$$\frac{\$100}{\$1,000} = 0.1 = 10\%$$

The $100 is your return. The 10 percent is your rate of return. A 10 percent rate of return is more than banks generally pay their depositors.

Suppose banks are paying 4 percent interest on deposits. Your rate of return from investing in the bicycle business is 6 percent higher. The opportunity to earn this higher rate of return is the reason you did not deposit your money in an insured bank account.

Risk/Return Pyramid

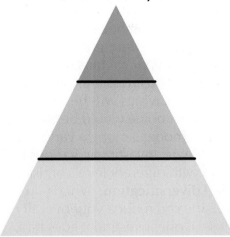

You did well with your investment in the bicycle business this year. There is no guarantee, however, that the business will continue to succeed. Next year, the business may have new competition. Its costs may increase or its sales may fall. It could earn no profit at all. If so, you may receive little or no return on your investment. If the business fails, you could even lose the $1,000 you invested.

Evaluate Your Risks

A general rule of investing is *the higher the potential rate of return, the greater the risk.* If an investment is risky, the potential rate of return must be high to make it worth the risk.

For some investment options, the risk may be greater than you are willing to accept. Then you should choose not to invest in that option, no matter how high the possible rate of return. Remember that when you invest in something other than an insured account, you are not just risking your potential earnings. You could lose your entire investment as well.

© Getty Images/PhotoDisc

289

Limit Risk Through Diversification

Imagine that you have sacrificed to save for your retirement. You chose to invest all your savings in one business. If that business fails, all of your retirement savings will be lost.

A better choice would be to distribute your money among a variety of investments. Investing in various businesses with different levels of risk is called **diversification**. When you diversify, you reduce your overall risk of loss. If one investment goes bad, the others may do well, and you can still end up with a good overall return.

Suppose you place part of your savings in an investment that probably won't provide a large return, but there is little chance you will lose your money. To balance this low-risk, low-return investment, you can invest another part of your savings in a way that involves greater risks and a higher potential return.

As your financial needs change during your life span, you will probably want to invest a different percentage at different levels of risk. If you are young and have many income-earning years left, you may want to take more risks. You have more time to recover from any losses. If you are older and have most of the money you will need for retirement, you may not need or want to take many risks. Don't make risky investments with money you can't afford to lose.

CheckPoint

Why is investing your savings a better choice than hiding it under your bed? How are risk and rate of return related? How can you limit your risk?

$MATH OF MONEY

Suppose you bought 150 shares of stock at $2.50 per share last year. The corporation paid a $0.15 dividend per share for the year. At the end of the year, you sold the stock for $3.00 per share. What was the total return on this investment if you disregard fees? What rate of return did you earn on your initial investment?

SOLUTION

150 shares × $2.50 per share = $375 initial investment

150 shares × $0.15 dividend per share = $22.50 total dividend

150 shares × $3.00 per share = $450 price of stock sold

$450 price of stock sold − $375 initial investment = $75 capital gain

$75 capital gain + $22.50 total dividends = $97.50 total return

$97.50 total return ÷ $375 initial investment = 0.26 = 26% return

How to Make Investment Choices

There is no one right way to invest. Which investment choices are right for you depends on your personal financial situation.

Your Financial Situation

You may have few financial responsibilities now, but your life-span goals require money. If you lose your savings in a risky investment now, you may not quickly recover the lost money if you don't have a job or are working only part-time.

For some people, however, taking some financial risks makes sense. If you make a good salary and have a substantial amount to invest, risking some of your money for the chance at a high rate of return may be a good choice. If you lose your money on the risky investment, you will still have plenty left over. Your good salary also will help you recover your losses.

Nadine, for example, is a 36-year-old chemical engineer. She earns an excellent salary and has invested her savings regularly for many years. Nadine's low-risk investments are worth about $150,000. In Nadine's

VOTE Your Wallet

When you invest in a company, your investment choice is a vote in favor of the way that company operates. For years, environmental groups, civil rights groups, and consumer groups of all kinds have been telling their supporters to "put your money where your mouth is."

What do you feel strongly about? Animal testing? Recycling? Companies that contribute to your community?

Whatever you would like to support, you can find companies that share your values. Advocacy groups such as the Sierra Club publish the records of companies as well as candidates for office on certain issues. So if you have a strong belief about how companies should operate, check their records before you invest in, or vote for, them.

situation, it makes sense to accept more risk with *some* of her savings.

She might invest $5,000 in a new business that may or may not succeed. If the company is successful, she might earn a large return. Many new businesses fail, however, so the investment is risky. Even if Nadine loses all of her $5,000 investment, she will not be financially ruined. She has plenty of financial cushion to fall back on. She also has many working years left to save and invest for a comfortable retirement.

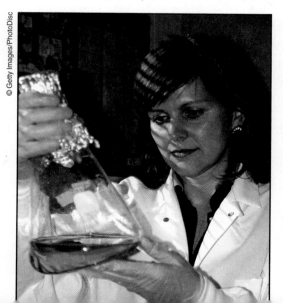

© Getty Images/PhotoDisc

Your Risk Tolerance

People tolerate risk differently. Some like to make risky choices and are comfortable with the uncertainties of risky investments. Others like to be safe and make the most conservative choices, avoiding the uncertainties of risky investments. Most people fall between these two extremes.

When you choose how to invest your savings, consider your risk level of comfort. If taking risks makes you nervous, make safer investments. Low-risk investments can make a good rate of return. No matter where you fall on the risk-tolerance scale, you can make investment choices that fit your comfort level.

Your investment risks are important to your family. Suppose that in ten years, you have a good job, are married, have three children, and want to help support your grandparents. If you have invested wisely, you will be better able to help them. If you have taken many risks and lost money, however, you might not even have enough to make ends meet. When you invest, remember

to consider more people than just yourself.

Your Values

You may want your investments to reflect your values. If your community is important to you, support it by investing in a business that builds new homes there. If you value social responsibility, you might invest in a company that uses recycled products. When you invest, remember your values. A financial return is not the only benefit from an investment.

IN CLASS ACTIVITY

List decisions you think are risky and those that aren't. What kind of investor would you be? Why?

CheckPoint

Why should you consider your financial situation, values, and risk tolerance in choosing investments?

TRY THESE

1. What is the difference between saving and investing?

2. What is an investment's rate of return, and how is it measured?

3. What is the relationship between risk and rate of return?

4. How does diversification limit your overall risk?

5. Why is your financial situation important to consider in making investment decisions?

6. If you don't like taking risks, what kinds of investments should you make?

7. What other benefits can you receive from an investment besides a monetary return?

THINK CRITICALLY

8. **CONSUMER ACTION** Tyra wants to earn more on her $20,000 savings than her savings account pays. She is not a big risk taker but is willing to take some risks. Explain to Tyra the trade-off between risk and rate of return. How can she minimize her investment risk?

9. Why do you think risky investments offer a higher potential rate of return? What would happen if a risky investment had only a small potential rate of return?

10. **MATH OF MONEY** You invested $2,500 in Awesome Software, Inc. The company did well that year, and you received a check for $300. What was your rate of rate of return on this investment?

11. Suppose you are thinking about making some risky investments. What should your financial situation be for risky investments to be a good choice?

12. **COMMUNICATE** Write about three values that would guide your investment strategy. What types of companies would you support? What types of companies would you avoid? Why? E-mail your answers to your teacher.

13. If you had money to invest, would you diversify your investments? Why or why not? What does this say about your risk tolerance?

14. **COMMUNICATE** Explain this general rule of investing: *The higher the potential rate of return, the greater the risk.*

DECISION MAKING PROJECT

SPECIFY · **SEARCH** · **SIFT** · **SELECT** · **STUDY**

SPECIFY What are your life-span goals for investing? How much will you need and when will you need it? How comfortable are you with risk? How will your values affect your investment decisions? Will you diversify?

Life-Span Plan

© Getty Images/PhotoDisc

9.2 How to Invest in Corporations

Corporate Stocks

By investing, you can actually become a part owner of a corporation. One way to invest in a corporation is to buy its stock. A **share of stock** is a unit of ownership in a corporation. **Stockholders** are the investors who own the corporation because they own shares of its stock. Even if you buy only one share, you are an owner of the corporation.

Corporations sell shares of stock to investors to raise money for the business. As an investor, you would buy shares of stock in the hope of earning a return on your investment. You probably believe that the corporation will make a profit. If it does, you may expect to receive part of the profit as a *dividend*. Dividend payments and any increase in the price of the shares of stock are both part of your return.

The amount of your return depends on how much profit the corporation makes, the price of the stock, and on how much stock you own. The more stock you own, the

CONSUMER ACTION

Mija's aunt gave her $5,000 on her twenty-first birthday. Mija decided to invest her gift in stocks. She had heard that she could make a higher rate of return by investing in stocks, but when she talked to a stockbroker, she was confused by all of the choices. What types of stock should she consider? Would bonds be a better option for her? What investment options should she choose?

more return you will receive if the corporation makes a profit. If it does not make a profit, you may get no return, and your investment may even become worthless.

Other people or businesses currently own almost all of the shares of stock you could buy. The first time a corporation sells shares of stock is the only time it receives any money from the transaction. After that, investors buy and sell shares of stock among themselves.

How Stock Exchanges Work

Investors can buy and sell stocks in two ways: through a stock exchange or an electronic system called *NASDAQ*.

Transactions, sales or purchases of shares, are usually conducted through a stock brokerage firm or a stockbroker. A **stockbroker** is a person who handles the transfer of stocks and bonds between buyer and seller. A **brokerage firm** is a company that specializes in helping people buy and sell stocks and bonds. Brokerage firms charge fees for their services. For small trades, these fees are typically between $50 and several hundred dollars. The fees are usually a small percentage of the total value of the transaction.

A **stock exchange** is where orders to buy or sell stock are sent and carried out. The largest is the New York Stock Exchange (NYSE), which is located on Wall Street in New York City.

Suppose you want to buy 100 shares of IBM stock. You could place your order at a local office of a brokerage firm, such as Merrill Lynch. The firm owns a membership in a

stock exchange that allows it to carry out trades on the exchange. Your buy order would be wired to the company's office at the NYSE in New York City.

© Getty Images/EyeWire

Now suppose another person owns 100 shares of IBM she wants to sell. She might place her sell order with a different brokerage firm. The order would be sent to that firm's office at the NYSE. Both brokerage firms would take their orders to a trading desk at the NYSE where IBM transactions are made. After the exchange is completed, both you and the seller would be notified.

In recent years, some online brokerage firms have offered to complete stock trades for as little as $7 per transaction, much lower than most brokers charge. These firms provide no investment advice to customers. Investors who use these online services must make their own investment decisions.

GUESS WHAT

There are days when more than two billion shares of stock are traded on the NYSE.

How to Trade on the NASDAQ

Developments in computer technology have resulted in a new way to buy and sell stock. In the 1990s, the National Association of Securities Dealers Automated Quotation System (NASDAQ) became the most common way to trade stock. **NASDAQ** electronically links brokerage firms.

Through this system, stocks can be bought or sold without using a central location.

NASDAQ has many advantages. It is less expensive to operate because users do not need to pay the cost of maintaining a central stock exchange. It is not limited by the space of a single building. Investors can trade more kinds of stock using NASDAQ. It is also able to operate for longer hours.

How can you buy stock in a corporation?

How Stockholders Earn Returns

If you own stock, you can earn returns from your investment in two ways: as dividends and by selling the stock. If the company makes a profit, you will probably receive a dividend as a return on your investment.

You can also earn a return by selling the stock. Suppose you bought 100 shares of stock for $2 per share. The total you invested is $200. A few months later, the stock is selling for $3 per share. If you sell the stock at $3 per share, you will earn a profit of $100 on the transaction, not including fees.

$3 × 100 shares = $300 selling price
$300 − $200 = $100 profit

The profit you earn from selling stock at a higher price than you paid for it is called a **capital gain**. For you to earn a capital gain, the stock must increase in value after you buy it.

What In The World?

For many years, China had a command economy. Businesses were owned and run by government. This changed in the 1980s when Chinese citizens and then foreigners were allowed to buy stock in these businesses. Millions of U.S. investors accepted large risks with these stocks.

The value of Chinese stocks fluctuated widely. The average value grew by 50 percent between May of 2003 and 2004. But in the four years prior, the value of Chinese stocks declined in every year. Many investors lost half of their investments. Is an investment in Chinese stocks right for you? Why, or why not?

That is, the selling price must go up. Your stock could decrease in value instead. If you sell your stock at a lower price than you paid for it, you lose money. The amount you lose is called a **capital loss**.

Why Stock Prices Change

The price of a corporation's stock at any point in time depends on what other people are willing to pay to buy it. Suppose a company is successful and earns large profits. Large profits usually mean high dividends. Because the dividends are high, more people want to own a company's stock. They are willing to pay more, so the price of its shares grows. The owners of the stock enjoy a capital gain if they sell their stock.

When a company is not successful, however, dividends are smaller and fewer people want to own its stock. To sell shares, current owners must offer to sell their stock at lower prices. If they sell their stock at a lower price than they paid for it, they take a capital loss.

Dollar Cost Averaging

Regular investing allows you to "dollar cost average." **Dollar cost averaging** means investing roughly equal amounts of money at regular intervals. Stock prices may move up or down, but when you spread your purchases out like this, you get more shares when the price is down. As a result, you will buy most of your shares at a price lower than the average price. The table illustrates how it works if you invest $25 a month for a year in Stock A.

The average cost per share ($300 ÷ 17.058 shares = $17.59) is less than the average price per share ($213 ÷

12 months = $17.75). The value of those 17.058 shares at the year-end price of $20.50 is $349.69. Since you paid $300 for them, you made $49.69, or a 16.56 percent gain.

Types of Stock

You can buy two types of corporate stock. Both make you a part owner in the corporation.

Preferred Stock

A nonvoting share that pays a fixed dividend is called **preferred stock**. No matter how well the company performs, preferred stockholders receive the same dividend unless the company suffers a loss. Preferred stockholders do not have the right to vote on how the company is run.

Common Stock   A voting share that does not pay a set dividend is called **common stock**. Each corporation's board of directors sets the dividend for common stock from year to year. The board of directors is chosen by the stockholders to oversee the operation of a company. The dividend that the board sets depends on the corporation's profits and its need for money to reinvest in the business.

Suppose a corporation's board wants to buy new equipment or develop new products. It might limit dividend payments so that it

Month	Amount Invested in Stock A	Stock Price	Shares Bought
1	$25.00	$15.00	1.666
2	$25.00	$15.50	1.612
3	$25.00	$16.00	1.562
4	$25.00	$16.50	1.515
5	$25.00	$17.00	1.470
6	$25.00	$17.50	1.428
7	$25.00	$18.00	1.388
8	$25.00	$18.50	1.351
9	$25.00	$19.00	1.315
10	$25.00	$19.50	1.282
11	$25.00	$20.00	1.250
12	$25.00	$20.50	1.219
Total	$300.00		17.058
Average	$25.00	$17.75	$17.59

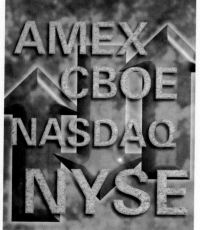

© Getty Images/PhotoDisc

has money to spend on these other uses. This choice should benefit stockholders in the long run. If investing in equipment or new products improves the corporation's profits, it will pay higher dividends in the future. Also, its success could cause its stock value to grow, and investors would benefit from the capital gain.

Common stockholders have the right to vote on important corporate decisions. They normally have one vote for each share they own.

What Should You Consider?
Preferred stock is less risky than common stock. If the company fails, or goes out of business, preferred stockholders receive their share of the company's assets before common stockholders. If no assets are left after paying preferred stockholders, common stockholders get nothing. Because it is somewhat riskier, however, common stock generally has a better return than preferred stock in the same corporation.

The price of common stock tends to change more than the price of preferred stock. Because of the frequent price changes, you have a better chance of earning a capital gain or suffering a loss with common stock than preferred stock.

When you invest in either common or preferred stock, keep in mind that the corporation is never required to repay your original investment. The only way you can get cash for your stock is to sell it to another investor.

How to Earn Returns

Corporations are not all equally successful. Some earn good profits. Some don't. Some corporations grow while others decline or fail. Some corporations fail even after a long period of good profits. Corporations operate in an ever-changing world. Mergers, new technology, new competition, and many other factors affect a corporation's performance.

There is no way to be sure which corporations will be successful and which will not. When you buy corporate stock, you cannot be sure what

Buy the Numbers?

The GMX Corporation owns a number of gold mines in the western United States. Its profits change with the price of gold. Imagine that gold is at its lowest price in many years. GMX is trying to raise funds by selling bonds, preferred stock, and common stock. The bonds will pay 9 percent interest. The preferred stock will pay a fixed dividend of 10 percent of its face value. Its common stock's dividends have decreased in recent years. Three years ago, the company paid dividends of $1.00 per share. The firm has not done well recently, so it pays only $0.50 a share now. The common stock is being offered at a price of $6.00 per share.

Consider each of these investment opportunities (bonds, common stock, preferred stock). What are the risks involved in each one? Which would you choose if you had money to invest? Why?

return you will earn. If you investigate the financial histories of different corporations, however, you will probably make better investment choices. While past success does not guarantee future success, a corporation's past performance is one way you can judge its chances for future success.

There are two general classes of stock. One pays most of its returns in dividends. The other is more likely to increase in value.

Blue Chip Stocks   Shares in large, well-established corporations are called **blue chip stocks**. These businesses have histories of steady sales and profits. Some pay dividends every year, and their dividends usually grow over time.

Their stock values generally do not change rapidly. Buying blue chip stocks involves lower risk than other stocks. Companies such as Procter and Gamble, Ford, and General Motors are examples of blue chip stocks. Much of the return from blue chip stock comes from its dividends.

Growth Stocks   The sales and profits of smaller or younger corporations that produce new products may increase rapidly. These businesses often pay no, or very small, dividends. They use their profits instead to purchase new equipment and research new products. Stock in a corporation that is expected to experience rapid growth is called **growth stock**.

Investors buy growth stocks because they hope to earn a large capital gain. If the business succeeds, it may earn high profits in the future. It could then pay especially good dividends, and the value of its stock could grow faster than a blue chip stock. When such a company does succeed, the return can be impressive. Intel and Microsoft are examples of growth stocks that made their early investors spectacular returns. A growth company, however, also has a greater chance of failure than a well-established company.

© Getty Images/PhotoDisc

CheckPoint

How may you receive a return on your investment in stock? What would you consider in choosing which stock to buy?

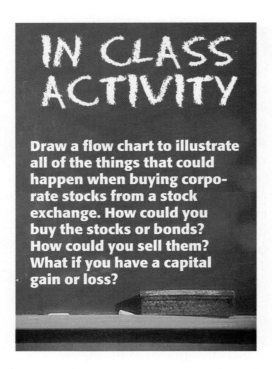

IN CLASS ACTIVITY

Draw a flow chart to illustrate all of the things that could happen when buying corporate stocks from a stock exchange. How could you buy the stocks or bonds? How could you sell them? What if you have a capital gain or loss?

Corporate Bonds

Another way to invest in corporations is to buy the bonds they sell. A bond is a written promise to pay a debt by a specified date. This definition applies to corporate and government bonds. Bonds are a form of borrowing rather than a share of ownership in the corporation.

Many corporations raise money by selling bonds. Corporate bonds usually pay a fixed rate of interest and are paid after a specific term. Like most government bonds, you can sell your corporate bonds to other investors. Stockbrokers handle bonds as well as stock transactions.

Why Own Corporate Bonds? When you buy a corporate bond, you are lending money. Corporations must make interest payments and repay their bonds on time, even if they earn no profit. This makes bonds less risky than stock. Unless the corporation fails, you will be paid. If it does fail, you will receive your money before stockholders get any of theirs. Because they are less risky than stocks, bonds generally pay a smaller return.

Junk Bonds Some corporate bonds are high-risk investments. Businesses in financial difficulty sometimes sell bonds to raise money. They offer high interest rates to encourage people to buy. Because the corporation is unstable with a high probability of failure, however, the investment is highly risky. These high-return, high-risk bonds are **high-yield bonds**. They are also referred to as *junk bonds* because of their high-risk status.

Bond Rating Services How can you judge the difference between high- and low-risk corporate bonds? One easy way is to look at the bond's rate of return. The higher the promised rate of return, the greater the risk.

If you want a thorough evaluation of a corporate bond, you can turn to a bond rating service. Moody's and Standard and Poor's are two of the most popular services. Both organizations evaluate corporations' financial situations and rate them according to their ability to pay their

© Getty Images/EyeWire

debts. Bonds sold by the safest firms are rated AAA by Moody's and by Standard and Poor's. The riskiest bonds have ratings of C or D. Ratings in between tell you the risk of one corporation's bonds relative to another's.

You can find bond ratings from these services in your local library or stockbroker's office. Both services also offer rating information through the Internet. Some are free and some require a small fee.

CheckPoint

What is the difference between stocks and bonds? Why does this difference matter to you as an investor?

TRY THESE

1. Why do corporations sell stock?

2. What are the differences in how a stock exchange and NASDAQ work?

3. What are the two ways for you to earn a return from owning stock?

4. What are the differences between preferred and common stock?

5. Why are blue chip stocks less risky than growth stocks?

6. Why do corporations sell bonds?

7. Why should you invest only part of your money in highly risky stocks?

8. Why does buying a corporate bond involve less risk than buying stock in the same corporation?

9. How do Moody's and Standard and Poor's help investors choose which corporate bonds to buy?

THINK CRITICALLY

10. **CONSUMER ACTION** What types of stock could Mija choose? Should she consider bonds? What investment options would you recommend to Mija? Why?

11. Why should you consider a corporation's past performance in making your investment decision? Why should past performance not be the only thing you consider? E-mail your answer to your teacher.

12. **MATH OF MONEY** Suppose you bought 50 shares of stock for $17.50 each last year. You also paid a $10 fee for this transaction. The stock paid a $0.20 dividend per share. One year later, you sold the

stock for $19.50 per share and again paid a $10.00 fee. What was your rate of return on your investment?

13. If you had $10,000 to invest, how would you diversify your portfolio?

14. You have a total of $2,000 in your savings account. You are thinking about investing it in either a blue chip stock that has been paying a 5 percent dividend over the last several years or a corporate bond that offers an 8 percent return. What would you consider in making this decision? Which decision would you make? Why?

© Getty Images/EyeWire

9.3 How to Invest in Mutual Funds

Mutual Funds—An Easy Way to Diversify

What if you have little savings to invest or don't want to investigate stocks to invest in? The answer could be mutual funds.

A **mutual fund** is a business that accepts deposits from many people to invest in various ways. A mutual fund's investors, in effect, own a portion of the stocks or bonds that the fund purchases. The value of their investment changes with the value of the fund's stocks or bonds. The fund employs investment professionals to make buy-and-sell decisions. This is an important benefit if you don't want to "follow the market." You might also have other reasons for investing in a mutual fund.

1. You can diversify your investment even if you have limited savings. Because the mutual fund pools money from many investors, it can buy from a wide selection of stocks.

CONSUMER ACTION

Latoya has saved $1,000 that she wants to invest in corporate stocks. She doesn't have much interest in researching stocks or keeping track of any stocks she buys. How can Latoya invest in stocks without having to manage her investments herself? What other benefits would she receive by investing this way? What costs would she pay?

2. Many mutual funds are managed to delay owners' taxes. When these funds sell stocks that have increased in value, they also sell others that have fallen. This eliminates or reduces current capital gains. The result delays taxes on capital gains until owners redeem their investment.

Mutual funds usually require a minimum investment of $1,000 or more. Your investment's value changes with the value of the stocks or bonds the fund purchased. Your return is a share of the fund's dividends or capital gains or losses.

Costs of Mutual Funds

All mutual funds charge annual maintenance fees for their services. You should consider these fees when choosing a fund. They can be from 0.2 or 3.0 percent or more of the value of your investment.

Besides maintenance fees, some mutual funds have a load. A **load** is a sales fee paid for investing in a mutual fund. You pay a *front-end load* when you buy shares or a *back-end load* when you sell them. The load amount is typically 5 to 6 percent of the funds invested or received from the sale of shares. The fee goes to the salespeople who market the fund.

No-load funds do not charge a sales fee because they have no salespeople. To invest in a no-load fund, request an order form, complete it, and return it with your payment.

You can buy mutual funds through brokerage firms such as Merrill Lynch and TD Waterhouse. To request information about their mutual funds, call their toll-free numbers or visit their web sites. Mutual funds are also advertised in *The Wall Street Journal* and many other financial publications.

GUESS WHAT

In 2004, investors could choose from more than 10,000 different mutual funds.

CheckPoint

How can investing in a mutual fund benefit you?

© Getty Images/PhotoDisc

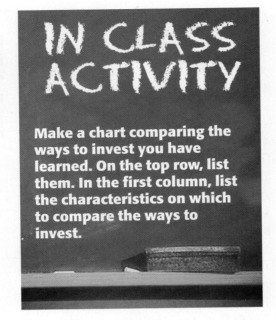

Make a chart comparing the ways to invest you have learned. On the top row, list them. In the first column, list the characteristics on which to compare the ways to invest.

Mutual Fund Investment Objectives

Every mutual fund has investment objectives, often based on the risk-versus-return trade-off the fund is willing to make. Like all stocks, the higher the potential rate of return, the greater the risk.

Some mutual funds aim for a high degree of safety, so they invest in safe stocks such as blue chips and expect somewhat low but steady return. Others aim for high rates of return, so they invest in riskier stocks, such as growth stocks and some high-risk stocks. Some aim for risk and rate of return somewhere in the middle.

All mutual funds clearly state their objectives in their informational literature so that you can select the fund that best fits your own investment objectives. Funds generally fall into four categories of investment objectives. Growth funds invest in new businesses likely to grow. Growth and income funds invest in established, profitable businesses still growing rapidly. Income funds invest in established firms that pay a good return. Tax-exempt funds purchase municipal bonds that pay tax-free interest. These categories provide different trade-offs between risk and expected return.

As the risk/return pyramid illustrates, potential risk and return of mutual fund categories range from the highest, growth funds, to the lowest, income funds and tax-free funds. When you shop for a mutual fund, select one matching your risk level or invest in a variety of funds with different risk levels.

Also consider whether you want returns now in dividends or possible higher returns later, as capital gains. Funds toward the top of the pyramid tend to invest in stocks that pay smaller dividends but perhaps larger capital gains later. Toward the

Risk/Return Pyramid for Mutual Funds

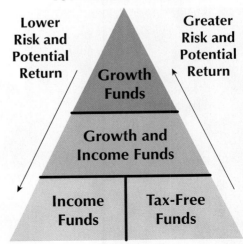

Lower Risk and Potential Return

Greater Risk and Potential Return

Growth Funds

Growth and Income Funds

Income Funds

Tax-Free Funds

bottom, the funds pay higher current dividends but aren't expected to increase much in value.

Some mutual funds have objectives other than certain risk/return levels. Here are some other common investment objectives.

▶ Global funds buy stock in businesses located in many nations.

▶ Index funds invest in all the stocks that an index is based on. For example, the *S&P 500 Index* is a group of stocks that economists use to judge the overall performance of the stock market. An index fund based on the *S&P 500* invests in all the *S&P 500* stocks.

▶ Social responsibility funds buy stock in businesses that have good records in giving back to the community.

▶ Environmental funds buy stock in businesses that have good records in protecting the environment.

CheckPoint

How are mutual funds categorized? How can these categories help you select a fund that is right for you?

TRY THESE

1. What is a mutual fund?

2. What benefits do mutual funds offer investors?

3. What is the difference between a load and a no-load fund?

4. What are several investment objectives mutual funds follow?

5. How can your own investment objectives help you select a mutual fund?

THINK CRITICALLY

6. **CONSUMER ACTION** Latoya wants to invest $1,000 in stocks but without the hassle of researching or keeping track of them. How can a mutual fund meet her need? What costs should she expect to pay?

7. Some corporations not doing well sell *junk bonds*. These bonds pay high interest rates to encourage investors to buy them. The firm could fail, however, causing investors to lose their money. E-mail a description of the type of investor who should consider buying junk bonds to your teacher.

8. What could cause you to be willing to pay the 6 percent sales fee to buy a load mutual fund?

9. On the risk/return pyramid, which category of mutual funds would you expect to have the greatest increases and decreases in price over time? Why?

10. Suppose you have $10,000 to invest, and you want to buy three different mutual funds. What types of funds would you choose? Why?

GOALS

IDENTIFY
sources of investment
information

DISCUSS
signs of dishonest
investment schemes
and how to protect
yourself

© Getty Images/PhotoDisc

9.4 Research Investments

How to Find Investment Information

Before you invest in any stock, investigate your alternatives. The more information you consider, the better your decision is likely to be.

Printed Sources of Information

Many newspapers, magazines, and other printed materials provide information about stocks, bonds, and mutual funds. Probably the most widely known financial newspaper is

The Wall Street Journal, published every business day. It contains articles about businesses, the government, banks, and foreign nations. *The Wall Street Journal* quotes stock, bond, and mutual fund prices. It often presents graphs that show trends of individual prices.

Mutual Funds   Major financial publications, such as *Fortune, Forbes, Kiplinger's Personal Finance Magazine,* and *Money,* evaluate and compare mutual funds at least once

CONSUMER ACTION

Norman has $10,000 in certificates of deposit that earn 5 percent. Last week, Norman received a call from a person who said he was an investment specialist. He encouraged Norman to buy stock in a new golf resort. He promised the stock would earn a 25 percent rate of return in six months. What clues should make Norman suspicious about this offer? What should he do to check it out before investing?

a year. Their articles group mutual funds according to their objectives. They also report and rank mutual fund returns for the past one to five years. The fees the funds charge are included, along with their telephone numbers and web addresses.

Another valuable source of information about mutual funds is the *Morningstar Report,* which you can find in most public libraries. This monthly publication explains investment policies of mutual funds and rates their success.

Stocks Each stock has a company abbreviation made up of several letters called a *ticker symbol.* You can identify a particular stock by its ticker symbol.

Magazines that report financial news include *Kiplinger's Personal Finance Magazine, Forbes, Fortune,* and *Money.* They provide in-depth evaluations and comparisons that can help you judge investments in particular corporations. You can also find information in *Moody's Reports* and *Value Line.* These printed sources are available in larger public libraries.

Information on the Internet

The most current information is on the Internet. Financial information can be posted within minutes.

All major mutual funds maintain web sites that provide information about their funds. For example, on some web sites you can find information about index stock funds that could be purchased, their return over many years, and even their investment philosophy just by clicking on an individual fund. Index funds

INTERNET ACTIVITY

Investigate a local corporation with stock traded on the NYSE or NASDAQ. Use financial information from its web site, other online sites, or your library to evaluate its financial success. Decide whether you would invest in this firm. Exchange your findings with another student by e-mail. Decide whether you agree with the other student's opinion of the firm he or she investigated. Send your opinions to your teacher by e-mail.

© Comstock Images

automatically purchase a selection of stocks that are the same as those in a market index such as the 500 Index or Total Market Index.

On mutual funds web sites, you can track whether funds had a good year. Keep in mind, however, that these numbers don't tell the whole story. If you are thinking about investing in a fund, you should also look at the long-term performance. Then compare the numbers to those of other similar funds during the same time period.

During a period when the value of most stocks is going up, a comparison of funds will show a lot of positive numbers. Remember, there is some risk in owning any stock funds. In years when the economy is good, their value is likely to increase, but in bad years, they will probably fall. You can limit your risk by carefully choosing which fund, or funds, to purchase.

Many financial Internet sites, such as American Express Financial Direct, Yahoo! Finance, and TD Waterhouse, allow you to follow stock prices. Using a stock's ticker symbol, you can find the stock's price up to the minute. Even opening screens of some browsers, such as Yahoo! Finance, allow you to request a current stock price.

If you want stock quotes sent to your computer automatically, you can sign up for the service with your Internet service provider. Most will allow you to specify the stocks you want to follow, and the provider will display the current prices on your opening screen each day.

You can even buy and sell stocks online. Most major stockbrokers maintain web sites that allow online transactions. These sites are also a rich source of company information and financial news.

The major financial print publications also have a web presence. You

PRIMARY SOURCES

When you choose to save in a way that earns income, you are investing. Some people may believe they don't have enough "extra" money to invest. Maggie Lena Walker believed that big things can come from small starts.

Walker was born into poverty in Virginia just after the Civil War. Through careful and determined study, she opened a bank for African-Americans in 1903. She was the first woman president of a bank in the country.

Ms. Walker taught poor people how to make their money make money. She said, "Let us have a bank that will take the nickels and turn them into dollars."

What did she mean by turning nickels into dollars? How could her statement be put into action in today's world? How can you apply her teaching to your own life?

can find *The Wall Street Journal* at www.wsj.com and *Value Line* at www.valueline.com.

To find out about a company from the company's point of view, you can check out its own web site. Most large corporations provide data about their sales, profits, and products on their site.

Request Information from Companies

You can request investor information from any company whose stocks or bonds are being traded in a stock exchange or on NASDAQ. It may send you the company's annual report or other information you can use to evaluate the company and its stock and bond performance.

All mutual funds are required by law to provide investors with a publication that describes how the fund is operated, the fund's investing objectives, and the fees that it charges. This publication is called a **prospectus**.

The easiest way to get a prospectus is to request it from the funds that interest you. You can find toll-free phone numbers for mutual funds in ads or articles in financial publications. You can also request a prospectus from the fund's web site.

CheckPoint

What is a prospectus? How can you get one?

Ask a Stockbroker

A *stockbroker* is a person who handles the transfer of stocks and bonds between buyer and seller. If you need advice on how to invest your money, you can ask a full-service broker.

A *full-service broker* is a stockbroker who provides information and advice in addition to trading stocks and bonds for customers. The broker inquires about your financial goals and situation and recommends appropriate investments for you. To receive this advice, you pay a fee when you buy or sell stocks and bonds using the broker.

If you don't have the time or the interest to research stocks thoroughly yourself, then getting this expertise from a full-service broker may be well worth the fee to you. You should realize, though, that full-service brokers make their money by making trades. The more transactions they make for investors, the more money they make in fees. Just use common sense to evaluate the advice you receive from a full-service broker.

Some stockbrokers do not provide information or advice about stock purchases. They simply carry out the transactions for their customers. These *discount brokers* charge smaller fees because they spend less time with customers than full-service brokers. If you do your own research about stocks and make your own decisions, then a discount broker would be your best choice.

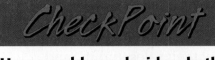

How would you decide whether to go to a full-service broker or a discount broker?

Imagine that a person calls you with the following sales pitch:
  "Good evening. My name is Gregory White. I represent the Imperial Securities Corporation. We have been informing a few select people of a wonderful investment opportunity. The Manitoba Coat Company is about to buy Great Western Furs, but no one knows yet. If you agree to buy GWF stock now, I can get it for you at $3 a share. Next week, GWF shares are going to sell for $10 or more. May I put you down for 1,000 shares?"
What clues do you see in this presentation that should make you suspicious? What would you want to find out from other sources to evaluate this offer?

Make an Investment Plan

An investment plan is a basic part of any life-span plan. You know that almost every life-span goal requires money to succeed. As you grow older, you should have more income and savings to invest. Fortunately, by then, you should also know more about investment choices you can make.

Many people are comfortable making investment decisions. Some are not. If you are not comfortable making investments on your own, you can rely on a stockbroker to give you advice. You may worry about this choice, however. Most stockbrokers earn income from fees when consumers trade stock or make investments. Unethical brokers may encourage people to make investments just to earn more fees. Whether the investor earns a good return or not, the broker still does well.

As an alternative, you could employ a financial advisor who earns income that does not depend on how you choose to invest. Many *financial planners* charge a flat fee to give you investment advice. They evaluate your budget, discuss your life-span goals, and make recommendations for how you should invest. Their fee is the same no matter what you do with your funds. To find a financial planner you may look in the yellow pages of your telephone book, ask friends, or search online. When you choose a financial planner, be sure to find out how he or she earns income. If the planner receives income for getting you to make a particular investment, that person may not give you the best advice.

Everyone needs a financial plan. Whether you make your own or receive help, your financial plan should help you reach your life-span goals. When you carry out your financial plan, avoid making mistakes that can cost you much of your hard-earned money.

© Getty Images/PhotoDisc

Investment Schemes

You work hard for your money, so don't throw it away on get-rich-quick investment deals. Any promise of a large return at low risk should make you suspicious. Such offers are most often dishonest and can cost you your savings.

There is risk in any investment, even legitimate ones. Sometimes even the best investments lose value, but don't take unnecessary risks by investing in deals that seem too good to be true. If someone tells you that an investment will double your money in two weeks, it is either a very high-risk investment or fraud.

Information about investments is easy to find. Experts talk and write about investment opportunities. Consumers research investments through published information. No one is likely to find an investment opportunity before everyone else. So if someone tells you about a great deal that only he knows, it is probably fraud. If such an opportunity existed, other people would know about it too.

CheckPoint

As an investor, would you be most comfortable making your own investment decisions, relying on a stockbroker, or hiring a financial planner? Why?

Check Out Investment Offers

Before you make any investment decision, you should evaluate the offer. Here are some ways you can protect yourself from dishonest investment offers.

1. Invest through large, well-established stock brokerage firms. These firms grew large by satisfying customers. If they were dishonest, they would probably have disappeared long ago. This does not mean all offers made by large firms are right for you. Investments still involve trade-offs between risk and return. Even large businesses sometimes make mistakes or employ dishonest people.

2. Ask the name, address, and telephone number of any company that contacts you about an investment offer. Then check out the company before investing.

3. Ask for a copy of investment offers in writing. These contracts should be written in words you can understand. If you are not sure you understand a document, ask for an explanation. You should never make an investment that is not clear to you.

4. Financial conditions do not often change quickly. In the long run, it usually makes little difference whether you invest today or next week. Hard-sell salespeople who demand that you decide *now* are likely to be dishonest.

5. Salespeople who say they know something that others don't are probably dishonest. It is against the law to use insider information to make investments.

6. Demands for immediate payment are often a sign that the deal is not honest. Investors generally have five days to pay for financial transactions.

The best way to protect your savings is to use common sense. You can easily learn about investments offered by reputable businesses. Avoid investments that promise a higher rate of return for a lower risk than seems reasonable. As in most consumer choices, if it looks too good to be true, it probably is.

CheckPoint

What are the clues that an investment may be dishonest? How can you protect yourself from shady deals?

Investment Regulation

You must be able to trust your stockbroker to deal with you honestly. To help gain your trust, stockbrokers have their own professional organization that certifies and oversees its members. To help protect consumers, the federal government also has established an agency to regulate the investment process.

Stockbroker Self-Regulation

Most businesses that buy and sell stocks for consumers are members of the National Association of

Securities Dealers (NASD). This is the group that organized and runs NAS-DAQ. It also polices the behavior of its members.

NASD tests and certifies people who wish to become stockbrokers. Most brokerage businesses employ only people who have passed the exam and are registered with NASD. You should not deal with an unregistered broker.

NASD maintains a listing of complaints that have been filed against its registered brokers. This is called a Central Registration Depository Record (CRD). You can request copies of CRDs for registered brokers on the Internet by searching for the NASD Regulation web site.

Although CRDs are useful, they have limitations. Dishonest people who say they are brokers but aren't registered will have no CRD. Also, brokerage businesses don't always report the complaints they receive.

You can also inquire about brokers with your state's office of the attorney general. This office maintains files of complaints about investment businesses and their employees. From this information, you can find out whether complaints have been filed about a brokerage business or if it is being sued.

Securities Exchange Commission

In 1929, the stock market crashed. In a few months, stocks traded on the New York Stock Exchange lost as much as two-thirds of their value. Some businesses and banks failed. Many people lost their investments. One possible reason for this crash was the limited power of the government to regulate stock trading. To try to prevent a crash in the future, Congress created the **Securities and Exchange Commission (SEC)**.

Congress has given the SEC the responsibility for enforcing the laws concerning the trading of stocks and bonds. It also licenses stockbrokers and investment advisors. In addition, the SEC has the final authority on matters of financial reporting, but it has given the job of determining required financial accounting procedures to use when preparing financial reports to the accounting profession. Sometimes, however, the SEC has overruled decisions of the accounting profession.

SEC Protections The SEC works to reduce the number of dishonest investment offers made to consumers. It employs nearly 1,000 regulators who investigate consumer complaints. When it

© Getty Images/EyeWire

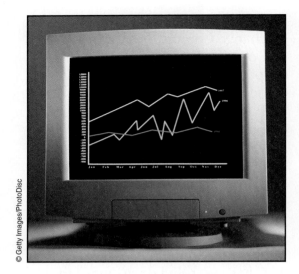

© Getty Images/PhotoDisc

Recent Investment Scandals

In 2001–2003, accounting scandals, such as those plaguing WorldCom, Enron, Tyco International, and other companies, caused concern about the accuracy of the information corporations report to the SEC.

"The WorldCom disclosures confirm that accounting improprieties of unprecedented magnitude have been committed in the public markets," the SEC said in a prepared statement. It filed a lawsuit against WorldCom, charging the company with fraud and asking a court to block the payment of extraordinary bonuses to executives.

Insider Trading

One important job of the SEC is to prevent insider trading. **Insider trading** is trading stocks based on information that is not available to the general public.

For example, suppose a manager at ABC Corporation helps her company plan to buy the XYZ Corporation. Before the deal is announced, she buys 10,000 shares of XYZ at $10 per share. Later the announcement of the deal causes the stock's value to increase to $25 a share. She sells her stock and earns $150,000. This is unfair to other investors. It is also against the law. Investors can be fined and sent to jail for insider trading.

finds a dishonest operation, the SEC has the power to close it and prosecute its operators.

The SEC requires that publicly traded companies submit for its review the documents that disclose information about the companies' financial condition and business practices.

Investors can go to the SEC's web site to review these financial documents through its Electronic Data Gathering, Analysis, and Retrieval (EDGAR) system. The site also provides information identifying companies that the SEC has sued or has taken other actions against.

INTERNET ACTIVITY

On the Internet, research the payment of extraordinary bonuses to Enron executives. E-mail what you learn to another student. Agree on what you believe should have been done to these people, and e-mail your opinion to your teacher.

CheckPoint

How does stockbroker self-regulation work? Why was the SEC created and what does it do?

TRY THESE

1. What kinds of information can you get from *The Wall Street Journal* or from financial magazines?

2. What kinds of sites on the Internet provide financial information?

3. What are the differences between a full-service broker and a discount broker?

4. Why should you look at a fund's performance over more than one year?

5. What are several ways that you can tell that an investment offer may be dishonest?

6. How can you find out if complaints have been made about a stockbroker?

7. What is the SEC and how does it benefit you?

8. What is insider trading, and why is it illegal?

THINK CRITICALLY

9. **CONSUMER ACTION** Norman received an investment offer that promised a much larger return than his current investment. Why is this offer likely to be dishonest? Where should Norman go for information to evaluate this offer?

10. Why would you want to know the current price of stock you own?

11. **COMMUNICATE** Write a paragraph describing the advantages that the Internet has over print material as a source of investment information. E-mail your answer to your teacher.

12. Why do you believe the SEC has taken steps to improve its regulation of the accounting practices of large corporations?

DECISION MAKING PROJECT

 SPECIFY   SEARCH   SIFT   SELECT   STUDY

SEARCH Assign one investment option, such as corporate stocks or mutual funds, to each group member. Find out the following:

1. What is the history of this investment option?

2. What is its risk level?

3. What is your anticipated rate of return?

4. Why should you invest in this option?

5. How does this option fit with your investment goals?

GOALS

DISCUSS
the advantages and
trade-offs of retirement
investment plans

DESCRIBE
the risks of and ways
to earn a return on
uncommon investment
options

© Getty Images/PhotoDisc

9.5 Retirement and Other Investments

Plan Your Retirement

In the past, some companies had pension plans for their employees funded completely by the company. After spending most of their working years at one company, workers retired and lived on their pension.

Today, employer-funded pension plans are less common. Instead, workers must take more responsibility for their own retirement savings. Many companies offer investment plans in which their employees can participate. Self-employed workers and workers whose companies do not offer a retirement plan have other investment options.

CONSUMER ACTION

While Leonard was searching the attic of his house, he found a box of old comic books. His father told him they had belonged to him when he was young. There were Superman, Archie, and Batman comics in nearly perfect condition. Leonard realized they might be worth hundreds or maybe thousands of dollars to collectors. Leonard began to think that collecting might be a great way to invest for retirement. He could buy popular collectibles now and sell them for a big profit when he is old enough to retire. Are collectibles a good investment strategy? What should Leonard learn about collectibles before investing? What other ways might he invest for his retirement?

Trade-Offs of Retirement Planning

One main benefit of many retirement plans is that they allow you to put off paying tax on part of your income until you retire. In this way, you earn a return on money that you would otherwise pay in taxes.

The trade-off for receiving a tax advantage is that you can't easily withdraw money from these plans before you reach retirement age. Early withdrawal usually costs a penalty, although some plans allow withdrawals without penalty for children's college tuition or medical emergencies. You should try to include in your life-span financial plan at least some investments that allow you to put off paying taxes until you retire.

401(k) Plans

A 401(k) plan is a tax-deferred retirement plan that some employers offer their employees. Only the company's employees may participate in its 401(k) plan.

Usually you can designate a portion of each paycheck to your 401(k) plan. Your employer automatically withholds it and invests it in a professionally managed investment account. The money is then invested in the stock market, mutual funds, or other options.

Employer Matching Programs

Some employers match employee's 401(k) savings as much as 50 cents per dollar invested up to a designated maximum. For example, if with each paycheck you designate $100 to your 401(k) account, your employer might add $50. If you work for a company that offers a match, you should accept it. The amount matched is free money! Try to save at least the maximum amount the company will match.

If the company does not match your 401(k) savings, the plan is still an excellent way to save for retirement. Because it is tax deferred, you can save a significant amount on income taxes during your working years. When you retire, your income may be lower, so the tax rate may be lower when you withdraw money from your plan. In the meantime, you earn a return on the income instead of paying it in taxes.

Unlike pensions, 401(k)s are portable. If you change jobs, you can take your 401(k) savings with you. This is a significant advantage over traditional pensions since people seldom spend their entire career with one company.

© Getty Images/PhotoDisc

Investing in a 401(k) plan does not eliminate the need to evaluate investments. Many employers choose the firm that runs the 401(k) plans, but they may allow participants a voice in how to invest the funds. Be sure that any 401(k) investments you make are diversified. Employees of the Enron Corporation, for example, lost more than $1 billion when that firm failed in 2001. Many of them had invested all of their retirement funds only in Enron stock. The Enron bankruptcy led to new government rules on how 401(k) funds may operate.

IRA Plans

In addition to an employer-sponsored pension or retirement plan, most people can set up an **individual retirement account (IRA)**, a savings plan with special tax benefits.

Savings in a *traditional IRA* are tax deferred. Those in a *Roth IRA* are not, so when you withdraw the money at retirement, you pay no income tax on it. Its tax benefit is not paying taxes on the amount earned on your investment.

A Roth IRA is often a good choice for young people because they have many working years left to earn tax-free returns on their investments. A financial advisor can help you decide which type is best for your financial situation.

The law specifies the maximum amount you can put into an IRA in one year. Married people can jointly invest more funds in their IRA accounts than single people. IRAs are not employer-sponsored, so they have no matching funds, and you make your own investment decisions.

Life-Span Plan

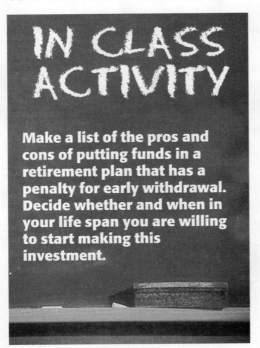

IN CLASS ACTIVITY

Make a list of the pros and cons of putting funds in a retirement plan that has a penalty for early withdrawal. Decide whether and when in your life span you are willing to start making this investment.

CheckPoint

What are the advantages of investing in a 401(k)? Under what circumstances would you invest in an IRA instead of a 401(k)?

Other Investment Options

There are a variety of less common ways to invest. If you enjoy researching investments, you might join an investment club. As always, investigate your investment options with care.

Investment Clubs

Investment clubs can be an enjoyable way to share knowledge of investments and earn a return. They also offer socialization with people who have similar interests.

When you join an investment club, you invest the amount the club requires. The club pools its members' money and invests it as the majority decides. Usually everyone is expected to research investment opportunities and make recommendations.

You should never invest all of your money in a club. Members are not investment professionals, so the club will likely not always make the best decisions. Limit your investment to only what you can afford to lose.

The National Association of Investors Corporation (NAIC) helps people organize investment clubs. Its publications explain the processes and provide forms to use to make clubs legal. Clubs can use the NAIC's software to keep their accounts and print out members' holdings.

If your club joins this organization, you will receive the monthly magazine *Better Investing*. It identifies and evaluates a wide variety of investment opportunities. You can find information about NAIC at its web site.

Real Estate

Your Home as an Investment

The largest investment you are likely to make in your lifetime is buying a home. Houses are different from other investments in important ways. Part of the return you receive is the value of having a place to live. Real estate also often increases in value over time. This is not always true,

COMMUNICATE

Caroline purchased more than 200 CDs by her favorite artists over the years. She thinks of her CD collection as an investment. Write a one-page essay that evaluates her point of view. Is her CD collection an investment? Why or why not?

but many people have made large capital gains by selling their homes.

To encourage homeownership, the government passed a law that allows married couples to earn up to $500,000 of capital gains on the sale of their home without having to pay federal income tax on it. You may also be able to deduct the property taxes and interest you pay on your home loan.

Investing in Other Types of Real Estate You can also invest in real estate that you will not use as your home. Real estate is land and the buildings on it. You can invest in real estate by buying property that you intend to rent. For example, you

© Getty Images/PhotoDisc

In 1986, the U.S. Treasury began to produce and market gold coins called American Eagles. They are made only from gold mined within the U.S. More than one million of these coins are sold each year.

could own and rent out an apartment building or a vacation home. You can also invest in land that you hope will increase in value.

You can earn a return on your real estate investment in two ways. First, the rent you receive can help you pay for the property. Second, if the property increases in value over time, you can sell it to earn a capital gain.

Real Estate Risks and Responsibilities

If you buy rental property, you have to find renters. You must pay the loan on the building whether or not you are receiving rental income. You are also responsible for maintaining the property. When you need a new roof or something breaks, you—not your renters—must arrange to have it fixed and pay for the repairs.

If you are unlucky in your choice of renters, you could have problems collecting rent and expensive repairs and upkeep due to careless tenants. If you consider investing in real estate, be sure that you are prepared to invest the time and money required to maintain it and have patience to handle problems.

Real estate doesn't always increase in value. If property values go down or if you have to sell your property before the value goes up, you will take a capital loss on the sale.

Never invest money that you could need in a hurry in real estate. It usually takes many years to increase in value if it does at all. Be sure to investigate the history of property values in the area before you invest.

© Getty Images/PhotoDisc

Collectibles

Collecting can be fun, but it can also be a form of investing. Some collections increase in value over time.

Collecting for profit is a very risky business. People who do it seriously are experts. They know how to judge the quality and value of the items they collect. They also know how to determine whether or not an item, such as an antique, is real or an imitation.

To earn a return on collected items, you have to find someone willing to pay more for it than you paid to buy it initially. There is no guarantee that the value of collectibles will go up. Collecting antique Coke trays may be popular now, so the trays bring a high price. In the future, people may be less interested in collecting Coke trays. If so, you may not be able to find a buyer willing to pay enough for your trays to make a profit.

Unless you plan to put in the time and effort to become an expert, don't invest more in your collection than you are willing to lose.

Always remember that any investing, whether in stocks, bonds, mutual funds, real estate, or collectibles, includes the chance that your investment will decrease in value. The higher the potential rate of return, the greater the risk. Remember, too, that investing your money in different places provides a better chance of earning a return than investing in one place. Finally, never take big risks with money you're not willing to lose.

CheckPoint

How could you benefit from joining an investment club? How can you earn a return from real estate?

TRY THESE

1. How can a 401(k) plan benefit you?

2. What does *tax deferred* mean?

3. How is an IRA different from a 401(k) plan?

4. What is the difference between a traditional IRA and a Roth IRA?

5. If you are thinking about investing in less common ways, why should you be especially careful to investigate your choices?

6. What are the benefits of joining an investment club?

7. How can you earn returns from investing in real estate?

8. What are the risks and responsibilities involved in real estate investing?

THINK CRITICALLY

9. **CONSUMER ACTION** Leonard is considering investing in collectibles. How would you describe the risks of this type of investment to him? What other investments would you suggest?

10. What benefits might a company receive in helping its employees invest in a 401(k) plan?

11. Ask several adults who are approaching retirement age what they have done to prepare financially for their retirement and family financial security.

12. If you had the money, would you choose to invest in an apartment building? Why or why not?

DECISION MAKING PROJECT

SPECIFY　　SEARCH　　SIFT　　SELECT　　STUDY

Life-Span Plan

SIFT Have all group members present their methods of investing. Put the options on a comparative chart. Make sure to include what the members estimate their investment options will be worth when they want to have their money.

Chapter 9

ASSESSMENT

KEY IDEAS

Investing Basics

1. Investing is saving in a way that earns income. The income you earn on an investment is your return.
2. In general, the higher the potential rate of return, the greater the risk. To reduce your overall risk, you should diversify your investing among a variety of risk levels.
3. In making investment decisions, you should consider your current financial situation, your risk tolerance, your values, and your family's needs.

How to Invest in Corporations

4. A share of stock is a unit of ownership in a corporation. Stockholders are investors who own the corporation because they own its stock. To raise money for the business, corporations sell stock to investors.
5. You earn a return as dividends or by selling your stock. If you sell your stock for more than you paid for it, you earn a capital gain. If you sell it for less, you take a capital loss.
6. You can buy and sell stocks through a stock exchange or NASDAQ.
7. There are two basic types of stock: preferred and common. Stocks may also be classified as blue chip or growth.
8. Corporate bonds are a form of borrowing—a loan to, rather than a share of ownership in, a corporation.

How to Invest in Mutual Funds

9. Mutual funds pool investors' money to buy a variety of stock and give the benefits of diversification and professional investment managers.
10. Mutual funds charge an annual maintenance fee. Some also charge a load, which is a sales fee.
11. Mutual funds generally fall into four categories of investment objectives: growth funds, growth and income funds, income funds, and tax-free funds.

Research Investments

12. You can find information about corporations and their stocks from print publications, the Internet, and stockbrokers.
13. The Internet provides the most up-to-date stock information, web sites for most companies, and the option to conduct online stock trades.
14. A stockbroker is a person who handles the transfer of stocks and bonds between buyers and sellers.
15. All mutual funds state their investment objectives in their prospectus.
16. Avoid investments that promise a higher rate of return for a lower risk than seems reasonable.
17. The SEC enforces laws concerning the investment process, licenses stockbrokers, and investigates investor complaints. Stockbrokers have the NASD to regulate the behavior of its members.

Retirement and Other Investments

18. One of the main benefits of retirement plans is their tax advantage.

19. Many companies offer their employees a 401(k) retirement plan. If your company doesn't offer a retirement plan, you can set up your own individual retirement account (IRA).

20. You could learn about investing by joining with an investment club.

21. Investing in a home may provide a return, a tax advantage, and a place to live.

22. You can also invest in land or rental property to receive a return.

23. Collectibles such as coins and antiques can earn capital gains when you sell them.

TERMS REVIEW

Match each term on the left with its definition on the right.
Some terms may not be used.

a. 401(k) plan

b. blue chip stock

c. brokerage firm

d. capital gain

e. capital loss

f. common stock

g. diversification

h. dollar cost averaging

i. growth stock

j. high-yield bond

k. individual retirement account (IRA)

l. insider trading

m. investing

n. load

o. mutual fund

p. NASDAQ

q. preferred stock

r. prospectus

s. return

t. risk

u. Securities and Exchange Commission (SEC)

v. share of stock

w. stock exchange

x. stockbroker

y. stockholder

z. transaction

1. chance that an investment will decrease in value

2. distributing funds among a variety of investments to minimize overall risk

3. a unit of ownership in a corporation

4. using savings in a way that earns income

5. electronic stock-trading system that links brokerages

6. profit earned from selling stock at a higher price than you paid for it

7. stock of an established and historically successful corporation

8. a tax-deferred retirement savings plan offered to employees by their employer

9. a person who handles the transfer of stocks and bonds between buyer and seller

10. a company that specializes in helping people buy and sell stocks and bonds

11. stock in a corporation that is expected to experience rapid growth in sales and profits

12. income earned on an investment

13. a voting share of ownership in a corporation for which the dividend varies as determined by the corporation's board of directors

14. a group of investments owned by many investors and managed by investment professionals

15. investor who owns a corporation because he/she owns shares of its stock

16. a legal document provided by all mutual funds that describes the fund's operations, its investing objectives, and its fees

17. a location where orders to buy or sell stock are sent and carried out

18. a retirement savings plan with special tax benefits that you may set up if your employer does not offer a retirement plan

CONSUMER DECISIONS

19. Your company has a 401(k) plan, and it matches employees' investments 50 cents for each dollar. After you have paid all your living expenses, you have $400 left over each month. Would you put all of the $400 in the 401(k) plan each month? Why or why not? What would you consider in making this decision?

20. You have decided to save for your retirement by investing $1,000 each year in an account that pays 6 percent interest. You are 16, expect to retire at 65, and expect to live to 90. Use the Retirement Planner to calculate how much you would be able to withdraw each year from this account when you retire.

21. Leanne rents one side of a duplex. The other side is vacant. She pays $500 each month to rent her half of the duplex. The landlord offered to sell her the building. The payments would be $900 each month. If Leanne could rent the other half of the building for $500, then she would have to pay only $400 each month instead of the $500 she was paying, and she would own the building. Should Leanne accept this offer? What should she consider in making this decision?

THINK CRITICALLY

22. Eduardo is 28 years old and has been saving a portion of each paycheck in his company's 401(k) plan for seven years. He now has $10,000 in the plan. The company offers a selection of mutual funds from which Eduardo may choose to invest his 401(k) funds. The selection includes one fund option in each of these categories: growth, growth and income, and income. Eduardo can choose to put it all in one type of fund or put portions in more than one type. Should he put it all in one type? If so, which one? If not, which ones should he choose to divide his money among? How much should he put in each type? Explain your choices.

LOOK IT UP

23. Identify a large corporation whose products are sold in your community. Find out what has happened to the value of its stock and the dividends it pays over the past three years. Has this been a good investment? Would you buy its stock if you had savings to invest?

WHICH IS THE BEST DEAL?

Ryan has saved nearly $3,000. He does not like to take risks, but he wants to earn more than the 2 percent return his bank is paying. He has identified three investments he might make. What are the advantages and disadvantages of each option? Which one would you recommend to Ryan? Why?

Alternative 1   Buy stock in a large, established corporation that usually pays a 2 percent dividend. Its stock, on average, has increased in value 3 percent per year over the past 10 years.

Alternative 2   Buy stock in a new company that is searching for a cure for cancer. It pays no dividends. If successful, its stock could double or triple in value.

Alternative 3   Buy a mutual fund that invests in foreign stocks. Last year, it earned a 34 percent return. The year before, its value fell by 13 percent. Over the past ten years, its average return has been 17 percent.

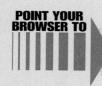

POINT YOUR BROWSER TO

www.ee4c.swlearning.com
Complete the activity for Chapter 9.

24. Visit the web site of a family of mutual funds, such as Vanguard, Fidelity, American Express, or Putnam. Identify one fund in each category of the risk/return pyramid.

25. Many financial publications, such as *Forbes, Fortune,* and *The Wall Street Journal,* report mutual fund returns at the end of each year. Search the Internet or use a library to identify the funds that performed the best in each category of the risk/return pyramid. What reasons did the publication give for the success of these funds?

26. People who collect coins, stamps, or other items often form groups that maintain web sites. Choose a collectible that interests you. Search the Internet for the sites of groups that share this interest. What do the sites tell you about buying and selling this collectible?

INSIDE THE NUMBERS

27. Curtis is considering the purchase of 100 shares of IBM. He has identified two brokers he might use to buy the stock. One is a full-service broker. He will charge $150 if Curtis decides to purchase the stock. The other is a discount broker. She will complete the transaction for $39. Why might Curtis choose to spend the extra $111 to use the full-service broker? How could he benefit from this extra expense?

CURRICULUM CONNECTION

28. **HISTORY** A number of famous people gained much of their wealth from investing in the stock market. Among these were John D. Rockefeller, Cornelius Vanderbilt, and J.P. Morgan. Read a brief biography of one of these people in an encyclopedia or other book. How much risk did the person you studied take? What smart investment decisions did this person make?

JOURNAL RECAP

29. After reading this chapter, review the answers you wrote to the questions in the Journal Journey. Have your opinions changed?

DECISION MAKING PROJECT

SPECIFY   **SEARCH**   **SIFT**   **SELECT**   **STUDY**

SELECT Discuss your findings with your group. Decide which investment option you think will best fulfill your needs. Write a short paragraph stating how your group chose this option. What did you consider in addition to the potential rate of return? Include your calculations.

STUDY Present your paragraph on the process your group went through to choose an investment. Did any other group have the same requirements for investing that your group had? Did any other group choose the same investment? Did other groups have the same reasons?

Life-Span Plan

Chapter 10

CREDIT
YOU'RE IN CHARGE

WHAT'S AHEAD

EXPLODING MYTHS

Fact or Myth?
What do you think is true?

1. You should avoid borrowing money if you possibly can.

2. Financial mistakes you make when you are young are wiped clean when you turn 21.

3. Banks are no more likely to lend you money in the future if you have repaid loans on time in the past.

JOURNAL JOURNEY

WRITE IN YOUR JOURNAL ABOUT THE FOLLOWING.

WHEN TO USE CREDIT When is using credit a good idea? How can you tell when taking out a loan is not a good idea?

TO QUALIFY FOR CREDIT Why can some consumers get credit more easily than others? What can you do to convince lenders to lend to you?

USE CREDIT RESPONSIBLY What does it mean to use credit responsibly? What can you do to avoid getting into financial difficulty from using credit?

DECISION MAKING PROJECT

SPECIFY   SEARCH   SIFT   SELECT   STUDY

GIVE YOURSELF CREDIT Your group will decide on a good or service you will buy using credit. You will then research the various forms of credit available and fill out an application to borrow the money you need. Plan how you will fit the payments into your budget, how long it will take to pay the money back, and how much interest you will pay.

GOAL

To learn how to plan to use credit wisely

PROJECT PROCESS

SPECIFY	Lesson 10.1
SEARCH	Lesson 10.3
SIFT	Lesson 10.4
SELECT	Lesson 10.5
STUDY	Chapter Assessment

© Stockbyte

10.1 What Is CREDIT?

Why Borrow?

The ability to borrow money in return for a promise of future repayment is **credit**. Future repayment usually includes interest.

When you save, you are giving up spending now for the ability to spend in the future. When you use credit, you are making the opposite trade-off. You are giving up the ability to spend in the future in order to spend now. Because you must pay interest on borrowed money, you also are giving up *more* future spending than the amount of the loan.

For example, suppose you use credit to buy an outfit for $100. If the interest rate is 15 percent per year, you must repay $115 at the end of the year.

$$\$100 \times 0.15 = \$15$$
$$\$100 + \$15 = \$115$$

So you are really giving up $115 worth of future spending for the ability to spend $100 now. Your opportunity cost of using credit to buy this outfit is whatever you would have bought for $115 one year later.

CONSUMER ACTION

Ryan's take-home pay is $1,700 a month. His credit card payments are $100 per month. He would like to buy a new car that he saw at the local dealer. To have enough money to buy it, he would have to get a loan with payments of $400 a month. He really wants the car. Should he buy it?

CheckPoint

What is credit? What is the opportunity cost of using credit?

For Your Goals

Credit can help you buy the things you want earlier than you could get them by saving. When your income is too small to pay for something you want, you could choose to buy it on credit. Is this a wise choice? The answer depends on your financial situation. Never borrow more money than you can easily repay.

Sometimes borrowing is almost a necessity. Some items, such as a house or car, are too expensive for most people to buy with savings.

Using credit can be a good decision. Suppose you are moving into your first home. You need many products to set up housekeeping—appliances, furniture, kitchen utensils, linens, and so on. If you are young, you probably can't buy all of these products unless you borrow. If you are just starting out in life, your income and savings probably aren't very high.

As you grow older, your earnings will likely increase. You will gain experience and advance in your career. As your salary increases, making your loan payments will be easier. As long as you use credit responsibly and you don't borrow more than you can easily repay, using credit makes sense.

For a Home

Owning a home is part of the American dream. The average cost of buying a home is more than $230,000. In some parts of the country, the average is more than $400,000. Few people can pay for a home without borrowing. Even saving for a down payment is often a challenge. Without credit, most Americans could never own a home. By borrowing to buy the house, you get the benefits of living in it while you are making the loan payments.

The interest on a home loan can be staggering, but owning a home can make good financial sense. Most people who do not own a home are renters. For example, Maria and Raymond have lived in an apartment for seven years. They pay their landlord $700 every month. In the seven years, they have paid their landlord $58,800.

$700 × 12 months = $8,400 per year
$8,400 × 7 years = $58,800

Maria and Raymond have nothing to show for their payments, however. They received the benefit of having a place to live, but they own nothing in exchange for their money.

GUESS WHAT

In 2002, Americans had borrowed more than $6.0 trillion to purchase homes.

A Home as an Investment

What if Maria and Raymond had instead bought a home for $90,000? They could have made a down payment of $20,000 and borrowed $70,000. Their payments would have been a little larger, but they would own something of value.

Equity *Equity* is the difference between the amount owed on a home and the home's value. After seven years, Maria and Raymond might still owe $60,000. The value of their home, however, could have grown to $100,000. If it had, their equity would be $40,000.

$$\$100,000 - \$60,000 = \$40,000$$

If Maria and Raymond decided to sell their home, they would receive $100,000 from their buyer. They would use $60,000 of this to pay off their loan, and the rest, $40,000, would be their equity.

© Getty Images/PhotoDisc

Homes are different than most property you can buy. Home values often increase over time, so a home is an investment. You will often receive more when you sell your home than you paid for it. This is not true of most consumer goods. The value of cars or appliances falls over time. If you sell these items, you will get less than you paid for them.

Taxes and Home Ownership

Another good reason to borrow for a home is the tax advantage home ownership provides. Property taxes and interest paid for home loans are deductible on income tax form 1040. Homeowners can save hundreds of dollars in taxes each year.

Renters also pay these costs indirectly. They are built into the rent they pay. Landlords can deduct these expenses, but renters receive no tax advantage from their spending for housing.

For Your Education

Higher education or training is expensive. Tuition, fees, and other expenses can cost many thousands of dollars a year, even at the least-expensive schools. Private schools can cost $30,000 a year or more. Few people can afford to pay these costs without borrowing.

Investing in yourself pays off. Statistics show that people with more training or education have higher average incomes. Suppose a high school graduate earns an associate degree. On average, this person's yearly income will increase by more than $9,000. A four-year degree allows people to earn an average of $21,000 more per year than a high school diploma. For

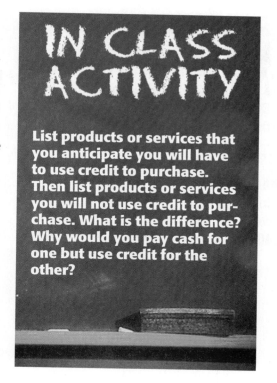

IN CLASS ACTIVITY

List products or services that you anticipate you will have to use credit to purchase. Then list products or services you will not use credit to purchase. What is the difference? Why would you pay cash for one but use credit for the other?

most people, borrowing to pay for education makes good financial sense.

For Your Health

The cost of being ill is often very high. These costs involve more than the price of treatment. When people are sick, they often cannot work. They may have insurance to pay their doctors, but medical insurance does not pay the rent. If you become ill, you may have to borrow to pay your living expenses until you can earn a salary again.

CheckPoint

What are some good reasons to borrow? What are the benefits of owning a home over renting?

© Getty Images/PhotoDisc

Plan Your Borrowing

Most adults borrow money at one time or another in their lives. Borrowing creates fixed expenses that you must pay. To be useful, your budget must take borrowing and repayment into account.

When to Borrow

Some people do not use credit wisely. They borrow for what they *want*. Then, when they really *need* to use credit, they are unable to get a loan, or they take on more debt than they are able to repay. Before you borrow, ask yourself four questions.

1. Is it important that I buy the good or service I want now?

2. Do I have to borrow to buy the product?

3. Can I afford to make the payments on the loan?

4. Will I be able to buy other products I want more if I borrow to buy this product?

If you answer *yes* to all of these questions, you may continue to evaluate your borrowing alternatives.

How Much to Borrow

The first rule of borrowing is to buy responsibly. Make good buying decisions, and don't spend more than necessary. It's easy to overspend. Salespeople often encourage you to buy more—this is their job. Besides, you just have to pull out your credit

© Getty Images/EyeWire

card, and the product is yours. It can almost seem like play money.

Remember, however, that the payments are real, and they get larger as you buy more on credit. Plus, the amount you pay in interest increases with each new credit purchase. Interest is money out of your pocket. Before you buy on credit, make sure that what you are buying is worth giving up the products you could have bought with the interest money.

A basic rule of thumb is that your total debt payments (excluding housing costs) should be no more than 20 to 25 percent of your take-home pay. For example, if your take-home pay is $500 per month, your total debt payments should be no more than $125 per month.

$$\$500 \times 0.25 = \$125$$

If your payments require more than 20 to 25 percent of your take-home pay, they will start seriously affecting your daily life. To pay your bills, you could have to cut back on some flexible expenses, such as going to the movies or having a hamburger with your friends. Living this way is uncomfortable. Be smart—use credit responsibly.

CheckPoint

Why should you include borrowing in your budget? Why should you be careful not to take on more debt than you can easily repay?

TRY THESE

1. What trade-off do you make when you use credit?

2. How does interest on credit affect your ability to spend in the future?

3. How can borrowing help you achieve your goals?

4. What are some benefits of owning a home?

5. What four questions should you ask yourself before you decide to borrow?

6. What is the general rule for the amount of debt payments you can handle?

7. What kind of budget expense would be immediately affected if you used credit?

THINK CRITICALLY

8. **CONSUMER ACTION** Ryan wants to buy a new car but isn't sure if he should. What do you think? Would Ryan be able to handle the loan payments? Why or why not? How could he make the car more affordable?

9. Suppose you were interested in a career in computer information services. Courses at night for a degree would cost $20,000. You are currently earning $25,000 a year. Salaries for entry-level information service jobs requiring a degree start at $35,000. Would you go into debt to get this degree? Why or why not?

10. **COMMUNICATE** Think of a product you would like to own in the future. Explain whether you think using credit to purchase this product would be a wise choice. What would you have to give up to do this? Send your answer to your teacher in an e-mail.

11. **MATH OF MONEY** You have decided to borrow $5,000 to buy a used car. The dealer will arrange a 6 percent loan that you must repay over 48 months. Use the Loan Planner to calculate your monthly payment, total of all payments, and total interest cost for this loan.

12. What does it mean to use credit responsibly?

PLANNING TOOLS

DECISION MAKING PROJECT

SPECIFY   SEARCH   SIFT   SELECT   STUDY

SPECIFY Decide on a good or service that you would have to use credit to purchase. Why is it necessary to buy this good or service on credit? Estimate what you think it will cost. Assume for this project you can afford to spend only $100 a month to repay the loan.

© CORBIS

GOALS

EXPLAIN
how lenders judge
your creditworthiness

DESCRIBE
the factors that go into
your credit rating

10.2 How to Qualify for Credit

Your Creditworthiness

To get a loan, you must demonstrate your creditworthiness to lenders. **Creditworthiness** is a measure of your reliability to repay a loan. To be creditworthy, you must have the ability and willingness to pay your debts.

Lenders judge creditworthiness on three factors: character, capacity, and capital. These are *the three C's of credit.*

Character

Your **character** is a measure of your sense of financial responsibility. Are you dependable? Do you take your obligations seriously? One way that lenders try to judge your character is to look at your credit history.

Your **credit history** is a record of your past borrowing and repayments. If you paid your bills on time in the past, lenders will be more likely to

CONSUMER ACTION

Derrick has worked hard to make his business a success. He installs driveways for a living. Derrick thinks he's rich. He buys almost everything he wants. He always charges purchases on his credit cards. Derrick owes more on his credit cards than he earns in a year. What recommendations would you make to Derrick if you could? What problems is he likely to have if he does not change his spending habits?

lend to you in the future. Paying your bills on time *always* is the most important factor in being able to get credit in the future.

What if you are looking for your first loan and have no credit history? Lenders look at the way you live your life for other signs of responsibility. If you have worked at the same job for a long time, you appear more reliable to lenders than if you switch jobs often. Living at the same address for a long time, having good school and work attendance, and saving regularly all suggest good character to lenders.

One way that a young person can get credit for the first time is to ask an older person, usually a parent, to **cosign a loan**. By cosigning a loan, your parent would be agreeing to pay the debt if you don't. If your cosigner is creditworthy, the lender will feel safe in lending to you because the cosigner is just as responsible as you are for making the payments.

Cosigning is a serious step that should not be taken lightly. If someone asks you to cosign a loan, you must be very sure that you can trust that person to make the payments. If you cosign, the loan is legally as much your responsibility as it is the borrower's. If the borrower misses payments, a court will require you to make the payments. In addition, the borrower's lack of responsibility will appear in your credit history as well as in the borrower's.

Capacity

Your **capacity** is a measure of your financial ability to repay a loan. Is your income sufficient to make the payments? How many other fixed expenses do you have that your income must cover? Are you already financially overextended?

When you apply for a loan, the lender will require you to state your other debt payments. The lender will then calculate this as a percentage of your income to judge whether or not your income can support another payment.

Capital

Your **capital** is the value of what you own, including savings, investments, and property. If necessary, you could cash in your stock or sell your house to pay the debt. The more capital you have, the safer it is for a lender to give you a loan.

© Getty Images/PhotoDisc

CheckPoint

How would you judge your own creditworthiness? What evidence could you give lenders to show them that you have good character?

Your Credit Rating

Where do lenders get all of this information about you? One source is your application form. Lenders can also get a report of your credit history from a credit bureau.

Loan Applications

When you want to borrow, you will be required to complete an application form. The information you provide on the form helps the lender determine your creditworthiness.

Look at the loan application to see the information you must supply. In the section on financial information, you must list your assets and liabilities. Your assets are your *capital*—the things of value you own. Your liabilities are your debts.

From your list of liabilities, the lender can see how many other payments you are obligated to make each month. Then the lender can look at the income you list on the form and judge whether or not your income can support another debt payment.

Credit Bureaus

Besides your application form, lending institutions also get information about you from a credit bureau. A **credit bureau** is a company that collects information about consumers' credit history and sells it to lenders.

Credit bureaus have records on just about every adult who has ever made payments on anything. They

get the information from stores, banks, utility companies, and court records. If you have ever bounced a check, missed a rent payment, or were sued, most likely this information is in your file at a credit bureau. The three largest credit bureau companies are Trans Union, Equifax, and Experian.

© Getty Images/PhotoDisc

Sample Credit Application

Loan Application

Our Towne Bank

APPLICANT

Date	Taken By – Ext. #	Amount Requested	Purpose of Loan (Specific Reason)	
2/5/--		$1,000	furniture	☐ Secured ☒ Unsecured

Full Name	Date of Birth	Social Security No.	Home Phone
Peter L. Chase	4/16/75	123-12-1234	555-1234

Present Street Address	City	State	Zip Code	County	Lived There Years / Months
123 Oak Street	Hometown	ST	12345	Cook	4 / 10

Rent by Mo. ☒ Lease ☐ Own ☐	Mortgage Payment or Rent $	Landlord or Mortgage Holder Name	Previous Address	Lived There Years / Months	No. of Dependents
	500.00	Towne Prop.	123 Elm	2 / 0	0

Present Employer And Address	Occupation	Phone Number	How Long
Chase Concrete	President	555-2345	6 yrs

Previous Employer and Address	Occupation		How Long
Tom's Driveways	Apprentice, foreman		2 yrs

Name, address, and phone number of nearest relative not living with you
1) John Chase 234 Elm 555-6789

Name, address, and phone number of personal friend
2) Tony Lazzo 456 Elm 555-5432

CO-APPLICANT

Full Name	Date of Birth	Social Security No.	Home Phone

Present Street Address	City	State	Zip Code	County	Lived There Years / Months

Rent by Mo. ☐ Lease ☐ Own ☐	Mortgage Payment or Rent $	Landlord or Mortgage Holder Name	Previous Address	Lived There Years / Months	No. of Dependents

Present Employer and Address	Occupation	Phone Number	How Long

Previous Employer and Address	Occupation		How Long

Name, address, and phone number of nearest relative not living with you
1)

Name, address, and phone number of personal friend
2)

FINANCIAL INFORMATION

Assets	Amount	Liabilities	Monthly Payment	Amount
Cash (list Name of Institutions)		Credit Cards, Dept. Stores, & Other		
Checking Acct. Our Towne Bank	600	MasterCard		
Savings Acct. Our Towne Bank	2,000	VISA	75	3,000
Securities Owned (Market Value)				
Autos (Year & Model) 04 Ford Focus	9,400	Auto Loans	304	8,200
Home (Market Value)		Mortgage on Home		
		Home Equity Loan		
Other Real Estate Owned		Mortgage – Other Real Estate		
Personal Property (Market Value)		Installment Contracts Payable		
		Contingent & Other Liabilities		
TOTAL	$12,000	TOTAL	$379	$11,200

INCOME

Please indicate below your GROSS income, which is your income before taxes and other payroll deductions.	Applicant	Please indicate below your GROSS income, which is your income before taxes and other payroll deductions.	Co-Applicant
Salary: (If you are self-employed, please attach complete copies of your last two (2) federal income returns.) Monthly ☐ Annually ☒	$60,000	Salary: (If you are self-employed, please attach complete copies of your last two (2) federal income returns.) Monthly ☐ Annually ☐	
OTHER INCOME: Income from alimony, child support, or separate maintenance payments need not be revealed if you do not choose to have it considered as a basis for repaying this obligation. Other income not disclosed above: _____ per _____ SOURCE:		OTHER INCOME: Income from alimony, child support, or separate maintenance payments need not be revealed if you do not choose to have it considered as a basis for repaying this obligation. Other income not disclosed above: _____ per _____ SOURCE:	
TOTAL INCOME	$60,000	TOTAL INCOME	

IN CLASS ACTIVITY

List all of the products and services you obtain for which you must give your Social Security number, address, and telephone number. What does this tell you about the possibility of someone getting financial information about you?

Credit Ratings

When you apply to borrow, the lending institution will buy your credit record from a credit bureau. The lender will then analyze this information and give you a credit rating. A **credit rating** is a measure of your creditworthiness. It is a judgment about whether or not you have the ability and willingness to pay your bills on time.

Lenders often compute a numerical credit rating by using a computerized scoring system called *FICO*. Based on your credit report data, the FICO system will give you a score between 100 and 800. The score is based on certain factors from your credit report.

1. **Payment history**   This is the most important factor in your score. Even just a few late payments will lower your score dramatically.

2. **Current debt**   Do you already have as much debt as you can handle? If so, you most likely won't be able to borrow more.

3. **Length of credit history**   If you have a long history of financial responsibility, lending to you is less risky, and your rating will be higher.

4. **New accounts and inquiries**   Every time you apply for a loan or credit, the lender will ask the

---

PRIMARYSOURCES

Gus Constantin Geraris came to America from Greece in 1921. Read what he had to say about America and credit. Mr. Geraris made his comments more than 60 years ago! Is credit still easy to get? Have you experienced easy credit yourself? Do the benefits of easy credit outweigh the dangers?

"America is a land of easy money. There is more money in America and, strange to say, more suffering than in the old countries. The trouble in America is easy credit. It is so easy for a [person] making $25 a week to try to live like [someone] making a hundred dollars a week. You can buy a suite of furniture for a dollar down and a dollar a week; a radio or a suit of clothes the same way. You can buy an automobile on time, trading in your old car as down payment. Credit is too easy."

credit bureau for your report. If you have many such inquiries, it is a bad sign.

5. **What kind of credit do you use?** Having a credit card or two that you use responsibly is good, but having many credit cards lowers your score. Having too many credit cards gives you too much opportunity to get into financial trouble.

Your credit rating is really up to you. Always pay your bills on time. Don't take on more debt than you can easily repay. If you do these things, your credit rating will be excellent, and you will have no trouble borrowing within your means to repay.

CheckPoint

What kinds of information is a credit bureau collecting about you? Where does it get the information? How is it used to compute your credit rating?

TRY THESE

1. What are the three C's of credit?

2. How can a lender judge your character?

3. How can a lender judge your capacity?

4. How can a lender judge your capital?

5. What is a credit history?

6. Where can a lender get your credit information?

7. What does cosigning a loan mean for the cosigner?

8. What kinds of information about you can a lender get from your loan application form?

9. What do credit bureaus do and where do they get their information?

10. What factors go into a FICO credit rating?

THINK CRITICALLY

11. **CONSUMER ACTION** Derrick is deeply in debt. What trouble do you see ahead for Derrick? What advice would you give him? Why?

12. **COMMUNICATE** Write three paragraphs in which you evaluate your own creditworthiness. What are your character, capacity, and capital? What can you do now to improve your creditworthiness in the future? E-mail your answer to your teacher.

13. Why is a good credit rating important?

14. Imagine where you will be financially when you are 25. Fill out a loan application for yourself. Estimate your expenses or what you think they will be at that time. What will your income be in your job at that time? Where and how will you live? What do you expect to purchase using credit?

GOALS

IDENTIFY
different options for
getting credit

DESCRIBE
the benefits and costs
of credit cards

© Getty Images/PhotoDisc

10.3 Sources of Consumer Credit

Types of Consumer Borrowing

Consumer borrowing takes two basic forms: loans and credit card accounts. When you get a loan, you receive an amount of money all at once to make your purchase. You then must make specified payments to repay the loan, with interest, by a certain date.

When you use a credit card, the amount of your purchase is added to your account. You then pay whatever amount you want each month, as long as you pay at least the required minimum. The account has no specified payoff date. As long as you continue making the minimum required payments, you can keep adding purchases to your account up to your credit limit. This arrangement is dangerous, as you will see later in this lesson.

Secured Loan

A loan can be secured or unsecured. A **secured loan** is backed by something of value pledged to ensure

CONSUMER ACTION

Tracy wants to borrow $600 to buy a kayak. She has always made the payments on her credit card account on time. She works part-time and thinks she earns enough to take on the new debt. Where should she go to get the loan? What are her options? How can she decide which is best?

payment. For example, if you own a house, you can pledge your house as your assurance that you will repay a loan. If you fail to make your payments, your house could be sold to pay your debt. The property pledged to back a loan is called **collateral**.

A secured loan is safe for the lender because the lender can be sure that your debt will be repaid. This type of loan is not as safe for you. For you to get a secured loan, you risk losing the property you pledge.

Most secured loans are also installment loans. An **installment loan** is repaid in a certain number of payments with a certain interest rate. For example, most car sales are financed by installment loans of 36 months or more. Because installment loans are made at one time and for one amount, installment loans may be called *closed-end credit*.

Unsecured Loan

An **unsecured loan** is not backed by any collateral. The lender grants you credit based on your credit-worthiness alone. If your credit history is good, you can probably get an unsecured loan.

One drawback to unsecured loans is that they generally require you to pay higher interest rates than secured loans. Remember that the lender is taking a greater risk in making this type of loan.

Most credit cards are considered unsecured loans because they are loans for an unspecified amount up to the customer's credit limit. This is

sometimes referred to as *open-end credit* since the balance does not have to be paid by a specific date.

Banking Institutions as Sources of Loans

The most common sources of consumer loans are banks, savings and loan associations, and credit unions. Banks and credit unions make loans for all kinds of purchases, large or small. Savings and loans specialize in loans to buy real estate, but most lend money for other purchases as well.

Not all banks charge the same interest rates. Shop around for a loan. Start with the bank where you keep your savings and checking accounts. Then move on to other banks in your community. You may be surprised at the differences in their lending costs.

Also, look for special deals advertised in newspapers. Some banks have "loan sales." Some banks could offer lower interest rates to new customers. Saving 1 percent on a loan of $5,000 is saving $50 per year.

© Getty Images/PhotoDisc

Other Sources of Consumer Loans

Generally, a bank, credit union, or savings and loan should be your first choice for obtaining a loan. They often have the best rates. There are other options, but be careful! Except for life insurance companies, these other sources of loans are more expensive and in some cases *much* more expensive than borrowing from a bank.

Finance Companies Many young people get their first loans from finance companies. Finance companies are usually more willing to lend to people with no credit history or a poor credit rating. Loans to people like this, however, are riskier for the lender. Because of the additional risk, finance companies charge higher interest rates than banks.

Life Insurance Companies If you own a life insurance policy, you may be able to use it as collateral for a loan. Borrowing against a life insurance policy is safe for the insurance company. If you don't pay back the loan by the time you die, the company simply deducts the amount you owe from the insurance benefits. Because of the safety of such a loan for the company, the interest rate is usually lower than for other types of loans, and the loan is easy to get.

Credit Card Cash Advances Within limits set by your bank, you can borrow money on your credit card account as a *cash advance*. When you use an ATM, one of your choices is to receive a cash advance. If you select this option, the machine will give you the cash and then add it to your credit card bill.

In many cities and towns, you can see big signs that advertise check cashing services. They will give you cash for your paycheck now. If you don't have enough to cover the check, a bank will make you wait three days or so until the check clears before you can have the cash.

What's the cost of having your cash now? *The Detroit News* reported a typical case. Chad got his federal tax refund check for $2,334, and he wanted the cash now. He took it to a check cashing service and received $2,194 in cash. How much did Chad pay for the convenience of getting cash now instead of going to a bank and waiting until the check cleared? Do you think that using a check cashing service is a smart choice?

The interest rate on a cash advance is quite high—often between 17 and 24 percent per year. Because of the interest rate, it is an easy way to get into financial trouble.

Pawnbrokers To get a loan from a pawnbroker, you must turn over personal property, such as jewelry or a TV. To get your property back, you must pay back the loan plus a fee. The rates are always very high.

Rent-to-Own Companies

Suppose you don't have $125 to buy a DVD player, so you rent one. Your payments are $8.95 a month for two years, and all payments will be applied to the purchase. As a renter, you are technically paying no interest. How much are you *really* paying to buy this machine? If you rent until you own it, you will have paid $214.80 for a $125 player!

$8.95 × 24 months = $214.80

In addition, until you make the final payment, you don't own the player. If you stop paying at any time, the company will just take it back.

CheckPoint

What is the difference between a secured and an unsecured loan? Why are banks, credit unions, and savings and loans generally the best choices for a consumer loan?

© Getty Images/PhotoDisc

Credit Cards

When you use a credit card, you are borrowing money. To open a credit card account, you must fill out an application. If your application is approved, you will receive a credit card that represents your account. A credit card looks much like an ATM card. It has information about your account stored on a piece of magnetic tape on its back.

To buy something with your credit card, simply present it to the salesperson when you are ready to make a purchase. The salesperson will run the card through a computerized system, which will make sure your credit account is still open and you have credit available. Then the amount of the purchase is added to your account.

Regular Charge Accounts

Some credit cards do not allow you to carry a balance from one month to the next. With a **regular charge account**, you must pay your balance each month in full within a specific amount of time. There is no stated interest rate since you are not borrowing money with this type of account. Regular charge accounts are offered by American Express, Diner's Club, and some department stores.

Revolving Charge Accounts

When you think of a credit card, you are probably thinking of a revolving charge card. A **revolving charge account** allows you to carry a balance from one month to the next. You pay interest on this type of account because you are borrowing money for a while. You can pay any amount over the minimum each month. If you pay only the minimum each month, the balance could take months or years to pay off.

Sources of Credit Cards

More than a billion credit cards are in use in the United States. Some large stores offer their own cards to encourage buying from them. A few large organizations, such as VISA, MasterCard, American Express, and Discover, issue most credit cards.

Banks put their names on the cards they provide to their customers.

Credit cards are also available through some charities, gasoline companies, universities, credit unions, and special interest groups.

Credit Card Incentives

Some organizations offer incentives to use their card. For example, some gas companies offer free gasoline for purchases using their cards. Use of other credit cards earns free airline ticket points. Others, such as Working Assets, donate a percentage of payments to charity.

$MATH OF MONEY

Ted owes $720 on his credit card. He plans to make the minimum required payment of $20 this month. His interest rate is 18 percent per year. What is his monthly interest rate? How much of his payment will be interest? If he doesn't charge anything else, how much will his $20 payment reduce his debt?

▌SOLUTION

0.18 per year ÷ 12 months = 0.015 = 1.5 percent per month

Ted pays 1.5 percent interest each month.

$720.00 × 0.015 = $10.80

The monthly interest rate is applied to Ted's unpaid balance of $720.00, so the monthly interest is $10.80.

$20.00 − $10.80 = $9.20

Ted's minimum payment this month reduces his debt by only $9.20. Since interest is charged on and added to the unpaid balance, his debt will decrease by a little more than this amount in following months. At this rate, it will take him more than five years to pay off his debt. If he charges anything else in that five years, it will take even longer to pay off the debt. From these numbers, you can see that Ted could get into debt trouble easily by making only the minimum payment each month.

INTERNET ACTIVITY

List the types of credit that businesses in your community offer. Also, look for credit card offers on the Internet. Which have higher and lower interest rates? Why are interest rates higher for some than others? E-mail your final list and answers to your teacher.

All of these incentive programs are designed to encourage you to sign up for a particular card and then run up your credit account balance. The credit card company earns much of its income from the interest you pay on the money you borrow. It is in the credit card company's best interest to encourage you to use the card.

Credit Card Costs

The cost of owning and using credit cards varies widely. The fact that a card was issued through an organization you support doesn't automatically make it a good choice. Evaluate the costs of your alternatives before you choose a credit card.

Annual Fees   A card's annual fee can be as little as $15 or as much as $100. Some banks offer cards without an annual fee to customers who have other accounts with minimum balances. Other banks offer cards that have no fee in the first year.

Information about fees can be confusing. Be sure you understand what you are required to pay before you open any credit account.

Interest   All credit accounts charge interest on unpaid balances.

Interest rates vary widely, so shop around. Introductory offers may charge 3.9 percent or less, but low rates are usually short lived. Typical rates after the special promotion period can be as high as 24 percent.

You can avoid paying these high interest charges by paying your entire debt before the end of your grace period. A **grace period** is the time between the billing date and the payment due date when no interest is charged. For most cards, the grace period is between 15 and 25 days.

If you do not pay your entire debt within the grace period, interest will start accumulating from the date of your purchase. With a few exceptions, the interest rate will be high. Your best choice is to pay off your credit balance every month to avoid the interest charges.

Limits and Penalties   Each account has a **credit limit**. This is the maximum amount you are allowed to charge. If you go over your limit, you will have to pay a penalty.

© CORBIS

For example, suppose your card has a $1,000 limit. If your total debt in the account rises above $1,000, you will typically have to pay a penalty of $20 to $40 per month. A similar fee is charged if you fail to pay your bills on time. Some banks earn almost as much in penalty fees as they do in interest from credit cards. Keeping good records of your purchases is the best way to avoid a penalty for charging over your limit.

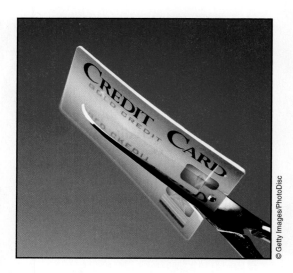

© Getty Images/PhotoDisc

Control Credit Card Costs

Interest is the greatest cost of using a credit card. Except for introductory offers of discounted rates to get you to sign up, interest rates for credit cards are higher than almost any other type of consumer credit.

A Loan as an Alternative

One way to control your credit costs is to choose a loan instead of a credit card for your purchase. Suppose you charged $1,250 on your credit card. When you receive your bill, you can pay only $500 of this debt. You will be charged 18 percent per year on the remaining $750 balance.

You do have an alternative. You could borrow $750 from your bank. The bank's loan interest rate is likely to be closer to 9 percent per year. By using your loan to pay your credit card debt, you can reduce your interest cost. The lower interest charged by the bank would save you about $5 the first month and a little less per month thereafter as your balance decreases.

The Minimum Payment Trap

Most people add many months to their credit card payments by paying only the minimum payment each month. A large part of the minimum payment is interest, so your debt doesn't decrease much with each payment. Since interest is charged on your unpaid balance each month, the quicker you can reduce the balance, the less interest you will pay overall.

Choose the Least Expensive Card

Choosing a credit card is easier if you never intend to pay credit card interest. If you always pay your entire balance, you need to consider only the annual fee and any incentives.

The best credit situation is to pay your balance each month. If you know that you won't be able to pay off your balance each month, compare rates among cards. Even a small difference in interest rate can make a big difference in the total interest you will pay over your lifetime.

CheckPoint

How can you avoid paying credit card interest? What should you compare when shopping for a credit card?

TRY THESE

1. Why is a secured loan safer for a lender than an unsecured loan?

2. Why would you pay more in interest for unsecured credit than for secured credit?

3. Why should you try to get a loan at a bank before considering a finance company?

4. What is the difference between a regular and a revolving charge account?

5. What are some things to consider before applying for a certain credit card?

6. Why do some organizations offer incentives with their credit cards?

7. What kinds of charges would you typically have to pay for having and using a credit card?

8. How can you control your credit card expenses?

THINK CRITICALLY

9. **CONSUMER ACTION** Tracy wants to know where to go to get a $600 loan to buy a kayak. What options does she have? Which option would you advise her to choose? Why?

10. Why do you think people use rent-to-own companies? If you wanted to buy a stereo but didn't have the money to pay cash, what other options would you consider rather than renting it from a rent-to-own company?

11. Why is making the minimum payment on your credit card account each month a trap?

12. Why do you think most credit cards have limits?

13. **MATH OF MONEY** Your credit card balance is $1,500. You decide to make the minimum payment of $45 each month so that you will have more cash to spend on other things. The interest rate is 24 percent. How much of this month's payment will be interest? How much will this month's payment reduce your debt? What do these numbers tell you about the wisdom of your decision to pay the minimum each month?

DECISION MAKING PROJECT

 SPECIFY **SEARCH** SIFT SELECT STUDY

SEARCH Have group members find the following information and request an application for different credit options available in your area.

1. What is the interest rate?

2. Is it secured or unsecured credit?

3. How long will it take to repay the loan for your purchase?

4. How much will you pay in interest on your purchase?

GOALS

DISCUSS
ways that laws protect
your credit rights

DESCRIBE
how to take responsi-
bility for your own
financial health

Photo by Eric Von Fischer/ Photonics

10.4 Credit Rights and Responsibilities

Consumer Credit Rights

As a borrower, you have rights that enable you to make good credit choices and help to solve credit problems. When you use credit, you need clear, accurate information to evaluate your alternatives. You need protections from discrimination in obtaining credit and from abusive collection practices. If there are errors in your bill or in your credit record, you need ways to fix them. Consumer protection laws help to protect you from these and other credit-related problems.

Truth in Lending

In the past, banks provided credit information written in complicated language. Interest rates and fees were calculated in many different ways. Many consumers were unable to make rational decisions because it was difficult to determine how much a loan actually cost.

To help solve this problem, the government passed the Truth in Lending Act in 1968. This law requires all banks to calculate credit costs in the same way. They must

CONSUMER ACTION

Eric is 24 years old. He has held the same job for five years, saves regularly, and always pays his bills on time. He has never overdrawn his checking account. Last week, Eric applied for an $8,000 loan to buy a jet ski. The bank turned him down. What should Eric do? What are his consumer rights?

provide two types of information about the cost of every loan: the finance charge and the annual percentage rate.

The **finance charge** is the total cost a borrower must pay for a loan, including all interest and fees. The **annual percentage rate (APR)** is the finance charge calculated as a percentage of the amount borrowed.

Even if you don't understand how these numbers are determined, you can use them to evaluate your alternatives. Since all banks must calculate these numbers exactly the same way, you can compare finance charges and APRs to determine the best deal.

Suppose you visit two banks and ask to borrow $1,000 for a year. The first bank tells you its APR is 8.9 percent. The second's APR is 8.5 percent. Since both banks must calculate APR the same way, you know that the second bank has the lower rate for the loan.

The law does not guarantee that you will pay the lowest amount possible when you use credit. It requires only that lenders give you clearly stated, accurate information. Using this information to get the best deal is up to you.

Equality in Lending

At one time, banks had different credit policies for different consumers. Women, members of racial minority groups, and older Americans often found it difficult to get credit. The Equal Credit Opportunity Act, passed in 1975 and amended in 1977, made it illegal to refuse credit on the basis of race, color, religion, national origin, gender, marital status, or age.

VOTE Your Wallet

The Truth in Lending Act requires all lenders to calculate their finance charges the same way. The same is not true of grace periods and penalties. In recent years, many lenders have reduced the number of days in the grace periods they give borrowers to make payments and increased the amount of penalties charged for late payments.

At one time, 21-day grace periods were the norm and penalties ranged from $10 to $20. Today, 15-day grace periods are typical and penalties can be as high as $40. Some lenders make almost as much from penalties as they do from interest.

Some legislators have suggested that the Truth in Lending Act should be amended to standardize grace periods and limit penalties. Others believe that this would be too much government regulation. How would you vote?

Protect Your Credit History

If your credit history shows that you made your payments on time for past loans, you will probably be able to borrow again.

Credit bureaus collect credit information about almost every U.S. adult consumer. When this information is accurate, it can help people get the credit they want. What happens if it is not?

In 1971, the Fair Credit Reporting Act gave consumers a way to check their credit reports. This law requires lending organizations to identify the credit bureau that supplied the information used to make their lending decision. If you have been refused credit, you have 30 days to request a free copy of your file. Even if you weren't denied credit, you can request a copy of your file for a small fee, usually around $8.

In 1996, Congress passed the Consumer Credit Reporting Reform Act, which makes it easier for consumers to correct mistakes in their credit reports. This law requires the credit bureau to investigate disputed items on a credit report within 30 days. If the bureau can't verify the information within that time, the item must be removed from the record.

If you think you were refused credit unfairly, here is what you should do.

1. Get the contact information for the credit bureau from the lender that denied you credit.

2. Write to the credit bureau and request a copy of your credit report.

3. Study the report for inaccuracies.

4. If you find errors, report them to the credit bureau in writing. The credit bureau must, by law, look into your claim within 30 days.

5. If you find no errors but you believe your credit problems were caused by unusual circumstances, write an explanation of the circumstances surrounding the late or unpaid account on your record. The law allows you to have a 100-word statement attached to your credit report.

If your credit history is corrected for any reason, check it again after six months. Credit bureaus share information. Sometimes information that one credit bureau removes gets re-entered into the record when a second credit bureau shares its uncorrected report.

Never assume that the credit bureau will take care of a problem for you. Usually it will, but mistakes can still happen. Your best choice is to take responsibility for defending your own credit history.

Resolve Billing and Product Quality Problems

The Fair Credit Billing Act, which is part of the Truth in Lending Act, helps consumers correct credit card billing mistakes.

Imagine you receive a credit card bill of $119.43 for clothes you never bought. Under the law, you have the

right to refuse to pay the bill. Within 60 days, you must write to the company that issued your credit card and explain why you believe the bill is wrong. The company must reply to your letter within 30 days and resolve the dispute within 90 days.

During this time, you may not be charged interest. If it turns out that you really owe the money, you can be charged interest later.

The law also gives you a way to resolve problems related to product quality. If you believe a product you bought with a credit card was of inferior quality, you must first try to settle the problem with the merchant. If you cannot resolve the problem with the merchant, you may withhold payment to the company that issued your credit card until the matter is settled.

Protection from Abusive Collection Practices

The Fair Debt Collections Practices Act was passed in 1977 to stop debt collection agencies from using abusive practices. The law prohibits harassment or abusive conduct, such as threatening phone calls or deceptive means to get information. The law applies to agencies in the business of collecting debts for others, not to individuals or businesses trying to collect their own accounts.

© Getty Images/PhotoDisc

> ## CheckPoint
>
> **How do the different laws pertaining to consumer credit protect your rights and help you make good credit decisions?**

Consumer Credit Responsibilities

Borrowing money carries responsibilities as well as rights. You are responsible for your own financial health. Credit is a privilege, not a right. If you use it responsibly, it can help you buy the things that add enjoyment to your life.

Accept Responsibility

You may think that if a lending institution is willing to lend you money, you must be financially able to handle the payments. Not so! Although lending institutions have access to your credit record and know how much you owe in other debts, they will not necessarily limit your credit.

Lenders are in business to make money. They are not trying to protect you from financial difficulties. You must take responsibility for borrowing only what you can afford to repay.

Know Your Debt Capacity

When you are thinking about taking on more debts, you should consider your other fixed expenses as well as your debt payments. A little arithmetic and some common sense can help you determine whether you can afford to take on more debt.

Suppose your take-home pay is $1,000 a month. Fixed expenses for your car loan and insurance, rent, and utilities total $600. Subtract your debt payments and other fixed expenses from your take-home pay.

$1,000 - $600 = 400 left per month

The result is the amount of income you have left each month to spend as you like, save, or take on new debt.

Now apply common sense. Is this enough to pay for all the food, clothes, gas, personal-care items, and entertainment you want each month and have some to save? If increasing your debt payments would cause you to give up important types of flexible spending or saving, don't do it!

Credit and Family

Like saving or investing, your borrowing affects other family members. Your future income will probably help support other people: a spouse, children, or perhaps your parents. When you borrow, you trade current spending for future spending. Going far into debt now could mean you won't be able to meet your future financial obligations. A bad credit history can make borrowing difficult when it is really needed. One of your life-span goals could be owning a home. If you don't use credit wisely, banks probably won't give you a mortgage. Remember the basic credit rule: Never borrow more than you can comfortably repay.

Self-Control with Credit

Pay More than the Minimum Credit card spending can easily get out of hand. Since you can choose how much to pay each month, as long as you pay at least the minimum, it is tempting to pay the least amount possible. But paying just the minimum each month is a trap that you can't easily escape.

Make a better choice: Pay more than the minimum every month. Plan a payment that will pay your balance off. Then stay within your budget.

Avoid Too Many Credit Cards Credit card offers in the mailbox are common. Each card may offer another $1,000 or $2,000 of credit. Be smart. Resist the temptation to have too many credit cards. One or two should be enough. A good strategy is to have one card for small purchases you plan to pay off every month and another for large purchases and emergencies.

Pay Cash Because you have a credit card doesn't mean you have to use it for everything. Credit isn't free. Make a habit of paying cash for small purchases such as those under $25. Paying cash gives you a better sense of when you're spending too much.

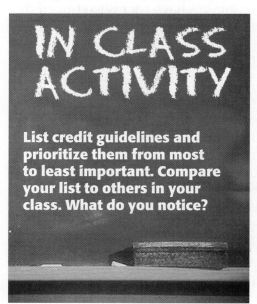

IN CLASS ACTIVITY

List credit guidelines and prioritize them from most to least important. Compare your list to others in your class. What do you notice?

Keep Accurate Records

When you use your credit card to make purchases, keep the receipts. Each month you will get a credit card statement that lists each purchase. Always check the statement for accuracy. If you find an error, you will have the receipt to back up your claim. Plan to pay off the balance shown on your statement.

CheckPoint

Describe a common sense approach for determining whether you can handle more debt.

TRY THESE

1. How does the Truth in Lending Act benefit you?

2. What is the difference between the finance charge and the annual percentage rate (APR) on a loan?

3. If you order a product using a credit card and the product turns out to be defective, what can you do?

4. How do the two credit reporting acts help you protect your credit history?

5. If you believe you were refused credit unfairly, what should you do?

6. Why must you take responsibility for your own financial health?

7. What are some ways to keep your credit card spending under control?

THINK CRITICALLY

8. **CONSUMER ACTION** Eric was turned down when he applied for credit even though his credit history seems to be good. What can Eric do?

9. When you apply for credit, your bank will show you a finance charge and an APR. Which one will be higher? Why? Which one should you use to compare rates at different lending institutions?

10. Why is credit a privilege rather than a right? What should you do to be worthy of the privilege?

11. **COMMUNICATE** Kathy buys all her clothes with her credit card. She pays the minimum amount each month but doesn't understand why her balance keeps going up. Write a short letter to Kathy explaining why this occurs. E-mail your letter to your teacher.

DECISION MAKING PROJECT

 SPECIFY SEARCH SIFT SELECT STUDY

SIFT Have group members present their credit options. Put the options on a comparative chart. Include what each person estimates the total interest paid will be for the purchase.

GOALS

EXPLAIN
how to establish a
positive credit history

DISCUSS
how to avoid credit
problems and how to
get help if you need it

© Getty Images/PhotoDisc

10.5 Maintain a Good Credit Rating

Establish Your Credit History

If you want the option of using credit when you need it, you must earn and maintain a good credit history. To earn it, you must show in your financial dealings that you are a responsible consumer and borrower.

Start Small

If you have never used credit or paid regular bills before, the credit bureau probably has no credit history file on you. You have to start somewhere to build a positive record.

Start small. Apply for a department store credit card. This type of card is easier to get than a major credit card. Make small purchases at the store, and pay off the balance on time every month.

Do Not Miss a Payment! If you make even one payment late at this early stage, the department store may close your account. Also, you will have created a bad entry in your credit history that will take you a long time to overcome.

CONSUMER ACTION

Last month, Stacy was billed for several credit card purchases she didn't make. At first she thought little of it. She wrote the credit card company and asked to have the problem investigated. Then Stacy received a bill for a refrigerator she never bought. The next day, she was billed for a cellular telephone she does not own. Now she is really worried. What should she do?

As you continue to make payments on time, your credit history will strengthen.

Save Regularly Making regular deposits in a savings account will also show the bank that you can manage your money and will encourage the bank to extend you credit in the future.

Credit for Married People

If you are married, it is important that you establish your own credit history apart from your spouse. When you apply for a credit card, either get one with both names on it or get a card in each name separately. When you take out a loan, use both of your names.

By doing these things, you will have a credit record in your own name at the credit bureau. Then, if you ever need to borrow money on your own, you will have a credit history for the lender to evaluate.

Be aware, though, that loans or credit cards in the names of you and your spouse together count equally toward each person's credit history. If either of you misses a payment, it will affect both of your credit ratings.

© Getty Images/PhotoDisc

Avoid Common Credit Mistakes

It is easier to destroy a credit history than to build a good one. Always pay bills when they are due. Never ignore bills when you are short on money. If something unusual happens, such as unemployment or illness, that would cause you to miss a payment, contact the lender to discuss the situation. Lenders will usually be flexible if you contact them as soon as there is a problem.

Records stay in your credit history for many years. Especially when you are young and have only a short history of payments, a mistake could prevent you from getting credit for years.

Read What You Sign

You are legally bound by the contracts you sign. If you do not fulfill your obligations under a contract, you can be taken to court and might even lose your property.

Read every contract and make sure you understand it. If you don't understand something, ask the lender for an explanation. If you are uncomfortable with any part of the contract, don't sign it. Once you sign, you are legally obligated to uphold your end of the deal.

Acceleration Clause Some credit contracts include an **acceleration clause** that says the entire debt is immediately due if you miss a single payment. Suppose you borrow $1,000 to buy a small fishing boat. You agree to pay $50 every month for two years. Your loan contract has an acceleration clause.

You make your payments faithfully for a year, but one time you forget to make a payment. The following month, the boat dealer demands that you pay the remaining $500 you owe. If you don't have the funds, the store can take back your boat. In spite of all the payments you made, you would have no boat, and it's perfectly legal.

When you read a credit agreement, be careful to look for an acceleration clause. If it has one, ask the lender to remove it. If the lender refuses, don't sign the contract.

Balloon Payment Some contracts have a clause that requires you to make a final payment that is much larger than the regular payments. This large final payment is called a **balloon payment**, and it is legal in most states. Suppose you bought a TV on credit and have been making regular $25 payments each month for a year. When your final payment is due, you find out that your final payment must be $200, or your TV will go back to the store. You may have to take out another loan just to pay off the first one.

Balloon payment clauses are not always bad. They do result in low payments until you get to the final one. Sometimes this is what you need.

Suppose you just started a new career with a low starting salary. You are offered a home loan with low monthly payments and a balloon payment after 15 years. You expect your salary to rise over the years so you can save for the balloon payment and/or be eligible to refinance the loan. Still, a loan with a balloon payment is risky. If your income does not rise as you hope, you could lose your house.

Bankruptcy

The lure of "the good life" sometimes causes consumers to get themselves hopelessly in debt. Using credit until

CYBER CONSUMER

Nolo Press, a publisher of law books, sponsors a self-help law center on the Internet. Look for this site and click on *Debt & Bankruptcy* in the Nolo Legal Encyclopedia. There you'll find all kinds of advice about responsible use of credit, debt repayment strategies, and the consequences of ignoring your debt.

you cannot possibly pay off the debt is the worst credit mistake you can make. At its most extreme, out-of-control debt can force you into bankruptcy.

Bankruptcy is a legal process in which people who cannot pay their debts must surrender most of their property. The court then sells the property to help pay the debts. In exchange, the consumer is not required to pay the rest of the debt.

The price of bankruptcy is very high. You could be left with almost no property. Your credit history will carry the report of your bankruptcy for ten years.

During that time, you will probably not be able to get any credit. You might have trouble finding someone to rent you a place to live. Most likely, you will have to pay cash for everything, so making big purchases, such as a car, might be impossible.

If you get into such severe financial trouble, bankruptcy will give you a chance for a new start, but it can be a very painful process.

True-Name Fraud

A new type of fraud has become a serious problem for American consumers. **True-name fraud**, or identity theft, involves using someone else's identity to get cash or buy products using credit.

How "They" Become "You"

All criminals need is your Social Security number, your driver's license, or even your credit card number to open charge accounts in your name. They don't even have to give a real address; a post office box will do.

If your identity is stolen, the businesses that extended the credit are responsible for the debts. However, records of these transactions can ruin your credit history.

How to Protect Yourself

The best way to protect yourself from true-name fraud is to guard your personal documents. Never give your Social Security number to anyone unless it is absolutely necessary. Keep your personal documents in a safe place. Keep track of your bills. If you receive a bill for any charge you did not make, contact the business immediately.

CheckPoint

What things should you look for when you read a credit agreement? What are the costs of bankruptcy?

What In The World?

The U.S. population is about twice that of Japan, yet bankruptcies in the United States are more than 16 times the number in Japan. Why the big difference? The answer lies in the different attitudes toward bankruptcy in the two cultures. A recent magazine article told the story of a man who had moved from Tokyo to work on a farm after he filed for bankruptcy. When asked why he had done this, the man answered that he could not face his friends after the shame of bankruptcy.

How do you think the U.S. attitude toward bankruptcy differs from that of the Japanese? Would U.S. consumers be better off if society adopted a point of view on bankruptcy more like the Japanese have? Would Japanese consumers be better off if their attitude were more like that of Americans? Why?

Help for Credit Problems

It is far better not to get into credit trouble at all. If you do, however, some options can help you get back on your feet.

Debt Consolidation Loans

Many small debts can add up to a sizable part of your income when you pay bills. Each payment by itself doesn't seem like more than you can handle, but taken together, these payments can be overwhelming. Banks and finance companies offer a **debt consolidation loan** designed to pay off all the smaller loans and give you one payment to make each month. Payments on the new loan are extended over a longer period of time, so the amount of the payment is smaller than the monthly total of the old payments. If you shop around for the best APR, you might even be able to get the loan at a lower rate than you were paying for the smaller loans.

Cost of a Debt Consolidation Loan   The result of the debt consolidation loan is a lower monthly payment, but this doesn't mean that you pay less. In fact, you pay *more* because you are making payments over a longer period of time.

For example, suppose you have a car loan, owe on several credit cards, and make regular payments to a furniture store. Together, your debts total $9,000 and your interest rate averages 24 percent. Each month, you must make payments of $475. If you can make them, your debts will be paid in about two years. Such payments might not leave you enough money, however, to pay your rent and other expenses.

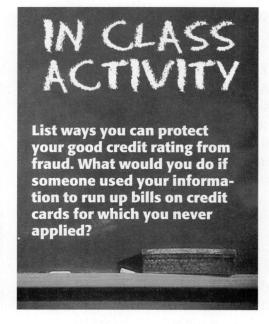

IN CLASS ACTIVITY

List ways you can protect your good credit rating from fraud. What would you do if someone used your information to run up bills on credit cards for which you never applied?

You could borrow $9,000 from a bank and use this money to pay your debts. This could reduce your interest rate to 15 percent and your monthly payment to $250 for four years.

This appears to be a great saving, but the longer you make payments, the more interest you pay. Without the consolidation loan, your total interest would be $2,420. With the consolidation loan, you would pay a total of $3,023 in interest. You will pay $603 more in interest for the loan.

It's a Bandage, Not a Cure
If you take a debt consolidation loan, be aware that you are making the best of a bad situation. Don't use the lower payments as an opportunity to spend more. Recognize and stop the problem that got you into debt in the first place—overspending.

Credit Counseling Services

If you see yourself heading for financial trouble, seek help. Many

PAID IN FULL

communities have an office of the National Foundation for Consumer Credit (NFCC). This is a non-profit service that helps consumers create budgets and pay their bills.

Other groups offer credit help in many communities. Most of these organizations are honest, but check them out as you would any other business. Check the Better Business Bureau for complaints. Be sure you understand any fees. Some so-called credit clinics charge excessive fees to people desperate for credit. If any part of the deal seems too good to be true, go somewhere else for help.

CheckPoint

If you find yourself sinking into debt trouble, what can you do?

TRY THESE

1. How can you start to establish your credit history?

2. Why should you read and understand credit agreements?

3. What are bankruptcy and its consequences?

4. What is true-name fraud, and how can you protect yourself from it?

5. How can a debt consolidation loan help you if you get too far in debt?

6. Where can you get help for financial problems?

THINK CRITICALLY

7. **CONSUMER ACTION** Stacy received bills for purchases she did not make. What should Stacy do in this situation? What steps can she take to prevent this from happening again?

8. How could bankruptcy affect you?

9. If you can get a debt consolidation loan with a lower total monthly payment and interest rate than the smaller loans it pays off, how could it actually cost you more than the smaller loans?

DECISION MAKING PROJECT

SPECIFY   SEARCH   SIFT   SELECT   STUDY

SELECT Discuss your findings with your group. Decide which credit option you would choose. Write a short paragraph stating how your group chose this option and what you learned about credit. Have each group member practice filling out an application for this credit option.

ASSESSMENT

KEY IDEAS

What Is Credit?

1. If you use credit, you give up the ability to spend in the future in order to spend now. Because you must pay interest, you are giving up *more* future spending than the amount of the loan.

2. Using credit can be a good choice as long as you do not borrow more than you can comfortably repay.

3. Homes usually increase in value over time, creating equity. The interest and property taxes also are deductible from federal income taxes.

4. Investing in your training or education usually results in higher income.

5. When you use credit, don't take on more debt payments than 20 to 25 percent of your take-home pay.

How to Qualify for Credit

6. To get a loan, lenders judge creditworthiness on the three C's of credit: character, capacity, and capital.

7. Lenders buy your credit record from a credit bureau and analyze it to give you a credit rating.

8. If you pay your bills on time and don't take on more debt than you can handle, your credit rating will be fine.

Sources of Consumer Credit

9. You can get loans through banks, savings and loans, credit unions, your life insurance policy, finance companies, pawnbrokers, and rent-to-own companies and as cash advances on your credit card.

10. A credit card is one of the most expensive forms of borrowing.

Interest rates are high and you often must pay an annual fee.

11. Control your credit costs by shopping for cards with low interest rates and annual fees, paying on time, and not overcharging your credit limit. Pay off your balance every month or pay more than the minimum.

Credit Rights and Responsibilities

12. The Truth in Lending Act requires all banks to state their finance charge and annual percentage rate (APR) for each loan and to calculate these costs in a standard way. You can compare finance charges and APRs to find the best deal.

13. Two laws protect your credit history. The Fair Credit Reporting Act requires the credit bureau to give you your credit report if you were refused credit. The Consumer Credit Reporting Reform Act requires the credit bureau to investigate any items you dispute on your credit report within 30 days and remove any item that can't be verified.

14. The Equal Credit Opportunity Act makes it illegal to refuse credit on the basis of race, color, religion, national origin, sex, marital status, or age.

15. The Fair Credit Billing Act helps you correct credit card billing mistakes and resolve problems with inferior-quality products bought with a credit card. The Fair Debt Collections Practices Act prohibits debt collection agencies from using abusive practices.

16. Judge your capacity for new debt carefully.
17. Practice self-control with your credit cards. Make more than the minimum payment each month.

Maintain a Good Credit Rating
18. If you have no credit history, start small. Follow a regular saving plan.
19. Read credit agreements before you sign them.
20. The consumer is left with little property plus the difficulty of getting credit for the ten years that a bankruptcy remains in a credit history.
21. True-name fraud is using another person's identity to buy products through the use of credit.
22. A debt consolidation loan is designed to pay off your smaller loans and give you one payment to make each month.
23. The National Foundation for Consumer Credit (NFCC) is a non-profit service that helps consumers create budgets and pay their bills.

TERMS REVIEW

Match each term on the left with its definition on the right.
Some terms may not be used.

a. acceleration clause
b. annual percentage rate (APR)
c. balloon payment
d. bankruptcy
e. capacity
f. capital
g. character
h. collateral
i. cosign a loan
j. credit
k. credit bureau
l. credit history
m. credit limit
n. credit rating
o. creditworthiness
p. debt consolidation loan
q. finance charge
r. grace period
s. installment loan
t. regular charge account
u. revolving charge account
v. secured loan
w. true-name fraud
x. unsecured loan

1. a measure of your ability and willingness to repay a loan
2. using another person's identity to get cash or buy products using credit
3. a contractual agreement to pay a debt if the borrower does not pay it
4. a measure of financial ability to repay a loan
5. a company that collects information about your credit history and sells it to lenders
6. property pledged to back a loan
7. the ability to borrow money in return for a promise of future repayment
8. the total amount a borrower must pay for a loan, including interest and fees
9. the finance charge calculated as a percentage of the amount borrowed
10. a measure of your creditworthiness, often computed as a numerical score using the FICO scoring system to analyze your credit history
11. a statement in a credit contract that requires you to repay the entire loan immediately if you miss a payment
12. the time between the billing date and due date when no interest is charged
13. a final loan payment that is much larger than the regular monthly payments
14. the maximum amount that you may charge on your credit account
15. a record of your past borrowing and repayments
16. a large loan used to pay off a number of smaller loans

CONSUMER DECISIONS

17. Imiko would like to borrow money from her bank to buy a used car. The payments would be $200 per month. She doesn't have any other debts. Still, she isn't sure whether she can afford it. Her take-home pay is $1,200 per month. Would you advise Imiko to borrow the money? Why or why not?

18. Ann wants to buy new furniture for her home on credit. She can borrow the $2,000 from her bank at a 12 percent rate. The store that she intends to buy from is running a special promotion. It will give her a 10 percent discount if she opens a credit account there. How should Ann decide which offer of credit to accept?

19. Carlos has always paid his bills on time. Last week, he applied to buy a new stereo system on credit. The store turned down his application. What should Carlos do?

20. Ted was injured in a bicycle accident a few months ago. His medical expenses have made it impossible for him to make his credit card payment this month. He expects to have problems making payments for a few months because of his injury. What should Ted do?

THINK CRITICALLY

21. Corey has been a construction worker for several years with a company that supplies the tools to do the job. Corey has received an offer to work for another company that does not supply tools. He would earn $20 more per week at the new job, and his wage could increase a little each year if he does a good job. Also, he has a chance to be promoted to foreman in a few years if he does well. To take this job, Corey would have to borrow $3,000 to buy the tools he needs. The payments would be $100 per month for three years. Would you advise Corey to take the job? What should he consider in the decision?

LOOK IT UP

22. The Internet offers a number of debt calculators that will automatically calculate monthly payments and interest for different loan amounts. Search on the key words *debt calculator.* Find a calculator that figures the interest. How much interest would you pay on a $4,000 loan at 18 percent interest for three years? How much interest would you pay for the same loan for four years? What do these numbers tell

WHICH IS THE BEST DEAL?

Jerome wants a high-definition TV for a Super Bowl party he is planning for next month. The one he wants costs $2,000. He is considering several options. What are the pros and cons of each alternative? Which do you think he should choose? Why?

Alternative 1   Wait to buy the set until he has saved the money to pay cash for it. He determined that the most he can save each month is $100.

Alternative 2   Rent the set now from a rent-to-own company that offers the set for $70 a month for 48 months. After he makes the final payment, the set will be his.

Alternative 3   Borrow $2,000 from a local bank for $90 per month for two years.

Alternative 4   Choose a smaller, less expensive TV set.

you about paying debts for different periods of time?

23. You can find loan rates in your local newspaper or *The Wall Street Journal* and by calling local financial institutions. Find a current APR from a bank, a finance company, and a credit card company as a cash advance. Compare the rates you found. Which is highest? Which is lowest? What does your research tell you about shopping for rates?

24. A number of web sites talk about the FICO scoring system. Search on the key word *FICO* and read about how the system determines credit ratings. What kinds of things raise your score? What kinds of things lower your score?

25. Look for three credit card offers in magazines or newspapers, in mail sent to your house, or on the Internet. What differences do you see in the offers? How is each one trying to attract consumers?

INSIDE THE NUMBERS

26. Joan carries a balance on her three credit cards. She is thinking of taking out a debt consolidation loan for $3,000 so she can pay off all her credit cards. If she does, she will pay 12 percent in interest for the next five years. Her payment will be half of what her monthly credit card payments are now. The interest rates for the

three cards are between 16 and 18 percent. Should Joan take out the debt consolidation loan? Why or why not? Will she pay more interest?

CURRICULUM CONNECTION

27. **HISTORY**   In England in the 1700s, people who could not pay their debts were put in poorhouses or debtor's prisons. They were forced to stay there until their families paid their debts. Investigate the use of credit in the 1700s. How were the rules different from the way consumers use credit now? How has the use of credit evolved from that time?

28. **PHILOSOPHY**   Many philosophers have discussed the ethics of borrowing or lending money. Find a book that summarizes the ideas of several philosophers. Compare the ideas of two of them on the subject of borrowing or lending. Which do you agree with most? Explain.

JOURNAL RECAP

29. After reading this chapter, review the answers you wrote to the questions in your Journal Journey. Have your opinions changed?

DECISION MAKING PROJECT

SPECIFY   **SEARCH**   **SIFT**   **SELECT**   **STUDY**

STUDY   Present your paragraph on the process your group went through to choose a credit option. Did other groups learn the same things that your group did about credit? If they learned something different, would this information have affected your choice of credit?

Chapter

11

BUDGET ESSENTIALS
FOOD, CLOTHES, AND FUN

WHAT'S AHEAD

EXPLODING MYTHS

Fact or Myth?
What do you think is true?

1. You will get all the nutrition you need by taking vitamin pills daily.

2. Designer clothes are the best-quality clothes on the market.

3. If you want to take up a new sport, buy the best equipment to get the most enjoyment out of it.

JOURNAL JOURNEY

WRITE IN YOUR JOURNAL ABOUT THE FOLLOWING.

FEELING GOOD Does what you eat affect how you feel? How could you improve your diet?

LOOKING GOOD How important is your appearance? How do your clothes affect the way you feel about yourself? What do you look for in the clothes you buy?

GOING PLACES What activities do you like to do most? What vacation destinations would give you the opportunity to do these activities? If you could vacation anywhere in the world, where would you go? Why?

DECISION MAKING PROJECT

SPECIFY   **SEARCH**   **SIFT**   **SELECT**   **STUDY**

SHOP 'TIL YOU DROP The semiformal dance is coming up, and each member of your group has saved $400 for a new outfit, a new suit, or a tuxedo rental. This amount must also cover your date's flowers, transportation, and any other related expenses. Shop for the best deals in town so you can go to the dance in style!

GOAL

To learn how to buy clothes and recreation

PROJECT PROCESS

SPECIFY	Lesson 11.2
SEARCH	Lesson 11.3
SIFT	Lesson 11.4
SELECT	Chapter Assessment
STUDY	Chapter Assessment

© Getty Images/PhotoDisc

11.1 Nutrition Facts

A Balanced Diet

To operate properly, your body needs **nutrients**—chemical substances from the foods you eat. Six basic nutrients help your body run: carbohydrates, protein, fats, vitamins, minerals, and water. Some nutrients supply energy. Others help body processes function properly.

Nutrients That Supply Energy

Three nutrients—carbohydrates, protein, and fats—supply energy to your body. **Calories** are a measure of the amount of energy that foods contain.

Carbohydrates are sugars and starches. They break down quickly, releasing energy for the body. Sugars are simple carbohydrates. They contain few nutrients, so your body doesn't need much sugar.

Starches are complex carbohydrates. They come from plants, such as whole grains, vegetables, and fruits. Complex carbohydrates are a better source of nutrients than simple carbohydrates.

CONSUMER ACTION

Kelly likes to sleep late in the morning. She has to be at school by 7:15, but she gets up at 6:30. This doesn't leave her much time for breakfast. Most days, Kelly eats a candy bar or bag of chips on her way to school. What advice would you give Kelly? What problems could her eating habits cause her?

Some complex carbohydrates also contain **fiber**. Fiber contains no nutrients, but it is essential to moving food through your digestive system.

Proteins help the body build and repair cells and also supply energy. They are the body's main building materials. You get proteins in such foods as meat, fish, eggs, dried beans, and nuts.

Fats are nutrients that your body needs, but they contain the most calories per gram of food. Fats come from foods such as butter, oils, and meat. **Cholesterol** is a substance found in animal fat. It can build up in your blood vessels and cause heart disease.

Nutrients That Aid Body Processes

The other three nutrients—vitamins, minerals, and water—do not supply energy. Instead, they help control your body processes.

Vitamins are nutrients that help your body react in essential ways. For example, vitamin D strengthens your bones and teeth and helps your body absorb calcium.

Minerals, such as calcium and iron, help your body grow and work. For example, phosphorous helps your body use energy from food. Some minerals keep the water balance in your body stable, and others help you fight diseases.

You need only small amounts of vitamins and minerals. But your body needs one nutrient in large quantities each day—water. Your body is made up mostly of water. You need water to digest food and transport nutrients to your cells. Water helps keep your body temperature stable and move waste prod-

The Food Guide Pyramid

Fats, Oils, and Sweets
USE SPARINGLY

Milk, Yogurt, and Cheese Group
2–3 SERVINGS

Meat, Poultry, Fish, Dry Beans, Eggs, and Nuts Group
2–3 SERVINGS

Vegetable Group
3–5 SERVINGS

Fruit Group
2–4 SERVINGS

Bread, Cereal, Rice, and Pasta Group
8–11 SERVINGS

ucts out of your body. To stay healthy, you should drink 48 to 64 ounces of water each day.

The Food Guide Pyramid

To be healthy, you need to eat a **balanced diet**. This means choosing foods that give you the right amounts of all six nutrients. But how can you make the right choices to balance your diet?

To help consumers achieve a balanced diet, the U.S. Department of Agriculture (USDA) created the **Food Guide Pyramid** based on scientific research on foods and nutritional needs. This guide divides foods into groups. Each group provides some, but not all, of the nutrients you need each day. A healthy, balanced diet requires foods from all groups in the pyramid.

The Food Guide Pyramid illustrates how much you need from each food group in terms of servings. A **serving** is the amount of food that you would probably eat during one meal or snack. The number of servings shown for each food group on the pyramid tells you how much food you need to eat from that group each day.

The guide is arranged in the form of a pyramid to show that you need more foods from some groups than others. The larger base of the pyramid emphasizes that you should choose more foods from the bottom than from the smaller top of the pyramid. In 2003, the USDA began revising the Food Guide Pyramid.

Here are some tips for making good food choices, based on the Food Guide Pyramid.

1. Eat a variety of foods each day.

2. Choose foods that are low in fat and cholesterol.

3. Eat plenty of fruits, vegetables, and whole-grain products.

4. Limit your consumption of sugar and salt.

CheckPoint

What is the Food Guide Pyramid? How can it help you get the nutrients your body needs?

Avoid Dietary Problems

Eating a balanced diet can be a challenge. Fast-food restaurants tempt you. Candy and ice cream taste too good to pass up. You don't have to deprive yourself of all life's treats to stay healthy—just use self-discipline and make good choices.

Fast Food

Fast-food restaurants are part of American culture. In fact, they are popping up in many other countries as well. They offer foods at low prices. It's easy to fall into the habit of stopping for a burger when you are out with your friends. Be aware that most fast food is very high in fat, calories, and cholesterol.

You don't have to give up fast food to stay healthy. You can eat fast food in moderation and make good choices from the menu. All major fast-food chains provide an analysis of their food's nutritional value if you ask. Sometimes the information is displayed on a wall chart.

If you look at this information, you will see that some food choices are more healthful than others. Hamburgers and hot dogs are high in fat, calories, and cholesterol. But you can choose a grilled chicken sandwich or salad pita instead. If you choose mustard instead of mayonnaise, you can make your sandwich more healthful as well. To reduce the amount of sugar in your fast-food meal, you can select orange juice instead of a soft drink.

© Getty Images/PhotoDisc

© Getty Images/PhotoDisc

Dieting

A recent survey showed that more than half of all American teenagers think they weigh too much. At any given time, about one-third of the U.S. population is trying to lose weight. This has created an enormous market for diet products.

Dieting aids are substances that are supposed to suppress your appetite, so that you can lose weight. They can take several forms, such as pills or drinks.

Often, dieting aids don't work, or work only temporarily. You may lose some weight this way, but if you don't change your eating habits, you will quickly regain the weight. Plus, taking a dietary aid for a long time can be harmful to your health. You are probably not getting the nutrients you need. If you use a dieting aid, diet under the supervision of a doctor.

Eating Disorders

Dieting taken to a dangerous extreme is an eating disorder that can threaten your life. **Anorexia nervosa** is a disorder characterized by a fear of obesity, a distorted self-image, an aversion to food, and severe weight loss. **Bulimia** is binge eating followed by purging through vomiting or use of laxatives. With either of these disorders, your body does not get the nutrients it needs. And without nutrients, your body cannot function.

Obesity means weighing above your ideal body weight by more than 20 percent. Your ideal weight depends on your height and whether you are male or female. You can find ideal weight tables in a health reference book, on the Internet, or by asking your doctor.

Being a little overweight is probably not life threatening, but being

---

☐ **PRIMARY**SOURCES

The ease with which we can find food today, and the abundance in our choices of food, would have been unimaginable to our ancestors. Read the following diary entry from a Western pioneer woman.

"Our living at first was very scanty—mostly corn coarsely ground or made into hominy. After we had raised a crop of wheat and had some ground, we would invite the neighbors, proudly telling them we would have 'flour doings.' Next it was 'chicken fixings.' And when we could have 'flour doings and chicken fixings' at the same meal we felt we were on the road to prosperity."

What does her writing indicate about a balanced diet? From what you know about the settling of the West, did the people get any exercise? What might this woman think of fast-food restaurants?

obese is. It can put a serious strain on your heart and other organs. It increases your chances of heart disease and stroke, as well as diabetes and other diseases.

If you have any of these eating disorders, seek medical help immediately. Your life depends on it.

Balanced Diet and Exercise

The only truly effective way to lose weight, keep it off, and remain healthy is to eat a balanced diet and exercise regularly. Choose healthful snacks from the Food Guide Pyramid. Eat junk food only in moderation. If you make good food choices, you don't have to starve yourself. What you eat is just as important to losing weight as how much you eat.

Many food manufacturers offer choices that are lower in fat, sugar, or calories than their regular foods. For example, diet soft drinks contain a sugar substitute that makes them sweet without the calories in regular soft drinks. Some cheeses are manufactured with less fat than others. Such low-fat and low-calorie diet foods can help you lose weight. Use them as part of, but not as a substitute for, a balanced diet.

Losing weight requires a change in your overall eating and exercise habits, not a one-time crash diet. You gained the

© Getty Images/PhotoDisc

This ad is typical of ads for body-building supplements on the Internet. Whom do you think this ad targets? What dangers can you see in such substances? What would you like to know about these products that you don't find in this ad?

weight over a long period of time. It makes sense that you would have to lose it over time as well. After a while, you will find that eating right makes you feel happier and more energetic.

CheckPoint

What is the difference between dieting and an eating disorder? What are the keys to maintaining a healthy body weight?

Investigate the nutritional value of foods offered at fast-food restaurants in your community. This information can be found on the Internet for most national fast-food chains. Assign a different restaurant to each member of your group. Exchange information found by e-mail. As a group, decide which restaurants offer the most healthful menus. Which restaurants appeal to children, young adults, or to the elderly? Send your findings to your teacher in an e-mail.

TRY THESE

1. What are nutrients, and what do they do for your body?

2. What are calories?

3. Why is fiber important in your diet?

4. Why is water important in your diet?

5. What is a balanced diet?

6. What are carbohydrates?

7. What are three common eating disorders?

8. What is the purpose of the Food Guide Pyramid?

9. How can you eat at fast-food restaurants and maintain a healthful diet?

10. What is the best way to lose weight? Why?

THINK CRITICALLY

11. CONSUMER ACTION Kelly has chosen to eat junk food for breakfast. What problems could this choice cause her? What other options does she have? What other choices would you suggest to her?

12. What are your greatest challenges in trying to eat a healthful diet? List three things you can do in your daily life to improve your eating habits.

13. COMMUNICATE Visit a local fast-food restaurant. Ask for information about the nutritional value of the foods it serves. Write a list of menu items that you think would result in a balanced meal. Then, in two or three paragraphs, explain why you made these selections.

14. COMMUNICATE Describe either your experience, or that of a friend, in trying to lose weight. Was the diet successful? Why or why not? What could have made the effort easier or more successful?

15. COMMUNICATE Write a paragraph or two about why you think so many teenagers have eating disorders. List as many possible causes as you can. Then evaluate each possible cause.

16. COMMUNICATE Write a short comparison of your current eating habits to those suggested in the Food Guide Pyramid. Based on this comparison, would you change your diet? Why or why not?

© Stockbyte

GOALS

DESCRIBE
how to plan a food shopping trip

DISCUSS
how to use the information available at the store to make rational buying decisions

11.2 Shop for a Healthful Diet

Have a Plan

It's easy to overspend in a grocery store. To make sure you leave the store with the food you need, not just junk food and impulse purchases, you need to plan before you go.

Determine Your Budget

If you have been keeping an overall budget, you will have a category for food. If you budgeted $400 for food this month, and you shop weekly, then you have approximately $100 to spend on this trip. To make sure you don't overspend, take only $100 with you.

Make a List

One good strategy is to plan your meals for the week and make a list of items you need for each meal. Then list the nonfood necessities, such as toothpaste and napkins. If you still have room in your budget, you can add more items.

When you list things to buy, be sure to consider other members of

CONSUMER ACTION

Brandon is doing the family's food shopping this week. His mother gave him a general list, so he thought the task would be easy. But when he got to the grocery store, the number of choices he had to make seemed overwhelming. His family wants to eat balanced meals, and his father is watching his weight. Plus, he must make all the purchases with the $75 his mother gave him. How can he decide what to buy?

VOTE Your Wallet

In the early 1990s, some people suffered food poisoning as a result of eating undercooked beef or chicken. These and other meats sometimes contain salmonella germs, which can cause illness. Salmonella can kill young people and people already in poor health.

One way to eliminate the danger of salmonella is to bombard food with radiation. The radiation kills the germs. Irradiation of foods to kill germs was approved by the FDA in 1997. This process has reduced the chance of salmonella poisoning. But some people worry about the effects the radiation might have on the food.

Would you vote to support irradiation? What other information would you want to consider? Do you believe irradiated foods should be labeled?

Look for Coupons and Advertised Specials

Most grocery stores advertise in local newspapers or distribute circulars. These ads tell you what the store has on sale. Often, they also include coupons that reduce the price of some items. Some stores even double the amount of manufacturers' coupons.

Clip the coupons for items your family might want. When you are ready to shop, pick out coupons for the items you plan to buy. Check the coupon expiration date. Be careful not to let coupons influence you to buy something you won't really use or that is too expensive for your budget.

Remember, though, that a coupon doesn't guarantee that the product is the best deal. You will have to subtract the amount of the coupon from the price and then compare the adjusted price with the other alternatives.

Don't Shop When You're Hungry

When you are hungry, everything looks good. It's hard to stick to a list with so many temptations.

GUESS WHAT

In 2004, more than 340 billion manufacturers' cents-off coupons were distributed to consumers.

your family. Bananas may not be your favorite fruit, but your sister may like them. Although you may be fond of Little Debbie snacks, you should not buy them if it means you can't afford necessities such as milk or bread. Shopping is always a trade-off. You can't buy everything you want, so buy the things your family needs the most.

© Getty Images/PhotoDisc

IN CLASS ACTIVITY

Make a list of dinners that you might make for your family for one week. Make sure the meals are well balanced. Then make a shopping list for this menu. How much do you think this will cost at the store?

Avoid shopping just before dinner time or just before holidays. These are the most crowded times at grocery stores. Go when you can take the time to compare your options.

Take Advantage of Sales

When you find special prices at the store for items that keep well and your family uses regularly, stock up on these items, within the limits of your budget and storage space.

Resist Impulse Purchases

Stick to your list. The store will have many attractive displays to entice you to buy. Be sure to make rational

© Getty Images/PhotoDisc

buying decisions. Remember, your money is limited. Buying one item means giving up something else. Make sure you buy what you need for a balanced diet before considering impulse purchases.

CheckPoint

Why do you need to make a plan before you shop? What can you do to help yourself stick to your plan?

Information in the Store

You arrive at the grocery store with your list and coupons in hand. You know what foods you want, but how do you make sense of all the options? Most of the information you need is on the product packages and store pricing labels.

Understand the Language

You know you want a loaf of bread, but which one? One wrapper says "enriched." Another says "fortified."

To protect consumers from misleading claims, the government has passed laws to establish a standard meaning for many of these terms. Food manufacturers must make their products conform to these definitions if they want to print the claims on the package.

▶ fresh: product must not have been precooked, altered, or frozen

▶ low fat: 3 grams or less of fat per serving

▶ sugar free: less than 0.5 grams of sugar per serving

▶ reduced calories or *light:* no more than ¾ of the calories of the product to which it is compared

▶ *more* of an ingredient: at least 10 percent must have been added

▶ high fiber: 5 grams or more of fiber per serving

▶ cholesterol free: less than 2 milligrams of cholesterol and 2 grams or less of saturated fat per serving

▶ low sodium: less than 5 milligrams of sodium per serving

▶ fortified: vitamins and minerals have been added

▶ enriched: vitamin B complex and iron have been added

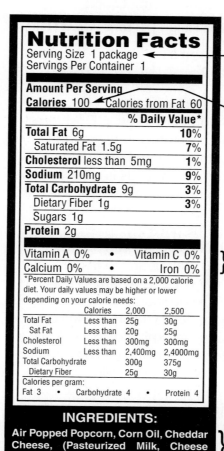

Serving size that provides the nutrition amounts on the label

Calories per serving

Daily values of vitamins and minerals, stated as percentages

Ingredients the product contains, listed from most in the product to the least

Nutrition Labels

The nutrition labels on food packages provide much of the information you need to make a rational buying decision. The Fair Packaging and Labeling Act requires certain information to appear on every food package, and the information must be stated in a standard way. You can use this information to compare the nutritional value of different products.

Serving Size In the illustration of a nutrition label, notice that the first item listed is the serving size. The Food and Drug Administration (FDA) sets standard serving sizes for most food products. The rest of the nutrition information on the label is based on this serving size. If you eat more than the serving size stated, then you will get more of each substance.

Daily Values Scientific research has determined how much

of each nutrient the human body needs each day. These are called **daily values**. By law, food labels must report the percentage of daily values that each serving contains.

For example, if the label says "Vitamin A: 15%," then one serving provides you with 15 percent of the Vitamin A you need for the day. You would have to get the other 85 percent from the other foods you eat that day.

For some substances, consuming less is better. Too much fat, especially saturated fat, cholesterol, and sodium or salt can harm your health.

Ingredients By law, food labels must show the ingredients in the product. Also, the ingredients must be listed according to the amount the product contains—from most to least.

Unit Pricing Labels

West's Corn Flakes	Toni's Corn Flakes
Price per ounce	Price per ounce
12 oz. 20.8	14 oz. 19.6
$2.50	$2.74

Freshness Date

Foods don't last forever. Fresh products such as milk and eggs spoil sooner than canned or frozen products, but all products go bad at some time. To make sure you can use the product before it spoils, look for a date on the package.

Not all packages carry dates, and the dates may be stated in different ways. An **expiration date** is the date by which you should use the product. For example, if you are buying canned soup and the expiration date is a year from today, then you can be sure that the soup will be good for a while.

Sometimes, instead of an expiration date, the package shows when the product was manufactured or packaged. This date gives you an idea of how old the product is. Often, though, it is stated in a code that is hard to interpret. Look for a stamp or numbers cut into the packaging that appear to form a date. For example, 061905 probably means June 19, 2005. Stores often use this type of date to know when to take the product off the shelves.

Unit Pricing

By law, grocery stores must state not only the full price of each product but also the price of one unit of the product. For example, if the product is measured in ounces, the store label must show the price for one ounce of the product. The price of one standard unit of a product is called its **unit price**.

To know which box of corn flakes gives you the most for your money, you can compare the unit price of one to the unit price of another. But you don't have to do the arithmetic. The unit pricing label does it for you.

Psychology of Store Layout

Businesses pay professionals to design stores in a way that will encourage consumers to spend more. Basic food products such as milk, meat, and bread are stocked in the rear of the store. To reach them, you must pass through aisles filled with snacks, specialty foods, and other products that are more profitable for the store.

The most profitable products are often placed on the shelves at eye level, where you will probably look first. Products that might attract your children's attention, such as candy

Buy the Numbers?

Suppose you are looking for a large bottle of baby shampoo at a grocery store. Both the name brand and the store's brand have 20-ounce bottles. The price of the name brand baby shampoo is $2.99, and the unit price is $0.15 per ounce. The store's brand of baby shampoo costs $2.39, and its unit price is $0.12. You have a coupon for $0.40 off the name brand of baby shampoo. Which bottle would you buy? Why? What factors other than price would you consider?

and children's cereal, may be located at their eye level.

In the checkout line, you probably look at the magazines or the candy and other small items in the racks next to you. These items are located by the checkout counters intentionally. They are high-profit items and items that many people buy on impulse.

CheckPoint

How can you compare the nutritional value of products? What is the easiest way to compare prices?

TRY THESE

1. What is the purpose of a shopping list?

2. What are coupons and what should you consider when you use them?

3. What are some claims you are likely to see on product packages, and what do they mean?

4. What are daily values?

5. How can you use information on product labels to select nutritious selections?

6. How do unit prices benefit you?

7. How does the store layout help the store increase its profits?

THINK CRITICALLY

8. **CONSUMER ACTION** Advise Brandon how to make nutritious food choices, stay within his $75 budget, and choose food that will help his father watch his weight.

9. **MATH OF MONEY** You have a coupon for $0.35 off a pound of Hearty Bird turkey, and the store will double coupons up to $1.00. When you get to the store, you find that Hearty Bird turkey costs $2.29 per pound and Big Value turkey is on sale for $1.65 per pound. Which is the better deal?

10. **COMMUNICATE** Your job is to choose the food products to stock in a convenience store that is located near a retirement community. Most of its customers are in the final stages of their life cycle. Write an essay that describes how the products stocked in this store may be different. Send your essay to your teacher in an e-mail.

DECISION MAKING PROJECT

SPECIFY   SEARCH   SIFT   SELECT   STUDY

SPECIFY Each member needs to decide how to spend the $400. You can spend it on any combination of clothes, flowers, taxi rides, limousine rides, or anything else. Plan how much you will spend on each item on your list.

GOALS

IDENTIFY
trade-offs in clothes-buying decisions

EXPLAIN
how to judge fabrics, tailoring, and fit to make good buying decisions

11.3 Evaluate Clothes Choices

Trade-Offs in Buying Clothes

Americans spend more than $325 billion each year on clothing. When you buy clothes, you are really choosing among three benefits: utility, style, and value.

Utility

Utility is a measure of something's usefulness. The utility of your clothes depends on how you use them. Suppose you accept a summer job as a camp counselor. You will be taking children on nature walks—rain or shine. When you buy a waterproof jacket and hiking boots for this purpose, you may have to give up some style to get the sturdy qualities you want.

If you work in a restaurant serving meals to customers, you want clothes that don't stain easily and comfortable walking shoes. For uses such as these, utility should be the most important factor in your buying decision.

CONSUMER ACTION

Leon wants new pants and shirts for school and new shoes for his job as a stock clerk at the grocery store. He doesn't have much money, so he needs to choose carefully. How can he plan his shopping trip so that he doesn't overspend his budget? How can he make good choices at the store?

Style

Often when you buy clothes, utility is not your main priority. You want a garment with a certain look or style. A garment's **style** is its characteristics that distinguish it from other garments. Styles change from year to year. Styles that go in and out of fashion quickly are called **fads**. Styles that stay in fashion for a long time are **classics**.

Designer clothes are styles created by a famous designer. When you buy a shirt by Tommy Hilfiger or a skirt by Liz Claiborne, be aware that you are paying extra for the name and for the advertising that helped make the designer famous. You will not necessarily get superior quality.

When you buy the most popular designer jeans, you are making a trade-off. You will most likely pay more than you would for jeans that are useful but not particularly stylish. Such a choice is fine, as long as you can afford to make this trade-off and are willing to give up other purchases you could make if you bought less expensive jeans.

Value

Getting what you pay for does not necessarily mean always buying the most expensive product. One good way to approach a buying decision is to look for the best value—the most you can get for the price.

© Getty Images/PhotoDisc

COMMUNICATE

Some schools require students to wear uniforms. Do you think school uniforms are a good idea? Write one page describing the benefits and drawbacks of uniforms from the students' point of view.

Your level of satisfaction depends on a number of factors. Quality is one of them. If your new sweatshirt loses its color in just a few washings, then it probably wasn't worth the price. Maybe the best choice would have been to spend a little more to get better quality.

Style is also part of satisfaction. Suppose that you feel equally in fashion wearing Brand A jeans or Brand B jeans. You find Brand A jeans at $40 and Brand B jeans at $30. In this case, the Brand B jeans are the better value. You are getting the same amount of satisfaction at a lower price.

But what if Brand A jeans are more in style than Brand B? Which is the better value? You would have to judge whether Brand A would be worth the extra $10 to you.

CheckPoint

How can you decide whether to look for utility or style? How is value different from just a low price?

Clothes Shopping

Know What You Want Before you set out for the mall, be sure you know what you want. To really know what you want, you must first know what you have. Then look for items that fit with the rest of your wardrobe.

Know How Much You Can Spend Check your budget to decide how much you can spend. Clothing choices come in a wide range of prices. If you buy an expensive shirt, you may not be able to also buy the pants you want. Prioritize. If you want a high-quality jacket for a job interview, then perhaps selecting a relatively expensive jacket is a better choice for you now than buying a cheaper jacket.

Know Where to Shop Department stores offer a wide range of clothes and prices and can be a good source for many of your clothes purchases. Specialty clothes shops

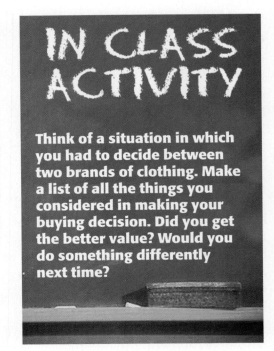

IN CLASS ACTIVITY

Think of a situation in which you had to decide between two brands of clothing. Make a list of all the things you considered in making your buying decision. Did you get the better value? Would you do something differently next time?

can be more expensive, since they often specialize in designer brands. But don't forget about discount stores, such as factory outlets and thrift shops. You can often get great

SMATH OF MONEY

Terri is looking for a new winter parka. She has identified two she likes. One sells for $50 and has polyester fill for insulation. The other is made with goose down and usually sells for $130. It is on sale at 20 percent off its regular price this week. How much would Terri save by purchasing the less expensive coat this week? What other factors should she consider when she makes her decision?

SOLUTION

She will save $54 if she buys the less expensive coat.

$130	$130	$104 sale price
×.20	− 26	− 50 less expensive parka price
$26 discount	$104 sale price of expensive parka	$54 saving

deals on the same clothes you would find at a department or specialty store.

When you go to a discount store, be sure to check carefully for quality. Also, just because it is a discount store doesn't mean that all of its prices are low. Compare prices from several stores.

Catalogs, either printed or on the Internet, make price comparisons easy, and usually you can depend on reputable catalog companies to maintain a quality standard.

Natural Fibers

Natural fibers come from plants or animals. The natural fibers most often used in clothes are cotton, flax, wool, and silk.

Cotton   The world's most popular fiber is cotton, which comes from the boll of the cotton plant. It is washable and durable and holds up well after many launderings. It also breathes and absorbs moisture, which makes it feel cool against the skin in hot, humid weather. Cotton tends to shrink and wrinkle. Manufacturers often preshrink cotton fabrics to minimize the amount of shrinkage after you buy the product. Wrinkle-resistant finishes and blends with synthetic fibers help to make cotton fabrics easier to care for.

Linen   Linen, the oldest known textile, is actually made of fibers from the flax plant. At one time, linen was used extensively for

bedding, which is the reason people refer to sheets and towels as linens. Its light weight and cool qualities make linen a popular fabric for summer clothes. It wrinkles easily, so it is often blended with synthetic fibers to minimize this property.

Wool   For the cool days of fall, winter, and early spring, clothes made from wool are a good choice. Wool comes from the fleece of animals, most commonly sheep, but can come from camels, llamas, alpacas, or vicunas.

Wool absorbs and evaporates moisture well. It is very resilient and returns to its previous shape after stretching, making it wrinkle resistant. Air pockets in woven wool fabrics give clothes a natural insulation, making them especially warm. You can buy wool clothing in different weights, depending upon the amount of warmth you want.

Wool is soft, but can feel scratchy against the skin, so make sure you like the feel before you buy wool clothes. Also, wool clothes usually must be dry cleaned.

Silk   Silk is a secretion from the silkworm that it uses to build its cocoon. Silk has a luxurious feel and a unique luster that gives an elegant look to fine garments. It has insulation properties that make the wearer feel cool in summer and warm in winter, so it is often used in thermal underwear. Silk clothes are durable but tend to be expensive. Also, pure silk garments often require dry cleaning or hand washing.

GUESS WHAT

There are about nine pairs of shoes sold for every person in the United States per year.

Manufactured Fibers

Fibers that are made rather than naturally occurring are **manufactured fibers**. Clothes made from manufactured fibers or a blend of manufactured and natural fibers usually hold their colors and resist stains and wrinkles better than natural fibers alone.

Rayon   One of the most versatile manufactured fibers is rayon. It is not synthetic because it is made from living materials—the cellulose of wood pulp, cotton, and other vegetable matter. It is soft, lustrous, and blends well with other fibers. Rayon is becoming more expensive as wood prices rise.

Acetate   Acetate is a popular, less expensive alternative to rayon. Both are made from cellulose. Although not as strong as rayon, acetate is soft and lustrous, and provides easy-care properties.

Nylon   Nylon is a synthetic fiber in that it is made from a polymer rather than from living matter. Though it is one of the strongest and most durable synthetics, nylon feels soft and silky. It is washable and colorfast, and seldom requires ironing.

Polyester   Like nylon, polyester is a synthetic fiber made from a polymer. It is the most widely used manufactured fiber in the world. It is prized for its highly wrinkle-resistant nature. It is often blended with natural fibers to give them easy-care properties. Polyester is used in many kinds of clothing and is often the reason that some clothes can be labeled *permanent press*.

Labels

By law, all clothing sold in the United States must have content and care labels, which identify the types of

Content and Care Labels

65% POLYESTER 35% COTTON MADE IN TAIWAN R.O.C **M** FABRIQUE A TAIWAN OVER FOR CARE

MACHINE WASH COLD **GENTLE CYCLE** WITH SIMILAR COLORS ONLY NON-CHLORINE BLEACH WHEN NEEDED TUMBLE DRY LOW REMOVE PROMPTLY WARM IRON AS NEEDED

Clothes Shopping Checklist

✔ Does it fit properly?

✔ Is it well constructed?

✔ Does it fit into your wardrobe?

✔ Does it reflect your personality?

✔ Will it stay in style for a while?

✔ Will it be easy to maintain?

✔ Do you want it more than any other items you could buy for the money?

✔ Have you evaluated alternatives to find the best price?

fibers that make up the fabric. Often, fiber content appears on the front of the label, along with the size, and care instructions appear on the back. Always check the care instructions before you buy clothes. Dry cleaning can be very expensive. For clothes you plan to wear and clean often, you may want to select items that can be machine washed.

Tailoring

The construction or tailoring of a garment is important to your overall satisfaction with your clothing. To judge quality, here are some signs of good tailoring to look for.

1. stitching that is neat and even

2. seams that are well finished at the edge to prevent fabric unraveling

3. extra fabric at the seams to prevent them from pulling out

4. patterns or prints in the fabric that match well

5. double stitching in places that will be under extra stress from movement

6. buttons that are firmly attached and neatly finished buttonholes

7. garments that hang evenly when you try them on

Fit

To be attractive, clothes must fit you well. Sizes give some indication of which clothes will fit, but sizes can vary. If an item feels loose or tight in places, try another size. Move around in the garment. Look in the mirror. Does it look good on you? Take the time to find clothes that make you look and feel good.

How should you evaluate your clothing options?

TRY THESE

1. What are several ways in which clothes can give you satisfaction?

2. How do different fabrics affect your buying decisions?

3. What useful information can you get from clothes labels?

4. What signs of quality tailoring should you look for in evaluating clothes?

THINK CRITICALLY

5. **CONSUMER ACTION** What can Leon do before he goes shopping that will help him make good choices? What trade-offs will he have to make? Once at the store, how can he evaluate his alternatives?

6. Describe how your clothing choices are likely to change as you pass through your life cycle.

7. **COMMUNICATE** Is it better to purchase a few high-quality clothes than many poor-quality clothes? In a page or less, explain your point of view. Send your answer to your teacher in an e-mail.

8. **MATH OF MONEY** Michael is 14 and already 6 feet tall. Last year, he grew 4 inches. He could buy off-brand jeans for $24 or designer jeans for $38. How much more will he pay if he purchases 4 pairs of the more expensive jeans? What else should he consider?

DECISION MAKING PROJECT

SPECIFY   SEARCH   SIFT   SELECT   STUDY

SEARCH Every person in the group should shop individually. Bring in photos or descriptions of clothing options. Bring in ideas for corsages or boutonnieres. Bring in your choices for transportation. Make sure to have prices for each good or service.

© Getty Images/PhotoDisc

GOALS

EXPLAIN
how to budget, prioritize, and evaluate alternatives for buying recreation

DESCRIBE
how to plan a vacation and minimize its costs

11.4 Recreation and Travel

Recreation

The value of money lies in the power it gives you to buy things to help you enjoy life. Suppose you earn a good income. Each month, you pay for food, shelter, and clothing. You put some money aside for the future. How will you use the rest?

Budget

The income you spend for recreation means giving up other products you might want. Spending always involves trade-offs. So after you cover the necessities, including saving, you can use what's left for recreational activities.

Set Your Priorities

Once you know how much you can spend for recreation, prioritize your activities. Remember, you are prioritizing your time, not just your spending. You may like to play golf, go sailing, and work out. But before you

CONSUMER ACTION

Rhonda was tired as she drove home from work. As she was passing a travel agency, she noticed a sign in the window advertising vacations to Hawaii. Rhonda always wanted to visit Hawaii, so she turned in and immediately bought a vacation package for $2,899. Now she isn't sure she made a wise decision. What should Rhonda have done before making this purchase?

go out and buy golf clubs, a sailboat, and a treadmill, think realistically about how much you really have time to do. Target your spending toward the activities that you like most and truly have time to do.

Equipment Equipment for leisure activities can be expensive. Hockey equipment costs hundreds of dollars. The same is true of golf. A good-quality basketball may cost $50, and shoes can run another $100. You could find a tennis racket for $25, but a good one will cost about $150.

Facilities Most communities have municipal facilities, such as tennis courts, available free to residents. But if you live in a cold climate, you would have to join a club to play year round. Usually racquetball courts require a membership as well. Club memberships plus hourly court fees can run into hundreds of dollars.

Save for What You Want As you can see, sports can be expensive. Fortunately, you have options in all price ranges, from a free walk in the woods to expensive club memberships. If your favorite activities are expensive, you will probably have to plan and save to purchase the equipment or membership. Saving for these future purchases means giving up spending now.

Start Small

Before you spend much on any sport, make sure it is something you really want to do. If you have never played a sport, borrow or rent equipment and try it before you spend money to buy equipment.

Fitness clubs and other recreational facilities often allow free trial memberships. You may be able to try out the equipment and atmosphere at a

© Getty Images/PhotoDisc

club for a month before making a decision to join.

If you decide that you like the activity and want to buy your own equipment, start small. You don't need the best that money can buy.

Look for second-hand equipment in newspaper classified ads and in stores that specialize in it. You can often pick up used equipment in good condition for a fraction of the price of the same product new.

Evaluate Your Alternatives

When you shop for recreational equipment, look for the level of quality that matches your level of skill and interest. The finest racing bicycles sell for more than $10,000. Unless you are planning to become an international bike racer, this is more quality than you need. If you plan to use your bike to get to school and occasionally to the mall, you can be happy with a bike that costs less.

Read Labels Like fibers in clothes, different materials provide different benefits. For example, tennis rackets are generally made of graphite or graphite with titanium. If you are strong and need more shot control, your best choice would be a stiff graphite racket with a smaller head. For players who need more power and lighter weight, a racket made of graphite with titanium and a larger head is a better choice.

Ask a knowledgeable salesperson to explain the benefits of the different materials. Then choose the product that fits you best.

Look for Bargains   Look around different stores and on the Internet for good deals. Always compare prices. Recreational equipment prices vary a lot. Discount stores and catalogs can offer bargains as well. You can often find the best deals at the end of a sports season. Skis, for example, may be purchased for half price in February or March.

Compare Apples to Apples Different brands of equipment vary widely in quality and price. When you compare prices, make sure you are looking at equipment of comparable quality and features. Are the alternatives you are comparing made

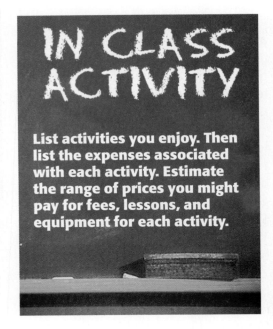

IN CLASS ACTIVITY

List activities you enjoy. Then list the expenses associated with each activity. Estimate the range of prices you might pay for fees, lessons, and equipment for each activity.

of similar materials? Do they have the same features, such as 30 gears on a bicycle?

More features usually mean a higher price, so don't pay for some-

What In The World?

How does advertising influence your spending? Would you be more likely to use a Visa card because Visa helps pay for international athletic events? Visa International apparently believes consumers throughout the world will, because it has committed to giving $40 million to the International Olympic Committee (IOC) from 2008 through 2012.

Visa undertook its program of Olympic support in 1986. Some of the money was given to specific teams, but more was contributed directly to the IOC. Jacques Rogge, president of the IOC, stated, "Visa International. . . has shown that Visa is not only a global leader in finance but in sports sponsorship." Would you be more likely to apply for and use a Visa card because of this organization's sponsorship of the Olympics? Why, or why not?

thing you won't really use. Unless you plan to bike up a mountain, you probably will use only a few gears.

Make Good Choices Like designer clothes, sports equipment that bears the name of a famous person often costs more than a similar product without the name.

Choose a product based on quality and features, not based on name. Your best choice is the product that most fits the way you plan to use it at the lowest price.

CheckPoint

How can you keep the price of a recreational activity low? What should you consider when buying sports equipment?

Vacations

You have to budget for transportation to your destination, accommodations, food, and activities for vacations.

You'll also need to budget your time. Even if you are going only 100 miles away, you'll want to spend at least a weekend to make the trip worth the transportation expenses.

If you work, your company probably allows you a certain number of vacation days. You need to prioritize your destination alternatives, so that you use this limited time to go where you want to go most. And, if your company doesn't offer paid vacation, then the opportunity cost of your vacation time includes the wages you are giving up.

Because of the costs and time involved in a vacation, it pays to plan. With careful planning, you can get all the enjoyment out of your vacation at a lower overall price.

Destinations

What do you like to do on vacation? Hike? Kayak? Shop? What you like to do and how much you have to spend determine the travel destinations you should consider. If you like to hike, look for destinations with many hiking trails in settings you enjoy most. Then, narrow your choices to the destinations you can afford.

Travel Guides Your local library or bookstore is a good place to start to learn about destinations. Well-known names like *Fodor's* and *Frommer's* have guides for almost every destination you can think of.

CYBER CONSUMER

Vacation web sites are among the most popular on the Internet. Search engines usually have shortcuts to the best sites they have found. To research travel on the Internet, write down key words to describe the kind of vacation you want. Then use these key words to see what your search engine turns up! Would you use the Internet to find vacation information? Would you trust the Internet to make travel reservations?

You can also learn about destinations from books on your favorite activities. Books about windsurfing usually suggest the best places to go for the sport. Another approach is to look for publications about national and state parks.

The Internet A vast amount of travel information is available on the Internet. Tourist bureaus in most locations have web sites that you can find by searching by state or city name. The National Park Service has an extensive site that describes the highlights of every park.

You can also search by activity key words, such as *ski* or *sail.*

The major search sites on the Internet have a travel channel. Clicking on *travel* sends you to destination and activity links all over the Internet.

Transportation

By Car The cost of driving a car, on average, is about 50 cents per mile. When a family of four travels, this is not expensive compared to buying four airfares.

By Bus Travel by bus is not often quick and may not be as comfortable as other options. But it does offer a number of advantages. Buses are inexpensive and go many places not served by train or air.

By Train Taking a train is usually faster than a bus and a little more expensive. You can walk around on a train. The number of locations that you can travel to, however, is limited.

By Air Flying is the quickest way to travel between distant locations but may not be the fastest way to get somewhere close. A trip by bus or train from Boston to New York City, for example, takes about five hours. When you add up all the time to travel

Vacation Cost Cutters

Here are some tips for minimizing your vacation costs.

1. Avoid making spur-of-the-moment decisions.

2. Take vacations during a destination's off-season when possible.

3. Look for transportation bargains in the newspaper and online.

4. Choose accommodations close to the activities, but not right in the prime (and most expensive) spot.

5. Picnicking is cheaper than eating at restaurants.

to and from the airport, check in, fly, and get your luggage, flying between close locations can take longer.

Tickets Always shop for the best price. Airfares change almost daily. Some travel agents on the Internet will send you weekly rate updates by e-mail if you sign up for this service. You can also buy the tickets online.

If your schedule is flexible, you can usually save by flying mid-week. Business travelers usually choose to fly from Friday through Monday. As a result, airlines charge lower prices on Tuesdays, Wednesdays, and Thursdays to help fill their mid-week flights.

Accommodations

You should make reservations for a place to stay before you go on vacation. Many of the best hotels, parks, and campgrounds sell out in advance.

Rooms in chain hotels or motels are likely to be much the same no matter where they are. Local hotels and motels can be more interesting.

You may prefer the charm of a bed-and-breakfast (B&B). B&Bs are rooms for rent, often in the owner's home, that include breakfast for one price. People who operate B&Bs can give personal advice about local places to go and sights to see.

Resorts are accommodations that also include activities of interest to travelers. Golf, tennis, horseback riding, and beach resorts are common. These accommodations tend to be expensive.

For young people, youth hostels are simple, inexpensive accommo-dations available across the U.S. and abroad. They can cost as little as $10 a night, but you may have to supply your own sleeping bag.

CheckPoint

What costs should you budget for when planning your vacation? How can you minimize the costs?

TRY THESE

1. What costs are involved in recreational activities?

2. When you are thinking about taking up a sport, how can you start small?

3. How can you evaluate alternatives in sports equipment?

4. What are some sources of travel information?

5. What advantages do bus and train travel have over travel by air?

6. What should you consider when choosing accommodations?

THINK CRITICALLY

7. **CONSUMER ACTION** What advice would you give Rhonda for planning her vacation next time?

8. **MATH OF MONEY** Vicky plans to visit her Aunt Louise who lives 323 miles away. Vicky could drive her car at a cost of about 50 cents per mile, or she could take a bus. Louise could pick her up at the terminal. A round-trip ticket costs $69. How much could Vicky save by taking the bus? Why might she choose to drive her car instead?

9. Explain why buying a top-of-the-line tennis racket at 25 percent off its regular price may not be a rational decision.

DECISION MAKING PROJECT

● SPECIFY ● SEARCH ● SIFT ● SELECT ● STUDY

SIFT Have group members present their choices. Are some group members considering sharing the cost for transportation? Are you going to be able to stick to your original plan for spending?

Chapter 11

ASSESSMENT

KEY IDEAS

Nutrition Facts

1. To operate properly, your body needs nutrients. Carbohydrates, protein, and fats are nutrients that provide energy. Vitamins, minerals, and water are nutrients that help control your body processes.
2. A balanced diet means eating foods that give you the right amounts of all six nutrients.
3. Diet aids designed to suppress your appetite often don't work or work only temporarily.
4. Dieting taken to a dangerous extreme is an eating disorder that can threaten your life.
5. The only truly effective way to lose weight, keep it off, and remain healthy is to eat a balanced diet and exercise regularly.

Shop for a Healthful Diet

6. Before you go grocery shopping, make a plan. Determine how much you can spend. Make a list of the items you want. Look for coupons and advertised specials.
7. Most of the information you need to make good food choices is on the product packages and store pricing labels.
8. By law, food must have labels showing nutritional content stated as the percentage of daily values per serving.
9. A unit price is the price of one standard unit of the product, such as per ounce or per pound.

Evaluate Clothes Choices

10. When you select clothes, you are making a trade-off among three benefits: utility, style, and value. The benefit that is most important for a particular purchase depends on how you plan to use it.

11. Utility is a measure of something's usefulness. Style is a garment's characteristics that distinguish it from others. Good value means getting the most satisfaction you can for the price.
12. Before you shop, know what you want, how much you can spend, and where you can go to get what you want.
13. Understanding the qualities of different fibers can help you select the right garment for your purpose. Natural fibers come from plants or animals. Manufactured fibers are made rather than occurring naturally.
14. By law, clothes must carry labels that show their fiber content and how to care for them. Also, look for signs of good construction and good fit.

Recreation and Travel

15. Recreation requires money for sports equipment and sometimes for facilities, such as court fees or club memberships. Before you spend on a new sport, borrow or rent equipment to make sure you enjoy it.
16. Buy equipment with the level of quality that matches your level of skill and interest in that sport.
17. What you like to do and how much you have to spend determine the vacation destinations you should consider. You can learn about destinations from guide books, from books on your favorite activities, and by searching the Internet.
18. Air travel is the fastest way to get to a distant location, but may not be for close locations. Car travel can be economical when you travel in

groups, but expensive when you travel alone. Buses and trains can be good, inexpensive alternatives for some trips.

19. Make reservations for accommodations in advance.

TERMS REVIEW

Match each term on the left with its definition on the right.
Some terms may not be used.

a. anorexia nervosa

b. balanced diet

c. bulimia

d. calorie

e. carbohydrate

f. cholesterol

g. classic

h. daily value

i. designer clothes

j. expiration date

k. fad

l. fat

m. fiber

n. Food Guide Pyramid

o. manufactured fiber

p. mineral

q. natural fiber

r. nutrient

s. obesity

t. protein

u. serving

v. style

w. unit price

x. utility

y. vitamin

1. chemical substance in food that your body needs to function properly
2. style that stays in fashion for a long time
3. nutrient that the body needs but contains the most calories per gram of food
4. price of one standard unit of a product
5. eating foods that give you the right amounts of all six nutrients
6. guide to help consumers achieve a balanced diet, created by the USDA from research on foods and nutritional needs
7. measure of the amount of food that you would probably eat during one meal or snack
8. amount of each nutrient that the human body needs each day
9. fiber that is made rather than naturally occurring
10. style that doesn't stay in fashion long
11. weighing above your ideal body weight by more than 20 percent
12. date by which you should use a product to avoid spoilage
13. fiber that comes from plants or animals
14. substance in some complex carbohydrates that contains no nutrients but helps food move through the body's digestive system
15. measure of something's usefulness
16. sugars and starches that break down quickly to provide energy to the body
17. measure of the amount of energy a food will supply
18. clothes styled by a famous designer
19. nutrient that helps the body build and repair cells and that also supplies energy

CONSUMER DECISIONS

20. Keep track of the food you eat for several days. Compare your record with the Food Guide Pyramid. Are you eating a healthful diet? What could you do to make your diet more balanced?

21. Manuel wants to buy a can of soup for lunch. He wants either cream of chicken or tomato, whichever is the more nutritious choice. He looked at the labels on page 392. Compare these labels. Which soup do you think

Cream of Chicken Soup

Nutrition Facts	Amount / serving	%DV*	Amount / serving	%DV*
Serv. Size 1/2 cup (120mL) condensed soup	**Total Fat** 8g	**12%**	**Total Carb.** 11g	4%
Servings about 2.5	Sat. Fat 3g	**15%**	Fiber 1g	4%
Calories 130	**Cholest.** 10mg	**3%**	Sugars 1g	
Fat Cal. 70	**Sodium** 890mg	**37%**	**Protein** 3g	
*Percent Daily Values (DV) are based on a 2,000 calorie diet	Vitamin A 10% • Vitamin C 0% • Calcium 2% • Iron 2%			

Tomato Soup

Nutrition Facts	Amount / serving	%DV*	Amount / serving	%DV*
Serv. Size 1/2 cup (120mL) condensed soup	**Total Fat** 0g	**0%**	**Total Carb.** 18g	4%
Servings about 2.5	Sat. Fat 0g	**0%**	Fiber 2g	4%
Calories 80	**Cholest.** 0mg	**0%**	Sugars 10g	
Fat Cal. 0	**Sodium** 730mg	**30%**	**Protein** 2g	
*Percent Daily Values (DV) are based on a 2,000 calorie diet	Vitamin A 10% • Vitamin C 4% • Calcium 2% • Iron 4%			

is more nutritious? Why? What is not so nutritious about the one you chose?

22. Identify a type of garment that you often wear. Visit a store that has a wide selection of that type of garment. Compare the quality of high- and low-priced brands of this garment. What differences do you see? Which brand would you buy? Why?

23. Investigate different ways of traveling to visit a friend or relative in a city that is at least 500 miles from your home. List the benefits and costs of each type of transportation. How would you choose to travel?

THINK CRITICALLY

24. Jenny is concerned about her weight. She isn't really fat, but she does weigh about 15 pounds more than she would like. Using the Food Guide Pyramid, plan a week's menu for Jenny that would help her lose weight and stay healthy. Include meals for breakfast, lunch, and dinner. Explain why you made the food choices on your menu. What other advice would you give Jenny that would help her lose weight?

25. Identify a famous person whom you admire. Examine several photographs of this person. Does this person's manner of dress have anything to do with your feelings about him or her? Would you pay more to buy similar clothing? Explain.

LOOK IT UP

26. Identify a sport or recreational activity that you have not tried but think you might enjoy. Find out

WHICH IS THE BEST DEAL?

A shop near Kendra's home stocks designer fashions. A factory-outlet store 10 miles from her home sells many of the same fashions at discounted prices. All garments at this store are marked down at least 25 percent. A round-trip bus ticket to the factory-outlet store costs $4. About half the time, Kendra can't find anything she wants to buy there.

Kendra wants a new dress for her graduation in June. She found one she likes at the nearby store for $120. This store usually has a sale in May and marks some items down 20 percent. What should Kendra do? Explain.

Alternative 1 Buy the dress now for $120.

Alternative 2 Visit the outlet store now to see if she can find a better deal.

Alternative 3 Wait until May to see if she can get the dress on sale.

POINT YOUR BROWSER TO

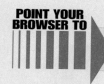

www.ee4c.swlearning.com
Complete the activity for Chapter 11.

what equipment you would need for this activity. What is the smallest amount you could spend to buy this equipment?

27. Visit a local grocery store. Find the location of basic foods such as bread, milk, and meat. When you walk to their locations, what kinds of items do you pass? Why do you think the store is arranged in this way?

28. Identify a location you think you might like to visit on a vacation. Use the Internet to investigate this place and determine what you would like to do there. Did your research change your mind about this place in any way? Explain.

INSIDE THE NUMBERS

29. Francine is on a tight budget. She tries to save money by purchasing food in bulk. Calculate how much she saves by purchasing bulk foods.

Food	Amount	Bulk Price	Brand Price
Sugar	5 lbs.	$0.32 / lb.	$0.41 / lb.
Pasta	6 lbs.	$0.69 / lb.	$0.99 / lb.
Rice	2 lbs.	$0.49 / lb.	$0.69 / lb.
Flour	5 lbs.	$0.27 / lb.	$0.36 / lb.
Raisins	1 lb.	$1.29 / lb.	$1.59 / lb.

30. Gregg tries to play 27 holes of golf every weekend unless it rains. Gregg pays $25 for each nine holes he plays. One course is offering a special deal.

For $500, Gregg can become a summer member and play as often as he wants for the next 12 weeks. Gregg has to work, so he can play only on weekends. How much might Gregg save by becoming a summer member? Why are his actual savings likely to be smaller? What do you think he should do? Explain.

CURRICULUM CONNECTION

31. **HEALTH**   Different vegetables are particularly good sources of different nutrients. Find out what nutrients these vegetables provide in abundance: carrots, broccoli, and spinach.

32. **SCIENCE**   Increased participation in athletics has resulted in the growth of a field called sports medicine. This field of medical care specializes in treatment of sports-related injuries. Investigate injuries that may result from participation in your favorite sport. How are these injuries treated? How can you minimize your risk of injury when you participate in that sport?

JOURNAL RECAP

33. After reading this chapter, review the answers you wrote to the questions in Journal Journey. Have your opinions changed?

DECISION MAKING PROJECT

SPECIFY   SEARCH   SIFT   **SELECT**   **STUDY**

SELECT   Your plan for spending $400 might have changed by now. Write how you plan to spend it now that you have actual costs. Remember not to go over your budget!

STUDY   Present a paragraph on the process you and your group went through to choose how to spend $400 on the upcoming dance. What did you learn?

Chapter 12

TRANSPORTATION
HOW WILL YOU GET THERE?

WHAT'S AHEAD

EXPLODING MYTHS

Fact or Myth?
What do you think is true?

1. In today's society, you must have a car.

2. The price listed on a new car's sticker is the price you should expect to pay for the car.

3. As long as you put gas and oil into your car, you don't need to do anything else with it.

JOURNAL JOURNEY

WRITE IN YOUR JOURNAL ABOUT THE FOLLOWING.

OWNING A CAR What responsibilities come with owning a car? What are some benefits and drawbacks of owning a car? What other options do you have?

BUY OR LEASE? Would you buy or lease a car? What is the difference between buying and leasing? How would you decide which method is right for you?

MAINTAINING A CAR What would you have to do to maintain your car? What can you do yourself? What would you like to learn to do? How can you find a good mechanic?

DECISION MAKING PROJECT

SPECIFY   SEARCH   SIFT   SELECT   STUDY

GOT TO GET THERE You will decide what car you would recommend to a friend whose transportation budget per month is $400. You'll create your friend's list of needs and wants. Then you'll use this list to do some research and make a recommendation.

GOAL

To learn how to buy a car

PROJECT PROCESS

SPECIFY	Lesson 12.2
SEARCH	Lesson 12.3
SIFT	Lesson 12.4
SELECT	Lesson 12.5
STUDY	Chapter Assessment

GOALS

DESCRIBE
the importance of transportation in American society

DISCUSS
transportation alternatives to cars

12.1 Transportation Basics

Transportation and Society

Americans travel more than people in any other nation. You may take a bus to school. Other members of your family may drive to work. You could take a train or bus to visit relatives in another state. More than ten million commercial passenger flights take off in the United States each year. It seems as if Americans are always going somewhere.

When Do You Use Transportation?

Most Americans use some form of transportation every day through all stages of their life cycle. You may ride your bike to school. Your parents could carpool or take the subway to work. Your grandparents might ride in a *senior van* to go shopping or visit a community center. It's difficult to think of anyone who does

CONSUMER ACTION

Holly is a junior in high school. Most of the time, her parents let her use the family car after her father gets home from work. But she wants to take a summer job at a downtown shoe store, which is three miles from her house. She needs a reliable way to get to her job. She doesn't have enough money to buy a car. What are some inexpensive options she should consider?

VOTE *Your Wallet*

Owning a car will do you little good if our roads are falling apart. Many roads and bridges are crumbling from age, and urban areas suffer from traffic congestion. Highway construction and maintenance are paid for from tolls and gasoline taxes. In 2003, the U.S. Chamber of Commerce pointed out that these taxes had not been increased in 10 years. Spending on highways has not kept pace with inflation or transportation needs. If you were given a chance to vote, would you support increased spending on our roads? Higher taxes? Consider positive and negative results of your position. What tradeoffs must our nation make?

your local community and state and federal governments have offices that monitor transportation conditions. For example, some people who work for these offices make sure that traffic lights are working properly. Others remove snow from roadways so you can get to school. Some repair streets and interstates.

CheckPoint

How important is transportation in the American lifestyle?

Transportation Options

To many Americans, transportation means a car. But you really have many options for getting where you want to go. Most are less expensive than owning a car. So check out your transportation options.

Individual Transportation

Bicycles Americans spend well over a billion dollars every year to purchase bicycles. You could pay as little as $25 to buy a used bicycle or as much as $10,000 for a competition racer. Most bicycles cost between $100 and $400.

Before you shop for a bicycle, think about how you plan to use it. This will help you decide what quality and features you want. Bicycles designed for riding on paved roads in a city will not work well for cross-country treks. Racing bicycles are built for speed and the

not rely on transportation in some way to achieve life-span goals.

Americans take many trips, but most of them are relatively short. Most people don't live more than a few miles from their school, place of employment, or the stores where they shop. Studies show that more than 90 percent of trips are less than ten miles long.

Local, State, and Federal Transportation Offices

Since transportation is an important part of daily life in the United States,

© Getty Images/PhotoDisc

smooth surfaces of paved tracks. They may fall apart if you ride them on bumpy roads.

Once you know the type of bicycle you want, your next step is to identify brands and models to examine. Several publications rate bicycles. You can find information about specialized bicycles in *Bike, Mountain Biker,* and *Women's Sports and Fitness.*

For more ordinary bicycles, *Consumer Reports* is a good source. Check the index on the last page of any issue to find the most recent report. These articles identify specific brands and models you can buy. They provide the list price and explain special features or problems you should know about.

Prices for the same bicycle vary from store to store, so be sure to compare. You may be able to negotiate a slightly lower price with a store. Or you may be able to get free equipment, such as a tire pump, water bottle, or set of tools, as an incentive to buy from that store.

In-line Skates In-line skates first became popular in the late 1980s. These skates can help you move quickly in urban areas. And, they have no parking problem. All kinds of people use them, from secretaries to corporate executives.

GUESS WHAT

There is one private automobile or truck for every 1.3 licensed drivers in the United States.

What In The World?

In China, there is one bicycle for every two people—that's more than 500 million bicycles! Even today with its growing economy, bicycles remain the most common form of transportation. To supply its demand, China manufactures more than 35 million bicycles each year. The price of a typical one-speed Chinese bicycle is about $40. Ten-speeds go for about $90. Very few racing bicycles are used in China. The Chinese do not see using a bicycle as a sport or means of exercise, but as an inexpensive means of transportation. Why don't people in the United States rely as much on bicycles? If you ride a bicycle, why have you made this transportation choice?

In-line skates can be purchased for as little as $29. But if you are serious about them, you will pay $150 or more to buy a good pair.

In evaluating in-line skates, look particularly at the wheels, bearings, and fit and construction of the boots. Large wheels roll faster, but smaller wheels are more stable. Wheels of 72mm or less are best for beginners. Often wheels are graded for hardness. Harder wheels last longer but don't grip as well. A medium hardness will provide a good combination of speed and maneuverability.

Good-quality bearings will have an ABEC rating on the bearing itself, or on the box or tag. The ratings will be ABEC-1, -3, or -5. The higher the number, the better the bearing. But any ABEC-rated bearing causes the wheels to spin more smoothly than a nonrated one.

The boots should fit more snuggly than street shoes, but your toes should not hit the ends. When you bend your knees, your heel shouldn't lift. When the boots are laced tightly, your ankles shouldn't wobble.

When you begin to use in-line skates, expect to fall. Practice in a place with no hills, no traffic, and few other people until you know how to stop and turn.

Motorcycles There are more than four million motorcycles and motorbikes registered in the U.S. They are less expensive to buy and maintain than a car but can be expensive to insure. In fact, motorcycles with powerful engines can be as expensive to insure as a car.

You must have a license to drive a motorcycle on public roads. You must pass a test. Also, getting a license depends on the size and power of the engine. Many states have lower requirements for motorcycles with five horsepower or less. If you are considering a motorcycle, check your state's requirements.

Statistically, you have more than three times the chance of being seriously injured while driving a motorcycle than while driving a car. Motorcycles can tip over or lose traction on loose gravel. They do not have a body to protect their drivers. Because a motorcycle is small compared to a car, car drivers may not see it. A "fender-bender" for a car could be fatal for a motorcyclist. So always be aware of your surroundings while you are riding. Watch out for unexpected moves from other drivers.

If you decide to drive a motorcycle, get training. A nonprofit organization called The Motorcycle Safety Foundation offers training courses in all 50 states. Check its web site for locations. Or ask the dealer to recommend a program in your area.

When shopping for a motorcycle, evaluate the trade-off between price and the features you want. Because insuring a powerful motorcycle is as expensive as insuring a car, select a smaller engine if you are looking for inexpensive transportation.

Safety Equipment When you use a bicycle, motorcycle, or in-line skates, always wear a helmet. More than 600,000 people are injured in

© Getty Images/PhotoDisc

bicycle accidents each year. Roughly 700 of these accidents result in death. It is estimated that helmet use could prevent a third of these fatalities. Most states have laws requiring helmets for motorcyclists. Some also require helmets for bicycling.

For motorcyclists, a full-face helmet offers the best protection. It covers your chin and much of your face. A three-quarters or open-face type does not protect your face and jaw. Smaller helmets that cover just the top of your head are likely to fall off in an accident.

Make sure you understand how to wear the helmet properly. Bicycle

© Getty Images/PhotoDisc

helmets are designed to cover your forehead, not just the back of your head. Buy a helmet that fits snuggly, so that it will stay in place during an accident. Helmets for bicycling and in-line skating often have padding that can be adjusted for a good fit.

A helmet is just the minimum protection you should have. For in-line skating, you should also have elbow and knee pads and wrist guards. When riding a motorcycle, you should wear over-the-ankle boots, long pants, a good jacket, and gloves.

Public Transportation

Most cities and suburban areas have public transportation systems. These may include buses, streetcars, subways, trains, ferries, and taxis. Public transportation has some important benefits over owning a car.

▶ **Cost** Compared to owning a car, public transportation is very inexpensive. You pay for it only

when you need it. You don't have to buy gas or insurance, pay for repairs, or pay to park.

▶ **Convenience** Public transportation is designed to go to the most popular destinations in an area, such as downtown offices and major shopping districts. You don't have to find a place to park.

▶ **Speed** Public transportation can be a faster way than cars to get to your destination. Subways and ferries don't have to compete with cars on a congested freeway. Large cities often have bus lanes that allow buses to bypass the traffic.

Environmental Benefits

Emissions from gasoline-powered vehicles pollute the air. When people use public transportation, fewer pollution-causing vehicles are on the road.

Using public transportation, however, does require you to plan ahead. Some lines may not run late at night, or they may run infrequently. All public transportation systems publish a schedule so that you can plan to be at the pick-up points at the right times.

Taxis are the most expensive forms of public transportation. For most trips by taxi, you must pay by the mile as well as pay a tip.

A taxi can be a good option if you are in a place where you are unfamiliar with the public transportation system. If you will be there awhile, though, look into the less expensive public transportation options. Your taxi expenses can add up quickly.

You can reduce the price of a taxi by sharing one with others and splitting the fare. For example, suppose you fly into an unfamiliar city and want transportation to your hotel. Other people at the airport's taxi pick-up point may be going to the same hotel or another in the same area. You can ask if any of them would like to share a taxi with you.

IN CLASS ACTIVITY

Who in the class has used public transportation? What did they think of the experience? What other options to driving a car do you use regularly?

Carpooling

A *car pool* is an arrangement to share private transportation. If other people in your neighborhood work near your job and work similar hours, you can take turns driving everyone to your mutual destinations. By sharing transportation, you are significantly reducing the cost of gas and vehicle maintenance for everyone. Plus, you are benefiting the environment by reducing the number of cars on the road. To encourage people to carpool, large cities often provide a carpool lane on expressways.

CheckPoint

What methods of transportation can you choose besides owning a car?

TRY THESE

1. Why are most trips Americans take relatively short?

2. What roles does the government play in transportation in the United States?

3. What are some benefits to using a bicycle for transportation?

4. What are some benefits of safety equipment?

5. What should you consider when deciding whether to buy a motorcycle?

6. What are some benefits to using public transportation?

THINK CRITICALLY

7. **CONSUMER ACTION** What choices does Holly have? What are the benefits and drawbacks of each option?

8. If most forms of public transportation pollute the air just as cars do, why is taking public transportation better for the environment than driving a car?

9. Why do you think the government requires you to get a license to drive a motorcycle?

10. How will your need for transportation change as you pass through your life cycle?

© Getty Images/PhotoDisc

GOALS

EXPLAIN
how to determine
whether you can afford
a car

DESCRIBE
how to evaluate your
choices in new and
used cars

12.2 How to Choose a Car

Should You Buy a Car?

A car or truck is the second most expensive purchase most Americans make, next to a home. The purchase price is just part of the cost of owning a car. Insurance, gas, oil, maintenance, parking, and other costs can add up to nearly as much as your monthly loan payment. So before you decide to buy a car, make sure you can afford to own it.

Can You Afford a Car?

As a general rule, you can afford a car loan payment of no more than 20 percent of your take-home pay. But this means that all of your other living expenses—housing, food, clothes—plus savings—must be covered by the remaining 80 percent of your paycheck. Your housing expense (rent or house payment) is likely to be 30 percent of your take-

CONSUMER ACTION

Philip is learning to be a carpenter and needs a way to get to work. He never works at the same location for long, so he has decided to buy a car. Although Philip is excited, he is a little worried too. He realizes he doesn't know much about cars. He wants a car that is reliable and large enough to carry his tools to work. But he doesn't make much money yet. How can he determine how much he can afford to pay? How can he choose a vehicle that is right for him?

home pay. That leaves 50 percent for everything else. And don't forget the cost of gas, car insurance, and car maintenance.

Your first task in determining whether you can afford a car is to determine your other expenses. Include in your expense calculation an amount to save each month. After adding all your monthly expenses and savings, subtract this figure from your take-home pay. This is the most you can afford for a car payment.

An average new car costs about $20,000. To buy this average new car, you may have a cash down payment of $4,000. To get a loan for the remaining $16,000 for a term of 48 months at 9 percent interest, your monthly payment would be $398.16. Could you afford the average new car?

New or Used Car?

Owning a new car has many advantages. The sleek new design, bright paint, spotless interior, and quiet ride are quite enticing. New cars also may have new technology that improves their safety or gas mileage.

Reliability Probably the most important advantage of new cars is the reliable transportation they provide. New cars generally have fewer mechanical problems than used cars. When a new car does have mechanical problems, the warranty may cover the cost of repair.

Dealers usually provide a limited warranty on used cars and offer an extended warranty option. When you buy from an individual, you usually do not receive a warranty.

Cost A new car is much more expensive than the same car bought

MATH OF MONEY

Suppose you want to buy a $15,000 car. You have $3,000 for a down payment. Your bank told you that your monthly loan payment would be $240. Your monthly take-home pay is $1,200. You have estimated your monthly expenses as follows. Can you afford to buy this car?

Rent: $380   Entertainment: $50   Car insurance: $90
Food: $80   Clothes: $50   Gas & maintenance: $50
Utilities: $70   Personal needs: $40   Savings: $50
Phone: $20

SOLUTION

Yes. You will have $320 left per month after paying living expenses.

$380 + $80 + $70 + $20 + $50 + $50 + $40 + $90 + $50 + $50 = $880 monthly expenses

$1,200 − $880 = $320 income remaining after paying monthly expenses

© Getty Images/PhotoDisc

used. As soon as you drive a new car off the lot, it loses value. Studies show that most cars lose almost 25 percent of their value each year. So if you bought a new car for $20,000, it would be worth only $15,000 next year.

This loss of value benefits the used-car buyer. You might be able to buy someone else's $20,000 car for $15,000 when it is a year old.

Mileage The value of a used car also depends on the number of miles it has traveled. Its mileage, indicated on the car's **odometer**, is a measure of wear. Cars wear out, as other products do. The more miles a car has traveled, the more repair costs you can expect as parts begin to wear out. Still, you can afford to spend quite a bit on repairs for the large amount you saved initially by choosing a used instead of a new car.

CheckPoint

What should you consider in deciding how much car you can afford? What are some advantages and disadvantages of new versus used cars?

How to Choose a Car

Cars come in an array of styles, sizes, features, and options. Before you start shopping, do your homework. Learn about different cars. Decide which features and options are most important to you.

What Class of Car?

Manufacturers design different classes of vehicles to appeal to different consumer tastes and uses. These are vehicle classifications.

- ▶ Economy cars
- ▶ Midsize cars
- ▶ Full-size cars
- ▶ Luxury cars
- ▶ Sport utility vehicles
- ▶ Vans
- ▶ Sports cars
- ▶ Pick-up trucks

The class of vehicle that is right for you depends on how you plan to use it. For example, suppose you plan to do a lot of off-road driving. A sport utility vehicle might be a good choice. If your budget is tight, perhaps a fuel-efficient economy car would be a good way to get around.

Be realistic. Choose a class that best fits your lifestyle and wallet.

Which Model?

After deciding which class of vehicle you want, start searching for information about the different models in that class offered by different manufacturers. There are many printed sources of information about cars. Most of these publications can be found in public libraries.

A good place to begin is the December issue of *Kiplinger's Personal Finance Magazine*. Every year, it describes most automobile models sold in the U.S. It won't tell you which car to buy, but it can help you decide which to investigate further. *Edmund's New Car Prices* and *Kelley Blue Book* will give you a general idea of what you should expect to pay for specific models.

For information about sporty and luxury cars, try magazines such as *Motor Trend, Car and Driver,* and *Road and Track.* An excellent all-around source of car information is *Consumer Reports.* Each April, it devotes an entire issue to evaluating new cars. It summarizes tests of specific models each month and publishes a *New Car Yearbook* at the end of each year. Much of this information can be found online.

Features and Options

The characteristics of a particular model of car that offer benefits to the owner are **features**. For example, one model of sedan might feature leather seats and cup holders. Some features come with the car as standard equipment and are included in the price. Others are options.

Options are features that you can choose to include or not include on the car. Options add to the price of the car. For example, a four-cylinder engine may be standard on the model you want. A six-cylinder engine may be offered as an upgrade. If you choose the larger engine, the price of the car will increase.

The cost of options adds up quickly. So before you head to the car dealer, decide what features and options you want on your car. Then

CYBER CONSUMER

A vast amount of car information is available on the Internet. Search the Net using the key word *automobile*. Try *Autobytel, CarPoint,* or *Edmund's Online*. Many sites provide calculators that can help you determine what you can afford to pay for a car.

prioritize your list, with the options you want most at the top. You will probably have to make trade-offs to keep the price affordable.

Features and Options Checklist

Which are most important to you?
- ✓ Air conditioning
- ✓ Sunroof
- ✓ Convertible top
- ✓ Automatic or manual transmission
- ✓ Cruise control
- ✓ Leather interior
- ✓ Cup holders
- ✓ Number of doors
- ✓ Power locks, windows, and seats
- ✓ Airbags (driver and passenger)
- ✓ Anti-lock brakes
- ✓ Anti-theft package
- ✓ Engine size (4, 6, or 8 cylinder)
- ✓ Sound system

Dealer Add-Ons Dealers offer options that they install in their own shops. These include rust proofing, special paint sealers, and treatments to make upholstery resist stains.

IN CLASS ACTIVITY

Write a list of the features, options, and add-ons you would like to have on the first car you might buy. Next, prioritize this list into needs and wants.

Extended Warranty   The basic warranty for most new cars lasts for three years or 36,000 miles. For as much as $1,200 or more, you can have this extended, usually to seven years or 70,000 miles.

Safety Features   Safety may be an important concern when you choose a car. Size more than any-thing else determines a vehicle's safety. Larger cars surround their pas-sengers with more protective mater-ial than smaller cars. But size alone doesn't make a car safe. Check *Consumer Reports* or another infor-mation source for results of crash tests on different car models.

Studies have shown that airbags significantly reduce deaths and injuries in crashes. Because airbags can cause injuries to children and small adults, you may want to learn more about airbag safety.

Recent studies indicate that anti-lock brakes are not reducing the number of accidents. They have the potential to make a car safer, but you must learn how to use them properly.

How to Evaluate a Used Car

More than two-thirds of the cars sold in the United States each year are used. You can buy a used car from a dealer or from an individual.

You should inspect a used car carefully before buying. Here are some things to look for when you evaluate a used car.

1. Look for mismatched paint and exterior panels that don't fit together well. These are signs that the car has been in an accident.

2. Check for rust. Look in less obvious places, such as under the doors and carpeting, and inside the trunk.

3. Look for stains on upholstery and carpeting and for a moldy smell.

4. Look on the ground under the car for fluid drips.

5. Check all controls and lights.

6. Drive slowly on a level road that is not busy and briefly let go of the steering wheel. The car should not pull to the left or right.

7. Step on the brake firmly to make sure the car stops easily and without pulling to one side.

8. On a car with manual transmis-sion, make sure the gears shift without grinding or slipping out of gear.

9. When you let off of the acceler-ator, look for blue smoke from the tailpipe. This is a sign that the car is burning oil. Small amounts of white smoke are normal, but large clouds mean serious engine problems.

10. With the engine idling, pull the automatic transmission dipstick. The fluid should be cherry red with no burn smell or bubbles.

After you have made your own evaluation of the used car, take it to a mechanic you trust as a final check before you buy.

CheckPoint

How can you decide what type of car is right for you? Where can you find information to help you narrow your choices?

TRY THESE

1. What is the maximum percentage of monthly take-home pay that you should consider paying for a car loan?

2. Why is a used car's mileage important in determining its value?

3. What are some advantages of buying a used car?

4. What are some sources of information about car models?

5. Why should you make a list of features and options you want and prioritize it before shopping for a car?

6. What are some things to look for when evaluating a used car?

THINK CRITICALLY

7. CONSUMER ACTION Write an essay describing how Philip can determine how much he can afford to pay. List some of the things he should consider in selecting a vehicle.

8. Suppose you are calculating how much you can afford for a car. Why should you include savings in your calculation of expenses?

9. MATH OF MONEY Suppose your take-home pay is $800 a month. The monthly payment on a used car is $140. Your monthly expenses total $155. Can you afford the car? Why or why not?

10. List all the ways you would use a car now and in the near future. What class of car would best fit your life stage?

DECISION MAKING PROJECT

SPECIFY   **SEARCH**   **SIFT**   **SELECT**   **STUDY**

SPECIFY   Create a list of needs and a list of wants for your friend's car. Does this person want certain features? Decide on an amount that this person can afford to use as a down payment. Other than the car payment, what are other costs to consider?

GOALS

EXPLAIN
the difference between buying and leasing a car

DESCRIBE
the sales contract

12.3 To Buy or Lease?

Finance Options

More than 80 percent of the people who buy new cars in the United States use credit to finance their purchase. All car dealers have financing plans to offer their customers. In some cases, dealers make agreements with local banks to provide financing for the cars they sell.

Some automobile manufacturers extend credit through special divisions of their businesses. General Motors Acceptance Corporation (GMAC), for example, will provide credit for cars sold by GM dealers.

Convenience is probably the biggest advantage of using credit offered through dealers. Lower

CONSUMER ACTION

Amy has decided she wants a new car. Unfortunately, she doesn't have much to spend. When she visited a dealership, she expected to buy a basic model with few options. But a salesperson told her how she could drive a more expensive model. She could enjoy luxuries without making a larger monthly payment. All she has to do is agree to lease a car instead of purchase one. Amy likes the idea of driving a nicer car, but she isn't sure this is a wise choice. How should she evaluate her alternatives? What benefits will she receive if she agrees to lease a car? What costs will she pay?

interest rates are generally available from other sources, such as credit unions. Remember, you do not have to borrow through the dealer. Before you sign you should investigate your credit alternatives. This can be done by visiting local banks or by using the Internet. Try searching the Web using the key words *car loans.*

Sometimes dealers offer special low interest rates as a promotion. Or you may be able to choose a **rebate**, a partial refund of the purchase price. This offer could be better or worse than the special rate reduction. Do the math to figure out which option will be the least expensive.

Leasing

For consumers, **leasing**, or renting, automobiles has become a common way to purchase transportation. Until the 1970s, mostly businesses leased vehicles, so they could deduct the cost of their leases to reduce their taxes. Consumers were not allowed this deduction, so they usually bought new or used cars. Then conditions changed.

The price of new automobiles went up rapidly in the 1970s and 1980s. Manufacturers worried that sales of new cars would fall. Leasing was promoted as a way for people to buy the use of more expensive cars. Today, more than one-third of new cars driven in the U.S. are leased.

How a Lease Works

Before you decide to lease a car, you should learn how a lease works. Consumers who lease automobiles are paying for the use of the car. They own nothing. When a lease agreement is made, the manufacturer is paid for the car with money

© Getty Images/PhotoDisc

borrowed by the leasing business. Payments made by consumers and the money received from the sale of returned cars are used to repay this debt. Consumers often do not realize it, but leasing a car is much like a loan. They are required to make payments over time. The biggest difference is that at the end of the agreement, they have nothing to show for their payments.

Lease Terms

Salespeople use special terms to describe lease agreements.

▶ *Gross capitalized cost* This is the price you would pay for the car, and you should negotiate it just as if you were buying the car.

▶ *Capitalized cost reduction* This is the cash down payment.

▶ *Acquisition fee* This is a payment to cover the cost of setting up a lease. It often includes a security deposit that should be refunded at the end of the lease.

▶ *Residual value* This is the predicted value the car will have at the end of the lease. It is also what you will be expected to pay if you purchase the car at that time.

▶ *Money factor* This is an indication of the interest rate that you would pay for financing the lease of the car. Multiply it by 24, for instance, for a 24-month lease to calculate the approximate annual interest rate.

▶ *Monthly payment* This is the amount you will pay each month during the lease.

▶ *Mileage allowance* This is the number of miles you will be allowed to drive the car without paying an extra charge per mile.

▶ *Excess wear fee* This is an amount charged for damage to the car that is beyond that which could reasonably be expected. It is determined by the dealer when a car is returned. Find out how any excess wear will be determined before you sign the lease.

▶ *Disposition fee* This is an amount that is paid when the car is returned at the end of the lease. It is supposed to cover the cost of getting the car ready to sell to someone else.

Steps to Leasing

Step One — Negotiate the Price of the Car Suppose you negotiated the price of a car with the dealer as $15,000. This is the gross capitalized cost.

© Brand X Pictures

Betty is considering leasing a car. She read the dealer's proposed agreement and believes it is generally a fair offer. There is only one problem. The contract calls for a mileage allowance of 10,000 miles per year. In most years Betty drives over 15,000 miles. There is a $0.15 charge for each excess mile that is driven. Why should Betty be concerned about this part of the agreement? What should she do?

Step Two — Know the Residual Value The residual value of the car could be 60 percent. This means that the leasing business is guaranteeing that the value of the car will be at least 60 percent of its current value after the term of the lease.

You will pay the remaining 40 percent because you are paying for the value of the car that you will use up.

40% × $15,000 = $6,000

Step Three — Down Payment and Security Deposit You might pay a $1,000 down payment, or capitalized cost reduction, and an acquisition fee. The security deposit is part of the acquisition fee. This fee will be refunded to you after you return the car if you follow the terms of the lease. It is usually equal to one monthly lease payment.

PRIMARYSOURCES

Very few people pay cash for a car—especially if the car is new. But financing a car is a long-term commitment for an item whose value diminishes rapidly. Read the opinion of a South Carolina woman in 1939.

"And there's that old car. I'll be glad when it's paid for. I ain't never gonna buy another one, 'less I've got the spot cash to pay for it with the day I get it. I'll walk first. This thing of having to plank out your good money for a good-for-nothin' old car every time a check comes in don't suit me a-tall."

Do you or your friends and family members have car payments? What else could you be doing with that money? Would you ever be willing to give up your car and take a less costly means of transportation?

Step Four — Financing The amount of your down payment is subtracted from the $6,000.

$$\$6,000 - \$1,000 = \$5,000$$

This is the amount that you will finance at a specified money factor. The money factor is calculated the same way as an interest rate for a car loan. This money factor, 0.0029 in this instance, is used to calculate your monthly lease payment. Multiply 0.0029 by 24 months for a 24-month lease. This lease is comparable to a 7% APR loan.

$$0.0029 \times 24 = 0.07 = 7\%$$

Another factor that will affect how your monthly lease payment is calculated is your mileage. Each lease has a maximum allowance for mileage during the term of the lease. Usually this maximum is 12,000 miles driven in a year. If you know that you are going to drive more miles than the maximum, you can pay for the extra mileage before the lease or pay for it at the end of the lease.

Step Five — Before You Return Your Leased Car Before you return a leased car, find out and record its condition. Have a mechanic go over the car to see if anything serious is wrong with it. If there is a problem, it could be less expensive to have the car repaired before you return it. Have the mechanic write down any problems or defects in the exterior or interior of the car.

Step Six — Return Your Leased Car After the lease term is over, the dealer will check the car for excess wear and tear, as well as for excess mileage. You will have to pay for repairs or excess mileage.

When you signed your lease, the leasing company guaranteed that the car would be worth 60 percent of its value new, or $9,000. If the car is now worth $8,000, you should not have to pay the $1,000 difference.

If the car is now worth $10,000, some leasing businesses will allow you to use the $1,000 difference as a down payment on another car lease or purchase.

You may choose to buy the car you have leased. Try to negotiate the car's residual value. The dealer may be willing to sell it to you for less.

If you no longer want to lease a car, you can simply pay the disposition fee and leave the dealership.

Who Should Consider a Lease?

Choosing to lease a car makes more sense for some people than for others. You probably should not lease a car if you:

▶ can pay cash for a new car

▶ drive many or very few miles each year

▶ keep your cars for many years

▶ are particularly hard on your cars

People who can't pay for new cars, replace cars regularly, or drive about 12,000 miles per year are better candidates for leases.

CheckPoint

How does a lease agreement work? What are the steps in leasing a car?

© Getty Images/PhotoDisc

The F&I Office

Whether you are buying or leasing a car, you will go to the Finance and Insurance (F&I) office after you have negotiated the price with the salesperson. Here you will complete the paperwork for the purchase and financing.

Financing

If you did not get financing from a bank or other source before you went to the dealership, the F&I manager can contact lending institutions for you. If you get your financing through the dealership, the F&I manager will usually add an extra percent or two to the interest rate or money factor as a commission for arranging the loan or lease. This may not be disclosed to you, so be sure to ask.

Insurance

The F&I manager will offer a number of insurance policies to you. These are some commonly sold policies.

▶ *Accidental Death and Dismemberment* pays off the balance of your lease or loan if you accidentally die or are dismembered.

▶ *Gap protection* pays the difference between what you owe and what your car is worth if it is totaled in an accident. Suppose that at the time your car is wrecked, it is worth $16,000. But you still owe the bank $17,500 on the loan. Your insurance company will pay you $16,000, but you still have to pay the remaining $1,500 on your loan. Gap protection will cover this remaining amount.

▶ *Extended warranty protection* will extend the manufacturer's warranty on certain parts or services. You can buy warranty protection by yearly increments.

Some insurance policies are from the vehicle's manufacturer and some are from another source. If you are considering buying any insurance, check out the company as you would for any other type of insurance.

The price of some policies can be added to the purchase price of your vehicle and financed. Be aware of what coverage you want before you go to the dealership. For instance, gap protection is important to have, but many auto insurance policies contain this protection already.

Optional Products

If you are interested in such extras for your vehicle as pin striping, rust protection, or a security system, the F&I manager will have product information and prices.

The F&I manager earns income from selling the added options and insurance. The income may come in the form of a bonus, a percentage, or other compensation.

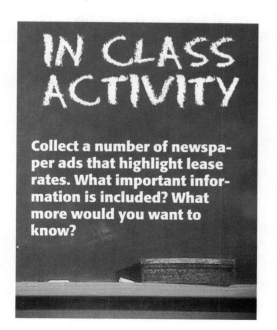

IN CLASS ACTIVITY

Collect a number of newspaper ads that highlight lease rates. What important information is included? What more would you want to know?

Sample Sales Contract

Vehicle Purchase Price	$14,800.00
Other Options	+ 500.00
Subtotal	$15,300.00
Sales Tax (5%)	+ 765.00
Total Cash Price	$16,065.00
Down Payment	1,000.00
Trade-in	− 0.00
Unpaid Cash Balance	$15,065.00
Insurance Premiums:	
Credit Life	
Gap Protection	
Other Insurance	0.00
Principal Amount Financed	$15,065.00
Finance Charge	+ 2,588.74
Total Cost of the Loan	$17,653.74
Interest Rate	8%
Length of Loan	48
Monthly Payment	$367.79

The Sales Contract

Of all the documents you will sign in the F&I office, the sales contract is by far the most important. It may look intimidating, but if you know what to look for, you can be sure you know what you are signing.

Cash Price This should be the purchase price that you negotiated with the salesperson. The cash price is the price you would pay if you were not financing the purchase. Suppose you negotiated a price of $14,800. The dealer then adds any optional extras you wanted to buy. The sum of the negotiated cash price and the extras is then taxed at your state's sales tax rate. Suppose your state sales tax is 5 percent and that you wanted the dealer to pinstripe your car for $500.

$14,800 + $500 = $15,300

$15,300 × 0.05 = $765

$15,300 + $765 = $16,065

The sales contract should also include title, license, and document fees.

© Getty Images/PhotoDisc

Down Payment The down payment should be listed. Any amount that you negotiated for a trade-in should also be listed separately. Suppose you paid a $1,000 down payment and you had no trade-in.

Unpaid Cash Balance To figure the amount to be financed, subtract your down payment and amount of trade-in from the cash price of the car. You will take out a loan for this unpaid cash balance.

$$16,065 - \$1,000 = \$15,065$$

Insurance Premiums If you purchase any insurance from the dealer, such as gap protection, the premiums would be listed on your sales contract. The sales contract should indicate that the certificate for your insurance policies should be sent to you within 25 days. Suppose you bought no insurance from the dealer.

Other Costs Different states have different laws as to allowable other costs. These, however, should also be listed on your sales contract.

Principal Amount Financed This is the sum of the unpaid cash balance, any insurance premiums, and other costs. In this case, your principal amount financed would be $15,065.

Finance Charge This is the total amount of interest you will pay over the term of your car loan. If it is not listed, ask that the F&I manager write the interest rate for the loan on the contract before signing it. Remember, you must be told the APR of any loan.

Be sure to ask what the term of the loan is. The longer the loan, the more you pay in interest. Suppose your car loan is for 48 months. Check the F&I manager's math. Many stores and the Internet offer calculators that can help you figure monthly loan payments.

Suppose you have a loan at 8 percent for 48 months.

The total finance charge for this loan is $2,588.74. Remember, this is not calculated as simple interest.

Total Cost of the Loan This is the total amount you will pay for the car loan. It is the sum of the principal amount and the finance charge.

$$15,065 + \$2,588.74 = \$17,653.74$$

Payment Schedule Here the contract will state how many payments you are responsible for, and the amount of the payments. Again, check the math. If something doesn't add up, don't sign the contract. According to the math you have checked, your monthly payment will be $367.79.

$$17,653.74 \div 48 = \$367.79$$

Different states have different laws governing the car sales contract. Other parts to the sales contract may list the specific provisions for your liability for damage, making payments on time, and your rights as a buyer. Read these as well. If you are being pressured for time, ask to take it home to read it before you sign.

CheckPoint

What kinds of products will the F&I manager want to sell you? What are the parts of a sales contract?

TRY THESE

1. List some businesses that offer financing for car loans or leases.

2. What is a rebate? What is often offered as its alternative?

3. What is leasing?

4. What is a leased car's residual value?

5. What is the money factor of a lease?

6. Describe the steps in leasing a car.

7. What is the F&I office, and what happens there?

8. How is an F&I manager paid?

9. Why is it important to know about the parts of a car sales contract?

THINK CRITICALLY

10. **CONSUMER ACTION** Amy was encouraged to lease a car that was more expensive than one she had expected to buy. How can Amy determine if leasing is right for her?

11. Martha is considering leasing a car for two years. She has examined the agreement and is troubled by just one thing. The money factor is 0.00571. She thinks this is a bit high, but the salesperson says it's nothing to worry about. He says, "How can 571 hundred-thousandths of anything be important?" Should Martha be concerned?

12. Should someone who drives only 5,000 miles a year consider leasing a car? Explain.

13. Why do you think insurance is sold at dealerships?

DECISION MAKING PROJECT

SPECIFY SEARCH SIFT SELECT STUDY

SEARCH Have each group member look in the newspaper, go online, or visit dealerships to research appropriate new and used car choices for your friend. Have your list of needs, wants, and monthly transportation budget handy. Each group member will investigate one possible car choice.

12.4 The Car-Buying Process

Determine a Fair Price

You know what you want, what you can afford to pay, and how you want to finance your purchase. Now you have one more bit of research to do before you are ready to hit the showroom.

The Invoice Price

To effectively negotiate a price with a dealer, you should know ahead of time the invoice price for models you are considering. The **invoice price** is the amount the dealer paid to buy the car from the manufacturer.

From this information, you can calculate a fair price.

You can find invoice information for specific car models from *Consumer Reports,* by mail, or from online sources, such as *Edmund's, Kelley Blue Book,* or *Microsoft CarPoint.* By phoning *Consumer Reports* at 1-800-348-2028, you can order a report for a particular model that includes the invoice price, dealer cost for each available option, and current rebates or other dealer incentives. This report will cost a

CONSUMER ACTION

Carmello wants to buy his first new car. He has narrowed his choices to three models that he can afford. But how can he know what is a fair price for these models? He wants some special options. What should he expect to pay for these? How can he negotiate for a good deal?

small fee (approximately $12 per report). For an additional small fee, *Consumer Reports* will tell you what your old car is worth if you plan to sell it yourself or trade it in.

You can get similar information from online sources. Search for these sites by their company name or a key word, such as *car*. Popular search sites such as Yahoo will take you directly to *Edmund's, Kelley,* or *CarPoint* through their site links. Be sure to get the dealer's cost for the options you are considering and information about current rebates and dealer incentives.

Sticker Price

Every new car will have a price tag in the window, detailing the prices of the car's options and the total price, or **sticker price**. The sticker price is the manufacturer's suggested retail price (MSRP). The sticker price is almost always higher than the dealer expects consumers to pay for the car. Typically, the sticker price is 9 to 11 percent above the invoice price. By knowing what the car and each option actually cost the dealer, you can estimate the price the dealer might accept.

How to Calculate a Fair Price

Car dealers must make a profit to stay in business. But they don't have to make an excessive profit. A fair profit is about 3 percent of the invoice price of the car plus options.

To calculate a fair price to shoot for in your negotiations, begin with the invoice price of the car. Add to it the invoice prices of all the options you want. Subtract any rebates or dealer incentives. Then add 3 percent

© Getty Images/PhotoDisc

of this adjusted invoice price as the dealer's profit.

The result of these calculations is a fair price for the car. This gives you an idea of the price you should target in your negotiations with the dealer. You may not be able to get exactly this price, but at least you know what is reasonable.

Your Trade-In

You will get the best price for your old car if you sell it yourself. But if you want to trade it in to avoid the hassle, determine its value before going to a dealer.

In determining the value of your trade-in, start with the value for this model and year of car listed by *Consumer Reports* or one of your other sources. Take a little off if there is excessive mileage or flaws, like rust, old tires, and needed repairs.

CheckPoint

How can you determine a fair price for the car you want? Where can you get the information you need to calculate this price?

The Buying Process

You have done your homework. You are ready to go car shopping.

Where to Shop

Your best choice is to go to several dealers, not just one. Size and location of a dealership don't really determine where you will get the best price. All dealers pay the same invoice price from the manufacturer.

Ask friends and family members about their experiences with particular dealers. Do they think they got a fair deal? Would they buy another car from that dealer?

A dealer who has been in business a long time may be a better choice than a new dealer. A well-established dealer probably gained its success by treating customers fairly.

New dealers are a bit riskier since they haven't had time to establish their reputation.

No-Haggle Dealers Saturn and some others advertise themselves as "no-haggle" dealers. This means that the price on the sticker is non-negotiable. It is already discounted from the MSRP, and it is the price you will pay to buy from that dealer.

No-haggle dealers can be a good option if you really find the process of negotiating distasteful. Their sticker price is discounted, though it will almost always be higher than the fair price you calculate from invoice prices. But the difference between the sticker and fair price will be much less with a no-haggle dealer than with dealers who expect you to negotiate.

Buying on the Net On the Internet, you can find service companies that will negotiate with dealers in your area for you. Some of these

$MATH OF MONEY

Eric wants to buy a particular model of car. He learned that the invoice price is $20,000. He wants to upgrade to a 5-speed transmission (invoice $700) and sunroof (invoice $600). The dealer is giving a $1,000 rebate now. What is a fair price that he should seek in his negotiations with the dealer?

SOLUTION

Car invoice price	$20,000	$20,300 × 0.03 = $609 dealer profit
5-speed transmission	$ 700	
Sunroof	+$ 600	Adjusted invoice $20,300
TOTAL INVOICE	$21,300	Plus dealer profit +$ 609
Minus rebate	−$ 1,000	TARGET PRICE $20,909
ADJUSTED INVOICE	$20,300	

services, such as *Autobytel,* are free. They get paid by charging a small membership fee to area dealers. Other Internet services will charge you a small fee. These services will shop all local dealers, not just their members.

At the service's web site, you register, then enter the model of car and options you want. The service will contact local dealers, find the car you want, and get back to you with the lowest price. You can then go to that dealer and buy it at the price the service quoted.

When to Shop

Dealers may be "hungrier" for your business at some times more than others. Salespeople are typically paid at the end of the month. By shopping then, you may find a salesperson who wants one more commission that month.

In cold climates, winter months are often a good time to buy. Fewer consumers head to showrooms in bad weather, so dealers may be more willing to reduce their prices to get your business.

At the beginning of a new model year, usually September, dealers often receive an incentive bonus from manufacturers to sell previous-year models to make room for the new models. This is a good time to negotiate for the older models.

The months of August and December are typically slow at car dealers. You may be able to get a better deal during these months.

Test Drive

A salesperson will approach you. Ask questions when you have them, but don't allow the salesperson to distract you. Don't talk about price yet.

Examine First   Before you take your chosen model out for a spin, look at it carefully inside and out. It should be flawless. Panels should align smoothly. The paint should have no defects.

Sit in the driver's seat. Is the seat comfortable? Try the controls. Does everything work? Turn on the radio to make sure you like the sound. Sit in the back seat. Will your passengers be comfortable?

Open the trunk. Think about the kinds of things you expect to haul. Do you regularly carry luggage? Tools? Will these fit in the trunk?

Then Drive   During the test drive, concentrate on the car's

Buy the Numbers?

You've seen or heard the ads many times...

"We'll give you $3,000 for your trade-in. Push it in. Drag it in. Just get it here by midnight tonight, and we'll give you $3,000 toward the purchase of any new car on our lot!"

How do you think car dealers can make such an offer? What should you do to make sure you get a good deal?

INTERNET ACTIVITY

Using the Internet, research the car-buying and negotiating process. Write a brief essay describing your findings. Share your essay with other students by e-mail. Review the essays you receive in exchange, and make a list of car-buying tips. Summarize what you learn in an e-mail to your teacher.

performance and sounds. Try it in different driving situations. Test its acceleration, braking, shifting, and handling by driving as you normally drive.

How to Negotiate the Deal

You've selected the car you want, and you are now ready to negotiate.

Always remember that you are in charge. Don't allow the salesperson to pressure you. Be prepared to walk out if you don't like the price or the way you are treated. There are other dealers.

Don't tell the salesperson the price or monthly payment you can afford. Let the salesperson know that you are aware of the invoice price of the car and all options, and about any rebates or dealer incentives. Tell the salesperson that you intend to shop around for the best deal. You will come back later to buy if this price is the lowest.

Negotiate the price of the car only, not the monthly payment. Negotiate the value of your trade-in separately. Otherwise, the salesperson might give you a great price on the new car but then try to increase the dealer's

© Getty Images/PhotoDisc

profit by offering too little for your trade-in. Know and be firm on your trade-in's wholesale value.

Round 1   Make your first offer at just a little above invoice but below your calculated target price. Do not reveal your target price! Also, do not make another offer until you get a counteroffer from the salesperson. That counteroffer should be below the sticker price. If it is not, stick to your first offer until the salesperson comes down.

No matter what the counteroffer is, respond by saying that your initial offer was fair, and you would pay it today. See if the salesperson will make a lower counteroffer.

Round 2   Your next offer should be a bit higher than your first but still below your calculated target price. Wait for a counteroffer. With each new offer and counteroffer, you and the salesperson should be getting closer to your target price.

How close you can get to your calculated target price depends on supply and demand. Greater demand for a product means a higher price. When you are negotiating for a car that is in high demand right now, the dealer won't have to reduce the price as much. Other consumers may be willing to pay more.

The Final Price   After you settle on a price, you can expect to pay a few additional charges.

▶ Sales tax

▶ Destination fee (the cost of shipping from the manufacturer to the dealer, which is legitimate and non-negotiable)

▶ License and registration

▶ Documentation fee (not more than $50 to $100)

The salesperson or F&I manager will try to sell you a number of "extras." You are not required to pay for administrative and advertising costs. If you want add-ons, you will have to pay for them, such as fabric protection, rust proofing, and extended warranties.

Read All Paperwork Always read everything before signing. Don't depend on the F&I manager's explanation. Check the figures. Make sure that everything you agreed on is in writing. Make sure no options or fees appear that you didn't agree to. Remember, you are signing a legal contract.

In your own words, describe the negotiation process.

TRY THESE

1. Where can you get information about dealer costs?
2. How should you determine a fair price for the car you want?
3. What is a no-haggle dealer?
4. How can the Net help you buy a car?
5. How should you examine a car on the lot and in a test drive?
6. What additional costs should you avoid paying?

THINK CRITICALLY

7. **CONSUMER ACTION** How can Carmello calculate a fair price for these cars and options? What advice would you give him about negotiating with the dealer?
8. **MATH OF MONEY** Your report from an online service told you that the new car you want cost the dealer $15,000. The invoice price for the optional anti-lock brakes is $500, and the cassette player is $150. The dealer is giving a $500 rebate. What price should you target in your negotiations?
9. Why should you determine a fair price for the car before going to a dealer?
10. Why should you be prepared to walk away from a deal you don't like? Send your answer to your teacher in an e-mail.

DECISION MAKING PROJECT

SPECIFY   SEARCH   SIFT   SELECT   STUDY

SIFT Have group members present their car choices. Make a table to compare the features of each possible car choice against the list of your friend's needs, wants, and monthly budget.

© Getty Images/PhotoDisc

12.5 How to Maintain a Car

Every Car Needs Maintenance

Once you have bought a car, protect your investment by maintaining it properly. A car is a complex machine. It needs regular care to stay in good working order.

Your Owner's Manual

Learn about how your car works by reading the **owner's manual**. All new cars come with a manual. Many used cars still have theirs in the glove box.

If you buy a used car without a manual, you may order one through a dealership that sells that model of car.

Your owner's manual will show you where all the controls are located and how to operate them. It will tell you such things as how to read the gauges and what the warning lights mean. It also provides detailed instructions for doing minor maintenance tasks yourself, such as changing a tire or checking your oil.

CONSUMER **ACTION**

When Shauna turned 18, her grandfather gave her a car. She loves the car, but it is six years old and has 87,000 miles on it. Her grandfather told her that all it needs is a little "love and care." What can Shauna do to keep her car in good condition? When she needs repairs, how can she find a good repair shop? What can she expect when she takes her car for repairs?

Different systems on your car need to be checked and parts replaced at regular intervals. The manufacturer provides a detailed **maintenance schedule** in your owner's manual. It is a timetable for checking systems and replacing parts.

Following this schedule is important because it will keep your car in good working order for the longest possible time. Also, failure to follow this schedule is likely to void your car's warranty.

Having your car serviced at regular intervals can help you catch little problems before they become big (and expensive) ones. Something simple, such as replacing a worn fan belt, may cost $15 to $30 at a repair shop. But if the belt breaks when you are miles from a service station, it can cost much more.

Routine Preventive Tasks

Car parts wear out in normal use and must be replaced. You can check and even replace many parts yourself.

Tires   Make sure your tires are properly inflated. The manufacturer specifies the proper pressure for your tires in your owner's manual or on a sticker attached to the inside of the glove box or edge of the car door. Maintaining proper tire pressure will help your tires last longer and will save gas.

Check the tread on your tires every few months. Uneven tread patterns can be caused by improper inflation or misalignment. If you see uneven wear, you need to fix the problem or the tires will be damaged further.

Tread helps your tires grip the road. When the tread is worn to less than one-sixteenth of an inch, tires are no longer safe and must be replaced.

COMMUNICATE

Your friend Colin just got a used car. He doesn't have much money, so he plans to have problems repaired when they break rather than pay for routine maintenance. Write Colin a memo, explaining why his plan may be shortsighted.

Oil   Oil lubricates your engine's moving parts. Make sure your engine always has a sufficient amount of oil. Running out of oil can ruin your engine.

You can easily check the oil level yourself using a dipstick. The **dipstick** is a metal measuring stick with a handle. Your owner's manual will tell you where the dipsticks are located for checking different fluids in your car.

To check a fluid level, pull out the dipstick, wipe it clean with a clean rag, and put it all the way back in its slot. Then remove it again. The dipstick will be moist with fluid up to some point. Compare where the moisture ends to the measurements on the dipstick.

When oil wears out, it can no longer efficiently lubricate your engine. Replacing your oil according to your car's maintenance schedule is one of the most important things you can do to avoid costly repairs.

Other Fluids   You can also check the levels of your transmission fluid and brake fluid using their dipsticks. Antifreeze often has a transparent reservoir with the proper level marked. Check these fluids every few months and fill them as necessary. Don't overfill.

Your antifreeze will need to be flushed out of your cooling system and replaced every two or three years. Like oil, antifreeze wears out and loses its ability to cool your engine.

Tune-ups Consider a tune-up to be your car's physical exam. Get your car tuned on schedule. If you don't, your engine will likely start running roughly. A **tune-up** generally means replacing the spark plugs, but can also include replacing the air filter, fuel filter, and other parts.

Brakes Brakes usually last about 40,000 miles. But if you drive in city traffic, pull a trailer, or live in a hilly area, you will need to have your brakes checked more often.

Other Routine Checks Every couple of months, inspect the belts and hoses in your engine. If you see any bulges, cuts, or frayed edges, replace them. Check your windshield wipers for signs of wear. If they don't wipe away water well enough for you to see clearly through the windshield, you need to replace them.

Look under your car for signs of leaking fluids. If you see a puddle, take your car in for repair. While you are under the car, check the exhaust pipe to make sure its supports are holding it firmly in place. When your exhaust

© Getty Images/EyeWire

pipe has a hole, you'll know by the constant loud noise.

Exterior Maintenance To keep your car's finish sparkling, wash it regularly with a mild soap. Road grime and salt can damage your paint and lead to rust.

At least once a year, apply car wax. You'll know that the wax is working when you see rainwater forming round droplets on the surface. When rainwater starts looking more like sheets than droplets, it's time to apply another coat of wax.

CheckPoint

How can your owner's manual help you maintain your car ? What routine tasks can you do yourself?

Repair Services

Eventually every car needs repairs. Make sure to find a good repair shop and build a good working relationship with its mechanics.

How to Choose a Repair Shop

Choosing a reliable mechanic can be as important as choosing a car. Technological advances have brought many benefits to car owners, but they have also made car repair more complicated.

New car dealerships repair the car models they sell. If the problem with your car is covered by the warranty, you should have the repair done by a dealer.

Dealers are often more expensive than independent shops. Start your search by getting recommendations from people you know. If other people have had several positive experiences at a shop, then it is probably a good shop.

Check Them Out When you have identified several possibilities, check with the Better Business Bureau for complaints on file. Then visit each shop. The facilities should be reasonably neat and well organized and should have modern equipment. It should have clearly posted policies regarding labor rates, guarantees, and payment methods.

Also look for posted training certificates from organizations such as the National Institute for Automotive Service Excellence (ASE) and I-Car. These certificates show that the mechanic has completed courses to stay up to date on new automotive technology. Certificates of membership in professional organizations such as the Better Business Bureau and Chamber of Commerce also suggest that the shop is legitimate.

Build a Relationship Once you find a mechanic you trust, build a relationship with that shop. Let the shop know that you will continue to take your business there if you are satisfied with the work.

Doing Business with a Repair Shop

The time will come when you know there is something wrong with your car.

Describe the Problem
Before calling your repair shop for an appointment, make a list of the symptoms. Note unusual sounds, odors, leaks, or smoke. List changes

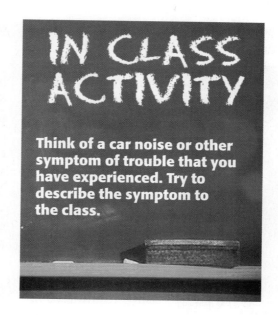

IN CLASS ACTIVITY

Think of a car noise or other symptom of trouble that you have experienced. Try to describe the symptom to the class.

in performance. When do these things occur—when accelerating, braking, or turning? Where do noises or leaks seem to be coming from?

Be prepared to describe these symptoms to your mechanic in detail.

Get an Estimate The repair shop must give you a written price estimate before making the repairs. This estimate should list the services to be performed and the price for labor and parts. If you think the estimate is too high, get an estimate from another shop.

When you sign the estimate, you are authorizing the shop to do the work. Then you are legally obligated to pay for the work up to the specified amount.

Sometimes a problem requires further diagnosis before the shop can quote a price. In this case, you can leave your car at the shop. A technician will call you later and

GUESS WHAT

According to the Better Business Bureau, problems with car repairs are the second most common form of consumer complaint.

describe the repairs needed and the price. You can then give verbal authorization. The shop may not perform repairs beyond those you authorized without further consent.

Guarantees

Ask about guarantees. Repair shops are not required to guarantee their work, but most good shops do provide some guarantees on parts and labor. Get any guarantees in writing.

Check and Pay for Repairs

When the job is finished, you will receive an invoice. The invoice should show the name and address of the shop and list all work done, including warranty work performed at no charge. Labor and parts must be listed separately. The invoice must note if any parts the mechanic installed were **rebuilt** or **reconditioned**. These are used parts that were repaired or restored to working order.

By law, the shop must return your old parts if you request them. However, repair shops return some old parts to the supplier as partial payment for the rebuilt parts installed in your car. In this case, you will have to pay more to have the old parts returned to you.

Before paying the invoice, check to see if the problem is solved. When checking requires a test drive, the mechanic may want to go with you, which is good. Then if you think the problem was not fixed, you can show the mechanic what is wrong.

Save Your Receipts After paying the invoice, you will get a receipt. Keep all repair and maintenance receipts with other car papers. You might need your receipts to make a claim under a guarantee or to help keep track of routine maintenance. If a major repair is needed later, your warranty company may want proof of proper maintenance. When ready to sell, your receipts will show good care to potential buyers.

To Resolve Problems

If you are dissatisfied with the repair, discuss the situation with the manager of the repair shop. Most problems can be worked out in a reasonable manner. Show copies of the estimate and any other paperwork to support your position. Be prepared to compromise on a fair solution.

If you can't resolve the problem directly with the repair shop, your next step is to ask for help from an arbitrator organization such as the Better Business Bureau or AUTO-CAP. If this kind of intervention fails, you can resort to small claims court.

Lemon Laws

All states have **lemon laws** that protect consumers who buy defective new cars. The laws vary from state to state. But generally a car is defined as a *lemon* if it has

► a defect that cannot be fixed after four attempts

► continued major problems that keep it in the shop for 30 days during the warranty period

► numerous major problems

© Getty Images/PhotoDisc

If your car qualifies as a lemon, you have a choice. You can have the car replaced or your money refunded. A refund should include the purchase price and all the money you spent on repairs.

Manufacturers must report to the state the vehicle identification numbers (VINs) of all lemons they take back. Sometimes these cars are resold without disclosing their past problems to the buyer. This is fraud. If you suspect you bought a resold lemon, look for the VIN printed on your dashboard or on your title documents. Several web sites will check state listings for your VIN, or you can call your state attorney general's office.

CheckPoint

How can you find a good repair shop? What can you expect from the shop when you take your car for service?

TRY THESE

1. What kinds of things can you learn from your owner's manual?

2. How can you check your oil and other fluid levels?

3. What can you do to help your mechanic identify your car's problem?

4. How can you evaluate repair shops?

5. Why should you save your repair receipts?

6. What are lemon laws, and how do they protect you?

THINK CRITICALLY

7. CONSUMER ACTION What can Shauna do to maintain her car? What can she expect when she takes the car in for repair?

8. Suppose you need new tires. You visit a tire store expecting to pay $60 each for tires rated to last 35,000 miles. But you discover that for $100 each, you can buy tires guaranteed to last 70,000 miles. What would you consider in deciding which to buy?

DECISION MAKING PROJECT

SPECIFY   SEARCH   SIFT   SELECT   STUDY

SELECT   Use the table to help make a group decision on a recommendation for your friend. Write an explanation of how your car choice would benefit your friend.

ASSESSMENT

KEY IDEAS

Transportation Basics

1. Because of the importance of transportation in American life, the local, state, and federal governments all have offices responsible for maintaining transportation systems.
2. You have many transportation options that are less expensive than owning a car.

How to Choose a Car

3. As a general rule, you can afford a car loan payment of no more than 20 percent of your take-home pay. But to really determine what you can afford, you should total your monthly expenses and savings, and subtract this total from your take-home pay.
4. The advantages of a new car are its reliability, warranty, new technology, and the enjoyment of driving a new car. Used cars are less expensive to buy but will probably have more maintenance problems.
5. The class of vehicle that is right for you depends on how you plan to use it.
6. There are many sources of information about car models in the library and online.
7. Before buying a used car, have a mechanic check it.

To Buy or Lease?

8. When you lease a car, you are renting and essentially paying only for the value of the car that you will use up during the lease period.
9. To lease a car, you will pay a capitalized cost reduction (down payment), an acquisition fee, and monthly payments. When you return the car, you may have to pay an excess wear fee, a disposition fee, and an excess mileage fee. At that point, you may be able to pay the residual value to buy the car.
10. Steps in leasing are (1) negotiate the price, (2) know the residual value, (3) pay your down payment and acquisition fee, (4) arrange financing and determine the monthly payment, (5) check the car's condition before returning it, and (6) return it.
11. When you buy or lease a car, you will complete the paperwork in the Finance & Insurance (F&I) office. The F&I manager may offer you financing, several types of insurance, and optional products such as pin striping, rust proofing, and fabric protection.
12. Read the sales contract carefully before signing. Make sure that all costs match what you agreed to.

The Car-Buying Process

13. A fair price lies between the sticker and invoice price.
14. You can find out the invoice price for the car and its options from *Consumer Reports* and from Internet sources, such as *Microsoft CarPoint, Edmund's,* and *Kelley Blue Book.*
15. To calculate a fair price to target in negotiations with the dealer, first add the invoice prices of the car and all options you want. Subtract any rebates or other dealer incentives. Then add 3 percent of this figure as a fair profit for the dealer.
16. To get the best price for your old car, sell it yourself. If you prefer to trade it in, first determine its value by consulting one of your online sources or *Consumer Reports.*

17. Compare prices at several dealers.
18. Before taking a test drive, examine the car inside and out. When driving, try the car in different driving situations.
19. Begin negotiations with a price just above invoice. With each new offer and counteroffer, you should be getting closer to your target price.

How to Maintain a Car

20. Your car's owner's manual tells you how to operate controls and care for your car. It contains a maintenance schedule that tells you when to service different car systems.
21. You should make several routine maintenance checks on your car.
22. To find a good repair shop, start with recommendations from acquaintances. Find out if the Better Business Bureau has complaints on file for these shops.
23. Visit the shops and look for modern equipment, general neatness and organization, and posted policies and certificates from training or professional organizations.
24. When your car needs repair, describe the symptoms to the mechanic as precisely as possible. The shop must provide an estimate for your authorization. At completion, make sure the problem is fixed. Keep a copy of the invoice with your car records.
25. Lemon laws require manufacturers to replace or buy back some cars.

TERMS REVIEW

Match each term on the left with its definition on the right.
Some terms may not be used.

a. dipstick
b. feature
c. invoice price
d. leasing
e. lemon law
f. maintenance schedule
g. odometer
h. option
i. owner's manual
j. rebate
k. rebuilt (or reconditioned) parts
l. sticker price
m. tune-up

1. instrument in a car that measures miles traveled
2. amount the dealer paid to buy the car from the manufacturer
3. timetable for checking systems and replacing parts on a car
4. metal measuring stick for checking fluid levels in a car
5. manufacturer's suggested retail price, listed on a sticker in a new car's window
6. used parts that were repaired or restored to working order to be installed as replacements
7. feature that you can choose to include or not include on a car, but if chosen, will add to the price of the car
8. partial refund of the purchase price
9. characteristic of a particular model of car that offers benefits to the owner

CONSUMER DECISIONS

10. Imagine that you are the parent of a 16-year-old high school student. She has saved her babysitting income and birthday gifts for years. You have always thought this money would help pay for her education. Now, she wants to use her savings to buy a used car. What would you say to her? Would you agree to her decision? It is her money, but you have to cosign the loan and help her buy insurance.

11. Describe the features of three different cars you would choose at different times in your life cycle. The first should be for an unmarried young adult who has just accepted a new job. The second should be for a married couple with three young children. The last should be for an older married couple looking to retire soon.

12. You would like to buy a car that will cost $350 a month. You earn $900 twice a month, after taxes are deducted. Your monthly expenses include rent ($500), food ($90), utilities/phone/cable ($130), entertainment ($100), insurance and gas ($160), savings ($50), and other ($200). Can you afford this car?

13. You live in Minnesota. You just got a job downtown, which is 3 miles from your home, and want a way to get there. You can't afford a car. A bus runs by your house every hour and stops five blocks from your job. You also have an old bicycle. A friend who works downtown, too, is willing to give you a ride but sometimes she works different hours. What are the pros and cons of each option? Which would you choose? Why?

14. Francisco has an old car that has been driven more than 100,000 miles. It still runs, but it makes strange noises and burns a little oil. Right now, the car needs new brakes. He could have them fixed for about $400. He wonders if the car is worth fixing. What should he do to make a rational decision?

LOOK IT UP

15. Select a make and model of vehicle that you like. Use a library or the Internet to look up information about its quality and price. What good points and bad points did you discover about this vehicle? Would you still like to own it? Explain.

16. Find out how much your family car would be worth as a trade-in on a new car you would like to own. If your family does not own a car, do this research for a friend's car. Why do dealers offer more for trade-ins on expensive new cars than for basic models?

17. Investigate different lease offers advertised by car dealers in your community. Do they provide all the information you should have to make a rational decision to lease a car? What information, if any, is missing?

WHICH IS THE BEST DEAL?

You have researched car models and selected one you want to buy or lease. The terms are stated below. How much would each alternative cost? Which of these alternatives would you choose? Why?

Alternative 1 Purchase the car for $500 down and $430 a month for 36 months.

Alternative 2 Lease the car for $250 a month for 36 months. You would have to pay an acquisition fee of $399 (that includes a security deposit), a down payment of $500, and a disposition fee of $300 at the end of the lease. The security deposit of $199 would be refunded when you turn the car in.

Alternative 3 Lease the car and buy it at the end of the lease. The residual value is calculated to be $12,000.

POINT YOUR BROWSER TO

www.ee4c.swlearning.com
Complete the activity for Chapter 12.

18. Investigate recent cases of car-repair fraud. You can do this by looking in magazines at your library or over the Internet. What can you do to protect yourself from being cheated when you take your car in for repair?

19. Find automobile loan agencies on the Internet. What do they offer? What do you think about their offers? Would you finance a car this way? Why or why not? How can you check them out?

INSIDE THE NUMBERS

20. You found out that the invoice price of the car you want to buy is $16,000. The dealer's costs for the options you want are security system ($160), four-speed transmission ($750), stereo cassette ($165), and anti-lock brakes ($445). The dealer is offering a $500 rebate. What price should you target in negotiating for this car?

THINK CRITICALLY

21. Last week while you were driving to work, you smelled a strange odor coming from your engine. Later that day, you took your car to your dealer, who told you everything was OK. The next day, it happened again. One reason you are worried is that you bought the car two years and eleven months ago. Next month your warranty will expire. What should you do?

CURRICULUM CONNECTION

22. **HISTORY** Look up facts about Henry Ford's Model T. Pretend you are Henry Ford's advertising manager. Write an ad promoting your Model T to appear in a 1920s newspaper. How would you convince consumers that this is the right car for them?

23. **INDUSTRIAL ARTS** Examine a current repair manual for a car or truck. What repairs do you think you could do yourself now? What other repairs could you do with further training? What kinds of tools would you need?

24. **BUSINESS** One indicator of the health of the U.S. economy is the health of the American automobile industry. Look in the business section of your local newspaper or online. Find information about car sales and car production. What does this tell you about the health of the national economy at this point in time?

JOURNAL RECAP

25. After reading this chapter, review the answers you wrote to the questions in Journal Journey. Have your opinions changed?

DECISION MAKING PROJECT

SPECIFY   SEARCH   SIFT   SELECT   STUDY

STUDY Present a paragraph on the process you and your group went through to recommend a car for a friend. What did you learn?

Chapter 13

HOUSING
A PLACE TO CALL HOME

WHAT'S AHEAD

EXPLODING MYTHS

Fact or Myth?
What do you think is true?

1. In an apartment, you are free to live any way you want.

2. If you can afford the monthly loan payments, you can afford to buy a house.

3. When you shop for an appliance, higher price always means better quality.

JOURNAL JOURNEY

WRITE IN YOUR JOURNAL ABOUT THE FOLLOWING.

A HOME OF YOUR OWN When do you expect to move to a home of your own? Why do you want to live independently? What costs do you expect to pay?

SHARING A HOME WITH A FRIEND Do you think living with a friend would be a good idea? What agreements would you like to make with your roommate before moving in together? What potential problems can you see in living with someone else?

BUYING A HOME How would you choose a home to purchase? What would your dream home be like? What aspects of your dream home would you be willing to give up to get a home you could afford?

DECISION MAKING PROJECT

SPECIFY   SEARCH   SIFT   SELECT   STUDY

RULE YOUR OWN ROOST Your group will decide what type of housing you could rent for $700 a month. You will also make a list of household chores and rules, adjust your budget to move in, and learn how to furnish your living space.

GOAL

To learn how to choose an apartment

PROJECT PROCESS

SPECIFY	Lesson 13.1
SEARCH	Lesson 13.4
SIFT	Lesson 13.4
SELECT	Chapter Assessment
STUDY	Chapter Assessment

© Getty Images/PhotoDisc

13.1 Your Housing Options

Types of Housing

What kinds of housing appeal to you? An apartment or a house? Quaint or trendy? Spacious or cozy? When you start life as an independent adult, you may not be able to afford your dream home quite yet. If you consider your options carefully and make good choices, however, you can find a comfortable place to live that fits your personality and budget.

When you finish school and are ready to start life on your own, you are in a transition period. You may not have a job yet. Even if you have started a job, you may not have saved much yet. Independent living can be difficult during this period.

Your Parents' Home

For some young people, remaining in the family home can be a wise choice for a while. If your parents or guardians allow you to continue sharing their home, you should contribute to the family's living expenses. You should also contribute your time and effort to the upkeep of the household.

CONSUMER ACTION

Raul just graduated from high school. He has started a full-time job, but he doesn't have much money saved yet. Right now, he is still living with his parents, but he is eager to live independently as soon as he can. What housing options does he have? What choices can he make that will help him move out of his parents' home in a short time?

Come to an agreement with your parents about what your responsibilities will be while you live there. As you work and earn money, you can save toward the goal of living independently.

Dormitories

If you decide to go to college, you may be required to live in a dormitory. **Dormitories** are buildings with rooms that colleges rent to students at reasonable prices, usually in large complexes. Often, two or more students share a room. Room rates usually include meals in a cafeteria.

Living in a dormitory has many advantages. By living so close to many other students, you can meet people and make friends. Also, you usually have no responsibilities for cooking or maintenance other than to take care of your own room.

Apartments

Your first home away from home is likely to be an apartment. Apartments come in many shapes and sizes and in a wide range of prices.

Apartment Building or Complex? You can find an apartment in a single building or in a building that is part of a larger complex. If you are very social, you may choose a complex, where you will be surrounded by more people. If you prefer more privacy, a single building might be your best choice.

An apartment complex often offers additional facilities for its residents, such as a pool, fitness equipment, and tennis courts. If you would use these facilities, you might want to consider a complex that offers them. Just know that you are paying for these extras in the form of higher

rent. Choose this type of complex only if you will take advantage of these facilities.

Large or Small? In general, you pay for space. You need to decide how much space you are willing to pay for. An **efficiency apartment** is the smallest and the least expensive type of apartment. It consists of one room that serves as the living area, bedroom, and kitchen, plus a bathroom. Apartments with a separate bedroom cost more, and the price increases with the number of bedrooms the unit contains.

If space is particularly important to you—and you can afford it—you might consider a duplex. A **duplex apartment** is an apartment with rooms on two floors of a building. A duplex can give you the feel of living in a house but at a lower cost.

Furnished or Unfurnished? When you are just starting out, you may not have much money to buy furniture. You can rent an apartment that provides basic furnishings, such as a living room set, kitchen table and chairs, bed, and chest of drawers. In effect, you are renting the furniture, so furnished apartments are more expensive than similar unfurnished apartments.

You do have less expensive options. Your parents or friends may have old furniture that they will lend you until you can buy some of your own. You can get good deals on used furniture at flea markets and thrift shops. Be creative! By renting an unfurnished apartment and saving the cost of renting furniture, you will be able to save and buy your own furniture.

Houses, Condos, and Mobile Homes

You may dream of owning your own home. Home ownership is expensive, and it brings with it many responsibilities.

A **condominium** is an apartment that you own rather than rent. It is often more spacious than a typical rented apartment. Buying a condo requires you to take on many financial responsibilities. Besides making loan payments, you will also be required to pay a monthly condo association fee. This fee pays to maintain the facilities and grounds shared by all residents in the complex. Like many apartment complexes, condominium complexes often have a pool, playground, and green space for everyone's enjoyment.

A mobile home can be a relatively inexpensive way to own a home. A **mobile home** is a small house on wheels, designed so that the owner can transport it to a rented space in a mobile home community. You can

What In The World?

Many people believe that buying a home is the best investment you can make. They argue that homeowners have a place to live and will gain from increasing values over time. While usually true, there are no guarantees.

Consider the housing market in Japan. From 1975–1990, home prices increased by 10 to 15 percent per year, far exceeding the rate of inflation. By 1990, a small two-bedroom home cost the equivalent of $1 million. Property values were expected to continue growing and interest rates were low, leading many people to borrow heavily to invest in property.

In 1991, the real estate bubble burst, and housing values began to decline. By the end of 2002, average home values had declined by 40 percent or more. Thousands found themselves owing more on their homes than their homes were worth. When many homeowners were unable to make their mortgage payments, several of Japan's largest banks went into crisis.

How can consumers protect themselves from housing bubbles? From falling values?

Buy or Rent?

Advantages of Renting

► *Lower cost* The money you save by renting instead of buying can be used for something else.

► *Less responsibility* No responsibility for upkeep or repair beyond normal cleaning.

► *Mobility* You can move out whenever you want as long as you give the required notice.

Advantages of Buying

► *Ownership* Monthly payments lead to eventual ownership.

► *Value* Houses and condos often increase in value over time, so you can often sell them for more than you paid.

► *Your own space* You get privacy, space, and perhaps your own yard.

► *Fewer restrictions* You can do whatever you want to on your property within the law.

► *Tax-deductible interest and property tax* The interest you pay on your home loan can decrease your income tax significantly.

Disadvantages of Renting

► *No ownership* Your monthly payments do not give you ownership of anything.

► *More restrictions* The property owner sets the rules for what you can do in and to your living space.

► *Shared space* Living closely with others means their conduct affects your tranquility.

Disadvantages of Buying

► *Down payment* You would need about 20 percent of the house price in cash, up front.

► *High cost* Houses are often expensive and monthly loan payments can be high.

► *Property taxes and insurance* You must pay for these.

► *Restricted mobility* You may have to sell the house when you want to relocate.

► *More responsibility* You must handle all maintenance and repairs, which can add significantly to the cost of ownership.

buy a mobile home for as little as $20,000. Unlike most houses and condos, mobile homes do not increase in value over time.

Renting a house is often the most expensive rental alternative. By renting a house, you are paying for the benefits of privacy and space without the responsibilities of ownership. A rented home generally has fewer limitations on what you can do than an apartment. You may be able to have outdoor parties, keep pets, or grow a garden. The downside to renting a house could be the expectation that you will tend the yard and do normal maintenance. Heat or electricity is usually more expensive for a house than for an apartment.

Choosing the best type of property to rent depends on your values and financial situation. Probably the greatest advantage to renting is the ability it gives you to move easily if you find you don't like where you are living.

CheckPoint

What kind of apartment appeals to you? Describe it in as much detail as you can. What does this description tell you about your personal tastes?

Shared Housing Costs

One way to minimize the high cost of housing is to share the cost with a friend. Living with someone, however, is far different from going to a movie together. To live together successfully, you and your friend should plan together and agree on rules of conduct to minimize conflict.

Agree on Rules of Behavior

You may like your friend's music, but not at 2 A.M. Discuss your living habits—what each of you likes to do at home and how these behaviors affect the other person. Be ready to compromise. Common house rules address neatness, house guests, quiet time, personal space, pets, and the use of TV, stereo, and phone.

Divide Responsibilities

Shared living requires shared responsibilities. What you do—or don't do—affects your roommate, too. Common responsibilities are cooking, dishwashing, cleaning, grocery shopping, paying expenses (rent, utilities, phone, groceries), and choosing and paying for apartment furnishings and decorations

A grocery fund can be convenient as long as you can agree on the kinds of food to buy and rules about sharing food with guests. You could agree to contribute $30 each to the fund each week and keep this

COMMUNICATE

Assume that you are a junior in college. You have been living in a college dorm for three years. For your senior year, you would like to rent an apartment, but to afford it, you need a roommate. Write an advertisement for a roommate to post on the dorm bulletin board. Briefly describe what you are looking for in a roommate. Also, say a little about yourself. Write the ad in a way that might encourage someone to share an apartment with you.

INTERNET ACTIVITY

You and a friend are thinking about renting an apartment. Search the Internet for tips on roommate etiquette. Share some of the tips in e-mail exchanges with your friend. Also describe your living habits. Include your good and bad habits and anything else you do that might bother others. Agree on three "house rules" that would help you live together. E-mail your rules to your teacher.

money in a specified location. Then, when one of you goes grocery shopping, you can use that money.

Make a Written Agreement

Even though you like and trust your friend, some agreements need to be in writing to protect both of you, particularly agreements involving money. It's best to keep your paychecks and budgets separate. Pool money only for expenses that must be shared, such as rent and utilities. The rules you make together for pooled funds should be in writing.

When you rent an apartment with someone, you are both legally and equally responsible for meeting the lease terms. The **lease** is a legal contract you sign that gives you the right to live in the apartment for a specific period of time as long as you pay the rent and follow the contract rules. If one of you moves out early or refuses to pay part of the rent, the other is legally bound to pay the rent for the rest of the lease.

To avoid financial problems, decide together how to part ways when the time comes. Put the agreement in writing, and sign it.

CheckPoint

Why is it important to discuss house rules with a prospective roommate before living together? Why is it important to put some agreements in writing?

TRY THESE

1. What are some advantages to living in a college dormitory?

2. What choices do you have in types of apartments?

3. Why might someone rent a furnished apartment?

4. What issues should you discuss with a prospective roommate to minimize possible conflict?

5. What is a lease?

6. What kinds of agreements with a roommate should you put in writing?

THINK CRITICALLY

7. **CONSUMER ACTION** Raul started his first full-time job and wants to live independently as soon as he can. What housing options should he consider? What choices would help him reach his goal shortly?

8. You are considering two apartments. One in a new high-rise building has one large room and a small kitchen and bath. The other is in an older home. It has three large rooms and a kitchen and bath. It is also a little closer to your job. The rent is the same. Which apartment would you choose? Why?

9. **COMMUNICATE** Assume that you just graduated from high school and took a job. You want to continue living at home, but your parents require you to contribute to the household. Write a contract including tasks you are willing to do and your financial contribution. E-mail it to your teacher.

DECISION MAKING PROJECT

SPECIFY   **SEARCH**   **SIFT**   **SELECT**   **STUDY**

SPECIFY Your monthly housing budget is $700. Brainstorm a list of housing options available in your area. Brainstorm a list of household chores. Finally, brainstorm a list of household rules you might make. You don't have to decide right now.

© Getty Images/PhotoDisc

13.2 How to Rent an Apartment

How to Find and Evaluate Apartments

Start your search by making a list of all the things you want in an apartment. Consider such things as location, convenience, space, facilities, and appearance. After you complete the list, prioritize it with the things you want most at the top and the least at the bottom.

Budget Trade-Offs

Before you start looking at apartments, narrow your search by determining the price range you can afford. Your rent should be no more than one-third of your monthly take-home pay. With this figure in mind as your upper limit, you can start making trade-offs.

Look at your prioritized list. The more of these items you get in an apartment, the higher the rent is likely to be. You should start by making judgments as to which items you are willing to pay for and which you will give up in order to get the rent down to your price range.

CONSUMER ACTION

Vanessa is ready to select her first apartment. She knows what features she wants her apartment to have. As she drives around town, stopping at apartment complexes that seem to have it all, she discovers that she can't afford to rent them. What can she do to find apartments in her price range? How can she decide which is right for her?

In general, the rent of an apartment depends on these factors.

▶ **Convenience** An apartment close to shops, jobs, schools, and public transportation or to areas such as a beach will cost more than the same apartment farther from these things.

▶ **Neighborhood** Some neighborhoods are safer and better maintained than others. Also, every neighborhood offers different amenities, such as parks. Apartments in more desirable neighborhoods are more expensive.

▶ **Environment** Rents usually reflect pleasures such as privacy, a nice view, and quiet surroundings.

▶ **Size and Condition** The larger and better maintained the apartment, the higher the rent.

▶ **Facilities** The more facilities—such as laundry equipment, cable hookups, furniture, and a pool—the higher the price.

▶ **Pets** Many apartments do not allow pets, but those that do often charge extra for the privilege.

To reduce your rent, decide where you want to make trade-offs among these factors.

Where to Find Leads

The vast array of apartments can make your search seem overwhelming. So, where do you start?

Family and Friends You may know people who have lived in apartments and can describe their experiences with particular buildings. You can ask them questions to determine whether a certain apartment might work for you.

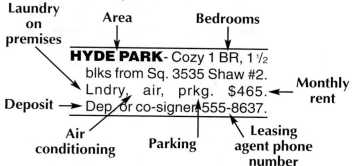

Sample Apartment Ad

Laundry on premises · Area · Bedrooms · Deposit · Air conditioning · Parking · Leasing agent phone number · Monthly rent

HYDE PARK - Cozy 1 BR, 1 ½ blks from Sq. 3535 Shaw #2. Lndry, air, prkg. $465. Dep or co-signer 555-8637.

Newspaper Ads Almost every local newspaper carries ads for apartments in its real estate or classified section. The ads describe the basic features and prices, so you can easily narrow the list to just those in your price range and with more of the features at the top of your priority list.

Since newspapers charge by the line for ads, the ads often contain abbreviations to keep them short.

Internet Apartment ads abound on the Internet. Most search engines, such as Yahoo! and Excite, have real estate or classified channels. Click on one and follow the links to apartments in the locations you are considering. Also look for listings on the web sites of local newspapers or real estate agencies.

Real Estate Agencies These agencies list apartments as well as houses. Visit or contact an agency to view the listings. Agencies can be very helpful if you are moving to an unfamiliar location.

Apartment Managers Apartment buildings often have managers who live there. These managers are responsible for showing apartments to potential renters and for solving maintenance and other problems. If you have targeted particular apartment buildings, you can call or visit the manager to find whether any apartments are available there. If you know the name of the apartments, you can get the manager's phone number from the Yellow Pages.

How to Evaluate an Apartment

After you have narrowed your list of apartment choices to just a few, it's time to tour them. Call the apartment manager and make an appointment to look at the apartment. Whenever possible, tour the actual apartment that is available, not a model or one like it. If the current renter, or **tenant**, has not moved out yet, ask the manager to set a time with the tenant when you can enter the apartment.

Go to the apartment prepared with a written list of questions to ask the manager. These are some typical questions.

1. What is the monthly rent?

2. Does the rent include heat, electricity, gas, and water?

3. How long is the term of the lease?

4. At the end of the lease, must I sign a new lease, or can I rent month-to-month?

5. What facilities do you provide? Laundry? Cable? Parking?

6. What rules or restrictions do you have?

7. Can I have pets? If so, is there an extra charge?

8. What type of security do you provide?

Prepare an evaluation checklist to take with you on every apartment tour. A typical checklist is shown on the next page. The purpose of a checklist is to make sure you inspect all the important features of every apartment you visit.

© Getty Images/PhotoDisc

Walk through every room. Take notes on your checklist. Include positive as well as negative impressions. Later, after you have seen all the apartments, you can easily compare notes.

If you are still interested in the apartment, come back later, without the manager, and talk to some current tenants who live near the available apartment. Ask these people about the building. Talking to your potential neighbors also gives you a chance to meet them and determine whether you would like living near them.

CheckPoint

What would be your top three requirements for an apartment? What are three features that you would like to have but would be willing to give up to reduce the rent?

Apartment Evaluation Checklist

Outside the Building and Grounds
- ☐ Does the neighborhood appear safe and well maintained?
- ☐ Did you see shopping and public transportation close by?
- ☐ Does the neighborhood offer a park or other facilities important to you?
- ☐ Are the apartment grounds well lit and well maintained?
- ☐ Is sufficient parking provided for residents and guests?

Inside the Apartment
- ☐ Does the apartment's entry door have a strong lock that works?
- ☐ Is the layout of rooms convenient and appealing?
- ☐ Are all rooms clean and well painted?
- ☐ Are the floors and carpeting clean and in good condition?
- ☐ Does the apartment have at least one working smoke detector?
- ☐ Could you hear noise from adjoining apartments?
- ☐ Do the windows open and close easily?
- ☐ Do all lights work?
- ☐ Do the heat and air conditioning work and can you control the temperature?
- ☐ Does the shower have good water pressure?
- ☐ Does the toilet flush?
- ☐ Is the bedroom large enough to fit the furniture you want?
- ☐ Is there a cable hookup, and is it in a convenient location?
- ☐ If the apartment is furnished, does it contain the basic pieces you need and are they in good condition?
- ☐ Do the refrigerator and stove work and are they clean?
- ☐ Does the kitchen have a microwave, dishwasher, or other useful appliances?
- ☐ Is the kitchen counter space sufficient for easy food preparation?

Common Areas Inside the Building
- ☐ Are the building's hallways clean and free of trash?
- ☐ If laundry facilities are available, do the machines work and is the room clean?
- ☐ If the complex offers other facilities, such as a pool or workout room, are the facilities clean and the equipment in good working order?
- ☐ Is there a working security system besides a lock?

The Lease and Moving In

You have selected your apartment. What do you do next?

Lease Terms: Rights and Responsibilities

The lease details your rights and responsibilities as a tenant and those of your **landlord,** the owner. Always read a lease carefully before signing. If you see a clause you don't like, ask if it can be changed. Get any changes in writing, signed by the apartment manager or landlord.

Lease Terms These are the kinds of terms that would be in your lease.

▶ Length of time the lease runs.

▶ Rent amount and due date.

▶ Amount of your **security deposit,** or money landlord holds to cover any damages to rental property.

▶ Who is responsible for paying utilities such as heat.

▶ Rights to use the facilities.

▶ Restrictions, such as whether or not you can have pets.

▶ Rules of conduct, such as rules concerning parties or loud music.

▶ Landlord's responsibility to make repairs.

▶ Conditions under which the landlord can enter your apartment. Must permission be asked before entering, except in an emergency?

▶ Notice you are required to give before moving out.

Condition Report You are responsible for keeping the apart-

© Getty Images/PhotoDisc

ment in good condition. If you damage the apartment, the landlord has the right to keep your security deposit. If you don't, you have the right to get it back.

To make sure you get your security deposit back, walk through the apartment with the landlord and make a list of any existing damage before you move in. Then both you and the landlord should sign the list as your agreement on the condition of the apartment when you moved in. Keep the original and give a photocopy to the landlord.

IN CLASS ACTIVITY

Make a list of the features you would like to have in your first apartment. Then look in the classified section of your local newspaper for apartment ads. Are there apartments available with the features you want? How would you decide which apartments you would look at from the ads?

Moving Expenses

How are you going to get your things to your new place? If you have the money, you can hire a moving company. Ask friends and family about companies they have used. Check out moving companies with the Better Business Bureau. Get bids from several reputable companies, and take the best deal.

A less expensive option is to rent or borrow a truck and move yourself. You might have some friends help you. Several weeks ahead, reserve the truck and your friends' time for your move date. If possible, avoid holidays. Rental trucks can be hard to get on holidays, especially Memorial Day and Labor Day when many college students are moving from or to school.

Packing There are many different ways to pack. Here are some useful guidelines.

▶ You can save money with a moving company if you pack the boxes yourself.

▶ You can often get empty boxes free from stores.

© Getty Images/PhotoDisc

▶ Start packing early.

▶ Packing to move is a good opportunity to get rid of all those old clothes and items you don't use anymore. If you don't need it, don't move it.

▶ Pack similar items together and label them. For example, you might pack all kitchen utensils together in several boxes and write "kitchen" on the boxes. Then when the boxes arrive at their destination, you will know what is in them and where to put them.

▶ Put items you will need immediately together in one box. You might include toilet paper, toothbrush and toothpaste, and a set of

---

■ PRIMARY SOURCES

Americans who migrated to the West in the mid-1800s often found their new houses very different from the ones they had left behind. In order to have shelter in a hurry, many settlers dug holes in the sides of hills or made "bricks" out of sod. Read the following description from a young woman who went west with her family. Discuss these and other challenges this family had. Do you worry about these things? Explain why or why not.

"Father made a dugout and covered it with willows and grass, and when it rained, the water came through the roof and ran in the door. After the storms, we carried the water out with buckets, then waded around in the mud until it dried up. Then to keep us all nerved up, sometimes the. . .snakes would get in the roof and now and then one would lose (its) hold and fall down on the bed, then off onto the floor."

sheets and towels. You may be too tired to unpack right away.

▶ Wrap breakable items in newspaper, tissue, or bubble wrap.

▶ Make sure to check the weight of boxes as you pack. Don't fill them beyond what you can pick up if you are moving yourself.

Mail A day or two before you move to your new apartment, you need to make a few arrangements. Go to the post office and fill out a change-of-address card so that your mail will find you. Usually the post office will forward mail sent to your old address for 30 to 60 days. You can also get a packet of cards from the post office to notify others of your new address, such as your

employer, your creditors, your doctor, and your insurance company.

Utilities You also need to have your utilities turned on. Call the gas and electric, phone, and water companies to set up your accounts. Some may charge an installation fee or a security deposit.

CheckPoint

Why should you read the lease carefully before signing? What things do you need to do to plan your move?

TRY THESE

1. What factors affect the price of an apartment?

2. How can you find out what apartments are available in an area?

3. How can a checklist help you evaluate apartments?

4. What are your rights and responsibilities regarding a security deposit?

5. What should you have the right to expect from your landlord?

6. How would you pack for your move?

THINK CRITICALLY

7. **CONSUMER ACTION** Vanessa knows what she wants in an apartment but can't find any in her price range. How can she identify available apartments without driving all over town? What advice would you give her for narrowing her choices to apartments she would like in her price range?

8. What would you look for in a prospective apartment to determine if you would feel safe living there?

9. Suppose that your elderly grandparents sold their home because it was too much work. They plan to move into an apartment. List what you think they would want their apartment to be like. Where would it be located? How would it be different from one that you would choose for yourself?

10. What expenses should you include in your budget for your first month in your new apartment?

© Getty Images/PhotoDisc

13.3 How to Buy a Home

How to Pay for a Home

An average house in the United States costs more than $150,000, which does not include other costs that come with home ownership. You will probably have to take out a loan to buy a home.

Costs of Home Ownership

A loan to buy real estate, such as land or a house, is called a **mortgage**. The property serves as collateral for the loan. If you don't repay your loan according to the terms of the mortgage, your property becomes the property of the lender.

Your mortgage payment is just one of the costs of home ownership. You will have to pay points and closing costs when you buy a home. You also will have to pay other costs, such as property taxes and insurance. Your income must be sufficient to cover all of these normal expenses.

Mortgage Payment A mortgage has two parts: principal and interest. The **principal** is the amount you borrow. To get a mortgage, you will have to pay a specified percentage of the purchase price up front as the **down payment**. Usually the

---

CONSUMER ACTION

Anna and Pedro think they are ready to buy their first home. They have saved enough for a down payment, but what other expenses should they expect? How much can they afford to pay? How should they go about locating a house they want to buy?

amount is around 20 percent. So, if you buy a $100,000 house, you would need $20,000 for the down payment.

$$\$100{,}000 \times 0.20 = \$20{,}000$$

The mortgage principal, then, would be $80,000.

$$\$100{,}000 - \$20{,}000 = \$80{,}000$$

The interest on the mortgage is a percentage of the principal remaining after each payment. Since you may be paying your mortgage over 20 or 30 years, the interest adds up to an impressive sum. For example, if your interest is 9 percent on a $100,000 loan for 30 years, you will pay a total of $189,663 in interest!

Points Most mortgage lenders charge a service fee in the form of **points**. Each point equals 1 percent of the principal. Points are a cost of obtaining a mortgage.

Closing Costs When you sign the final paperwork for the loan, you will be required to pay closing costs. **Closing costs** are a collection of fees to cover tasks the lender must do related to your loan. For example, the lender hires specialists to estimate the property's value.

© Getty Images/PhotoDisc

Consumer ALERT

Use of lead-based paint is now illegal, but it still exists in some older homes. Lead can cause nerve and brain damage in children who chew on the painted woodwork. Landlords and home sellers are required by law to inform you if the home you want to rent or buy has lead-based paint. However, they don't always do it. If lead-based paint is found in your home, no matter whether you are buying or renting, you should take responsibility to see that it is removed.

For more information, you can call the National Lead Information Center at (800) 424-LEAD.

Homeowner's Insurance

Lenders require you to carry homeowner's insurance, which helps protect you (and them) against loss from fire, theft, or other hazards.

Property Taxes Your local government charges property taxes based on the value of your property. The lender may require you to pay your taxes and homeowner's insurance proportionally each month with the mortgage payment. These amounts are held in an **escrow account** until the insurance and tax payments are due. Then the lender makes these payments for you out of the escrow account. Consider how this service is in the best interest of the lender.

Mortgage Insurance If you have a government-insured loan, your mortgage payment will also include a percent or two to pay for the required **mortgage insurance.** In exchange for this cost, you get a loan with a smaller down payment.

Types of Mortgages

There are several types of mortgages. Each has advantages and disadvantages.

Fixed-Rate Mortgages Some mortgages charge the same interest rate for the entire term of the loan. These are called **fixed-rate mortgages.** They usually last from 15 to 30 years.

The greatest advantage of a fixed-rate mortgage is that your payment does not change. If your first mortgage payment today is $536 a month, your last one 30 years from now will be $536. Knowing what your payment will be can help you plan your long-term budget.

Adjustable-Rate Mortgages Interest rates on some loans go up or down as rates in the economy rise or fall. These loans are called **adjustable-rate mortgages (ARMs).** The ARM contract specifies how often and by how much the rates can be adjusted.

In exchange for accepting the uncertainty of a changeable rate, you will get a lower beginning rate on an ARM than on a fixed-rate mortgage. The disadvantage is that these rates, and thus payments, can increase.

Adjustable-rate mortgages can make borrowing less expensive but not always. By taking out an ARM, you are predicting that rates will not increase too much. Since you never know what you will be paying next year, an ARM can make budgeting difficult.

VOTE Your Wallet

When you think of New York City, you probably visualize tall buildings and paved streets. Not all parts of New York City are like that. Staten Island is more like a rural community. It has only 43,000 homes, and parts of it are undeveloped. Many people want to keep it this way. Others would like to see new houses built.

Government leaders imposed a temporary building freeze on parts of Staten Island while they tried to decide what to do. One problem was the shortage of school space for additional children. More houses would mean more children. The schools were already full, so new housing would require taxpayers to pay for new schools.

If you could vote on this issue, would you support leaving Staten Island the way it is, or would you vote to allow additional houses to be built? Explain your decision.

Insured Mortgages If you are a first-time home buyer, you may qualify for an **FHA mortgage.** An FHA mortgage is a loan insured by the Federal Housing Administration, designed to reduce the down payment. You can get an FHA loan through a bank, savings and loan, or other financial institution. The insurance protects the lender, not you.

CYBER CONSUMER

Want to know how much a home loan costs? Search the Internet using the keywords *mortgage calculator*, or go to a realtor's site and follow the links to a mortgage calculator. Try different scenarios. Plug in different interest rates and down payments to see how they affect your monthly payments.

bank. Also, a builder may arrange a mortgage for a new home. Consider creative types of mortgages, but check them out carefully.

CheckPoint

What are some costs you should expect to pay as part of buying a home? What is the difference between a fixed-rate mortgage and an ARM?

However, because of this protection, the lender offers the loan for a 3 to 10 percent down payment instead of the more common 20 percent.

Other Mortgages If you are a military veteran, you may qualify for a **VA mortgage.** This loan is insured by the Veteran's Administration to help past and present military people buy a home. There are many other government-sponsored programs. Ask your lender if you qualify for one.

A **graduated-payment mortgage** allows you to make small payments for a few years and much larger ones later. This type of mortgage might be a good choice if you expect your income to increase significantly in the future.

Another type of mortgage would require you to renegotiate the loan every five years. In some cases, the property seller may provide a mortgage. Payments are made to the seller rather than to a

The Home-Buying Process

Buying a home is likely to be the biggest financial commitment you make in your life. Unlike most purchases, a home can also be a good investment. A house often **appreciates**—increases in value over time. When you sell your house, you may make a profit.

The loan interest and property taxes you pay are tax deductible. You are allowed to subtract these from your taxable income, which reduces your income taxes.

Equity is the difference between what a home is worth and what the buyer still owes on the mortgage. You can use the equity in your home as collateral to borrow money for other purposes. This

© Getty Images/PhotoDisc

is called a **home equity loan**. Interest on this loan is also tax deductible.

Homeownership involves a number of nonfinancial responsibilities as well. For example, you will have to cut the grass, rake leaves, shovel snow, clean gutters, paint, and fix whatever breaks.

Know What You Can Afford
A rule of thumb says you can afford a house that costs up to 2.5 times your annual gross income. Large debts reduce this amount. If your annual gross income is $50,000 and you have little current debt, you should be able to afford a $125,000 home ($50,000 × 2.5 = $125,000). This is a way to limit your search to affordable houses.

Know What You Want
As you do when apartment hunting, list the features you want in a house. Prioritize the list to narrow your choices to houses that meet your most important criteria.

Since you could live in your house for many years, buy in a neighborhood that offers the services and environment you will want during your life cycle. If you plan to have children, consider the quality of neighborhood schools. Being located near an expressway entrance can be important if you expect to drive to work daily.

Work with a Real Estate Agent
Real estate agents are experts at getting home buyers and sellers together. They know the features of houses on the market and can locate ones that best match your criteria and budget.

GUESS WHAT

There are more than 1,400,000 real estate agents in the United States.

$MATH OF MONEY

Shawn and Carol have found a house they want to buy. It costs $135,000. Together, their annual gross income is $55,000, and they have no debt. After the down payment and all closing costs, they will have the following ongoing expenses. Can they afford this house? What will their total monthly payment be?

▶ **$790 monthly principal and interest**

▶ **$210 homeowner's insurance due every 6 months**

▶ **$3,000 property taxes due every year**

SOLUTION

With Shawn and Carol's income, they can afford a house that costs $137,500.

$55,000 × 2.5 = $137,500

Their monthly payments will total $1,075.

$210 ÷ 6 months = $35 per month for homeowner's insurance

$3,000 ÷ 12 months = $250 per month for property taxes

$790 + $35 + $250 = $1,075 total monthly payment

Home sellers usually *list* their property with a real estate agent. Listed homes appear in a computerized database of homes for sale called a *multiple listing.* The database describes the prices and major features of each house, often with photos. Through your agent, you will have

access to the multiple listings of all agents in the area. The houses are grouped by location and price to focus your search.

After you have narrowed your choices to a few favorites, your agent will take you on a tour of them. When you make your selection, the agent will take care of all details for closing the deal. In exchange for these services, the seller pays the agent a percentage of the purchase price, usually around 6 percent.

© Getty Images/PhotoDisc

Tips for Evaluating Houses

Before you tour a home with your agent, list your most important features. Walk through all rooms, and note what you like and dislike about each house and each neighborhood. Be sure everything mechanical works. Look for signs of problems, such as water marks on the ceilings or musty odors.

When you find the house you want, hire a professional building inspector (see the Yellow Pages). The inspector will check parts of the house you may not be able to evaluate yourself, such as the furnace, electrical system, and roof.

How to Make an Offer

When you have chosen a house you want to buy, you make an offer for it. An **offer** is a proposal to buy the

house for a stated price. Generally, the price listed for a house is more than the seller expects to get for it. You should first offer several thousand dollars below the list price.

Your agent will present your offer to the seller in a formal document. If the seller accepts your price, you have a deal. But the seller may make a counteroffer of another price that is higher than your offer but lower than the original listed price. You continue to negotiate this way until you reach an agreement or decide not to buy the house.

How to Complete the Deal

After you and the seller agree on the purchase price, you will be expected to pay a deposit of $1,000 to $5,000. This deposit, or **earnest money**, is proof of your intention to buy at the agreed-upon price. If you change

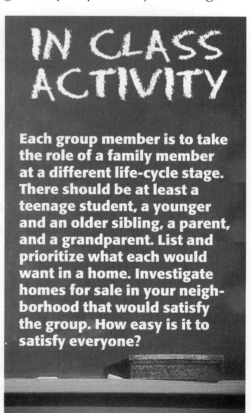

IN CLASS ACTIVITY

Each group member is to take the role of a family member at a different life-cycle stage. There should be at least a teenage student, a younger and an older sibling, a parent, and a grandparent. List and prioritize what each would want in a home. Investigate homes for sale in your neighborhood that would satisfy the group. How easy is it to satisfy everyone?

your mind, you forfeit this money to the seller. Otherwise, this amount becomes part of your down payment.

To complete the deal, you must locate financing. Mortgage rates are published regularly in the real estate section of local newspapers as well as on the Internet. Your real estate agent knows the current rates in the area and can guide you to the best deals.

When you find the mortgage you want, you fill out a loan application and wait for approval. Once your loan is approved, your agent sets a closing date. On this date, you, the seller, lender, agent, and perhaps the lender's lawyer meet to sign the final papers. You may want your lawyer there to review the contract. At the closing, you pay your down payment and all points and closing costs.

After all papers are signed and checks exchanged, you will receive the keys and title to your new property.

CheckPoint

How can a real estate agent help you buy a home? What should you do to prepare before you contact an agent?

TRY THESE

1. What is a mortgage, and what is included in it?

2. What costs, besides the mortgage, should you be ready to pay?

3. Why might you choose a fixed-rate mortgage, even if an ARM has a lower interest rate?

4. Explain why a home is an investment.

5. In general, how much can a buyer afford to pay for a house?

6. Why should you have an expert inspect the house before you agree to buy it?

THINK CRITICALLY

7. **CONSUMER ACTION** How can Anna and Pedro determine how much they can afford to pay for a house? What other expenses should they include in their budget? Write the steps they should take to locate, evaluate, and finally buy the home they want.

8. **MATH OF MONEY** Assume your gross income is $60,000 a year. How much can you afford to pay for a house?

9. **COMMUNICATE** Prepare a checklist to use when you tour a house you might buy in the next few years. Make additional lists suitable for people at different stages of the life cycle: one for a middle-aged couple with three children and another for a retired person who lives alone. How are these lists similar and different?

10. Suppose you rent an apartment for $500 a month. Your lease will run out in six months. You have found a house you want to buy. Your price offer was accepted, but the owner wants to close in one month. You want to close in six months to avoid paying both rent and mortgage payments. The owner says that it's now or never. What would you do? Explain.

Life-Span Plan

13.4 How to Furnish Your Home

Plan Your Place

It's easy to spend lots of money quickly when you are buying furnishings for your home. Furniture and appliances can be expensive.

Before you buy anything, make a plan. Write a list of everything you would like for your home, room by room. Think about things such as sheets and towels as well as furniture and appliances.

To help you think of everything, walk through your parents' home or the home of a friend, and notice the furnishings they have. It's easy to forget important items such as a vacuum cleaner or curtains.

Also consider what will realistically fit your space. Measure the rooms in your new home. Then measure a bed, couch, chairs, and other furniture. Plan where you will place each piece in your rooms. You can use string to mark the dimensions of furniture, or you can draw a plan on paper. Make sure you don't buy something that won't fit.

CONSUMER ACTION

Keneesha just signed a lease to rent her first apartment. It is unfurnished, and right now she doesn't own a single plate, spoon, or towel. She has no furniture or appliances. A stove and a refrigerator come with the apartment. Keneesha must supply everything else. She has only $2,000 to spend. How can she decide what to buy? How can she afford everything she needs?

Some items you will need now. Others can wait. Prioritize your wish list into three categories.

1. Things you need immediately

2. Things you want soon

3. Things you would like to have eventually

Next, determine how much you can spend now. Then plan your saving so that you can buy other furnishings on your list later.

What Can You Borrow?

Most households have boxes or closets full of old linens, dishes, and utensils. Often people's basements or attics contain tables and chairs they don't use anymore. Many times, the owners would be glad to get rid of these things. Even if you must return borrowed household goods, borrowing can help you furnish your new home with useful items before you can afford to buy them.

What Can You Buy Used?

You don't have to buy everything new. For a fraction of the cost, you can buy used furniture, dishes, and

appliances that are almost as good as new. Most communities have thrift stores that sell used household goods. Goodwill and the Salvation Army also sell inexpensive used goods. Garage sales sometimes offer the best bargains of all. Be practical.

How Can You Buy New Affordably?

After you have borrowed or bought all the used furnishings you can, other items on your wish list will have to be purchased new. Buying new always involves a trade-off between price and quality. In general, the higher the quality, the higher the price.

To make rational buying decisions, you need to determine how much quality is worth the price. Suppose one package of sheets is 250-count. Another is 180-count. With sheets, the higher the thread count, the softer the sheets. If you cannot tell the difference between thread counts, why pay for 250?

Don't forget about discount or outlet stores. You can save money by buying discontinued styles without giving up the benefits of a new product. Last year's curtain pattern will look just as good in your apartment as this year's and will cover your windows just as well.

CheckPoint

How can you plan your furnishings? What are some ways that you can reduce the cost of furnishing your home?

Furniture and Appliances

Shop for the quality that matches your purpose. Are you buying a couch to last for many years or to keep you off the floor until you can afford something better? If you want functional, don't pay for luxurious.

Materials

One of the major factors in the quality of furniture is the kind of wood used to make it. The highest quality is *hardwood,* such as maple and oak. *Softwood* comes from trees such as cedar and pine. Softwood furniture scratches more easily than hardwood but is less expensive, yet sturdy and attractive.

An economical choice is furniture made from *particleboard,* which is not solid wood. It is made of wood chips and shavings pressed together and bonded with an adhesive. The particleboard is then covered with a *veneer,* a thin layer of wood or other material that gives the piece a finished appearance. If you are looking for functional furniture that you plan to replace in a few years, particleboard can be a good choice.

Upholstered furniture is furniture with padding and a fabric covering. The padding can be foam rubber,

cotton filling, or metal springs. The best quality upholstery has heavy, durable fabrics and sturdy padding.

Construction

When you are shopping for furniture, look for sturdy construction. You can save money by choosing pieces made of less expensive materials, such as softwood or particleboard, but still be sure they are well constructed. Here is a checklist for judging quality construction.

▶ Does the furniture sit level on the floor without wobbling?

▶ Do the joints feel tight when you pull on them?

▶ Are major joints reinforced with blocks or braces glued or screwed into them?

▶ Do drawers and doors move easily and look even when closed?

▶ Does the fabric on upholstered furniture feel thick and strong?

© Getty Images/PhotoDisc

▶ Are wood surfaces finished smoothly without cracks or bubbles?

▶ Is the fabric treated to be stain resistant?

▶ Is the padding thick and evenly distributed?

▶ Do the springs feel firm without poking you?

One way to save money is to buy unfinished furniture and finish it yourself. Several mail-order businesses even offer furniture kits that you can assemble for yourself.

Appliances

An *appliance* is a device that is powered by electricity or gas and is designed to perform a specific function. Some appliances are labor-saving devices that are nice to have, such as a toaster or microwave. Others are necessities, such as a stove or refrigerator. Since appliances can be expensive, it is important to prioritize your appliance wish list to make sure you have enough money to buy the appliances you want most.

Consumer Reports The quality of appliances can be difficult to judge, since they are often complicated mechanical devices. One good way to find out about the strengths and weaknesses of different brands is to check the consumer publication *Consumer Reports*.

This magazine, available at most libraries and by subscription on the Internet, is a publication of the Consumers Union. This nonprofit organization tests products and publishes its results in its magazine. The reports evaluate different brands and provide extensive information about features and options.

Energy Labels The purchase price of major appliances, such as a furnace or water heater, is not their largest cost. A water heater can be purchased for $250 to $400. On average, a water heater lasts about

Buy the Numbers?

Suppose you want to buy new furniture for your home. If you saw this advertisement in your Sunday newspaper, would you investigate further? What additional information would you want? What potential problems do you see in accepting an offer like this?

15 years. Over that time, the energy to run it will cost between $700 and $1,000.

When you buy a major appliance, check the energy label, such as the one shown on this page. Energy labels predict the cost of running an appliance. By comparing labels, you can choose an appliance that is energy efficient, so it costs less to run.

For example, suppose you are shopping for a water heater. You find a model priced at $250. Its energy label predicts an annual energy cost of $75. A different model with better insulation is priced at $350. Its energy label predicts it will use $55 worth of energy per year. In this case, you would save by buying the more expensive model. Over its 15-year life, the $350 water heater would save more than the extra $100 you would spend to buy it.

Options A higher price does not necessarily mean a better-quality appliance. Two washing machines may be exactly the same except for their options. Some washing machines offer choices of water temperature, load size, and several fabric cycles. In general, the more options you get on an appliance, the higher the price. Don't pay for options you won't use.

Warranties As you learned in Chapter 3, a *warranty* is a guarantee that the product will fulfill the use for which it is intended. Appliances should come with written warranties. Compare warranties on different brands. Some cover the appliance for a longer period or cover more possible problems than others. Better warranties generally indicate better quality products. However, it is seldom necessary to pay extra for an extended warranty.

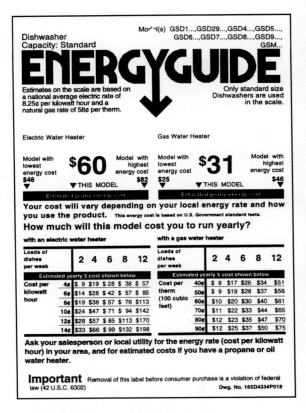

Bargains Look for appliance sales. Appliances commonly go on sale several times a year. Also consider buying floor models. These are new items that are reduced in price because they have been on display in the store. They may have surface flaws from customers inspecting them. Just make sure they still work properly and carry a full new product warranty.

CheckPoint

If you didn't have the money to buy both a dishwasher and a clothes washer, which would you choose? How would you select the brand to buy?

TRY THESE

1. How can you determine what furniture will fit in your new home?

2. How can you prioritize your wish list for furniture to make the best use of your funds?

3. What is the relationship between quality and price for new products?

4. How can you judge the quality of furniture construction?

5. How can you learn about the qualities of appliance brands?

6. Why is energy efficiency an important consideration in buying a major appliance?

THINK CRITICALLY

7. **CONSUMER ACTION** Write a plan for Keneesha. List what she needs to furnish her apartment. Recommend how she should spend her $2,000. Explain your recommendations.

8. Suppose that you have almost no money to spend on furniture right now. Think of some creative ways to make furniture that will serve the purpose until you have the money to buy real furniture. What materials could you use? Where could you get them? Describe your furniture.

9. Make a list of everything you would want to furnish a kitchen. Then prioritize the list into what you need now and what could wait until later. Explain how you set your priorities.

10. At a garage sale, you find a wood dining room table and four matching chairs. The owner is asking $250 for the set. How would you evaluate the quality of this furniture? How can you judge whether or not it is a good deal?

DECISION MAKING PROJECT

SPECIFY   SEARCH   SIFT   SIFT   SELECT

SEARCH Assign each group member to find out the following information for his or her own one-bedroom apartment.

1. What are the prices of available one-bedroom apartments? What are the features and benefits of each apartment?

2. What are some extra costs you will have to pay if you rent?

3. How much does it cost to move? Look into movers and rental trucks.

All group members should list furniture that they will borrow and that they will buy for their apartments. Include cost estimates.

SIFT Have each group member present his or her housing information. Put your options on a comparative chart. Make sure to include cost estimates. Remember that you have only $700 to spend each month.

KEY IDEAS

Your Housing Options

1. After you finish school, you might live with your parents or rent an apartment. You have many choices in apartments, such as in a single building or a complex.
2. Home ownership, mobile homes, and condominiums are other, more expensive, housing options.
3. Renting is less expensive and provides more mobility and freedom from responsibility. Buying gives you more freedom to do what you want in your living space but carries more responsibility and cost.
4. To avoid conflict with a roommate, you should agree upon rules of behavior and how to divide up responsibilities before moving in.
5. The lease legally binds you and your roommate, so you need to agree on how to fulfill the lease.

How to Rent an Apartment

6. Make a list of what you want in an apartment and prioritize it. Then make trade-offs to narrow your choices to apartments that cost no more than one-third of your take-home pay.
7. You can find out about apartments from friends and family, local newspapers, real estate agencies, or on the Internet.
8. Make an apartment evaluation checklist and use it to take notes when you tour apartments.
9. The lease document spells out your rights and responsibilities as a tenant and those of your landlord.
10. You can hire a moving company or rent or borrow a truck and move yourself.
11. Fill out change-of-address forms at the post office, and call utility companies to have utilities turned on.

How to Buy a Home

12. A mortgage is a loan to buy real estate. It consists of the principal, or amount borrowed, and interest.
13. You should expect to pay a percentage of the purchase price up front as a down payment. You will probably also have to pay points and closing costs when you sign the final purchase papers.
14. The most common types of mortgages are fixed-rate and adjustable-rate (ARMs).
15. A home is an investment that often appreciates or grows in value over time.
16. In general, you can afford a house that costs 2.5 times your annual gross income. A real estate agent can help you select a home.
17. Before you offer to buy a home, you should have an expert inspect it for you.

How to Furnish Your Home

18. Make a list of all the furnishings you want. Then prioritize it into what you need now, what you want soon, and what you want eventually.
19. To get more of your wish list now, borrow items from family and friends and buy some items used. When you buy new, you must make a trade-off between quality and price.
20. Test results published in *Consumer Reports* can help you compare appliance brands and features. By comparing energy labels, you can select major appliances that cost less to run.

TERMS REVIEW

Match each term on the left with its definition on the right.
Some terms may not be used.

a. adjustable-rate mortgage (ARM)

b. appreciate

c. closing costs

d. condominium

e. dormitories

f. down payment

g. duplex apartment

h. earnest money

i. efficiency apartment

j. escrow account

k. FHA mortgage

l. fixed-rate mortgage

m. graduated-payment mortgage

n. home equity loan

o. landlord

p. lease

q. mobile home

r. mortgage

s. mortgage insurance

t. offer

u. points

v. principal

w. security deposit

x. tenant

y. VA mortgage

1. apartment consisting of one room that serves as the living area, bedroom, and kitchen, plus a bathroom
2. collection of fees you must pay when you sign mortgage paperwork to cover tasks the lender must do related to your loan
3. home loan for which the interest rate remains the same throughout the term of the loan
4. legal contract that gives you the right to occupy property for a specified period of time, as long as you pay the rent and follow the rules specified in the contract
5. owner of rental property
6. loan to buy real estate, such as land or a home
7. grow in value over time
8. rooms that colleges rent to students at a reasonable price, usually in large complexes
9. amount borrowed
10. percentage of the purchase price that the borrower pays up front
11. apartment that a consumer owns rather than rents
12. someone who rents an apartment or other home
13. mortgage lender's service charge, each unit being equal to 1 percent of the principal
14. home loan for which the interest rate goes up or down as rates in the economy rise or fall
15. home loan insured by the Federal Housing Administration, designed to reduce the down payment
16. holding account used by a mortgage lender to accumulate the borrower's funds for taxes and insurance until these payments are due
17. deposit paid by a home buyer as proof of intention to buy at the price stated in the offer
18. money the landlord holds to cover any damages to rental property
19. an apartment with rooms on two floors of a building
20. allows you to make small payments for a few years and larger payments later

CONSUMER DECISIONS

21. You have found two apartments that you like. Apartment A costs $20 more per month, but is close to your job, would allow you to have a dog, and has a workout room. You have been meaning to start exercising, so this is your chance. Apartment B is five miles farther from your job but is on a bus line that stops near your office. It doesn't allow pets or have a workout room, but it does have laundry facilities, which Apartment A doesn't have. Which would you choose? Why?

22. You are reading the lease agreement on an apartment you want to rent. It says that pets are not allowed. You have a pet bird that you don't want to give up. It lives in a cage, so it wouldn't cause any damage to your apartment. You don't think the pet ban applies in your situation. What should you do?

23. You want to buy a house, so you contacted a real estate agent. The agent asked you what price range you want to consider. You make $38,000 a year. What should you tell your agent?

24. You are ready to buy a house and need a $75,000 loan. Your bank offers one at 7 percent fixed-rate interest or a $5\frac{1}{2}$ percent ARM. You can barely afford the 7 percent loan, but you expect your salary should increase yearly. Which mortgage would you choose? Why? If it is the ARM, how would an increase in interest rates to 9 percent affect you?

THINK CRITICALLY

25. Suppose you have found an apartment you want to rent. The owner will rent it unfurnished for $500 a month. She has also offered to furnish it if you will pay $625 a month. You have seen the furniture. It is old but usable. Which choice would you make? Explain your choice. If you paid for a furnished apartment, what would you still need to buy?

LOOK IT UP

26. Look through the real estate listings in your community's Sunday newspaper. Find an advertisement for an apartment you believe you might like to rent. Don't choose one that would cost more than you could reasonably pay. Write an explanation of why you chose this particular rental property.

27. Investigate types of home security systems. You can ask for

WHICH IS THE BEST DEAL?

Cynthia will graduate from high school in June. She plans to attend a local college in September. She would like to live on her own, but she doesn't make much money in her part-time job. Still, if she works more hours while she attends college, she could probably afford to rent an inexpensive place. Here are her options. Which would you choose? Why?

Option 1 Continue to live with her parents so she can save the money she earns and concentrate on her studies.

Option 2 Live in a college dormitory and work 10 hours a week in the dorm cafeteria to help pay for her dorm room.

Option 3 Rent an apartment off campus with a friend and work 20 hours a week at a local department store to pay the rent.

POINT YOUR BROWSER TO

www.ee4c.swlearning.com
Complete the activity for Chapter 13.

information at a local hardware store, call businesses listed in the Yellow Pages, or find companies on the Internet. Does a home security system seem worth the cost? Why or why not?

28. Find out what interest rates are being offered by local lenders for fixed-rate and adjustable-rate mortgages in your community. What other factors might you consider besides the interest rate in a mortgage?

29. Visit a local real estate office. Explain that you are completing a school assignment. Ask if you can look at the multiple listings. Write down the types of information you find there. How helpful would the multiple listings be if you were looking for a home to buy?

30. Examine appliance sales supplements to your Sunday newspaper. Evaluate the information they provide. Which ads impressed you? Why? Do any provide all the information you need to make a selection?

INSIDE THE NUMBERS

31. Sam found a small house he likes. The owner is willing to rent or sell it. The rent would be $650 a month. If Sam buys the property, he would have to make a $10,000 down payment, pay $900 in closing costs, and borrow

$50,000. His mortgage payment would be $525 each month, and he would have to pay $950 in property tax each year. What do you think Sam should do? Explain your recommendation.

CURRICULUM CONNECTION

32. **BUSINESS** Do you think you would like to be a landlord? If you owned an apartment building, you could probably rent the rooms for enough money to pay the mortgage on the building. What would your responsibilities be as a landlord? What kinds of problems would you have to handle? What risks are involved?

33. **HISTORY** Settlers in the American colonies used to join together to build homes or barns for each other. Some groups, such as the Amish, still follow this practice. Part of the reason is social. Read about people who followed this practice. Compare their way of life with the way your family lives.

JOURNAL RECAP

34. After reading this chapter, review answers you wrote to the questions in Journal Journey. Have your opinions changed?

DECISION MAKING PROJECT

SPECIFY   SEARCH   SIFT   **SELECT**   **STUDY**

SELECT Group members should decide on apartments, list their reasons, and draw floor plans with furniture. They should also make a list of the costs to move into and live in their apartments.

STUDY Present your group's housing options. Did other classmates consider options that your group didn't? What did you learn about renting in your area?

Chapter

14

AUTOMOBILE AND HOME INSURANCE
SHARING THE RISK

WHAT'S AHEAD

EXPLODING MYTHS

Fact or Myth?
What do you think is true?

1. Only wealthy people who own property they could lose need insurance.

2. Insurance on your home covers damage caused by any storm or natural disaster.

3. You can't do much to control the cost of the insurance you buy.

JOURNAL JOURNEY

WRITE IN YOUR JOURNAL ABOUT THE FOLLOWING.

INSURANCE   What is insurance? How does it work? How does it protect you?

AUTOMOBILE INSURANCE   Why do you need automobile insurance? Are some types more important than others?

HOME INSURANCE   What types of insurance should you buy for your home? If you rent rather than own your home, do you need insurance?

DECISION MAKING PROJECT

SPECIFY   **SEARCH**   **SIFT**   **SELECT**   **STUDY**

COVER YOUR WHEELS   Your group will investigate and choose an insurance company and policy for an automobile. Consider your state's laws and decide whether the state's minimums for insurance coverage are enough for you.

GOAL

To learn how to choose an auto insurance policy

PROJECT PROCESS

SPECIFY	Lesson 14.2
SEARCH	Lesson 14.3
SIFT	Lesson 14.4
SELECT	Chapter Assessment
STUDY	Chapter Assessment

14.1 Insurance Basics

How Insurance Works

Life is full of risks. In Chapter 9, you learned about one form of risk—the chance of losing money on an investment. Risk also means the chance of financial loss resulting from damage, illness, injury, or death.

Risk Management

You can't eliminate risk from your life, but you can manage it. *Risk management* means limiting possible financial losses to amounts you can handle. To manage your risk of financial loss from illness, injury, or damage, you can buy **insurance**. In exchange for this protection, you make a regular payment called a **premium** to the insurance company.

Shared Risk   You can manage investment risk by diversifying—spreading your funds over different investments. That way, investments that do well might balance your losses from those that don't. Managing risk of loss from illness, injury, or damage

CONSUMER ACTION

Lavonne recently moved into her first apartment. She spent almost every penny she had on furniture, dishes, linens, and a new television. Her parents gave her an old car that she uses to get to work. Lavonne knows it would take her years to replace these things if she lost them. What can she do to protect her property? What other risks should she consider in shopping for insurance?

works in a similar way. The difference is that the insurance company, not the consumer, does the diversifying.

When you buy insurance, you sign a legal contract called a **policy**. You then become the *policyholder*. Different policies protect you from different types of loss. The policy spells out the specific loss that it covers and the financial compensation the company will provide if you suffer that loss. If you do have a loss covered by the policy, you file a **claim**, a formal request for payment from the insurance company.

The insurance company diversifies the risk by selling policies to thousands of people. Each policyholder pays a premium that is small compared to the cost of the possible loss. For example, the premium to insure your home might be a few hundred dollars a year. But if your house burned down, the insurance company might pay $100,000 to rebuild or replace it.

Strictly speaking, insurance works by transferring funds from a large group to the relatively few who suffer losses. Insurance companies act as the intermediaries for transferring these funds. They collect premiums from all policyholders. Then they use these funds to pay policyholders who have losses. Through this method, all policyholders share the cost of losses. No single policyholder must bear the burden of a financially devastating loss. This is the concept of **shared risk**.

© Getty Images/PhotoDisc

Premiums and Statistics

Insurance companies use statistics from past events to predict how many losses are likely to occur within any large group of people. Statistics cannot predict whether a particular individual will break an arm. But statistics can show that, for instance, 100 out of every 100,000 people broke an arm in each of the

What In The World?

Palau is an island in the western Pacific Ocean, about 500 miles east of the Philippines. Palauan society is organized around extended families, or clans. Clan members support each other. Commercial insurance does not exist there. When one member of the clan suffers a loss, all other members are expected to help. If a house burns down, for example, the clan members gather to build another. Anyone who refuses to help becomes an outcast of the clan. How does this social system provide a form of insurance to its members? Does your family help out its members in a similar way?

last ten years. From these statistics, the company knows how many such losses to expect among its policyholders in the future.

Statistics can also help insurance companies estimate how much they will have to pay to reimburse particular types of losses. For example, suppose the average medical cost for treating a broken arm is $3,500. The company can estimate that it will have to pay out approximately $350,000 for every 100,000 policyholders per year to pay for broken arms.

Insurance companies have such statistics about all the types of losses they insure. They use this knowledge to set premiums. By charging a little more than the expected losses, insurance companies earn a profit.

© Getty Images/PhotoDisc

What Insurance Protects

The purpose of buying insurance is to protect against the loss of something of value. Insurance is designed to restore your financial position to where it was before the loss—not to allow you to profit from the loss.

To insure something, you must have an **insurable interest** in the item. That is, it must be something of value that, if lost, would cause you financial harm. So, for example, you can insure your own car but not your brother's. If your brother lost his car, you would not suffer financially.

Determining the Value of Insurable Interest Before you can insure your property, its value must be measured in financial terms.

Then, if you lose the insured item, the insurance company will compensate you based on its value.

When the value of property is not clear, you or the insurance company may have it appraised. An **appraisal** is an expert's determination of the value of a piece of property. For example, if you want to insure your diamond ring, you might have it appraised to make sure you buy enough insurance to cover its loss.

Home insurance does not automatically cover some particularly valuable items, such as a diamond ring. To insure it, you may have to purchase a rider for your policy. A **rider** is a special addition to an insurance policy that covers a specific type of loss.

Determining the Amount of Life and Health Insurance

Your life and health don't carry a price tag like property does. So life and health insurance is sold in different amounts. The greater the amount of coverage you choose, the higher the premiums.

Your life insurance premiums will also depend on your life expectancy. *Life expectancy* is an estimate of the average number of years remaining in people's lives based on their gender and current age and health.

For example, suppose you are an 18-year-old female, nonsmoker, in good health. From statistics, insurance companies know that people like you, on average, live to be 78.6 years old. At 18, then, your life expectancy is 60.6 more years.

The company uses this knowledge to calculate how much to charge you for each thousand dollars of life insurance you buy.

Your insurable interest in health insurance is your medical condition.

From statistics, insurance companies know how many people can be expected to need medical care in any year. They know how much each type of illness is likely to cost. Using this information, they determine your health insurance premiums.

The Insurance Trade-Off

Your goal in buying insurance should be to protect yourself from a loss that could put you in financial difficulty. It should not be to protect from *any* loss. The more insurance coverage you buy, the higher the premiums. At some point, the premiums themselves could put you in financial difficulty.

When you shop for insurance, decide how much of a loss you can reasonably cover yourself without too much financial hardship. Then buy just the amount of insurance needed to cover the losses you would have trouble paying for yourself. For example, if you agree to pay the first $1,000 of your medical

Using the Internet, research how your family should react to emergencies, such as a fire, sudden illness, or robbery, and create a plan. Exchange your plan with another student by e-mail. Evalute the plan you receive and e-mail your evaluation to the other student. Revise your plan and e-mail it to your teacher.

expenses each year, then your premiums will be lower than if you agree to pay just the first $100.

Role of Insurance in the Economy

Insurance provides security. It protects you from the risk of catastrophic loss. Insurance also benefits you indirectly. Many business activities wouldn't even be possible without insurance. A bank wouldn't lend you money to buy a home if you didn't insure the home. The transaction would be too risky for the bank. Your home is the collateral for the loan. If your home burned down, the bank could not recover the loaned funds.

Physicians usually don't practice without insurance to protect them from lawsuits. One lawsuit could ruin them financially. Businesses could not operate without insurance protecting their buildings and equipment and protecting them in case of injury to workers. Our economic system relies on sharing the risk through insurance.

© Getty Images/PhotoDisc

CheckPoint

How does insurance help you manage risk? How can you decide how much insurance to buy?

Types of Insurance

There are three basic types of insurance designed for consumers: property, liability, and personal.

Property Insurance

Insurance that protects you from financial loss when things you own are stolen, damaged, or destroyed is **property insurance**. Consumers typically buy property insurance for their homes, cars, and valuable possessions.

Property insurance is designed in two basic ways. It pays based on either the item's market value or its replacement value.

Market value is the amount an item is worth now. For example, a car that cost you $20,000 three years ago may be worth only $10,000 now. If someone stole the car, the insurance company would pay you its market value, $10,000. The company would not buy you a new car.

Replacement value is the cost of replacing the item, regardless of its market value at the time of the loss. For example, suppose you spent $600 for a couch five years ago. If you sold the couch today, you might get only $200 for it. That's its market value. But if your house burned down and you lost the couch, you would have to pay today's price, maybe $800, to buy a comparable new couch. If you insured the contents of your house for replacement value, then the insurance company would pay the replacement cost of $800.

Liability Insurance

Sometimes your actions cause losses to other people. For example, you may cause damage to someone else's car by bumping it in a parking lot.

Your actions may also injure someone else, requiring you to pay medical expenses. For example, suppose a delivery person tripped

PRIMARY SOURCES

One day in 1931, Paul Harrison opened up his dry cleaning shop and discovered something wrong. Read what happened. What would have been different in his life had he had insurance?

"Every garment that was ready for . . . delivery was gone. . . . The open window at the rear of the store told the grim story. I called the police department out but no trace of the burglars was ever found. The missing garments amounted to more than $1,000 and I didn't have a penny's worth of burglar insurance. I notified my customers. . . that I would reimburse them for all stolen articles. This must be done from my own funds but I couldn't do anything else."

over trash you left on your sidewalk and broke her leg. You would be responsible for her medical bills. Plus, she might sue you for her suffering.

Liability insurance protects you from losses that you cause others. Up to a stated maximum, it will pay the cost of damage, medical expenses, and legal fees if you are sued.

Personal Insurance

Insurance that protects you, your spouse, and your children against financial loss due to illness, disability, or death is *personal insurance*. Health and life insurance are two common examples of personal insurance. Often, employers pay part of the cost of health insurance for their employees.

Another form of loss is the loss of the income or services of someone who helps support the family. For example, suppose Brad and Susan are married. Brad works as a pharmacist, and Susan is a stay-at-home mom. If Brad died, the family would lose his income. If Susan died, Brad would have to hire someone to take care of the children and the house. In either case, life insurance could help the family financially survive the loss of a loved one.

CheckPoint

What are the three basic types of insurance? What does each one cover?

TRY THESE

1. What is the difference between eliminating risk and managing it?

2. What is the concept of shared risk?

3. How does an insurance company set premiums?

4. What is an insurable interest?

5. How does insurance help the economy operate?

6. What is the difference between market value and replacement value?

7. What does liability insurance cover?

THINK CRITICALLY

8. **CONSUMER ACTION** How can insurance help Lavonne? What other risks does she face besides loss of this property? What types of insurance should she consider buying?

9. **COMMUNICATE** Should you buy insurance to protect yourself from all losses? Write a few paragraphs explaining why or why not and e-mail to your teacher.

10. Your house is worth $90,000. Should you insure it for $120,000? Why or why not?

11. Suppose a hurricane destroyed most of the homes in a large part of your state. One local insurance company insured the majority of those homes. Explain, in terms of shared risk, how this kind of disaster might affect the insurance company.

GOALS

IDENTIFY
basic types of auto
insurance coverage

EXPLAIN
factors that contribute
to the cost of auto
insurance

14.2 Automobile Insurance

How to Choose Automobile Insurance

A car is a major investment. Not only is the purchase price high, but fixing damage to it is expensive. Plus, damage or injury caused by its use can result in medical expenses and lawsuits that could ruin you financially. Protect yourself and your investment by buying automobile insurance. In fact, state laws say you can't legally drive without it.

Types of Coverage

To protect you against financial loss, including the cost of your legal defense, when you are legally responsible for injuring other people in an automobile accident, you can buy **bodily injury liability coverage**. The amount of coverage is typically described by two numbers. They might be shown as $250,000/ $500,000, or without the last three

CONSUMER ACTION

Glenn has an older car that he bought for only $1,500. He could pay for a new car, but he worries what might happen to it. Glenn parks his car in a part of town where there is a lot of crime. Last week, Glenn received a $950 bill for his car insurance premium. He thinks it is higher than it should be. Glenn wonders whether he has the right amount and kinds of automobile insurance. What should Glenn do to evaluate his insurance coverage? How might he reduce his payments?

zeros, as 250/500. In both cases, the numbers mean:

1. Your policy will pay up to a maximum of $250,000 for injuries to any one person in a given accident. If one person has a $300,000 claim against you, your policy will pay only $250,000. You will be responsible for paying the remaining $50,000.

2. Your policy will pay up to a maximum of $500,000 total for all injuries to other people in a given accident. If three people are injured in the accident, and each has $200,000 in medical bills, the total is $600,000. Your policy will pay up to its per-accident limit of $500,000. You will be responsible for paying the remaining $100,000.

Property damage liability coverage pays for damage you caused to another person's property. It does not cover damages to your car.

You can buy this coverage in various amounts. The policy may state this number after the bodily injury numbers as, 250/500/50. The last number means that the company will pay up to $50,000 for damage to another person's property for any one accident.

Medical payments coverage pays medical and funeral expenses for you, your family members, and other passengers in your car because of injuries sustained in an accident—no matter who caused the accident.

Uninsured/underinsured motorist coverage pays medical and damage expenses for you and your passengers caused by a driver without insurance or with too little insurance to cover the loss. It does not cover the other driver.

Imagine yourself driving home from school in heavy traffic. Suddenly, a van traveling two cars in front of you slams on its brakes. The car you are following does the same. You are not able to stop and just bump this car. The van leaves the scene.

You exchange information with the driver of the other car and call the police. No one seems to be hurt. But later that day, the other driver goes to a clinic complaining of a sore neck. He threatens to sue for pain and suffering. Your insurance company is likely to settle to avoid the cost of going to court. Also, your insurance premiums will be increased.

You might think this was just an unfortunate accident. Maybe it was a scam called *swoop and squat*. In this scenario, the driver of the van and the car were working together to cause the accident. Insurance companies have found some individuals who have been accident "victims" as many as ten times in a single year.

© Getty Images/PhotoDisc

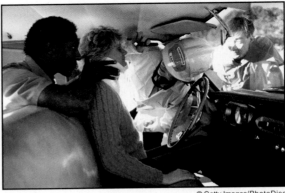

© Getty Images/PhotoDisc

Comprehensive coverage pays for damage to your car caused by something other than a collision. For example, it covers damage caused by earthquakes, fire, wind, hail, and floods. It also covers your losses if your car is vandalized or stolen.

This type of coverage may exclude some items in your car, especially something that is easy to steal, such as a car phone. Be sure you understand what your policy excludes. You may have to purchase a rider to cover these items.

Collision coverage pays for damage to your car caused by colliding with another car or object, such as a tree or fire hydrant. This coverage can be the most expensive portion of an automobile policy.

Comprehensive and collision coverage often carry a deductible. A **deductible** is the amount you pay before the insurance company pays anything. For example, suppose collision damage to your car costs $1,200 to fix. Your deductible is $500. You would have to pay the first $500, and the insurance company would pay the remaining $700.

Additional Coverage Options
Insurance companies offer several options in addition to standard coverage. You may wish to add provisions for a rental car while your car is being repaired and/or for towing services to a repair facility. If you install an expensive MP3 player, you may wish to add coverage for it.

Also, if you have a five-year car loan, you may owe more on the car than it is worth when it is destroyed in an accident. Because the insurance company will pay only the market value of the car, you may need additional insurance to cover the gap between what you owe and what the company will pay. Otherwise, you'll have to continue paying off the loan on a car you no longer have.

You can buy coverage for each of these situations. You must decide if protection from these types of losses is worth the additional premium.

How Much Insurance Should You Buy?

All states set a minimum amount of liability insurance that you must buy. For a few states, this amount is as low as 10/20/5. This is not enough protection even if it is legal. Today, many accidents result in costs that exceed hundreds of thousands of dollars. The least you should consider buying is 50/100/25.

Liability and Medical Paying for basic liability coverage is expensive. Increasing this to a larger amount does not cost much more. You should also purchase enough medical payments insurance to cover injuries that might result from an accident. With medical costs as high as they are today, $10,000 in medical payments coverage is not enough. You should consider $50,000 or more.

Collision and Comprehensive

The cost of collision and comprehensive insurance depends on the value of your car and the size of the deductible you choose. Insurance companies do not normally pay more than a car is worth. A five-year-old car that is worth $4,500 will not be insured for $10,000. The greater the market value of the car, the larger the premium will be.

If you have an old car, collision coverage may not even be worth buying. Ask the insurance company how much it would pay for the loss of your old car. If your car is worth only a thousand or two, you may pay more in premiums than you would ever get back from the insurance company. Just remember—if you choose not to carry collision coverage and you wreck your car, you will have to pay for the damage yourself or go without a car.

When you buy collision and comprehensive insurance for your car, you may choose the size of your deductible. The cost of coverage with a $250 deductible is more than the same policy with a $500 deductible. The reason is that the insurance company pays a smaller part of losses when there are larger deductibles.

CheckPoint

What are three types of injury coverage? What are three types of damage coverage? What should you consider in determining how much insurance to buy?

Cost of Automobile Insurance

Thirty years ago, a typical automobile insurance policy could be purchased for several hundred dollars a year. Prices of most products have risen over the years, but the cost of insuring a car has gone up faster than most other prices. There are several reasons for this trend.

Causes of Increasing Insurance Costs

One reason for the growing costs is that cars are more complicated today. New technology such as computer-controlled braking systems make cars better products, but it also makes them more expensive to repair.

Medical technology also adds to the cost of automobile insurance. New treatments save lives and improve quality of life, but medical equipment and drugs are expensive.

Many cars are more fuel efficient today. Much of this efficiency results from their reduced weight. Accidents involving lighter cars can result in more injury and damage than accidents involving heavier cars.

© Getty Images/PhotoDisc

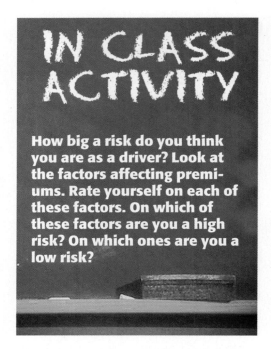

IN CLASS ACTIVITY

How big a risk do you think you are as a driver? Look at the factors affecting premiums. Rate yourself on each of these factors. On which of these factors are you a high risk? On which ones are you a low risk?

Today, Americans injured in automobile accidents are more likely to sue than in the past. And juries are awarding victims increasingly larger amounts. The number of personal injury lawsuits more than doubled between 1988 and 2000, even though the number of accidents increased by about only 15 percent. The average award for injuries suffered in an accident increased nearly 90 percent in the decade of the 1990s. By 2005, the average award for wrongful death in an automobile accident was over $1 million.

These awards may be fair and just. Their costs, however, are passed on to consumers in higher premiums. Insurance companies only transfer funds when they pay benefits. Policyholders bear the real cost of higher injury awards.

Factors Affecting Your Premium

From statistics, insurance companies know that certain characteristics make some policyholders bigger risks. From the insurance company's point of view, risk means the chance that the policyholder will have a loss that requires reimbursement. The company will charge higher premiums to risky policyholders.

Driver Classification Insurance companies classify policyholders by age, gender, and marital status. They charge different premiums using these classifications.

For example, from statistics, companies know that young males have more accidents than young females or older males. If you are a man under the age of 21, you will pay more for your insurance, even if you have a good driving record.

Married people average fewer accidents than single people. So single people pay more for insurance.

Rating Territory Statistics show that more claims come from some locations than others. Insurance companies divide states into rating territories, such as cities, parts of a city, or rural areas. If you live in a territory that generates more claims, then you will pay more for insurance.

For example, more accidents take place in urban than rural areas. Insurance companies take all location risk factors into account in determining your premium. A basic insurance policy in rural Nebraska can be purchased for less than $600 a year. The same policy in Boston, Washington, D.C., or Los Angeles costs more than $1,400.

Driving Record Your driving record is an official list of your accidents and traffic violations, and it has a lot to do with the cost of your premium. When a police officer gives you a ticket or you cause an accident, **points** may be added to your record with the state Bureau of Motor Vehicles.

When your insurance company reviews your policy for renewal, it will check your driving record. A point on your record can increase your premium about 10 percent. Two or three points can increase your premiums 25 to 100 percent.

CYBER CONSUMER

In a recent year, *PC Magazine* evaluated six popular web sites that offer financial services, including information about insurance policies. At that time, it rated *Quicken.com* as the best service. Check out the user-friendly Quicken web site. Also search the *PC Magazine* site to see if it has completed a new evaluation.

If you accumulate too many points, your insurance company will drop you, and you may have trouble finding another company willing to insure you. Because state laws require all drivers to carry auto insurance, your state will assign you to an insurance company if you cannot find one that will insure you. But as an **assigned risk**, you will have to pay very high premiums for coverage.

Type of Car Some cars are more expensive to repair or replace than others. Also, statistics show that thieves tend to steal popular cars more often than other types of cars. If you have one of these high-risk cars, your premiums will reflect this risk.

Claims History The more claims you make on your policy, the more you cost the company, so your premiums will be higher.

Reduce Your Premiums

You can reduce your premium costs by controlling some of the factors affecting your premiums. For

COMMUNICATE

Think about a car accident that you have been in or one that you observed. Write a description of what happened. Include as much detail as possible, including when and where it happened, what caused the problem, and who was at fault. Assume that you will give your description to the police officer who arrives at the accident scene.

Sample Auto Insurance Policy

Progressive Insurance Company
231 Main Street, Rivertown, MA 90000
1-800-555-1877

Declarations Page

Named Insured: Thomas Reid
Address: 510 Elm Street, Eastern City, TX 00000
Policy Number: 90076-5678
Effective Dates: January 1, 2005 to January 1, 2006

Description of Vehicle(s)

Year	Make	Model	Body Type	Vehicle Id Number	Annual Mileage
1993	Honda	Accord LX	4 Door	1Hond6189ry123489	15,000

Vehicle Usage	Lienholder Information
Work	Honda Motor Company, P.O. Box 111, City, ST, USA 00000

Coverages	Limits or Deductibles	Premiums
Bodily Injury Liability	$250,000/$500,000	$190.00
Property Damage Liability	$100,000	$100.25
Medical Payments	$10,000	$55.10
Uninsured/Underinsured Motorists		
Bodily Injury	$250,000/$500,000	$50.35
Property Damage	$100,000	$22.90
Comprehensive	$50	$135.00
Collision	$200	$260.35
Additional Coverage Options		
Rental Reimbursement	$900	$24.25
Towing/Labor	$100	$45.00
Emergency Road Service		$40.00
Electronic Equipment Protection	$1000	$90.30
Sound Reproducing Tapes	$100	$35.00
Auto Loan Lease Gap		$70.00
Subtotal with selected options		**$1,118.50**
Discounts		
Multi-policy (10%)		−$117.89
Safety equipment		−$15.00
Good driver		−$28.00
Anti-lock brakes		−$12.25
Anti-theft system		−$4.45
Driver training		−$14.10
Multi-car coverage		−0.00
Total Annual Premium		**$926.81**

example, your driving record reflects your skill and judgment behind the wheel. Drive carefully. Be a responsible driver. If you keep your record clean, you will save money on insurance.

You can choose to drive a moderately priced car. Also, as you can see in the auto policy shown on this page, insurance companies often give discounts for certain safety features on your car, such as air bags, and anti-lock brakes. When you are considering a car to buy, call your insurance company for an estimate of your premium for that particular car.

Some insurance companies give discounts to good students. A "B" average will earn you a 5 to 10 percent discount, or about $100 of savings per year. Take a driver's education course for another discount.

Sometimes living just outside city limits or in a safe neighborhood can save you 5 to 10 percent on your premiums.

Increasing the size of your deductibles is another way to reduce your premiums. The difference between the cost of a $250 and a $500 deductible is typically about $100 per year. It won't take long to save this entire amount if you have no claims.

CheckPoint

What do insurance companies consider in determining your auto insurance premium? What can you do to minimize your cost?

TRY THESE

1. What are the six basic types of automobile coverage that insurance companies offer?

2. On an automobile insurance policy, what does 50/100/25 mean?

3. What is the minimum amount of auto insurance you should buy?

4. What is a deductible?

5. Why do young drivers generally pay higher premiums than older drivers?

6. What happens if you have a bad driving record and cannot find a company to insure you?

7. Why do people who live in different communities often pay different premiums for the same amount of insurance?

8. What can you do to reduce your auto insurance premiums?

THINK CRITICALLY

9. CONSUMER ACTION How should Glenn evaluate the amount of coverage he has? What can he do to reduce his premium?

10. COMMUNICATE Tom's parents always carried 250/500/100 liability coverage for their car. When he bought his own car, he realized how expensive this coverage is. He can reduce the cost of his annual premium by $75 if he buys 25/50/10 coverage. Write Tom a letter evaluating his choices. What recommendation would you make to Tom to reduce his cost? Send your answer to your teacher in an e-mail.

11. Cheryl has a seven-year-old Ford Taurus. It isn't in great shape, but she likes it. Her insurance premium is higher than she can handle right now. She can get her premium down to where she wants it by either reducing her liability coverage to 20/40/10 or dropping her collision coverage. Which should she do? Why?

12. Suppose you are 18 years old and about to go shopping for your first car. You have a part-time job but don't make much money yet. What choices can you make in selecting a car that will help keep your insurance premiums low?

DECISION MAKING PROJECT

SPECIFY   SEARCH   SIFT   SELECT   STUDY

SPECIFY Decide what vehicle you will use to compare insurance rates. Specify make, model, and model year. If different engines are offered, such as a four-cylinder or six-cylinder, choose one. Next, decide on a driver profile. Include gender, driver classification, where the driver lives, and so on.

© Getty Images/PhotoDisc

14.3 Home Insurance Coverage

How to Choose Home Insurance

When you own a home, you can suffer financial losses in several ways. A storm could damage your house. A thief could steal its contents. A neighbor could slip on your front porch, sustain an injury, and sue you. Fortunately, you can buy insurance to protect yourself from all of these financial losses. **Homeowner's insurance** provides personal property and liability protection for your home.

Types of Coverage

Personal Property The personal property portion of homeowner's insurance covers damage to or loss of your house and its contents. It covers not only the physical structure of your house but also any unattached structures on your property, such as a separate garage or a storage shed.

In the interior of your home, the personal property coverage includes

CONSUMER ACTION

Matthew used most of his savings to make a down payment on a small house. It isn't in good condition. His idea is to fix it up and sell it to earn a profit. Matthew wants to buy new wall board, flooring, and cabinets for his house. This won't leave him much money to pay for insurance. Matthew wonders if there is any value in buying insurance for a house in this condition. What risks will he take if he doesn't buy insurance?

items such as furniture, appliances, curtains, and clothes. Depending on the policy you buy, it may also cover personal property stolen from your car and living expenses during repair if your house is uninhabitable after a loss.

Exclusions   Some items are specifically excluded or are not covered for their full value. Typical exclusions and limitations apply to stamp or coin collections, laptop computers, silverware, valuable jewelry, and cash. You may have to buy special riders to cover these items.

Liability   The liability portion of your homeowner's policy covers bodily injury or damage you cause to others while on your property or in other locations. For example, suppose you have been working on your roof. You leave the ladder up against the house while you go in for lunch. The child next door climbs the ladder and he falls, injuring himself. Your homeowner's liability coverage will pay the child's medical expenses and your legal expenses if the child's parents sue.

Your homeowner's liability insurance also covers damage you do to someone else's property. For example, if your homerun breaks your neighbor's window, your insurance will pay for the window.

The liability coverage also applies if you cause injury to someone else or damage to someone else's property when you are not at home. If you hit your homerun in a public park and the ball injures a spectator, you are covered. Homeowner's insurance, however, does not cover injuries you cause with your car.

Umbrella Policy

Every year, people are sued for amounts over a million dollars. Most homeowner's and automobile policies will not protect you from awards of this size. Coverage is typically limited to $200,000 to $500,000.

You may purchase additional liability coverage at relatively low cost. An **umbrella policy** provides additional liability protection beyond that included in an automobile or homeowner's policy. A $1 million umbrella policy generally costs less than $750 per year.

Special Risk Coverage

Many Americans live in locations that have special risks. Suppose you live near the ocean along the Florida coast where hurricanes are common. In California and other states, there is a risk of earthquakes or mudslides.

Ordinary homeowner's insurance does not cover these types of losses. If you live where there are unique risks, investigate insurance to cover these types of losses. Federal programs can help some people pay for this insurance. Your insurance agent will know what is available in your area.

© Getty Images/PhotoDisc

481

Homeowner's Policies—What Do They Cover?

Basic Form   Covers 11 perils named in the policy: fire and lightning; windstorm or hail; explosion; riot or civil commotion; vehicles; aircraft; smoke; vandalism; glass breakage; theft; and volcanic eruption.

Broad Form   Covers the 11 perils named for the basic form plus six more: falling objects; weight of ice, snow, or sleet; building collapse; leakage, overflow of water, or steam from plumbing, heating, or air-conditioning systems; freezing of plumbing, heating, or air-conditioning systems; damage to appliances caused by electrical surges; discharge of steam or water.

Comprehensive Form   Covers all perils except those specified. Most all-perils policies exclude nuclear accident, flood, earthquake, war, and other events specified in the policy. The difference between an all-perils policy and a named-perils policy is the burden of proof when there is a question about the cause of damage. In a named-perils policy, it is up to the homeowner to prove that damage was caused by one of the perils listed in the policy. In an all-perils policy, it is up to the insurance company to prove the damage was caused by something excluded from the policy.

Special Form   Provides the same protection for the dwelling as the comprehensive form but less extensive coverage for personal belongings.

Renter's Form   Covers the same perils as the broad form but is for tenants in a house or apartment. It provides personal property protection and liability coverage. There is no coverage for the dwelling since that is the landlord's responsibility.

Condominium Form   Covers only the space occupied. The condominium corporation usually insures the building itself.

Basic Forms of Homeowner's Insurance

Most insurance companies offer six basic forms of homeowner's insurance. The number and types of perils covered depend on the form you choose.

Renter's Insurance

If you rent your home, you have most of the same property and liability risks as homeowners. For example, suppose someone falls and breaks a wrist in your apartment. You are responsible for the medical expenses. Also, you can be sued.

Renter's insurance provides about the same property and liability coverage as a homeowner's policy. It just doesn't cover the structure itself or accidents that take place outside of your rented apartment or house. The owner of the apartment is responsible for these losses.

Renter's insurance is not expensive. A typical policy costs from $200 to $400 per year.

How Much Insurance Should You Buy?

To fully insure your house, you should buy coverage for 80 percent of its replacement value. You don't need to cover 100 percent because your land is included in the value of your house. If your house is totally destroyed, the land will still be there. Also, some parts would remain and wouldn't have to be replaced, such as your foundation and driveway. Rebuilding wouldn't cost the full amount of your house's value.

Buying at least 80 percent coverage is important for another reason. Insurance companies follow an **80 percent rule** in reimbursing losses. According to this rule, your insurer isn't required to reimburse you for the total amount of a loss unless your policy covers at least 80 percent of your home's actual replacement value at the time of your loss.

This rule applies to any loss, not just the total loss of your house. For example, if you buy coverage for only 40 percent of your house's replacement value, then you have only half the coverage you should have (40 percent instead of 80 percent). So if a tree falls on your house and causes $10,000 in damage, your reimbursement will be only half of the loss, or $5,000.

To avoid this problem, you can agree to let your insurance provider increase your coverage periodically. Your new premiums will take into account the current costs of rebuilding homes as well as your home's appreciation. If you don't want automatic coverage adjustments, then you should review your insurance every year or two to make sure it is still adequate.

VOTE Your Wallet

Liability insurance is expensive because of the large awards given to accident victims for their pain and suffering. Many people have received amounts well over $1 million. Several states have considered laws that would limit these awards to some maximum amount, such as $250,000. Such a limit would reduce the cost of insurance significantly.

Some people believe that limiting awards would not be fair to victims. They argue that victims of other people's mistakes should be paid for their pain. But insurance companies do not pay these awards themselves. They pass the cost on to consumers in higher premiums.

If you could vote on this issue, would you limit awards for pain and suffering? Explain your point of view.

© Getty Images/PhotoDisc

CheckPoint

What are the two basic types of coverage that homeowner's insurance provides? What special coverages should you consider?

Cost of Homeowner's Insurance

Like auto insurance, the premiums insurance companies charge for homeowner's insurance are based on statistics from past experience. Insurance companies collect and evaluate data about claims filed in the past. This tells them about the probability of similar losses occurring in the future.

Factors Affecting Your Premium

Location Statistics show that losses occur more frequently in some places than in others. Some neighborhoods have more crime. Even the distance to your neighbor's house can make a difference in your premium. Fire is less likely to spread from house to house when houses are more than 20 feet apart.

Age of the House Statistics show that newer homes are less likely to burn than older homes. Therefore, your insurance company will take the age of your home into account in determining your premium.

Distance to a Fire Station or Hydrant If you live close to a fire station or hydrant, a fire can be put out more quickly, causing smaller losses. Your insurance company will likely give you a break on your premium in this case.

$MATH OF MONEY

Suppose you purchased $40,000 in homeowner's coverage. Then, a storm caused $20,000 worth of damage to your house. At the time of the loss, your house was worth $100,000. How much will you be reimbursed for your loss?

SOLUTION

According to the 80 percent rule, you should have $80,000 worth of coverage.

$100,000 × 0.80 = $80,000

But you have only half of what you should have.

$40,000 ÷ $80,000 = 0.5

Therefore, the insurance company will reimburse only $10,000.

$20,000 × 0.5 = $10,000

IN CLASS ACTIVITY

Think about your home. List factors that would increase the homeowner's premium and factors that would decrease the premium.

Reduce Your Premium

You can reduce your homeowner's or renter's insurance premium in several ways.

Increase Your Deductible

A typical deductible for the personal property portion of homeowner's insurance is $250. By increasing this deductible to $500, you can usually lower your premium by $50 to $75 per year. If you make few claims, this will save you money in the long run. But you will lose money by increasing the deductible if, on average, you make one claim every three years.

Upgrade Your Home

Older homes that still have their original plumbing and wiring are more prone to losses. Old pipes may freeze and break more easily than newer pipes, causing water damage. Old wiring can cause a fire. You can save money on insurance by replacing your old wiring and plumbing. You can also upgrade your house's construction in other ways to reduce your chance of loss.

If you are building a home, you can choose metal siding and interior supports, which are safer than those made of wood. Although these choices will increase your construction costs, they can lower your insurance premium by about 20 percent.

Install Smoke Detectors

You can buy a smoke detector for as little as $15. Not only will this purchase save money on your homeowner's insurance, it may also save your life. In most states, smoke detectors are required by law. Make sure you have at least one on every floor. A few extra detectors and a fire extinguisher might reduce your premium even more.

Install More Security

Deadbolt locks are more secure than other locks, and they are inexpensive. Also, a home security system can help lower your premium, since your home has good protection against theft.

Special Discounts

Some insurance companies give discounts to nonsmokers. If no one smokes in the home, then fires are less likely.

You may also receive a discount if a member of your family does not work outside the home. When someone stays at home, fires and thefts can be reported more quickly. This reduces the possibility of loss.

CheckPoint

What are ways you can reduce your insurance premium for your home? Why do these actions make you less of a risk to your insurer?

TRY THESE

1. What do the property and liability portions of homeowner's insurance cover?

2. How much coverage should you buy for your home to be fully insured?

3. What is the purpose of an umbrella policy?

4. What factors does the insurance company consider in determining your insurance premium?

5. Why would you need insurance if you rent an apartment?

6. What can you do to reduce your homeowner's premium?

THINK CRITICALLY

7. **CONSUMER ACTION** Matthew is considering not buying any insurance for his home. What risks would he take if he makes this choice? What advice would you give him?

8. **MATH OF MONEY** You have a house worth $125,000. Suppose you purchased $75,000 worth of coverage. A few months later, fire did $20,000 worth of damage to your home. How much would your insurance company reimburse you for this loss?

Which of the situations in exercises 9-11 is covered under the personal property portion of a homeowner's policy? Which is covered under liability? Explain.

9. A storm destroys the gazebo in your back yard.

10. A delivery person walks up your driveway, and your dog bites him.

11. You are riding your bike and accidentally run into another biker, causing her to fall and break her arm.

DECISION MAKING PROJECT

SPECIFY   SEARCH   SIFT   SELECT   STUDY

SEARCH Find out your state's insurance minimums from your teacher. Assign group members different insurance companies to contact. Inform these companies that you are working on a project for school and would like to have an insurance quote for a class. Also, ask the following questions.

1. How much would it cost to insure the driver you profiled at your state's minimum levels?

2. What discounts do you offer? Do you offer a discount if both auto and home insurance are purchased?

3. How can these premiums be reduced?

4. How much does the next higher level of coverage cost?

© Getty Images/PhotoDisc

14.4 Providers and the Claims Process

How to Choose an Insurance Provider

Insurance is a service. Unlike a product that you buy once and you own it, insurance is an ongoing relationship that you must depend on for years, even a lifetime. In exchange for your premium, you expect prompt reimbursement for losses and a courteous, knowledgeable insurance agent who will look out for your interests. It is important to shop for a good agent as well as a reliable insurance company.

Using the Internet, you can do comparison shopping for insurance quickly and easily. You can visit the web sites of many insurance companies and agents in a single afternoon. They will provide you with specific information about their policies.

Remember, the fact that a company offers a low price does not mean you should buy from that company.

How to Choose an Agent

An insurance agent sells insurance to consumers. This person will explain

CONSUMER ACTION

Soon-ye and Tran are buying a house, and they want to insure it. How should they go about searching for an insurance policy? Soon-ye collects antiques and has a lot of other furniture. Tran is restoring a classic car. They want to make sure all of their personal property is fully insured. How can they do this?

your options and help you match a policy to your needs. This is just the beginning of your relationship. Your agent then becomes your service provider. When you have questions or a claim, you call your agent for help.

Your insurance needs will change over the years. For example, when your daughter turns 16, you may want to add her to your automobile policy. If you buy a new laptop, you may want additional coverage for it. Your agent is the person you must depend on to help you keep your coverage current.

There are two types of insurance agents: agents who work for one insurance company and *independent agents* who represent many insurance companies. An agent who works for one company can sell insurance offered by only that company. To comparison shop, you must talk to several agents to find the price and policy you want.

© Getty Images/PhotoDisc

Since an independent agent sells insurance offered by many companies, the agent can do some comparing for you. You should still shop around, however, to make sure you get the best deal.

Probably the best way to look for an agent is to ask family members and friends about their experiences with their agent. Ask how they rate their agent on certain characteristics.

► Ability to explain insurance language and policy options

► Quality of advice about amount and kinds of coverage to buy

► Availability in time of need

► Helpfulness in guiding you through the claims process

► Speed in getting claims paid

► Overall friendly, patient, and cooperative nature

Insurance agents earn income according to the amount of insurance they sell. Typically, they receive 2 to 4 percent of the premiums their clients pay. This means that the more insurance they sell, the more income they receive.

Keep this in mind when you talk to an agent. Someone who tries to pressure you to buy more insurance than you want may not have your best interests in mind.

How to Choose an Insurance Company

An insurance policy is no better than the company that issues it. Since the policy represents a promise to reimburse for future losses, it won't be worth much if the company goes out of business or is financially unable to pay a claim when you have one.

Financial Health After you have narrowed your selection to a few policies, check out each company. One good way to gather information about insurance companies is to check *Best's Insurance Reports* in most libraries. This publication rates insurance companies according to their financial health, history, and strengths and weaknesses.

Standard & Poor's and Duff & Phelps offer ratings online for free. You can also get ratings for specific companies through the A.M. Best Company web site for a fee.

Claims Service Another important consideration in choosing a company is the speed and ease of claims processing. You want a company that will reimburse your loss quickly, fairly, and with a minimum amount of hassle.

Probably the easiest way to check the quality of a company's claim service is to use *Consumer Reports* online or in your library. Every few years, it evaluates consumer satisfaction with major insurance companies. You can compare how long it takes companies to settle claims and how many are disputed. Many smaller insurance companies, however, are not included in these reports.

CheckPoint

What does an insurance agent do for you? Why is it important to check out the insurance company before buying a policy?

How to File a Claim

The purpose of buying insurance is to receive reimbursement for a loss. However, you must pay your deductible for each incident before your insurance will pay anything.

If your loss is less than the amount of the deductible, there is no need to contact your insurance company. You will have to pay the full amount of the loss. But if you have a larger loss, call your insurance company to report it and to file a claim. All members of a family should know how to contact insurance providers in case of an emergency.

Homeowner's Claims

For any claim, you will have to supply information about your loss. For your home, this means planning ahead.

Home Inventory You probably could not make a list of everything you own from memory. So if your house were destroyed, how would you tell the insurance company what you lost? Also, how would you prove to the company that you even owned those items? The answer is to

Buy the Numbers?

The government-sponsored National Flood Insurance Program provides insurance to people in flood-prone areas at reduced cost. Private insurance companies sell it for the government.

Suppose you own a home that would cost $100,000 to rebuild. It is located near a river that floods every few years. Would you spend an extra $260 a year to purchase flood insurance? Would this be a good deal? Why do some people think the government is wrong to offer flood insurance at low cost? What problems might low-cost flood insurance cause?

create a thorough inventory of everything in your house—*before* you have a claim.

You should go through your home room by room, recording everything in each room. The illustration on the next page shows a sample inventory checklist for a kitchen and dining room area. Record approximately how much you paid for each item and when you bought it. Leave the Current Value column blank. If you have a loss, you can use this column to estimate the value of each lost item at that time.

It's also a good idea to take pictures or a video of each room. These pictures will help prove to the insurance company what furniture and other items were in the room if you have a loss.

For particularly valuable items not fully covered by a standard homeowner's policy, such as antiques and collections, have the items appraised. Ask your insurance agent how much extra you would have to pay to insure these items. If you decide to have them insured, have the agent list them separately on the policy, along with their appraised value. Be sure to take pictures of each one for your inventory record.

© Getty Images/PhotoDisc

Update your inventory list and pictures every few years and as you make major new purchases. Keep the list and pictures in a safe place outside of your home. That way, your inventory won't be lost along with your house in a disaster. A bank safe deposit box would be a good choice.

Claims Process   Suppose a storm blew off part of your roof. The rain was pouring in the hole and damaging your floor and furniture. Your first responsibility is to protect against further damage.

Cover the hole as quickly as you can. Even if you can just get some heavy plastic over it, do it to keep your loss to a minimum. Your insurance company requires this kind of responsible behavior, or it may not pay for the additional damage that you could have prevented.

Then, call your insurance agent to report the loss. Your agent will send an *adjuster* to assess the damage and determine the amount of reimbursement. If you don't know a contractor who does home repairs, your adjuster may recommend one.

To prove your loss, show your inventory list and pictures to the adjuster. Check off the items that were lost or damaged. Fill in your best estimate of how much each item was worth at the time of the loss.

Since you are the insured person, the reimbursement check will have your name on it. You will be responsible for paying the contractor. Some companies, however, will make out the check to you and the contractor jointly, to make sure the repairs are done.

Automobile Claims
When a Loss Occurs   If you have an accident or your car is stolen or damaged by vandalism, call the police. It is particularly important to call the police if you have an accident involving another

INVENTORY RECORD FORM

Dining/Kitchen Area

Item	How Many	When Purchased	Original Cost	Current Value
Air conditioner, fans				
Buffet, hutch, desk				
Cabinet contents				
Chairs				
China, dishes, crystal, glassware				
Clocks				
Dishwasher				
Electrical appliances				
Food (average kept on hand)				
Household utensils				
Lamps, lights				
Mirrors, pictures, etc.				
Radio, VCR, etc.				
Refrigerator, freezer				
Rugs				
Shelving, bookcases, etc.				
Silverware				
Stove				
Tables				
Table linens				
Television				
Window drapes/shades				
Other: Attach a separate list				

vehicle. The police report will help protect you in case your account of the accident and the other driver's disagree.

Ask for the other driver's name, phone number, and insurance company name. If the person will not supply this information, you can get a copy of the police report, which will give this information.

Then call your insurance agent and supply this information. Your agent will also want your account of the accident. Be prepared to tell the agent when and where the incident happened and the name of the police department that responded to your call. Ask the officer at the scene if you don't know.

Your agent will contact an adjuster to assess the damage. If your car is driveable, your agent will probably ask you to get at least two estimates of the cost of repair from different repair shops. If it is not driveable, then you can have it towed to a repair shop. The adjuster will inspect it there.

If you are unhappy with the repairs, or if the repair shop finds more damage than originally estimated, talk to your adjuster. The adjuster will work with the repair shop to get the repairs done right.

No-Fault Insurance Often, automobile claims involve more than one insurance company. If you have an accident involving someone else, which company pays depends on who was at fault. When responsibility is unclear, time-consuming and costly lawsuits can result. Meanwhile, injured people need their medical expenses paid and cars need to be repaired.

To speed up claims payments and reduce the number of lawsuits, many states have adopted no-fault insurance laws. Under **no-fault insurance**, each person's insurance company pays for that person's losses, no matter who caused the accident.

Insurance Fraud

Studies suggest that 20 percent of insurance claims involve some amount of fraud. Suppose you park your car at a grocery store. Ten minutes later, you return to find a dent in the door. You think it probably would cost $200 to repair. Since you

© Getty Images/PhotoDisc

would have to pay a $250 deductible, you might just forget it.

Several weeks later, you back your car into a post, causing extensive damage. When you get an estimate to have it fixed, would you include the damage to your door? Legally, this is unrelated damage. It should not be included with your claim. If you do include it, you are committing fraud. If you are caught, your insurance company will drop you. Plus, you're breaking the law.

The insurance company doesn't pay for this type of dishonesty. Fraudulent claims increase the costs of providing insurance protection. Eventually, these costs are passed on to all policyholders in higher premiums. To be a law-abiding citizen and help keep insurance costs down, report your losses honestly.

CheckPoint

What kinds of information do you need to supply when you have a homeowner's or an automobile claim? What could happen if you make a dishonest claim?

IN CLASS ACTIVITY

Make a list from memory of everything of value in your living room and bedroom that might be lost in a fire. When you go home, compare your list to what you actually see there. What did you forget? What does this exercise tell you about the value of an inventory?

TRY THESE

1. What characteristics should you look for in a good agent?

2. How do insurance agents earn their income?

3. How can you compare insurance companies?

4. Why keep a home inventory?

5. When your home is damaged, what is your first responsibility?

6. When you are involved in an automobile accident, what steps should you follow to make your claim?

7. What does an insurance adjuster do?

THINK CRITICALLY

8. **CONSUMER ACTION** What steps should Soon-ye and Tran follow in finding a good agent and a reliable insurance company? How can they make sure their property and valuable possessions will be covered?

9. Your tent is stolen from your car's trunk. Your insurance covers your loss. This may be your opportunity to get the sleeping bag you want. After all, it makes sense that if you had a tent in the trunk, you might also have had a sleeping bag. What

would you do? Explain your choice in an e-mail to your teacher.

10. You have had a collision with another car. Both you and the other driver think the other was completely at fault. He refuses to give you his name, phone number, and insurance company. He proposes that you both just pay for your own damage, rather than get the police or insurance companies involved. What would you do?

DECISION MAKING PROJECT

 SPECIFY   SEARCH   SIFT   SELECT   STUDY

SIFT Have group members present their insurance policies and quotes. Make a grid so your group can compare the quotes.

KEY IDEAS

Insurance Basics

1. Insurance helps you manage risk by limiting possible financial losses to an amount you can handle.

2. Insurance operates on the concept of shared risk, so no one policy-holder will suffer a devastating loss.

3. Insurance companies use statistics to set premiums. By charging a little more than the expected losses, they earn a profit.

4. To insure something, it must be something of value that, if lost, would cause you financial harm.

5. Your goal in buying insurance should be to protect yourself from a loss that could put you in financial difficulty.

6. Most businesses couldn't operate without insurance protection.

7. The three basic types of insurance are property, liability, and personal.

Automobile Insurance

8. Automobile insurance policies offer six basic types of coverage: bodily injury liability, property damage liability, medical payments, uninsured/underinsured motorist, comprehensive, and collision.

9. Automobile insurance costs are rising rapidly because cars are more costly to repair, medical costs are high, and awards in lawsuits for personal injury are becoming larger.

10. In determining your premium, insurance companies consider your driver classification, rating territory, driving record, type of car, and claims history.

11. You can reduce your premiums by such actions as maintaining a good driving record, taking a driver's education class, and increasing your deductibles.

Home Insurance Coverage

12. Homeowner's insurance provides personal property and liability protection for your home.

13. Most insurance companies offer six basic forms of homeowner's insurance: basic, broad, comprehensive, special, renter's, and condominium.

14. You can buy special insurance to cover risks not covered in a standard policy.

15. To fully insure your home, you should buy coverage for 80 percent of its replacement value.

16. Three factors affecting the amount of your premium are your home's location, its age, and the distance to a fire station or hydrant.

17. You can reduce your premium by increasing your deductible, upgrading the plumbing and wiring in your home, installing smoke detectors, and installing deadbolt locks.

Providers and the Claims Process

18. In exchange for your premium, you expect prompt reimbursement for losses and a knowledgeable agent who will look out for your interests.

19. Before buying a policy, research the insurance company's financial health by checking a rating service.

20. Make an inventory of the contents of each room in case of a loss.

21. When your home is damaged, act to avoid further damage. Then contact your insurance company. An adjuster will assess the damage and determine the reimbursement.

22. When you have a car accident, call the police and get the other driver's name, phone number, and insurance company name.

TERMS REVIEW

Match each term on the left with its definition on the right.
Some terms may not be used.

a. 80 percent rule

b. appraisal

c. assigned risk

d. bodily injury liability coverage

e. claim

f. collision coverage

g. comprehensive coverage

h. deductible

i. homeowner's insurance

j. insurable interest

k. insurance

l. liability insurance

m. market value

n. medical payments coverage

o. no-fault insurance

p. points

q. policy

r. premium

s. property damage liability coverage

t. property insurance

u. renter's insurance

v. replacement value

w. rider

x. shared risk

y. umbrella policy

z. uninsured/underinsured motorist coverage

1. insurance that pays for damage you caused to another person's property

2. insurance principle of using premiums from many policyholders to reimburse the losses of a few, so that no one suffers a financially devastating loss

3. something of value that, if lost, would cause you financial harm

4. an expert's determination of the value of a piece of property

5. formal request made to an insurance company for payment for a loss

6. insurance contract

7. laws adopted in some states that require each person's automobile insurance company to pay for the insured's losses, no matter who caused the accident

8. bad marks recorded on a person's driving record because of traffic violations and accidents

9. special addition to an insurance policy that covers a specific loss not covered in the standard policy

10. insurance that protects you against financial loss, including the cost of your legal defense, when you are legally responsible for injuring other people in an automobile accident

11. risk management tool that limits financial loss due to illness, injury, or damage in exchange for a premium

12. insurance that pays for damage to your car caused by something other than a collision. It includes damage from storms, vandalism, and theft.

13. regular payment required to purchase insurance

14. amount you pay for a loss before the insurance company pays anything

15. driver who has been assigned an insurance company by the state because a bad driving record makes every other company unwilling to insure the person

16. insurance that provides additional liability protection beyond that included in an automobile or homeowner's policy

17. amount an item is worth now

CONSUMER DECISIONS

18. Suppose you bought some land in a wilderness area for $10,000 and built a cabin on it. The lumber and other materials cost you about $5,000. But you spent at least 200 hours working on it. To have someone else build it would probably have cost $15,000 in addition to the materials. You want to insure your property. How much protection should you buy?

19. Paula lives in San Francisco. She owns her own home, which is located on a steep hill. She could purchase earthquake insurance for an extra $490 per year. How should she decide whether to buy this type of coverage?

20. Sonya was driving her friend Darien to football practice when she missed a stop sign and collided with another car. Sonya already has one accident on her driving record this year. This accident will probably cause her to lose her license. Darien offered to tell the police officer that he was driving. He has no points, so the accident won't cause him as much trouble. What should Sonya do? Explain.

21. Tamasa and Imiko want to buy one of two houses. One is in a safe neighborhood near a good school for their children. But since it is an old home that needs a lot of work, the insurance premium is very high. The other house is in a less convenient location, and the schools aren't quite as good. But since the house is new and has a security system, the insurance premium is much lower. Which should they choose? Why?

THINK CRITICALLY

22. Trampolines were very popular in the 1960s. Trampoline centers rented time on their trampolines for about $2 for 30 minutes. Many people were injured on them because they did not know how to use them safely. After a few years, most trampoline centers closed. Why do you think these businesses failed?

LOOK IT UP

23. Investigate a liability case that has recently been in your local news. What loss took place? How much money was involved in the case? What was the final resolution? How important was it for the parties involved to have liability insurance?

24. Find the Edmunds.com web site. Look up the crash-test results for the type of car that you or your family members drive. What do the test results tell you about the safety of your car or your family's car? Look at the results for other cars. Based on what you find, what cars would you consider buying in the future?

WHICH IS THE BEST DEAL?

Diego is 17 years old. He bought a 10-year-old used car for $1500, and he is investigating automobile insurance. Here are the insurance alternatives he can afford. Which should he choose? Why?

Alternative 1 10/20/5 plus collision and comprehensive coverage with a $200 deductible.

Alternative 2 50/100/25 and no collision or comprehensive coverage.

Alternative 3 No insurance, since he wouldn't lose much if he totaled his car.

POINT YOUR BROWSER TO

www.ee4c.swlearning.com
Complete the activity for Chapter 14.

25. Investigate laws in your state that determine how and when drivers become assigned risks. How long does it take to be removed from this status? How is it done?

26. Use the Internet to investigate the insurance company your family uses for its automobile, homeowner's, or renter's insurance. What did you learn?

27. Investigate new legislation in your state that will regulate what insurance companies are able to do. What did you learn? Do you believe these new laws will help consumers if they are passed? Explain.

INSIDE THE NUMBERS

28. In the early 1990s, the state of California required insurance companies to reduce their premiums for automobile insurance. The rates did go down. Afterward, many policyholders complained that they had difficulty getting reimbursed for their claims. Suppose you are a manager of an insurance company and the state requires you to lower premiums 30 percent. What alternatives would you have? Remember, your job is to earn a profit for your company.

29. You bought a leather reclining chair for $300 eight years ago. It looks its age, so you could probably sell it for only about $50 now. A similar chair bought today would cost $400. A fire just destroyed the chair. The contents of your house are insured for their replacement cost. How much will the insurance company pay to replace your chair?

CURRICULUM CONNECTION

30. **HISTORY** Early insurance companies were started to protect shipping companies. Storms and pirates made shipping a very risky type of business. But the rewards were great when ships returned to port, laden with goods. Investigate the origins of Lloyd's of London, which was the first insurance organization in England.

31. **GOVERNMENT** Many states have passed no-fault insurance laws. Investigate the reasons for these laws and how well they have worked.

JOURNAL RECAP

32. After reading this chapter, review the answers you wrote to the questions in Journal Journey. Have your opinions changed?

DECISION MAKING PROJECT

SPECIFY   **SEARCH**   **SIFT**   **SELECT**   **STUDY**

SELECT Based on your comparison, decide which policy and coverage levels would be the best for the driver you created. List at least two reasons for your choice.

STUDY Present your grid and reasons to the class. Compare your driver profiles, and note how much of a difference the driver profile made in determining a premium.

Chapter

15

HEALTH AND LIFE INSURANCE
YOUR PERSONAL SECURITY

WHAT'S AHEAD

EXPLODING MYTHS

Fact or Myth?
What do you think is true?

1. A good health insurance policy will cover all of your medical expenses.

2. You can choose any doctor, and your insurance company will pay the cost, as long as the doctor is licensed.

3. Life insurance has value only if the insured person dies.

JOURNAL JOURNEY

WRITE IN YOUR JOURNAL ABOUT THE FOLLOWING.

HEALTH CARE Who pays for your visits to your doctor? If you are young and healthy, do you need health insurance? Why or why not?

YOUR HEALTH CARE RIGHTS What rights do you have to receive medical treatment? What health care costs should insurance cover? Why?

LIFE INSURANCE What is the purpose of life insurance? If you stay home to take care of your children and home, do you need life insurance? Why or why not?

DECISION MAKING PROJECT

SPECIFY SEARCH SIFT SELECT STUDY

AN APPLE A DAY Assume that you are 21 years old, and you and the members of your group must find health insurance coverage. Decide on what levels of coverage you want, and shop for the best premium, agent, insurance company, and policy. You don't have to choose the same policy as other group members.

GOAL

To learn how to choose heath insurance coverage

PROJECT PROCESS

SPECIFY	Lesson 15.3
SEARCH	Lesson 15.4
SIFT	Lesson 15.5
SELECT	Chapter Assessment
STUDY	Chapter Assessment

15.1 Health Insurance Basics

What Health Insurance Covers

Advances in medical technology, just within your lifetime, have been nothing less than miraculous. New drugs, medical equipment, and treatment procedures mean that your generation can expect to live longer and healthier lives than previous generations.

These benefits carry a huge price tag, however. Research that creates new drugs and new treatments is expensive. This cost is part of the high price you pay for medical care.

A hospital stay can cost more than $1,000 a day!

Also adding to the rising cost of health care are lawsuits against health care providers. Doctors are human and can make mistakes. Unfortunately, their mistakes can result in permanent physical damage or even death. When a court determines that the doctor or hospital was at fault for a death, the average settlement exceeds $1 million.

CONSUMER ACTION

Derrick wants to buy his first health insurance policy. He got copies of policies from several insurance companies. They all seem so different from each other that he doesn't know how to compare them. What standard coverages should he look for in each one? What types of health insurance should he consider that are probably not in the standard plans?

To protect themselves against such a devastating loss, doctors buy **malpractice insurance**. This insurance can cost doctors as much as $150,000 per year. These costs are passed on to you in the form of higher prices for health care services.

How can you afford the benefits of modern medicine—by sharing the risk through health insurance.

Basic Coverages

Any insurance policy you choose should include coverage for hospital stays, surgical procedures, physician services when you are not in the hospital, major illnesses, and injuries. Health insurance, like any other insurance, involves cost sharing. When you require medical care, you pay part of the expense and the insurance company pays the rest. The portion that each of you pays depends on the policy you choose. The larger the insurance company's share, the higher your premium.

Hospitalization A stay in the hospital involves a number of expenses. Your policy's hospitalization coverage will pay a fixed daily amount for a stated number of days in the hospital per year. This payment covers room and board, routine nursing care, and medical supplies, such as dressings and syringes. It should also cover the use of hospital facilities, such as laboratory testing, an operating room, and X-ray equipment.

Surgery The surgical part of your insurance plan will cover the surgeon's fee, whether the operation takes place in a hospital or in the doctor's office. Most plans pay the total cost of the surgeon up to an amount that the insurance company considers appropriate for that surgical procedure. If your surgeon charges more than that amount, you would have to pay the difference.

Outpatient Services Outpatient coverage, also known as *physician's expense insurance,* pays some portion of doctors' fees for nonsurgical care in their office, in a hospital, or in your home. It covers visits to your doctor for routine health care. It also covers the cost of X-rays and laboratory tests when you are not hospitalized.

Major Medical Major medical coverage pays a share of the enormous costs resulting from a serious illness or accident. It will pay for extended hospital stays, long-term physical therapy, or multiple operations. Some policies have no limit, but most typically range from $500,000 to $2,000,000.

Additional Coverage Choices

Medications Drugs can be very expensive. A single prescription for a month's supply of a common medication can cost over $100. Most insurance plans offer options for covering part of the cost of prescription medications.

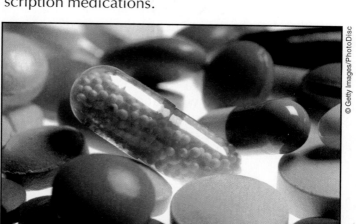

© Getty Images/PhotoDisc

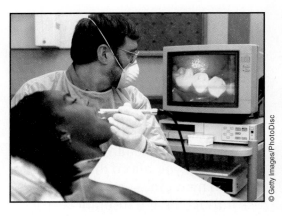

In most policies, however, some types of medications are excluded from coverage. Often excluded are medications to treat depression, contraceptives, diet drugs, and experimental drugs.

Most plans require the use of generic drugs when they are available. **Generic drugs** are medications that have the same composition as their name brand counterparts but are less expensive.

Dental Care For an additional charge, you can buy coverage for a wide variety of dental services. Dental coverage usually pays for preventive services, such as routine checkups, cleaning, and X-rays, and some portion of the expense of fillings, crowns, dental surgery, and repair of teeth damaged in an accident. Insurance that covers the costs of orthodontia is particularly expensive.

Vision Care Most basic insurance plans cover eye injuries and diseases but do not cover routine exams or eyewear. For an additional premium, you can buy vision coverage that usually pays for one eye exam per year. Often it also provides discounts for glasses and contact lenses if purchased from participating providers.

What's Not Covered

Health insurance is designed to help people pay for necessary medical services. Very few policies cover procedures that you elect to have done. For example, few policies

Buy the Numbers?

Some people believe that insurance companies refuse to pay for experimental treatments just to avoid their cost. Insurance companies say they are protecting their policyholders from unproven and therefore potentially harmful treatments.

One example of this controversy is a treatment for sickle cell anemia, a genetic disease that affects about 1 in 400 Americans of African heritage. Most people who suffer from sickle cell anemia live only into their thirties.

During the 1990s, an experimental treatment for this disease through bone marrow transplants was being tested. Each of these treatments cost more than $100,000. Side effects of the procedure often left patients in worse physical condition than when they started. About 10 percent of people who received the transplant died of complications. The people who died would have lived longer had they not had the transplant.

Do you think insurance companies should have paid for this treatment? Why or why not?

IN CLASS ACTIVITY

Have you ever been a patient in the hospital or visited someone there? Think back on this experience. Make a list of all the services, equipment, supplies, etc., that you think the hospital used to provide care. What does this list tell you about the high cost of health care?

CheckPoint

What should you expect your basic health insurance policy to cover? What other types of coverage should you consider?

cover cosmetic surgery that isn't necessary to correct damage caused by injury or disease.

Some plans may not cover regular checkups if you don't have a medical problem. Most policies cover complications resulting from pregnancy, but some do not cover normal childbirth.

Experimental drugs and surgical procedures are often excluded from coverage as well. Many plans now cover organ transplants, but some transplants may still be defined as experimental and excluded.

Insurance companies do not pay duplicate benefits. If both you and your spouse have a policy, your total benefits will not exceed the actual cost of the medical service.

Carefully read any policy you are considering. Look at the details of what is covered and what is excluded.

Insurance for Special Health Needs

Basic insurance plans cover the most common health care needs, but some health crises require care beyond the limits of a basic plan. Special types of insurance are available to fill these additional needs.

Catastrophic and Specified-Disease Insurance

Basic health insurance plans set limits on the amount they will pay over your lifetime. Sometimes, this limit is too low. A catastrophic illness that requires months of hospital treatment or many operations could exceed your limit. A catastrophic insurance policy provides additional protection by extending the lifetime maximum. These policies generally carry a very high deductible, such as $15,000 or more.

Some policies offer coverage for specific dreaded diseases, such as cancer. These policies cover medical expenses for only the diseases specified in the policy.

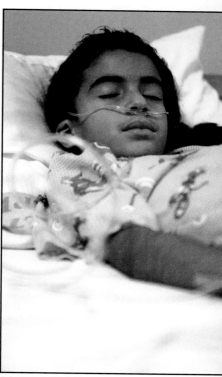

Long-Term Care Insurance

A chronic illness or disability could leave you unable to care for yourself for an extended period of time. You may require more medical, nursing, and personal care than your regular insurance covers. If you suffer a stroke, for example, you may need long-term care in a nursing home. This care could cost $80,000 per year or more. Even if you can remain at home, you may need home care from a nurse, health aid, speech therapist, or physical therapist.

Long-term care insurance is designed to cover the costs of these types of services. It pays a set amount per day for care in a nursing home and a smaller amount per day for home health care. Since the costs of long-term care are rising rapidly, you should expect the premiums for these policies to be relatively high. Look for a policy that adjusts its benefits for rising prices.

Disability Income Insurance

If you were injured and unable to work for an extended period of time, how would you live? How would you pay your bills? Disability income insurance is designed to replace your lost income when you cannot work because of an accident or illness.

Look for a policy that covers disability because of illness as well as accidents. Some plans define disability as being unable to work in your customary occupation. Others define it as being unable to work in any occupation. Be sure you know which definition your policy uses.

Typical plans pay 60 percent of your income at the time you

Today, many hospitals advertise their services, particularly for high-tech treatments that are expensive to provide, such as magnetic resonance imaging (MRI). Why would hospitals want to encourage consumers to use their MRI facilities? Would this type of advertising influence your decision about where to go for health services? Why doesn't this ad include information about the cost of the service it offers? Why does it recommend that patients discuss MRI services with their doctors?

purchased the policy. There is generally a waiting period of one to six months after you are disabled before benefits begin. A shorter waiting period will cost more in premiums. Select a waiting period that you can reasonably cover with other funds. For example, if you think you can continue to pay your bills for six months from your savings or other income, you can save money on disability insurance premiums by selecting a six-month waiting period.

Benefit periods vary. You probably won't need income replacement beyond your working years. But it's generally a good idea to insure yourself up to age 65.

CheckPoint

If you have basic insurance that covers hospitalization, why might you also need catastrophic, specified-disease, or long-term insurance? What is the purpose of disability insurance?

TRY THESE

1. Why is health insurance expensive?

2. What types of expenses should every policy cover?

3. What does the outpatient portion of a policy cover?

4. What is the difference between major medical and catastrophic coverage?

5. Why are some medical expenses excluded from coverage?

6. What does long-term care insurance cover?

7. What are some variations in disability income insurance?

THINK CRITICALLY

8. **CONSUMER ACTION** Derrick is trying to compare several insurance policies. What types of coverage should he compare in each one? What types of coverage might he need in addition to a standard policy?

9. Make a list of the new drugs and medical treatments that you think were developed within the last 20 years. Ask your parents for any they know of to add to your list. Go to the library or the Internet and see if you can find out how much some of them cost to develop. Are these advances worth higher premiums?

10. Why do you think a typical health insurance plan covers the cost of injury to your eyes but does not cover the cost of glasses?

11. Why is the definition of disability important in a disability income insurance policy? How might that definition affect the cost of the policy?

GOALS

DESCRIBE
the two main types of
health insurance plans

DISCUSS
the common forms of
managed care plans

© Getty Images/PhotoDisc

15.2 Health Insurance Plans

Fee-for-Service Plans

There are two basic types of health insurance plans: fee-for-service and managed care.

Both types of health plans cover medical, surgical, and hospital expenses. Many also offer prescription drug and dental coverage. To buy either type, you pay premiums, usually monthly. The differences lie mostly in the degree of freedom you have in choosing your health care providers and how the providers are paid.

With any type of plan, the cost depends on the amount and types of coverage you choose. No plan pays all of your medical expenses.

Under a **fee-for-service plan**, also known as an *indemnity plan,* you pay for health services as you receive them. Then you or your doctor's office submits a claim to the insurance company for reimbursement. For most services, you will be reimbursed for a portion of the cost, depending on the policy you choose.

CONSUMER ACTION

Sharon started a business working from her home. She needs to buy insurance for herself, but she doesn't know the first thing about her choices of plans. What types of plans are available? What are the differences among them? She has a regular family doctor whom she likes. Which plans will allow her to continue seeing her current doctor?

Costs

All fee-for-service plans have a deductible. As with homeowner's and automobile insurance, the *deductible* is the amount of a covered expense you pay before the insurance company pays anything. For health insurance, the deductible is an amount you must pay for the year, not for each incident as with homeowner's or car insurance.

Deductibles commonly range from $100 to $300 for individuals and $500 or more for a family. If your policy carries a $200 deductible, then you have to pay the first $200 of your health care expenses each year before the insurance company begins to pay a portion. The higher the deductible you choose, the lower your premium.

After you have paid your own expenses up to the deductible

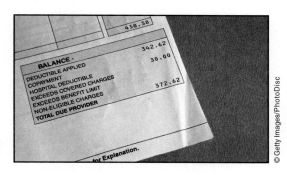

© Getty Images/PhotoDisc

amount for the year, you and the insurance company will share the remaining expenses. Usually the insurance company pays 80 percent of covered expenses, and you pay the other 20 percent. This is called **80/20 coverage**. The portion you pay—in this case, 20 percent—is your **coinsurance**.

With a fee-for-service plan, you may choose any health care provider. However, the insurance reimbursement is based on **reasonable and customary charges**. For each

$MATH OF MONEY

Suppose your fee-for-service insurance policy carries a $200 deductible and 80/20 coverage. You just had an illness that cost $5,000 in medical expenses. This was your only claim this year. How much of this cost will you have to pay? How much will the insurance company pay?

SOLUTION

You will pay $1,160.

$5,000 − $200 = $4,800

$4,800 × 0.20 = $960

$200 + $960 = $1,160

The insurance company will pay $3,840.

$4,800 × 0.8 = $3,840 or $5,000 − $1,160 = $3,840

medical treatment, these are the fees that the insurance company determines are normal in your geographic area. If your doctor charges more than the reasonable and customary fee, you will pay the additional amount.

For example, suppose you have 80/20 coverage and you have already met your deductible. You receive a medical treatment for which your doctor charges $100. If the reasonable and customary charge for the service is $100, you pay 20 percent of that ($20) and the insurance company pays 80 percent of it ($80). If your doctor charges $110, however, you have to pay the additional $10. You will pay $30 and the insurance company will pay $80.

Limits

Most fee-for-service plans set a maximum that you will have to pay in any one year. For example, if your maximum out-of-pocket amount is $5,000, then after you have paid a total of $5,000 that year, the insurance company will pay 100 percent rather than 80 percent of any additional charges. You no longer have to pay coinsurance that year.

The plan will also set a maximum that the insurance company will pay over your lifetime. A common maximum now is $2 million. You should look for a plan that has a maximum of at least $1 million.

CheckPoint

What costs do you pay for with a fee-for-service health insurance plan? What costs does the insurance company pay?

Managed Care Plans

Managed care plans are also called *prepaid plans* because you pay for health care coverage in advance instead of paying for services as you use them. Your premium is your prepayment. There is less paperwork with managed care than fee-for-service plans because you don't have to submit claim forms.

Managed care plans cover the same kinds of health care services as fee-for-service plans. As with any insurance plan, the amount of coverage varies, depending on the policy.

How Managed Care Works

Under managed care, the insurance company controls the cost of health care by negotiating fees with providers who want to participate in the plan. Then you must choose doctors and hospitals that are in the plan, or you will have to pay all or a large part of the cost yourself.

© Getty Images/PhotoDisc

Many managed care plans control costs by paying doctors and hospitals a fixed amount per year for each insured patient, no matter what services they provide. This payment policy is known as **capitation**. Your doctor, for example, might receive $350 each year to serve you. If you are healthy and never see the doctor, this amount is the doctor's profit. But if you are ill and see your doctor many times, the payment will be the same.

Most managed care plans require you to obtain preapproval from the insurance company for nonemergency hospitalization. For example, if you need surgery for a heart problem, your doctor would have to notify the insurance company and explain why the operation is necessary. The insurance company may require you to get a

Comparison of Health Care Plans

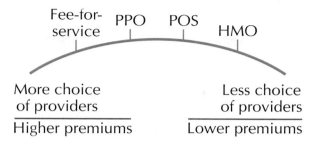

second opinion from another doctor before the company approves the procedure. The company usually pays 100 percent of the cost of your examination from the second doctor.

Managed care plans usually require a **copayment**. This is a specific amount you pay for particular services, regardless of the cost of those services. For example, you might pay $10 each time you visit your doctor and $12 for each prescription.

What In The World?

People throughout the world want health insurance. Medical care and health insurance, however, have been difficult to find in many developing nations. Recently, a prepayment plan was introduced in Zaire (now Congo). Under the Abota plan, villages collect funds and pay them to a hospital or health care facility. These funds are used to pay health care workers and purchase medical supplies. In exchange, health care workers visit the village on a regular schedule. They provide treatment at no additional charge. People who require specialized care are transported to a hospital located in a city.

Hundreds of villages have joined the Abota system, and it is spreading to other nations in Africa. Would you want your village to join this plan if you lived in rural Africa? In what ways is this system similar to the health insurance you can buy in the U.S.?

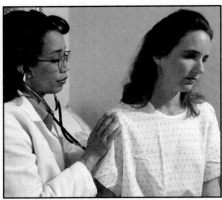

© Getty Images/PhotoDisc

There are three basic types of managed care plans: health maintenance organizations (HMOs), preferred provider organizations (PPOs), and point-of-service (POS) plans. The main difference among them is the amount of freedom you have to choose your health care providers.

Health Maintenance Organizations

A health maintenance organization (HMO) is a managed care plan that charges a set amount for each member each year. In return, members are covered for most medical services at no extra cost or for a small copayment, no matter how often you see your doctor.

Some HMOs operate their own clinics. They employ the doctors, and you visit them in the central location. Other HMOs contract with doctors in private practice to care for HMO members. With this kind of HMO, you visit doctors at their own offices.

IN CLASS ACTIVITY

Make a table or a chart to show similarities and differences between fee-for-service plans and the three managed care plans.

In an HMO, you must choose a doctor in the plan to be your **primary care physician**. This doctor coordinates your care. When you have a medical problem, you must see your primary care physician first. If needed, this doctor will refer you to a specialist.

HMOs will pay for services provided only by doctors and hospitals in the plan. If you go outside the plan for care, you will pay the complete cost. If you stay within the plan, an HMO is generally the least expensive of the health insurance options.

Preferred Provider Organizations

A preferred provider organization (PPO) is the managed care plan that is most like a fee-for-service plan. The PPO contracts with doctors, hospitals, and other health care providers to offer care to its members at reduced costs. However, you can choose to go outside the plan for your care if you pay a larger part of the cost. You aren't required to choose a primary care physician. You can refer yourself to a specialist if you want.

If you go to a doctor within the plan, you will have to pay a small copayment, often $5 to $15 per visit. Outside the plan, you will have to meet a deductible and pay coinsurance that is larger than the in-plan copayment. Also, you may have to pay the difference between what the doctor charges and what the plan will pay.

Point-of-Service (POS) Plan

A point-of-service (POS) plan combines some aspects of an HMO and some of a PPO. As with an HMO, you must select a primary care physician within the POS plan, but like a PPO, you can go outside the POS plan for health care. However, your primary care physician must refer you to a provider outside the plan in order for the insurance company to pay a large part of the cost.

Although a POS plan gives you some freedom to choose a provider, you pay more of the cost of going outside the plan than with a PPO. The cost structure of a POS is designed to encourage you to stay within the plan. For services within the plan, there is no deductible or coinsurance. If you go outside the plan, you must pay a deductible and coinsurance.

CheckPoint

How is managed care different from fee-for-service plans? How do the managed care plans differ from each other?

TRY THESE

1. What are the major differences between the two basic types of insurance plans?

2. What is the difference between a deductible and coinsurance?

3. What limits do fee-for-service plans set?

4. Why are managed care plans also called *prepaid plans*?

5. How do managed care organizations control the health care costs?

6. What is the purpose of a primary care physician?

7. How is a PPO different from a POS plan?

8. What is capitation?

9. What is a copayment?

THINK CRITICALLY

10. **CONSUMER ACTION** Sharon wants to buy health insurance. What basic types of plans are available to her? What are their main differences? Which plans allow her to keep seeing her current doctor?

11. **MATH OF MONEY** Suppose you have a fee-for-service insurance policy with 80/20 coverage. Your deductible is $300. In February, you had a claim for $150 for medical treatment. Now, four months later, you have an injury that will cost $1,500 for treatment. How much of this new claim will you have to pay? How much will the insurance company pay?

12. Under an HMO plan, you pay one price per year to cover medical expenses for the year. If you had to pay a $25 copayment each time you visited your doctor, how would this affect your use of health care services?

13. Managed care organizations negotiate with doctors to offer services to their members at reduced prices. How does this arrangement benefit doctors, managed care companies, and consumers? What possible drawbacks might this arrangement produce?

© Getty Images/PhotoDisc

GOALS

IDENTIFY
the major sources of health insurance

DISCUSS
how to evaluate health insurance options

15.3 Choose a Health Plan

Sources of Health Insurance

Health insurance is available through groups and, for qualifying individuals, through government programs. You also can buy your own individual policy.

Group Health Insurance

Large groups, such as large employers, unions, and professional organizations, often offer health insurance to their members. Most Americans get their health insurance through their employers. As a benefit for their employees, companies often pay part or all of the premium.

In general, premiums are lower for group than for individual insurance. Large groups can negotiate more favorable rates with insurance companies. Also, because of the large number of people in one plan, group plans are less expensive to administer.

CONSUMER ACTION

Tracy has been offered two jobs. One is a position as a clerk for a car dealership that would pay $8 per hour and provide employer-paid health insurance. Tracy thinks this would be boring. Her other choice is to take a job setting up clothing displays for a large department store at $9 per hour. Tracy knows she would enjoy this job, but it offers no health insurance benefits. What advice would you give Tracy? What other information should she consider to make a rational decision?

Employer-Sponsored Plans

You can usually enroll in your employer's plan when you begin your job at the company or during a specified period each year called **open enrollment**. Some employers offer employees a choice between a fee-for-service plan and a managed care plan. However, your choices are limited to the plans your company offers.

Part-time workers generally receive no health insurance from their employers. They may be allowed to pay to join a company-sponsored plan. Even if you are a part-time employee and have to pay the entire premium, joining the company plan could be your best choice. Because it is a group plan, you can take advantage of the lower premiums.

COBRA   If you leave your job, voluntarily or otherwise, the Consolidated Omnibus Budget Reconciliation Act (commonly known as **COBRA**) requires your employer to offer to continue your health coverage for 18 months after you leave. If you want to accept this offer, you must notify your employer within 60 days of leaving. You must also pay the entire premium. However, COBRA coverage can be very

important while you are looking for a job or are not yet covered by a new employer's health plan.

Pre-Existing Conditions

When you change health insurance plans because you are changing jobs or for any other reason, it is important that you maintain continuous coverage. Under the Health Insurance Portability Act of 1997, your new insurance plan must cover any pre-existing conditions without a waiting period if you have been insured continuously the previous 12 months.

A **pre-existing condition** is a medical condition diagnosed or treated before you joined a new insurance plan. If you have a pre-existing

---

COMMUNICATE

Suppose you were a congressperson when the Health Insurance Portability Act was being debated. Write a persuasive speech for or against such an act.

PRIMARYSOURCES

Attitudes toward health care have changed dramatically over the years. Read the following words from Bessie Gray, a woman who lived on a farm in Florida during the 1930s. How is her opinion different from our present-day opinion? Do you agree with her that people depend too much on professional care? Why or why not?

"In olden time people didn't know what a doctor was. Every time you turn around now, it has to be a doctor for this and a doctor for that. They cut you open for the least little pain. I don't see no sense in it, no I don't."

condition and have not had continuous coverage, your new insurance may not cover the expenses for that condition until after a waiting period of a month or more. According to the law, the waiting period must be no more than 12 months. After that time, the new plan must cover the pre-existing condition.

Individual Health Insurance

If your employer does not offer a health plan or you are self-employed, you can purchase an individual health insurance policy. Buying your own policy gives you more flexibility than does a group plan because you can choose the coverage that works best for you from any insurance company.

Individual policies are generally more expensive than group policies. Costs and coverage vary widely among insurance providers, so shop carefully. Consider a higher deductible or larger copayments to keep premiums down.

Most colleges and universities require their students to be insured. Students who don't have their own coverage can purchase a basic policy through their school. The policy could cost as little as $100 to $200 a semester. Schools often extend these low-cost policies to their recent graduates as well. Buying this insurance can be a good idea right after you graduate as you are looking for a job.

Government-Sponsored Health Insurance

Federal and state governments have established programs to provide health insurance for certain qualifying groups of Americans.

Medicare The federal government's Medicare program is designed to provide low-cost medical insurance for older Americans. To qualify, you must be age 65 or older or have certain disabilities.

During your working years, you contribute to the Medicare plan automatically by payroll deduction. Your employer matches your contributions. These taxes help pay the health care costs of the current generation of Medicare recipients. The recipients pay a portion as well. When you reach the federal retirement age, which is now 65, the contributions of younger workers and their employers will help support your Medicare costs.

Medigap Medicare recipients in most states can choose between a managed care and a fee-for-service plan. But no matter which plan you choose, Medicare insurance is very basic and doesn't cover everything. To fill some of the gaps in Medicare coverage, many older Americans purchase a supplemental insurance called **Medigap**. This coverage is sold by private insurance companies, not the government.

Medicaid Americans with low incomes or disabilities, regardless of age, may qualify for **Medicaid**. Medicaid helps ensure that people without the means to pay for health insurance can receive health care.

The Medicaid program is supported by both the federal and state governments but is run by the states. Therefore, the coverage varies from state to state, but all are based on federal guidelines. In general, people who qualify for welfare assistance probably qualify for free treatment through this program.

Workers' Compensation All states require employers to contribute to an insurance program to pay expenses for work-related injuries, illnesses, and death. This program is called **workers' compensation**. Injured workers generally receive two-thirds of their salary while they are disabled. In case of work-related death, the workers' compensation program provides cash benefits to the worker's family.

Workers' compensation programs are run by the states, so coverage varies from state to state. Even if you have other health insurance, you will be covered for work-related claims by workers' compensation if you are employed.

CheckPoint

What are the benefits of a group health plan? How does the government help people who otherwise may not be able to afford it to obtain health care services?

How to Shop for Health Insurance

When you are considering different health insurance plans, compare them carefully. Read the policies themselves, not just the sales brochures. Ask your insurance agent or your company's benefits coordinator what each plan covers.

Like auto and homeowner's insurance, health insurance is only as good as the company that provides it. Check the *A.M. Best* and *Standard & Poor's* ratings for the companies you are considering. These ratings indicate the financial strength of insurance companies, which is an indication of their ability to pay your health care costs. You can get the ratings at your library or online.

Remember that your objective in buying any insurance is not to cover every possible expense but to protect yourself from expenses that are too high for you to pay on your own. Like any insurance, health insurance is a trade-off. The greater the coverage, the higher the premiums. You will have to make choices to keep

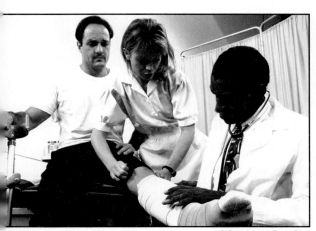

© Getty Images/PhotoDisc

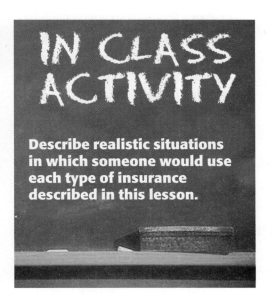

IN CLASS ACTIVITY

Describe realistic situations in which someone would use each type of insurance described in this lesson.

the premiums affordable. Consider your own situation. A plan that is right for someone else may not be right for you. For example, if you have young children, you may need more coverage for family preventive care and routine checkups than would someone without children. Decide what is most important for you. Then compare plans according to their coverage of these important aspects.

Questions to Ask Yourself

Here are some questions to ask yourself to help determine what health care coverage is most important to you.

▶ Do you need coverage for your family or just yourself?

▶ Will you have any major life-cycle changes in the near future, such as starting a family?

▶ Do you need coverage for any chronic illnesses or disabilities?

▶ Do certain medical conditions run in your family that may require coverage down the road?

▶ Would you prefer to pay for preventive care and routine checkups as your family needs them or pay a higher premium for coverage of this care?

▶ How much can you afford to pay in premiums?

▶ How comfortable are you with having a limited selection of health care providers?

▶ How important is convenience in access to health care?

▶ Is your doctor in the plan?

Insurance Provider Concerns

To help you compare health plans, find out how each one handles specific situations.

▶ Physical exams and health screenings

▶ Preventive care

▶ Care by specialists

▶ Prescription drugs

▶ Hospitalization

▶ Dental and vision care

▶ Extended care for long-term illnesses and disabilities

▶ Physical therapy and rehabilitation

▶ Chiropractic care

▶ The number of doctors and specialists participating in the plan

▶ The hospitals that participate in the plan

▶ The policy for going outside the plan for care

▶ The procedures in case of emergency and how the company defines emergency

▶ The plan's limits and exclusions

CheckPoint

When you want to buy health insurance, why is it important to decide first what is important to you?

TRY THESE

1. How does an employer-sponsored health plan benefit employees?

2. What are the benefits and drawbacks of an individual health plan?

3. How does COBRA help you if you are between jobs?

4. What is the difference between Medicare and Medicaid?

5. When shopping for health insurance, why should you read the actual policy rather than just look at the sales brochure?

6. What are some important health insurance questions to ask yourself?

7. What are some important questions to ask to help you compare plans?

THINK CRITICALLY

8. **CONSUMER ACTION** Tracy is trying to decide between two jobs. One provides health insurance. The other doesn't. What information should Tracy gather to help her make her decision? What other factors should she consider in making her decision?

9. Assume that you have diabetes and require regular medication and frequent visits to the doctor. Your employer's insurance plan currently covers these medical expenses, but you are thinking about changing jobs. How does the Health Insurance Portability Act affect this decision? If the law didn't exist, would your decision be different?

10. If you needed to choose a health insurance plan for your own family, what would you consider to be most important? Make a list and prioritize it. Which type of plan—fee-for-service or managed care—is likely to fit your family best? Explain your answer.

11. **COMMUNICATE** Do you think the government should provide health insurance for all Americans? Write a letter to your congressional representative stating your point of view. Explain why you believe such a program would or would not be worth the extra taxes required to pay for it. E-mail your answer to your teacher.

DECISION MAKING PROJECT

● SPECIFY ● SEARCH ● SIFT ● SELECT ● STUDY

SPECIFY Make notes about health insurance coverage you think you may want or need. Think of your financial situation at 21. Write your answers to *Questions to Ask Yourself.* Next, write questions you want to ask an insurance agent from *Insurance Provider Concerns,* adding any you think necessary. Discuss your questions with a group. Create a common list of insurance concerns and questions.

© Getty Images/PhotoDisc

15.4 Health Care Rights and Responsibilities

Patients' Bill of Rights

For many years, Congress talked of creating a **patients' bill of rights** to specify consumers' health care rights and responsibilities. In 2001, the Senate and the House of Representatives passed different versions of this law but couldn't agree on its exact terms. Thus, the final bill was not voted on. Even without a law, many insurance companies and health care providers voluntarily follow the guidelines included in the proposed legislation.

Your Proposed Rights

1. *You have the right to receive accurate, easily understood information about health plans, professionals, and facilities.* This information should include covered benefits, cost sharing, and procedures for resolving

CONSUMER ACTION

Walter ate a hamburger at a party. Later that night he didn't feel good, had a 103 fever, and was in pain, so his wife took him to an emergency room. The doctor gave him medicine and sent him home after a few hours. The hospital filed a $325 claim with Walter's health insurance provider, which denied the claim, saying this wasn't an emergency and he hadn't been preapproved as his plan requires. The hospital expects Walter to pay the bill. What are his rights?

complaints. You should have access to information about the qualifications and experience of your health care providers.

2. *You have the right to a choice of health care providers that is sufficient to ensure access to appropriate high-quality health care.* Health plans should provide sufficient numbers and types of providers to ensure that all covered services will be accessible without unreasonable delay. Women should be able to choose a qualified provider for routine women's health screenings. Consumers with serious medical conditions should have direct access to a qualified specialist and an adequate number of covered visits.

3. *You have the right to access emergency health care services when and where the need arises.* Health plans should educate their members about the availability, location, and appropriate use of emergency services. Health plans should cover emergency services without prior authorization.

4. *You have the right and responsibility to fully participate in all of your health care decisions.* Consumers unable to fully participate in treat-

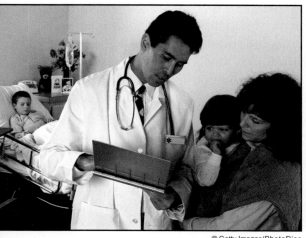

ment decisions have the right to be represented by family members or guardians. Health care professionals should provide patients easily understandable information and the opportunity to decide among treatment options. Professionals should discuss risks and benefits of different options and abide by the patient's decisions.

5. *You have the right to considerate, respectful care from all members of the heath care system and nondiscrimination in delivery of services.* Providers may not discriminate on the basis of race, ethnicity, national origin, religion, sex, age, mental or physical disability, sexual orientation, genetic information, or payment source.

6. *You have the right to communicate with health care providers in confidence and to have confidentiality of your health care information protected.* You have the right to review your medical records and request amendments to them. Your records may be used for health purposes only, except with written consent.

7. *You have the right to a fair and efficient resolution to differences with your health providers, including an appeals system.* The appeals system should provide timely notification of decisions to deny, reduce, or terminate services or deny payment for services. It should also provide timely resolution of your appeals of those decisions. In addition to a review of your appeal by your service providers, a system for an outside, independent review of your appeal should be available.

Your Responsibilities

The proposed patients' bill of rights implies responsibilities that you, as a consumer of health services, should accept. You should take the responsibility to:

▶ Practice healthful habits, such as exercising, not smoking, and eating a healthful diet.

▶ Become involved in health care decisions.

▶ Work with your health care providers to develop and carry out your treatment plans.

▶ Inform your providers of information relevant to your care and communicate your wants and needs.

▶ Use your health plan's complaint and appeals process to address your concerns.

▶ Avoid knowingly spreading disease.

▶ Recognize the risks and limits of the science of medical care and the human fallibility of the health care professional.

▶ Be aware of a health care provider's obligation to be reasonably efficient and fair in providing care to other patients.

▶ Become knowledgeable about your health plan coverage and options.

▶ Show respect for other patients and health workers.

▶ Make a good-faith effort to meet your financial obligations.

▶ Abide by the procedures of your health providers.

▶ Report wrongdoing and fraud to authorities.

VOTE Your Wallet

As of 2005, Congress was still debating a patients' bill of rights. If you were a supporter of the bill, what would you say are its most important benefits? If you were an opponent, what possible problems would you point out in this proposal? Would you vote for it? Why or why not?

CheckPoint

How would you summarize the kinds of rights and responsibilities offered by the patients' bill of rights?

Take Charge of Your Health Care

Insurance is a business. Most companies that provide health insurance intend to earn a profit. Although most do a good job providing protection, you are the one most concerned about your health. Be a responsible consumer of health care services.

To get the protection you pay for, you must first understand how your insurance plan works. Know the rules and follow them. If you are

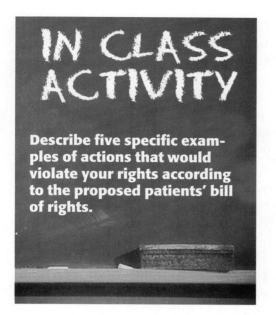

IN CLASS ACTIVITY

Describe five specific examples of actions that would violate your rights according to the proposed patients' bill of rights.

dissatisfied, know your plan's procedure for filing a complaint.

Almost equally important is ensuring that all family members know what to do in a medical emergency—a fall from a ladder or a sudden, serious illness. Your family should plan where to go and what to do in this case. Unless you reach an emergency room quickly, the best medical insurance won't help. Family members must know the location of insurance cards, medical information, and family doctors' names. Teach even young children to dial 911 for help.

Referrals

Under many managed care plans, you must get a referral before seeing a specialist. A **referral** is a request from your primary care physician for services from a particular specialist. Even if you want to see a specialist, you must go to your primary care physician first. That doctor will decide whether or not you need to see a specialist and, if so, will direct you to one. If you go to a specialist without this referral, your plan may not pay the cost of your treatment.

In effect, this referral policy requires you to see two doctors. The insurance company will pay for both visits. So why would the company have such a policy?

Specialists generally charge high fees. Insurance companies know that many people choose to see specialists for conditions that a primary care physician can treat equally well. Under a referral system, the primary care physician will treat these problems, and the company will save the cost of a specialist. Overall, the insurance company will save more by avoiding unnecessary visits to a specialist than it will pay in visits to two doctors.

A problem with this policy is that it makes it more difficult for you to see a specialist when you truly need one. It takes time to schedule two appointments. Meanwhile, your condition could be getting worse. Also, the primary care physician could misjudge the condition and not give you a referral when you need one.

When you believe you need to see a specialist right away, your best choice is to be persistent. If your primary care physician has no appointments available soon, ask to be squeezed in, or you may ask to see a different primary care physician in the plan.

In-Plan Providers

Managed care plans provide a list of doctors, hospitals, and other health care providers who participate in the plan. These are the providers who have agreed to serve you for the prices negotiated with the insurance company. To keep costs in line, the company requires you to choose your providers from among those in the network or plan.

Your managed care plan will state the consequences of going outside the plan for care. Some pay a smaller amount for these services. Others pay nothing at all. Know what your plan's policies are. Suppose you need an operation and you want to have it at a hospital near your home, but the hospital is not in your plan. You might have to pay the entire amount to go there. If you want to go outside your plan often, then you probably have the wrong plan.

Pre-Approvals If your plan requires pre-approval for nonemergency operations, then you must follow this rule or risk paying the entire cost of the operation. Often, insurers require a second opinion from a different doctor before approving the procedure for coverage.

Second Opinions
Second opinions can benefit both you and the insurance company. Whenever you are considering a serious treatment, such as an operation, it is a good idea to get another doctor's opinion. Medicine is an inexact science. One doctor may know something that the other doesn't or may offer other options that may benefit you. Perhaps the proposed treatment isn't even necessary. Naturally, you want the solution that is right for you.

The insurance company saves as well. Inappropriate treatment may

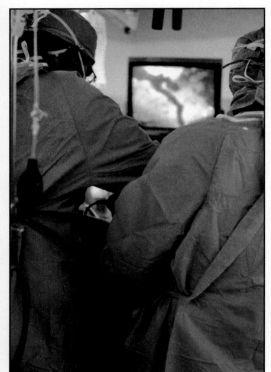
© Getty Images/PhotoDisc

require the company to pay for additional care. If you discover that the operation is unnecessary, the company saves the price of the operation.

Be aware, though, that the insurance company benefits from lower-cost treatments. You may want to get a third opinion if the two doctors disagree or if you are uncomfortable with their ideas. Make sure you are satisfied that the treatment is the right one before you agree to it.

Pre-Existing Conditions
Federal law prohibits insurance companies from excluding pre-existing conditions from coverage for more than 12 months. If you have been continuously covered under a different plan for the last 12 months, a new plan must cover you without a waiting period.

Most insurance companies follow the law. Unfortunately, some get around the law with policies that effectively discriminate against people with pre-existing conditions. They may refuse to insure groups that include people with costly conditions. They also may increase the premiums beyond a reasonable amount for people with these conditions, so they cannot afford the insurance.

Some people with pre-existing conditions have reported difficulty in finding employment. Companies may not hire them because they are worried that their health insurance premiums will increase.

If you believe you are being discriminated against because of a pre-existing condition, contact your state attorney general's office. Someone there will be able to either help you or tell you who can.

Experimental Treatments

It takes time to fully research new drugs and treatment procedures. Even if they work, most are expensive. Insurance companies often classify new treatments as experimental and refuse to pay for them. If the treatments are not proven effective, they cannot justify the cost.

In fairness, if insurance companies pay for every new treatment, their costs and your premiums could sky-rocket.

Court cases over the years have ruled that some treatments previously considered experimental should be covered. For example, organ transplants used to be classified as experimental and not covered. As transplants became more common and more successful, many insurance plans covered them.

The Appeals Process

Every health plan has an appeals process. If you are dissatisfied with your care, follow the set process.

If you are unhappy with your primary care provider, change doctors. Also, your employer may offer more than one plan, and you can switch plans at certain times of the year.

Start with the Company

First, find the coverage information in your policy to be sure a service is covered. If you think that your plan unfairly refused to provide or pay for covered services, call the member services department of your insurance company. Ask why the service was refused.

If your policy states that the service is covered, check with the representative to make sure the company has the correct diagnosis, your deductible was calculated correctly, and you got the proper pre-authorizations.

Ask the representative to review your claim. Then the representative should advise you on how to follow the plan's formal appeals process.

Keep written records and all correspondence. Take notes of phone conversations, including the names, dates and times, and the nature of your discussion. Also keep all claim forms and copies of bills.

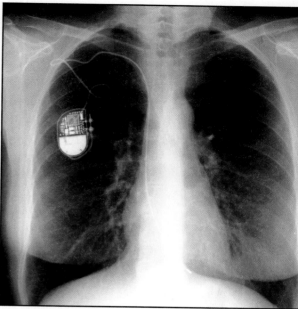
© Getty Images/PhotoDisc

If You Still Aren't Satisfied

Most disagreements can be solved directly with the insurance company. If you are still dissatisfied after appealing to the company, however, take your complaint to your state insurance commissioner or state department of health. All states have procedures to settle disputed insurance claims that can impose a settlement on insurance companies.

Your final resort is court action. Suing an insurance company is expensive, so do it only if you have a strong case.

CheckPoint

What are some ways that you can take charge of your own health care? Why is it important to know how your plan works?

TRY THESE

1. If your plan offers a list of approved providers, what rights do you have to choose a doctor, according to the proposed patients' bill of rights?

2. What rights do you have under the proposed patients' bill of rights if you have a dispute over a claim with your health insurance company?

3. What responsibilities do you have in working with your doctor?

4. Why do patients often need to have referrals to see a specialist?

5. How can insurance companies get around the law requiring them to cover pre-existing conditions?

6. What steps should you take if you think your claim was denied unfairly?

7. How do second opinions help you and your insurance company?

THINK CRITICALLY

8. **CONSUMER ACTION** Who do you think is right, Walter or the insurance company? What are Walter's rights according to the proposed patients' bill of rights? How should Walter appeal this decision?

9. Suppose that a deadly disease runs in your family. A DNA test would give you prior warning whether you inherited this disease. If your employer had access to your medical records, would you still get this test? Why or why not?

10. One of your responsibilities as a consumer of health services is to "recognize the risks and limits of the science of medical care and the human

fallibility of the health care professional." What do you think this means? Why is this responsibility important in health care?

11. How could the requirement to get pre-approval for an operation potentially lead to lower quality health care?

12. Discuss the drawbacks of referrals and explain what to do if the referral process is taking too long.

13. Write a letter to a friend who is having trouble finding insurance because of a pre-existing condition. Explain what you know about the problem and what she can do about it. E-mail your answer to your teacher.

DECISION MAKING PROJECT

SPECIFY   SEARCH   SIFT   SELECT   STUDY

SEARCH Assign group members different health insurance companies to contact. Inform these companies that you are working on a project for school and would like some insurance information for a class. Then ask the questions from your common list. Have one group member look up the reliability of the insurance companies you will contact.

© Getty Images/PhotoDisc

GOALS

EXPLAIN
why life insurance should be part of your financial plan

DISCUSS
differences among basic types of life insurance

15.5 Life Insurance

The Value of Life Insurance

The purpose of life insurance is to protect you and your family from financial hardship that could result from the death of a family member. About three-quarters of all American families own some type of life insurance.

What Is Life Insurance?

A person's death causes various problems for those left behind. It is sure to bring a sense of loss and a change in family responsibilities. The most serious short- and long-term problems are likely financial. When a wage earner dies, his or her income is lost to other family members. They may have to work more hours to pay bills or lower their standard of living.

The death of a person who did not work outside the home can still cause financial hardships. Most family members contribute to their family's financial health, even when they do not earn wages. They may care for children, keep family records, and maintain their home. When these

CONSUMER ACTION

David and Marcy have been married for just over a year. Last week, Marcy's doctor told her that they will be parents in about seven months. David and Marcy want to do the best that they can for their new son or daughter. They have already adjusted their budget to include buying baby furniture, clothing, diapers, and formula. Should their financial plan include life insurance? What benefits could life insurance provide them?

people die, other family members must take over these jobs or hire others to do them. This will create new costs for the family.

Even the death of a child results in some costs. Funeral expenses can run more than several thousand dollars. Life insurance cannot eliminate the tragedy of an unexpected death, but it can protect people from the resulting financial hardships. Buying life insurance should be part of almost everyone's life-span plan.

How Life Insurance Works

When you buy life insurance, you specify who will receive the payment, or **death benefit**, if you die. The person you specify is your **beneficiary**. You may specify several beneficiaries in your policy if you want. You then pay regular premiums for your coverage.

From statistics, life insurance companies know, on average, how many people of any age will die in each year. They often consider policyholders' sex, type of employment, and lifestyle. This knowledge allows them to calculate how much to charge for the coverage they sell.

Types of Life Insurance

There are two basic types of life insurance: term and permanent. The main difference is that term life is pure insurance. It pays a benefit for a covered loss but has no value at the end of its term. Permanent life insurance includes a savings component, so it has value beyond protection against financial loss.

Term Life Insurance

Term life insurance pays a death benefit if the policyholder dies within a specified period of time, its *term*. If the policyholder does not die, the policy terminates at the end of its term and has no remaining value.

This type of life insurance is often a good choice for young people, because it is a less expensive insurance option. Also, insurance companies can charge less for young people because young people are less likely to die during the term of the policy. Older people have to pay higher premiums for a term policy.

If you are young and are supporting a family, you may want to protect your family against the loss of your

CheckPoint

How does life insurance protect a family's financial well-being? How do insurance companies decide how much to charge for this type of protection?

income during your working years. You may choose a policy that lasts 5 years, 10 years, or even up to age 65.

You may want a term policy for a special purpose. For example, you may want a small policy to cover your funeral expenses if you die or a term policy to ensure that your child has enough money to go to college if you die.

There are several types of term life insurance available.

© Getty Images/PhotoDisc

Level Term Life Insurance

Level term policies pay a fixed benefit for a fixed premium over a specified number years. Terms for this type of policy typically run 5, 10, 15, or 20 years. A five-year policy with a death benefit of $20,000 would pay $20,000 no matter when the policyholder died within the term of the policy.

An advantage of level term life insurance is that your premiums do not increase as you grow older. You will pay a higher premium overall for a longer term, however, than for a shorter one.

Renewable Term Life Insurance

At the end of its term, most level term policies turn into renewable term policies. Renewable term insurance allows you to renew your policy each year regardless of your health and without a physical examination. Premiums will increase each year when you renew to reflect your current age and life expectancy.

The major advantage of this type of policy is that it cannot be canceled if you become ill or as you grow older. It will continue for as long as you choose to renew and continue to pay the premiums, up to its expiration date—typically age 65 or 70.

Convertible Term Life Insurance

Most term life policies contain a convertible option. This means that, at any time during the term, you can choose to convert the term policy into a permanent policy without evidence of insurability. Evidence of insurability would include things such as a physical examination and information about your lifestyle. The earlier in the term you choose to convert, the lower the premiums.

Being able to renew or convert term policies into permanent protection without evidence of insurability is an important benefit. If you have had a serious illness, such as cancer, you would pay a much higher premium for a life insurance policy if the company knew about your illness. In some cases, you would not be able to buy insurance at all. If you took up a high-risk hobby, like sky-diving, insurance companies may not sell you a policy either.

Permanent Life Insurance

All life insurance pays a death benefit. **Permanent life insurance** provides a death benefit plus a savings plan, and the coverage lasts throughout the policyholder's life. Because this type of policy has value besides a death benefit, it is often called *cash value life insurance.*

Some of every premium payment you make pays for your death benefit. The rest goes into a savings or cash value account that earns dividends throughout your lifetime. Because of the savings component, your premiums will be higher than for a term life policy with similar death benefits. Your policy cannot be canceled as long as you pay your premiums as specified in the insurance contract.

When you die, your beneficiaries will receive the amount specified as your death benefit plus the value of your savings. Many permanent policies allow you to withdraw your savings at any time. If your child goes to college, you may choose to use the cash value of your permanent life insurance policy to pay school expenses. You may use the cash value as your retirement fund. Many plans even allow you to borrow funds with your insurance policy's cash value as collateral.

Whole-Life Insurance The most common and least expensive type of permanent policy is *whole-life insurance.* As the name implies,

CYBER CONSUMER

Life insurance companies offer many types of term and permanent insurance, besides the common ones described in this lesson. Find two companies on the Internet that sell life insurance. Describe a policy from each one that is somewhat different from the policies described in this lesson. How are they different?

this type of policy is yours for life. You pay a fixed premium that cannot be increased over your lifetime as long as you pay the planned amount.

You can choose to receive dividends from the earnings of your cash value account or apply the dividends to your premium. You can also borrow against the cash value. However, you do not have the flexibility to change the amount of your savings contribution, change the amount of coverage (death benefit), or determine how your funds will be invested.

Variable Life Insurance If you prefer to decide how your savings will be invested, a variable life policy could be right for you. Like a whole-life policy, it is yours for life, but it allows you to select from several investment options.

This is a riskier plan than whole-life. Your death benefit will vary with how well your investments do. Also, you may not withdraw from your cash value account during your

© Getty Images/PhotoDisc

lifetime or change the amount of your coverage or premium.

Universal Life Insurance A permanent life policy that has more flexibility than either whole- or variable life is universal life. You can borrow against or withdraw from your

cash value account during your lifetime. You can even change the amount of your coverage and your premium, but you can't choose how your savings are invested, as you can with a variable life policy.

Life Insurance as an Investment

All permanent life insurance premiums are higher than term policies that have the same death benefit. The reason is the cash value component of permanent policies. With each premium, you are investing. You must decide whether life insurance is a good way to invest your money. The answer isn't always clear.

Funds invested in permanent insurance policies generally do not earn high returns over time. Suppose Sara is 20 years old. She pays a $600 annual premium for a universal life insurance

Comparison of Common Life Insurance Options

	Term Life	Whole Life	Variable Life	Universal Life
Premiums	start low; increase as renewed	stay level	stay level	policyholder may change them
Coverage	generally renewable only to age 70 or 75	permanent	permanent	permanent
Death Benefit	fixed	fixed	varies with investment returns	policyholder may change it
Cash Value Account	no	yes	yes	yes
Ability to Withdraw Cash Value	NA	yes	no	yes
Ability to Borrow	no	yes	yes	yes

policy. Forty years from now, Sara will be able to withdraw the policy's $50,000 cash value.

Alternatively, she could purchase a term policy for $200 per year with the same death benefit. If she invested the extra $400 herself, she would likely accumulate more than $50,000 in the next 40 years.

Before you invest in a permanent life policy, check your investment options. You may be better off buying term insurance and investing your remaining funds yourself.

How Much Life Insurance Should You Buy?

There is no right amount of life insurance. The amount that is best for you depends on your family and financial situation. Here are some factors to consider when you make your life insurance decision.

Your Family Responsibilities

People who have children or provide the primary income for their family should have more life insurance than single people with no dependents. A husband or wife who does not work outside the home still contributes to a family's financial well-being. You need to insure against the loss of this person's contribution as well.

Your Financial Situation

Most young people don't have much income to spend on life insurance. Still, if others depend on your income, you should buy some life insurance, no matter how young you are. The sooner you start buying life insurance, the smaller your premiums will be. Later, you may have more income and be able to pay for more coverage.

Your Future   Although you may not have children now, you may have in a few years. Buying small amounts of life insurance when you are young may guarantee that you will be able to buy more in the future. Remember, though, that many employers and Social Security offer some life insurance protection. When you decide how much life insurance to buy, consider what you have from these other sources.

Your Special Needs   Many people have special situations in their lives that cause them to purchase extra life insurance. For example, if you were the parent of a disabled child, you might want enough extra life insurance to care for your child if you died. You might have a large college loan. Extra life insurance could pay this debt if you died so that your spouse would not have this financial burden.

© Getty Images/PhotoDisc

CheckPoint

What are the major differences between term and permanent life insurance? What should you consider in deciding which type and how much to buy?

TRY THESE

1. From what kinds of financial hardships does life insurance protect you?

2. Why are the premiums higher for permanent than for term life insurance?

3. Why might you buy a term life policy?

4. What is the difference between renewable and convertible term life insurance?

5. How is universal life insurance more flexible than either whole-life or variable life insurance?

6. How can you decide whether permanent life insurance is a good investment?

7. What should you consider in deciding how much life insurance to buy?

THINK CRITICALLY

8. CONSUMER ACTION Why should David and Marcy consider adding life insurance to things they want to buy? What benefits could it provide them and their new family?

9. COMMUNICATE Which type of insurance would you recommend to David and Marcy, term or permanent? Write a letter to them, explaining your recommendation. E-mail your answer to your teacher.

10. Nathan was diagnosed with diabetes at age five. Now he is 22. Even though he eats right and is quite healthy, he cannot buy life insurance at a reasonable price. Do you think this is fair? Explain.

11. Describe how buying life insurance provides financial security to families as they pass through different stages of the life cycle.

DECISION MAKING PROJECT

SPECIFY **SEARCH** **SIFT** **SELECT** **STUDY**

SIFT Have group members present the information they received from their assigned insurance company. Make a grid so your group can compare insurance premiums and policies. Then compare these factors against the reliability ratings of the insurance companies.

Chapter 15

ASSESSMENT

KEY IDEAS

Health Insurance Basics

1. Your health insurance policy should include coverage for such things as hospital stays, major illnesses, and injuries. Health insurance, like any insurance, is cost sharing.
2. Check your policy for exclusions.
3. You can buy separate policies to cover special health needs.

Health Insurance Plans

4. The two basic types of health insurance plans are fee-for-service and managed care.
5. Under a fee-for-service (or indemnity) plan, you pay for medical services as you receive them and submit a claim to the insurance company for reimbursement. Under managed care, you pay for services in advance.
6. The most common managed care plans are HMOs, PPOs, and POS plans.
7. For HMO and POS plans, you must select a primary care physician in the plan to coordinate your care. You may refer yourself in a PPO plan, but you will pay more.

Choose a Health Plan

8. You can obtain health insurance through membership in a group, through the government if you qualify, or by buying an individual policy.
9. If you leave your job, you can continue coverage under your previous employer's plan under COBRA.
10. If you have had continuous coverage for the previous 12 months, your new plan must cover your pre-existing condition without a waiting period.
11. Before shopping for insurance, decide what is most important to you in health coverage. Ask questions about different health situations.

Health Care Rights and Responsibilities

12. Under the proposed patients' bill of rights, you have the right to (1) information, (2) sufficient choice of providers, (3) emergency services, (4) make decisions concerning your care, (5) considerate and nondiscriminatory care, (6) confidentiality, and (7) a fair appeals process.
13. Among your responsibilities under the proposed patients' bill of rights are to (1) practice healthy habits, (2) be involved in your own care, (3) understand and follow your plan's procedures, (4) be sensitive to the limitations of modern medicine, and (5) meet your financial obligations.
14. Start any appeal with the insurance company. Then, if unsatisfied, call the insurance commissioner or health department before you consider suing.

Life Insurance

15. Life insurance protects against financial loss caused by the death of the insured.
16. Term life insurance pays a death benefit if the policyholder dies within a specified period of time.
17. Renewable term policies allow you to renew for another term at a higher premium. Convertible term policies allow you to convert your term policy to a permanent policy.

18. Permanent life insurance is yours for life. Common permanent plans are whole-life, variable life, and universal life.

19. The amount of life insurance you need depends on your family and financial situation.

TERMS REVIEW

Match each term on the left with its definition on the right.
Some terms may not be used.

a. 80/20 coverage

b. beneficiary

c. capitation

d. COBRA

e. coinsurance

f. copayment

g. death benefit

h. fee-for-service (or indemnity) plan

i. generic drugs

j. health maintenance organization (HMO)

k. malpractice insurance

l. managed care plans

m. Medicaid

n. Medigap

o. open enrollment

p. patients' bill of rights

q. permanent life insurance

r. point-of-service (POS) plan

s. pre-existing condition

t. preferred provider organization (PPO)

u. primary care physician

v. reasonable and customary charges

w. referral

x. term life insurance

y. workers' compensation

1. managed care health insurance plan that allows you to choose providers outside the plan if you pay a larger part of the cost and does not require you to get referrals from a primary care physician

2. government-sponsored health insurance designed for people with low incomes or disabilities, regardless of age

3. fees for each medical treatment that the insurance company determines to be normal in your geographic area

4. health insurance coverage that you pay for in advance instead of paying for services as you use them

5. under managed care health insurance, the specific amount you pay for particular services regardless of the cost of those services

6. under fee-for-service health insurance, the portion of covered medical expenses you must pay, after meeting the deductible

7. doctor in a managed care health plan that you select to coordinate your care and refer you to specialists

8. life insurance that pays a death benefit if the policyholder dies within a specific time period but has no remaining value at the end of this time

9. medications that have the same composition as their name brand counterparts but are less expensive

10. specified time each year when employees may sign up for the employer-sponsored health insurance plan

11. type of health insurance in which you pay for health services as you receive them and submit a claim to the insurance company for reimbursement of covered expenses

12. medical condition diagnosed or treated before you join a new insurance plan

13. life insurance that provides a death benefit plus a savings plan and lasts for the policyholder's lifetime

14. employer-paid insurance program that covers expenses for work-related injuries, illnesses, and death

CONSUMER DECISIONS

15. Your doctor just told you that you have high cholesterol. You know nothing about this problem. Your doctor gave you some suggestions for exercising and changing your eating habits. According to the proposed patients' bill of rights, what are your responsibilities for dealing with your problem?

16. Your employer gives employees a choice. The company will pay $4,000 toward the cost of your health insurance, or it will pay you the $4,000 as an increase in your salary. Which choice would you make? Explain.

17. You are a self-employed management consultant who makes around $80,000 a year. You are looking for disability income insurance protection. One policy will reimburse you 60 percent of your current income if you become disabled and unable to work as a management consultant. Another policy will reimburse 70 percent of your current income if you become disabled and unable to work at all. Which would you choose? Why?

18. Suppose your sister has a serious illness. A new treatment is being developed that might help her. It would cost about $100,000. Your family's health insurance company has refused to pay for it because the treatment is classified as experimental. What would you do?

THINK CRITICALLY

19. Patients who belong to plans with copayments (of $5 or $10) visit doctors about 40 percent less often than do people whose visits are entirely paid. How can you explain this fact? Do you think this difference affects the patients' overall health?

LOOK IT UP

20. Obtain a list of local doctors and hospitals that participate in a particular managed care insurance plan. Do you think this plan offers you enough choices to cover whatever services you need?

21. Investigate the financial condition of a health insurance company that serves your community. You can find this information in *Best's*

WHICH IS THE BEST DEAL?

You are 25 years old and have two small children. You are the only member of your family who works outside the home. You don't make much money, and your savings wouldn't sustain your family for more than a couple of months if you died. You would like to protect your family against the loss of your income. Here are the alternatives you have identified. Which choice would you make? Why?

Alternative 1 Buy a level term life insurance policy for $220 per year for 5 years with a death benefit of $100,000.

Alternative 2 Buy a renewable term life insurance policy for $240 per year for 10 years with a death benefit of $100,000.

Alternative 3 Buy a whole-life policy for $780 per year for life with a death benefit of $100,000 and a cash value account that will likely build to around $50,000 by the time you are 65.

Alternative 4 Buy no life insurance and promise yourself that you will start a regular savings plan to help your family if you die.

Insurance Reports, Standard & Poor's, or *Moody's.* These publications are available in larger public libraries and on the Internet. Would you feel safe buying insurance from this company?

22. Search the Internet for an insurance service that will give free instant online quotes for term life insurance. Supply the requested information and select a coverage amount. How much did it cost? Now change the way you answered a key question but keep the same coverage. For example, if the questionnaire asked if you smoke, you said no. Then change the *no* to *yes* and note the rate changes. Do this with other key questions. What does this tell you?

23. Ask your local pharmacist what the differences are, if any, between generic and name brand medications. Would the pharmacist recommend that you use generic medications?

INSIDE THE NUMBERS

24. In 1980, just over 9 million Americans belonged to managed care health insurance plans. This number now exceeds 100 million. Write a few paragraphs that explain why you think this change in health insurance coverage has occurred. How do you think this trend toward managed care has affected the cost and quality of health care? Explain.

CURRICULUM CONNECTION

25. **SCIENCE**   Investigate a recent scientific breakthrough that has improved medical treatments. How has it benefited patients? What was the cost of this scientific achievement? What process did developers have to follow to get it approved for use in the United States?

26. **SOCIAL STUDIES**   Many consumer groups have formed to advocate for particular health care issues. Search the Internet for a group concerned with one such health issue. What is this group currently lobbying for? What are some of the actions it is taking to try to reach its goals?

JOURNAL RECAP

27. After reading this chapter, review the answers you wrote to the questions in Journal Journey. Have your opinions changed?

DECISION MAKING PROJECT

SPECIFY   SEARCH   SIFT   SELECT   STUDY

SELECT   Based on your comparison, decide which policy and coverage levels would be the best for the you. List at least two reasons for your choice.

STUDY   Present your policy and reasons to the class. Did anyone else choose the policy and premium from the same company that you chose? Why?

CHOOSE SERVICES
WHEN YOU NEED HELP

EXPLODING MYTHS

Fact or Myth?
What do you think is true?

1. You must buy your glasses from the doctor who examined your eyes, because that doctor wrote the prescription.

2. As long as you obey the law, you won't need a lawyer.

3. The purpose of welfare is to provide food, shelter, and medical care for poor people throughout their lifetimes.

JOURNAL JOURNEY

WRITE IN YOUR JOURNAL ABOUT THE FOLLOWING.

CHOOSING A DOCTOR   How would you choose a doctor? What qualities would you want your doctor to have?

CHOOSING A LAWYER   Why might you need a lawyer? What kinds of questions would you want to ask a lawyer before deciding to hire one?

GOVERNMENT ASSISTANCE   Do you have to be poor to receive government assistance? How does the government provide some degree of economic security to its citizens?

DECISION MAKING PROJECT

SPECIFY   **SEARCH**   **SIFT**   **SELECT**   **STUDY**

IS THERE A DOCTOR IN THE HOUSE?   The Washington family just moved into your town. Your group belongs to the "welcome wagon" and has offered to help the family settle into your community. The family needs information on a medical insurance provider, family doctor, and a local hospital. Eight-year-old Nancy has diabetes. Her father suffers from high blood pressure. Her grandfather had a stroke and still needs physical therapy. Mrs. Washington and her teenage son are in good health.

GOAL

To learn how to choose a medical professional

PROJECT PROCESS

SPECIFY	**Lesson 16.1**
SEARCH	**Lesson 16.2**
SIFT	**Lesson 16.3**
SELECT	**Chapter Assessment**
STUDY	**Chapter Assessment**

© Getty Images/PhotoDisc

GOALS

DESCRIBE
how to choose a
doctor and hospital

EXPLAIN
differences among
dental and eye care
professionals

16.1 Health Care Providers

How to Choose a Physician

The medical profession has a whole array of specialties and subspecialties. How can you choose a doctor to fit your needs? The key qualities to look for in any doctor are competence, compassion, and the ability to communicate.

Primary Care Physicians

Your primary care physician will serve as your main doctor. This should be someone with whom you can feel comfortable and who can serve your needs for many years.

Most adults choose a primary care physician who is either an internist or family practitioner. Both of these specialties cover a broad range of care, which is why they are good choices for your main doctor.

An **internist** is a specialist in internal medicine, a branch of medicine

CONSUMER ACTION

Liz has recently accepted a job working for a newspaper. Her employer provides health insurance through a preferred provider organization (PPO). When Liz was hired, she was given a list of hundreds of physicians who participate in this PPO. Unfortunately, her family doctor was not among them. To avoid paying out-of-plan costs, Liz must choose a primary care physician in the plan. She doesn't know anything about the approved doctors. How can she evaluate her options?

that deals with the long-term, comprehensive management of both common and complex illnesses. A **family practitioner** is trained in the prevention, diagnosis, and treatment of a wide variety of ailments in patients of all ages.

Women often select an obstetrician/gynecologist in addition to their primary care physician. An **obstetrician/gynecologist (OBGYN)** specializes in the diagnosis and treatment of diseases of the female reproductive system and care and treatment during pregnancy, labor, delivery, and just after delivery.

For your child's primary care physician, you may want to choose a pediatrician. A **pediatrician** is specially trained in the physical, emotional, and social health of children from birth to young adulthood.

Competence

More than anything, you want your doctor to be skillful. This quality is hard to judge, but with a little research, you can uncover some indicators of competence.

Ask Other Health Care Professionals Probably the best way to find out the quality of a doctor is to get some inside information. Ask others working in the same medical field. For example, ask nurses or other hospital workers you know to recommend doctors. Hospital workers often know the reputations of different doctors.

If you are looking for a specialist, your primary care physician's

---

Other Common Medical Specialists

Allergist/Immunologist specialist in evaluating, diagnosing and managing disorders involving the immune system. This type of doctor treats conditions such as asthma, adverse reactions to food or bee stings, and diseases that affect your body's natural defenses.

Cardiologist specialist in diseases of the heart and blood vessels. You would need a cardiologist if you had a heart attack, abnormal heart beats, or problems with blood circulation.

Neurologist specialist in the diagnosis and treatment of diseases or impaired function of the brain, spinal cord, and nervous system.

Oncologist specialist in the diagnosis and treatment of all kinds of cancer.

Orthopedist specialist in the prevention or correction of injuries or disorders of the skeletal system. If you break a bone, you may want to see this type of doctor. Specialists in sports medicine are often orthopedists.

Osteopath doctor of osteopathy, a branch of medicine that emphasizes treatment of the body as a whole. Osteopaths believe that problems in the musculoskeletal system affect other body parts, causing disorders that can be corrected by manipulative techniques in conjunction with conventional medical procedure.

Surgeon specialist in treating medical problems by manual or instrumental means. Surgeons often subspecialize in certain areas of the body.

Dermatologist specialist in the diagnosis and treatment of disorders of the skin. Dermatologists treat such problems as acne and skin cancer.

Radiologist specialist in the diagnostic and therapeutic applications of radiation. For example, a radiologist reads x-rays, and some administer radiation treatment to cancer patients.

recommendations are usually dependable. You can also call the hospital unit for that specialty and ask for recommendations.

For example, if you are looking for a cardiologist, you can call the cardiac care unit of your local hospital. Don't ask for negative information about a particular doctor. You probably won't find anyone willing to give you that information. Instead, ask for recommendations.

If the doctor you are considering works at the hospital you called but is not among those recommended, try another doctor. When possible, call more than one hospital. It may take a few calls to find someone who will give you a recommendation, but getting this inside information is worth the time spent.

Check Credentials Is the doctor board certified? **Board certified** means that the doctor has completed a training program in a specialty and has passed an exam in that specialty. To find out if a doctor you are considering is board certified, you can call the American Board of Medical Specialties at (866) 275-2267 or visit its web site.

Another good source for checking a doctor's credentials is the American

Consumer ALERT

The Internet can be a rich source of health-related information that can be as good as you'll find in a medical library. You can find articles from *The Journal of the American Medical Association* and from consumer groups concerned with health matters. You can even join an online newsgroup made up of people coping with the same disease who are exchanging information about it with each other.

But remember, the Internet is a wide-open forum. Anybody can post anything to the Web. Newsgroups of people battling chronic or life-threatening illnesses are full of advertisements for questionable cures. For example, a posting in a cancer support newsgroup tried to sell readers something to "build back up the immune system" by preventing the excretion of "co-cancerogenic K factor."

Why do you think newsgroups for people with serious diseases are a good target for questionable remedies? How would you check out a remedy you found online?

Medical Association. For information on training, specialties, and board certification of over 650,000 U.S. physicians, you can contact the AMA at (800) 621-8335 or check out the Physician Select section of its web site. The AMA's *Medical*

Directory is also available in some libraries.

Negative information about a doctor is more difficult to find. See if your library carries the publication *Questionable Doctors,* published by the Public Citizen Health Research Group. This publication lists discipline reports from medical boards in all 50 states. However, it takes many years for such reports to become public record, so no publication is likely to have a complete list of problem doctors.

What Hospital Does the Doctor Use? Doctors aren't automatically allowed to work at a hospital. They must apply for hospital privileges and meet the hospital's criteria to become part of the staff. You can safely assume that doctors on staff at a large, prestigious hospital in your area will be competent doctors. For small community hospitals, it's harder to judge. If your area has several hospitals and the doctor you are considering is on staff at more than one, then this can be an indication that the doctor is competent.

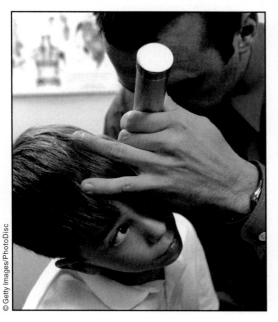

© Getty Images/PhotoDisc

COMMUNICATE

The ability to explain is a very important quality for a doctor. How difficult is it to explain something complicated in language someone else can understand? Think of a video game you played recently. In one page or less, write instructions for playing this game. Then test your communication skills. Ask a friend who has never played the game to read your instructions and try to play the game. What do you notice?

Compassion

You want a doctor with whom you feel comfortable. You want someone who will take the time to get to know you as a person. This kind of relationship is particularly important for a primary care physician. For a specialist whom you may not use often, compassion may not be as high a priority.

When you are narrowing your search, recommendations from friends and family members can help. Such recommendations can be an indication of a doctor's competence, but they may be a better reflection of the doctor's bedside manner.

Ask your friends and family if the doctor took time with them and seemed to really care. After your first visit with the doctor, evaluate for yourself. Did the doctor take the time to answer your questions? Did the doctor seem genuinely concerned? Don't be afraid to choose another doctor if you're uncomfortable with your primary care physician.

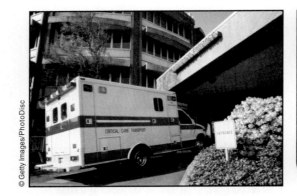

© Getty Images/PhotoDisc

Ability to Communicate

The ability to communicate includes good listening skills as well as the ability to explain clearly.

▶ Does the doctor really listen to your concerns and ask you questions to get to information you may not have thought to say?

▶ Are the doctor's explanations clear and easy to understand?

▶ Is the doctor willing to repeat the information in a different way if you do not understand?

▶ Does the doctor provide easy-to-understand written information about particular concerns?

These are all questions you can ask someone you know who currently sees that doctor. After your first visit, you can judge for yourself.

In working with your doctor, you can help the communication process by coming to the office prepared. It's easy to forget to tell the doctor something relevant to your condition, especially if you aren't feeling well.

Before your appointment, list your symptoms and anything about your medical history that the doctor should know. Include your questions and concerns. Remember, you have a responsibility to actively participate in your health care.

Hospital, Dental, and Vision Providers

Most people need dental and eye care services during their life spans. To make good choices, you should know the differences among the specialties. You may also need a hospital at some time. You have several ways to check the quality of hospitals in your area.

How to Choose a Hospital

If your community has only one hospital, then you have no choice. Also, your choices are limited to hospitals where your doctor has privileges and that are accepted by your health insurance plan. But if you have a choice after satisfying these constraints, check out your options before you need a hospital.

1. *Does the hospital meet national quality standards?* Most hospitals choose to be surveyed by the Joint Commission on Accreditation of Healthcare Organizations (JCAHO). Hospitals that meet JCAHO's quality standards receive accreditation. **Accreditation** is official recognition that the person or organization met certain quality standards for their profession. You can get a copy of a hospital's performance report by calling JCAHO at (630) 792-5000 or by visiting its web site.

2. *How does the hospital compare with others in the area?* Some states and consumer groups create hospital report cards. Some groups gather information on hospital performance and patient satisfaction. Consumer groups publish guides to hospitals. To find out what information is available for your area, call your state department of health, health care council, or hospital association.

3. *Does the hospital have experience with your condition?* For common medical problems, all hospitals have sufficient experience. But some hospitals specialize in certain less common procedures. For example, one hospital may do most of the heart surgery in your area. Hospitals that do the same types of procedures many times tend to have better success with them. Your doctor can tell you which hospitals have the most experience with your situation.

Dental Service Providers

Dental hygiene and regular checkups with a dentist are important to your overall health. The term **dentist** usually refers to someone trained in general dentistry. A dentist is like a primary care physician for your teeth. Your dentist is concerned with the overall health of your mouth and can fill cavities, extract teeth, and replace lost teeth.

Many dental offices employ a *dental hygienist.* This person is an assistant who is trained and licensed to

take x-rays and clean your teeth to help prevent gum disease and tooth decay.

The dental profession has a number of specialists as well.

▶ A *pedodontist* specializes in dentistry for children.

▶ An *orthodontist* specializes in straightening teeth that are out of normal position, usually by applying metal and wire structures called *braces.*

▶ An *oral surgeon* specializes in removing wisdom teeth, as well as more difficult surgical techniques.

▶ A *periodontist* specializes in diseases of the gums and bones that support the teeth. Gum disease is a serious problem that causes more tooth loss than any other dental problem.

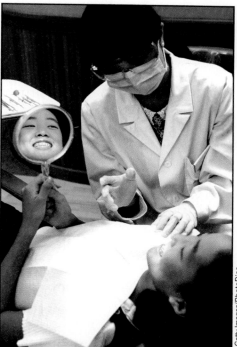

© Getty Images/PhotoDisc

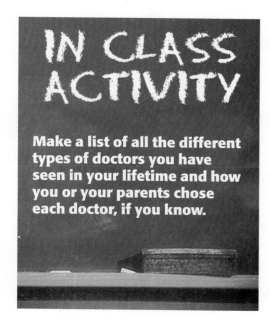

IN CLASS ACTIVITY

Make a list of all the different types of doctors you have seen in your lifetime and how you or your parents chose each doctor, if you know.

▶ An *endodontist* specializes in root canal procedures.

▶ A *prosthodontist* specializes in replacing teeth or missing jaw structures with artificial devices.

Eye Care Professionals

People often confuse the three most commonly used providers of eye care: ophthalmologist, optometrist, and optician. The difference lies in the amount of training and, therefore, the extent of the services they can provide.

Choosing the Right Provider

Only ophthalmologists and optometrists can issue prescriptions for glasses or contact lenses.

Ophthalmologists are physicians who specialize in diagnosing and treating diseases of the eyes. They can prescribe drugs, examine for eye disease, and perform eye surgery.

Optometrists are not physicians. They have a doctor of optometry degree (O.D.), which qualifies them to examine for vision problems and eye disease and prescribe eyewear. For serious diseases, optometrists will refer patients to an ophthalmologist.

Opticians fill prescriptions for eyewear written by an ophthalmologist or optometrist. They may not examine eyes or prescribe lenses.

The greater the amount of training, the higher the fee. Ophthalmologists are the most expensive provider. So if you have no serious disease and only want a routine exam or prescription for lenses, choose an optometrist.

Filling Your Prescription

You don't have to buy your glasses or contacts from the optometrist's office. This may be expensive. Federal law requires eye doctors to give you your eyeglass prescription

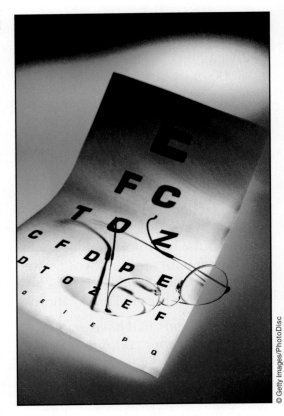

© Getty Images/PhotoDisc

and your contact lens specifications, but you may have to ask.

To fill your prescription inexpensively, compare prices among different opticians. If your prescription is fairly common, an eyewear store can be a good choice. But for complicated prescriptions, such as unusual corrections, bifocals, or trifocals, an optician may be able to provide more precise lenses than can an eyewear store.

CheckPoint

How can you judge the hospitals in your area? Why is it important to understand the differences among eye care professionals?

TRY THESE

1. What types of doctors generally serve as primary care physicians?

2. Name three medical specialties, and briefly describe what each does.

3. What are some indications that a doctor is competent?

4. What is communication, and why is it important in choosing a doctor?

5. What is compassion, and why is it important in choosing a doctor?

6. Why is a hospital's experience important in choosing a hospital?

7. What services does a dental hygienist provide?

8. Name two dental specialties and briefly describe what each does.

9. How can you decide whether to go to an ophthalmologist, optometrist, or optician?

THINK CRITICALLY

10. **CONSUMER ACTION** Liz wants to select a primary care physician from among those participating in her PPO. What qualities should she look for in a doctor? How can she evaluate doctors based on these criteria?

11. Imagine that your primary care physician, whom you have been seeing for ten years, recently joined a group with six other doctors. The policy of this group is to schedule patients for whichever doctor is free. What are the benefits of such a policy? What are its drawbacks? What would you do in this situation? Explain why.

12. **COMMUNICATE** Suppose that you have been having severe back problems, and your doctor recommends surgery. Prepare a list of questions you would want to ask your doctor. E-mail your list to your teacher.

13. Your area has two hospitals. You need to select one for your back operation. Hospital A is close to your home, and your doctor is on staff there. Hospital B is 20 miles from your home, and your doctor is not on staff there, but this hospital has a team of specialists in the kind of back surgery you need. What other information would you want to know before making a choice? Which would you choose? Why?

DECISION MAKING PROJECT

SPECIFY   **SEARCH**   **SIFT**   **SELECT**   **STUDY**

SPECIFY Pick a locally popular medical insurance plan that the Washingtons could join. Then list some important medical considerations that the Washington family has. Discuss how these considerations will affect its search for doctors and hospitals in your area.

© Getty Images/PhotoDisc

16.2 Legal Service Providers

What Lawyers Do

Television often portrays lawyers in spectacular court battles. In reality, the vast majority of legal work occurs outside of court. Most legal services involve preparing legal documents and settling disputes between individuals. You will find there are many situations in your life span when you may need a lawyer.

When You Need a Lawyer

One type of legal document that you encounter constantly in daily life is a contract. A **contract** is an agreement between two or more people that can be enforced by a court. When you apply for a credit card, rent an apartment, or take out a car loan, you must sign a contract.

You don't need a lawyer for most routine contracts you sign. But for some contracts and other legal matters, a lawyer can guide you through the maze of paperwork and procedures. For example, you may want a lawyer to help:

CONSUMER ACTION

Leonard paid $899 to have an above-ground swimming pool installed. The job was done while he was at work. When he got home, he found ruts in his lawn, and someone had driven a truck right across a flower bed and broken many of his bushes. Now the pool leaks. When Leonard called the company to complain, he was told someone would come to look at his property. No one ever came. Leonard thinks he should sue the company. What do you think he should do?

▶ prepare a premarriage agreement between you and your fiance.

▶ adopt a child.

▶ settle divorce and child custody agreements.

▶ settle a dispute with your insurance company.

▶ transfer ownership of real estate.

▶ settle a disagreement with your landlord.

▶ prepare a will.

▶ plan or settle the transfer of an estate (property) to the children upon the parents' death.

▶ sue if you are injured by someone else.

▶ defend you if you are sued.

▶ defend you if you are accused of a crime.

CYBER CONSUMER

Search the Internet for Intuit, a company that offers legal software for home use. Read about the legal services its software provides. Then check out reviews of this software at the *PC World* site or at another online software store. How much does this software cost compared to what you think you might have to pay a lawyer for such services?

© Getty Images/PhotoDisc

When You Don't Need a Lawyer

Sometimes, you can handle uncomplicated legal matters without hiring a lawyer. For example, a **will** is a written declaration of how you want your property divided when you die. If you own a large amount of real estate and investments, you may want to have a lawyer prepare your will. But if you own about as much as a typical American, you can prepare your own will.

For $20 to $30, you can buy software that will walk you through the steps in preparing a will. For $50 to $60, you can buy software that helps you with a will plus many other routine legal documents, such as estate planning, lease agreements, and purchase agreements. Or for only a few dollars, you can buy paper forms from office supply stores.

After you prepare your own will or other legal document, you may want to hire a lawyer to review it to make sure everything is legally enforceable. This kind of review is much less expensive than having the lawyer prepare the document itself.

Other types of professionals can handle some legal matters for you without a lawyer. Accountants can deal with your routine tax issues. Your banker or financial planner can help you plan your estate.

Real estate agents are trained in the process of transferring ownership of real estate from seller to buyer. If you are uncomfortable with the legal documents provided by the real estate agent, you can get a lawyer's review. When you buy or sell a house without a real estate agent, however, you will need a lawyer to help you transfer ownership. Banks usually require you to have a lawyer at your closing when you get a mortgage.

© Getty Images/PhotoDisc

About Fees

Lawyers usually charge in one of three ways: hourly, a flat rate, or a percentage of the proceeds. An hourly rate is most common. Be aware, though, that when you are paying by the hour, you will likely pay for phone calls, even brief ones, plus photocopying or any other routine office task related to your matter.

Flat Fees   Flat fees are often charged for preparing routine legal documents, such as a will or house purchase agreement. This type of payment is less risky because you will know the costs up front.

Percentage Fees   To settle an estate, sometimes lawyers charge a percentage of the value of the estate. If the property and assets in the estate have a high value, this percentage can amount to a huge sum. Try to avoid this kind of payment plan. It will generally cost you more than you would pay by the hour.

Contingency Fees   Another type of percentage payment plan is a **contingency fee**. This is a percentage

MATH OF MONEY

Laura's mother passed away, leaving her a house worth $120,000 and investments totaling $40,000. Laura is looking for a lawyer to help her through the legal process of settling the estate. One lawyer she talked to offered to do the job for 25 percent of the estate. Another would charge a flat fee of $30,000. Which lawyer should she hire? How much would she save by hiring this lawyer?

SOLUTION

By hiring the lawyer who charges a flat fee, she would save $10,000.

$120,000 + $40,000 = $160,000 total value of the estate

$160,000 × 0.25 = $40,000

$40,000 − $30,000 = $10,000 total saving

of the cash award in a lawsuit, such as for personal injury. In effect, the lawyer is sharing the risk. If you win the case, the lawyer gets a percentage. If you lose, you pay only expenses, which should be specified upfront.

A contingency arrangement can make it possible for people to get legal services who might otherwise be unable to afford them. The percentage deducted from the award, however, can leave you with very little after expenses are paid. Be careful about accepting this kind of fee arrangement. If possible, make sure that the expenses are deducted before the lawyer takes a percentage, so that the expenses don't come out of your portion alone.

CheckPoint

What kinds of legal matters could you reasonably handle yourself? When would it be wise to hire a lawyer?

How to Choose a Lawyer

Each state has its own *bar,* which is the body of lawyers licensed to practice in the state. To receive a license, lawyers must graduate from an accredited law school and pass the state's bar examination.

Many lawyers have a general practice. They provide a wide variety of legal services, from drawing up a bill of sale to handling common kinds of court cases. Some lawyers, particularly in big cities, specialize in a branch of law. They may be experts in law related to corporations, the government, or criminal prosecution.

A lawyer in general practice can provide most of the services that a typical consumer might want. But if you own a business or have a complicated financial situation, you may need a specialist in business or tax law.

Get Recommendations

The best way to find a good lawyer is to start with recommendations from friends, family, and coworkers. You might also ask for recommendations

Buy the Numbers?

Your apartment repeatedly flooded due to faulty plumbing. You are angry with your landlord, and you have proof of his negligence. Your renter's insurance covers damage to your property, but your deductible is $500. The property loss you suffered totaled $2,500. If you file a claim with your insurance company, your premium will go up about $20 a year. Your insurance company will probably sue your landlord to recover its losses.

According to state laws, you can sue for damages in small claims court. The filing fees and court costs are $200. You might not win, but your case is strong. Also, even if the small claims court rules in your favor, you will have to get the landlord to pay the damages. What would you do?

from other professionals with whom you have worked, such as your accountant or real estate agent.

Make up a list of recommended lawyers and call their offices. Ask if they have handled cases similar to yours, if they are taking new clients, and whether they charge for an initial consultation.

After you have narrowed your list with these questions, look into their backgrounds. By calling your local bar association, you can confirm that a particular lawyer is licensed to practice. Your local bar association may also have a web site with information about lawyers in your area.

Your library is likely to have a legal directory, such as the *Martindale-Hubbell Law Directory* or another that is commonly used in your area. This kind of directory can tell you when lawyers were licensed, where they went to school, and sometimes their areas of expertise.

Some states have disciplinary agencies associated with the state bar association or state supreme court. In these states, the disciplinary agencies will tell you if the lawyers you are considering have any complaints lodged against them. Look in your phone book for the state court offices or bar association.

© Getty Images/PhotoDisc

Ask Questions

Set up interviews with several possible choices. Be sure there is no charge for an interview. Before going to the interviews, prepare a list of questions similar to these.

▶ How have you handled matters similar to mine?

▶ What are the possible outcomes?

▶ How long do you expect this matter to take?

▶ How will you keep me informed?

▶ How do you charge—flat fee, hourly, or on contingency?

▶ If you charge by the hour, what is your hourly rate?

▶ Will an assistant handle some of the work at a lower rate?

▶ If you charge a flat fee, what is it, and what happens if something unforeseen occurs?

▶ If you charge on contingency, what percentage of the settlement would you charge, and can that percentage be taken after expenses have been deducted?

▶ What is the total bill likely to be?

▶ Can I do some of the work to help reduce the cost?

▶ What other information do you need from me to help you do your job?

When you are talking to the lawyer, evaluate how well the lawyer communicates. Does the person listen and explain well and treat you with respect? If not, remove that lawyer from your list. Then choose a lawyer you feel comfortable talking with and who seems to approach your case the way you want.

Working with Your Lawyer

The law and the lawyer's code of ethics protect the confidentiality of your communications with your lawyer. Lawyers cannot be required to reveal any information provided to them by their clients. This legal right allows you to speak with your lawyer openly and honestly.

To get the best advice possible, you must give your lawyer complete and accurate information. In return, your lawyer is ethically bound to look out for your interests.

When you meet with your lawyer, come prepared. Know the facts. Bring copies of all relevant documents. Have a list of questions that you want to ask. If you are paying by the hour, good preparation will save you money as well as help your lawyer do a good job for you.

Remember that you hired the lawyer, so you are the boss. Your lawyer should not make important decisions without consulting you. You should hold up your end of the deal by communicating all relevant information completely and honestly.

Sources of Low-Cost Legal Services

Legal-Services Plans   Check with your employer, union, or other organizations to which you belong to see if they offer a legal-services plan. This type of plan is similar to a managed-care health insurance plan. Legal advice is relatively inexpensive, but your choice of lawyer and amount of coverage are restricted. Still, if the plan offers lawyers with a wide range of specialties, the plan may be worth joining.

Legal Aid   The term **legal aid** refers to any of several programs that provide legal services for people who cannot afford a lawyer. Legal-aid agencies are sponsored by charitable organizations, law schools, bar associations, and the federal, state, and local governments.

Legal-aid agencies handle contracts and disputes between individuals, such as adoptions, bankruptcies, divorces, and job and rent disputes. The law prohibits legal-aid agencies from using federal funds in criminal cases.

PRIMARYSOURCES

Women and other minorities have not always been part of the professional world, the legal world included. Clara Shortridge Foltz became California's first female attorney in 1878, after pushing through legislation to allow women to practice law. She met much resistance. Apply Ms. Foltz's thinking to other minorities and the law. How can knowing the law help ethnic minorities?

Women today? Those in poverty? Immigrants?

"But we are told that if women go into the legal profession, it will destroy our homes.... Think you that knowledge of law will destroy our homes? That is not the legitimate effect of knowledge of any kind. On the contrary, a knowledge of the law of our land will make women better mothers, better wives, and better citizens."

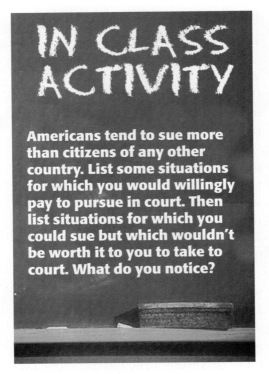

IN CLASS ACTIVITY

Americans tend to sue more than citizens of any other country. List some situations for which you would willingly pay to pursue in court. Then list situations for which you could sue but which wouldn't be worth it to you to take to court. What do you notice?

Public Defender   By law, people accused of a crime have a right to legal counsel. For those unable to pay for a lawyer, the court will appoint and pay for a **public defender** to represent them. Public defenders often are new lawyers who accept this kind of low-paid work to gain experience. They provide an important service by defending people who otherwise could not afford a qualified lawyer.

Legal Clinics   Millions of middle-income Americans cannot afford to hire a lawyer. Yet they do not qualify for the free legal-aid services available to the poor. To help solve this problem, some lawyers in large cities have set up legal clinics. These clinics offer routine legal services at reduced rates.

Mediation or Arbitration Lawsuits can be very expensive to settle in court. A less expensive and often faster alternative is to take your dispute to a mediator or arbitrator. In mediation, you and the other person try to work out your dispute yourselves with the help of a neutral third party called a **mediator**. The mediator does not pass judgment. Instead, this person listens to both sides and makes suggestions.

An **arbitrator** is also a neutral third party chosen by both sides. But an arbitrator has the power to make a decision in the case. The disputing parties may or may not be required to abide by the arbitrator's decision. You can find qualified mediators and arbitrators through the American Arbitration Association or the Better Business Bureau.

Small Claims Court   In Chapter 3 you learned that for disputes involving relatively small amounts of money, you can avoid lawyers' fees altogether by taking your suit to a small claims court. The amount considered a small claim varies from state to state. The upper limit could be $1,000 in one state and $10,000 in another.

Small claims courts often deal with such issues as a homeowner suing a builder, a tenant suing a landlord, or a buyer suing a seller. However, if you win, it is up to you to collect. So before you file a suit with small claims court, try to determine whether the person you are suing actually has the means to pay.

CheckPoint

What steps would you follow to select a lawyer? What are some less expensive ways to obtain legal services?

TRY THESE

1. Name five common legal services for which consumers hire lawyers.

2. What kinds of legal tasks can you do yourself?

3. What are three ways that lawyers charge for their services?

4. Why should you interview lawyers before you choose one?

5. What is confidentiality between lawyer and client, and why is it important?

6. What is the difference between a mediator and an arbitrator?

7. What is legal aid? Who might need their services?

THINK CRITICALLY

8. **CONSUMER ACTION** Leonard is dissatisfied with the installation of a pool in his backyard. What options does he have? What do you think he should do?

9. **MATH OF MONEY** Antonio and Carlotta want to hire a lawyer. Lawyer A charges $100 per hour but will charge $45 per hour for his assistant's time. He estimates that the legal process will take about six hours of his time and two hours of his assistant's time. Lawyer B will charge a flat fee of $750. Which lawyer should they choose? How much would they save by choosing this lawyer? What else should they consider in their decision?

10. Suppose you left a pan on your stove and forgot to turn off the burner. The pan overheated causing a fire. Your insurance company didn't pay as much for the damages as you thought they should according to your policy. You hired a lawyer to help you sue the company. You know the fire was your fault. Should you tell your lawyer how the fire started? What could happen if you do? What could happen if you don't?

11. Some people believe that contingency fees should be legally limited to 25 percent. Evaluate this idea. Do you believe it would serve the best interests of consumers? Explain your answer.

DECISION MAKING PROJECT

 SPECIFY SEARCH SIFT SELECT STUDY

SEARCH Have one group member contact the recommended insurance plan to ask for a provider list. Let them know you are calling for information for a class. Then ask how a family like the Washingtons should go about getting care for important medical considerations. Assign one recommended medical provider or hospital to each group member to research. Look for information about competence, compassion, and communication.

© Getty Images/PhotoDisc

GOALS

DESCRIBE
various welfare programs

DISCUSS
two major social insurance programs

16.3 Government Assistance

Welfare

The general term for government programs that provide money, medical care, food, housing, and other necessities for people who cannot afford them is **welfare**.

Government welfare programs are also called *public assistance.* To be eligible for welfare benefits, a family's income and other financial resources must be near or below the amount defined by the federal government as the poverty line. The government establishes the **poverty line** for families of different sizes and revises the amount each year.

Americans may find themselves living in poverty for a variety of reasons. Some people lack skills necessary to earn a *living income* that would allow them to escape poverty. Others suffer from chronic illnesses that prevent them from working. Victims of crime may fall into poverty because of physical or mental trauma they have suffered. The same may happen to the families of those convicted of a crime. It is difficult to support your family when you are serving time in jail. Recent immigrants may live in poverty

CONSUMER **ACTION**

Leona is a single mother of two children. She worked as a checker for a grocery store until she was laid off last week. Leona doesn't know how she will pay the rent or put food on the table. She wants to look for work but can't pay anyone to watch her children. What government assistance may Leona receive? How should she go about finding help?

while they adjust to life in their new country. The largest group of people who live in poverty, however, are children. Often they belong to households with only one parent. It can be difficult for a single parent to both earn a living income and take care of children.

TANF

Before 1996, families below the poverty line received assistance through the Aid to Families with Dependent Children (AFDC) program.

The Personal Responsibilities and Work Opportunity Reconciliation Act (PRWORA) in 1996 eliminated AFDC and replaced it with a program called **Temporary Assistance for Needy Families (TANF)**. TANF changed the welfare system to one that requires work in exchange for public assistance and limits the length of time people may receive assistance. In most cases, able-bodied people receiving assistance must be working within two years. Adults in the family may receive assistance for no more than five years throughout their lives.

The goals of TANF are to promote work, responsibility, and self-sufficiency. Previously, poor families could receive assistance indefinitely, which influenced some people not to work.

Each state receives federal funds to operate the TANF program. The states are then responsible for developing and administering their own TANF programs based on federal guidelines. By granting money to the states, the federal government gives the states the flexibility to design programs that can best serve the needs of their population.

VOTE Your Wallet

The 1996 Personal Responsibilities and Work Opportunity Reconciliation Act (PRWORA) eliminated food stamp benefits for legal immigrants in the United States. The purpose of this change was to discourage people who were unable to support themselves from coming to the United States. Public pressure, however, caused Congress to restore food stamp benefits to legal immigrants in 1998. This decision benefited about 250,000 people at an estimated cost of $800 million per year.

Who do you think is paying for this benefit? Was this the right thing for the government to do?

Food Stamps

For over 40 years, the federal government has issued coupons called **food stamps** to low-income people to help them buy food. The PRWORA requires states to convert from paper coupons to an electronic system. This transition was taking place in 2004. The Act also limits the time that recipients without dependents may receive food stamps.

SSI

The welfare program that aids low-income people who are at least 65 years old, blind, or disabled is called **Supplemental Security Income (SSI)**.

This program is funded and administered by the federal government and supplemented by some states.

A major difference between SSI and Social Security is the income qualification. To receive SSI, the family's income must be below the poverty line. Social Security provides benefits to participants, regardless of their income.

Programs for Families with Children

Several government programs are designed to help low-income mothers keep their children healthy. The **Women, Infants, and Children (WIC) Program** provides nutrition education and coupons for free healthful foods for pregnant women, new mothers, and children up to age 5. The food coupons can be exchanged only for food that meets WIC's standards for nutrition.

The national **Head Start** program provides developmental and learning activities for low-income preschool children, ages 3 to 5. The program emphasizes parental involvement in the child's activities. Each child in the program also receives medical and dental services.

The **National School Lunch Program** provides low-cost or free nutritionally balanced lunches for needy school children. School districts that participate get cash subsidies from the federal government to purchase food, and they get surplus food products donated by the Department of Agriculture.

Other government services designed to aid low-income families with children include childcare while parents work, child protective services against abuse and neglect, and foster care. The Administration

What In The World?

Sweden has an extensive welfare program. Everyone receives free medical services. Families raising children receive cash allowances. Newly married couples can get financial aid to buy home furnishings. Swedes who lose their jobs receive a large percentage of their former wages in unemployment benefits. After retirement, most Swedes receive annual pensions of about 65 percent of their average earnings during their 15 highest paid years. In exchange for all these benefits, Swedes pay very high taxes. What do you think of this system? Would you be willing to give up a larger portion of every paycheck in taxes to receive these benefits?

What does poverty mean to you? Make a list of characteristics of the lives of poverty-stricken people. Search the Web for poverty statistics. Send your definition along with these poverty statistics to your teacher in an e-mail.

for Children and Families, part of the Department of Health and Human Services, runs these family-oriented programs.

Housing

The Department of Housing and Urban Development (HUD) makes funds available to local housing authorities to provide public housing. **Public housing** is housing built specifically for low-income people. Local housing authorities first determine the need for public housing in their area, and then plan, create, and manage the housing projects.

The housing authorities may construct new buildings or buy and rehabilitate existing buildings. They may also lease housing rather than buy it. Low-income people then rent these homes at reduced rates. HUD pays the difference between the amount the renters can afford and the true cost of the housing. A family pays no more than 30 percent of its income for rent.

Mortgage insurance is another way that HUD helps people afford housing. The Federal Housing Administration (FHA), an agency of HUD, insures mortgages so that

lenders will be more willing to make loans with low down payments to people with lower incomes.

CheckPoint

What kinds of government assistance are available to people in financial need?

Social Security

Welfare differs from another government financial program called *Social Security*. Unlike welfare, Social Security provides benefits to people regardless of their income.

Social Security, also called *social insurance*, provides cash payments to help replace income lost as a result of retirement, unemployment, disability, or death. The purpose of Social Security is to give workers, retired workers, and their families some amount of economic security.

Programs established by the Social Security Act of 1935, include:

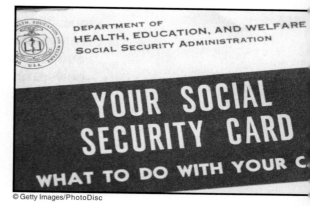

DEPARTMENT OF HEALTH, EDUCATION, AND WELFARE SOCIAL SECURITY ADMINISTRATION

YOUR SOCIAL SECURITY CARD

WHAT TO DO WITH YOUR C

© Getty Images/PhotoDisc

▶ old-age, disability, survivors, and health insurance

▶ unemployment compensation

▶ workers' compensation

Throughout your working years, you will pay into the Social Security system through payroll taxes. Your employer will contribute an equal amount. When you reach retirement age, you will be entitled to Social Security benefits. The amount of your benefits depends on:

▶ the amount you have contributed into the system.

▶ your age at retirement.

The normal retirement age to receive full social security benefits is currently 65, but will gradually increase to 67 for people born in 1960 or later. You may retire and collect benefits as early as age 62, but your benefits will be reduced.

Social Security was never meant to provide all the funds a retired worker needs to live. It was created to *supplement* workers' savings.

Unemployment Compensation

The government-sponsored insurance program designed to provide income for people who have lost their jobs through no fault of their own is **unemployment compensation**. If you quit your job or are fired for good reason, you probably won't qualify for unemployment compensation. But you may qualify if you are laid off.

Most of the funding for the program comes from employers. The rules and benefits vary widely from one state to another. Generally, if you are laid off, you will receive approximately half your former salary up to a maximum weekly amount. Your benefits may last for up to 26 weeks. During times when an unusually large number of people are unemployed, the government may extend the benefit period. This happened in March of 2002.

© Getty Images/PhotoDisc

When you apply for benefits at the state unemployment office, you must also apply for help in finding work. During the time you are unemployed, you must be actively seeking work to continue receiving benefits.

How to Apply for Government Benefits

To receive any kind of government benefits, you have to meet the program's qualifications and fill out an application. The location and phone number of each state's department of social services can be found in your telephone book. The listing will appear in either a special government office section or in the white pages under your state or local government.

Qualifications for welfare assistance vary from state to state. If you need help buying the basic necessities of life, call your local social services office. Explain your situation and ask what programs might help you. Find out what the qualifications are for the assistance you need.

Bring Documents Ask what documents you must bring with you to the office. You are likely to need your Social Security number, birth certificate, birth certificates of your spouse and children, savings and checking account information, and recent tax forms to show your income. If you are applying for disability benefits, you will also have to provide medical records.

Waiting Periods Social Security disability benefits have a five-month waiting period. The waiting period for unemployment compensation varies from state to state but is usually one week. Your Social Security benefits have a three-month waiting period.

If You Are Turned Down If you are unfairly turned down for assistance, ask for an explanation of the decision. If you are not satisfied with the explanation, ask to see the social service representative's manager. Some social service offices have client advocates who will help people. As a final resort, enlist the support of your elected officials.

CheckPoint

How do Social Security programs help people gain some economic security?

TRY THESE

1. How has TANF changed the U.S. welfare system?

2. What is a major difference between SSI and Social Security?

3. What are some programs available to help low-income women and children?

4. What are some possible links between crime and poverty?

5. What is the difference between welfare and social insurance?

6. What is the main purpose of the retirement benefits under Social Security?

THINK CRITICALLY

7. **CONSUMER ACTION** Leona lost her job and now needs help making ends meet. Describe some of the government programs for which she might qualify. What must Leona do to receive this assistance?

8. There is a national debate over whether workers who go on strike should receive unemployment compensation or welfare. What do you think? Explain your position.

9. Why are immigrants among those groups of people that are more likely to find themselves living in poverty? Should the government offer assistance to immigrants? If so, what kind of assistance?

10. Why do you think the government has many welfare programs designed for women and young children?

DECISION MAKING PROJECT

● SPECIFY   ● SEARCH   ● SIFT   ● SELECT   ● STUDY

SIFT Have all group members present the information they received from their assigned provider or hospital. Make a grid so your group can compare the providers or hospitals on the criteria of competence, compassion, and communication.

ASSESSMENT

KEY IDEAS

Health Care Providers

1. The key qualities to look for in any doctor are competence, compassion, and the ability to communicate.
2. Most adults choose an internist or family practitioner as their primary care physician because these doctors provide a broad range of care.
3. Hospital workers often know the reputations of doctors, so they are a good source of recommendations.
4. You can check a doctor's credentials by contacting the AMA and American Board of Medical Specialties.
5. Check the hospital's accreditation and performance report card.
6. You should have a regular dentist for routine checkups and preventive care.
7. For serious eye disease, see an ophthalmologist. For routine exams, see an optometrist. An optician can fill your prescription.

Legal Service Providers

8. You may need a lawyer for such things as a premarriage agreement, divorce, a will, or settling disputes.
9. If your situation is uncomplicated, you can prepare some legal documents yourself.
10. Lawyers may charge by the hour, a flat fee, a percentage fee, or a contingency fee.
11. A lawyer in general practice can handle most of your legal needs.
12. Consult a law directory to make sure the lawyers are licensed and have experience in the work you want.
13. Low-cost legal services may be available from a legal clinic or legal-services plan offered by an organization you belong to. If you are below the poverty level, you may get services from a legal-aid agency or public defender.

Government Assistance

14. *Welfare* is a general term for government programs that provide money, medical care, food, housing, and other necessities for people who otherwise cannot afford them.
15. The Temporary Assistance for Needy Families (TANF) program requires work in exchange for public assistance and limits the amount of time people may receive assistance.
16. Food stamps are coupons issued by the federal government to low-income people to help them buy food.
17. Supplemental Security Income (SSI) is a welfare program for low-income people who are at least 65 years old, blind, or disabled.
18. The WIC Program provides nutrition education and food for women and young children. Head Start offers a variety of developmental and learning experiences for low-income preschool children. The National School Lunch Program provides nutritious lunches to needy school children.
19. HUD helps low-income people obtain affordable housing.
20. Social Security is social insurance that provides cash payments to help replace income lost as a result of retirement, unemployment, disability, or death.
21. To receive government benefits, you must qualify according to the program's criteria, and you must apply at a social services office.

TERMS REVIEW

Match each term on the left with its definition on the right.
Some terms may not be used.

a. accreditation

b. arbitrator

c. board certified

d. contract

e. contingency fee

f. dentist

g. family practitioner

h. food stamps

i. Head Start

j. internist

k. legal aid

l. mediator

m. National School Lunch Program

n. obstetrician/gynecologist (OBGYN)

o. ophthalmologist

p. pediatrician

q. poverty line

r. public defender

s. public housing

t. Social Security

u. Supplemental Security Income (SSI)

v. Temporary Assistance for Needy Families (TANF)

w. unemployment compensation

x. welfare

y. will

z. Women, Infants, and Children (WIC) Program

1. welfare program to aid low-income people who are at least 65 years old, blind, or disabled

2. specialist in the physical, emotional, and social health of children from birth to young adulthood

3. written declaration of how you want your property divided when you die

4. lawyer appointed and paid by the court to defend someone accused of a crime who is unable to pay for legal representation

5. general term for government programs that provide money, medical care, food, housing, and other necessities for people who otherwise cannot afford them

6. income level, established by the federal government, that helps determine who is eligible for welfare benefits

7. welfare program that requires work in exchange for public assistance and limits the amount of time people may receive assistance

8. physician who specializes in diagnosing and treating diseases of the eyes

9. lawyer's fee arrangement in which the lawyer receives a percentage of the cash award in a lawsuit

10. any of several programs that provide legal services for people who cannot afford a lawyer

11. government-sponsored insurance program designed to provide income for people who have lost their jobs through no fault of their own

12. agreement between two or more people that can be enforced by a court

13. someone trained in general dentistry

14. neutral third party that listens and makes suggestions in a legal dispute

CONSUMER DECISIONS

15. A new doctor just moved into your community. She recently finished her training and wants to develop a practice quickly. To attract new patients, she is offering free flu shots to anyone who visits her for a physical examination. These shots are not normally covered by health insurance plans. Would you go for an exam? How would you decide whether to become her patient?

16. You moved out of an apartment into a new home. You left the apartment in good condition, and your landlord said he would return your $800 deposit in a month. Now, two months later, the landlord refuses to return the deposit, saying that you didn't give enough notice before you moved out. What are your alternatives? What would you do?

17. Suppose you are a single parent of two children. You have been receiving welfare benefits under the TANF program for the past year. These benefits amount to nearly $600 a month. They will run out one year from now. You have been offered a job that will pay $900 a month. How would you decide whether or not to accept this job offer?

THINK CRITICALLY

18. Imagine that you are in charge of your state's public assistance program. The governor has asked you to reduce your agency's spending by 10 percent. You have identified the following alternatives. Each would reduce spending by 5 percent. Which ones would you choose? Explain your answer.

Eliminate all payments to single people who are physically able to work.

Eliminate any extra payments to women who receive welfare now and have more children.

Reduce all welfare payments by 5 percent.

Stop making any exceptions to the two-year limit on receiving benefits.

Lay off 20 percent of your case workers.

LOOK IT UP

19. TANF has now been in use for several years. One of its main goals is to encourage people to get off welfare. Investigate how well it is achieving this objective.

20. Find out what legal services are offered by the American Civil Liberties Union. Search the

WHICH IS THE BEST DEAL?

Imagine that you are married, run a business, and have a child. You and your spouse want to prepare a will. You have talked to two lawyers and have identified the following alternatives. Which would you choose? Why?

Alternative 1 Hire lawyer A, who will do the will for a flat fee of $500.

Alternative 2 Hire lawyer B, who will charge $80 per hour and estimates that it may take about four hours but says that figuring out how to include the business might create some additional complications.

Alternative 3 Spend $60 for a software program to use in preparing the will yourself.

POINT YOUR BROWSER TO

www.ee4c.swlearning.com
Complete the activity for Chapter 16.

Internet or your library, or check your telephone book to see if there is a local office you may call.

21. Investigate the requirements of becoming a doctor or lawyer. Are there differences among the states? What are the requirements in your state? Would you choose either of these as your career goal?

22. Each state sets its own upper limit for the amount of a claim that can be settled in small claims court. Find out what that limit is in your state.

23. Find out the income figure that the federal government has established as the poverty line for a family of four this year.

INSIDE THE NUMBERS

24. Unusually high birth rates just after World War II created a large pool of workers in the U.S. These workers' taxes have been supporting social security benefits for the relatively smaller population of current retirees. Now, this "baby boom" generation is starting to retire and draw Social Security benefits. What does this mean to the generation of young workers now entering the labor force? What problems might this cause? What changes could be made in the Social Security system to deal with these problems?

CURRICULUM CONNECTION

25. **GOVERNMENT** Many political leaders in the United States became lawyers before they went into politics. Identify and study the life of one such leader. How did that legal training contribute to a successful political career?

26. **WORLD STUDIES** All developed nations have public assistance programs. Choose a foreign nation and investigate its welfare system. Compare it with the U.S. system. What are the similarities and differences? Do you think that country's system would work in the United States? Explain.

JOURNAL RECAP

27. After reading this chapter, review the answers you wrote to the questions in Journal Journey. Have your opinions changed?

DECISION MAKING PROJECT

 SPECIFY SEARCH SIFT SELECT STUDY

SELECT Based on your comparison, make a recommendation on a provider and hospital that would be in the Washingtons' health plan. Write a letter to the family explaining your recommendations. Include your comparison grid.

STUDY Present your letter and grid to the class. Did anyone else choose the provider and hospital that your group chose? Did anyone else decide against a provider or hospital you chose? Why?

Chapter

17

GLOBAL ECONOMY
WHAT IT MEANS TO YOU

WHAT'S AHEAD

EXPLODING MYTHS

Fact or Myth?
What do you think is true?

1. How well the economy works is determined by business and political decisions, not by consumers.

2. International trade harms U.S. consumers.

3. Poor countries cannot trade with other nations because they have nothing of value to trade.

JOURNAL JOURNEY

WRITE IN YOUR JOURNAL ABOUT THE FOLLOWING.

ECONOMIC GROWTH What does a "growing economy" mean? What causes an economy to grow? How does a growing economy affect you and your family?

INTERNATIONAL TRADE Why does the U.S. trade with other nations? As a consumer, how do you benefit from trade?

INFLATION What is "inflation"? How does inflation affect you as a consumer?

DECISION MAKING PROJECT

● SPECIFY ● SEARCH ● SIFT ● SELECT ● STUDY

IT'S A SMALL WORLD Your group will compare the cost of a fast-food meal in the United States to the cost of one in another country. Then decide whether you would buy a fast-food meal if you lived in the other country.

GOAL

To learn about how currency exchange works

PROJECT PROCESS

SPECIFY	Lesson 17.1
SEARCH	Lesson 17.2
SIFT	Lesson 17.3
SELECT	Lesson 17.4
STUDY	Chapter Assessment

GOALS

DISCUSS
what international
trade is and why
nations trade

DESCRIBE
ways that nations limit
or promote trade

© Getty Images/PhotoDisc

17.1 The Nature of International Trade

What Is International Trade?

Are you wearing athletic shoes? If you are, there is better than a 99 percent chance that your shoes were not produced in the United States. Almost all athletic shoes, along with many other products Americans purchase, are imports. An **import** is a good or service that one country *buys* from another country.

A good or service that one country *sells* to another is an **export**. So, for example, Nikes made in China and sold in the United States are *exports* for the Chinese and *imports* for Americans. Computer software made in the United States and sold in China are *exports* for Americans and *imports* for the Chinese.

CONSUMER ACTION

Harold has a cup of coffee with his cereal and sliced bananas every morning. Then he drives his Toyota to work. His fiance, Carol, is a photographer for the paper. She uses a Nikon camera and Fuji film for her work. On Fridays, Harold and Carol go to their favorite restaurant and order chicken lo mein. Later they watch DVDs on Harold's television. Sometimes they just sit and talk. One of their favorite topics is U.S. trade with other nations. They believe that the United States could get along quite nicely without other countries. What do you think? How do Harold and Carol benefit from trade? How would their lives change without it?

Balance of Trade

A country has a **trade deficit** when it spends more on imports than it earns from exports. When a country earns more from exports than it spends on imports, it has a **trade surplus**.

Nations trade services as well as goods. In trading services, the United States sells more than it buys. In 2004, the U.S. had a trade surplus in services of about $60 billion.

The value of all of a country's exports minus the value of all of its imports is the country's **balance of trade**.

exports − imports = balance of trade

When the result of this calculation is a negative number, the country has a balance of trade deficit. When it is positive, the country has a balance of trade surplus.

In 2004, the United States imported about $1,260 billion worth of goods and services. In recent years, the value of U.S. exports has approached $720 billion. The United States spends $640 billion more to buy imported goods and services than it earns by selling exported goods and services. This difference is the U.S. trade deficit.

Countries trade with each other because they benefit from trade. All countries can make some products more efficiently than other products. In production, *efficiency* means achieving the most output for the resources used. By making and selling the products they make efficiently, countries earn money they can use to buy products they can't make as efficiently.

Absolute and Comparative Advantage

There is always a single country that is most efficient at producing each product. Suppose Italy is able to manufacture microwave ovens at a lower cost than any other nation. It is absolutely the most efficient producer of this product. If this is true, Italy might specialize in producing microwave ovens. It could trade its ovens for other products that it cannot produce as efficiently. In this way, it would maximize the quantity of microwave ovens it is able to produce. Economists would say that Italy has an **absolute advantage** in producing microwave ovens.

© Getty Images/PhotoDisc

What is the situation for nations that are not the most efficient producer of any product? Economic theory says they can still benefit from trade. Suppose Peru does not have an absolute advantage in producing any product. Other countries produce every product that Peru can make using fewer resources. Peru can still benefit from trade according to the theory of **comparative advantage**.

Imagine that workers in Peru produce high-quality leather shoes. They are not as efficient in producing shoes as people in some nations. The production of shoes, however, is the most efficient use of their resources. When it comes to making products that are not shoes, Peruvians are much less efficient than people in other countries. Logic tells us that people in Peru should use their resources to produce shoes. They should trade shoes for products that they cannot make as efficiently. Peru has a comparative advantage in producing shoes because this is the most efficient use of its resources.

By specializing in producing shoes and trading for other products, the people of Peru will be better off.

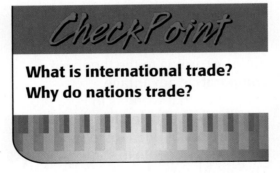

CheckPoint

What is international trade? Why do nations trade?

Trade Barriers and Agreements

Free trade is a nation's economic policy of permitting its citizens to buy and sell where they please without restrictions. In practice, trade is hardly ever completely free. For various reasons, countries impose barriers that restrict trade. The most common trade barriers are tariffs and quotas.

Tariffs   A **tariff** is a tax on imported goods. Tariffs make imported goods more expensive to buy. The higher the tariff on a product, the higher the price to consumers. The higher the price, the less consumers will buy. Fewer sales will then cause less of this product to be imported.

For example, suppose there was a 10 percent tariff on cars imported into the United States. A car produced in Germany might have a value of $15,000 when it is shipped to this country. It would be taxed 10 percent, or $1,500, when it entered the United States. This tax would increase its price to U.S. consumers. Similar U.S.-made cars would then be less expensive than the German import, causing consumers to buy more U.S. cars and fewer German imports. Lower sales would result in fewer German cars being imported. This is how tariffs act as barriers to trade.

Quotas   Nations sometimes set a limit on the amount of a product that can be imported. This trade barrier is called a **quota**. Quotas are most often used when a country produces some, but not all, of a product that it wants.

For example, suppose the United States is able to grow half the sugar Americans consume, 10 million tons each year. It could set a limit of another 10 million tons that could be imported. This quota would protect U.S. sugar farmers. They would be assured that they would have half of the U.S. sugar market.

Quotas are most often used for raw materials and agricultural products. They are barriers to trade because once a product's quota is reached, no more of that product may be imported.

Why Nations Create Trade Barriers

The theory of comparative advantage indicates that nations benefit from free trade. Why, then, do they create trade barriers? Why limit something that helps people have more of the things they want? Doing so is called **protectionism**. Economists have identified three basic reasons for this policy. Each of these theories limits international trade to protect the nation's own self-interest.

To Help Young Industries

When industries first operate, they are expensive and often inefficient to run. They could fail if they must compete with developed industries in other nations. For this reason, nations often protect their new industries with tariffs to give them a chance to develop into successful, competitive businesses.

About 50 years ago, Brazil wanted to develop its automobile industry. The cars and trucks produced there then were expensive

© Getty Images/PhotoDisc

and of low quality. Without protection, Brazil's auto industry could not compete.

To help its auto industry, Brazil's government placed high tariffs on imported vehicles that made them so expensive that few people could pay for them. Most Brazilians bought cars made by their own factories. Brazilian consumers paid more for lower-quality cars, but this policy

What In The World?

In recent years, Japan's imports of foreign food products have grown by as much as 50 percent per year. These imports have contributed to lower food prices in Japan. Some of Japan's political leaders worry that their nation may be too dependent on imported food. But there isn't enough good farm land in Japan to grow food for all its people, and fewer young Japanese want to be farmers than in the past.

If you lived in Japan, would you buy imported food? How does this situation demonstrate comparative advantage?

helped Brazil's automotive industry grow and become more efficient.

To Support National Security

Some products are important for nations to produce themselves, even inefficiently. They may need the products to run their economy or defend their country. Even if they can buy these products for less from other countries, they may want to produce at least a portion of them at home to reduce dependency on other nations for such critical products.

Steel and aluminum are often considered critical products. If too many of these products are imported, it could put U.S. producers out of business. If war breaks out, the United States wouldn't have the materials to produce the weapons to defend itself. The United States might even be at war with the countries that it depends on for steel and aluminum. Protectionists believe that nations should use tariffs and quotas to protect defense-related industries in the country.

To Protect Jobs
Some people believe that tariffs should be put on products imported from nations with low wage rates. The average factory hourly wage is $15 in the United States, about $3 in Mexico, and in some Caribbean nations and in parts of Asia less than $1. Such low wages make some products less expensive to produce and to buy.

It can be difficult for U.S. businesses to compete with companies that pay their workers such low wages. To do so, U.S. businesses may have to reduce workers' wages or send production to countries where wage costs are lower, causing some U.S. workers to lose their jobs.

Tariffs on goods produced in low-wage countries would raise the prices of these goods to U.S. companies and consumers. The tariff would make their prices closer to those made in the United States, helping U.S. companies compete.

Trade Agreements

Trade barriers work both ways. If the United States imposes quotas on products made in Japan, Japan is likely to do the same on the U.S. products it imports.

All countries can benefit from trade. To help reduce trade barriers, many nations have negotiated trade agreements with each other.

World Trade Organization

In 1947, 23 countries, including the United States, signed the *General Agreement on Tariffs and Trade (GATT)*. More than 100 countries have participated in GATT. One of its goals was to reduce tariffs and quotas among trading partners.

In 1993, the *World Trade Organization (WTO)* replaced GATT. The WTO now provides a forum for member nations to discuss trade issues and resolve disputes.

NAFTA In 1993, the United States, Canada, and Mexico signed the **North American Free Trade Agreement (NAFTA)**. Under it, tariffs on most goods produced and sold in North America will be eliminated gradually by 2009.

Opponents of the NAFTA agreement argued that without tariffs on Mexican products, U.S. companies would move to Mexico to take advantage of its low wage rates, resulting in lost U.S. jobs. Supporters argued that U.S. workers are more productive than Mexican workers. They believed that this productivity would compensate for the higher U.S. wages.

People don't agree on whether NAFTA has been good or bad for the U.S. economy. Its impact has been felt most in states that border Mexico and Canada. The value of goods crossing the Mexican border into Arizona, California, New Mexico, and Texas has more than tripled since 1993. In the same time period, U.S. trade with Canada increased by about 85 percent. Trade experts believe that NAFTA's full implementation in 2009 will cause trade to grow even more quickly. There also is talk of including other countries from Central and South America in the agreement. Western Hemisphere

nations are moving toward more integration of their economies.

VALUE OF U.S. TRADE WITH CANADA AND MEXICO, 1993 & 2002 (Values in millions of dollars)		
	U.S. Exports To	**U.S. Imports From**
Canada		
1993	$100,442	$111,218
2002	180,922	200,087
Mexico		
1993	$ 41,587	$ 39,915
2002	97,470	134,815

European Union The **European Union (EU)** is an organization of 25 Western European countries that agree to economic and political cooperation among member nations. Its forerunner, the European Community (EC), cooperated only on economic and trade issues. In 1992, EC members signed the *Maastricht Treaty,* extending its agreement and creating the EU.

The EU is a major trading block. The combined value of its imports and exports exceeds that of any single country in the world. Its members impose no tariffs on each other. And together they set a common tariff on goods imported from other countries.

Euro For years, the EU has worked to create a single European currency. On January 1, 1999, the EU launched the *euro,* the single currency that replaced the currencies of the 11 EU members that agreed to participate. At first, euros were used just for international banking and stock transactions. Since January 1, 2002, however, euro notes and coins have replaced

national currencies and have become the legal currency for all transactions in EU countries.

As a result, Germans no longer have to exchange marks for francs to buy products in France.

CheckPoint

What is protectionism? How do countries help promote free trade?

TRY THESE

1. Why do countries trade?

2. What types of products does comparative advantage suggest nations should produce?

3. What are the two basic types of trade barriers?

4. How do tariffs restrict trade?

5. Why do countries create trade barriers?

6. What is the purpose of NAFTA?

7. What is a euro?

THINK CRITICALLY

8. **CONSUMER ACTION** From what you know about Harold and Carol from the opening scenario, how would their lives be different without trade? What do you think: Do U.S. consumers benefit from international trade?

9. Comparative advantage suggests that when each country produces the products it makes most efficiently, total world production will be larger. Why do you think this is so?

10. The U.S. depends on other nations for much of its supply of oil. Oil is an important resource for the U.S. economy. What would happen if the U.S. put a high tariff on imported oil? Do you think this would be a good idea? Why or why not?

11. Why are many electronic devices assembled in less developed nations? Why are many parts for these devices made in developed nations?

DECISION MAKING PROJECT

SPECIFY   **SEARCH**   **SIFT**   **SELECT**   **STUDY**

SPECIFY Your group will have to make four decisions: (1) decide on a fast-food restaurant chain, (2) decide what you would order for a meal from this restaurant, (3) identify another country that has your chosen restaurant chain, and (4) decide whether you would purchase this food if you lived in that country.

© Getty Images/PhotoDisc

17.2 U.S. Economy and World Trade

Trade and U.S. Consumers

The United States is one of the world leaders in the area of international trade. Exports and imports affect not only what U.S. consumers can buy but also their jobs, incomes, and quality of life. Consider the products that the United States imports each year.

U.S. Imports

Motor Vehicles You would probably not be surprised to learn that motor vehicles and parts account for more U.S. imports than any other single product. Think of the people you know who drive cars or trucks from foreign companies.

CONSUMER ACTION

Cindy works as a clerk for a discount store. Her father worked for a textile mill. The mill closed because it could not compete with products imported from other nations. Cindy's parents are bitter. They think her father lost his job because of "cheap foreign imports." Cindy sees a different side to the story where she works. Every day, customers buy inexpensive goods that were imported from other countries. Cindy can't decide how she should feel about selling these items. Should she be angry because her father lost his job? Should she be happy that she and other consumers don't have to pay higher prices? What advice would you give Cindy?

Americans spend more than $170 billion each year to buy these products.

Where do you think most cars imported into the states come from? Japan? Not so! Most come from Canada and Mexico. The majority of these cars and trucks are produced by U.S.-owned companies, but they are not considered U.S. cars in international trade statistics. Because the cars were assembled in foreign countries, they are considered imports, even if they are Ford cars.

A key question involves what a U.S. car is. U.S. manufacturers buy more than $30 billion worth of automobile parts from other countries each year. They use these parts for assembling cars and trucks in this country. When 40 percent of a car is made from parts produced in another country, is it still a U.S. car?

For that matter, what is a Japanese car? Toyota operates eight manufacturing plants in the United States. These plants produce nearly 800,000 Toyota vehicles each year. Are the vehicles produced in these plants Japanese or American? They are made mostly by U.S. workers.

Appliances The second largest category of U.S. imports is electrical appliances. Most of the televisions, DVD players, digital cameras, and

© Getty Images/PhotoDisc

CD players you or your friends own were manufactured in other countries. Americans spend more than $120 billion each year on these products. Think about how your life would be different if you could not buy these products.

Electronics Imported computer equipment and software run a close third at over $80 billion a year. This category includes many computer games. Telephones and other communications equipment add another $30 billion to the total.

Oil Another important category of imports includes oil and petroleum products. The value of these products totals almost $80 billion each year. The price of gasoline to U.S. consumers is relatively low because more than half of the oil is imported. Other countries, such as Saudi Arabia and Kuwait, can produce oil more efficiently. The United States can buy from these countries at a lower price than it can produce oil itself. By importing oil, the United States can hold down the price of gasoline to consumers.

U.S. Exports

Machinery The largest category of U.S. exports is machinery. U.S. businesses sell more than $260 billion worth of machinery products each year.

Electronics Electronics products represent this nation's second most important export. U.S. sales of computer and telecommunications equipment annually totals about $140 billion.

Transportation U.S. sales of motor vehicles and parts abroad are substantial. These exports have a value of more than $90 billion per

© Getty Images/PhotoDisc

year. The U.S. is also the world's largest producer of commercial aircraft. U.S. aerospace businesses annually sell more than $50 billion worth of airplanes to other countries.

Agriculture Agricultural products are also big sellers, bringing in almost $50 billion per year.

Trade in Services

Many people think of trade as only an exchange of goods. In reality, about 30 percent of U.S. exports are services. *Services* are tasks performed for someone else. For example, dry cleaning, air transportation, education, health care, and amusement park rides are all services. Service industries provide services as their product instead of a physical product.

Service industries are becoming an increasingly large segment of the U.S. economy. The United States now has more service companies than manufacturing companies. Service companies employ about two-thirds of the country's workers.

U.S. service industries sell to people in other nations as well as to Americans. The value of exported U.S. services annually exceeds $290 billion. The United States also imports services, but the value is about $60 billion less than the value of services the U.S. exports each year.

The Trade Debate

Economists believe that international trade benefits the world overall. When each country uses its resources as efficiently as possible, world consumers will have more products to buy. More production means more jobs. More jobs mean more income, so that consumers can afford to buy more of what they want. In addition, worldwide competition forces companies to produce higher quality products at lower prices.

Public opinion varies on the issue of trade, however. For example, as the United States moves more toward a service economy and away from manufacturing, service jobs are created, but manufacturing jobs are lost. In the broader view, this is a shift of productive resources from an area in which the United States is becoming less competitive to an area where it has comparative advantage.

For individual workers, this transition often isn't easy. An auto assembly line worker can't immediately become a computer programmer. To take advantage of lower wages in other countries, some U.S. manufacturing plants close and move elsewhere, putting U.S. workers out of work. These workers may need additional training to prepare them for the new jobs being created in other growing sectors of the economy.

International trade creates many jobs in this country. Expanding world markets for computer products keep U.S. high-tech companies scrambling to find workers qualified to make their products. Millions of U.S. jobs depend on exports of services to other countries. The United States exports billions of dollars worth of legal, accounting, and financial services each year.

Foreign investment also creates many jobs for U.S. workers. In its U.S. plants and dealerships, Toyota employs more than 100,000 workers.

CheckPoint

How does international trade affect the lives of U.S. consumers?

Exchange Rates

When you buy a product from a U.S. retailer, you pay for it in dollars. People in England, for example, pay for purchases in pounds. If you want to buy a product imported from England at a U.S. store, do you pay for it in dollars or pounds?

You pay in dollars, which the U.S. business deposits in its bank. To pay its bills, it has its bank trade dollars for pounds. The number of pounds it receives for its dollars depends on the exchange rate. It then sends the pounds (probably electronically) to the business in England that produced the product you bought.

Some consumers prefer to buy goods produced in the United States. They are often willing to pay higher prices for U.S.-made products. To achieve their objective, however, they must be able to identify when a product is, or is not, made in this country. Product labels can help but not always. Consider the following clothing label. What does it say about the product? Is the garment really made in this country? Where was the cotton grown?

100% Cotton
Made from textiles produced in the United States

Assembled in Ecuador

The **exchange rate** is the price of one currency in terms of another currency. For example, suppose the exchange rate between the British pound and the U.S. dollar is 1 pound = $1.50. You are traveling in England and find a coat you want to buy. It costs 40 pounds. To find out how much the coat costs in terms of dollars, multiply the British price by the dollar equivalent.

40 pounds × $1.50 = $60

To buy the coat, you must exchange $60 for 40 pounds. Similarly, importers who are buying thousands of dollars worth of products from other countries must exchange currencies to pay for the products.

How Exchange Rates Are Determined

Each country's currency is like a product for sale, and exchange rates are the prices for these products. Like most products, when many people want to buy a country's currency, the price (exchange rate) tends to go up. When fewer people want the currency, the price tends to go down.

The price of a country's currency rises and falls in relation to world demand for that currency. This is the concept of **floating exchange rates**. Anything that causes people to trade one currency for another will cause the value of the desired currency to increase and the price of the currency given up to decrease.

People may want to exchange one currency for another for many reasons. For example, a U.S. importer may want to exchange dollars for pounds to pay for a shipment of Jaguar cars to sell in the United States. If British banks are paying high interest rates for deposits, Americans may want to exchange dollars for pounds to deposit in British banks. Or, suppose a U.S. company wants to build a factory in England. It will need to trade dollars for pounds to pay for the land.

All of these situations will push the exchange rate for pounds up and for the dollar down. Instead of an exchange rate of, for example, 1 pound = $1.50, it may become 1 pound = $1.60. It will then take more dollars to buy pounds than it did before. The price of the pound has gone up.

$MATH OF MONEY

You are planning a trip to Germany and want to have euros in your pocket to spend while you are there. The exchange rate is $1 US = 0.77 euros. You decide to exchange $1,500 for euros. How many euros will you have to spend in Germany?

When you get back from your trip, you have 220 euros left that you want to exchange back into dollars. How many dollars will you have after the exchange if the exchange rate is still the same?

▌SOLUTION

You will have 1,155 euros to take to Germany.

$1,500 × 0.77 euros = 1,155 euros

When you return, you can get $285.71 US for your remaining euros:

220 euros ÷ $0.77 = $285.71

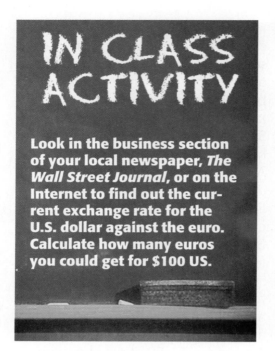

IN CLASS ACTIVITY

Look in the business section of your local newspaper, *The Wall Street Journal*, or on the Internet to find out the current exchange rate for the U.S. dollar against the euro. Calculate how many euros you could get for $100 US.

takes more dollars to buy pounds. When the value of a nation's currency goes down, the prices of the goods it imports go up.

Because exchange rates affect the prices of imports and exports, they have a great influence on international trade. A change of a fraction of a percent in an exchange rate can cause an importer's large shipment of goods to cost thousands of dollars more or less. Depending on exchange rates, a country's products may be relatively expensive or relatively inexpensive for other countries to buy.

© Getty Images/PhotoDisc

Effects of Floating Exchange Rates

As exchange rates change, the prices of imported and exported goods also change. Suppose an American wants to buy a British painting that costs 100 pounds. When the exchange rate was 1 pound = $1.50, she would have paid $150. When the rate changed to 1 pound = $1.60, the price of the painting became $160. The value of the dollar had decreased against the pound. It now

Exchange Rates and the U.S. Economy

Exchange rates change constantly. Between 1985 and 1994, the value of the dollar fell against most other currencies. This made imported goods more expensive to U.S. consumers. After 1994, the value of the dollar increased. This made imported goods less expensive for U.S. consumers at that time.

The increase in the value of the dollar wasn't good news for everyone. It caused U.S. products to be more expensive for people in other nations to buy. The number of products the

Buy the Numbers?

Many businesses along the border between Canada and the United States depend on foreign customers. This is particularly true of restaurants. In a recent year, the Canadian dollar was officially worth 0.74 of a U.S. dollar (74 cents). A U.S. restaurant advertised that it would accept Canadian dollars with this exchange rate.

$5 Canadian = $4 US

Was this a good deal for Canadian citizens? Explain. How could U.S. consumers take advantage of this offer?

United States was able to export fell. This harmed businesses that depended on exporting to earn a profit. U.S. farmers, for example, suffered a 12 percent decline in the amount of their foreign sales. Because exports make up a large portion of farm income, this decrease in foreign sales caused great financial hardship.

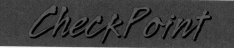

CheckPoint

How do floating exchange rates affect international trade?

TRY THESE

1. What products are major imports for the United States?

2. What industries are becoming an increasingly large segment of the U.S. economy?

3. What are some of the benefits of international trade?

4. How can international trade disrupt some people's lives?

5. How are exchange rates determined?

6. Why would people want to exchange one currency for another?

7. How do exchange rates affect prices?

THINK CRITICALLY

8. **CONSUMER ACTION** Cindy isn't sure whether importing products into the United States is good or bad. Explain to Cindy the benefits and costs of international trade.

9. **MATH OF MONEY** You want to exchange $150 for Mexican pesos for your trip to Cancun. The exchange rate is $1 = 9.522 pesos. How many pesos will you have?

You spend 1,200 pesos. When you return, you want to change your pesos into dollars. The exchange rate is 1 peso = $0.1050. About how many dollars can you return to your savings account?

10. Describe the effect on your life if the value of the U.S. dollar fell by 25 percent. E-mail your answer to your teacher.

DECISION MAKING PROJECT

SPECIFY **SEARCH** **SIFT** **SELECT** **STUDY**

SEARCH Your group must now find out how much your meal would cost at your local fast-food restaurant. Your group must also find out how much the same meal would cost in another country at the same restaurant chain. This will probably be expressed in terms of the local currency. Your last search will be for the current exchange rate between the U.S. dollar and the local currency of your selected country.

17.3 Government and the Economy

Flow of Economic Activity

An economy grows when it produces goods and services at an increasing rate. A growing economy can improve the standard of living for its citizens. Increased production means more products to buy, more jobs for workers who produce the products, and more income for consumers to buy the products.

Measuring Economic Performance

Governments use several measurements to keep track of how their economy is doing. These measurements help them decide what actions to take to help the economy grow. Businesspeople are also interested in the health of the economy.

CONSUMER ACTION

Robert was laid off from his job at a company that produces computer chips. His job was to pack chips in boxes to be sent to businesses in the United States and other countries. Robert's supervisor said he was sorry to lay him off. He knows Robert works hard and does a good job. But, he explained, chip sales are down 30 percent from last year. Foreign sales have almost disappeared. Robert also knows many other people who have lost their jobs recently. Robert wonders what is wrong with the economy. How has he been affected by the business cycle? What steps might the government take to help Robert and the economy recover?

They make investment decisions based on the strength of the economy and estimates of its future growth.

Gross Domestic Product

The most frequently used method for measuring economic performance is the **gross domestic product (GDP)**. This is the current value of all goods and services produced in a country in a year. It includes new goods and services consumers buy, such as clothes, movie tickets, and haircuts. It also includes business spending on things such as equipment and buildings and government spending on things such as highways, military equipment, and government employee salaries.

Studying changes in the GDP over several years can give a general idea of a nation's economic strength. When GDP is growing, the country is producing more goods and services. Greater production generally means more jobs, more income for consumers to spend, and a higher standard of living. When GDP falls, fewer products are being produced, workers may be losing their jobs, and consumers overall have less money to spend.

Inflation To evaluate changes in GDP, analysts must adjust the values for inflation. **Inflation** is a general increase in the average level of prices in a nation's economy. Inflation reduces the value of money because it reduces money's *purchasing power.* Suppose you make $40 a week mowing lawns. Last week, a video game you wanted cost $40. This week, it costs $45. Because the price went up, your earnings can't buy as much.

If prices, in general, are going up, an increase in GDP could be caused by an increase in prices rather than by greater production of goods and services. For example, suppose the GDP is 5 percent larger this year than it was last year. Does this mean the economy is producing 5 percent more goods and services? Maybe, but maybe not. You can't be sure unless you also know what happened to prices in general.

Suppose GDP increased 5 percent last year while prices in general went up 3 percent. Then only about 2 percent more goods and services were produced. This is the *real* change in GDP because it has been adjusted for inflation. Using **real GDP** gives a more accurate picture of what is happening in the economy.

Measuring Inflation A common method for measuring inflation is the **Consumer Price Index (CPI)**. The CPI measures monthly changes in the price of about 400 goods and services that people buy regularly, such as food, clothing, and housing.

The prices of these products are combined in a certain way each month to produce a figure representing overall prices for the month. To calculate the CPI, analysts compare the figure for this month to a similar

GUESS WHAT

In 1980, GDP in the United States totaled $2.708 trillion. Only 24 years later, this total had risen to $11.447 trillion.

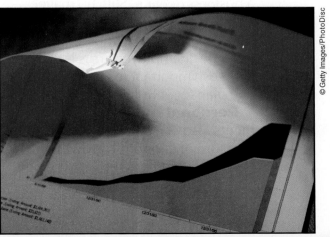

© Getty Images/PhotoDisc

measure of prices at a specific time in the past, called a *base year*.

Differences between these two measures indicate the general change in prices between the base year and the present. The changes are expressed as a percentage of the base year's prices. For example, if the CPI is 180 now, prices have gone up 80 percent from the base year.

Unemployment Rate Another measure of a nation's economic health is its **unemployment rate**, which is the percentage of people who are able and looking for work but don't have jobs. High unemployment rates indicate that the economy is not growing fast enough to create jobs for the people looking for work.

During the depression of the 1930s, unemployment in the United States and other nations reached almost 25 percent. In the early 1980s, it was more than 10 percent. By 2000 it had fallen to just over 4 percent, but it rose to more than 6 percent in the 2001–2002 economic downturn. Unemployment doesn't affect all groups equally. Workers with transferable skills through training or education usually suffer less unemployment and often find other work quickly if they are laid off. Government data show that younger and older workers are unemployed more often than middle-aged workers. Those recently hired are often the first to be laid off in a business decline. Still, no matter where you are in your life cycle or how carefully you planned, you could become unemployed. This is one of the most important reasons to save and plan for your future.

Personal Income Governments also use personal income as a measure of economic growth. *Personal income* is the income peo-

VOTE Your Wallet

When you listen to candidates for national office, you will likely hear the word *economy* frequently. Voters often judge the performance of their national representatives by the economy. When voters think they are better off now than before, they are likely to return incumbents (current office holders) or their party to office. When voters think they are worse off, incumbents often lose the next election.

Why do you think incumbents often lose during economic downturns? How would you judge whether you are economically better or worse off now than in the past? Would you use your assessment of the economy to judge your representative's performance?

ple receive through wages, profits, dividends, interest, and from other sources. It is a good indication of how much people are able to spend and save. When personal income grows, consumers have more money to spend or save. Consumer spending and saving spurs production, helping the economy grow.

The Business Cycle

Economies don't grow at the same rate every year. Sometimes, they don't grow at all. In the early 1980s and in 1991, business activity

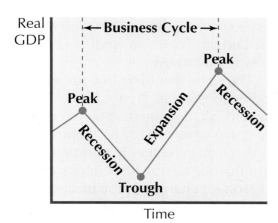

Real GDP

← Business Cycle →

Peak

Peak

Recession

Expansion

Recession

Trough

Time

slowed. Consumers bought less. As sales fell, businesses produced less and laid off many workers. Some people lost their homes or cars because they couldn't make their payments. A few years later, business activity picked up. Sales grew, unemployment dropped, and businesses were generally making good profits. Activity slowed again in 2001 only to recover in 2003.

Over time, an economy's GDP resembles a roller coaster, with many upswings, peaks, and downturns. This recurring pattern of ups and downs in a nation's business activity is called the **business cycle**. When an economy is generally growing, it is in a period of **expansion**. When it is generally falling, it is in a **recession**.

The level of economic activity in other nations may differ from that in the United States. All nations have business cycles. Because nations trade with each other, changes in business activity in one nation affect the others.

Suppose many businesses in Japan experience falling sales. They lay off workers and cut back on their spending. Japanese people and businesses buy fewer products from the United States This causes sales in the United States to fall.

To stimulate sales, Japanese businesses may lower their prices. Americans may then buy more Japanese goods and fewer U.S.-made goods, causing U.S. sales to fall further. Workers in the United States may be laid off as U.S. businesses cut back production.

When Japan's economy recovers, its prosperity helps other nations as well. The Japanese would buy more imported goods and charge more for the goods they sell. Sales of products made in other countries would then increase, helping their economies expand. Because of this economic interdependence, most nations move through their business cycles at about the same time.

Consumer Confidence and the Business Cycle

Consumers often make their buying decisions according to the state of the economy. They are more willing to spend when they are confident in the future. Consumers spend less when they are worried. Taken as a whole, the nation's confidence level affects the overall amount of buying and selling, therefore influencing the business cycle.

Imagine that you work for a company that produces gold jewelry. Your company sells some of its jewelry in the United States and exports some. For most consumers, gold jewelry is a luxury item. People may want gold jewelry, but they don't *need* it.

© Getty Images/PhotoDisc

583

INTERNET ACTIVITY

The government pays close attention to the University of Michigan's monthly study of consumer confidence. Search the Internet for information on this study and write an essay about recent consumer confidence. E-mail it to your teacher.

When consumers have good incomes and believe their jobs are secure, they buy more gold jewelry. Suppose your employer's sales have grown by 25 percent from last year. Your boss asks you to work extra hours, and the company is hiring new workers. Still, the company is having a hard time keeping up with consumer demand. All of this makes you and other employees confident. You decide this is a good time to borrow $20,000 to buy a new car.

Consumer confidence passes from person to person and from nation to nation. As consumer confidence spreads, consumers buy more, creating more economic growth, which breeds more confidence. Confidence in the economy knows no borders. When consumers are confident, they buy more products, regardless of where the products were produced.

Lack of confidence works the same way. Suppose the world's economy was in a recession. Consumers would feel their jobs are less secure. Fewer consumers would feel confident enough to buy luxury items such as gold jewelry. Your employer's sales would decrease at home and abroad. Instead of being asked to work extra hours, you might be laid off. Then you would not borrow to buy a new car.

The same would be true for many other consumers. New car sales would fall, and the recession would become worse. Many economists believe that changes in consumer confidence are the most important reason for changes in the business cycle.

CheckPoint

How does the government measure economic activity? How do consumers affect the economy?

Government Efforts to Stabilize the Economy

Most experts agree that everyone is better off if the swings in the business cycle are as small as possible. **Depression**, a deep, extended decline in a nation's economy, can cause severe unemployment and financial hardship. Steep expansions in the past have created inflation, causing consumers' purchasing power to decline.

Governments everywhere carry out policies to try to minimize the swings in the economy. The main goal of a government's policies is to promote economic growth and high employment with a minimum increase in prices. The government's primary tools for accomplishing this goal are fiscal and monetary policies.

Fiscal Policy

The government's decisions on taxing and spending are called **fiscal policy**. If the economy is declining, the government can try to stimulate growth by reducing taxes. This puts more money in the hands of consumers, encouraging them to buy more products. More consumer spending increases sales and production, making the economy grow.

The government can also attempt to slow a decline by increasing its own spending. It can institute programs to build more highways, put more police on the streets, and initiate other public works programs. Government spending on these programs creates jobs and increases consumers' income, increasing consumer spending and economic growth.

When the economy is expanding too rapidly, the government can try to slow it down by doing the opposite with fiscal policy. It can increase taxes or decrease government spend-

ing. These changes would reduce consumer spending power, slowing production and reducing inflation.

© Getty Images/PhotoDisc

Monetary Policy

The government's efforts to help stabilize the economy by managing interest rates, the availability of loans, and the supply of money is called **monetary policy**. Monetary policy decisions are carried out by a country's central bank. The central bank in the United States is the *Federal Reserve System (Fed)*.

To fight an economic downturn, the Fed can reduce interest rates. This makes loans less expensive, so more people will borrow. This increase in borrowing gives consumers more money to spend. As consumers spend more, businesses produce more products to satisfy this demand, and employ more workers

PRIMARY SOURCES

Sometimes, what's good for business in one country is not good for business in another country. Read the following comments of Bill Knox, a knifemaker who was put out of business in the 1930s. His competition was knives made in other countries. Does Mr. Knox's experience have any similarity to the U.S. workplace today? If so, think of three specific examples. Is the United States taking any manu-

facturing away from other countries? Does the United States lead in any product or service areas?

"'Twas the …foreign knives and the new machinery. Between the two of them. And now there's a …good trade all shot to [pieces], and nothin' to take its place. Ole punks like me havin' to go on relief. We could be workin' if the trade was any good yet, and teachin' it to our kids."

to make the products. All of this activity causes the economy to grow.

When the economy is growing too fast, causing too much inflation, the Fed can do the opposite with monetary policy. It can increase interest rates, making loans more expensive. Fewer people will borrow, and spending and production will slow down.

CheckPoint

What can governments do to help influence economic growth?

TRY THESE

1. How does a growing economy increase the standard of living of its citizens?

2. What is included in the measurement of gross domestic product?

3. How does inflation decrease the value of money?

4. What does the unemployment rate indicate about growth in the economy?

5. What is the business cycle?

6. How does consumer confidence influence the business cycle?

7. How can the government use monetary and fiscal policy to reduce the size of the swings in the business cycle?

8. What is the Consumer Price Index?

9. What is a depression?

THINK CRITICALLY

10. **CONSUMER ACTION** Robert has been laid off from his job. Explain how his personal problem has resulted from a larger problem in the world's economy. What can the government do to help?

11. Suppose GDP increased by 7 percent last year. The CPI went up 2.5 percent. Approximately how large was the increase in real GDP?

12. If you were thinking about buying a new home, how could economic conditions affect your decision?

13. Suppose unemployment across the nation rose by 2 percent. How could this affect people in your community, the nation as a whole, and residents of foreign countries?

14. Comment on the state of the U.S. economy at this time.

DECISION MAKING PROJECT

SPECIFY   SEARCH   SIFT   SELECT   STUDY

SIFT To compare local currency amounts to dollar amounts, use the current exchange rate to convert the cost of the meal in the local country to U.S. dollars. Check that country's income level. Can most residents afford to buy U.S. fast food?

© CORBIS

GOALS

DESCRIBE
ways that companies
do business in the
global marketplace

DISCUSS
ways that nations
depend on each other

17.4 It's a Global Economy

Business in a Global Economy

Some people talk of the global economy as if it were new. In fact, economics has influenced world events in all history. Ancestors of most U.S. citizens came here for economic reasons. Many immigrated to find jobs or land. Some were brought against their will as a source of cheap labor. Now, as in the past, most of the steady flow of immigrants to the United States come here to gain freedom and economic opportunity.

Economics has caused exploration, colonization, and many wars throughout history. Columbus was seeking a new trade route to Asia when he accidentally "found" the

CONSUMER ACTION

Eduardo is proud to be a U.S. citizen. His parents came to the United States from Mexico in the 1970s. They worked as farm laborers and went to night school to learn about America and become naturalized citizens. Now they both have good jobs. Eduardo and his parents often visit their relatives across the border in Matamoras. He sees how much better his family lives in the United States. In school, Eduardo heard that the world is a *global economy.* He wonders what this means to his relatives. Will people who live in less developed nations catch up with consumers in the United States? If they live better, will Americans live worse, or will the global economy help everyone live better?

New World. Francisco Pizarro was looking for gold when he landed in Peru and conquered the Incas.

Important inventions affected economies worldwide. Development of the steam engine in the early 1800s revolutionized production and transportation worldwide. The telegraph, radio, television, and satellites followed each other as cutting-edge communications technology. Today, messages that took weeks to send in the 1700s arrive in seconds over the Internet. Such technological advances have made business transactions between nations faster and easier, turning the world into one big marketplace.

Economic problems are global, too. The depression of the 1930s may have started in the United States, but it quickly spread to other nations. The war in the Persian Gulf in 1990–91 pushed oil prices up throughout the world. The list goes on and on. In spite of national boundaries, events in one nation do affect the economies of others.

IN CLASS ACTIVITY

List historical events not mentioned in the book that were caused by economic conditions.

a business that is based in one country but has branches or plants in other countries.

In 1998, Chrysler merged with Daimler-Benz of Germany, becoming DaimlerChrysler. Daimler-Benz was almost twice as large as Chrysler at that time. Management of the new corporation is shared, but the German owners probably have a larger share. Is it a German company now?

Actually, was Daimler-Benz really a German company? Americans have been free to invest in this company for years, and many did by buying stock. So did people in other countries. The same was true of Chrysler. The owners of any corporation are its stockholders. Because of such shared ownership that crosses national boundaries, it is difficult to say that any large company truly belongs to just one nation.

Employment and Multinationals   Multinational corporations are in business to earn a profit as is any other company. Labor is always a large part of the cost of production. Lower labor costs help

© Getty Images/PhotoDisc

Multinational Corporations

Do you believe the Chrysler Corporation is a U.S. business? In some ways it is, but in others it isn't. Chrysler, like many large companies, is a multinational corporation. A **multinational corporation (MNC)** is

companies produce products more cheaply. As a result, they can charge lower prices for their products, increasing sales and profits.

Imagine that you are the manager of a large multinational corporation. You have factories throughout the world where you can produce your products. Would you want to produce more goods where labor costs are $15 per product or $5 per product?

Many multinational corporations have expanded production in places where employees work for less. For example, factories in Mexico along the U.S. border manufacture many products for U.S.-based companies. These factories, called *maquiladoras,* have become an important part of Mexican industrial growth. They manufacture products such as automobile engines, kitchen appliances, computers, and televisions.

Some labor groups believe that U.S. MNCs have increased unemployment at home by locating factories in other countries. However, some studies have indicated that MNCs have preserved or created more jobs for U.S. citizens than they have eliminated.

One fact of life in a global economy is that workers are no longer competing for jobs just within their own borders. The labor market is worldwide. Jobs that require little skill or experience are likely to go to the workers who will accept the lowest wages, wherever they may be. To earn a high wage, workers must have a valuable skill to sell.

Technology and Multinationals Think of some of the U.S. inventions that had a major impact on business. Henry Ford

CYBER CONSUMER

ExxonMobil is one of the largest multinational corporations in the world. Go to the ExxonMobil web site and find out about five countries in which it operates. What kinds of business activities does ExxonMobil perform outside the United States?

invented the production line, substantially reducing the cost of producing automobiles. The lower costs made car prices affordable for the average American.

You can probably think of many other U.S. inventions that revolutionized business: Eli Whitney and the cotton gin, James Morse and the telegraph, Steven Jobs and the Apple computer.

In the past, a U.S. invention gave U.S. businesses an advantage over businesses in other nations, helping the U.S. economy grow. Similarly, inventions made in other nations gave their businesses a competitive advantage.

© Getty Images/PhotoDisc

Today, many inventions are shared throughout the world—almost immediately. The reason is that multinational corporations fund much of the research and development that takes place in the world. Suppose a new medicine is discovered in Sweden. Swedish researchers may have been collaborating with researchers in France and the United States, all working for the same multinational corporation.

Other Ways to Enter Foreign Markets

A company doesn't have to be a multinational corporation to do business globally. Even small and medium-size companies can take advantage of the global marketplace. The easiest way is through exporting: making products in one country and selling them in another.

Licensing Another way to sell in other countries is through licensing. A company in one country can allow a company elsewhere to sell its products for a licensing fee.

One form of licensing arrangement is *franchising*. The company sells the right to use its name and sell its products in a specific territory. For example, if you travel in Europe, you will see many KFC locations. They are managed locally by owners of the franchise, although KFC sets quality standards.

© Getty Images/PhotoDisc

COMMUNICATE

Over the centuries, advances in transportation technology have been astonishing. The first engine-powered vehicles were developed in the late 1700s and early 1800s. The first commercial airlines went into service in Europe in 1919. Ships progressed from the sailing ships of the Pilgrims to the giant tankers of today. Write about how you think advances in transportation have affected the global economy.

Partnerships Companies can also enter foreign markets by establishing a local marketing subsidiary. That is, the company can rent space in a foreign country, hire local staff, and ship products to the subsidiary to sell in that country. The company could partner instead with a foreign firm in a joint venture. In a joint venture, the company often buys a percentage of its partner company in the country where it wants to do business.

CheckPoint

What are some ways that economics has influenced historical events? Why do companies do business in other countries?

Sharing Resources

The world's nations interact with each other in more ways than just buying and selling products. Funds and knowledge flow easily across national borders. People all over the world share knowledge through electronic communications. The world is realizing that economic success in any nation helps all nations prosper.

© Getty Images/PhotoDisc

International Flow of Funds

At one time, borrowing and investing occurred primarily within single countries. Interest rates were most important to each country's consumers and businesses. Now funds freely flow across national borders. Businesses compete for investors worldwide. Investors can buy stock in a German company, or any other they believe will earn high profits. Borrowers can shop for the best rates anywhere in the world.

Suppose you are the manager of a large business. You want to build a new factory in Alabama requiring you to borrow $10 million. You don't have to borrow that money in the United States. If interest rates are lower in France, you can take out a loan there. You can borrow euros and trade them for dollars. You also can borrow some of the many dollars Americans have sent out of the United States to pay for imported goods.

U.S. banks compete with banks in other nations for deposits and borrowers. Billions of dollars worth of funds can be transmitted around the world with several keystrokes on a computer.

International Flow of Knowledge

Students travel throughout the world to gain knowledge and understanding. This is nothing new. It has been going on for generations. What is new is the ability to "travel" to other nations over the Internet.

Suppose you want to learn about Scottish history. You can find the University of Scotland's web site. It will lead you to the university's library. It also can put you in touch with faculty members who teach history. You might even have an electronic conversation about the topic with one of them.

Electronic communications also allow rapid global exchange of information between businesses and governments. U.S. tourists in Rome can access their savings accounts at an Italian ATM. Farmers can learn the price of grain in London. Customs agents can investigate shipments of oil or other products.

This rapid flow of information helps all nations. For example, researchers in different countries are often working on the same problem at the same time. Suppose that researchers in France and the United

© Getty Images/PhotoDisc

States are looking for a cure for cancer. Before communications were easy, these researchers could have been working in isolation, perhaps wasting time on something that others had already discovered to be ineffective. Now the researchers can work together, sharing their findings as they go along. By collaborating, they may solve the problem more quickly and at a lower cost.

The Global Environment

Environmental problems affect people around the world. Pollution, global warming, and damage to the ozone layer respect no international borders.

In 1997, the United States and many other nations met in Kyoto, Japan, to discuss the dangers of global warming. It resulted in an agreement meant to reduce carbon dioxide (CO_2) emissions by 2012. The United States' goal was to cut its CO_2 emissions by 40 percent from 1997 levels. Doing this would require extensive changes in factories, power plants, vehicles, and furnaces, estimated to raise energy costs by 50 percent.

Meeting Kyoto targets, however, will not solve the problem. A large part of the CO_2 released comes from nations that did not participate in the Kyoto conference. China, for example, emits almost as much CO_2 as the United States and at first refused to meet a reduction quota. Also, a large part of the CO_2 entering the atmosphere is from natural sources, such as animals, that cannot be eliminated.

President Bush announced in 2001 that the United States would not meet its CO_2 reduction goals. He said that doing so would harm the U.S. economy and trade position. He stated that instead the U.S. government and businesses would work together to reduce CO_2 emissions in ways that would not harm our economy. Some people in the United States and the world disagreed with this decision. Severe storms and droughts in recent years are suggested as signs that global warming is changing the earth's weather patterns.

The Spread of Prosperity

Prosperity is no longer limited to a few nations. It is not like a pie that is cut into smaller and smaller pieces. Prosperity in the world is the result of greater production of goods and services everywhere. When people in developing nations produce more and better products, they earn more income. This allows them to buy more goods and services and to increase their standard of living. When individual nations prosper, all nations prosper.

CheckPoint

What are some ways that nations can work together to promote prosperity in the global economy?

TRY THESE

1. How has economics influenced historical events?

2. What is a multinational corporation?

3. Why is it difficult to identify just one nation to which a multinational corporation belongs?

4. How can workers compete for jobs in a global labor market?

5. What are some ways that small and medium-size companies can take advantage of the global marketplace?

6. What causes funds to cross national borders?

7. How does increasing prosperity in a developing country help the world economy grow?

THINK CRITICALLY

8. **CONSUMER ACTION** Eduardo wonders if his relatives in Mexico will ever be able to live as comfortably as his family in the United States. He wonders whether increased prosperity for people in developing nations would mean less prosperity for Americans. Explain to Eduardo what the global economy might mean for his family.

9. **COMMUNICATE** Does a multinational corporation benefit or harm the economy of its home country? Write a one-page paper explaining your position on this issue.

10. Why do you think it is so difficult for countries to agree to reduce the pollution that their businesses and vehicles release into the air?

11. **COMMUNICATE** Imagine you have made a discovery that can reduce the cost of generating electricity by 25 percent. If your invention were used only in the United States, it would give U.S. businesses an advantage in competing with companies in other nations. If you made the invention available to every nation in the world, all people would live better. How would you choose to distribute your invention? Write an explanation of your choice.

12. **COMMUNICATE** Imagine you meet people your own age who are from another country. How would you explain the term *global economy* to them? E-mail your explanation to your teacher.

DECISION MAKING PROJECT

SPECIFY   SEARCH   SIFT   <u>SELECT</u>   STUDY

SELECT Most fast-food chain restaurants offer the same quality no matter where they are. Based on your comparison, which meal is more expensive, the one in the United States or the one in the other country? If you lived in the foreign country, would you be willing to buy U.S. fast food?

KEY IDEAS

The Nature of International Trade

1. An *import* is a product that one country *buys* from another country. An *export* is a product that one country *sells* to another country.
2. The value of all of a country's exports minus the value of all of its imports is its balance of trade.
3. When a country can produce a product at a lower cost than any other nation, it has an absolute advantage.
4. Comparative advantage is a country's production of a product that makes the most efficient use of the resources it has.
5. Nations create trade barriers to protect their young industries from competition, to protect national security, and to protect domestic jobs.
6. Trade agreements reduce trade barriers and help promote trade.

U.S. Economy and World Trade

7. Major U.S. imports are motor vehicles and parts, electrical appliances, electronics, and oil. Major exports are machinery, electronics, motor vehicles, airplanes, and agricultural products.
8. Service industries are a growing segment of the U.S. economy. The United States also exports services.
9. Worldwide competition increases product quality and lowers prices.
10. For individual workers, world trade can cause difficult transitions.
11. The exchange rate is the price of one currency in terms of another. The rate rises and falls in relation to world demand for that currency.

12. As exchange rates change, the prices of imported and exported goods also change.

Government and the Economy

13. An economy grows when it produces goods and services at an increasing rate.
14. Inflation is a general increase in the price level. It reduces the value of money by reducing money's purchasing power.
15. The business cycle is the recurring pattern of ups and downs in a nation's business activity.
16. Consumer confidence has a major influence on the business cycle.
17. Governments attempt to minimize the swings in the business cycle through monetary and fiscal policy.

It's a Global Economy

18. Economics has influenced world events throughout history.
19. A multinational corporation (MNC) is a business that is based in one country but has branches or plants in other countries.
20. To compete successfully in the global labor market, workers must have a valuable skill to sell.
21. Small and medium-size companies can take advantage of the global marketplace by exporting, licensing, or franchising their products or by entering partnerships with companies in other countries.
22. People and businesses can invest, borrow, or deposit funds in any nation, not just their own.
23. When individual nations prosper, the world economy grows.

TERMS REVIEW

Match each term on the left with its definition on the right.
Some terms may not be used.

a. absolute advantage

b. balance of trade

c. business cycle

d. comparative advantage

e. Consumer Price Index (CPI)

f. depression

g. European Union (EU)

h. exchange rate

i. expansion

j. export

k. fiscal policy

l. floating exchange rates

m. gross domestic product (GDP)

n. import

o. inflation

p. monetary policy

q. multinational corporation (MNC)

r. North American Free Trade Agreement (NAFTA)

s. protectionism

t. quota

u. real gross domestic product (GDP)

v. recession

w. tariff

x. trade deficit

y. trade surplus

z. unemployment rate

1. business that is based in one country but has branches or plants in other countries
2. value of all of a nation's exports minus the value of all of its imports
3. organization of 25 Western European countries that agree to economic and political cooperation
4. government's efforts to help stabilize the economy by managing interest rates, the availability of loans, and the supply of money
5. tax on imported goods
6. limiting international trade to protect the nation's own self-interest
7. the result when a country earns more from exports than it spends on imports
8. price of one currency in terms of another currency
9. good or service that one country buys from another country
10. general increase in the average level of prices in a nation's economy
11. value of all goods and services produced in a country in a year, adjusted for inflation
12. limit on the amount of a product that can be imported
13. common measure of inflation that tracks monthly changes in the price of 400 goods and services that people buy regularly
14. recurring pattern of ups and downs in a nation's business activity
15. period of general decline in a nation's economy
16. government's taxing and spending decisions that are intended to help the economy work better
17. when a country can produce a product at a lower cost than any other nation
18. good or service that one country sells to another

CONSUMER DECISIONS

19. Would you be in favor of eliminating all tariffs on imported clothing? How would this affect your life? Do you believe other people would have opinions different from yours? Explain.

20. Denise has $10,000 she wants to deposit in a savings account. She has checked with local banks and banks in other countries. The best rate she could find was at a bank in Mexico that was paying 20 percent for deposits. By changing her dollars for Mexican pesos, she could take advantage of this high rate. Do you think she should deposit her money into the Mexican bank? What would happen if the value of pesos fell by 25 percent compared to dollars?

21. How would decisions U.S. consumers make be affected if the value of the U.S. dollar fell by 20 percent compared to other currencies? Would Americans probably buy more or fewer foreign products? Explain.

22. Kirsten is planning a trip to England in six months. The economy in England is booming at present. Would it be better for her to trade her dollars for pounds now, or should she wait? Explain.

THINK CRITICALLY

23. Economists believe that consumer confidence affects the business cycle. Why do you think this is so? What happens when consumers, in general, are optimistic about the future? What happens when they hear reports of layoffs at many companies?

24. What do you think would happen to the price of autos made in the United States if a 50 percent tariff was placed on imported cars?

25. If the value of the U.S. dollar increases, what will happen to the price of goods imported into the United States? Explain why.

26. Why do you think countries make trade agreements with each other?

LOOK IT UP

27. Find out which countries are current members of the EU. Which of these switched to the euro?

28. Investigate changes in the U.S. gross domestic product in the last five years. Do the changes show

WHICH IS THE BEST DEAL?

You are shopping at a store in Canada, just across the U.S. border from your home in Minnesota. You see a sweatshirt you like that costs $45 Canadian including tax. You have only U.S. dollars in your pocket. The exchange rate is $1 Canadian = $0.75 US. Here are your alternatives. Which is the best deal?

Alternative 1 The store clerk said he would sell you the sweatshirt for $40 US.

Alternative 2 You could go to a bank down the street and exchange your U.S. dollars for Canadian dollars so that you could purchase the sweatshirt for $45 Canadian.

Alternative 3 You saw the same sweatshirt in a store at home for $35, but you will have to pay 6 percent more in sales tax if you buy it there.

POINT YOUR BROWSER TO

www.ee4c.swlearning.com
Complete the activity for Chapter 17.

that the economy has been in a recession or an expansion?

29. Choose any country in South America and identify its major exports and imports. Why do you think this country exports and imports these particular products?

30. Investigate the value of U.S. exports and imports in the past three years. What has happened to the U.S. balance of trade? You can find this information in *Survey of Current Business* or *Economic Indicators* in most public libraries. You might also find these figures on the Internet.

31. Many inventions occurred in countries other than the U.S. Find out about an important invention by a non-U.S. citizen. How did this invention impact the world economy?

32. Find out what has happened to the value of the U.S. dollar compared to the Japanese yen in the past three years. How do you think these changes in exchange rates have affected the ability of U.S. businesses to export goods and services?

INSIDE THE NUMBERS

33. In a recent year, U.S. citizens took about 7.5 million trips to Europe for pleasure and business. It is estimated that they spent more than $15 billion on their travels. Explain why these numbers are important to the world's global economy and to that of the United States in particular.

CURRICULUM CONNECTION

34. **HISTORY** In 1930, Congress passed the Hawley-Smoot Tariff Act. Investigate the reasons for the passage of this law and its results. Do you believe we have anything to learn today from the results of this law? Explain.

35. **SOCIAL STUDIES** Taiwan has few natural resources. Its economy depends heavily on manufacturing and foreign trade. Why do you think manufacturing and trade are such a large part of Taiwan's economy?

JOURNAL RECAP

36. After reading this chapter, review the answers you wrote to the questions in Journal Journey. Have your opinions changed?

DECISION MAKING PROJECT

SPECIFY   SEARCH   SIFT   SELECT   **STUDY**

STUDY Prepare a presentation to the class. Include the information you gathered. What do you think would happen if the price for the meal in the United States became the same as the price of the meal in the other country? Would you buy more or fewer meals at the restaurant? What do you think would happen to restaurant chains nationwide at these prices?

Tying It All Together

In the past few months, you have learned about consumers and their role in the U.S. economy. Some of the topics you studied concerned society as a whole. Others centered on your family or you as an individual. You learned that your values and goals, which change throughout your life cycle, affect your decision making process when making consumer choices.

It is time to put what you have learned to use. By establishing goals, you will be better prepared to make rational consumer decisions. Your final assignment is to construct your own life-span plan.

A Life-Span Plan for James

To help you do this, consider James, a high school student who has also used this text. James wanted to apply what he learned to his own life. To do this, he used the life-span timeline in Chapter 1 on page 7 and adapted it to create his own life-span plan. He included short- and long-term goals

© Getty Images/PhotoDisc

that he wants to accomplish during his life span. His life-span timeline is shown on page 599.

To begin, James identified six central life-span goals that he wants to achieve over the next 50 years. These goals fit in well with his values, aptitudes, interests, and personality. They are to

1. Gain education and training needed to repair computers

2. Own and operate a computer repair business

3. Get married, have children, and own a house in a nice neighborhood

4. Become financially secure

5. Be active in his church and local government

6. Be able to retire and take up other interests by age 65

Many of the central life-span goals James has chosen are the same ones he identified when he investigated career choices earlier in this course. By talking with a person employed in the computer repair business, James learned how to prepare for this career. He realizes that he needs advanced training and experience. This will force him to make sacrifices in other parts of his life. James and his future wife have agreed to put off getting married and having a family for several years. He needs to construct a budget that allows him to save much of his current income. James has decided to ask for financial help from his grandparents. James expects to do extra work at their home to begin to pay them back for their help.

Related Goals James' central life-span goals are related to each other. Saving and investing to achieve financial security, for

James' Life-Span Plan

Birth ———————————————————————— Death

Infancy   Childhood   Young Adult   Mature Adult   Retired   Elderly

Time	Education	Career	Family	Financial	Community	Retirement
Next 2 years	Complete high school.	Find a job with a computer repair business.	Help elderly grandparents around their home.	Save to attend private technology school.	Be an active member of my family's church.	Nothing yet.
5 years from now	Graduate from private technology school.	Work to become supervisor with a computer repair business.	Find an apartment in a good location.	Save to get married and buy a home.	Become active in local government. Help a candidate run for office.	Buy term life insurance. Open a Roth IRA.
10 years from now	Get a small business management certificate at a local community college.	Work to become a computer repair business branch manager.	Get married. Take a nice honeymoon. Have our first child. Buy a small house in a neighborhood with good schools.	Save to buy a larger home and start my own business in a few years.	Continue role in local government. Attend Board of Education meetings.	Take trips to places we might like to live one day.
20 years from now	Take continuing education courses to keep up with computer technology.	Either buy into the business I work for or start my own.	Have another child. Expand our house or buy a larger one. Take family trips each year.	Save for children's education. Make annual contributions to IRA. Invest in stocks.	Be active in our children's schools. Run for a Board of Education position.	Buy permanent life insurance.
35 years from now	Teach continuing education classes at a community college.	Build a successful business I can be proud of. Look for a person to help run it.	Help children pay for their education. Buy a few luxuries for our home, maybe a pool.	Increase investments in stocks. Continue making IRA contributions.	Run for public office in City Council.	Try other types of work I could volunteer for later.
50 years from now	Take classes in French cooking and the French language.	Sell my business but agree to come in one day a week to help out.	Keep in touch with adult children and (hopefully) spend time with grandchildren.	Invest income from selling business to provide security. Take long trip to France.	Continue to be active in local government but don't hold office.	Volunteer to help young people study computers.

example, will help him pay for training and later start a business. If his business is successful, he will be able to afford the house he wants to own. Financial security will also allow James to enjoy a few luxuries. Nearly 200 years ago, his ancestors immigrated from France. Some day he would like to visit France to see where they lived. He would also like to learn to speak French. If his business is a success, he will be able to do these things.

James wants to achieve many short- and some long-term goals that are not his central goals in life. These include buying cars, televisions, and owning a fishing boat. Although

© Getty Images/PhotoDisc

these goals are important, they aren't among the things James cares most about in life and so aren't in his life-span plan. James had to differentiate between his wants and needs and set priorities.

Using a Grid for Organization

James organized his life-span goals in a grid. Across the top he placed six categories to represent his central life-span goals. On the left side he placed periods of time. These started with the next two years at the top and went fifty years in the future at the bottom. He then placed his goals in the grid according to when he would like to achieve them and how they contribute to his central life-span goals. In this way, he created a life-span plan that he believes will help him accomplish what he wants most in life.

James feels a sense of satisfaction with his work. He knows that he will almost surely revise his plan in the future, but he has a foundation on which to build. He can use his plan

to help make decisions now. When he makes his school schedule for next year, he will sign up for accounting, business management, and computer classes. He knows what type of job to look for and how to spend and save his income. Because he has definite goals, he is motivated to resist spending money for things he doesn't really need.

James' life-span plan is right for him. It fits his values and family situation. His plan, however, would not be right for most students, including you. You aren't James. You have other values, aptitudes, and interests. His personality is not your personality. His family is not your family.

Your Own Life-Span Plan

Using James' plan as a pattern, construct a life-span plan for yourself. To do this, you will want to reflect on what you've learned throughout this course. You have studied many topics and completed several activities that will help you develop your life-span plan. Many of these topics and

© Getty Images/PhotoDisc

Your Life Span

Birth						Death
Infancy	**Childhood**	**Young Adult**	**Mature Adult**	**Retired**		**Elderly**

School   Job   Career   Travel

Advanced Education   Care for Parents

Raise Children   Community Service

Home Ownership   Medical Care

activities were identified with the life-span icon. Examples throughout the textbook include the following.

- Lists of values, aptitudes, personality traits, and career goals in Chapter 4

- Budget worksheets in Chapter 6

- Saving and investing plans in Chapters 8 and 9

- Housing plans in Chapter 13

- Insurance and security needs in Chapter 15

In addition to these materials, you most likely have accumulated many other useful resources in the research you did throughout the course. Use all this material to help you write your goals (both short- and long-term). Base them on what you want from life for yourself, your family, and your community. Place your goals in your plan.

After you have finished your life-span plan, it would be helpful to interview a person in the career field you have chosen (or a school career guidance counselor) to discuss your choices and the feasibility of your plan. This person can offer advice and encouragement for achieving your goals. Putting your life-span plan into action is one of the most important steps you can take toward achieving the satisfaction you want during your life span.

GLOSSARY

401(k) plan   A tax-deferred retirement plan offered to employees by their employer

80 percent rule   Insurance company rule that you must buy homeowner's coverage for at least 80 percent of your home's actual replacement value at the time of your loss in order to receive full reimbursement for any loss

80/20 coverage   Common fee-for-service health insurance coverage in which you pay 20 percent of covered expenses, after meeting the deductible, and the company pays 80 percent

A

absolute advantage   A country's ability to produce a product at a lower cost than any other nation

acceleration clause   A statement in a credit contract that requires you to repay the entire loan immediately if you miss a payment

account balance   The total amount in your bank account at a specific date

accreditation   Official recognition that the person or organization met certain quality standards for their profession

adjustable-rate mortgage (ARM)   Home loan for which the interest rate goes up or down as rates in the economy rise or fall

allowance   A number that you calculate on a Form W-4 that reduces the amount withheld from your pay

annual percentage rate (APR)   The finance charge calculated as a percentage of the amount borrowed

annual percentage yield (APY)   The actual interest rate an account pays per year, calculated the same way by all banks

anorexia nervosa   A disorder characterized by a fear of obesity, a distorted self-image, an aversion to food, and severe weight loss

appraisal   An expert's determination of the value of a piece of property

appreciate   Increase in value over time

aptitude   A natural talent for learning some skills over others

arbitrator   A neutral third party in a dispute who has the power to make a decision in the case

assigned risk   A driver who has been assigned an insurance company by the state because a bad driving record makes every other company unwilling to insure the person

automated teller machine (ATM)   A computer terminal that you can use to make deposits, withdraw cash, transfer money between accounts, check your account balances, and pay some kinds of bills

automatic withdrawal   A bill-paying arrangement in which your bank removes money from your account at a specified time and sends it to a company to pay your bill

B

bait and switch The practice of "baiting" consumers with an advertised but nonexistent bargain and then "switching" them to a more expensive product when they arrive at the store

balance of trade The value of all of a nation's exports minus the value of all of its imports

balanced diet Eating foods that give you the right amounts of all six nutrients

balloon payment A final loan payment that is much larger than the regular monthly payments

bankruptcy Legal process for selling most of a consumer's property to help satisfy debts that he or she cannot pay in exchange for relieving the consumer of the debt obligations

barter Trading goods and services without using money

beneficiary Person specified in a life insurance policy to receive payment upon the death of the insured person

Better Business Bureau (BBB) A nonprofit, business-sponsored agency with local offices dedicated to educating consumers, helping to resolve disputes, and promoting honest business practices

blue chip stock Stock of an established and historically successful corporation

board certified Doctor who has completed a training program in a specialty and has passed an exam in that specialty

bodily injury liability coverage Insurance that protects you against financial loss, including the cost of your legal defense, when you are legally responsible for injuring other people in an automobile accident

bond A written promise to pay a debt by a specified date

brokerage firm A company that specializes in helping people buy and sell stocks and bonds

budget A plan for dividing your income among spending and saving options

budget worksheet A planning document on which you record your expected and actual income and spending over a short time, usually one month

bulimia Binge eating followed by purging through vomiting or use of laxatives

business cycle Recurring pattern of ups and downs in a nation's business activity

business tax Fee paid for a license, permit, or stamp to operate certain kinds of businesses (also known as a *license* tax)

C

calories A measure of the amount of energy that foods contain

canceled check A check with the bank's stamp on it, indicating that it has been paid

capacity A measure of financial ability to repay a loan

capital The value of what you own, including savings, investments, and property

capital gain Profit earned from selling stock at a higher price than you paid for it

capital loss Money lost from selling stock at a lower price than you paid for it

capitation Managed care cost-control policy in which doctors and hospitals are paid a fixed amount per year for each insured patient, no matter what services they provide

carbohydrates Sugars and starches that break down quickly to provide energy to the body

career An occupation to which you have made a long-term commitment

career connection The meeting you have with someone who works in your career choice

cashier's check A bank's own personal check, signed by the bank's cashier. Payment of this check comes from the bank's own funds.

CD-ROM A data storage disc that holds more data than a floppy disk but less than a DVD-ROM disc

cease-and-desist order An administrative or judicial order requiring a business to stop conducting unfair or deceptive practices, such as deceptive advertising

central processing unit (CPU) The heart of a computer that converts data into electronic codes and uses these codes to complete calculations, transfer information or images, or create sound

certificate of deposit (CD) A deposit in a savings institution that earns a fixed interest rate for a specified period of time

certified check A personal check that has been stamped and signed by a bank officer as a guarantee that your account has the funds to cover the check

character A measure of your financial responsibility, often based on your credit history

check An order to a bank to pay a specified sum to the person or business named on the check

check register A booklet provided by your bank for recording your checking account transactions

checking account A bank account that allows depositors to write checks to make payments

cholesterol Substance found in animal fat that can build up in your blood vessels and cause heart disease

claim Formal request made to an insurance company for payment for a loss

classics Styles that stay in fashion for a long time

closing costs A collection of fees you must pay when you sign mortgage paperwork to cover tasks the lender must do related to your loan

COBRA Federal law that requires your employer to offer to continue your health coverage for up to 18 months after you leave your job, although you must pay the entire premium

coinsurance Under fee-for-service health insurance, the portion of covered medical expenses you must pay after meeting the deductible

collateral Property pledged to back a loan

collision coverage Insurance that pays for damage to your car caused by colliding with another car or object

command economy An economic system in which the government owns most resources and makes most economic decisions

commercial bank A financial institution that serves individuals and businesses with a wide variety of accounts, loans, and other financial services

common stock A voting share of ownership in a corporation for which the dividend varies, as determined by the corporation's board of directors

comparative advantage A country's production of a product that makes the most efficient use of the resources it has

competition A contest among sellers to win customers

compound interest Interest paid on the principal and also on previously earned interest, assuming that the interest is left in the account

comprehensive coverage Insurance that pays for damage to your car caused by something other than a collision, such as damage from storms, vandalism, and theft

condominium An apartment that a consumer owns rather than rents

consumer Anyone who buys or uses products

consumer economics The study of the role consumers play in an economic system

consumer movement Efforts to protect and inform consumers by requiring such practices as honest advertising, product warranties, and improved safety standards

Consumer Price Index (CPI) A common measure of inflation that tracks monthly changes in the price of 400 goods and services that people buy regularly

Consumer Product Safety Commission (CPSC) A federal agency that protects consumers from dangerous products

consumer sovereignty The idea that consumer choices determine what goods and services are produced

contingency fee Lawyer's fee arrangement, in which the lawyer receives a percentage of the cash award in a lawsuit

contract Agreement between two or more people that can be enforced by law

cookies Files containing information about you that web sites store on your hard drive

cooling-off period A specified period of time within which a consumer can back out of an agreement to buy something

copayment Under managed care health insurance, the specific amount you pay for particular services, regardless of the cost of those services

cosign a loan A contractual agreement to pay a debt if the borrower does not pay it

cover letter A letter of introduction that you send with your resume to a potential employer

credit Ability to borrow money in return for a promise of future repayment

credit bureau Company that collects information about your credit history and sells it to lenders

credit history A record of your past borrowing and repayments

credit limit The maximum amount that you may charge on your credit account

credit rating A measure of your creditworthiness, often computed as a numerical score, using the FICO scoring system to analyze your credit history

credit union A financial institution that provides banking services to its members, who are people who share a common bond, such as a certain profession, church group, or labor union

creditworthiness A measure of your ability and willingness to repay a loan

currency Paper money and coins used for financial transactions

customs duties Taxes imposed on imported goods (also known as *tariffs*)

D

daily values The amounts of each nutrient that the human body needs each day

death benefit Payment made to the beneficiary of a life insurance policy upon the death of the insured person

debit card Card that transfers funds electronically from your checking account to the store's account to pay for a purchase

debt consolidation loan A large loan used to pay off a number of smaller loans

deductible (insurance) The amount you pay for a loss before the insurance company pays anything

deductions Any expenses you can legally subtract from your income when figuring your taxes

demand The quantity of a good or service that consumers are willing

and able to buy at various prices during a given time period

dentist Someone trained in general dentistry that serves as a primary care physician for your teeth

dependents For tax purposes, the people you support financially

depreciation A decline in a product's value

depression A deep, extended decline in a nation's economy

designer clothes Styles created by a famous designer

dipstick Metal measuring stick for checking fluid levels in a car

direct deposit Depositing an employee's pay into the employee's bank account electronically, instead of using a paper paycheck

diversification Distributing funds among a variety of investments to minimize overall risk

dividend Portion of a company's profits paid to the owners

dollar cost averaging Investing roughly equal amounts of money at regular intervals

dormitories Rooms that colleges rent to students at a reasonable price, usually in large complexes

down payment Percentage of the purchase price that the borrower pays up front

downsizing Terminating employees to cut expenses

duplex apartment An apartment with rooms on two floors of a building

DVD-ROM A data storage disc that holds much more data than a CD-ROM

E

earnest money   Deposit paid by a home buyer as proof of intention to buy at the price stated in the offer

economic system   The way a nation uses resources to provide goods and services

economics   The study of how economic systems work

efficiency   Achieving the most output of goods and services for the resources used

efficiency apartment   An apartment consisting of one room that serves as the living area, bedroom, and kitchen, plus a bathroom

electronic funds transfer (EFT)   The movement of funds from one account to another by computer

endorsement   Your signature on the back of a check, acknowledging that you received the funds or transferred your right to the funds to someone else

Environmental Protection Agency (EPA)   Federal agency responsible for enforcing laws that protect the environment

equilibrium price   The price at which the quantity supplied exactly equals the quantity demanded of a product

escrow account   A holding account used by a mortgage lender to accumulate the borrower's funds for taxes and insurance until these payments are due

estate tax   Tax on property received by the legal heirs when someone dies

European Union (EU)   Organization of Western European countries that have agreed to economic and political cooperation among member nations

exchange rate   The price of one currency in terms of another currency

excise tax   Tax included in the price of certain goods and services

expansion   A period of general growth in a nation's economy

expiration date   The date by which you should use the product to avoid spoilage

export   A good or service that one country sells to another country

F

face value   The dollar value printed on a bond

fads   Styles that don't stay in fashion long

family practitioner   Physician trained in the prevention, diagnosis, and treatment of a wide variety of ailments in patients of all ages

fats   Nutrients that the body needs but contain the most calories per gram of food

features (car)   Characteristics of a particular model of car that offer benefits to the owner

Federal Deposit Insurance Corporation (FDIC)   A federal government agency that insures deposits in banks

Federal Trade Commission (FTC)   Federal agency responsible for protecting consumers from unfair or deceptive business practices, such as misleading information in advertising or on product labels

fee-for-service (or indemnity) plan Type of health insurance in which you pay for health services as you receive them and submit a claim to the insurance company for reimbursement of covered expenses

FHA mortgage Home loan insured by the Federal Housing Administration, designed to reduce the down payment, so that more consumers can afford to buy a home

fiber A substance in some complex carbohydrates that contains no nutrients but helps food move through the body's digestive system

FICA (Federal Insurance Contributions Act) Federal law that requires workers to contribute to social security and Medicare

finance charge The total amount a borrower must pay for a loan

fiscal policy Government's taxing and spending decisions

fixed expenses Amounts you have already committed to spend

fixed-rate mortgage Home loan for which the interest rate remains the same throughout the term of the loan

flexible expenses Amounts that you can choose to spend or not spend

floating exchange rates A system that determines exchange rates in which the price of a country's currency rises and falls in relation to world demand for that currency

floppy disk A data storage disk that stores smaller amounts of data than CD-ROM or DVD-ROM discs

Food Guide Pyramid A guide to help consumers achieve a balanced diet, created by the USDA from research on foods and nutritional needs

food stamps Coupons issued by the federal government to low-income people to help them obtain food

Form 1040EZ The simplest of the basic income tax forms, often used by young people and others whose finances are fairly uncomplicated

Form 1099-INT A statement of the interest your bank paid on your savings that year

Form W-2 A summary of your earnings and withholdings for the year for a job

Form W-4 A form that you fill out to provide the information your employer needs to determine the proper amount to withhold from your paycheck

fraud Deliberate deception, designed to secure unfair or unlawful gain

full warranty A written promise that the company will repair or replace a defective product within a specified time period at no charge

G

generic drugs Medications that have the same composition as their name brand counterparts but are less expensive

gift tax Tax paid by the giver of gifts worth more than $11,000

goals The things you want to accomplish in your life

grace period The time between the billing date and the payment due date when no interest is charged

graduated-payment mortgage Home loan for which the payments start small and go up on a regular schedule over time

gross domestic product (GDP) The current value of all goods and services produced in a country in a year

gross income Amount you earn before taxes are withheld

growth stock Stock in a corporation that is expected to experience rapid growth in sales and profits

H

hard drive The computer's main storage area for electronic data

Head Start Welfare program that provides developmental and learning activities for low-income pre-school children, ages 3 to 5

health maintenance organization (HMO) Managed care health insurance plan that charges a set amount for each member each year in exchange for providing medical services at no extra cost or for a small copayment, no matter how often you see your doctor

high-yield bond A bond sold by corporations in financial difficulty that offers a high return but involves significant risk

home equity loan Loan that uses a home's equity as collateral

homeowner's insurance Insurance that provides personal property and liability protection for your home

HyperText Markup Language (HTML) Computer coding system that enables the use of graphics on the Internet

I

implied warranty An unwritten guarantee that the product is of sufficient quality to fulfill the purpose for which it was designed

import A good or service that one country buys from another country

impulse purchase A purchase made on a whim, without using the decision making process

income taxes Taxes you pay on most types of income you receive

individual retirement account (IRA) A retirement savings plan that has special tax benefits but is not employer-sponsored

inflation General increase in the average level of prices in a nation's economy

insider trading Trading stock based on information not available to the general public

installment loan A loan to be repaid in a certain number of payments with a certain interest rate

insurable interest Something of value that, if lost, would cause you financial harm

insurance Risk management tool that limits financial loss due to illness, injury, or damage in exchange for a premium

Internal Revenue Service (IRS) Federal agency responsible for collecting income taxes

Internet A worldwide network of millions of computer networks

Internet service provider (ISP) Businesses that relay messages across the Internet from computer to computer

internist Specialist in internal medicine, a branch of medicine that deals with the long term, comprehensive management of both common and complex illness

interview A face-to-face meeting with a potential employer to discuss your job qualifications

investing Saving in a way that earns income

invoice price Amount the dealer paid to buy the car from the manufacturer

J

job The set of tasks you accomplish while you work

L

landlord Owner of rental property

laptop computers Portable computers (also called *notebook computers*)

law of demand Economic law that says that consumers will demand more of a product at a lower price than at a higher price

law of supply Economic law that says that producers are willing to offer more of a product for sale at a higher price than at a lower price

lease (housing) Legal contract that gives you the right to occupy property for a specified period of time as long as you pay the rent and follow the rules specified in the contract

leasing (vehicle) Renting use of a vehicle by making specified payments over a stated period of time

legal aid Any of several programs that provide legal services for people who cannot afford a lawyer

lemon laws Laws that require car manufacturers to replace or buy back a car that cannot be fixed after repeated tries, has multiple major defects, or has defects that kept it out of service for 30 days

liability insurance Insurance that protects you from losses that you cause others

license tax Fee paid for a license, permit, or stamp to operate certain kinds of businesses (also known as a business tax)

life cycle A cycle made up of important events that take place during different phases of your life

life span The time between a person's birth and death

life-span goal Long-term goal that you want to reach during your life

life-span plan A plan to reach long-term goals within a person's life

limited warranty A written warranty that does not meet the standards of a full warranty because of specified limitations

load A sales fee that you pay when you invest in a mutual fund

long-term goal Something you hope to achieve over a period of years

loss leader A product priced below cost to attract customers to the store

luxury goods Goods that have special qualities that make them more expensive than alternative goods

M

maintenance schedule Timetable for checking systems and replacing parts on a car

malpractice insurance Insurance that health care providers buy to protect themselves against lawsuits resulting from their medical services

managed care (or prepaid) plans Health insurance coverage that you pay for in advance instead of paying for services as you use them

manufactured fibers Fibers that are made rather than naturally occurring

market economy Economic system in which the people, rather than the government, own the resources and run the businesses

market value Amount an item is worth now

mediator A neutral third party in a dispute who listens to both sides and makes suggestions but does not pass judgment

Medicaid Government-sponsored health insurance designed for people with low incomes or disabilities, regardless of age

medical payments coverage Insurance that pays medical/funeral expenses for you, your family members, and other passengers in your car because of injuries sustained in an accident—no matter who caused the accident

Medigap Private health insurance designed to pay for services that Medicare doesn't cover

microprocessor Device within a computer's CPU that carries out the computing functions

minerals Nutrients that help your body grow and work

mixed economy An economic system that has characteristics of a market and a command economy

mobile home A small house on wheels, designed so that the owner can transport it to a rented space in a mobile home community

modem A device that allows computers to communicate over telephone lines or television cables

monetary policy Government's efforts to help stabilize the economy by managing interest rates, the availability of loans, and the supply of money

money market account A deposit for which the interest rate changes over time as interest rates in the economy change

money order A check that draws on the funds of the bank or other financial business that issued it

monopoly A company that has an unfair advantage over competitors in an area of business

mortgage Loan to buy real estate, such as land or a home

mortgage insurance Government insurance on FHA and VA loans that protects the mortgage lender against loss if the buyer doesn't repay

multinational corporation (MNC) A business that is based in one country but has branches or plants in other countries

mutual fund A business that accepts deposits from many people to invest in various ways

N

NASDAQ An electronic stock-trading system that links brokerage firms

National School Lunch Program Welfare program that provides low-cost or free nutritionally balanced lunches for needy school children

natural fibers Fibers that come from plants or animals

needs Things you can't live without

net income Amount you receive after withholdings are subtracted from your gross pay

no-fault insurance Laws adopted in some states that require each person's automobile insurance company to pay for the insured's own losses, no matter who caused the accident

North American Free Trade Agreement (NAFTA) Agreement among the U.S., Canada, and Mexico to gradually eliminate tariffs on most goods produced and sold in North America

notebook computers Portable computers (also called *laptop computers*)

notice Official written notification that you are leaving the company

nutrients Chemical substances in food that your body needs to function properly

O

obesity Weighing above your ideal body weight by more than 20 percent

obstetrician/gynecologist (OBGYN) Specialist in the diagnosis and treatment of diseases of the female reproductive system and care and treatment during pregnancy, labor, delivery, and just after delivery

odometer Instrument in a car that measures miles traveled

offer Proposal to buy a house for a stated price

open enrollment Specified time each year when employees may sign up for the employer-sponsored health insurance plan

ophthalmologist Physician that specializes in diagnosing and treating diseases of the eyes

opportunity cost The value of your next best alternative whenever you make a choice

option (car) Feature that you can choose to include or not include on a car, but if chosen, will add to the price of the car

overdrawing Writing a check for more money than is deposited in your checking account

owner's manual Booklet provided with new cars that tells you where the controls are located, how to operate them, and how to maintain the car

P

patients' bill of rights Consumers' rights and responsibilities in the health care system, as proposed by the President's Advisory Commission on Consumer Protection and Quality in the Health Care Industry

payee The person or business to whom a check is written

payroll taxes A share of workers' earnings paid to the government by workers and their employers

pediatrician Specialist in the physical, emotional, and social health of children from birth to young adulthood

peripheral device Any hardware connected to the CPU

permanent life insurance Life insurance that provides a death benefit plus a savings plan and lasts for the policyholder's lifetime

personal identification number (PIN) Your secret number that identifies you to an ATM as the owner of the ATM card

personal interests Activities you find rewarding over an extended period of time

personality The unique blend of qualities that defines an individual

point-of-service (POS) plan Managed care health insurance plan that requires you to get referrals from a primary care physician within the plan but will pay part of the cost of providers outside the plan

points (driving) Bad marks recorded on a person's driving record because of traffic violations and accidents

points (mortgage) Mortgage lender's service charge, each point being equal to 1 percent of the principal

policy Insurance contract

poverty line Income level, established by the federal government, that helps determine who is eligible for welfare benefits

pre-existing condition A medical condition diagnosed or treated before you join a new insurance plan

preferred provider organization (PPO) Managed care health insurance plan that allows you to choose providers outside the plan if you pay a larger part of the cost and does not require you to get referrals from a primary care physician

preferred stock A nonvoting share of ownership in a corporation that pays a fixed dividend

premium Regular payment required to purchase insurance

primary care physician Doctor in a managed care health plan that you select to coordinate your care and refer you to specialists

principal (loan) The amount borrowed

principal (savings) Money on deposit

production The creation of goods and services

profit The difference between the money received from selling a product and the cost of producing that product

property damage liability coverage Insurance that pays for damage you caused to another person's property

property insurance Insurance that protects you from financial loss when something you own is stolen, damaged, or destroyed

property tax Tax on the value of real estate owned

prospectus A legal document provided by all mutual funds that describes the fund's operations, its investing objectives, and its fees

protectionism Limiting international trade to protect the nation's own self-interest

proteins Nutrients that help the body build and repair cells and supply energy

public defender Lawyer appointed and paid by the court to defend someone accused of a crime who is unable to pay for legal representation

public goods   Goods and services provided by the government that benefit all Americans

public housing   Housing built specifically for low-income people

puffery   Innocent exaggerations used to sell products

purchasing power   The amount of goods or services that your money can buy

pyramid scheme   A type of financial fraud in which people pay to join an organization in exchange for the right to sell memberships to other people

Q

quota   A limit on the amount of a product that can be imported

R

random access memory (RAM)   The computer's main workspace

rational buying decision   A choice made in an organized, logical manner, so that it will most likely fulfill your need or want

real gross domestic product   The value of all goods and services produced in a country in a year, adjusted for inflation

reasonable and customary charges   Fees for each medical treatment that the insurance company determines to be normal in your geographic area

rebate   Partial refund of the purchase price

rebuilt (or reconditioned) parts   Used parts that were repaired or restored to working order to be installed as replacements

recession   A period of general decline in a nation's economy

redress   To seek and receive a remedy to a problem

references   People the employer can contact to verify your training, experience, or character

referral (job)   A recommendation of a person for a job given to an employer by someone the employer knows

referral (medical)   A request from your primary care physician for services from a particular specialist

regular charge account   A charge account that requires the balance to be paid in full from one month to the next

renter's insurance   Insurance that protects renters from property and liability losses

replacement value   Cost of replacing an insured item, regardless of its market value at the time of the loss

resources   All the things used to create other goods or services

resume   A brief summary of your job qualifications, including your education, training, job skills, and work experience

return   Income earned on an investment

revolving charge account   A charge account that allows you to carry a balance from one month to the next, and you pay interest on the unpaid balance

rider Special addition to an insurance policy that covers a specific loss not covered in the standard policy

risk (investment) The chance that an investment will decrease in value

rule of 72 A compounding rule that says if an asset grows x% a year, its value will double in $72 \div x$ years

S

safe deposit box A box with a lock that you may rent from a bank for safe storage of important papers and valuable possessions

sales tax Tax added to the price of goods and services at the time of purchase

saving Trading current spending for the ability to spend in the future

savings account An account at a banking institution in which you may deposit money, earn interest, and withdraw your funds at any time

savings and loan association A financial institution that specializes in lending money to buy homes

savings bank A financial institution owned by its depositors

savings bonds U.S. government bonds issued for amounts of $50 to $10,000

scarcity The basic economic problem that consumers' wants are always greater than the resources available to satisfy those wants

secured loan A loan backed by something of value pledged to ensure payment

Securities and Exchange Commission (SEC) A federal government agency responsible for enforcing the laws concerning the trading of stocks and bonds

security deposit Money the landlord holds to cover any damage to rental property

serving A measure of the amount of food that you would probably eat during one meal or snack

severance pay A sum of money for which an employee is eligible upon termination

share of stock A unit of ownership in a corporation

shared risk Insurance principle of using premiums from many policyholders to reimburse the losses of a few, so that no one suffers a financially devastating loss

short-term goal Something you hope to achieve within a year

simple interest Interest paid one time per year at the end of the year on the average balance in the savings account

skill An aptitude developed through training and experience

small claims court A court that handles suits for small dollar amounts without the services of a lawyer

Social Security Government-sponsored insurance program that provides cash payments to help replace income lost as a result of retirement, unemployment, disability, or death

Social Security number Number that the government uses to identify you as a taxpayer and keep track of your earnings and tax records

spam Unwanted advertising distributed through e-mail

statement   A written record from your bank of all the transactions involving your account

sticker price   Manufacturer's suggested retail price listed on a sticker in a new car's window

stock exchange   A location where orders to buy or sell stock are sent and carried out

stockbroker   A person who handles the transfer of stocks and bonds between buyer and seller

stockholders   Investors who own a corporation because they own its stock

style   Particular characteristics that distinguish one garment from another

Supplemental Security Income (SSI)   Welfare program to aid low-income people who are at least 65 years old, blind, or disabled

supply   The quantity of a product that producers are willing and able to make available for sale at various prices over a given time period

T

tariffs   Taxes imposed on imported goods (also known as *customs duties*)

tax return   A set of forms that taxpayers use to calculate their tax obligation

taxable income   All the wages, tips, and interest on which you pay taxes

technological obsolescence   The process of new technology making products based on old technology out of date

temporary agencies   Private companies that specialize in supplying short-term employees to businesses

Temporary Assistance for Needy Families (TANF)   Welfare program that requires work in exchange for public assistance and limits the amount of time people may receive assistance

tenant   Someone who rents an apartment or other home

term life insurance   Life insurance that pays a death benefit if the policyholder dies within a specific time period but has no remaining value at the end of this time

third party checks   Checks made out to you that you sign over to someone else

trade deficit   The result when a country spends more on imports than it earns from exports

trade surplus   The result when a country earns more from exports than it spends on imports

trading up   The practice of pressuring consumers to buy a more expensive product than they intended

traditional economy   An economic system in which production methods are passed from one generation to the next

transaction (financial)   Buying or selling shares of stock, usually through a stockbroker

transferable skill   A skill that allows you to complete specific tasks in various careers

traveler's checks   Checks that you pay for in advance, and if they are lost or stolen, the issuing company replaces them

true-name fraud   Using another person's identity to buy products through the use of credit

tune-up   Service on a car that includes changing spark plugs, filters, and other parts to make the engine run better

U

umbrella policy Insurance that provides additional liability protection beyond that in an automobile or homeowner's policy

unemployment compensation Government-sponsored insurance program designed to provide income for people who have lost their jobs through no fault of their own

unemployment rate Percentage of people who are able and looking for work but don't have jobs

uninsured/underinsured motorist coverage Insurance that pays medical and damage expenses for you and your passengers caused by a driver without insurance or with too little insurance to cover the loss

unit price The price of one standard amount of a product

unsecured loan A loan not backed by any collateral

utility A measure of something's usefulness

V

VA mortgage Home loan insured by the Veteran's Administration to help past and present members of the military buy homes at favorable rates

values Your principles—the standards you use to judge what is right and wrong, good and bad, important and unimportant for you

vitamins Nutrients that help your body react in certain essential ways

W

wants Things that you would like to have but can live without

warranty A company's promise that its product will meet specific standards over a given time period, or the company will repair or replace it, or give a refund

web browser Program that gives users the ability to search the Web for information with just the click of a mouse button

welfare General term for government programs that provide money, medical care, food, housing, and other necessities for people who otherwise cannot afford them

will Written declaration of how you want your property divided when you die

wire transfer An electronic communication that moves funds from an account in one bank to an account in a different bank instantly

withholding Employer deductions from employees' earnings to pay employees' taxes

Women, Infants, and Children (WIC) Program Welfare program that provides nutrition education and coupons for free healthful foods for pregnant women, new mothers, and children up to age 5

workers' compensation Employer-paid insurance program that covers expenses for work-related injuries, illnesses, and death

World Wide Web (WWW or Web) Information retrieval system that organizes the Internet's resources in a graphical fashion

INDEX

F

G